KISETSU 1: HARUICHIBAN

Kazuo Tsuda

United Nations International School

New York, NY

Masatoshi Shimano

St. Paul's School

Concord, NH

KISETSU EDUCATIONAL GROUP
New York

Additional Writers

Timothy Vance

Sahe Kawahara

Kisetsu Educational Group Core Members

Kazuo Tsuda

Masatoshi Shimano

Geraldine Carter

Hiromi Yamashita

Supporter

Northeast Association of Secondary Teachers of Japanese

Photographs Donor

The Japan Forum

Publication Donor

Fuji Xerox Co., Ltd.

Kisetsu1: Haruichiban

ISBN4-907811-00-4

Published by Kisetsu Educational Group
c/o United Nations International School/Northeast Association of Secondary Teachers of Japanese
24-50 FDR Dr. New York, NY 10010 USA

Contents

Welcome to Japanese.
Welcome to Kisetsu.

Welcome, everyone! Opening this textbook is a small but significant step on the road to a prosperous and profitable relationship that may last a lifetime: a relationship with the Japanese language, culture, and people. Picking and choosing school courses is not always easy with all the choices and scheduling conflicts to consider, as well as the possible implications your selection may have for your future. So it is only natural if your are still wondering whether you made the right choice when you decided to begin studying Japanese. We think glancing at what immediately follows may clear this up for you. Take a look!

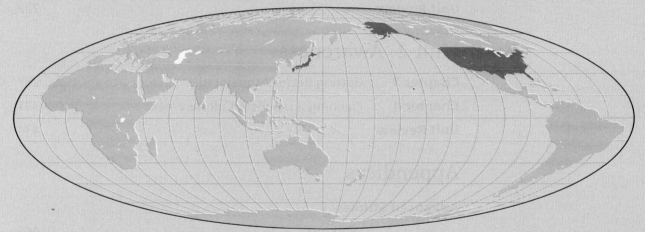

Gain an understanding of the language and culture of a neighbor across the Pacific.

Japan has become both a valuable friend and a fierce competitor of the United States in the past several decades. During this time the Japanese have embraced many aspects of the American popular culture, as well as its democratic values. They have also kept a close eye on our progress in computer technology and studied the American social infrastructure. Americans, on the other hand, examined the Japanese practice of consensus building, their efficient garbage recycling, and effective police system. They were also impressed by the possible connection between diet and longevity. Opportunities for collaboration and mutual enrichment between the people of these two countries have been abundant. However, dealings between the United States and Japan have been sort of a one-way traffic when it comes to studying each other's language and culture. While almost all school children in Japan study at least six years of English, the opportunity to study Japanese has not been readily available to their American counterparts. Although the United States is one of the countries most studied by Japanese, Japan remains an enigma to many Americans. To make our associations and interactions more mutually profitable, we need to increase the flow of traffic from our end. After all, they are a neighbor just across the Pacific.

Learn one of the ten most spoken languages in the world.

Japan is an island nation. The Japanese archipelago is believed to have been separated from the Asian mainland some 10,000 years ago. Naturally this explains the reason why the Japanese people only speak Japanese and why they have been isolated from foreign languages throughout their history. Despite this fact, Japanese is one of the ten most spoken languages in the world. This is, of course, understandable when the size of Japan's population (over 120 million) is taken into consideration, but the number of Japanese speakers outside Japan has been increasing noticeably as the global economy expands and travel and migration become more affordable and frequent.

Be a better learner and acquire skills you'll use for a lifetime.

Studying a language as different from English as Japanese will expand your mind and broaden your intellectual horizons. Gaining insight into and understanding of the cultural nuance, the mindset, and the thinking behind the language is a challenge that calls for involvement beyond just memorizing words and the sentence formulas. You will frequently have to examine and reflect during your learning process and make the necessary adjustments to render it more suitable to your own style and needs. You may have to strive to develop a good guessing ability to enhance your comprehension or become better organized to raise your efficiency. Whatever the adjustement, it is bound to make you an innovative, independent, and self-directed lifelong learner.

Wear a cool pair of glasses with bicultural lenses.

It's often said that one of best ways of learning about yourself and your heritage is to study something entirely different. Studying Japanese will allow you to see your own language and culture in a whole new way and lead to a renewed appreciation of them. In addition, you will gain the kind of perspective that enables you to see things more objectively and distinguish thoughtfully examined views, assumptions, and conceptions from those tinted with hasty stereotyping. Studying Japanese will also equip you with an ability to see things as if you were wearing a magical pair of glasses that give you a whole new view of the world. With these glasses you will see things, feel emotions and construct meanings the same way people who are growing up in Japan do. When you take them off you will realize how much we are alike in many respects. So give yourself a pair of glasses with bicultural lenses. The benefits and potential for you are unlimited.

Study of one of the fastest growing subjects in US precollege schools.

Japanese has been one of the fastest growing subjects in US schools for the past several decades. According to the Modern Language Association, the enrollment in college Japanese courses in 1990 was 45,717, a twenty-six-fold increase since1960, when a mere 1,746 students studied Japanese. By 1990, Japanese was the fifth most commonly studied foreign language in American colleges. Enrollment at the secondary level started showing a noticeable increase in the 1980s. According to the American Council on the Teaching of Foreign Languages, enrollment in Japanese language courses at public high schools alone went from 8,557 in 1985 to 25,123 in 1990. This figure increased an additional 70 percent to 42,290 over the next four years.

Prepare yourself for career opportunities that are truly stimulating and rewarding.

All the traffic and exchanges between the Uinted Sates and Japan, from official and diplomatic to individual and grass roots have strengthened the ties of friendship and mutual dependency between the two countries. The combination of this with the expansion of the global economy and international communication and the vital role both countries play on the world stage means that opportunities for a whole new set of careers and adventures are available to those who become proficient in the Japanese language and knowledgeable about Japanese culture.

Join an active, dynamic, and creative community of language learners.

In order to create a flowing movement in the textbook, the themes of the chapter link to one another. A series of projects and open-ended simulations will accompany each chapter and help you move on to the next level. Assistance from teachers will be kept to a minimum at this stage and you are expected to make plans, share tasks and monitor your progress with your peers. Learning here is neither an isolated effort for say, a perfect score on a vocabulary quiz, nor a passive absorption of knowledge. It's a dynamic, community activity.

Organization of the Textbook

Design of *Kisetsu*

Kisetsu is a series of Japanese-language textbooks for junior high and high school students. Kisetsu means "seasons" and the first volume is called Haruichiban (literally, First Spring Storm). Kisetsu aims to help a student become not only a successful communicator in Japanese but also a self-directed and reflective learner, a skillful problem solver and an active, sensitive and productive participant in the global community. Kisetsu also reflects the Standards for Foreign Language Learning in the 21st Century.

Organization of *Kisetsu*

A sequence of conceptual units has been developed in order to realize the aforementioned goals and objectives and these units facilitate a meaningful progression of learning throughout the program. The current volume, Haruichiban, contains two preliminary sections (Getting Started I and Getting Started II) and the first two of the conceptual units (Encounter and Awareness). The units are broken down into four thematically organized chapters. The accompanying chart allows users to see how the five goals of foreign language education identified in the Standards -- Communication, Cultures, Connections, Comparisons, and Communities -- are incorporated into the textbook.

Organization of *Haruichiban*

Getting Started

Getting Started I   Useful Daily Expressions

Getting Started II Simple Questions and Answers

Unit 1: Encounter

Chapter 1   Meeting Someone for the First Time

Chapter 2   Planning a Party

Unit Review

Unit 2: Awareness

Chapter 3   Getting Better Acquainted

Chapter 4   Planning Japanese Culture Week

Unit Review

Organization of the Chapters

Introduction-Mechanics-Application-Virtual Reality: Ultimate Progression!

This text book follows a progression of learning which is characterized by the four sequential sections captioned above and culminates in open-ended and project-based activities.

1. Introduction

The Introduction section gives you an overview of the chapter. It also lets you warm up with simple recognition drills, games and exercises utilizing useful learning and communication strategies. This section consists of the following segments.

1. Objectives: List of what you will be learning and what you will be able to do with it
2. Kisetsu Theater: A visual overview with compact descriptions
3. Warm-Up: A group of exercise emphasizing useful strategies
4. Basic Vocabulary: A pictorial introduction to selected basic words and expressions
5. Mechanics: Drills employing basic vocabulary
6. Games or songs

2. Mechanics

The Mechanics section reviews the Introduction section and introduces you to a new set of vocabulary. You will also learn communication skills through various drills and activities which concentrate on one or two items of importance at a time. This section is divided into several parts and it is accompanied by an additional segment which deals with one of the following topics.

1. Culture Note
2. Language Note
3. Pronunciation
4. Form (grammar and function)

3. Application

The Application section provides opportunities to integrate what you have learned in the Mechanics section into a more meaningful context. Often working in groups, you execute tasks using various functions and strategies including reading and writing. Although these tasks are not open-ended, they will encourage you to express your own ideas and help you become a successful communicator. This section is accompanied by an additional segment which deals with one of the following.

1. Vocabulary: A list of functional vocabulary and notional vocabulary
2. Kana and Kanji: Japanese syllabaries and Chinese characters

4. Virtual Reality

In this section you will participate in a comprehensive project where you will mobilize and integrate everything you learned to this point. Again, working with your peers, you will simulate situations that are open-ended and close to real world tasks as much as possible. The Virtual Reality section gives you opportunities to work on materials of your particular interest and facilitates both independent and group learning. The Virtual Reality section is supplemented by the following.

1. Assessments: A self-assessment or peer assessment to check your performance, knowledge and skills
2. Checklist: A set of questions asking you to evaluate your own progress and reflect upon your learning experience
3. Additional Vocabulary: An advanced list of words which will be useful for the Virtual Reality projects
4. Additional Information: Pictures depicting real Japanese life accompanied by photographs taken by Japanese students.

Acknowledgments

We would like to thank many individuals and organizations whose unfailing support and contributions have been vitally important to us over the five years that this book was in the making. Our first and foremost debt of gratitude is to Fuji Xerox Co.,Ltd. (Miyahara, Kawabe, Hattori, Shimizu, Kato, Ichinose, Ide) for their generous grant, and the Japan Forum (Nakano, Harashima, Jibiki, Ushijima, Takasaki, Takashima, Ito, Fujimaki, Mizuguchi) for making available their valuable resources, including many photos in this book. We are also very grateful to St. Paul's School (Hornor, Marshall, Anderson) and the United Nations International School (Blaney, Fuhrman, Wrye) for letting us use their facilities and equipment; to the Northeast Association of the Secondary Teachers of Japanese and its members for allowing us to establish our group.

Kanoya U.S. - Japan Committee (Yamazaki, Ino, Yotsumoto), Yamaguchi University (Hayashi, Ninomiya, Hayashi), Showa Women's University (Hitomi, Takamizawa), Boston Showa (Sakamaki, Ikuma, Provost), John Manjiro Center (Takahashi), Japan Foundation Language Center (Yokoyama, Furuyama, Kabutomori, Kaneda, Tsujimoto), Univesity of Colorado, Boulder (Lodd, Saegusa), Yamagata University (Takagi), U.S.-Japan Foundation, University of Massachusetts Amhesrt (Austin, Horiba), MIT (Miyagawa, Lavin, Torii) Kodansha America (Asakawa and Noma), Middletown High School (Magwire), Joba Group (Ogasawara, Mizuno, Deguchi, Shibuya, Nakano) Yokohama City Board of Education (Ueno, Ota, Takegoshi, Nagai, Isobe, Kishi, Kurisu) , Japanese Amercian Association of New York (Shirato, Samuel, Kodama), and students in Japanese classes of MIddletown High School (RI), St. Paul's School (NH) and United Nations International School (NY).

A great number of individuals have given us much-needed advice, feedback and encouragement. We would like to express our appreciation to Geraldine Carter, the core member of Kisetsu Educational Group , for her contribution for basic works; to Hiromi Yamashita, another core member of Kisetsu Educational Group for her devotion to teaching ideas; Timothy Vance for his contribution to the language and pronunciation section; Sahe Kawahara for her contribution of culture; and Kyoko Saegusa, Shinichi Hayashi, Erica Ma, TJF's commiitee members for feedback; to Cyrus Rolbin, Laura Kriska, Caryn Stedman, Jeffrey Johnson and Marcia Johnson for their valuable comments on earlier drafts of our manuscript; to Chiaki Kataoka, Shoji Sato, Chiaki Murakami, Jun Ono, Kyoko Iwasaki , Hiroko Nagai, Peter Henty, Fumiko Bacon, Shayne Gorga and Kayoko Tazawa for the work book draft; and Shiho Hagi, Fuhito Shimoyama, Atsuko Isahaya, Kanae Sakakibara and Kuniko Yokohata. Our special thanks also go to Kazuko Tsurumi, Sadako Ogata, Osamu Kamada, Carl Falsgraf, Hiroko Kataoka, Yasuhiko Tosaku, Seiichi Makino, Andre Hurtgen, Norman Masuda and Richard Kania who helped to develop our ideas and resources.

And finally, but not least importantly, we would like to acknowledge the contribution of the following technical staff: Dawn Lawson (chief editor), Lynda Crawford (editor), Mutsumi Kiyohara (editor in Japanese), Lisa Carter (editor for draft), Ichiro Sata (proofreader), Hitomi Ozaki (main illustrator and layout designer), Aka Chikazawa (illustrator), Hiromi Yamashita(illustrator), Yusuke Nakanishi (photographer), Alexandra Fallon (photographer), Lora Runge (photographer), Joan Greenfield (main layout designer), David Ascue (layout designer for draft), Mary Reed (proofreader), Kiyoshi Kanai (adviser for design), Minato Asakawa and Chikako Noma (adviser for textbook), Kei Ohara (paginator) and Fuji Xerox/Digital Workshop Shinagawa Staff (Shimizu, Okuda, Kato, Nishitani, Kishi). Their top-notch talent and creativity, as well as their patience, have been greatly appreciated.

This book could not have happened without the tremendous support we have received from those mentioned above. However, any errors or shortcomings in the manuscript are solely our responsibility.

Kazuo Tsuda
Masatoshi Shimano

Getting Started I

	USEFUL DAILY EXPRESSIONS	ACTIONS
STEP 1	Introducing each other	Standing and sitting
STEP 2	Leave taking	Counting to 20
STEP 3	Daily Greeting 1	Counting to 30
STEP 4	Expressing gratitude Requesting something	Counting to 50
STEP 5	Offering something to someone Before and after eating	Telling time Telling months Writing katakana letters
STEP 6	Sending someone off and welcoming them back	Counting things Putting things in containers
STEP 7	Drawing someone's attention Asking someone to speak in English Telling someone to wait	Telling the days of the month Erasing katakana words
STEP 8	Classroom Expressions 1	Adjusting volume and speed of one's speech Forming groups
STEP 9	Classroom Expressions 2	Counting to 500 Telling days of the week Writing katakana words
STEP 10	Classroom Expressions 3 Apologizing Praising	Counting to 100

KATAKANA	ACTIVITY	CULTURE AND REFERENCE
a-gyoo + long vowels	Bowing and handshaking	Objectives of Getting Started I Kisetsu Theater
ka-gyoo ga-gyoo + long vowels	"Throw ball around."	
sa-gyoo za-gyoo + long vowels	Scenario 1	
ta-gyoo da-gyoo small tsu + long vowels	"Give me ka."	Japan: Overview
na-gyoo + long vowels	"Thank you / no thank you."	
ha-gyoo ba-gyoo pa-gyoo	"I'm leaving"	
ma-gyoo + long vowels	Scenario 2	
ya-gyoo small ya,yu,yo + long vowels	Stroke order relay	
ra-gyoo wa-gyoo n + long vowels	Katakana bingo Expressions bingo	
Innovative combinations	Scenario 3 "Arrange them in the right order."	Additional Information: Colorful Japan School life

Getting Started II

	SIMPLE QUESTIONS	MIND-MAPPING
STEP 1	Asking what something is	Sports Seasonal events
STEP 2	Asking how much something costs	Beverage Fast food
STEP 3	Asking where something / someone is	Public facilities Famous places in the United States
STEP 4	Asking what time it is Asking what day of the week it is Asking what date it is	Japanese activities American holidays
STEP 5	Asking who someone is	Academic subjects
STEP 6	Asking one's likes and dislikes	Fruits Food
STEP 7	Asking if something exists / is available Asking one's destination	Items in the classroom Items in one's own room Classroom tasks
STEP 8	Asking if someone is present / available	Animals People in the school
STEP 9	Asking questions regarding one's personal character Asking one's preference regarding color	Personal characters Colors
STEP 10	Asking someone where she is going Asking someone with whom she is going Asking someone what she is going to do Asking someone where she is going to do	Places Family Daily activities

KATAKANA REVIEW	HIRAGANA	ACTIVITY	CULTURE AND REFERENCE
Italian food	*a-gyoo* + long vowels	"What is your fall sport?" (interview)	Objectives Kisetsu Theater
Baseball	*ka-gyoo* *ga-gyoo* + long vowels	"How much is it?" (information gap)	
US states	*sa-gyoo* *za-gyoo* + long vowels	"Where is it?" (team competition)	
Equipment, etc.	*ta-gyoo* *da-gyoo* small *tsu* + long vowels	"Event calendar" (information gap)	
Famous names	*na-gyoo* + long vowels	"Who is your teacher?" (interview)	Seasonal events
Food and beverages	*ha-gyoo* *ba-gyoo* *pa-gyoo*	"Do you like it?" (interview)	
Computers	*ma-gyoo* + long vowels	"Wheel of katakana." (game)	Cognate
Japanese abbreviated words	*ya-gyoo* small *ya, yu, yo* + long vowels	"Is there a big cat?" (card game)	
Colors	*ra-gyoo* *wa-gyoo* *n* + long vowels	"He is a nice person." (character description and perception comparison)	
Travel destinations	Innovative combinations	"Travel game." (game)	Additional information Seasonal events A day in the life of Japanese high school students

Chapter 1: Meeting Someone for the First Time
Conceptual Theme: Encounter

VOCABULARY	STRATEGY HIGHLIGHTS	COMMUNICATION HIGHLIGHTS
Notional **Functional**	**Affective** **Cognitive** **Language**	**Interpersonal** **Interpretive** **Presentational**
Greetings	Ensuring thorough acquisition of information	Oral Production Highlights
• First time greetings	• Partial repeating	Greeting
• Daily greetings	• Confirming with *desu ne*	
• New Year greetings	• Asking again	Social conversation
Numbers	Developing conversation with *ja*	Reading & Writing
• 0 – 10,000		
• Telephone numbers		Simple messages and lists
	Guessing	• Name cards
Schools		• Class list
• Type of school		• New Year's cards
• Grade levels	Appreciate the mindset/feeling associated with a first meeting	
Seasons		Design & Creation
Weather		Name cards
Sports		Class list
Year		New Year's cards
• Year by Common Era		
• Year by Japanese Era		
• 12 zodiac cycles		
Performing calculations		
• Division and multiplication		
Size of computer memory		
Currency units		
Question words: *nani, nan, nannen, nanban, nansai, nannensei, ikura*		

CULTURE & CONNECTION	COMPARISON	FORM	COMMUNITY
Culture Connection	**Language Pronunciation Kanji and kana**	**Grammar/Function**	**Assessments Community**
New Year Japanese currency Mathematics (division and multiplication) Computer Science (memory size) Biology (animals) Music (songs) Game & Song • *haru ga kita* • *musunde hiraite*	Short and long syllables The Japanese language in the modern world Kana Long vowels in katakana	Identifying things and people with the "be" verb – *desu.* Asking questions • Asking yes-no questions – *desu ka?* • Asking questions using question words (Part 1) – Q-word *desu ka?* • Asking for confirmation – *desu ne.* • Asking for repetition – *moo ichido onegaishimasu.* • Establishing a topic – Topic *wa* - *desu (ka?)* • Linking no uns – Noun A *no* Noun B	Self-assessment Sum up Video portfolio assessment High school social

Chapter 2: Planning a Party
Conceptual Theme: Encounter

VOCABULARY	STRATEGY HIGHLIGHTS	COMMUNICATION HIGHLIGHTS
Notional **Functional**	**Affective** **Cognitive** **Language**	**Interpersonal** **Interpretive** **Presentational**
Beverages	Cooperating	**Oral Production highlights**
Food	Cooperative decision making	Class meeting
• Japanese food		
• Non-Japanese food	Decision making	**Reading & Writing**
Events and activities		Simple messages and lists
School facilities	Hesitating	• Party posters
Time		• Restaurant menus
• On the hour and a half past		• Excursion itinerary
Days of the week		Notes and records
Months and days		• Writing on the board as a scribe in a meeting
Counting people		
Class meeting		**Design & Creation**
• Roles in the meeting		Party posters
• Items for discussion		Excursion itinerary
• Conducting the meeting		
Restaurants		
Question words: *dochira/dotchi, dore, nanji, nan'yoobi, nangatsu, nannichi, nannin, doko, itsu, ikutsu, naani*		

CULTURE & CONNECTION	COMPARISON	FORM	COMMUNITY
Culture **Connection**	**Language** **Pronunciation** **Kanji and kana**	**Grammar/Function**	**Assessments** **Community**
Japanese food Game & Song • janken Student Council (meeting & cooperative decision making) Graphic design (designing posters)	Japanese dialects topics Word Accent Kana Innovative katakana combinations	Asking preferences - *ga ii desu ka,* *(soretomo)* - *ga ii desu ka?* - *to - to dochira/dotchi ga* iidesu ka. - *to -to -to dore ga iidesu ka.* *Announcing decisions* *- ni shimashoo.* Declaring the beginning and the end of a meeting *miitingu o hajimemashoo.* [beginning] *kore de miitingu o owarimasu.* [end] Asking questions using question words (Part 2) • Requesting objects- *o kudasai.* - *o onegaishimasu.* Procedures for a meeting	Peer assessment Poster evaluation Sum up Video portfolio assessment High school student committee

Chapter 3: Getting Better Acquainted
Conceptual Theme: Awareness

awareness of oneself   *awareness of others*

VOCABULARY	STRATEGY HIGHLIGHTS	COMMUNICATION HIGHLIGHTS
Notional **Functional**	**Affective** **Cognitive** **Language**	**Interpersonal** **Interpretive** **Presentational**

VOCABULARY	STRATEGY HIGHLIGHTS	COMMUNICATION HIGHLIGHTS
Simple personal questions	**Awareness**	**Production Highlights**
Family terms	• awareness of oneself	
Academic subjects	• awareness of others	Interview
Colors		• Interviewer
Transportation	Memorization	• Interviewee
Countries		Speech
Languages and nationalities	Extending conversation	• Self-introductory speech
Personal characters	• Attribution tactic	
	• Analogy tactic	**Reading & Writing**
		Reflective writing
Self-introductory speech		• Brief personal account
• Structures of the speech		Subject writing
• Itemized contents of the speech		• Celebrity profile and interview report
• Connectors in the speech		Simple messages and lists
		• List of interview questions
		• List of pen pals
Common last names		Notes and records
Kanji: 一〜十、月、日、時、語、人		• Taking notes while interviewing
		Reading personal composition in Japanese style
		Design & Creation
		Celebrity posters
		Web page or magazine page for celebrity profile and interview report

CULTURE & CONNECTION	COMPARISON	FORM	COMMUNITY
Culture Connection	**Language Pronunciation Kanji and Kana**	**Grammar/Function**	**Assessments Community**
Schools in Japan	Standard languages	Asking simple questions	Self-assessment
Profile of a student		• (*o, go*) - *wa*. [abbreviated version]	Peer assessment
	Syllable-final consonants	• –*wa* Q-word *desu ka*?	
Japanese last names			Web evaluation
	Kana	Counting people	Sum up
	Writing hiragana		Video portfolio assessment
Game & Song		Describing features of things and persons with adjectives	
kaeru no uta, senro wa tsuzukuyo dokomade mo	Kanji		Celebrity
	Learning kanji	Link nouns to indicate examples	
		• Noun A ya Noun B	
Social Studies (Languages and nationalities, family)		Indicating means (of transportation, etc.)	
Music (song)		Means *de* (ie. *basu de*)	

Chapter 4: Planning a Japanese Culture Week
Conceptual Theme: Awareness
awareness of one's actions   awareness of culture

VOCABULARY	STRATEGY HIGHLIGHTS	COMMUNICATION HIGHLIGHTS
Notional **Functional**	**Affective** **Cognitive** **Language**	**Interpersonal** **Interpretive** **Presentational**
Describing daily activities	**Awareness** • awareness of one's actions • awareness of culture	**Oral Production Highlights** Telephone conversation
Useful words for writing event proposals		Committee meeting and presentation
Telephone terms		
	Changing topics and ending conversation	
Frequency of action	Self-monitoring comprehension while listening or reading	**Reading & Writing**
Terms for calculation • Addition and subtraction		Event proposals
Time • Minutes • Relative time きょう、あした、あさって		Simple messages and lists • Fliers • Schedule of events
Japanese system of counting		Reading proposals
Japanese arts • Fine arts • Performing arts • Japanese martial arts		**Design & Creation** Fliers for Japanese culture week Posters for Japanese culture week
Expressing existence		
Expressing possession		
School items		
Facial parts		
Kanji: 火、水、木、金、土、分、年、本、学、先、生		

CULTURE & CONNECTION	COMPARISON	FORM	COMMUNITY
Culture **Connection**	**Language** **Pronunciation** **Kanji and kana**	**Grammar/Function**	**Assessments** **Community**

Awareness of culture
 	
Japanese arts and martial arts
 	
Game & Song
 	
Traditional Japanese board and card games
 	
Social Studies (Japan)
 	
Mathematics (addition and subtraction)
	Related languages topics
	
	Vowel quality
	
	Long vowels in hiragana
		Describing motions with reference to direction or destination
		- *e/ni* verb.
		  (ie. -*e/ni ikimasu.*)
		
		Describing actions
		- *o* verb.
		  (ie. -*o tabemasu.*)
		
		Negating motions and actions
		- *masen.*
		
		Indicating time of action
		- Time *ni*
		  (ie. *nichiyoobi ni*)
		
		Structure of the Japanese sentence
		• Topic and comment
		• Basic word order
		
		Basic particles
			Self-assessment
			
			Peer assessment
			
			Sum up
			
			Portfolio assessment
			
			Japanese culture week

Getting Started

Getting Started I
Useful Daily Expressions

Getting Started I

Useful Daily Expressions

OBJECTIVES

At the end of this section, you will be able to:

- handle a variety of Japanese greetings successfully

- use body movements associated with greetings

- confirm the accuracy of information you have acquired

- become acquainted with your teacher and classmates and start building productive learning relationships with them

- enhance your listening skills by using various strategies such as guessing, monitoring, observing, and predicting

You will also learn:

- how to exchange greetings with others

- how to tell time, the date and the day of the week in Japanese

- how to follow the teacher's instructions, asking questions if necessary

- about Japanese geography and the Japanese school calendar

- how to count from 1 to 1,000

- how to recognize katakana characters

Useful Daily Expressions

Learning with 10 "Steps"

This section includes ten "steps." Each step consists of the following four segments.

1. Daily Expressions
2. Actions
3. Katakana
4. Activity

Listen, observe, guess and predict. Be resourceful!

In the "actions" segments, listen attentively to your teacher and carefully observe his or her actions.

However, don't get discouraged if you can't understand precisely what is being said. Mobilize every possible clue. You can guess meanings and predict upcoming directions.

Katakana

There are 46 katakana characters in use today. A single katakana typically represents one syllable.

Monitor, reflect and revise.
Take control of your own learning!

If your comprehension and predictions tend to be off the mark, reflect on your past practices and think about making some adjustments. For example, if you think you have a tendency to pay too much attention to one thing (e.g., individual words) and not enough attention to another aspect (e.g., the overall context), you may want to redistribute your attention. At any rate, you are in the driver's seat on your learning journey. Don't be a passive passenger, and keep trying!

USEFUL DAILY EXPRESSIONS

Pay attention to tone of voice, facial expressions and bodily movements. You will learn general greetings and expressions especially useful in classroom interactions. Bear in mind the vocal, emotional, and behavioral aspect of each expression or greeting. Practicing new expressions with these things in mind will help you learn better. Be theatrical!

"ACTIONS" segment and the "red tag" rule

This segment will give you abundant opportunities to listen and get accustomed to the sounds and flow of the language as well as to gain some recognition of words, commands and descriptions of actions in Japanese. During the course your teacher will be doing lots of talking and acting, sometimes while holding up a red tag. Concentrate, listen and observe while the red tag is up. Start responding and follow directions as soon as the tag is lowered.

KATAKANA:
You need this to spell
your name!

Japanese writing uses both kanji (Chinese characters) and kana (syllabaries). Japan started adopting kanji from China in order to equip itself with a system of writing around the 4th century. Two sets of kana letters were then created based on kanji: first came hiragana around the 8th and 9th centuries, followed by katakana. Katakana will be introduced in this section because it is used today primarily to write words adopted into Japanese from English and other foreign languages (except Chinese) as well as to spell the names of non-Japanese people and places.

ACTIVITY:
Get involved and enjoy the dynamics
of human interactions.

Activities not only drill you on what you have learned but also give you opportunities to get to know your classmates and teacher better while using new expressions.

STEP 1

DAILY EXPRESSIONS

ACTIONS

KATAKANA

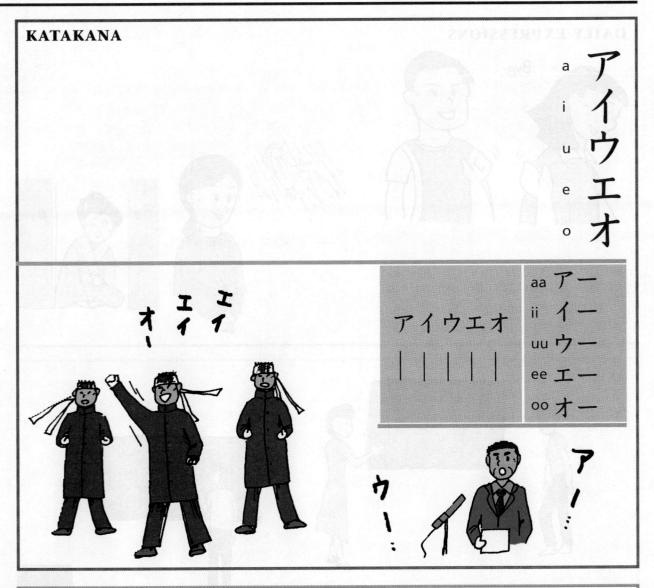

アイウエオ

a
i
u
e
o

aa	アー
ii	イー
uu	ウー
ee	エー
oo	オー

アイウエオ
｜｜｜｜｜

ACTIVITY

STEP 2

DAILY EXPRESSIONS

ACTIONS

KATAKANA

アイウエオ

ka	カ
ki	キ
ku	ク
ke	ケ
ko	コ

ga	ガ
gi	ギ
gu	グ
ge	ゲ
go	ゴ

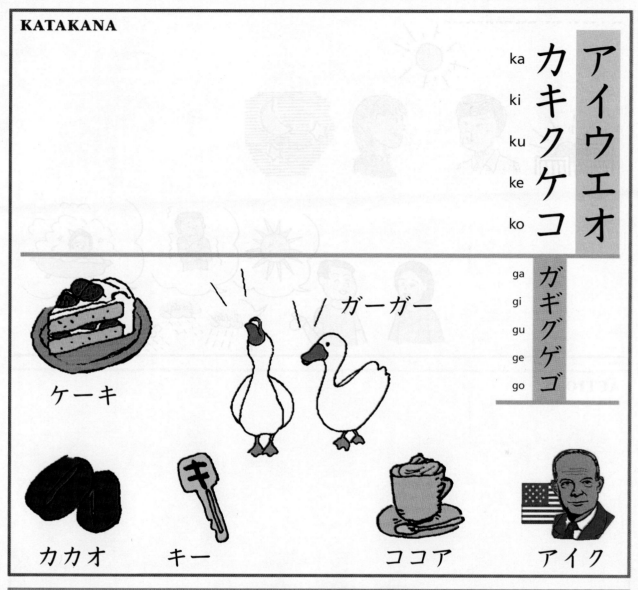

ガーガー

ケーキ

カカオ キー ココア アイク

ACTIVITY

11

STEP 3

DAILY EXPRESSIONS

ACTIONS

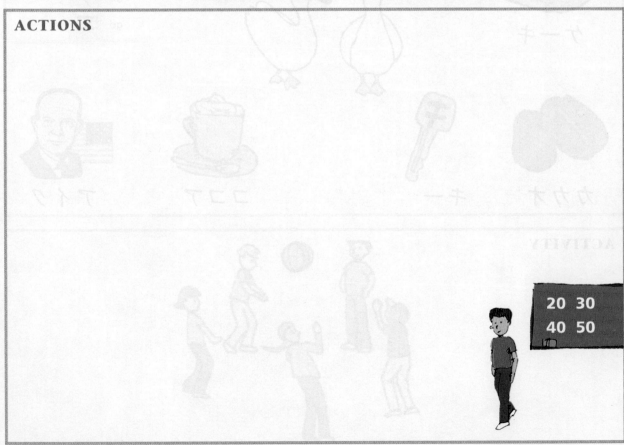

KATAKANA

アイウエオ
カキクケコ
サシスセソ
sa shi su se so

ガギグゲゴ
ザジズゼゾ
za ji zu ze zo

ソース

キス

スイス

サーカス

シカゴ (Illinois)

ソーセージ

ACTIVITY

シナリオ 1 (Scenario 1)

STEP 4

DAILY EXPRESSIONS

ACTIONS

KATAKANA

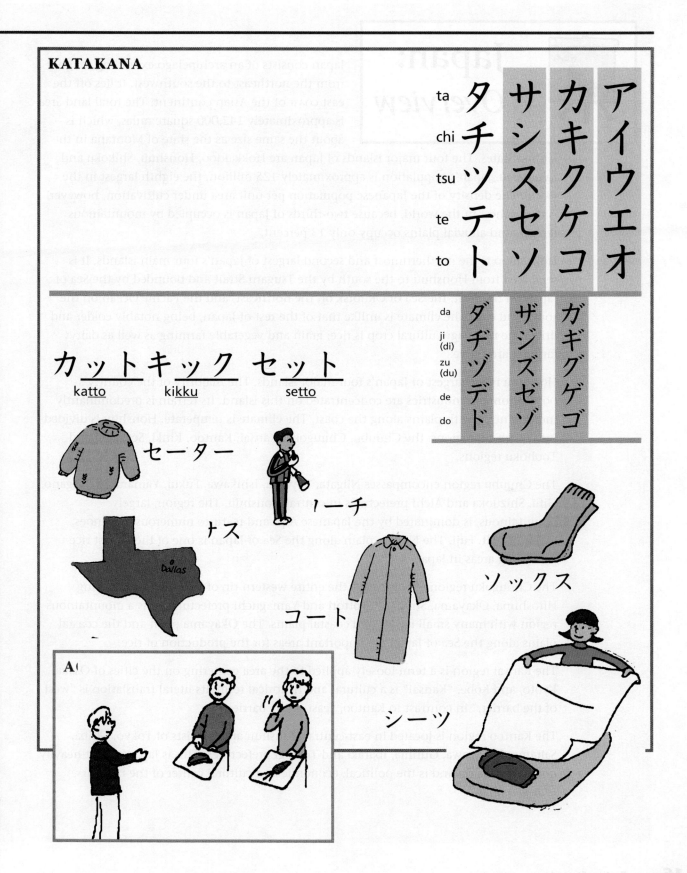

ta	タ	サ	カ	ア	
chi	チ	シ	キ	イ	
tsu	ツ	ス	ク	ウ	
te	テ	セ	ケ	エ	
to	ト	ソ	コ	オ	

da	ダ	ザ	ガ
ji (di)	ヂ	ジ	ギ
zu (du)	ヅ	ズ	グ
de	デ	ゼ	ゲ
do	ド	ゾ	ゴ

カット　キック　セット
katto　kikku　setto

セーター

ナス

ノーチ

ソックス

コート

シーツ

A(

Japan: Overview

Japan consists of an archipelago extending roughly from the northeast to the southwest. It lies off the east coast of the Asian continent. The total land area is approximately 142,000 square miles, which is about the same size as the state of Montana in the United States. The four major islands of Japan are Hokkaidoo, Honshuu, Shikoku and Kyuushuu. Japan's population is approximately 125 million, the eighth largest in the world. The density of the Japanese population per unit area under cultivation, however, is the highest in the world, because two-thirds of Japan is occupied by mountainous terrain, and alluvial plains occupy only 13 percent.

Hokkaidoo is the northernmost and second largest of Japan's four main islands. It is separated from Honshuu to the south by the Tsugaru Strait and bounded by the Sea of Japan on the west, the Sea of Okhotsk on the northeast, and the Pacific Ocean on the south and east. The climate is unlike that of the rest of Japan, being notably colder and drier. The main agricultural crop is rice; grain and vegetable farming as well as dairy farming are active.

Honshuu is the largest of Japan's four major islands. The majority of the country's population and industries are concentrated on this island. Its terrain is predominantly mountainous, with plains along the coast. The climate is temperate. Honshuu is divided into seven subregions: the Chuubu, Chuugoku, Kansai, Kantoo, Kinki, Setouchi and Toohoku regions.

The Chuubu region encompasses Niigata, Toyama, Ishikawa, Fukui, Yamanashi, Nagano, Gifu, Shizuoka and Aichi prefectures in central Honshuu. The region, largely mountainous, is dominated by the Japanese Alps and features numerous volcanoes, including Mt. Fuji. The Niigata plain along the Sea of Japan is one of the largest rice-producing areas in Japan.

The Chuugoku region encompasses the entire western tip of Honshuu, comprising Hiroshima, Okayama, Shimane, Tottori and Yamaguchi prefectures. It is a mountainous region with many small basins and coastal plains. The Okayama plain and the coastal plains along the Sea of Japan are important areas for the production of rice.

The Kansai region is a term loosely applied to the area centering on the cities of Osaka, Kyoto, and Kobe. "Kansai" is a cultural and historical term; its literal translation is "west of the barrier," in contrast to Kantoo, "east of the barrier."

The Kantoo region is located in east-central Honshuu and consists of Tokyo, Chiba, Saitama, Kanagawa, Gunma, Ibaraki and Tochigi prefectures. This is Japan's most heavily populated region and is the political, economic and cultural center of the nation.

The Kinki region, located in west-central Honshuu, consists of Osaka, Kyoto, Hyoogo, Shiga, Mie, Wakayama and Nara prefectures. It is the nation's second most important industrial region following the Kantoo region. The northern part of the region faces the Sea of Japan and is noted for its heavy snowfall.

The Setouchi region generally refers to the area that includes the southern part of the Chuugoku region facing the Inland Sea, the northern part of the Shikoku region, and the islands in the Inland Sea. It has placid seas and a mild climate, even in winter.

The Toohoku region encompasses the entire northern end of the island of Honshuu and consists of Aomori, Iwate, Akita, Yamagata, Miyagi and Fukushima prefectures. The region is largely mountainous, and the climate is highly seasonal, with short summers and long winters.

The Kyuushuu region consists of Kyuushuu, the third largest and southernmost of the four major islands of Japan and surrounding islands. The island of Kyuushuu comprise Fukuoka, Nagasaki, Oita, Kumamoto, Miyazaki, Saga and Kagoshima prefectures. Geographically divided into north, central, and south Kyuushuu, the region has a mountainous interior with numerous coastal plains, volcanoes and hot springs. The climate is subtropical, with heavy precipitation.

The Shikoku region is a region consisting of Shikoku, the smallest of Japan's four main islands and numerous surrounding islands. Shikoku lies to the south of western Honshuu, across the Inland Sea and across the Bungo Channel from northeastern Kyuushuu. It consists of Kagawa, Tokushima, Ehime and Kochi prefectures. Shikoku's high mountains and steep slopes severely limit agriculture, habitation and communication. The climate is subtropical, with short, mild winters and long, hot summers. On the Pacific Ocean side of the island there is heavy rainfall in the summer, and typhoons are frequent.

The Ryuukyuu Islands, in the broad sense, are a chain of islands extending southwest from Kyuushuu, usually called the Nansei Islands. The Ryuukyuu Islands encompass the main group of the Okinawa Islands and islands to the southwest, all of which are administered together as Okinawa Prefecture. These include the Miyako Islands and the Yaeyama Islands, which are often referred to together as the Sakishima Islands. The Ryuukyuu Islands are often struck by typhoons, and although rainfall is usually plentiful, they sometimes suffer from drought as well.

STEP 5

DAILY EXPRESSIONS

ACTIONS

KATAKANA

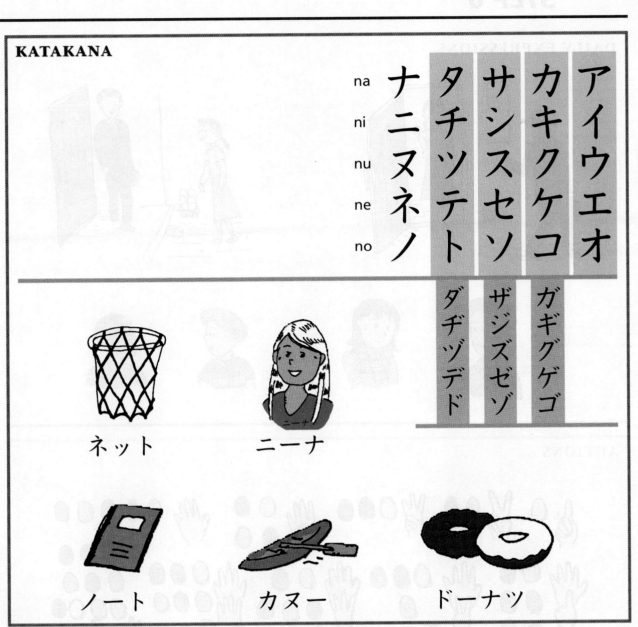

アイウエオ
カキクケコ
サシスセソ
タチツテト
ナニヌネノ

na
ni
nu
ne
no

ガギグゲゴ
ザジズゼゾ
ダヂヅデド

ネット　　　ニーナ

ノート　　　カヌー　　　ドーナツ

ACTIVITY

STEP 6

DAILY EXPRESSIONS

ACTIONS

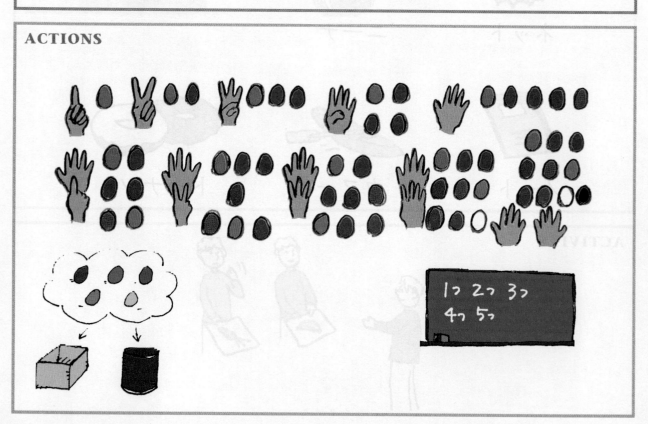

KATAKANA

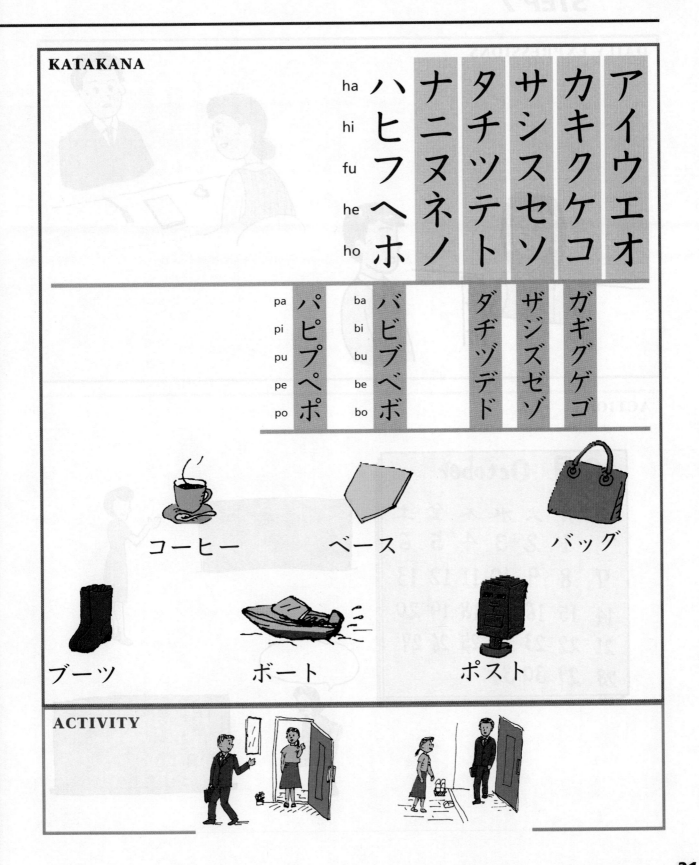

					ha	
ア	カ	サ	タ	ナ	ハ	ha
イ	キ	シ	チ	ニ	ヒ	hi
ウ	ク	ス	ツ	ヌ	フ	fu
エ	ケ	セ	テ	ネ	ヘ	he
オ	コ	ソ	ト	ノ	ホ	ho

	ガ	ザ	ダ	バ	ba	パ	pa
	ギ	ジ	ヂ	ビ	bi	ピ	pi
	グ	ズ	ヅ	ブ	bu	プ	pu
	ゲ	ゼ	デ	ベ	be	ペ	pe
	ゴ	ゾ	ド	ボ	bo	ポ	po

コーヒー

ベース

バッグ

ブーツ

ボート

ポスト

ACTIVITY

STEP 7

DAILY EXPRESSIONS

ACTIONS

KATAKANA

ma	マ	ハ	ナ	タ	サ	カ	ア
mi	ミ	ヒ	ニ	チ	シ	キ	イ
mu	ム	フ	ヌ	ツ	ス	ク	ウ
me	メ	ヘ	ネ	テ	セ	ケ	エ
mo	モ	ホ	ノ	ト	ソ	コ	オ

パ	バ	ダ	ザ	ガ
ピ	ビ	ヂ	ジ	ギ
プ	ブ	ヅ	ズ	グ
ペ	ベ	デ	ゼ	ゲ
ポ	ボ	ド	ゾ	ゴ

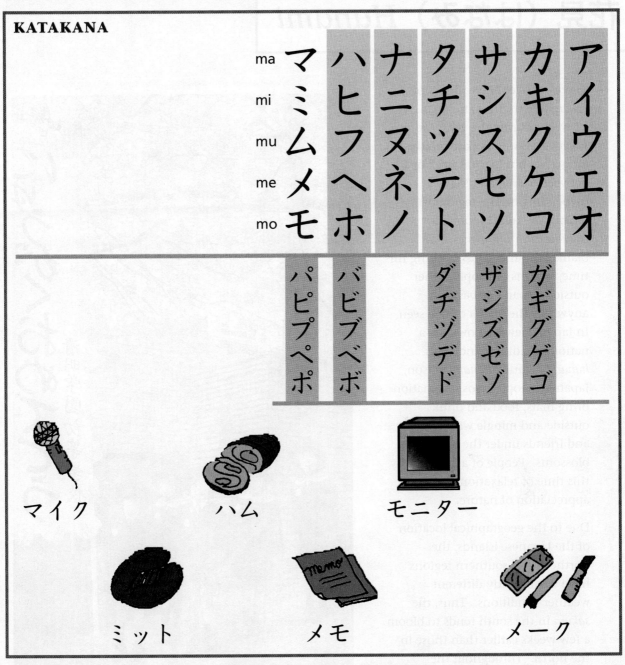

マイク　　　　　　ハム　　　　　　モニター

ミット　　　　　　メモ　　　　　　メーク

ACTIVITY

シナリオ　2 (Scenario 2)

23

花見（はなみ） *Hanami*

There are over 300 varieties of *sakura* (cherry trees) in Japan. For 51 weeks during the year, the *sakura* do not look particularly attractive, but for one week or so, between March and May (depending on the region of Japan), the trees bloom and transform into a spectacular blanket of pink petals. During this time, swarms of people gather outside in parks or basically anywhere the *sakura* can be seen. In Japan, viewing flowers is a national tradition known as *hanami*. During *hanami* season, Japanese people across the nation bring mats, food and drinks outside and mingle with family and friends under the cherry blossoms. People of all ages enjoy this time of relaxation and appreciation of nature.

Due to the geographical location of the Japanese islands, the northern and southern regions have significantly different weather conditions. Thus, the *sakura* in the south tends to bloom a few weeks earlier than those in the north. Throughout the country, though, cherry trees are considered Japan's national flower and a symbol of spring.

にゅうがくおめでとう

清明学園初等学校

The *hanami* season does not last very long, of course. Several days after the trees reach full bloom, the pink petals fall to the ground, carpeting the earth below. The brief *hanami* season symbolizes the fleeting nature of existence. The transient nature of the *sakura* has inspired Japanese poets for more than a thousand years. Kino Tomonori, a poet from the Heian period (794-1192 A.D.), wrote the following when he caught sight of pink *sakura* petals helplessly falling to the ground one spring morning.

ひさかたの　光のどけき　春の日に　しづこころなく　花の散るらむ

This perfectly still

Spring day bathed in soft light

From the open sky

Why do the cherry blossoms

So restlessly scatter down?

STEP 8

DAILY EXPRESSIONS

ACTIONS

KATAKANA

ya ヤ	マ	ハ	ナ	タ	サ	カ	ア
	ミ	ヒ	ニ	チ	シ	キ	イ
yu ユ	ム	フ	ヌ	ツ	ス	ク	ウ
	メ	ヘ	ネ	テ	セ	ケ	エ
yo ヨ	モ	ホ	ノ	ト	ソ	コ	オ

パ ピ プ ペ ポ	バ ビ ブ ベ ボ		ダ ヂ ヅ デ ド	ザ ジ ズ ゼ ゾ	ガ ギ グ ゲ ゴ

ヒャ hya / ヒュ hyu / ヒョ hyo	ニャ nya / ニュ nyu / ニョ nyo	チャ cha / チュ chu / チョ cho	シャ sha / シュ shu / ショ sho	キャ kya / キュ kyu / キョ kyo

ギャ gya
ギュ ju
ジュ

MONTHLY PLAN

	1	2	3	4	5
6	7	8	9	10	11	12
13	14	15	16	17	18	19
20	21	22	23	24	25	26
27	28	29	30			

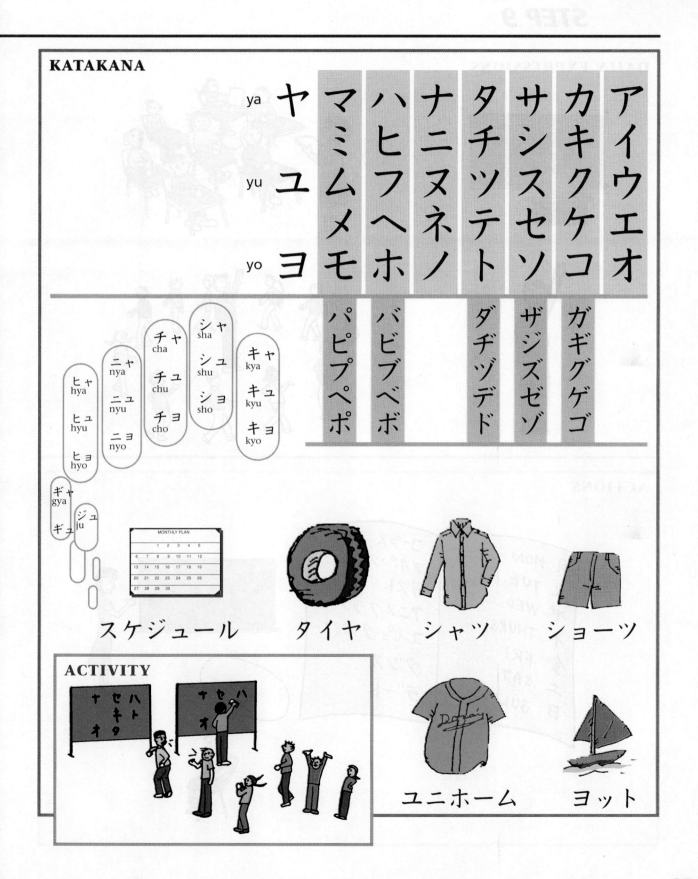

スケジュール　　　　タイヤ　　　　シャツ　　　　ショーツ

ユニホーム　　　ヨット

ACTIVITY

STEP 9

DAILY EXPRESSIONS

ACTIONS

KATAKANA

n ン	wa ワ	ra ラ	ヤ	マ	ハ	ナ	タ	サ	カ	ア
		ri リ		ミ	ヒ	ニ	チ	シ	キ	イ
		ru ル	ユ	ム	フ	ヌ	ツ	ス	ク	ウ
		re レ		メ	ヘ	ネ	テ	セ	ケ	エ
。 ヲ		ro ロ	ヨ	モ	ホ	ノ	ト	ソ	コ	オ

		パ	バ		ダ	ザ	ガ
		ピ	ビ		ヂ	ジ	ギ
		プ	ブ		ヅ	ズ	グ
		ペ	ベ		デ	ゼ	ゲ
		ポ	ボ		ド	ゾ	ゴ

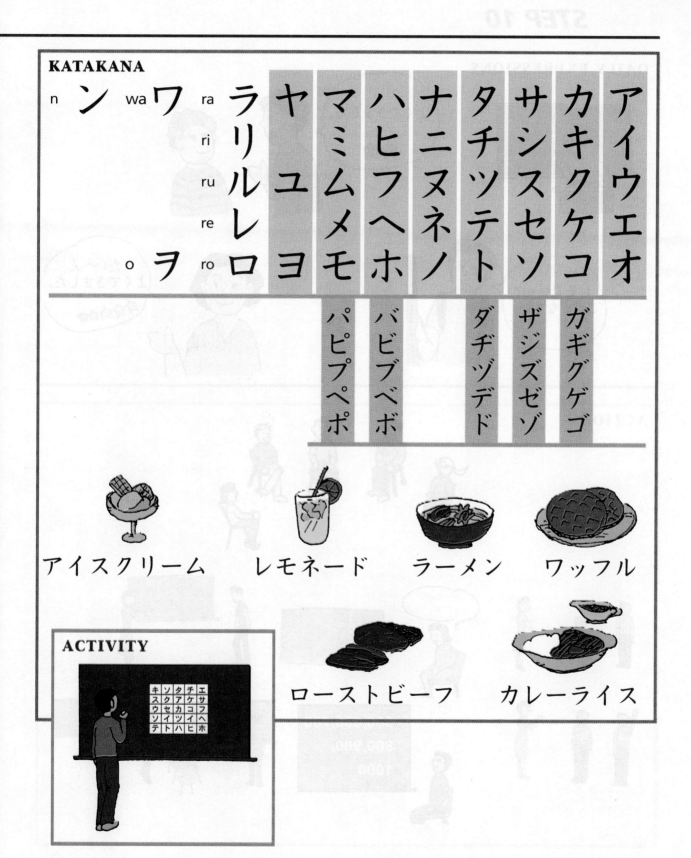

アイスクリーム　　レモネード　　ラーメン　　ワッフル

ローストビーフ　　カレーライス

ACTIVITY

29

STEP 10

DAILY EXPRESSIONS

ACTIONS

KATAKANA

ア		ヴァ ba	ファ fa					グァ gwa	クァ kwa	ア
イ		ヴィ bi	ウィ wi	フィ fi	ディ di	ティ ti				イ
ウ		ヴ bu								ウ
エ	イェ ye	ヴェ be	ウェ we	フェ fe	チェ che	ジェ je	シェ she		クェ kwe	エ
オ		ヴォ bo	ウォ wo	フォ fo					クォ kwo	オ
					デュ dyu					ユ

カフェ

フォーク

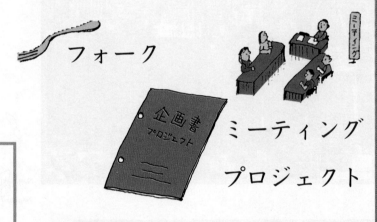

ミーティング

プロジェクト

ウィスコンシン

ミルウォーキー

キャンプファイアー

ACTIVITY

シナリオ　3

Colorful Japan

SEA OF JAPAN

Ishikawa • Toyama
Kanazawa • Toyama
Fukui
Fukui
Matsue • Tottori
Tottori
Gifu
Gifu
Shimane
Kyôto Shiga Nagoya
Okayama Hyôgo Kyôto Ôtsu Aichi
Hiroshima Okayama Kôbe Ôsaka Tsu
Yamaguchi Hiroshima Takamatsu Ôsaka Nara Mie
Yamaguchi Kagawa Nara
Fukuoka Matsuyama Tokushima Wakayama
Saga Fukuoka Ehime Tokushima Wakayama
Nagasaki Saga Ôita Kôchi
Ôita
Nagasaki Kumamoto Kôchi
Kumamoto Miyazaki
Kagoshima Miyazaki
Kagoshima

N

SEA OF OKHOTSK

Hokkaidô

•Sapporo

•Aomori
Aomori
Akita
•Akita   •Morioka
Iwate
amagata   Miyagi
•Yamagata   •Sendai
iigata
•Fukushima
Fukushima
Tochigi
•Utsunomiya   PACIFIC OCEAN
a   •Mito
itama   Ibaraki
rawa
kyô   •Tôkyô
ama•   •Chiba
nagawa   Chiba

kinawa

Naha

School Life

にゅうがくおめでとう
清明学園初等学校

1. **April:** The opening day of the new school year

2. Science class

3. Assembly

4. Regular class

5. Big sports tournaments

6. Big sports tournaments

7. Science fair

8. **October:** *Undookai* (Field Day)

9. **November:** *Bunkasai* (Culture Festival)

10. **December:** Ski trip

11. **February:** Interview practice for entrance exam

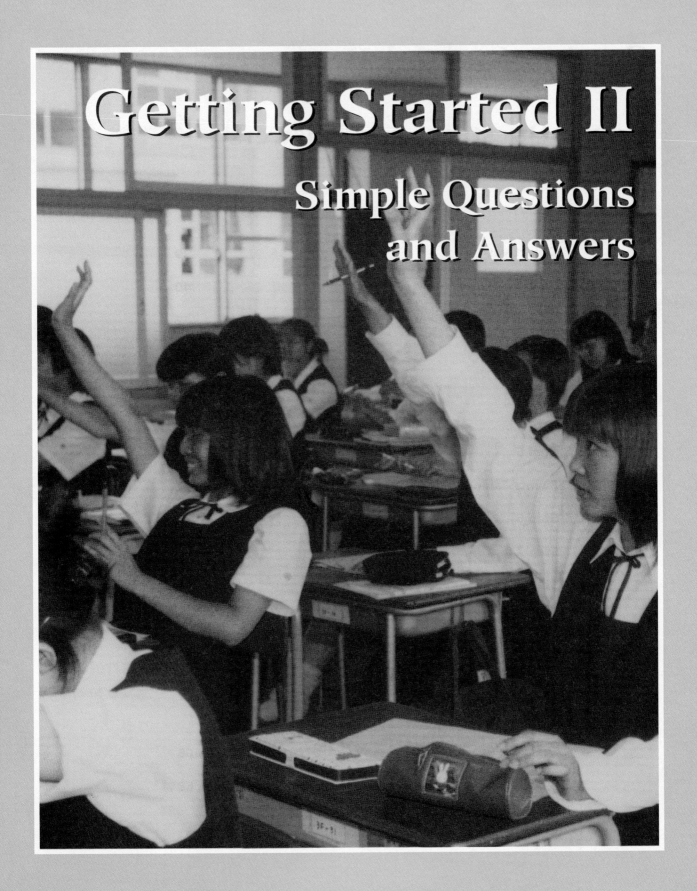

Getting Started II

Simple Questions
and Answers

Getting Started II

Simple Questions and Answers

OBJECTIVES

At the end of this section, you will be able to:

- handle a variety of Japanese simple questions and answers successfully
- better understand your teacher and classmates through interactive activities
- enhance your visualization skills
- express preferences
- construct and use mindmaps effectively to enhance your learning
- develop sets of useful categorical vocabulary

You will also learn:

- how to ask simple questions
- how to answer questions affirmatively
- how to describe colors, size and personalities
- about your own learning style
- about Japanese calligraphy, school subjects and Japanese events
- to recognize hiragana

Simple Questions and Answers

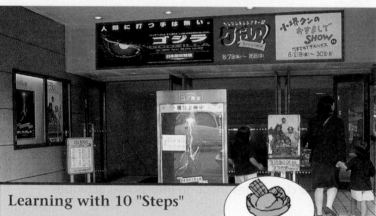

Learning with 10 "Steps"

This section includes ten "steps." Each step consists of the following four segments.

1. Simple Q and A

2. Mindmapping

3. Hiragana

4. Activity

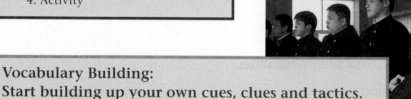

Vocabulary Building:
Start building up your own cues, clues and tactics.

The categories in the sample mindmaps have been selected with later chapters of this book in mind. Making your own maps of the same or similar categories and comparing them to those in the book will help you raise your conceptual awareness and lead to effective learning. Be aware that adding every word that appears in this section to your working vocabulary list is not the objective here. So free yourself from cramming mode. Focus on the larger picture, and see how you can start building up cues, clues and tactics that are useful in your own communication and learning. After all, research has shown that teenagers learn new words at an average rate of about 3,400 per year without even attempting to cram. This is, of course in their native language, but dealing with a foreign language may not be as different from this as you think.

Hiragana

Hiragana is the other Japanese syllabary. There are 46 characters in all, representing the same sounds in katakana.

波▶波▶波▶は

SIMPLE Q AND As:
Short and simple, but don't forget about contextualizing.

Q and As that are useful not only in everyday conversation but also in later chapters in this book. These question and answer sequences are all short and simple but can be used effectively in a wide variety of contexts.

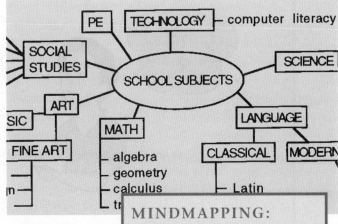

MINDMAPPING:
Increase your awareness of categories

Organizing isolated words by common categories, related notions or concepts will help you enhance your vocabulary.

HIRAGANA:
Appreciate the beauty of cursive writing

You will find that hiragana letters are roundish and contain many curvy strokes compared to their katakana equivalents, which are more square or angular in shape, with primarily linear strokes. This is because the former were derived from kanji written in cursive style, while the latter came from abbreviated kanji. Some hiragana letters are strikingly similar to their katakana counterparts, which means that they most likely originated from the same kanji.

The primary role of hiragana today is to write parts of sentences or words that are not written in kanji, either by nature or by convention. These include verb and adjective endings and some other grammatical elements. Children in Japan learn hiragana first and use it to write almost everything. However, it is gradually replaced by kanji as their literacy level increases.

ACTIVITY:
Take advantage of opportunities to put your creativity to use in interactions.

You will have plenty of opportunities to use the expressions introduced in this section. The activities and games here will also help you learn and retain katakana and hiragana characters as well as some other vocabulary items.

STEP 1

DAILY EXPRESSIONS

MINDMAPPING

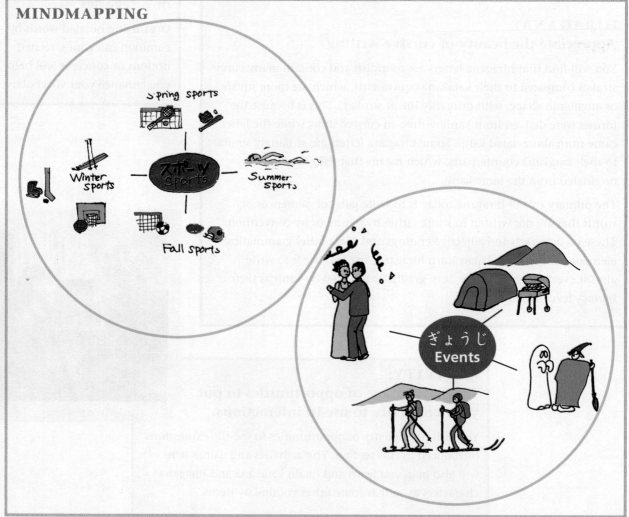

HIRAGANA

あいうえお

ア イ ウ エ オ

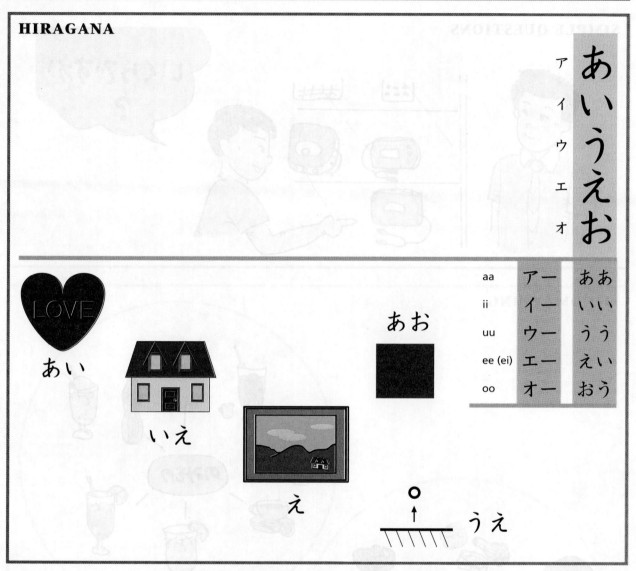

あー	aa
いー	ii
うー	uu
えー	ee (ei)
おー	oo

あ い う え お

あい

いえ

え

あお

うえ

KATAKANA REVIEW

パスタ

ピザ

チーズ

ACTIVITY

Spring sports

Winter sports

スポーツ Sports

Summer sports

Fall sports

STEP 2

SIMPLE QUESTIONS

MINDMAPPING

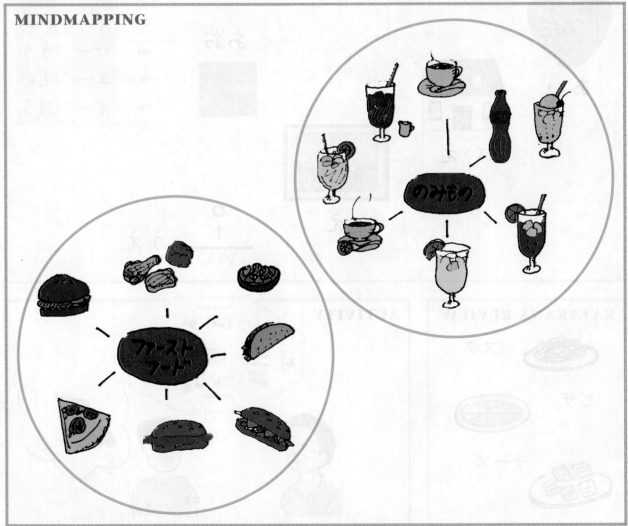

HIRAGANA

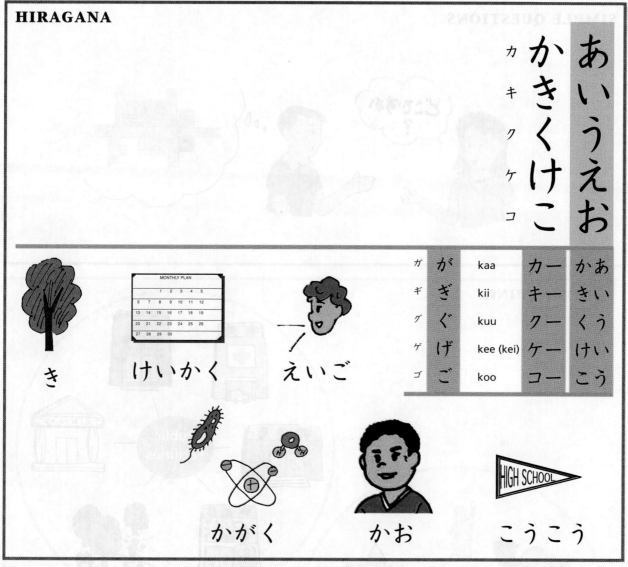

あいうえお

かきくけこ

カ キ ク ケ コ

		あ	カ		
ガ	が	あいうけこ	カーキークーケーコー	kaa	
ギ	ぎ	か	キ	kii	
グ	ぐ	き	ク	kuu	
ゲ	げ	う	ケ	kee (kei)	
ゴ	ご	け	コ	koo	

き

けいかく

えいご

MONTHLY PLAN

かがく

かお

こうこう

HIGH SCHOOL

KATAKANA REVIEW

ヘルメット
バット
ユニホーム
マスク
ミット
ボール
ホームベース

ACTIVITY

いくらですか？

STEP 3

SIMPLE QUESTIONS

MINDMAPPING

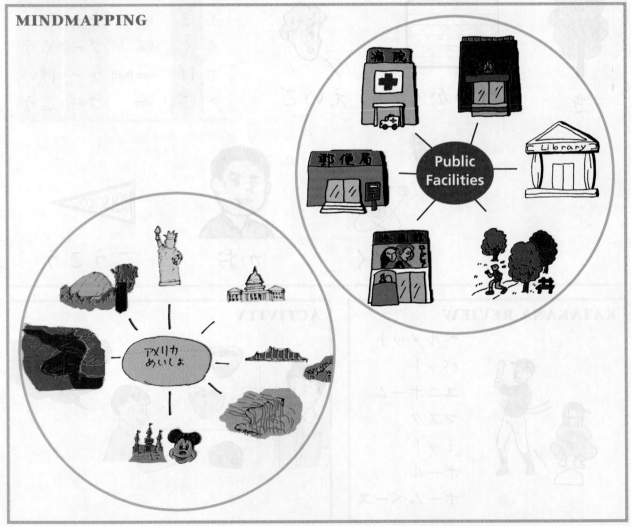

HIRAGANA

あいうえお
かきくけこ
さしすせそ
サ シ ス セ ソ

	saa	サー	さあ あ い う
	shii	シー	し す い う
	suu	スー	せ う
	see (sei)	セー	そ う
	soo	ソー	

ザ ジ ズ ゼ ゾ	が ぎ ぐ げ ご	ざ じ ず ぜ ぞ

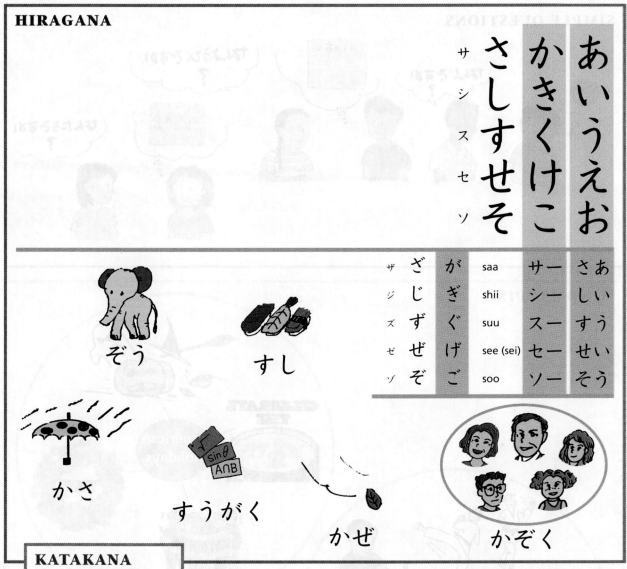

ぞう

すし

かさ

すうがく

かぜ

かぞく

KATAKANA REVIEW

① メーン
② ニューハンプシャー
③ ニューヨーク
④ コネチカット

ACTIVITY

どこですか？

STEP 4

SIMPLE QUESTIONS

MINDMAPPING

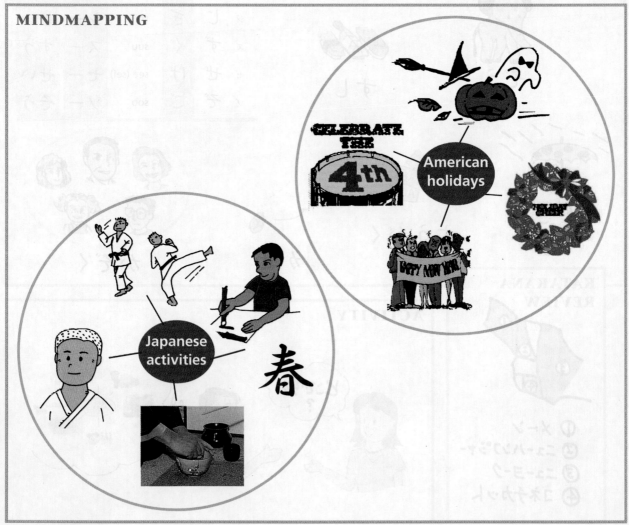

HIRAGANA

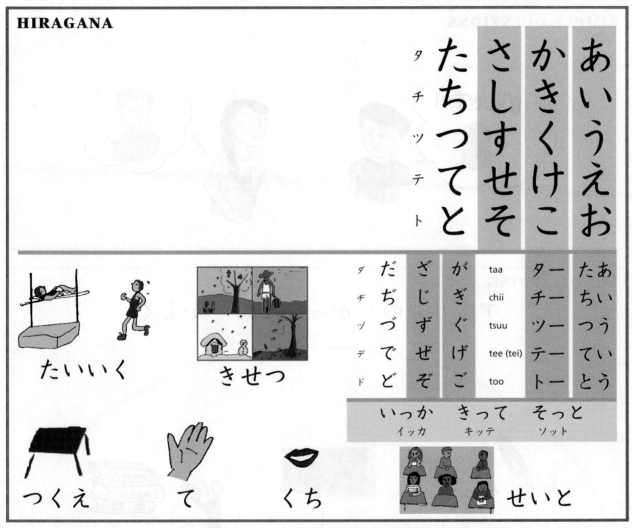

あいうえお
かきくけこ
さしすせそ
たちってと
タ チ ッ テ ト

		taa	ター	たあ
		chii	チー	ちい
		tsuu	ツー	つう
		tee (tei)	テー	てい
		too	トー	とう

がぎぐげご
ざじずぜぞ
だぢづでど
ダ ヂ ッ デ ド

| いっか | きって | そっと |
| イッカ | キッテ | ソット |

たいいく

きせつ

つくえ　　て　　くち　　せいと

KATAKANA REVIEW

アニメ

ビデオテープ

デジカメ

ACTIVITY

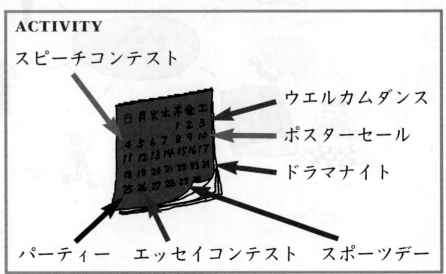

スピーチコンテスト

ウエルカムダンス

ポスターセール

ドラマナイト

パーティー　　エッセイコンテスト　　スポーツデー

STEP 5

SIMPLE QUESTIONS

MINDMAPPING

アメリカの　がっこうの　かもく

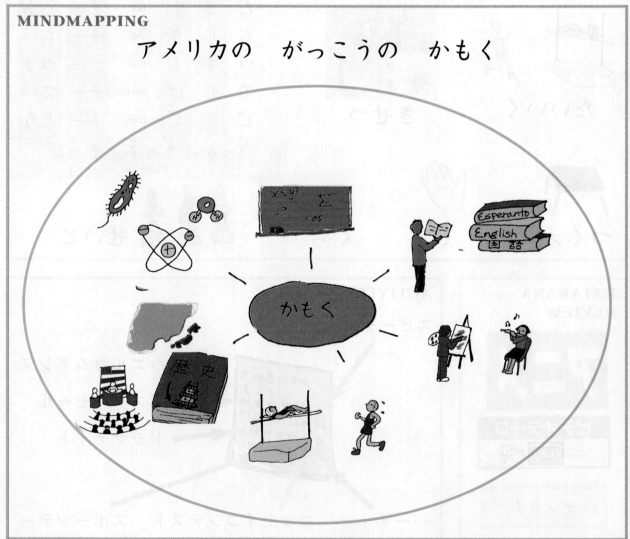

HIRAGANA

あいうえお
かきくけこ
さしすせそ
たちつてと
なにぬねの
ナニヌネノ

あいうえ おの	ナニヌネノー	naa nii nuu nee (nei) noo	がぎぐげご	ざじずぜぞ	だぢづでど
なにぬねの					

さかな

にく いぬ ねこ いのしし

KATAKANA REVIEW

だれですか。
ジョン・ケネディ
ヘレン・ケラー
マリリン・モンロー
ベーブ・ルース
ネルソン・マンデラ
パブロ・ピカソ

ACTIVITY

四季の行事と出来事(Events Calendar)

は

る

たうえ（6月）ちゃつみ（5月～6月） Rice planting (*taue*) is done mostly by machines these days. Tea-leaf picking (*chatsumi*) also takes place about this time.

ひなまつり（3月3日） The Doll Festival is observed on March 3 to celebrate girls. Dolls in ancient court costumes are displayed on a tier of shelves, and special meals and snacks are prepared.

こどものひ（5月5日） Children's Day, which originated from a holiday celebrating boys, is a national holiday. Special decorations include *koinobori*: carp streamers hoisted on a pole.

はなみ（4月） People gather around cherry trees talking, eating, dancing and appreciating the cherry blossoms, which come into full bloom in the beginning of April and start falling after only a week or so.

にゅうがくしき（4月） The Japanese school year begins in April. A special ceremony is held for entering students.

ゴールデンウィーク A stretch of time from the end of April to the beginning of May is known as "Golden Week" because it includes four national holidays.The weather is usualy pleasant around this time and many Japanese head for amusement parks, mountains and other attractions.

April 29	Greenery Day
May 3	Constitution Memorial Day
May 4	Additional holiday
May 5	Children's Day

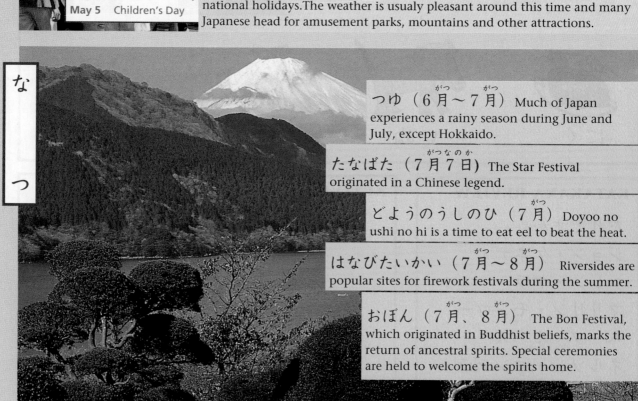

な

つ

つゆ（6月～7月） Much of Japan experiences a rainy season during June and July, except Hokkaido.

たなばた（7月7日） The Star Festival originated in a Chinese legend.

どようのうしのひ（7月） Doyoo no ushi no hi is a time to eat eel to beat the heat.

はなびたいかい（7月～8月） Riversides are popular sites for firework festivals during the summer.

おぼん（7月、8月） The Bon Festival, which originated in Buddhist beliefs, marks the return of ancestral spirits. Special ceremonies are held to welcome the spirits home.

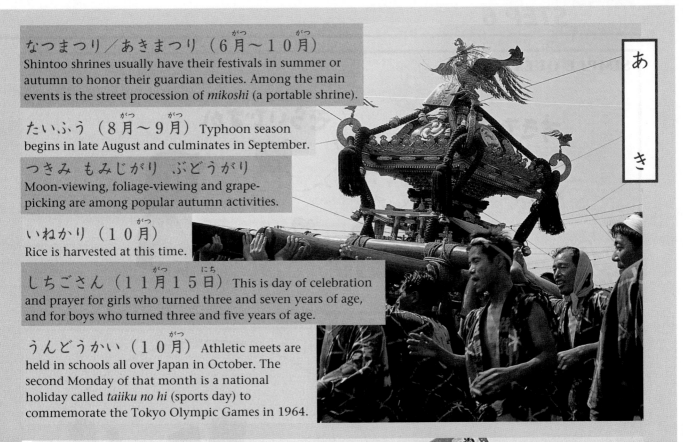

なつまつり／あきまつり（６月～１０月）
Shintoo shrines usually have their festivals in summer or autumn to honor their guardian deities. Among the main events is the street procession of *mikoshi* (a portable shrine).

たいふう（８月～９月） Typhoon season begins in late August and culminates in September.

つきみ もみじがり ぶどうがり
Moon-viewing, foliage-viewing and grape-picking are among popular autumn activities.

いねかり（１０月）
Rice is harvested at this time.

しちごさん（１１月１５日） This is day of celebration and prayer for girls who turned three and seven years of age, and for boys who turned three and five years of age.

うんどうかい（１０月） Athletic meets are held in schools all over Japan in October. The second Monday of that month is a national holiday called *taiiku no hi* (sports day) to commemorate the Tokyo Olympic Games in 1964.

あ

き

クリスマス Though the Christian population in Japan is less than 1 percent of the total, many Japanese have adopted the custom of exchanging Christmas presents.

せつぶん（２月３日）
A bean-throwing ceremony is observed on the evening of February 3. People scatter roasted beans while shouting "*Fuku wa uchi*" ("Luck, come in") and "*Oni wa soto*" ("Evil, go out")

しょうがつ（１月１日～３日）
The New Year is undoubtedly the most important holiday in Japan. It originated from a family custom of welcoming gods into the home, paying respect to ancestors and praying for a good harvest as a new year arrives. The New Year is celebrated with a variety of special events and activities.

ふ

ゆ

STEP 6

SIMPLE QUESTIONS

MINDMAPPING

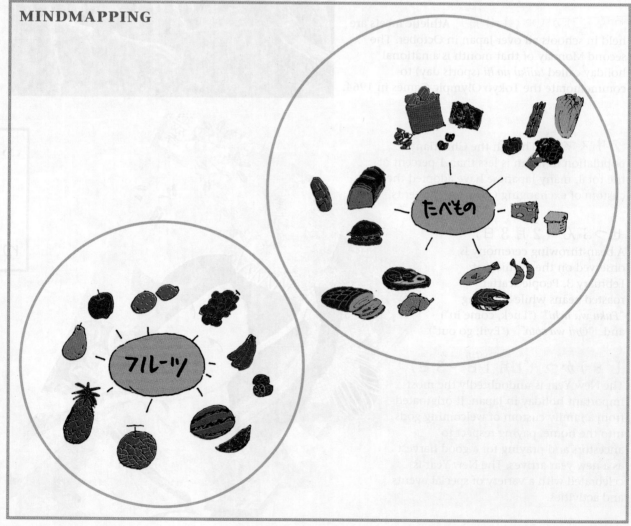

HIRAGANA

あいうえお
かきくけこ
さしすせそ
たちつてと
なにぬねの
はひふへほ
ハ ヒ フ ヘ ホ

				haa		あい
ぱ	ば	だ	ざ	が	ハー	あい
ピ	ビ	ヂ	ジ	ギ	ヒー	ひう
ぱ	び	ぢ	じ	ぎ	フー	ふう
ぴ	ぶ	づ	ず	ぐ	ヘー	へい
ぷ	べ	で	ぜ	げ	ホー	ほう
ぺ	ぼ	ど	ぞ	ご		
ぽ						

haa / hii / huu / hee (hei) / hoo

はな　　ひと　　ふね　　へび　　ほし

KATAKANA REVIEW

すきですか。
きらいですか。

ACTIVITY

アイスクリーム
アイスティー
ラーメン
コーラ
チキン
カレーライス
ハム
ワッフル
コーヒー

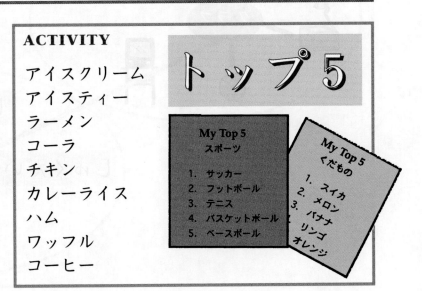

トップ5

My Top 5
スポーツ
1. サッカー
2. フットボール
3. テニス
4. バスケットボール
5. ベースボール

My Top 5
くだもの
1. スイカ
2. メロン
3. バナナ
　 リンゴ
　 オレンジ

STEP 7

SIMPLE QUESTIONS

MINDMAPPING

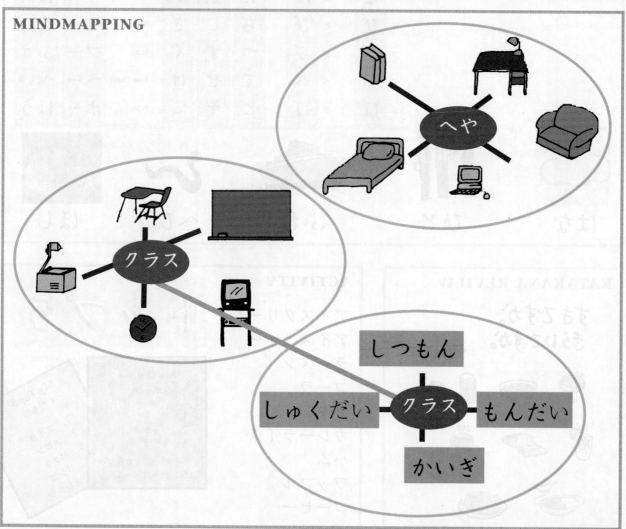

HIRAGANA

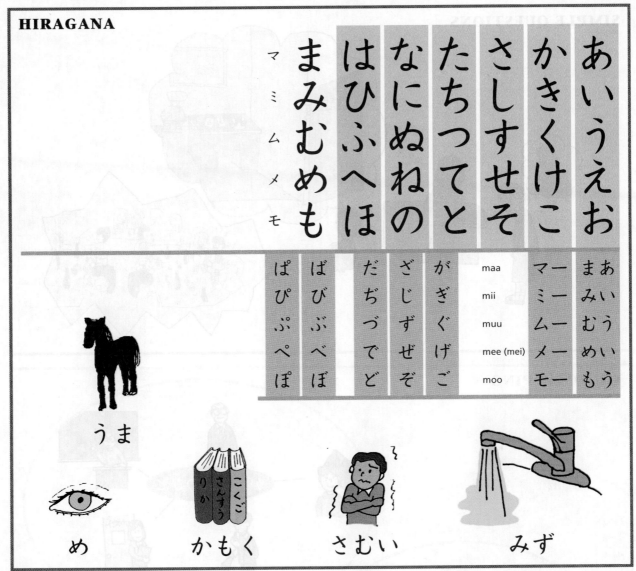

あ い う え お	か き く け こ	さ し す せ そ	た ち つ て と	な に ぬ ね の
は ひ ふ へ ほ	ま み む め も	マ ミ ム メ モ		

ぱ ぴ ぷ ぺ ぽ	ば び ぶ べ ぼ	だ ぢ づ で ど	ざ じ ず ぜ ぞ	が ぎ ぐ げ ご	maa mii muu mee (mei) moo	マー ミー ムー メー モー	まあ みい むう めい もう

うま

め

かもく

さむい

みず

KATAKANA REVIEW

コンピュータ
パソコン
モニター
ラップトップ
インターネット

ACTIVITY

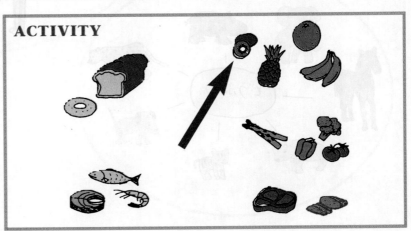

STEP 8

SIMPLE QUESTIONS

MINDMAPPING

HIRAGANA

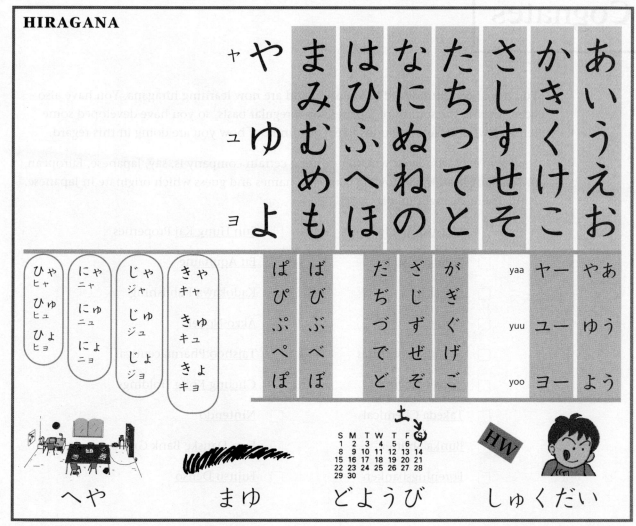

			あいうえお
			かきくけこ
			さしすせそ
			たちつてと
			なにぬねの
			はひふへほ
			まみむめも
ゃ			や
ゅ			ゆ
ョ			よ

きゃ キャ	じゃ ジャ	にゃ ニャ	ひゃ ヒャ
きゅ キュ	じゅ ジュ	にゅ ニュ	ひゅ ヒュ
きょ キョ	じょ ジョ	にょ ニョ	ひょ ヒョ

ぱぴぷぺぽ	ばびぶべぼ	だぢづでど	ざじずぜぞ	がぎぐげご	yaa ヤー やあ あ
					yuu ユー ゆう う
					yoo ヨー よう よ

へや　　　まゆ　　　どようび　　　しゅくだい

KATAKANA REVIEW

エアコン
プロレス
アメフト
カラオケ
リモコン
ポケベル
カーナビ

ACTIVITY

Cognates

You have been introduced to katakana and are now learning hiragana. You have also been hearing the sounds of Japanese on a regular basis, so you have developed some sense of what Japanese sounds like. Let's find out how you are doing in this regard.

Have you ever wondered whether or not a certain company is, say, Japanese, European, or Arabian? Read the following company names and guess which originate in Japanese. Hint: There are eight in all.

- ☐ <u>Matsushita</u> Electric
- ☐ <u>Treuhandstalt</u>
- ☐ <u>Hoechst</u>
- ☐ <u>Bradesco</u>
- ☐ <u>Nomura</u> Securities
- ☐ <u>Volker Stevin</u>
- ☐ <u>Takeda</u> Chemical
- ☐ <u>Bunka</u> Shutter
- ☐ <u>Foreningsbanken</u>

- ☐ <u>Sun Hung Kai</u> Properties
- ☐ <u>Elf Aquitaine</u>
- ☐ <u>Kadokawa</u> Publishing
- ☐ <u>Akzo Nobel</u>
- ☐ <u>Taishoo</u> Pharmaceutical
- ☐ <u>Cheung Kong</u> Holdings
- ☐ <u>Nintendo</u>
- ☐ <u>Den Danske</u> Bank Group
- ☐ <u>Fujitsu Denso</u>

Do you think some words commonly used in your native language are distinctively Japanese-sounding? If so, why do you think this is? They are certainly small in number, but some words in your English dictionary may be traced back to Japanese. Here are some of the dictionary definitions for words of such origin. Can you tell what they are?

1. An article of bedding consisting of a pad of tufted cotton batting or similar material, used on a floor or on a raised frame as a mattress or comforter. _____

2. Small cakes of cold cooked rice wrapped in seaweed, dressed with vinegar and topped or wrapped with slices of raw or cooked fish, egg or vegetables. _____

3. A long, wide-sleeved Japanese robe-like dress worn with an obi and often elaborately decorated. A loose robe worn chiefly by women.

    _____

4. A "sing-along" machine that plays background music for singing.

    _____

5. A Japanese lyric verse form having three unrhymed lines of five, seven, and five syllables, traditionally invoking an aspect of nature or the seasons. A poem written in this form. _____

6. A portable charcoal-burning brazier with a grill, used chiefly for cooking.

    _____

7. A very large ocean wave caused by an underwater earthquake or volcanic eruption. _____

STEP 9

SIMPLE QUESTIONS

やさしいせんせいは(wa)
だれですか。

すきないろは(wa)
なんですか。

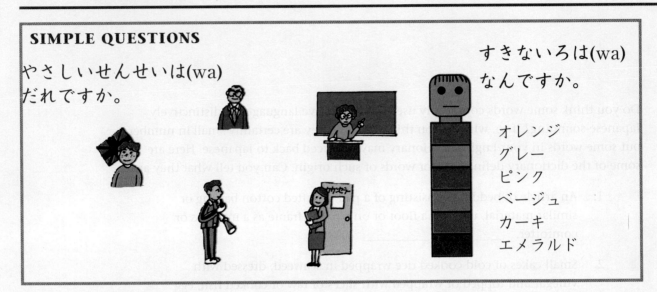

オレンジ
グレー
ピンク
ベージュ
カーキ
エメラルド

MINDMAPPING

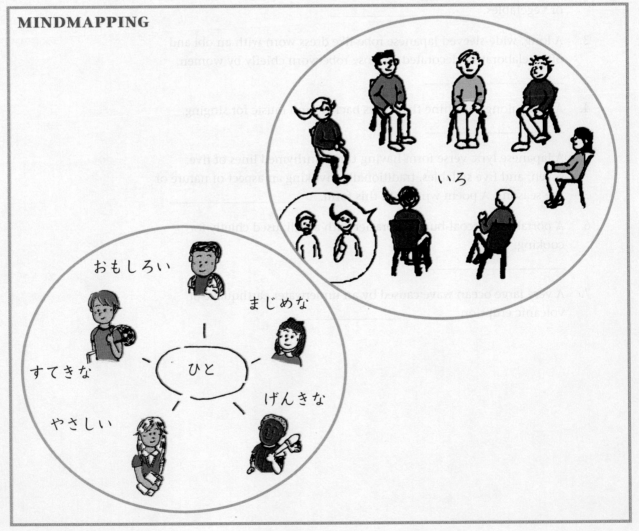

いろ

おもしろい
まじめな
すてきな
ひと
やさしい
げんきな

HIRAGANA

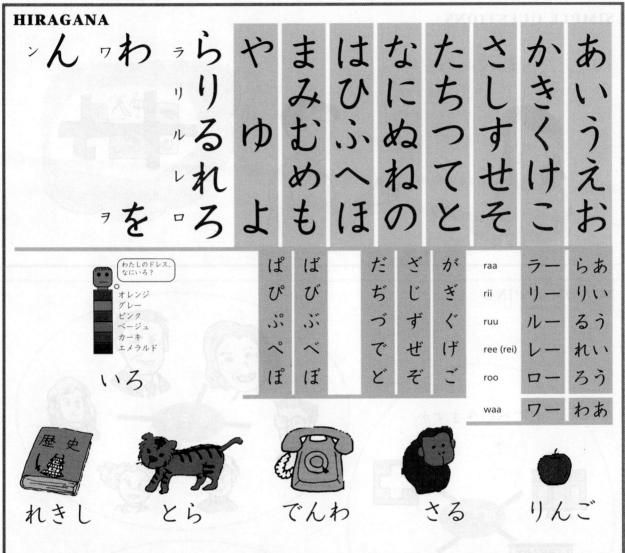

										ん	ワ わ		ら	
や	ま	は	な	た	さ	か	あ		ン	ラ り			
	み	ひ	に	ち	し	き	い			リ る			
ゆ	む	ふ	ぬ	つ	す	く	う			ル れ			
	め	へ	ね	て	せ	け	え			レ ろ			
よ	も	ほ	の	と	そ	こ	お		ヲ を	ロ			

ぱ	ば		だ	ざ	が	raa	ラー	らあ
ぴ	び		ぢ	じ	ぎ	rii	リー	りい
ぷ	ぶ		づ	ず	ぐ	ruu	ルー	るう
ぺ	べ		で	ぜ	げ	ree (rei)	レー	れい
ぽ	ぼ		ど	ぞ	ご	roo	ロー	ろう
						waa	ワー	わあ

わたしのドレス、なにいろ？

オレンジ
グレー
ピンク
ベージュ
カーキ
エメラルド

いろ

れきし　　　とら　　　でんわ　　　さる　　　りんご

KATAKANA REVIEW

わたしのドレス、なにいろ？

オレンジ
グレー
ピンク
ベージュ
カーキ
エメラルド

ACTIVITY

まじめな

げんきな

やさしい

すてきな

STEP 10

SIMPLE QUESTIONS

MINDMAPPING

HIRAGANA

TUESDAY ・

かようび　おおきい　ちいさい

わ ら や ま は な た さ か あ
　 り ゆ み ひ に ち し き い
　 る よ む ふ ぬ つ す く う
　 れ 　 め へ ね て せ け え
　 ろ よ も ほ の と そ こ お

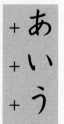

+ あ
+ い
+ う
+ い (1)
+ う (2)

(1) え (e) is used in a few words.
　 Ex. おねえさん（ネー）(older sister)
(2) お (o) is used in a few words.
　 Ex. とおか（オー）(the tenth day of
　 the month)

おかあさん　おとうさん　おねえさん　おにいさん

ACTIVITY

ああ（アー）いい（イー）うう（ウー）えい（エー）おう（オー）
かあ（カー）きい（キー）くう（クー）けい（ケー）こう（コー）
さあ（サー）しい（シー）すう（スー）せい（セー）そう（ソー）
たあ（ターー）ちい（チー）つう（ツー）てい（テー）とう（トー）
なあ（ナー）にい（ニー）ぬう（ヌー）ねい（ネー）のう（ノー）
はあ（ハー）ひい（ヒー）ふう（ラー）へい（ヘー）ほう（ホー）
まあ（マー）みい（ミー）むう（ムー）めい（メー）もう（モー）
やあ（ヤー）ゆう（ユー）よう（ヨー）
らあ（ラー）りい（リー）るう（ルー）れい（レー）ろう（ロー）
わあ（ワー）

KATAKANA REVIEW

トラベルゲーム

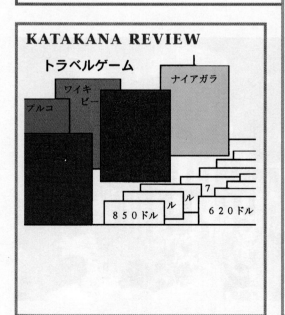

ナイアガラ
ワイキキ
ビー
プルコ

８５０ドル　ル　ル　７　６２０ドル

Seasonal Events

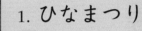

1. ひなまつり
2. たうえ
3. こどものひ
4. ゴールデンウィーク
5. つゆ
6. たなばた
7. はなび
8. おぼん

1. まつり
2. しちごさん
3. たいふう
4. うんどうかい
5. もちつき
6. じょやのかね
7. しょうがつ
8. せつぶん

A Day in the Life of High School Students in Japan

1. しんぶんはいたつ
2. しゅくだい
3. ゲームセンター
4. けいたい
5. インターネット
6. カラオケ

1. アルバイト
2. じはんき
3. リサーチ
4. まんが
5. ファーストフード
6. がっこう/じゅく

Unit 1:
Encounter

"Encounter." Don't be misguided by the not-so-peaceful nuance of this English word. In fact its Japanese equivalent, であい (*deai*), literally means "come forward and meet" and implies nothing hostile or difficult. On the contrary, to many Japanese this word carries the connotation of anticipation, hope, and even nostalgia. After all, when one looks back on one's life, it is possible to recount at least a few *deai* that have had a significant impact on the way things have turned out. The often accidental and often incidental nature of *deai* makes such an occurrence all the more precious. All in all, *deai* may be one of the most fascinating aspect, of human life.

The two chapters in this unit revolve around *deai*. In Chapter 1 you will be right in the middle of *deai*, experiencing them firsthand. In Chapter 2, on the other hand, you will be facilitating *deai* for others. By the way, we hope your *deai* with Kisetsu will turn out to be a fruitful and memorable one.

Chapter 1

Meeting Someone for the First Time

Chapter 1

Meeting Someone for the First Time

1.1 Introduction

OBJECTIVES

At the end of this chapter, you will be able to:

- exchange basic personal information with others

- understand and appreciate the mindset and feelings associated with a first meeting

- confirm information by repeating part of what was said and having the person who said it repeat it fully

- use guessing to enhance your communication

- read and write a New Year greeting card in Japanese

- count up to 10,000 and express ages and days of the year

You will also learn:

- how to affirm or deny information given to you

- how to connect two nouns with the particle *no*

- how to establish a topic with the particle *wa*

- how to use different modes of speech

- how to say your telephone number and grade

- how to develop conversation with *ja*

- how to write kana

- about the Japanese school system the Japanese New Year, and the zodiac year

Meeting Someone for the First Time

Meeting someone for the first time: How do the Japanese do it?

Whether in Japan or America, almost all first meetings begin with greeting and introducing one another according to customs widely accepted and practiced in the culture. For example, the act of shaking hands, making eye contact, and introducing yourself by saying "Nice to meet you" is a common custom in America. In Getting Started I you have had some exposure to Japanese greetings. Let's extend this topic and deal with a wide range of Japanese customs for greeting. This includes engaging in small talk and exchanging basic personal information. Learning about these customs will further expand your cross-cultural understanding.

Need a cure for "choppy" conversation? Knowing how to use "*ja*" may help.

When you are having a light social conversation with someone, you do not want to prolong it unnecessarily, but you do not want to end it too abruptly either. The use of "*ja*" enables you to further extend or develop a new thread of conversation without a jarring transition or an awkward silence. Let's master "*ja*" and become engaging speakers.

Exchanging telephone numbers:
Equip yourself with helpful strategies!

Do you often verbally exchange telephone numbers with people? Are you good at catching and remembering those numbers? What if you cannot keep pace with the rapid speech of a person giving you her number? You can safely assume that Japanese people are not immune to all the difficulties associated with exchanging information like phone numbers and that they may use certain strategic formulas to overcome such difficulties. "Partial repeating" and "confirming with *desu ne*" are among the useful strategies you will learn in this regard.

Nengajoo (New Year Greeting Cards):
Reading and writing simple messages

Exchanging *nengajoo* in Japan is similar to exchanging Christmas, Hanukkah and Kwanza cards in the United States, even though *nengajoo* have less religious meaning than their American counterparts, and people usually receive their cards on the first day of the new year. In this chapter you will learn to read and write *nengajoo*. You will see that the Japanese writing system can go either from left to right or from top to bottom, and you will also pick up some important information related to Japanese New Year's, such as *eto* (the twelve signs of the Chinese zodiac).

Dollars vs. yen:
Let's see if you can make a quick calculation for conversion

Many of you may already know that the currency unit used by the Japanese is the yen (*en* in Japanese). After all, the media often referred to Japan as "the land of the rising yen" during Japan's economic boom in the 1980s. What is the value of yen versus the dollar, anyway? Actually, the exchange rates "float" in currency markets and may change daily. During the last two decades of the 20th century, one dollar could buy as little as 78 yen at one time and more than 250 yen at another. Despite the volatility of the rates, you need to know how to convert back and forth and keep a rough idea in your mind of the current ones.

WARM-UP

これはなんですか？ *What is this?*
(Try to guess. The answers are on page [464].)

1. **When you meet Japanese people, can you determine their age? If the person is older than you, how do you say "good morning"? You have already learned that "good morning" is** 「おはようございます。」 **"ohayoo gozaimasu." Now let's practice guessing people's ages. Choose the answer that fits the picture above it.**

1.
☐ older than you
☐ younger than you
☐ same age
☐ cannot tell

2.
☐ older than you
☐ younger than you
☐ same age
☐ cannot tell

3.
☐ older than you
☐ younger than you
☐ same age
☐ cannot tell

4.
☐ older than you
☐ younger than you
☐ same age
☐ cannot tell

2. **The katakana flash cards below are covered by colored Post-Its™. Can you recognize what the katakana cards say? Fill in the blanks with the appropriate katakana character.**

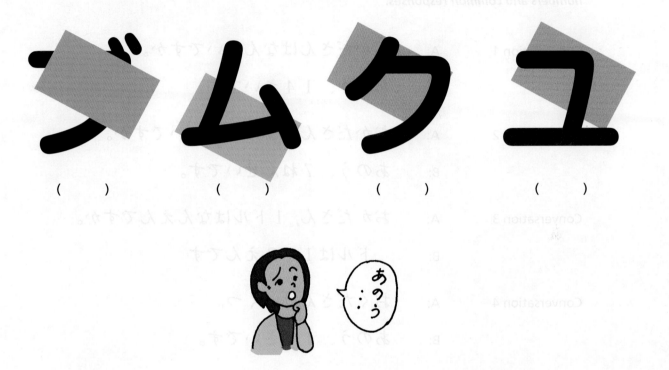

ゴ　ム　ク　ユ

(　　　)　　　(　　　)　　　(　　　)　　　(　　　)

3. **The shopping list below was painted over by your brother. Do you recognize which items are on the list? Fill in the blanks with the missing katakana characters.**

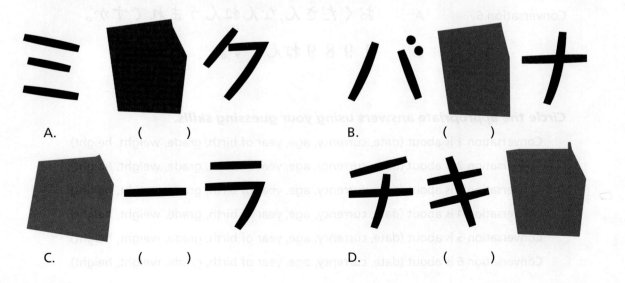

ミ　ク　バ　ナ

A.　　(　　　)　　　　　　B.　　(　　　)

ー　ラ　チ　キ

C.　　(　　　)　　　　　　D.　　(　　　)

4. *You have not yet studied the following conversations. (You will study them later in this chapter.) Try to guess what they are about using what you understand, such as numbers and common responses.*

Conversation 1   A: おかださんはなんさいですか。

B: あのう、１４さいです。

Conversation 2   A: おかださんはなんねんせいですか。

B: あのう、７ねんせいです。

Conversation 3   A: おかださん，１ドルはなんえんですか。

B: ドルは１１２えんです

Conversation 4   A: おくださんはいくつ。

B: あのう、１６さいです。

Conversation 5   A: おくださんのがくねんは。

B: あのう、１１ねんせいです。

Conversation 6   A: おくださん，なんねんうまれですか。

B: １９８９ねんです。

Circle the appropriate answers using your guessing skills.

Conversation 1 is about (date, currency, age, year of birth, grade, weight, height).
Conversation 2 is about (date, currency, age, year of birth, grade, weight, height).
Conversation 3 is about (date, currency, age, year of birth, grade, weight, height).
Conversation 4 is about (date, currency, age, year of birth, grade, weight, height).
Conversation 5 is about (date, currency, age, year of birth, grade, weight, height).
Conversation 6 is about (date, currency, age, year of birth, grade, weight, height).

BASIC VOCABULARY

はじめまして。
どうぞ　よろしく
おねがいします。

はい、ありがとうございます。

はい、どうぞ。

いいえ、けっこうです。

おげんきですか。

はい、ありがとうございます。

さようなら。

さようなら。

でんわ　　　　　でんわばんごう　　　　でんわばんごう

0〜20

0	れい、ゼロ
1	いち
2	に
3	さん
4	し、よん
5	ご
6	ろく
7	しち、なな
8	はち
9	きゅう、く
10	じゅう

11	じゅういち
12	じゅうに
13	じゅうさん
14	じゅうし、じゅうよん
15	じゅうご
16	じゅうろく
17	じゅうしち、じゅうなな
18	じゅうはち
19	じゅうきゅう、じゅうく
20	にじゅう

12ねんせい	こうこう	こうこう 3ねんせい
11ねんせい		こうこう 2ねんせい
10ねんせい		こうこう 1ねんせい
9ねんせい	ちゅうがっこう	ちゅうがく 3ねんせい
8ねんせい		ちゅうがく 2ねんせい
7ねんせい		ちゅうがく 1ねんせい
6ねんせい	しょうがっこう	しょうがく 6ねんせい
5ねんせい		しょうがく 5ねんせい
4ねんせい		しょうがく 4ねんせい
3ねんせい		しょうがく 3ねんせい
2ねんせい		しょうがく 2ねんせい
1ねんせい		しょうがく 1ねんせい

アメリカ
-grader

がっこう
SCHOOL

にほん
-grader

9ねんせい
ちゅうがく
3ねんせい

6ねんせい
しょうがく
6ねんせい

11ねんせい
こうこう
2ねんせい

3ねんせい
しょうがく
3ねんせい

20～99

にじゅう	20
にじゅういち	21
にじゅうに	22
にじゅうさん	23
にじゅうし、にじゅうよん	24
にじゅうご	25
にじゅうろく	26
にじゅうしち、にじゅうなな	27
にじゅうはち	28
にじゅうきゅう、にじゅうく	29
さんじゅう	30
よんじゅう	40
ごじゅう	50
ろくじゅう	60
しちじゅう、ななじゅう	70
はちじゅう	80
きゅうじゅう	90
きゅうじゅうきゅう、きゅうじゅうく	99

100～1000

ひゃく	100
にひゃく	200
さんびゃく	300
よんひゃく	400
ごひゃく	500
ろっぴゃく	600
ななひゃく	700
はっぴゃく	800
きゅうひゃく	900
せん	1,000

Calendar Years

なんねん
うまれですか。

せんはっぴゃくろくじゅうはちねん	1868ねん
せんきゅうひゃくよんじゅうごねん	1945ねん
せんきゅうひゃくきゅうじゅうきゅうねん	1999ねん
にせんねん	2000ねん
にせんいちねん	2001ねん
にせんひゃくじゅういちねん	2111ねん

つだうめこ
1864ねんうまれ

おざわせいじ
1935ねんうまれ

てづかおさむ
1928ねんうまれ

MECHANICS

5. *Circle the greeting that corresponds to the picture.*

1.
こんにちは　おはよう　こんばんは

2.
こんにちは　おはよう　こんばんは

3.
こんにちは　おはよう　こんばんは

6. **Fill in the blanks with the number of the greeting that corresponds to the picture.**

　（　　）　　　　（　　）　　　　（　　）　　　　（　　）

1. さようなら。
2. おげんきですか。
3. どうぞ。はい、ありがとうございます。
4. いいえ、けっこうです。
5. いいてんきですね。

7. **Fill in the blanks with the letter of the sport that corresponds to the picture.**

A. いち
B. ご
C. きゅう
D. じゅういち
E. ろく

1. （　　）　2. （　　）　3. （　　）

4. （　　）　5. （　　）

8. **Let's make mindmaps. Mindmapping can help you learn new information by organizing it with visual images.**

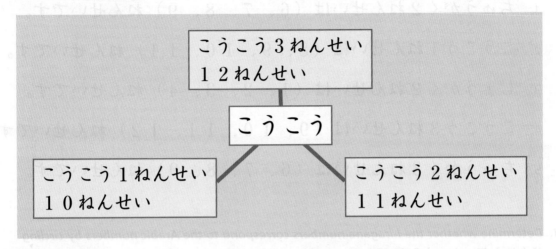

9. **Practice making mindmaps of school levels and grade levels with your partner.**

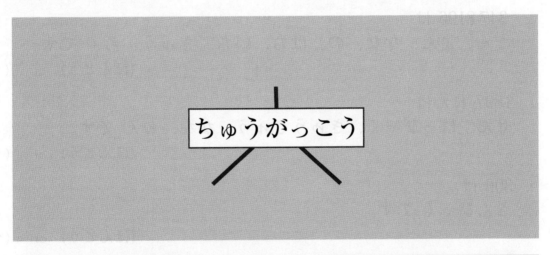

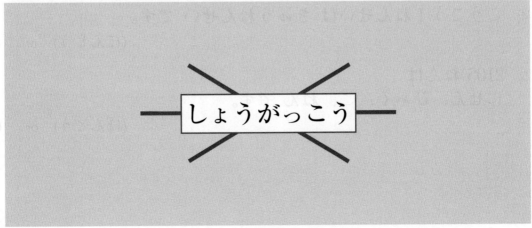

MECHANICS (continued)

10. *Circle the number that correctly completes each sentence below.*

1. ちゅうがく２ねんせいは（６、７、８、９）ねんせいです。

2. こうこう１ねんせいは（８、９、１０、１１）ねんせいです。

3. しょうがく２ねんせいは（１、２、３、４）ねんせいです。

4. こうこう３ねんせいは（９、１０、１１、１２）ねんせいです。

5. ちゅうがく３ねんせいは（６、７、８、９）ねんせいです。

11. *Determine whether the hiragana numbers correspond to the Arabic numbers by circling* ほんとう *(True) or* うそ *(False).*

1. 347-8196 は
   さん、よん、なな、の、はち、いち、きゅう、ろく です。

   （ほんとう） or （うそ）

2. 1897 ねんは
   せん、はっぴゃく、きゅうじゅう、なな、ねん です。

   （ほんとう） or （うそ）

3. 300 は
   さんひゃく です。

   （ほんとう） or （うそ）

4. こうこう１ねんせいは きゅうねんせい です。

   （ほんとう） or （うそ）

5. 2105 ねんは
   にせん、ひゃく、ご、ねん です。

   （ほんとう） or （うそ）

SONGS

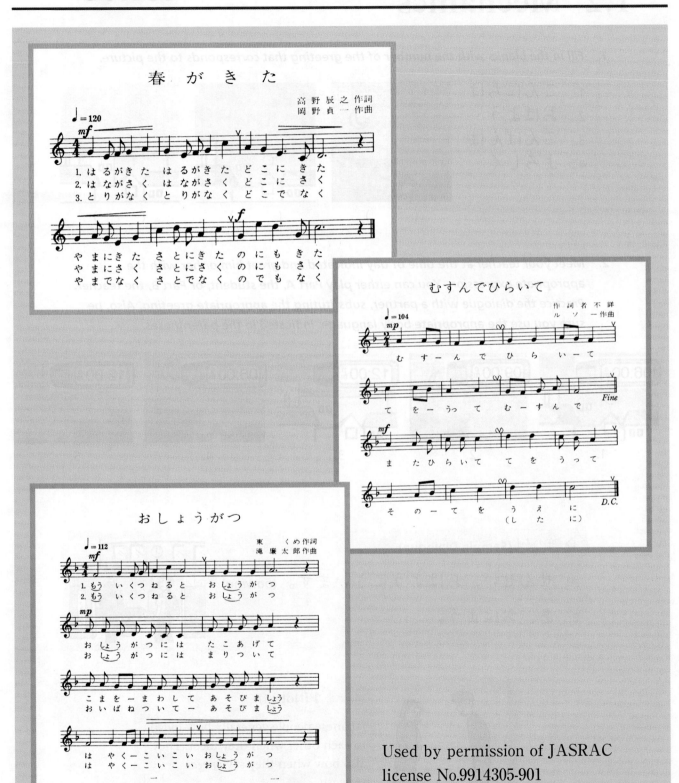

1.2 Mechanics

1. **Fill in the blanks with the number of the greeting that corresponds to the picture.**

1. こんにちは
2. おはよう
3. こんばんは
4. よろしく

(　　) 　　(　　) 　　(　　)

2. **Meet your teacher at the time of day indicated and greet him or her with the appropriate expression. You can either play Part A, the student, or Part B, the teacher. Practice the dialogue with a partner, substituting the appropriate greeting. Also, be sure you use the appropriate body language, indicated in the parentheses.**

1. 　　　　2. 　　　　3. 　　　　4. 　　　　5.

会話の例 (Sample Dialogue)

A: せんせい、おはようございます。(bowing)

B: あ、おはよう。

ノート**1 (Note 1):**

Japanese people generally bow (*ojigi*) to each other when they meet. They also bow when they say *onegai shimasu*.

3. **Exchange greetings with the following people. Their ages are given in parentheses and you should adjust your greeting expressions as well as your body language accordingly. You can either play Part A, the questioner, or Part B, the person who is pictured.**

かとう ゆみ (7)　　すずき よしお (50)　　たなか さちこ (17)　　かとう あみ (17)　　ほし まさこ (24)

会話の例 (Sample Dialogue)

A: <u>おはよう</u>。(*bowing*)

B: <u>おはようございます</u>。(*bowing more deeply than A*)

4. **Introduce yourself and say your name during your first encounter with someone. You can either play Part A, the questioner, or Part B, the person who answers. Practice the sample dialogue with a partner, substituting the person's name. Be sure you also use the appropriate body language, indicated in the parentheses.**

会話の例 (Sample Dialogue)

A: はじめまして、＿＿＿＿＿ です。
どうぞよろしく。(*bowing*)

B: はじめまして、＿＿＿＿＿ です。
どうぞよろしく。(*bowing*)

or　(*more politely*)

B: はじめまして、＿＿＿＿＿ です。
どうぞよろしくおねがいします。(*bowing*)

5. **Role Play: In this activity, you and your classmate will each choose one of the role cards. If you take Card A, you will perform the actions indicated on Card A. Your partner will perform the role on Card B. Follow the model below. Also be sure to use the appropriate body language, indicated in the parentheses.**

Card A (High School Student)

It's 11:00 a.m. and you are in charge of the registration desk at a high school fair. Greet an adult visitor and find out his or her name.

Card B (Adult/Parent)

It's 11:00 a.m. and you have come to the registration desk at a high school fair. Answer the receptionist's questions.

なまえ

ノート **2** (Note 2):

Japanese names are given with the last name first followed by the first name. However, non-Japanese names are usually given with the first name first. Compare the personal names on page 101.

会話の例 (Sample Dialogue)

A: こんにちは。

B: こんにちは。

A: あのう (hesitating)、おなまえは。

B: ＿＿＿＿ です。

A: (smile)

ノート **3** (Note 3):

あのう is similar to the English "well..." and "er..." but is more frequently used than its English counterparts. It is especially useful when initiating a question or a request, trying to get someone's attention, searching for the right word, or simply starting a conversation.

Counting to Twenty in Japanese　ノート4 (Note 4):

There are two ways to pronounce the numbers from 1 to 10 in Japanese. One was originally borrowed from China and the other is of Japanese origin. The former is used for mathematical computation, and that is the set that will be introduced at this time.

れい、ゼロ	0		
いち	1	じゅういち	11
に	2	じゅうに	12
さん	3	じゅうさん	13
し、よん	4	じゅうし、じゅうよん	14
ご	5	じゅうご	15
ろく	6	じゅうろく	16
しち、なな	7	じゅうしち、じゅうなな	17
はち	8	じゅうはち	18
きゅう,く	9	じゅうきゅう、じゅうく	19
じゅう	10	にじゅう	20

6. **Draw lines to connect the Japanese numbers on the right with their Arabic numeral counterparts on the left.**

1	*	*	に	4	*	*	じゅうさん
2	*	*	じゅうきゅう	18	*	*	じゅうはち
19	*	*	なな	13	*	*	よん
7	*	*	いち	20	*	*	にじゅう

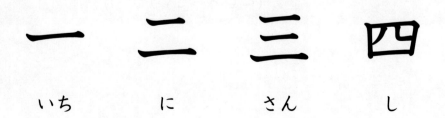

一　　二　　三　　四

いち　　に　　さん　　し

7. Practice saying the following numbers.

A.	1	I.	6
B.	4	J.	10
C.	5	K.	13
D.	9	L.	14
E.	3	M.	19
F.	7	N.	20
G.	8	O.	11
H.	2	P.	15

Counting age in Japanese　ノート**5 (Note 5):**

The counter for age is *sai*.

れいさい, ゼロさい	0 (years old)		
いっさい	1 (year old)	じゅういっさい	11 (years old)
にさい	2 (years old)	じゅうにさい	12 (years old)
さんさい	3 (years old)	じゅうさんさい	13 (years old)
よんさい	4 (years old)	じゅうよんさい	14 (years old)
ごさい	5 (years old)	じゅうごさい	15 (years old)
ろくさい	6 (years old)	じゅうろくさい	16 (years old)
ななさい	7 (years old)	じゅうななさい	17 (years old)
はっさい	8 (years old)	じゅうはっさい	18 (years old)
きゅうさい	9 (years old)	じゅうきゅうさい	19 (years old)
じっさい	10 (years old)	はたち、にじっさい	20 (years old)
(じゅっさい)		(にじゅっさい)	

8. **Indicate whether the numbers in hiragana correspond to the numerals by circling True** （ほんとう） **or False** （うそ）.

1. なおこさんは７（なな）さいです。　　　*True* （ほんとう） *or False* （うそ）

2. さやかさんは１１（いっ）さいです。　　*True* （ほんとう） *or False* （うそ）

3. ごろうくんは１８（じゅうはっ）さいです。*True* （ほんとう） *or False* （うそ）

ノート6 (Note 6):

〜さん
〜くん

Japanese names are given with the last name followed by the first name. When you call someone's name, you will usually say the last name followed by *san* (Mr., Ms., Miss, Mrs.). When you address a female friend, you can use the first name with or without *-san*. When you address a male (boy), you can use the first name with or without *-kun*. Try to watch a Japanese video in order to find out how to say names with *-san* or *-kun*.

---

9. **Practice asking someone's age as well as responding to an age question using the people pictured below as examples. Then do the same with your actual classmates.**

ジェニー
１７

ニコール
１５

サム
１３

ダリル
１６

ホゼ
１４

ヒュンジュン
１０

アヤナ
１８

ロサ
１１

会話の例 (Sample Dialogue)

A: <u>ジェニーさん</u>はなんさいですか。

B: <u>１７</u>さいです。

10. Fill in the blanks with the number of the greeting that corresponds to the picture.

A.

(　　) (　　)

(　　) (　　)

1. ごちそうさまでした。
2. ごめんなさい。
3. いいえ、けっこうです。
4. はい、ありがとうございます。
5. いただきます。

B.

(　　) (　二　)

(　　) (　　)

1. おやすみなさい。
2. いいてんきですね。
3. あのう、すみません。
4. どうも、ありがとうございます。
5. いただきます。

C.

 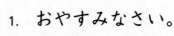

(　　) (　　)

(　1　) (　1　)

1. ごちそうさまでした。
2. さようなら。
3. げんき。
4. おかげさまで。
5. いただきます。

The expressions on the picture cards, which you learned in the preparation units, are useful for high school social situations. You will use these expressions a lot when working on the Virtual Reality sections with members of your group.

11. Paired work with picture cards: Form a pair with a classmate, each choosing one of the picture cards. You can either play Part A, the questioner, or Part B, the person who answers. Be sure you also use the appropriate body language, indicated in the parentheses.

Picture Card A.
Practice seeking someone's attention as well as responding to attention-seeking words.

会話の例 **(Sample Dialogue)**

A: あのう、すみません (bowing)

B: はい、なんでしょう。or なんでしょうか。

Picture Card B.
Practice making small talk (about the weather).

会話の例 **(Sample Dialogue)**

A: いいてんきですね。
(bowing)

B: はい、そうですね。

Picture Card C.
Practice using expressions for offering food as well as accepting it during a party. You can either play Part A, the host, or Part B, the guest.

会話の例 **(Sample Dialogue)**

A: はい、どうぞ。 (offering something politely)

B: はい、ありがとうございます。(bowing)
or はい、いただきます。(bowing)
or はい、すみません。(bowing)

Picture Card D.
Practice using expressions for offering food as well as rejecting it.

会話の例 (Sample Dialogue)

A: はい、どうぞ。(offering something politely)

B: いいえ、けっこうです。(shaking head)

Picture Card E.
Practice using expressions for ordering food as well as serving it.

会話の例 (Sample Dialogue)

A: ～をおねがいします。(asking politely)
or ～をください。(asking politely)

B: はい、どうぞ。(offering something)

Picture Card F.
Practice using expressions for saying "thank you" as well as answering "you're welcome."

会話の例 (Sample Dialogue)

A: ありがとうございます。(bowing)

B: いいえ、どういたしまして。(nodding)

Picture Card G.
Practice using expressions for apologizing after making a mistake (e.g., you step on someone's foot) as well as responding to an apology.

会話の例 (Sample Dialogue)

A: すみません。(bowing)
ごめんなさい。(bowing)

B: いいえ。(nodding head)

会話の例 (Sample Dialogue)

A: <u>いただきます</u>。 (bowing)

会話の例 (Sample Dialogue)

A: <u>ごちそうさまでした</u>。 (bowing)

Picture Card H and I.
Practice expressing gratitude for food before or after eating.

Picture Cards J, K and L.
Practice using expressions for ordering food as well as serving it.

会話の例 (Sample Dialogue)

A: <u>おやすみなさい</u>。

B: <u>おやすみなさい</u>。

会話の例 (Sample Dialogue)

A: <u>しつれいします</u>。 (bowing)

会話の例 (Sample Dialogue)

A: <u>さようなら</u>。

12. *Practice making small talk (about the weather). You can either play Part A, the questioner, or Part B, the person who answers. Substitute the appropriate weather condition in the underlined section.*

会話の例 (Sample Dialogue)

A: <u>いいてんきですね</u>。 (bowing)

B: はい、そうですね。

99

13. Practice using informal expressions for general greetings in formal situations (e.g., you meet your friend's parent) and familiar situations (e.g., you meet your friend). You can either play Part A, the questioner, or Part B, the person who answers.

ノート**7** (Note 7):

Formal and Informal Speech Styles

There are two different speech styles in Japanese: formal and informal. Formal speech is used with people of different social status, such as between teacher and student, or between your friend's parents and you. Informal speech, or casual speech, is used among friends and people of the same social status.

会話の例
(Sample Dialogue A: Formal)

A: <u>おげんきですか</u>。

B: <u>おかげさまで</u>。 (bowing)

A: <u>さようなら</u>。 (bowing)

B: <u>しつれいします</u>。 (bowing)

会話の例
(Sample Dialogue B: Informal)

A: <u>げんき</u>。 (upbeat)

B: <u>うん、げんき</u>。

A: <u>じゃ、また</u>。

B: <u>じゃ</u>。

Counting from 20 to 100 in Japanese　ノート**8** (Note 8):

にじゅう	20	よんじゅう	40
にじゅういち	21	ごじゅう	50
にじゅうに	22	ろくじゅう	60
にじゅうさん	23	しちじゅう／ななじゅう	70
にじゅうし／にじゅうよん	24	はちじゅう	80
にじゅうご	25	きゅうじゅう	90
にじゅうろく	26	きゅうじゅうろく	96
にじゅうしち／にじゅうなな	27	きゅうじゅうしち／きゅうじゅうなな	97
にじゅうはち	28	きゅうじゅうはち	98
にじゅうきゅう／にじゅうく	29	きゅうじゅうきゅう／きゅうじゅうく	99
さんじゅう	30	ひゃく	100

14. Circle the appropriate answer.

A. 21 は (にいちじゅう、にじゅういち、じゅうにいち) です。

B. 40 は (よんじゅう、よじゅう、さんじゅう、ごじゅう) です。

C. 100 は (はく、びゃく、いちじゅう、ひゃく、じゅうじゅう) です。

15. Practice saying the following numbers.

A.	21	I.	26
B.	64	J.	90
C.	25	K.	33
D.	95	L.	100
E.	23	M.	49
F.	73	N.	55
G.	28	O.	51
H.	82	P.	75

16. Practice asking someone's age as well as giving your own using the people pictured below as examples. Then do the same with your actual classmates.

ほし　まさこ (24)

すずき　よしお (50)

ケビン　ブラウン (17)

きた　しろう (72)

会話の例 (Sample Dialogue)

A: <u>ほし</u>さんはなんさいですか。

B: <u>24</u>さいです。

A: ありがとうございました。

お正月 <ruby>しょうがつ</ruby> New Year Events

The term しょうがつ (or おしょうがつ, with the polite prefix お) originally meant the month of January, but today it is used to indicate only the first week of that month. しょうがつ is undoubtedly the most important holiday season in Japan. People pay respect to their ancestors and pray for a good harvest as they observe the arrival of the new year. The Japanese celebrate the new year with a variety of special events and activities. Most take place during the first week of January, especially during the first three days, at which time government offices, private companies and schools are closed.

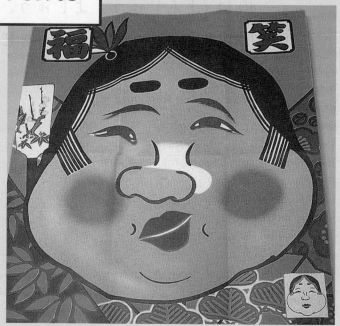

New Year is the time for many Japanese to practice their calligraphy skills. They take up their ふで, or calligraphy brush, and compose or copy a poem or a phrase in すみ, India ink. Schoolchildren are often asked to submit these poems and phrases when they return to school from vacation. The first calligraphy writing of the year is called かきぞめ.

あけまして おめでとうございます。 (Happy New Year!)

This is the greeting that Japanese people exchange when they see each other for the first time after a new year begins. It can be used, however, only during the first two weeks or so of the year. あけましておめでとうございます literally means, "We are happy that New Year's Day has dawned." A similar expression, しんねん おめでとうございます literally means, "We are happy to have the new year," and is used under the same circumstances. These greetings are often followed by another expression, ほんねん も どうぞ よろしく おねがいします, which literally means is "Please continue to be kind to me this year." ことしも どうぞ よろしく おねがいします has the same meaning but is slightly less formal.

すごろく

はごいた

<ruby>元日<rt>がんじつ</rt></ruby>／<ruby>元旦<rt>がんたん</rt></ruby>
New Year's Day

Most Japanese welcome the new year in a solemn yet cheerful atmosphere. Family members gather for a special New Year's meal. Traditional New Year's cuisine includes ぞうに and おせちりょうり. ぞうに (or おぞうに) is a soup of rice cakes and other ingredients, such as chicken and vegetables.

Early in the morning on がんじつ, or New Year's Day, ねんがじょう, or New Year's cards, are delivered to each home. Most Japanese send ねんがじょう to their friends and acquaintances before the end of the year, but post offices hold them until New Year's Day and deliver them all at once.

おとしだま is a tradition that children look forward to. It is a gift of money that parents customarily give to their young children on がんじつ.

Most Japanese pay a visit to a じんじゃ(a Shinto shrine) or an おてら(a Buddhist temple) sometime during the first three days of the year to pray for happiness and good fortune throughout the year. This practice is called はつもうで. The earliest groups of visitors arrive during the night of おおみそか, or New Year's Eve, and most of Japan's major shrines are packed with people by midnight. Public transportation in large cities remains in service throughout the early morning hours to accommodate these visitors. Many Japanese women go to shrines and temples in traditional kimono.

じんじゃ

1.3 Mechanics

Telephone Numbers ノート**9** (Note 9):

ゼロ さん （の） さん なな はち ろく （の） きゅう ごう よん にい

When giving telephone numbers in Japanese, each digit is pronounced individually. Note in the table below that the pronunciations よん、なな、and きゅう are used for 4, 7, and 9, and にい (2) and ごう (5) have elongated pronunciations to match the length of the other numbers.

0	ゼロ、れい
2	にい
4	よん
5	ごう
7	なな
9	きゅ

1. Indicate whether the hiragana numbers correspond with the Arabic numbers by circling ほんとう *(True)* or うそ *(False)*.

1. ４０７-８１９６
   は(よん、れい、なな、はち、いち、きゅう、ろく)です。

   (ほんとう) or （うそ）

2. ４２５-８３７６
   は(よん、にい、ごう、の、はち、さん、なな、ろく)です。

   (ほんとう) or （うそ）

3. ２１２-３７４-５１９０
   は(にい、いち、にい、の、さん、なな、よん、
   の、ごう、いち、きゅう、れい)です。

   (ほんとう) or （うそ）

4. ２０２-４４８-２２００
   は(に、ゼロ、に、の、し、し、はち、に、に、
   れい、　れい)です。

   (ほんとう) or （うそ）

2. Practice saying the following telephone numbers.

A.	03-3814-5722
B.	203-288-3273
C.	0120-123-9870
D.	0994-46-4629
E.	0839-33-2430
F.	800-375-2872
G.	0489-22-3838
H.	0473-65-2188
I.	212-959-0704
J.	052-745-3255

ノート **10 (Note 10):**

When Japanese people read a telephone number, they use (の) *no* to indicate a hyphen. For example, 212 の 567 の 8912.

3. **Practice exchanging phone numbers with your classmates using the model below.**

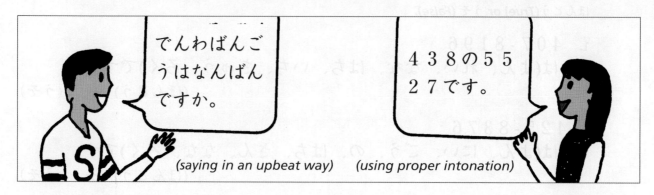

でんわばんごうはなんばんですか。

438の5527です。

(saying in an upbeat way)   *(using proper intonation)*

4. **Practice reading the following telephone numbers.**

会話の例 (Sample Dialogue)

A: <u>ギフトセンター</u>はなんばんですか。

B: <u>680の3288</u>です。

ノート **11** (Note 11):

なんばん means "what number."

Counting hundreds (100–2000) ノート **12 (Note 12):**

Study the pronunciations of 300, 600 and 800.

ひゃく	1 0 0
にひゃく	2 0 0
さんびゃく	3 0 0
よんひゃく	4 0 0
ごひゃく	5 0 0
ろっぴゃく	6 0 0
ななひゃく	7 0 0
はっぴゃく	8 0 0
きゅうひゃく	9 0 0
せん	1,0 0 0
にせん	2,0 0 0

5. *Circle the appropriate answer.*

A. （にせん、せん、いちせん、さんぜん）は 1,0 0 0 です。

B. （はちひゃく、しちせん、しっせん、はっぴゃく）は 800 です。

C. （さんひゃく、さんびゃく、さんぴゃく、さっぴゃく）は 300 です。

D. （ろくはく、ろくひゃく、ろっぴゃく、ろくびゃく）は 600 です。

E. （ごはく、ごっぴゃく、ごひゃく、ごびゃく）は 500 です。

6. *Practice saying the following numbers.*

A.	100	H.	300	O.	351	V.	1,669
B.	102	I.	600	P.	675	W.	2,010
C.	105	J.	800	Q.	247	X.	2,002
D.	107	K.	433	R.	829	Y.	2,103
E.	112	L.	1,000	S.	2,000		
F.	156	M.	549	T.	1,999		
G.	208	N.	755	U.	1,864		

7. **You know that the exchange rate of the US dollar and the Japanese yen changes every day. When you talk about the exchange rate, you must also calculate it. Here, use a simple exchange rate, $1.00 = 100 yen. Practice saying the following numbers.**

１ドルは１００えんです。

1. ２ドルはいくら（なんえん）ですか。
2. ８ドルはいくら（なんえん）ですか。
3. １０ドルはいくら（なんえん）ですか。
4. ６００えんはいくら（なんドル）ですか。
5. ９００えんはいくら（なんドル）ですか。

いくら （なんえん） （なんドル）	**ノート13 (Note 13):** You already learned いくら (*ikura*). The English equivalent is "how much?" You will be able to use なん (nan) to attach a currency counter such as えん en (Yen), ドル doru (dollar), セント sento (cent), and ポンド pondo (pound) to indicate the number of (yen, dollars, cents, and pounds).

Use division and multiplication to calculate the exhange rate between the dollar and the yen. ノート14 (Note 14):

100	×	6	=	600
(ひゃく)	(かける)	(ろく)	(は)	(ろっぴゃく)
(*hyaku*)	(*kakeru*)	(*roku*)	(*wa*)	(*roppyaku*)

300	÷	100	=	3
(さんびゃく)	(わる)	(ひゃく)	(は)	(さん)
(*sanbyaku*)	(*waru*)	(*hyaku*)	(*wa*)	(*san*)

会話の例 (Sample Dialogue)

A: ２ドルはいくら（なんえん）ですか。

B: ２ドル(×)かける109えんは218えんです。

A: ２００えんはいくら（なんドル）ですか。

B: 200えん(÷)わる100えんは２ドルです。

Strategies to make sure you have the correct number
ノート **15** (Note 15):

What do you do when you don't understand everything
someone tells you, as when they tell you a phone number?
Try these strategies to help you figure it out.

Strategy 1
Partial Repeating

Strategy 2
Confirming （ですね）

Strategy 3
Asking Again

8. *Keeping the strategies just introduced in mind, find out your classmates' telephone numbers using the model below.*

会話の例 (Sample Dialogue)

A: あのう、でんわばんごうは
　　なんばんですか。

B: <u>695の　1082</u>です。 (*using proper intonation*)

A: <u>695</u>の………。 (*extending the last sound*)

B: <u>1082</u>です。 (*pronouncing clearly*)

A: ありがとうございました。 (*saying in an upbeat way*)

9. *Practice asking someone their grade level as well as responding to such a question using the people pictured below as examples. Then do the same with your actual classmates.*

ジェニー
11th

ニコール
9th

サム
7th

ダリル
10th

ヒュンジュン
5th

アヤナ
12th

ホゼ
8th

ロサ
6th

会話の例 (Sample Dialogue)

A: <u>ジェニー</u>さんはなんねんせいですか。

B: <u>11</u>ねんせいです。 (*A looking puzzled*)

　　<u>こうこう2</u>ねんせいです。

Counting thousands (1,000–10,000)　ノート16 (Note 16):

Study the pronunciations of 2,000 and 8,000.

せん	1,000	にせん	2,000
さんぜん	3,000	よんせん	4,000
ごせん	5,000	ろくせん	6,000
ななせん／しちせん	7,000	はっせん	8,000
きゅうせん	9,000	いちまん	10,000

10. Indicate whether the hiragana numbers correspond to the Arabic numbers by circling ほんとう (True) or うそ (False).

1. 8,496は (はっせん　よひゃく　きゅうじゅう　ろく)です。

　　　　　　　　　　　　　　　　　　　　(ほんとう) or （うそ）

2. 3,375は (さんせん　さんびゃく　ななじゅう　ご) です。

　　　　　　　　　　　　　　　　　　　　(ほんとう) or （うそ）

3. 5,190は (ごせん　ひゃく　きゅうじゅう)です。

　　　　　　　　　　　　　　　　　　　　(ほんとう) or （うそ）

4. 12,200は(いちまん　にせん　にひゃく)です。

　　　　　　　　　　　　　　　　　　　　(ほんとう) or （うそ）

5. 17,050は(いちまん　ななぜん　ごじゅう)です。

　　　　　　　　　　　　　　　　　　　　(ほんとう) or （うそ）

11. Practice saying the following:

1.	$2,000 \times 1 = 2,000$	9.	$109 \times 80 = 8,720$
2.	$500 \times 2 = 1,000$	10.	$2,560 \div 8 = ?$
3.	$1,300 \times 4 = 5,200$	11.	$369 \times 10 = ?$
4.	$3,300 \div 11 = 300$	12.	$2,300 \div 115 = ?$
5.	$2,400 \div 6 = 400$	13.	$7 \times 522 = ?$
6.	$6,600 \div 22 = 300$	14.	$6,000 \div 120 = ?$
7.	$90 \times 80 = 7,200$	15.	$1,120 \div 112 = ?$
8.	$100 \times 80 = 8,000$		

12. **When you talk about computers, you must use many special terms (kilobytes, megabytes, gigabytes). You already know that I gigabyte equals 1,000 megabytes, 1 megabyte equals 1,000 kilobytes, and 1 kilobyte equals 1,000 bytes. Practice saying the following:**

1ギガは1,000メガです。　　1メガは1,000ケイです。
1ケイは1,000バイトです。

1. 2ギガはなんメガですか。
2. 8メガはなんケイですか。
3. 10ケイはなんバイトですか。
4. 100ギガはなんメガですか。
5. 2,000メガはなんギガですか。

6. 3,000ケイはなんメガですか。
7. 5,000バイトはなんケイですか。
8. 8,000メガはなんギガですか。
9.. 1,000ギガはいくらですか？

会話の例 (Sample Dialogue)

A: <u>2ギガ</u>はいくら（なんメガ）ですか。

B: <u>2</u>（X）かける<u>1,000メガ</u>は<u>2,000メガ</u>です。

A: <u>2,000メガ</u>はいくら（なんギガ）ですか。

B: <u>2,000メガ</u>（÷）わる<u>1,000</u>は<u>2ギガ</u>です。

Calendar Year　ノート17 (Note 17):

The Gregorian calendar was originally borrowed from the West. People in Japan use this calendar year and the Japanese imperial reign year.

1970ねん：せんきゅうひゃくななじゅうねん

1980ねん：せんきゅうひゃくはちじゅうねん

1990ねん：せんきゅうひゃくきゅうじゅうねん

2000ねん：にせんねん

2010ねん：にせんじゅうねん

1868=	めいじがんねん
1900=	めいじさんじゅうさんねん
1912=	たいしょうがんねん
1917=	たいしょうろくねん
1926=	しょうわがんねん
1945=	しょうわにじゅうねん
1980=	しょうわごじゅうごねん
1989=	へいせいがんねん
2000=	へいせいじゅうにねん

13. *Ask someone their year of birth and give your own, using the model below.*

てづか　おさむ
１９２８ねんうまれ

おざわ　せいじ
１９３５ねんうまれ

つだ　うめこ
１８６４ねんうまれ

会話の例 (Sample Dialogue)

A: てづかさんはなんねんうまれですか。

B: １９２８ねんうまれです。

A: ああ、そうですか。(saying in an upbeat way)

14. *Practice exchanging age and birth year with your classmates using the model above.*

Language Note

The Japanese Language in the Modern World

Geographically, Japan is an archipelago consisting of four main islands (Hokkaidoo, Honshuu, Shikoku and Kyuushuu) and many smaller ones. It includes the Ryuukyuu chain, which stretches from just south of Kyuushuu to just north of Taiwan.

Almost all native speakers of Japanese live in Japan, and almost everyone who lives in Japan is a native speaker of Japanese. According to the 1999 *World Almanac*, the population of Japan in 1998 was approximately 126 million, and this number is a good estimate of the number of native speakers. The nearly perfect match between Japanese language and Japanese nationality is unusual. English is the dominant language not only in England but in several other countries as well. Hindi has more native speakers than Japanese, but most of the people in India are native speakers of some other language.

Of course, some native speakers of Japanese do live outside Japan. In the early 20th century, thousands of people emigrated from Japan to what is now the United States (mostly Hawaii and California), to Canada (mostly British Columbia), and to several Latin American countries (especially Brazil). Needless to say, the original emigrants were native speakers of Japanese, and most of their children grew up bilingual in Japanese and the dominant language of the country where they were born. Emigration from Japan has slowed to a trickle in recent years, though, and most second-generation Japanese-Americans are now elderly. Most third- and fourth-generation Japanese-Americans don't know Japanese, so the number of native speakers is dwindling. The same thing is happening in Canada and Latin America. On the other hand, the recent international expansion of Japanese businesses has led to the development of small, transient communities of expatriate Japanese native speakers in almost every major city in the world.

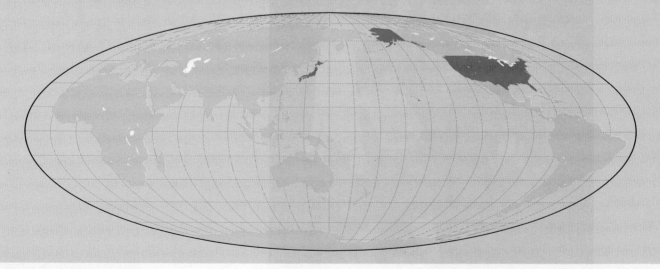

There are also native speakers of Japanese who live in Japan but are not of the Japanese nationality, although they account for less than one percent of the total population. Most of these people hold North or South Korean passports and are the descendants of Koreans who were brought to work in Japan during the period when Korea was under Japanese colonial rule (1910–1945). The rest are mostly the children of long-term foreign residents who have come to Japan in small numbers for a wide variety of reasons.

Japanese as a foreign language

Although Japanese ranks ninth in the world in terms of the number of native speakers, it isn't widely used as an international language. In recent years, though, the number of people studying Japanese as a foreign language has grown enormously.

For one thing, Japan has attracted large numbers of foreign students, especially from nearby Asian countries. According to a survey by the Japanese Ministry of Education, there were about 54,000 foreign students studying at Japanese institutions of higher education in 1995. Over 91 percent of these students were from Asia, and 77.7 percent were from one of three nearby countries: China, South Korea, and Taiwan. Students from Europe and North America combined accounted for only 4.8 percent of the total.

At the same time, there have been dramatic increases in the number of students studying Japanese as a foreign language in their home countries. The table below shows the number of college students who were studying Japanese in the United States in 1960, 1970, 1980, and 1990.

The number of college students who were studying Japanese in the United States

YEAR	1960	1970	1980	1990
NUMBER	1,746	6,620	11,506	45,717

SOURCE: Modern Language Association

The number of public high school students who were studying Japanese in the United States

YEAR	1982	1985	1990	1994
NUMBER	6,246	8,557	25,123	42,290

SOURCE: American Council on the Teaching of Foreign Languages

College Students Studying Japanese in the United States

As you can see, more than 25 times as many college students were studying Japanese in 1990 as in 1960. In fact, Japanese was the fourth most commonly studied language in 1997, trailing only Spanish, French, and German. There's been a similar trend in American secondary schools, and now you're part of it.

1.4 Mechanics

1. Practice developing a conversation with じゃ／じゃあ using the model below.

会話の例 (Sample Dialogue)

A: こうこう１ねんせいですか。

B: はい、そうです。

A: じゃ、<u>１０ねんせい</u>ですね。

B: はい、そうです。 *(saying in an upbeat way)*

ノート18 (Note 18):

じゃ (*ja*) and じゃあ (*jaa*) are used to develop conversation based on what the other person said. They can be roughly translated as "well, then," "in that case," and "that being so."

ノート19 (Note 19):

の (*no*) is a particle used to modify and relate nouns. Noun X *no* Noun Y means that Noun X modifies Noun Y. For example にほんのたべもの (*Nihon no tabemono*) means the foods of Japan.

2. Practice asking someone's age and giving yours using the chart and model below.

ニコール
14/15 yrs. 9th

ジェニー
16/17 yrs. 11th

サム
12/13 yrs. 7th

ダリル
16/17 yrs. 10th

ヒュンジュン
10/11 yrs. 5th

ロサ
11/12 yrs 6th

会話の例 (Sample Dialogue)

A: <u>ニコール</u>さん、<u>ちゅうがく３ねんせい</u>ですか。

B: はい、そうです。

A: じゃ、<u>１５さい</u>ですね。

B: いいえ、ちがいます。<u>１４さい</u>です。

A: ああ、そうですか。 *(saying in an upbeat way)*

アヤナ
17/18 yrs. 12th

ホゼ
13/14 yrs. 8th

Animal Years: えと **(The twelve signs of the Chinese zodiac)**
ノート20 **(Note 20):**

ねずみどし／ねどし	1924, 1936, 1948, 1960, 1972, 1984, 1996, 2008
うしどし	1925, 1937, 1949, 1961, 1973, 1985, 1997, 2009
とらどし	1926, 1938, 1950, 1962, 1974, 1986, 1998, 2010
うさぎどし／うどし	1927, 1939, 1951, 1963, 1975, 1987, 1999, 2011
たつどし	1928, 1940, 1952, 1964, 1976, 1988, 2000, 2012
へびどし／みどし	1929, 1941, 1953, 1965, 1977, 1989, 2001, 2013
うまどし	1930, 1942, 1954, 1966, 1978, 1990, 2002, 2014
ひつじどし	1931, 1943, 1955, 1967, 1979, 1991, 2003, 2015
さるどし	1932, 1944, 1956, 1968, 1980, 1992, 2004, 2016
とりどし	1933, 1945, 1957, 1969, 1981, 1993, 2005, 2017
いぬどし	1934, 1946, 1958, 1970, 1982, 1994, 2006, 2018
いのししどし／いどし	1935, 1947, 1959, 1971, 1983, 1995, 2007, 2019

ねずみ

うし

とら

うさぎ

たつ

いぬ

さる

へび

いのしし

とり

うま

ひつじ

117

3. **Fill in the blanks with the number of the animal that corresponds to the picture.**

A.(　　) B.(　　) C.(　　) D.(　　)

E.(　　) F.(　　) G.(　　) H.(　　)

1. うま
2. さる
3. ねこ
4. うし
5. いぬ

6. ねずみ
7. へび
8. とり
9. ひつじ
10. とら

4. *Developing a conversation with* じゃ／じゃあ. *Practice asking someone's animal year and giving yours, using the chart on the previous page and the model below.*

会話の例 (Sample Dialogue)

A: <u>うしどし</u>ですか。

B: はい、そうです。

A: じゃ、<u>１９８５ねん</u>うまれですね。

B: はい、そうです。 (*saying in an upbeat way*)

5. **Develop a conversation with** じゃ／じゃあ **using the chart on the previous page and the model below.**

1. 1982ねん　　2. 1975ねん　　3. 1969ねん　　4. 1995ねん　　5. 1952ねん　　6. 1945ねん

会話の例 (Sample Dialogue)

A: <u>１９８２ねん</u>うまれですか。

B: はい、そうです。

A: じゃ、<u>とりどし</u>ですね。

B: いいえ、ちがいます。<u>いぬどし</u>です。

A: ああ、そうですか。 (*saying in an upbeat way*)

6. **Developing a conversation with** じゃ／じゃあ**. Practice asking if a particular sport is played in a particular season using the pictures and models below.**

会話の例 (Sample Dialogue)

A: <u>あき</u>のスポーツは<u>バレーボール</u>ですか？

B: いいえ、ちがいます。 (*hesitating and making a hand gesture indicating that something is incorrect*)

A: じゃ、<u>サッカー</u>ですか。 (*widening eyes*)

B: はい、そうです。 (*saying in an upbeat way*)

7. **Developing a conversation with** じゃ／じゃあ**. Practice asking the exchange rate and giving it, and practice asking for the conversion between gigabytes, megabytes, and kilobytes using the model below.**

会話の例 **(Sample Dialogue A)**

A: あのう、<u>１ドル</u>はなんえんですか。

B: <u>１ドル</u>は<u>１１２えん</u>です。

A: じゃ、<u>２０ドル</u>は<u>２,２４０</u>えんですね。 (*widening eyes*)

B: はい、そうです。 (*saying in an upbeat way*)

会話の例 **(Sample Dialogue B)**

A: あのう、ハードディスクはなん<u>メガ</u>ですか。

B: <u>９ギガ</u>です。

A: じゃ、<u>９,０００メガ</u>ですね。 (*widening eyes*)

B: はい、そうです。 (*saying in an upbeat way*)

8. *In this role play, you and a classmate each choose one card. If you take Card O, you will perform the actions indicated on Card O and your partner will perform the role on Card M or Card F. If you take Card Y, you will perform the actions indicated on Card Y, and your partner will perform the role on Card M or Card F. Both of you should follow the model below. Also be sure to include the appropriate intonation, indicated in the parentheses.*

Card O (Teacher)

You are an American high school teacher. You see Mark. You ask him what fall sport he plays and the name of his coach.

Card M (Mark)

You are an American high school student. You see your teacher (use formal style) or Hiroko (use informal style), an exchange student, walking by. They ask you which fall sport you play and the name of your coach.

Card Y (Hiroko)

You are a Japanese exchange student. You see Mark. You ask him what fall sport he plays and the name of his coach.

Card F (Rachel)

You are an American high school student. You see your teacher (use formal style) or Hiroko (use informal style), an exchange student, walking by. They ask you which fall sport you play and the name of your coach.

会話の例 (Sample Dialogue)

Case I: Card O (Teacher) and Card M (Mark) or Card F (Rachel)

せんせい: マークさん／レーチェルさん、あきのスポーツはなんですか。

マーク／レーチェル: バレーボールです。

せんせい: じゃ、コーチはしまのせんせいですか。

マーク／レーチェル: はい、そうです。

Case II: Card Y (Hiroko) and Card M (Mark) or Card F (Rachel)

ひろこ: マーク／レーチェル、あきのスポーツなあに。(*rising intonation on the last word*)

マーク／レーチェル: バレーボール。

ひろこ: じゃ、コーチはしまのせんせい。(*rising intonation on the last word*)

マーク: うん、そうだよ。

レーチェル: うん、そうよ。

Formal and Informal speech ノート21 (Note 21):

Male and Female Speech Styles

As indicated in Note 7 on page 100, Japanese has two different speech styles: formal and informal.

Case I and Case II in Sample Dialogue are a formal-style example and an informal-style example respectively.

In addition, informal Japanese also has different speech styles for females and males. However, in formal speech, the differences between female and male speech styles are few.

9. Group Activity: Membership List Completion Game.

ドラマ クラブ		
なまえ	がくねん	でんわばんごう
George Albano	9	
James Berge	--	438-1725
Yu Sum Li	--	
Michael Bruno	11	
Fabian Galeano	--	854-0289
Kate Larkin	10	
Shawn Harris	--	
Melissa Esposito	9	

A. A group of five students forms a team.

B. Each receives a membership list for the same school club with different information missing.

C. Team members exchange information (regarding grades and phone numbers) among themselves and complete their list.

D. The team that completes the list accurately first is the winner.

Pronunciation

Short and long syllables

You already know that Japanese distinguishes long vowels from short vowels and long consonants from short consonants. This difference between long and short plays a very important role in the overall rhythm of Japanese. When you divide Japanese words into syllables, some syllables are long and some are short. A long syllable lasts approximately twice as long as a short syllable. Another way to say the same thing is to use the musical term **beat**. A short syllable has one beat and a long syllable has two beats.

Any syllable that ends in a short vowel is a short syllable (one beat), and any syllable that ends in a long vowel or in a consonant is a long syllable (two beats). The examples below will help you get the idea.

hamu	**ha**	(short syllable)	**+mu**	(short syllable)	ham
gitaa	**gi**	(short syllable)	**+taa**	(long syllable)	guitar
mitto	**mit**	(long syllable)	**+to**	(short syllable)	mitt
panda	**pan**	(long syllable)	**+da**	(short syllable)	panda

Notice that the syllable division comes in the middle of a long consonant; the two syllables in *mitto* are **mit** and **to**. The division between the two beats in a long syllable comes after the first vowel (which in many cases is the only vowel). Here are the same four words divided into beats.

hamu	**ha·mu**	2 beats
gitaa	**gi·ta·a**	3 beats
mitto	**mi·t·to**	3 beats
panda	**pa·n·da**	3 beats

You may have heard of a kind of Japanese poetry called **haiku**. People usually describe a haiku as consisting of seventeen syllables organized into three lines, with five syllables in the first line, seven syllables in the second line, and five syllables in the third line. In fact, though, what you count in a haiku isn't the number of syllables; it's the number of beats. A haiku has seventeen beats, but unless every single syllable is a short syllable, the number of syllables is less than seventeen.

Since each beat lasts approximately the same amount of time, the amount of time it takes to say a Japanese sentence depends on the number of beats it contains. Of course, people don't actually speak with this kind of ideal rhythm in real life. They do all kinds of things that disrupt it, such as hesitating when they can't think of a word, speeding up when they get excited, stretching out a word for emphasis, and so on. A person who spoke with every beat exactly equal to every other beat would sound like a robot. Even so, people come pretty close to this ideal rhythmic pattern when they recite poetry. It's very different from the ideal rhythmic pattern in English.

English doesn't make a distinction between long and short syllables, of course, and the general rhythmic principle is to equalize the intervals between syllables that are **stressed** (**accented**). Compare the following two sentences, in which the stressed syllables are in boldface.

Robb   has   five.

Rob|ert|son   pos|**sess**|es   fif|**teen**.

Now imagine that you're reciting these two sentences in time with a metronome. It's very natural to say each sentence in time with three ticks of the metronome. The first sentence has only three syllables, and each syllable is stressed, so it's easy to recite it so that **Robb** coincides with one metronome tick, **has** coincides with the next tick, and **five** coincides with the tick after that. The second sentence has seven syllables, but only three of them are stressed, and it's easy to recite it so that **Rob** coincides with one metronome tick, **sess** with the next tick, and **teen** with the tick after that. In other words, the ideal rhythmic pattern in English involves speeding up or slowing down the individual syllables to make the stresses come out at equal intervals.

If a Japanese speaker were to pronounce a Japanese sentence in time with a metronome, you'd expect the beats to coincide with the ticks. Given this dramatic difference in ideal rhythmic pattern, it's no wonder that English speakers sometimes say that Japanese sounds staccato, that is, like a series of equally timed short bursts of sound.

1.5 Mechanics

Listening Exercises

1. **You overhear several conversations between Japanese exchange students in your school. Choose the topic that corresponds to each.**

    1. (　)　　　　2. (　)　　　　3. (　)　　　　4. (　)

    (a) name
    (b) grade level
    (c) sports
    (d) telephone number

2. **You hear the self-introductions of Japanese exchange students in the classroom. Fill in their grade levels below.**

    1. (　) grade　　2. (　) grade　　3. (　) grade　　4. (　) grade

3. **You ask the telephone numbers of Japanese exchange students in your classroom. Choose the numbers that from the list below.**

1. (　) 647-7821	2. (　) 647-7834	3. (　) 647-7856	4. (　) 647-7879
1. (　) 647-7723	2. (　) 647-7814	3. (　) 647-7967	4. (　) 647-7634
1. (　) 647-8892	2. (　) 647-7754	3. (　) 647-6689	4. (　) 647-5579
1. (　) 647-6289	2. (　) 647-2759	3. (　) 647-5195	4. (　) 647-3961

4. **You ask the ages of Japanese exchange students in your classroom. Choose the ages from the list below.**

1. (　) 18	2. (　) 17	3. (　) 16	4. (　) 15
1. (　) 12	2. (　) 13	3. (　) 14	4. (　) 15
1. (　) 10	2. (　) 12	3. (　) 16	4. (　) 18
1. (　) 13	2. (　) 15	3. (　) 17	4. (　) 19

5. Ask the birth years and animal years of the Japanese exchange students in your class. Choose the numbers that correspond to each birth year and animal year.

    1. Year of birth (   )   Animal year (   )

    2. Year of birth (   )   Animal year (   )

    3. Year of birth (   )   Animal year (   )

    4. Year of birth (   )   Animal year (   )

6. American students talk about sports with Japanese exchange students in the classroom. Indicate the contents of their dialogues by answering the questions below.

    1. What sport does he play?

    2. What sport does she play?

    3. What sport does he play?

    4. What sport does she play?

7. You overhear conversations between Japanese exchange students in your school. What do think they are talking about? Choose the appropriate topics below.

    1. (   )   2. (   )   3. (   )   4. (   )

    (a) animal years

    (b) exchange rates

    (c) sports

    (d) telephone numbers

    (e) grade levels

    (f) computers

8. You overhear conversations between some Japanese exchange students and a Japanese teacher in your school. What do think they are talking about? Choose the appropriate topics below.

    1. (   )   2. (   )   3. (   )   4. (   )

    (a) animal years

    (b) exchange rates

    (c) sports

    (d) telephone numbers

    (e) grade levels

    (f) computers

FORM

1. Identifying people and things using the "be" verb

ギターです。　　　こうこうにねんせいです。

Gitaa desu.　　　*Kookoo ninensei desu.*

It is a guitar.　　　He is a second-year high school student.

The "be" verb *desu* is equivalent to the English "am," "is," "are." Noun + *desu* is used to identify people and things in Japanese.

2. Asking and answering questions

A. Asking yes-no questions

ギターですか？　　　こうこうにねんせいですか？

Gitaa desu ka?　　　*Kookoo ninensei desu ka?*

Is it a guitar?　　　Is he a second-year high school student?

Yes-no questions are made by simply adding *ka* at the end of the sentence following *desu*.

B. Answering yes-no questions

Answering yes

ギターですか。　　　はい、そうです。

Gitaa desu ka?　　　*Hai, soo desu.*

Is it a guitar?　　　Yes, that's right.

ギターですか。　　　はい、ギターです。

Gitaa desu ka?　　　*Hai, gitaa desu.*

Is it a guitar?　　　Yes, it's a guitar.

Answering no

ギターですか。　　　いいえ、ちがいます。

Gitaa desu ka?　　　*Iie, chigaimasu.*

Is it a guitar?　　　No, it's wrong.

ギターですか。　　　いいえ、ギターじゃありません。

Gitaa desu ka?　　　*Iie, gitaa ja arimasen.*

Is it a guitar?　　　No, it's not a guitar.

ギターですか。　　　いいえ、そうじゃありません。

Gitaa desu ka?　　　*Iie, soo ja arimasen.*

Is it a guitar?　　　No, that's not right.

Soo desu is a very useful expression for affirmatively answering a yes-no question.

Hai, gitaa desu would not be bad, but *Hai, soo desu* is preferred.

Iie, chigaimasu is also a very useful expression for negatively answering a yes-no question.

Other negative answers will be studied in Chapter 4.

C.　**Asking questions using question words**

In Japanese, yes-no questions and questions using question words share the same structure.

ギターです。	こうこうにねんせいです。	いち ばんです。
Gitaa desu.	*Kookoo ninensei desu.*	*Ichiban desu.*
It is a guitar.	She is a second-year high school student.	It is number one.

ギター ですか？	こうこう に ねんせいですか？	いち ばんですか？
Gitaa desu ka?	*Kookoo ninensei desu ka?*	*Ichiban desu ka?*
Is it a guitar?	Is she a second-year high school student?	Is it number one?

なん ですか？	こうこう なん ねんせいですか？	なん ばんですか？
Nan desu ka?	*Kookoo nannensei desu ka?*	*Nanban desu ka?*
What is it?	What grade is she in?	What number is it?

3.　*Asking for confirmation with* desu ne

こうこうにねんせいですね。

Kookoo ninensei desu ne.

You're a second-year high school student, aren't you?

By saying the information you remember and using special expressions (such as *desu ne* at the end of a sentence), the person you're talking to can confirm whether or not you understood or remembered accurately.

4.　*Asking for repetition*

Asking again	Partial repeating
もういちどおねがいします。	７７８の。
Moo ichido onegai shimasu.	*Nana nana hachi no...*
Could you say it again?	778-...

Saying *Moo ichido onegai shimasu*, "Please say it again," or saying the part you remember and pausing are strategies used to get the person you're talking with to supply you with the necessary missing information.

5. Establishing the topic with the particle wa

はやしさんは　じゅうどうのせんせいです。

Hayashisan wa juudoo no sensei desu.

Mr. Hayashi is a judo instructor.

でんわばんごうは３３４－５５７８です。

Denwa bangoo wa 334-5578 desu.

The telephone number is 334-5578.

たなかさんはなんねんせいですか？

Tanakasan wa nannensei desu ka?

What grade is Ms. Tanaka in?

In this XはYです (X wa Y desu) construction, the speaker establishes the topic (X) at the beginning of the sentence, indicating what he or she will be talking about. The particle *wa* follows the topic, and then the speaker gives information about the topic. In the first example sentence above, the topic is はやし せんせい (*Hayashi sensei*), and the information given is that はやしせんせいは じゅうどうのせんせいです (*Hayashi sensei wa juudoo no sensei desu*), Mr. Hayashi is a judo instructor.

6. Linking nouns with the particle no.

Description *no*

じゅうどうのせんせいです。

Juudoo no sensei desu.

He is a judo instructor.

Linking *no*

337の4789です。

San san nana no yon nana hachi kyuu desu.

It is 337-4789.

Possession *no*

マークのせんせいです。

Maaku no sensei desu.

He is Mark's teacher.

The [noun X + *no* + noun Y] phrase has several functions such as description, possession and linkage.

Noun X with particle の(*no*) is often used to modify or describe noun Y. In the first example, you see that じゅうどうの *juudoo no* describes or explains what kind of せんせい *sensei* (teacher) he is. He is a judo teacher.

Telephone numbers plus の(*no*) are discussed on page 105.

FORM (continued)

7. Counting numbers

A. There are two ways to count from 1 to 10 in Japanese. One was originally borrowed from China, and the other is of Japanese origin. The former is used for mathematical computation and is the set which will be introduced at this time. It is also the more extensively used. In Chapter 3, you will learn the Japanese system.

れい、ゼロ	(rei/zero)	0			
いち	(ichi)	1	じゅういち	(juuichi)	11
に	(ni)	2	じゅうに	(juuni)	12
さん	(san)	3	じゅうさん	(juusan)	13
し、よん	(shi/yon)	4	じゅうし、じゅうよん	(juushi/juuyon)	14
ご	(go)	5	じゅうご	(juugo)	15
ろく	(roku)	6	じゅうろく	(juuroku)	16
しち、なな	(shichi/nana)	7	じゅうしち、じゅうなな	(juushichi)	17
はち	(hachi)	8	じゅうはち	(juuhachi)	18
きゅう、く	(kyuu/ku)	9	じゅうく、じゅうきゅう	(juuku/juukyuu)	19
じゅう	(juu)	10	にじゅう	(nijuu)	20

にじゅういち	(nijuuichi)	21	ひゃく	(hyaku)	100
さんじゅう	(sanjuu)	30	にひゃく	(nihyaku)	200
よんじゅう	(yonjuu)	40	さんびゃく	(sanbyaku)	300
ごじゅう	(gojuu)	50	よんひゃく	(yonhyaku)	400
ろくじゅう	(rokujuu)	60	ごひゃく	(gohyaku)	500
しちじゅう／ななじゅう		70	ろっぴゃく	(roppyaku)	600
	(shichijuu/nanajuu)		ななひゃく	(nanahyaku)	700
はちじゅう	(hachijuu)	80	はっぴゃく	(happyaku)	800
きゅうじゅう	(kyuujuu)	90	きゅうひゃく	(kyuuhyaku)	900

せん	(sen)	1,000	ろくせん	(rokusen)	6,000
にせん	(nisen)	2,000	しちせん／ななせん	(shichisen/nanasen)	7,000
さんぜん	(sanzen)	3,000	はっせん	(hassen)	8,000
よんせん	(yonsen)	4,000	きゅうせん	(kyuusen)	9,000
ごせん	(gosen)	5,000	いちまん	(ichiman)	10,000

B. Japanese has many counters. In this chapter we learned the following counters. You will learn more counters later.

Year/Age/Grade			Currency			Computer memory		
ねん	nen	year	えん	en	yen	ギガ	giga	gigabyte
ねんせい	nensei	grade	ドル	doru	dollar	メガ	mega	megabyte
さい	sai	year old	セント	sento	cent	ケイ	kei	kilobyte
とし／どし	toshi/doshi	year (animal)	ポンド	pondo	pound	バイト	baito	byte
くみ	kumi	class						

1.6 Application

1. *Individual Activity: Making your own name cards (name tag, business card, and desk-top name sign).*

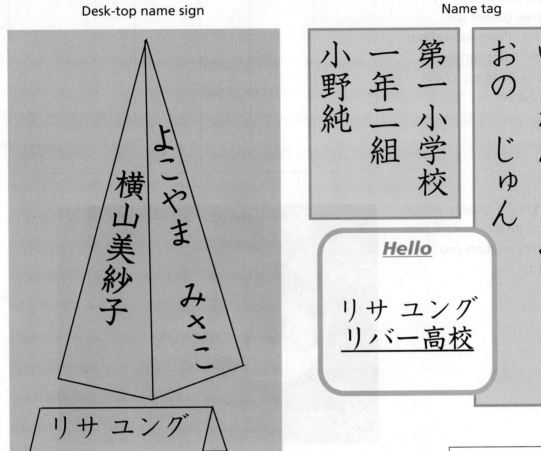

Desk-top name sign

Name tag

よこやま　みさこ

横山美紗子

リサ　ユング

第一小学校
一年二組
小野　純

だいいちしょうがっこう
いちねんにくみ
おの　じゅん

__Hello__

リサ　ユング
__リバー高校__

Business card

リバー高校

リサ・ユング

1 East 23rd St.
New York, NY 10010

Phone: (212) 696-0347
Fax: (212) 696-0347

山口高等学校
教諭　村上　春次
山口県川口市一番町三―二―八
電話〇八三九―二二―六二二二

Useful expressions: 高校: *kookoo* (high school), 高等学校: *kootoo gakkoo* (high school) (formal)

I2. Group Activity: Making and exhibiting a class list

A. Form a small group of about five students. Interviewing your group members and other classmates, gather the following information about everyone: name, grade, telephone number, school club and sport.

なまえ	がくねん	クラブ	スポーツ	でんわばんごう

B. Working in groups, design and produce a class list based on the information you have collected.

C. Have a peer evaluation exhibit in which all the class lists are evaluated according to their accuracy of information, user-friendliness and artistic creativity. A "peer evaluation sheet," such as the one on the right, should be used for tallying group scores.

Evaluation Sheet

	1	2	3
グループ 1	B	C	A
グループ 2	C	A	B
グループ 3			
グループ 4			
グループ 5			

1. Accuracy of information
2. User-friendliness
3. Artistic creativity

VOCABULARY

Functional Vocabulary

	Formal		Informal		English
Greetings	おはようございます	Ohayoo gozaimasu	おはよう	Ohayoo	Good morning
	こんにちは	Konnichi wa	こんにちは	Konnichi wa	Good afternoon
	こんばんは	Konban wa	こんばんは	Konban wa	Good evening
Introduction	はじめまして	Hajimemashite	はじめまして	Hajimemashite	How do you do? (lit., "It's the first time.")
	どうぞよろしくおねがいします		（どうぞ）よろしく		Nice to meet you.
		Doozo yoroshiku onegai shimasu		(doozo) yoroshiku	(lit., "Please look with favor upon me.)
Agreeing/	はい／ええ	Hai/Ee	うん	Un	Yes
Disagreeing	そうです	Soo desu	そう	Soo	That's right
	そうですね	Soo desu ne	そうね	Soo ne	That's right (confirmation)
	そうですよ	Soo desu yo	そう（だ）よ	Soo (da) yo	That's right (emphasis)
	あ、そうですか	A, soo desu ka	あ、そう	A, soo	Is that so?
	いいえ	Iie	ううん	Uun	No
	いいえ、ちがいます	Iie, chigaimasu	ううん、ちがう	Uun, chigau	No, that's incorrect
	いいえ、そうじゃありません		ううん、そうじゃない		No, it's not so
		Iie, soo ja arimasen		Uun, soo ja nai	
Asking for	なんですか	Nandesu ka	なあに	Naani	What? What is it?
and giving	なんばんですか	Nanban desu ka	なんばん	Nanban	What number?
information	なんねんせいですか	Nannen sei desu ka	なんねんせい	Nannensei	What school year/grade?
	なんねんうまれですか	Nannen umare desu ka	なんねんうまれ	Nannen umare	What year were you born in?
	おなまえは	Onamae wa	なまえは	Namae wa	What's your name?
	なんさいですか	Nansai desu ka	なんさい	Nansai	What's your age?
	なにどしですか	Nanidoshi desu ka	なにどし	Nanidoshi	What's your animal year?
	なんえんですか	Nan'en desu ka	なんえん	Nanen	How many yen is it?
	いくつですか	Ikutsu desu ka	いくつ	Ikutsu	How old are you?
Attracting	あのう…	Anoo...	あのう…	Anoo...	Er...Ummm...
attention	すみません	Sumimasen	すみ（い）ません	Su(m)imasen	Excuse me
Expressing	すみません	Sumimasen	すみ（い）ません	Sumimasen.	Excuse me (used when you
lack of				Sumimasen.	don't understand something)
comprehension					
Confirmation	-ですね	-desu ne	-（だ）ね	-(da)ne	—isn't it?
Developing	じゃ、（では）	Ja	じゃ、	Ja	(used to make a suggestion)
continuation					
of a conversation					
Asking for	もういちどおねがいします		もういちどおねがい		Could you say it again?
repetition		Moo ichido onegai shimasu		Moo ichido onegai	

	Formal		Informal		English
Leave-taking	おやすみなさい	*Oyasuminasai*	おやすみ	*Oyasumi*	Good night
	さようなら	*Sayoonara*	さよなら	*Sayonara*	Goodbye
	しつれいします	*Shitsurei shimasu*	しつれい	*Shitsuree*	Excuse me
	じゃ、また	*Ja,mata*	じゃ	*Ja*	See you again
Meals	いただきます	*Itadakimasu*	いただきます	*Itadakimasu*	I'll help myself, thank you.
	ごちそうさまでした	*Gochisoosama deshita*	ごちそうさま	*Gochisoosama*	Thank you for the delicious food/drink
Handing things over	はい、どうぞ	*Hai, doozo*	はい	*Hai*	Please
While receiving	はい、ありがとうございます		あっ、ありがとう	*Ah, arigatoo*	I accept the food/thing with gratitude
	Hai, arigatoo gozaimasu				
	はい、いただきます	*Hai, itadakimasu*	あっ、いただき	*Ah, itadaki*	I will receive the food/drink
	はい、すみません	*Hai, sumimasen*	あっ、すまない	*Ah, sumanai*	I'm sorry, but thank you
Rejecting	いいえ、けっこうです	*Iie, kekkoo desu*	いえ、けっこう	*Ie, kekkoo*	No, thank you
Requesting meals	～をおねがいします	*~o onegai shimasu*	～おねがい	*~ onegai*	I make a request ~
	～をください	*~o kudasai*	～をくれ	*~o kure*	Please give me ~
	すみませんが	*Sumimasen ga*	すまないが	*Sumanai ga*	Excuse me, but
Acceding to requests	はい、どうぞ	*Hai,doozo*	はい	*Hai*	Please
Gratitude	ありがとうございます	*Arigatoo gozaimasu*	ありがとう	*Arigatoo*	Thank you
Responding to gratitude	どういたしまして	*Doo itashimashite*	どういたしまして	*Doo itashimashite*	You're welcome
	いいえ	*Iie*	いや	*Iya*	Not at all
Apologizing	すみません	*Sumimasen*	すまない	*Sumanai*	I am sorry, excuse me
	ごめんなさい	*Gomennasai*	ごめん	*Gomen*	I am sorry, excuse me
Granting forgiveness	いいえ	*Iie*	いや	*Iya*	No
Simple greeting	おげんきですか	*Ogenki desu ka*	げんき	*Genki*	How are you?
	おかげさまで	*Okagesama de*	うん、げんき	*Un genki*	I'm fine (thank you)
Numeral Counter	ーえん ードル	*-en, -doru*	ーえん ードル	*-en, -doru*	-yen, - dollar
	ーさい	*-sai*	ーさい	*-sai*	- year old
	ーねん	*-nen*	ーねん	*-nen*	- year
	ーねんせい	*-nensei*	ーねんせい	*-nensei*	- grade
Weather	いいてんきですね	*Ii tenki desu ne*	いいてんき（だ）ね	*Iitenki (da) ne*	It's a nice day, isn't it?
	あついですね	*Atsui desu ne*	あついね	*Atsui ne*	It's a hot day, isn't it?
	むしあついですね	*Mushiatsui desu ne*	むしあついね	*Mushiatsui ne*	It's a hot and humid day, isn't it?
	さむいですね	*Samui desu ne*	さむいね	*Samui ne*	It's a cold day, isn't it?
	よくふりますね	*Yoku furimasu ne*	よくふるね	*Yoku furu ne*	It rains a lot, doesn't it?
Responding to requests	なんでしょう	*Nan deshoo*	なあに	*Naani*	What can I do for you?
	なんでしょうか	*Nan deshoo ka*	なんなの	*Nannano*	What can I do for you?
Describing State (topic)	～は～です	*~wa~desu*	～は～だ	*~wa ~da*	~ be (is, am, are) ~
Asking questions	～ですか	*~desu ka*	～か	*~ka*	[Be ~] ~ ?
	～は～ですか	*~wa~desu ka*	～は～か	*~wa ~ka*	Be (is, am, are) ~?

Notional Vocabulary

Telephone

でんわ	*denwa*	telephone
でんわばんごう	*denwa bangoo*	telephone number
なんばん	*nanban*	what telephone number
なまえ＋さん	*namae+san*	Mr., Ms., Mrs., Miss

School (used to address someone [general])

がっこう	*gakkoo*	school
しょうがっこう(しょうがく)		
	shoogakkoo (shoogaku)	
		elementary school
ちゅうがっこう（ちゅうがく）		
	chuugakkoo (chuugaku)	
		junior high school/middle school
こうとうがっこう（こうこう）		
	kootoo gakkoo (kookoo)	
		high school
せんせい	*sensei*	teacher
2くみ	*nikumi*	class 2

Grade

いちねんせい	*ichinensei*	1st grader
にねんせい	*ninensei*	2nd grader
さんねんせい	*sannensei*	3rd grader
よねんせい	*yonensei*	4th grader
ごねんせい	*gonensei*	5th grader
ろくねんせい	*rokunensei*	6th grader
ななねんせい／しちねんせい		
	nananensei/shichinensei	
		7th grader
はちねんせい	*hachinensei*	8th grader
きゅうねんせい	*kyuunensei*	9th grader
じゅうねんせい	*juunensei*	10th grader
じゅういちねんせい		
	juuichinensei	11th grader
じゅうにねんせい	*juuninensei*	12th grader

Club

ドラマクラブ	*dorama kurabu*	drama club

Season

きせつ	*kisetsu*	season
はる	*haru*	spring
なつ	*natsu*	summer
あき	*aki*	fall
ふゆ	*fuyu*	winter

Weather

いいてんき	*ii tenki*	nice weather
さむい	*samui*	cold
あつい	*atsui*	hot
むしあつい	*mushiatsui*	hot and humid
あめがふります／ふる		
	ame ga furimasu/furu	
		It rains
あめがよくふります／ふる		
	ame ga yoku furimasu/furu	
		It rains a lot

Sports

バレーボール	*bareebooru*	volleyball
ホッケー	*hokkee*	hockey
サッカー	*sakkaa*	soccer
アイスホッケー	*aisu hokkee*	ice hockey
フットボール	*futtobooru*	football
ゴルフ	*gorufu*	golf
バスケット（ボール）		
	basuketto(booru)	basketball
すもう	*sumoo*	sumo
じゅうどう	*juudoo*	judo
からて	*karate*	karate
テニス	*tenisu*	tennis
スケート	*sukeeto*	skate
やきゅう	*yakyuu*	baseball
スキー	*sukii*	ski

Animal Years (Oriental Zodiac)

ねずみどし/ねどし		
	nezumi doshi/ne doshi	
		(year of the rat)
うしどし	*ushidoshi*	(year of the cow)
とらどし	*toradoshi*	(year of the tiger)
うさぎどし/うどし	*usagidoshi/udoshi*	
		(year of the rabbit)
たつどし	*tatsudoshi*	(year of the dragon)
へびどし/みどし	*hebidoshi/mi doshi*	
		(year of the snake)
うまどし	*umadoshi*	(year of the horse)
ひつじどし	*hitsujidoshi*	(year of the sheep)
さるどし	*saru doshi*	(year of the monkey)
とりどし	*toridoshi*	(year of the bird)
いぬどし	*inudoshi*	(year of the dog)
いのししどし/いどし		
	inoshishidoshi/idoshi	
		(year of the boar)

Mathematics

かける	*kakeru*	multiply
わる	*waru*	divide
は	*wa*	equals

Number

いち	ichi	1
に	ni	2
さん	san	3
し／よん	shi/yon	4
ご	go	5
ろく	roku	6
しち／なな	shichi/nana	7
はち	hachi	8
きゅう／く	kyuu/ku	9
じゅう	juu	10
じゅういち	juuichi	11
じゅうに	juuni	12
じゅうさん	juusan	13
じゅうし/じゅうよん	juushi/juuyon	14
じゅうご	juugo	15
じゅうろく	juuroku	16
じゅうしち/じゅうなな	juushichi/juunana	17
じゅうはち	juuhachi	18
じゅうきゅう/じゅうく	juukyuu/juuku	19
にじゅう	nijuu	20
さんじゅう	sanjuu	30
よんじゅう	yonjuu	40
ごじゅう	gojuu	50
ろくじゅう	rokujuu	60
しちじゅう／ななじゅう	shichijuu/nanajuu	70
はちじゅう	hachijuu	80
きゅうじゅう	kyuujuu	90
ひゃく	hyaku	100
にひゃく	nihyaku	200
さんびゃく	sanbyaku	300
よんひゃく	yonhyaku	400
ごひゃく	gohyaku	500
ろっぴゃく	roppyaku	600
ななひゃく	nanahyaku	700
はっぴゃく	happyaku	800
きゅうひゃく	kyuuhyaku	900
せん	sen	1000
にせん	nisen	2000
さんぜん	sanzen	3000
よんせん	yonsen	4000
ごせん	gosen	5000
ろくせん	rokusen	6000
しちせん／ななせん	shichisen/nanasen	7000
はっせん	hassen	8000
きゅうせん	kyuusen	9000
いちまん	ichiman	10,000

Computer

ギガ	giga	gigabyte
メガ	mega	megabyte
ケイ	kei	kilobyte
バイト	baito	byte
ハードディスク	haadodisuku	hard disk

Year

めいじ	meiji	Meiji era
たいしょう	taishoo	Taisho era
しょうわ	shoowa	Showa era
へいせい	heisei	Heisei era
～ねんうまれ	~nen umare	birth year
がんねん	gannen	first year(of an era)

Currency Counters

ドル	doru	dollar
セント	sento	cent
えん	en	yen
ポンド	pondo	pound

New Year Greetings

あけましておめでとうございます
Akemashite omedetoo gozaimasu
(Happy New Year)

きんがしんねん *Kinga shinnen*
(lit., I humbly wish you a Happy New Year)

がしょう *Gashoo*
(lit., Celebrating a New Year)

げいしゅん *Geishun* (lit., Welcoming Spring + New Year)

ことしもよろしくおねがいします
Kotoshi mo yoroshiku onegai shimasu
(lit., I wish our cordial relationship to continue this year)

ことしもおげんきで *Kotoshi mo ogenki de*
(lit., Have a healthy and happy year)

えと *eto* (twelve signs of the Chinese zodiac)

VOCABULARY

1.7 Application

Let's Read New Year's Greeting Cards ねんがじょう

ノート22 **(Note 22):**

Japanese people customarily exchange New Year's greeting cards with relatives, friends and acquaintances. Post offices guarantee to deliver them to the addressees on the morning of New Year's Day if they are posted by a designated date in December. A typical ねんがじょう includes a New Year greeting, a short message, the date (January 1 = がんじつ or がんたん in Japanese), and some reference (mostly pictorial) to that year's えと (sign of the Chinese zodiac). For example, the year 2000 is the year of the dragon.

Popular New Year Greetings on Cards

あけましておめでとうございます。　(Happy New Year.)

きんがしんねん
謹賀新年　　　　　　　　　　　　(lit., I humbly wish you a Happy New Year.)

がしょう
賀正　　　　　　　　　　　　　　(lit., Celebrating a New Year)

げいしゅん
迎春　　　　　　　　　　　　　　(lit., Welcoming Spring = New Year)

Popular New Year Messages

ことしもよろしくおねがいします。　(lit., I wish our cordial relationship to continue this year.)

ことしもおげんきで。　　　　　　(lit. Have a healthy and happy year.)

えと**(Twelve signs of the Chinese zodiac)**

ねずみどし／
ねどし
1972, 1984,1996, 2008

うしどし
1973, 1985,1997, 2009

とらどし
1974, 1986,1998, 2010

うさぎどし／うどし
1975, 1987,1999, 2011

たつどし
1976, 1988, 2000, 2012

へびどし／みどし
1977, 1989, 2001, 2013

うまどし
1978, 1990, 2002, 2014

ひつじどし
1979, 1991, 2003, 2015

さるどし
1980, 1992, 2004, 2016

とりどし
1981, 1993, 2005, 2017

いぬどし
1982, 1994, 2006, 2018

いのししどし／
いどし
1983, 1995, 2007, 2019

1. Read the New Year's greeting cards below and find the corresponding animal years.

A.

あけまして
おめでとう
ございます
ことしもよろしく
おねがいします
二〇〇〇年　元旦

B.

謹賀新年

ことしもおげんきで

２００１年　元旦

やまだゆうじ

C.

賀正

平成１５年
１月１日

D.

迎春

A Happy
New Year

ニコール

Kana and Kanji

Long vowels in katakana

You've already learned that Japanese makes a distinction between short and long vowels (see p.123). In romanization, short vowels are spelled with single letters (*a i u e o*) and long vowels are spelled with double letters (*aa ii uu ee oo*). For example, the word chizu (with a short *i* sound) means "map," and the word chiizu (with a long *ii* sound) means "cheese." In katakana, long vowels are written with the symbol ー, which simply lengthens the preceding vowel.

ギター	*gitaa*	guitar		ケーキ	*keeki*	cake
スキー	*sukii*	ski		ソーダ	*sooda*	soda
プール	*puuru*	pool				

The technical term for the ー symbol is *choo-on kigoo* ("long sound symbol"), but the everyday name for it is just *boo* ("bar").

The words above divide into syllables and beats as follows, with the ー symbol representing the second half of a long syllable.

ギ|ター	*gi | taa*	2 syllables		ケー|キ	*kee | ki*	2 syllables
ギ・タ・ー	*gi· ta· a*	3 beats		ケ・ー・キ	*ke· e· ki*	3 beats
ス|キー	*su | kii*	2 syllables		ソー|ダ	*soo | da*	2 syllables
ス・キ・ー	*su· ki· i*	3 beats		ソ・ー・ダ	*so· o· da*	3 beats
プー|ル	*puu | ru*	2 syllables				
プ・ー・ル	*pu· u· ru*	3 beats				

Syllable-final consonants in katakana

A Japanese long syllable can end with a long vowel or with either one of two consonants. One of these syllable-final consonants is always written *n* in romanization and ン in katakana, as in the examples below.

パン	*pan*	bread	トンネル	*tonneru*	tunnel
ダンス	*dansu*	dance	ピンポン	*pinpon*	ping-pong

Since ン represents the second half of a long syllable, these words divide into syllables and beats as follows.

パン	*pan*	1 syllable	トン|ネ|ル	*ton|ne|ru*	3 syllables
パ・ン	*pa n*	2 beats	ト・ン・ネ・ル	*to n ne ru*	4 beats
ダン|ス	*dan|su*	2 syllables	ピン|ポン	*pin|pon*	2 syllables
ダ・ン・ス	*da n su*	3 beats	ピ・ン・ポ・ン	*pi n po n*	4 beats

The other syllable-final consonant is spelled in a wide variety of different ways in romanization (see p. 15), but it's always written in katakana with the symbol ッ, which is just the symbol ツ (*tsu*) reduced in size. This *chiisai tsu* ("small tsu") lengthens the beginning of whatever consonant comes right after it, as the words below illustrate.

サッカー	*sakkaa*	soccer	マッチ	*matchi*	match

Since ッ represents the second half of a long syllable, the words above divide into syllables and beats as follows.

サッ|カー	*sak|kaa*	2 syllables	マッ|チ	*mat|chi*	2 syllables
サ・ッ・カ・ー	*sa k ka a*	4 beats	マ・ッ・チ	*ma t chi*	3 beats

Stroke order in katakana

Of the three types of symbols in the Japanese writing system (katakana, hiragana, and kanji), katakana are the easiest to write. As explained earlier, each katakana symbol originated as an abbreviated kanji. The diagrams below show the kanji from which イ (*i*), ウ (*u*), and エ (*e*) developed.

伊→イ　宇→ウ　江→エ

Like kanji, katakana have to be written with a certain stroke order. Since katakana originated as parts of kanji, if you master the stroke order of katakana you'll have an easier time when it comes to learning kanji. Take katakana ウ (*u*). How many strokes does it have? And what order do the strokes comes in? The diagram below is one common way of showing stroke order. Since ウ has three strokes, the diagram shows three stages. These stages show how the symbol develops as each stroke is added in the correct order.

ウ：　ウ　ウ　ウ

In most cases, the strokes of a symbol are written high before low and left before right.

In addition to stroke order, the direction in which each stroke is written is also important. A stage-by-stage diagram like the one above doesn't provide this information. One common way of showing direction is with arrows:

In general, vertical strokes are written from top to bottom, and horizontal strokes are written from left to right. In curved or angled strokes, top to bottom usually takes precedence over left to right, although there are some exceptions.

1.8 Virtual Reality

I. Warm-Up

A. Match the expressions on the left with the situations on the right.

1. こんばんは
2. なんねんせいですか
3. おはようございます
4. こんにちは
5. おなまえは
6. いいえ、ちがいます
7. でんわばんごうはなんばんですか
8. おはよう
9. はい、そうです
10. あのう
11. はじめまして
12. じゃ

a. asking someone his/her name
b. greeting someone in the evening
c. pausing before asking a question
d. meeting someone for the first time
e. greeting in the afternoon
f. greeting an older person in the morning
g. developing a conversation
h. asking someone his or her grade level
i. confirming that what one just heard is correct
j. asking someone his or her telephone number
k. greeting a peer in the morning
l. saying that what one just heard is wrong

B. *Match the expressions on the left with the situations on the right.*

1.	あのう、すみません	a.	saying "thank you"
2.	いいてんきですね	b.	saying "you're welcome"
3.	はい、どうぞ	c.	attracting someone's attention
4.	はい、いただきます	d.	accepting food/things
5.	ありがとうございます	e.	offering food/things
6.	はい、すみません	f.	rejecting someone's offering of food or things
7.	いいえ、けっこうです	g.	appreciating someone's offering of food or things
8.	～をおねがいします	h.	referring to the weather when greeting someone
9.	～をください	i.	requesting food or things
10.	どういたしまして	j.	ordering food or things (more politely)
11.	いただきます	k.	apologizing after a violation
12.	ごちそうさまでした	l.	saying "thank you" before eating
13.	なんさいですか	m.	asking someone his or her animal year
14.	なんねんうまれですか	n.	saying "good night"
15.	ごめんなさい	o.	saying "thank you" after eating
16.	おやすみなさい	p.	planning to meet again
17.	しつれいします	q.	asking someone his or her age
18.	さようなら	r.	taking leave
19.	おげんきですか	s.	asking someone his or her birth year
20.	なにどしですか	t.	taking leave formally
21.	じゃ、また	u.	asking about someone's health

C. *Preparation for Main Activity: Making a list of questions.*

You are participating in a high school social. Make a list of questions you want to ask the other participants.

II. *Main Activity: Role Play*

Everyone plays a participant in a high school social. Each wears a name tag with a different color according to their age and host group (red, younger students; blue, older students; yellow, faculty advisers for school clubs and coaches for athletic programs; green, parents, citizens, senior citizens, Japanese parents, and the mayor). The participants circulate, introducing each other and exchanging information concerning telephone numbers, clubs, grades, ages, years of birth, animal years, currency, computers, sports, etc.

red: younger students	30% of participants
blue: older students	30% of participants
yellow: faculty advisers for school clubs and coaches for athletic programs	20% of participants
green: parents, citizens, senior citizens, Japanese parents, and the mayor	20% of participants

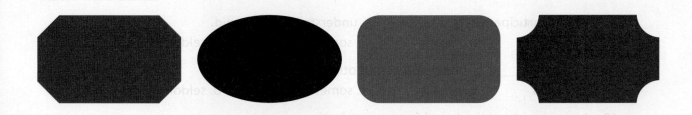

III. Wrap-Up: Self-evaluation

A. *How was the social? Did you get to know many people? Did everything go smoothly, or were there awkward moments? Think about your experience and complete the following multiple-choice questions.*

1. The atmosphere of the party was
   a. fun   b. tense   c. formal   d. other (_____)

2. I usually find meeting people
   a. enjoyable   b. boring   c. scary   d. other (_____)

3. This time I found meeting other participants
   a. enjoyable   b. boring   c. scary   d. other (_____)

4. In my interaction with others I was
   a. aggressive   b. smooth   c. shy   d. other (_____)

5. I would describe my role in communicating with other participants as
   a. leader   b. follower   c. mediator   d. other (_____)

6. I _____ that role.
   a. liked   b. did not like   c. felt neutral about

7. Throughout the party, I was _____ .
   a. confident   b. insecure   c. aloof   d. other (_____)

8. Other participants _____ understood what I said.
   a. always   b. usually   c. sometimes   d. seldom

9. I _____ understood what other participants said.
   a. always   b. usually   c. sometimes   d. seldom

10. Language strategies I used for communication were:
    a. comfirming with *desu ne*
    b. partial repeating
    c. asking again
    d. nonverbal signals
    e. developing conversation with じゃ
    f. pausing before a question with あのう

11. I still remember _____ of the information I collected.
    a. all   b. most   c. some   d. a little

B. *List the strengths and weaknesses of your performance in the role play and think about how you can improve your performance next time.*

ひゃくえん

ごひゃくえん

せんえん

ごせんえん

いちまんえん

Japanese Currency

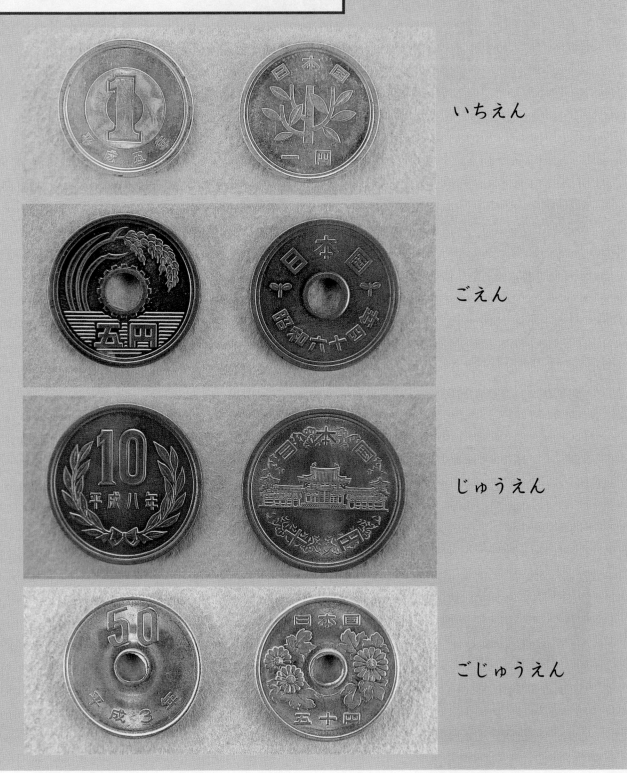

いちえん

ごえん

じゅうえん

ごじゅうえん

Chapter 2
Planning a Party

Chapter 2

Planning a Party

2.1 Introduction

OBJECTIVES

At the end of this chapter, you will be able to:

- handle successfully a variety of realistic situations involving decision making

- chair a class meeting and guide the class in making decisions

- participate in class meetings and cooperate with other participants in making decisions

- use hesitation noises effectively

- successfully handle a situation involving comparing things

- plan and talk about various school and teen activities

- obtain and disseminate information using basic sources written in kana

You will also learn:

- about the Japanese and American methods of decision making

- essential expressions for chairing a class meeting

- how to use basic question words

- how to compare two, three, or more items

- various ways of requesting something

- how to express dates, the time of day, and the day of the week

- how to count people

KISETSU THEATER

Planning a Party

Class meeting:
Experience the dynamics of cooperative decision making.

Chairing a class meeting successfully takes more than just language skills. You must be an efficient coordinator of discussion, an impartial sorter of conflicting opinions and interests, and a good consensus builder and decision maker. You also need to build trust in your leadership among participants and establish a cooperative relationship with people in other positions, such as board writer and note taker. What if you are a participant in the meeting? Should you pursue your own interests and insist on your opinions exclusively? Or should you aim for compromise and consensus building? In this chapter you will be playing a range of roles in mock class meetings in which you will be making various decisions about a party for Japanese exchange students.

Making a poster for the party:

Be artistic but make sure to include all the necessary information.

Your experience writing *nengajoo* should be useful here, since poster making also involves writing simple messages. In addition, you will be reminded of the importance of good planning and advance organization. Before designing your poster, make sure you know what piecess of information need to be included and which one should be presented to the audience in the most eye-catching fashion. Planning before writing is a habit you should certainly practice whenever you write anything.

Japanese food:
It's not all sushi and sashimi

Some Japanese foods, such as sushi, have become a fixture in restaurants in many cities throughout the United States. However, Japanese people eat a lot of other foods for supper in their homes. They enjoy a wide variety of "homey" dishes, to which you will be introduced in this chapter. The increase in the popularity of Japanese cuisine among Westerners has something to do with the fact that it is considered healthy. Do you think there is a connection between what Japanese people eat and their life expectancy being one of the longest in the world? If you are a health nut, this is a question you must explore! You will also learn to use chopsticks and find out that eating Japanese rice with them is not as hard as you may have imagined.

Board writing and scribing:
Not just neat handwriting

You will have an opportunity to play a board writer and/or scribe in your mock class meetings. Neat handwriting is not the only qualification for becoming a competent board writer. You must also be an effective organizer of the varying views expressed in the meeting. You need to be able to produce a quick summary of any opinion you hear and write it legibly on the board. Furthermore, you'll need to develop a feel for the dynamics of your particular group and be able to predict the amount of information you will be writing on the board during each phase of the meeting. This practice will help you use the available board space wisely and effectively. Finally, you must maintain good communication with the chair and have some say about the pace of the meeting. This way you can avoid having opinions be exchanged at a speed you can't keep up with. All this may seem taxing and overwhelming, but give it a try. Dive in. This may prove to be a fun, exciting, and rewarding learning experience.

WARM-UP

1. **Let's make mindmaps on transparencies.**

   Students work in groups of three to five. Each group creates a mindmap for the category they selected from the list given by the teacher.

   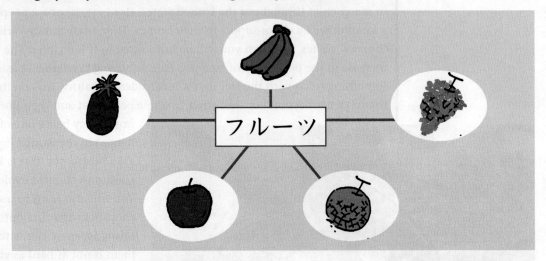

2. **Cooperative picture drawing.**

   You will do this exercise in small groups. No one is allowed to talk for the duration of the activity, which is set at ten minutes. All communication must be carried out nonverbally. You and your group work together to draw a picture conveying a theme. The theme can be anything from concrete (sports, flute, school) to abstract (love, friendship, peace), but bear in mind that you must remain silent during both the theme selection and the picture drawing. Each group will be given a large sheet of paper and may use markers or crayons of various colors. However, only one person in the group may draw at any given time. Take turns drawing so that everyone can participate in the production process as much and as equally as possible. And remember: You are collectively producing just one drawing with a designated theme, not a collection of completely different pictures drawn by each member. Stop working after ten minutes, but remain silent and choose a representative from your group, who will give a brief presentation about your drawing.

3.   *"Catch That Word?" Game*

A group of four constitutes a team in this game. One group plays the "performers" while the rest play the "observers" in any given round. Each round is completed in the following order; the teams should take turns assuming the performers' role in each round.

- The performers (**P**) receive a card on which a Japanese word is written from their teacher.

- **P** examine the word and count the number of its syllables/kana. One performer is assigned to each one of the syllables. (For example, if the word is それとも, someone will be in charge of そ while others will be assigned to either れ, と, or も. The number of performers should equal the number of syllables.)

- **P** then line up in front of the observers (**O**) and simultaneously and clearly pronounce their assigned syllables/kana.

- **O**, working in teams, must come up with the word that they think was uttered by **P** and write it on a sheet of paper.

- Each team shows its word to the rest of the class and then listens to **P** pronounce their assigned syllables/kana one by one in the proper order.

- Those teams that wrote the correct word earn a point.

Keep in mind that one of the key elements to success in this game is the degree of cooperation among team members.

BASIC VOCABULARY

パイナップル	バナナ
コーヒー	こうちゃ
ケーキ	クッキー
スープ	サラダ
ジャズ	ロック
ハンバーガー	ピザ
サッカー	テニス
ステーキ	チキン
えいが	ダンス
アイスティー	ソーダ

なんじ	**what time**
いちじ	one o'clock
にじ	two o'clock
さんじ	three o'clock
よじ	four o'clock
ごじ	five o'clock
ろくじ	six o'clock
しちじ	seven o'clock
はちじ	eight o'clock
くじ	nine o'clock
じゅうじ	ten o'clock
じゅういちじ	eleven o'clock
じゅうにじ	twelve o'clock

なんようび	**what day (of the week)**
にちようび	Sunday
げつようび	Monday
かようび	Tuesday
すいようび	Wednesday
もくようび	Thursday
きんようび	Friday
どようび	Saturday

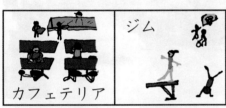

いちがつ　一月　January

にがつ　二月　February

さんがつ　三月　March

しがつ　四月　April

ごがつ　五月　May

ろくがつ　六月　June

しちがつ　七月　July

はちがつ　八月　August

くがつ　九月　September

じゅうがつ　十月　October

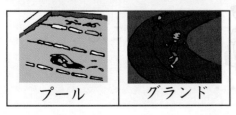

じゅういちがつ　十一月　November

じゅうにがつ　十二月　December

159

BASIC VOCABULARY (continued)

1st.	一日	ついたち
2nd.	二日	ふつか
3rd.	三日	みっか
4th.	四日	よっか
5th.	五日	いつか
6th.	六日	むいか
7th.	七日	なのか
8th.	八日	ようか
9th.	九日	ここのか
10th.	十日	とおか
11th.	十一日 じゅういちにち	
12th.	十二日 じゅうににち	
13th.	十三日 じゅうさんにち	
14th.	十四日 じゅうよっか	
15th.	十五日 じゅうごにち	
16th.	十六日 じゅうろくにち	
17th.	十七日 じゅうしちにち	

18th.	十八日 じゅうはちにち	
19th.	十九日 じゅうくにち	
20th.	二十日 はつか	
21st	二十一日 にじゅういちにち	
22nd	二十二日 にじゅうににち	
23rd	二十三日 にじゅうさんにち	
24th	二十四日 にじゅうよっか	
25th	二十五日 にじゅうごにち	
26th	二十六日 にじゅうろくにち	
27th	二十七日 にじゅうしちにち	
28th	二十八日 にじゅうはちにち	
29th	二十九日 にじゅうくにち	
30th	三十日 さんじゅうにち	
31st	三十一日 さんじゅういちにち	

ミーティングをはじめましょう。

トピックはパーティーです。

じゃ、２４かのきんようびにしましょう。

これでミーティングをおわります。

1, 2, 3, 4, 5, ・・・

なんにん？

ひとり、ふたり、さんにん、よにん、ごにん・・・

MECHANICS

4. *Fill in the blanks with the letter of the question word on the right that corresponds to the Japanese word on the left.*

    1. どこ　　　　( )　　a. which one (of three or more alternatives)
    2. どちら　　　( )　　b. which one (of two alternatives)
    3. どれ　　　　( )　　c. where
    4. いくら　　　( )　　d. what time
    5. なんじ　　　( )　　e. what day of the week
    6. なんようび ( )　　f. how much

5. *You are in charge of putting on a party for Japanese exchange students. You made a list of foods, beverages, and activities for the party. However, you put the list in your pocket and ended up washing it along with your shirt. Recompile the list.*

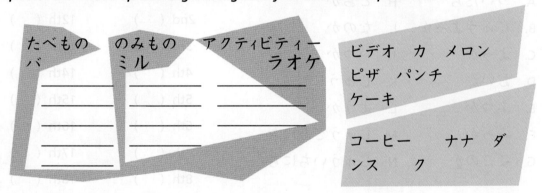

6. *Fill in the blanks with the letter of the time word on the right that corresponds to the Japanese word on the left.*

    1. にじ　　　　( )　　a. four o'clock
    2. よじ　　　　( )　　b. twelve o'clock
    3. はちじ　　　( )　　c. nine o'clock
    4. くじ　　　　( )　　d. what time
    5. なんじ　　　( )　　e. eight o'clock
    6. じゅうにじ ( )　　f. two o'clock

161

7. **Fill in the blanks with the letter of the day of the week below.**

A. きんようび

B. かようび

C. げつようび

D. もくようび

E. どようび

F. すいようび

G. にちようび

1がつカレンダー (January)						
1st	2nd	3rd	4th	5th	6th	7th
8th	9th	10th	11th	12th	13th	14th

8. **Fill in the blanks with the letter of the day of the month below.**

A. ついたち   H. とおか

B. じゅうよっか   I. なのか

C. よっか   J. いつか

D. むいか   K. じゅうににち

E. ふつか   L. ようか

F. みっか   M. じゅうさんにち

G. ここのか   N. じゅういちにち

1st ( )   11th ( )

2nd ( )   12th ( )

3rd ( )   13th ( )

4th ( )   14th ( )

5th ( )   15th ( )

6th ( )   16th ( )

7th ( )   17th ( )

8th ( )   18th ( )

9th ( )   19th ( )

10th ( )   20th ( )

9. **Determine whether the following expressions are used in a meeting situation. Mark them ほんとう (True) or うそ (False).**

1. ミーティングをはじめましょう。   (ほんとう) or (うそ)

2. これでおわります。   (ほんとう) or (うそ)

3. たってください。   (ほんとう) or (うそ)

4. てをあげてください。   (ほんとう) or (うそ)

5. いいおてんきですね。   (ほんとう) or (うそ)

6. いただきます。   (ほんとう) or (うそ)

7. どれがいいですか。   (ほんとう) or (うそ)

Janken Game

Janken is the Japanese equivalent of Rock-Paper-Scissors. Players chant *jan-ken-pon* in unison. On the last count, *pon*, each player puts out his or her hand in the form of a rock (closed fist), paper (open hand), or scissors (index and middle fingers spread out). Rock wins over scissors, scissors over paper, and paper over rock. When is a tie, the game is repeated, this time with the chant *aiko desho*. Japanese children play numerous variations of *janken*. Even adults use *janken* to decide things, the way Americans might decide to flip a coin.

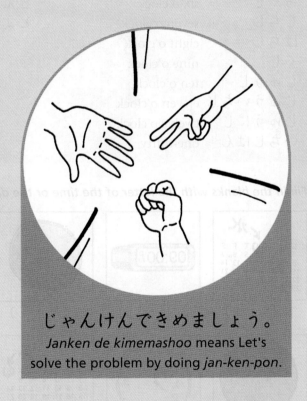

じゃんけんできめましょう。
Janken de kimemashoo means Let's solve the problem by doing *jan-ken-pon*.

163

2.2   Mechanics

Time expressions ノート1 (Note 1):

Hour, o'clock (Hours are given as – number + counter じ *ji*)		Days of the week (make for "day of week" is ようび *yoobi*)	
なんじ	what time	なんようび	What day of the week
いちじ	one o'clock	にちようび	Sunday
にじ	two o'clock	げつようび	Monday
さんじ	three o'clock	かようび	Tuesday
よじ	four o'clock	すいようび	Wednesday
ごじ	five o'clock	もくようび	Thursday
ろくじ	six o'clock	きんようび	Friday
しちじ	seven o'clock	どようび	Saturday
はちじ	eight o'clock		
くじ	nine o'clock		
じゅうじ	ten o'clock		
じゅういちじ	eleven o'clock		
じゅうにじ	twelve o'clock		
いちじはん	one-thirty		

1. *Fill in the blanks with the letter of the time or the day of the week below.*

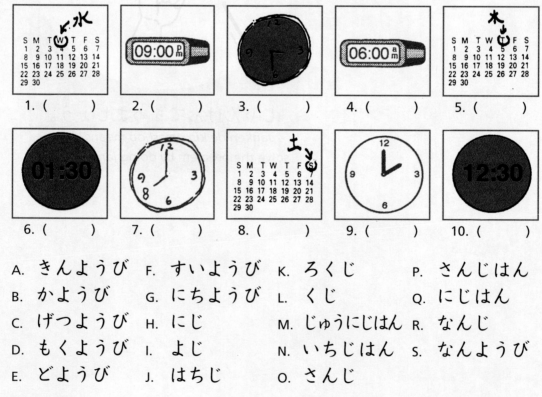

1. (   )   2. (   )   3. (   )   4. (   )   5. (   )

6. (   )   7. (   )   8. (   )   9. (   )   10. (   )

A. きんようび	F. すいようび	K. ろくじ	P. さんじはん
B. かようび	G. にちようび	L. くじ	Q. にじはん
C. げつようび	H. にじ	M. じゅうにじはん	R. なんじ
D. もくようび	I. よじ	N. いちじはん	S. なんようび
E. どようび	J. はちじ	O. さんじ	

2. **Read the following chart. Decide whether each of the statements is true or false. If it is true, write O in the parentheses. If it is false, write X in the parentheses.**

イベント　カレンダー			
イベント	ようび	じかん	ばしょ
アートフェア	すいようび	さんじ	アートセンター
アニメフェスティバル	かようび	はちじ	グラウンド
サイエンスフェア	げつようび	よじ	こうどう
ジャパニーズナイト	どようび	くじ	カフェテリア

1. (　　) Japanese Night will be held on Saturday at 9:00 in the classroom.

2. (　　) The Science Fair will be held on Friday at 4:00 in the gymnasium.

3. (　　) The Art Fair will be held on Tuesday at 3:00 in the art center.

4. (　　) The Science Fair will be held on Monday at 4:00 in the auditorium.

5. (　　) The Animation Festival will be held on Tuesday at 9:00 in the field.

3. **Practice asking your classmates the time using the model below.**

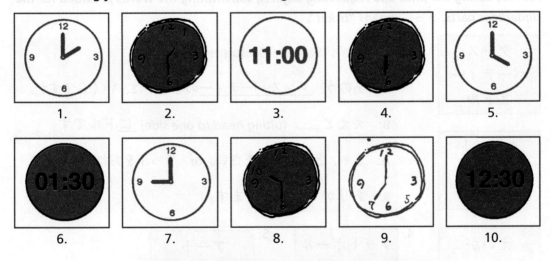

会話の例 (Sample Dialogue)

A: いまなんじですか。

B: <u>１０じはん</u>です。

A: ああ、そうですか。(*saying in an upbeat way*) どうもありがとう。

4. Practice asking your classmates the place and time using the model below.

会話の例 (Sample Dialogue)

A: あしたのパーティーはどこですか。

B: <u>カフェテリア</u>です。

A: ああ、そうですか。*(saying in an upbeat way)*
  パーティーは6じですね。

B: いいえ、ちがいます。<u>6じはん</u>です。

1.
6:30

2.
7:00

3.
8:00

4.
7::30

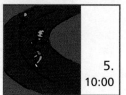

5.
10:00

ああ、そうですか
いいえ、ちがいます

ノート2 (Note 2):

ああ、そうですか。 corresponds to "Oh, I see." in English when expressing confirmation for the right answer. いいえ、ちがいます。 corresponds to "No, it isn't. " in English when expressing a different opinion from the one given.

5. Practice asking the price and requesting objects, substituting the words provided for the underlines parts. きっぷ means "ticket".

1.
ダンス
パーティー
2ドル

会話の例 (Sample Dialogue)

A: あのう、<u>ダンスパーティー</u>のきっぷは、いくらですか。

B: ええと……。*(tilting head to one side)* <u>に</u>ドルです。

A: じゃ、きっぷをください。or きっぷをおねがいします。

B: ありがとうございます。

2.
タレント
ショー
5ドル

3.
えいが
7ドル

4.
フットボール
20ドル

5.
アート
ショー
12ドル

ええと
あのう

ノート3 (Note 3):

Like あのう in the previous chapter, ええと is useful when searching for the right word. One can also show hesitation to give an answer by pausing for a while after ええと or あのう as shown in the conversation above.

6. Practice asking your classmates the day of the week using the model below.

1.   2.   3.

会話の例 (Sample Dialogue)

A: パーティーはなんようびですか。

B: すいようびです。

A: ああ、そうですか。 (*saying in an upbeat way*) どうもありがとう。

4.

5.

7. Practice asking your classmates the day of the week and time using the model below.

1.

会話の例 (Sample Dialogue)

A: なんようびのなんじですか。

B: すいようびのにじです。

A: ああ、そうですか。 (saying in an upbeat way) どうもありがとう。

2.

3.

4.

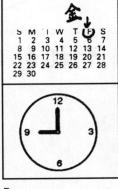

5.

8. **Group Activity: Weekly Schedule Completion Game**

A. A group of five students forms a team.

B. Each receives a weekly schedule of events with different information missing.

C. Team members exchange information among themselves and complete their schedule.

D. The team who accurately completes their schedule first is the winner.

イベント　カレンダー					
イベント	ようび	じかん	ねだん	ばしょ	でんわ
アートフェア	WED			アートセンター	
アニメフェスティバル		8:00	1.00		265-8097
サイエンスフェア	MON				233-1448
ジャパニーズナイト			ただ	カフェテリア	
スピーチコンテスト		4:00			
フォークダンス	SUN		2.00	グラウンド	451-9030
ロックコンサート		9:00	10.00	こうどう	

会話の例(Sample Dialogue)

A: あのう、<u>アート　フェア</u>はなんよ
　　うびですか。

B: <u>すいようび</u>です。

A: なんじですか。

B: ええと、<u>3じ</u>です。

A: <u>アートフェア</u>はいくらですか。

B: <u>2ドル</u>です。

A: それから、<u>アートフェア</u>はどこです
　　か。

B: <u>アートセンター</u>です。

A: それから、<u>アートセンター</u>のでん
　　わばんごうはなんばんですか。

B: <u>２７７－４５８９</u>です。

それから

ノート4 (Note 4):

それから in Sample Dialogue corresponds to "then" in English connecting the preceding statement with the one starting with a conjunction.

9. Practice asking and answering questions (agreeing and disagreeing), substituting the words provided for the underlined parts. Follow the models.

Example A

会話の例**A (Sample Dialogue A)**

A: <u>どようび</u>がいいですか。

B: そうですね。*(downbeat and quick)* <u>どようび</u>がいいですね。

1.   2.   3.   4.   5.   6.

Example B

会話の例**B (Sample Dialogue B)**

A: <u>かようび</u>がいいですか。

B: そうですねえ。*(upbeat and slow)* <u>かようび</u>はちょっと。

1.   2.   3.   4.   5.   6.

ちょっと

ノート**5 (Note 5):**

ちょっと in Sample Dialogue B above corresponds to "a little" in English. However, It is used when giving a rejection for an answer.

そうですね。

そうですねえ。

ノート**6 (Note 6):**

そうですね。(downbeat and quick) in Sample Dialogue A above corresponds to "That's right" in English when expressing confirmation for the right answer. そうですねえ 。(upbeat and slow) in Sample Dialogue B above corresponds to "it is wrong" in English when expressing reservation or doubt for the answer.

169

10. Practice asking and answering questions, substituting the words provided for the underlined parts. Follow the models.

Example A

会話の例A (Sample Dialogue A)

A: バナナがいいですか。それとも、りんごがいいですか。

B: りんごがいいです。

1.

2.

3.

Example B

会話の例B (Sample Dialogue B)

A: ハンバーガーとピザと、どちらがいいですか。

B: ピザがいいです。

1.

2.

3.

ノート7 (Note 7):

それとも in Sample Dialogue A above corresponds to "or" in English. It is used when giving an alternative or an additional choice. と in Sample Dialogue B is used when listing items for choices. See p.195 for further explanation.

11. *Practice asking and answering questions, substituting the words provided for the*
    underlined parts. Follow the models.

Example A, B

1.

2.

3.

会話の例 **A (Sample Dialogue A)**

A: <u>コーラ</u>がいいですか。<u>アイスティー</u>がいいですか。

それとも、(*hesitating*) <u>ソーダ</u>がいいですか。

B: ええと、<u>アイスティー</u>がいいです。

会話の例 **B (Sample Dialogue B)**

A: <u>コーラ</u>と<u>アイスティー</u>と<u>ソーダ</u>と どれがいいですか。

B: <u>アイスティー</u>がいいです。

171

12. Practice the following conversation, substituting the words provided for the first three underlined parts. Create your own response for the fourth underlined part.

会話の例 **(Sample Dialogue)**

A: ダンスは、<u>９じ</u>がいいですか、それとも、<u>１０じ</u>がいいですか。

B: ええと......。(*tilting head to one side*)

A: じゃ、<u>なんじ</u>がいいですか。

B: あのう、(*hesitating*) <u>８じ</u>がいいです。

Sample Responses

1. ９じ、１０じ、なんじ
2. ３じ、５じ、なんじ
3. げつようび、すいようび、なんようび
4. もくようび、きんようび、なんようび
5. カフェテリア、ジム、どこ
6. としょかん、きょうしつ、どこ

| ようび: _____ ようび |
| じかん: _____ じ |
| ばしょ: _____ |

13. Practice expressing a decision by substituting the words provided for the underlined parts.

Example

会話の例 **(Sample Dialogue)**

A: <u>コーラ</u>にしますか。

B: そうですね。(*down beat and quick*) じゃ、<u>コーラ</u>にしましょう。

1.　　　　2.　　　　3.　　　　4.　　　　5.

14. Role Play:

Card A (Host)

You have a guest visiting your home and want to find out her preferences with respect to fruit, drinks, and entertainment. You have two kinds of fruit (melon, oranges), three kinds of drinks (cola, juice, coffee), and two kinds of entertainment (video, karaoke).

Card B (Guest)

You are a guest at someone's house. Your host will ask you your preferences with respect to fruit, drinks, and entertainment. Respond with your choices.

会話の例 **(Sample Dialogue)**

A: メロンがいいですか。それとも、オレンジがいいですか。

B: メロンがいいです。

A: コーラとジュースとコーヒーと どれがいいですか。

B: ええと、(hesitating) コーヒーがいいです。

A: ビデオとカラオケと どちらがいいですか。

B: カラオケがいいです。

15. Cooperative Group Work: Construct a large picture.

Students should work in groups of three to five. Each group tries to construct a large picture with the colored cards given. The teacher distributes an equal number of colored cards to each group. Members of the groups try to exchange cards they don't need for cards they need with members of other groups, saying, for example, "みどりのカードをください／おねがいします。" (*Midori no kaado o kudasai./Onegai shimasu.*) "Can I have a green card?" The group that is able to complete their picture the fastest, wins.

Cooperative decision making with 〜に しましょう.ノート8 (Note 8):

〜に しましょう is used to announce a decision after some discussion of people's ideas. 〜に しましょう can be used for many kinds of decisions. It corresponds to "let's do such and such" or "let's make it such and such" in English. に is preceded by a noun.

会話の例 (Sample Dialogue)

A: スピーチコンテストは、げつようび で いいですか。

B: いいえ…… (looking away)。

A: じゃ、(rising intonation on "ja") なんよ うびが いいですか。

B: もくようびが いいです。

A: Cさんは、なんようびが いいですか。

C: もくようびが いいです。

A: じゃ、(rising intonation on "ja") もくよ うびに しましょう。

16. Role Play: Cooperative Decision Making

Do the role play below using the sample conversation as a model.

Card A (committee chair)

You are the chair of a committee for planning activities. Today you are talking with other committee members to finalize what day of the week, what time, and where to have a party. Ask the other members' opinions regarding this matter and make decisions as a leader. You suggest that the party will be on Saturday at 6:00 in the cafeteria.

Card B (committee member)

You are a member of a planning committee for school activities. Today your committee, under the leadership of its chair, is trying to finalize what day of the week, what time, and where a party should be held. Help the chair by contributing as much as you can. You'd prefer it to be on Friday at 7:00 in the auditorium.

Card C (committee member)

You are a member of a planning committee for school activities. Today your committee, under the leadership of its chair, is trying to finalize what day of the week, what time, and where a party should be held. Help the chair by contributing as much as you can. You'd prefer it to be on Saturday at 7:00 in the auditorium.

Japanese Food

When you think of Japanese food, what types of dishes come to mind? For many people, the most common initial responses to this question might be sushi, *sashimi*, *tempura*, and *sukiyaki*. However, it is important to note that most Japanese people do not eat these types of dishes daily. The main food in a Japanese meal is white rice, which it is eaten with a pair of chopsticks along with some side dishes. It is very important to know how to use chopsticks when eating Japanese food. Here is a quick explanation of how to use chopsticks:

1. Hold the chopsticks about one-third of the way from the top.

2. Lay the bottom chopstick against your ring finger and place the other one between your thumb, index finger, and middle finger.

3. Try to move the top chopstick.

Note: Do not hold the chopsticks too tightly. Relax and hold them gently.

Now, using a pair of chopsticks might sound fairly easy reading these instructions, but don't be too disappointed if you can't get it on your first try. Keep practicing, and eventually you will even be able to pick up a single grain of rice with your chopsticks!

Unlike Chinese white rice, in which each grain of rice can be individually isolated, Japanese white rice has a sticky texture. So technically it is easier to pick up Japanese rice with your chopsticks than Chinese rice. The side dishes eaten with rice include meat, fish, vegetables, different types of beans, and dried foods such as *hijiki* (brown algae) and *shiitake* (dried mushrooms soaked in water prior to cooking to make them soft again).

Japanese food is rarely very spicy, and the food is seasoned relatively lightly. However, the intensity of the seasoning varies according to the region. Food in the Kanto region is seasoned comparatively heavier than food in the Kansai region, for example.

Soy sauce is used in most Japanese dishes. This seasoning is made by adding *kooji* (a type of yeast obtained from the mold of steamed rice or barley) to soybeans and wheat and then fermenting the mixture. Other common seasonings used in Japanese cuisine include sugar, mirin (a sweet liquid made by adding glutinous rice and *kooji* to *shoochuu*, a distilled spirit made from rice and barley), sake (Japanese rice wine), and *miso* (a bean paste made by steaming soybeans or barley and fermenting it by adding salt and *kooji*).

In recent years, Japanese cuisine has become popular among Westerners because it is considered very healthy. The fact is that a lot of fish and vegetables are used in Japanese cooking and, compared to Western dishes, it has less calories. Also, many root crops, including taro and burdock, which Japanese often use in their cooking, contain plenty of fiber. Beans and tofu (bean curd), which are also common Japanese ingredients, contain large amounts of vegetable albumin. And eating miso soup everyday is said to prevent stomach cancer. For those of you who have never tried Japanese food, this is a good chance, so go for it!

2.3 Mechanics

> **ノート9 (Note 9):**
>
> Managing a meeting requires that the chairperson and the other members use various strategies. These strategies are explained below.

1. **Connect the Japanese meeting strategies on the left with their English counterparts on the right.**

ミーティングをはじめましょう。•   • deciding by vote

これでおわります。   •   • beginning of a meeting

てをあげてください。   •   • close of a meeting

トピックはパーティーです。   •   • wrapping up

じゃ、どようびにしましょう。   •   • announcing a topic of the meeting

>
>
> **ノート10 (Note 10):**
>
> The meeting you are starting, the meeting you are ending, and the something you are doing have to be followed by the particle を (o). Pay attention to the use of the particle を (o).

2. **Practice meeting strategy 1 (beginning a meeting) by substituting the words provided for the underlined parts.**

Example

会話の例 (Sample Dialogue)

Chair: じゃ、ミーティングをはじめましょう。

Chair: トピックは<u>パーティー</u>です。

1. コンサート

2. ダンス

3. フェスティバル

4. アスレチックデー

Time expressions ノート11 (Note 11):

Pay attention to the use of the months of the year and the days of the month which are colored.

Months are given as **number + counter** がつ *gatsu*   Days of the month: (1st day to 10th day)

なんがつ	What month	なんにち	**What day**
いちがつ	January	ついたち	1st day
にがつ	February	ふつか	2nd day
さんがつ	March	みっか	3rd day
しがつ	April	よっか	4th day
ごがつ	May	いつか	5th day
ろくがつ	June	むいか	6th day
しちがつ	July	なのか	7th day
はちがつ	August	ようか	8th day
くがつ	September	ここのか	9th day
じゅうがつ	October	とおか	10th day
じゅういちがつ	November		
じゅうにがつ	December		

3. **Connect the months of the year, on the left, and the days of the month, on the right, with their English counterparts in the middle.**

ごがつ •	• January 1st	•	• よっか
いちがつ •	• March 3rd	•	• ついたち
じゅうがつ •	• May 5th	•	• いつか
はちがつ •	• July 4th	•	• とおか
さんがつ •	• October 10th	•	• むいか
くがつ •	• August 6th	•	• みっか
しちがつ •	• September 7th	•	• ようか
しがつ •	• April 8th	•	• なのか

4. **Practice saying dates using the model below.**

   1. January 1st
   2. March 3rd
   3. May 5th
   4. July 4th
   5. October 10th
   6. August 6th
   7. July 7th
   8. April 8th
   9. February 9th
   10. September 2nd

会話の例 (Sample Dialogue)

A: パーティーは　なんにちですか。

B: <u>いちがつついたち</u>です。

ノート12 (Note 12):

As in English, when giving dates in Japanese, the month is given first followed by the day. In horizontal writing, either kanji or Arabic numerals are used to indicate the numbered parts. Only kanji is used in vertical writing. When asking the date, なんにちですか is used.

ノート13 (Note 13):

Pay attention to the use of the days of the month which are colored.

Days of the month: (11th day to 20th day) 　　　(21st day to 31st day)

じゅういちにち	11th day	にじゅういちにち	21st day
じゅうににち	12th day	にじゅうににち	22nd day
じゅうさんにち	13th day	にじゅうさんにち	23rd day
じゅうよっか	14th day	にじゅうよっか	24th day
じゅうごにち	15th day	にじゅうごにち	25th day
じゅうろくにち	16th day	にじゅうろくにち	26th day
じゅうしちにち	17th day	にじゅうしちにち	27th day
じゅうはちにち	18th day	にじゅうはちにち	28th day
じゅうくにち	19th day	にじゅうくにち	29th day
はつか	20th day	さんじゅうにち	30th day
		さんじゅういちにち	31st day

5. *Connect the days of the month on the left with their English counterparts on the right.*

くがつ　にじゅうさんにち　•　　• September 22nd

くがつ　にじゅうごにち　•　　• September 23rd

くがつ　にじゅうよっか　•　　• September 25th

くがつ　にじゅうににち　•　　• September 24th

　　　　　　　　　　　　• September 21st

6. *Practice saying dates using the model below.*

九月十三日	三月十日	六月二十五日	四 し
９月１３日	３月１０日	６月２５日	月 がつ
くがつじゅうさんにち	さんがつとおか	ろくがつにじゅうごにち	七 なの
			日 か

Example	1.	2.	3
September 13	March 10	June 25	April 7

会話の例 (Sample Dialogue)

A: ダンスは　なんにちですか。

B: 9がつ13にちです。

7. **Practice anking and answering questions based on the activities schedule below. Follow the model.**

ウエルカムダンス　　　　　　９月１３日

ポスターセール　　　　　　　９月２４日

ドラマナイト　　　　　　　１０月５日

スポーツデー　　　　　　　１０月１０日

ハロウィーンパーティー　　１０月３１日

スノーフェスティバル　　　　２月８日

スキートーナメント　　　　　３月６日

スピーチコンテスト　　　　　４月１日

エッセイコンテスト　　　　　５月１７日

会話の例 (Sample Dialogue)

A: <u>ハロウィーンパーティー</u>
はなんにちですか。

B: <u>１０月３１日</u>です。

8. **Practice Meeting Strategy 2 (board reading and board writing), substituting the words provided for each of the three categories below.**

ひにち: ２月１３日
じかん: ２時
ばしょ: こうどう
Example

ひにち: １月１５日
じかん: ６時
ばしょ: がっこう
1.

ひにち: ５月２１日
じかん: ５時
ばしょ: きょうしつ
2.

ひにち: ４月３日
じかん: １時
ばしょ: こうどう
3.

9. **Practice Meeting Strategy 2 (listening and board writing), listening to what your teacher says.**

ひにち: ９月２日
じかん: ４時
ばしょ: こうどう
Example

ひにち:
じかん:
ばしょ:
1.

ひにち:
じかん:
ばしょ:
2.

10. **Practice Meeting Strategy 3 (asking other's opinions and helping reach an agreement), substituting the words provided for the underlined parts.**

カニン：もくようび

Example

会話の例A (Sample Dialogue A)

Chair: パーティーは、なんようびがいいですか。

X:　　どようびがいいです。

Chair: <u>カニン</u>は？

Y:　　<u>もくようび</u>がいいです。

ジョアン：すいようび

1.

ジョン：かようび

2.

かおり：きんようび

3.

ジャネット

Example

会話の例B (Sample Dialogue B)

Chair: パーティーは、なんようびがいいですか。

X:　　どようびがいいです。

Chair: <u>ジャネット</u>さんは？

Y:　　わたしも、<u>どようび</u>がいいです。

ジョージ

1.

サン　ユン

2.

ジャック

3.

Counting people with 「人」 ノート14 (Note 14):

ひとり
一人 (one person)

ふたり
二人 (two people)

さんにん
三人 (three people)

よにん
四人 (four people)

ごにん
五人 (five people)

ろくにん
六人 (six people)

しちにん
七人 (seven people)

はちにん
八人 (eight people)

くにん
九人 (nine people)

じゅうにん
十人 (ten people)

When counting people, にん is placed after each number. However, as you can see, the first two, ひとり (one person) and ふたり (two people), are irregular. A word such as にん is called a "counter." In Japanese, different counters are used depending on the type and shape of the objects being counted.

11. Practice counting people with your classmates, using the model below.

会話の例 (Sample Dialogue)

Chair: <u>ピザのひと</u>。てをあげてください。

Chair: <u>ふたり</u>です。(after counting)

2 people

Example

5 people

1.

8 people

2.

7 people

3.

6 people

4.

9 people

5.

1 person

6.

4 people

7.

12. Practice Meeting Strategy 4 (deciding by a vote), substituting the words provided for the underlined parts.

Example

会話の例 (Sample Dialogue)

Chair: <u>どようびのひと</u>。てをあげてください。

Chair: <u>10</u>にんです。(*after counting*)

Chair: <u>きんようびのひと</u>。てをあげてください。

Chair: <u>8</u>にんです。(*after counting*)

1.

2.

3.

13. Practice Meeting Strategy 5 (wrapping up and deciding), substituting the words provided above for the underlined parts.

会話の例 (Sample Dialogue)

Chair: <u>どようびは10にん</u>です。<u>きんようびは8にん</u>です。

Chair: じゃ、<u>どようび</u>にしましょう。

Chair: これで、ミーティングをおわります。

Language Note | *Japanese Dialects* 方言（ほうげん）

Language Diversity

You've probably never suspected that there's any difficulty involved in deciding what exactly counts as Japanese, but it isn't as easy as you might think. The problem is that Japanese isn't homogeneous, and neither is any other language that has more than just a few speakers. As you know very well, native speakers of English don't all speak English exactly alike. Some of the differences are regional. For example, there are all kinds of obvious differences between the English of a person who grew up in New York City and the English of a person who grew up in Houston. Other differences are social. Imagine two people who both grew up in New York but had very different social statutes. You wouldn't expect a person who grew up in a wealthy family to interact with the same set of people as a person who grew up in a poor family, and you wouldn't expect them to speak exactly the same variety of English either. Different varieties of the same language are usually called dialects.

The differences among regional dialects in Japan are much more dramatic than the differences among regional dialects in the United States, although the 20th century has seen a trend toward greater homogeneity in both countries. The important point here is that when you see an estimate of the number of people who speak Japanese, the number includes everybody who speaks any dialect of Japanese.

Japanese and Okinawan

It's sometimes hard to decide whether two things are two dialects of the same language or two different languages. The usual criterion is mutual intelligibility; if two people can pretty much understand each other without having to learn anything new, they're speaking dialects of the same language. Most linguists regard the many Ryuukyuu dialects as a separate group rather than as dialects of Japanese. In fact, there's so much diversity within the Ryuukyuu varieties that some experts divide them into three different languages, each on a par with Japanese. But linguists aren't very influential, and most Japanese people refer to all the varieties spoken in the Ryuukyuu islands as Okinawan dialects of Japanese. The basis for this label is political rather than linguistic. Okinawa is the best known and most populous island in the Ryuukyuu chain, and the name of the prefecture that includes the whole chain is Okinawa Prefecture. Since Okinawa Prefecture is part of Japan, it's not surprising that people tend to call the languages spoken there dialects of Japanese. It's also important to know that the Ryuukyuu islands were independent of Japan until the 17th century, so labeling the Ryuukyuu languages dialects as Japanese can be understood as an indirect way of justifying the incorporation of the islands into Japanese territory. In any case, most citizens of Okinawa Prefecture today are native speakers of some variety of Japanese in addition to or instead of the Ryuukyuu dialect of the area where they live. As a result, an estimate of the number of native speakers of Japanese isn't significantly affected by whether or not the Ryuukyuu dialects are counted as Japanese.

2.4 Mechanics

1. ***Organize a Party: Practice conducting a class meeting, substituting the topics provided in the dialogue below and using the flow chart. Create your own response for each topic.***

   Situation: Your Japanese class will be having a party for the Japanese exchange students at your school, and you are on the party planning committee. Below is a list of tasks to be performed by the committee.

   1. Select a committee chair (ぎちょう), a blackboard writer, and a scribe (しょき).

   2. The chair opens the meeting.
      (じゃ、ミーティングをはじめましょう。)

   Topic 3. Discussion and decision making.

   4. The chair closes the meeting.
      (これでミーティングをおわります。)

ノート 15 (Note 15):

The particle も (mo) is used as an additional topic marker. It means "also" or "too."

イベント　プロポーザル			
	Plan A	**Plan B**	**Plan C**	**Plan D**
Time and Place	Sat. 6 PM こうどう	Fri. 7 PM ジム	Sat. 6 PM こうどう	Sat. 6 PM こうどう
Main Course	ピザ	パスタ	ピザ	ピザ
Dessert	アイスクリーム	ケーキ	アイスクリーム	アイスクリーム
Drinks	コーラ	コーラ	パンチ	コーラ
Main Activity	ダンス	ビデオ	ダンス	ダンス

1. Time (じかん) and place (ばしょ) of the party

2. Main course

3. Dessert (デザート)

4. Beverages

5. Main activity

Decision Making:
Flow Chart for the Meeting ／ー卜 16 (Note 16)

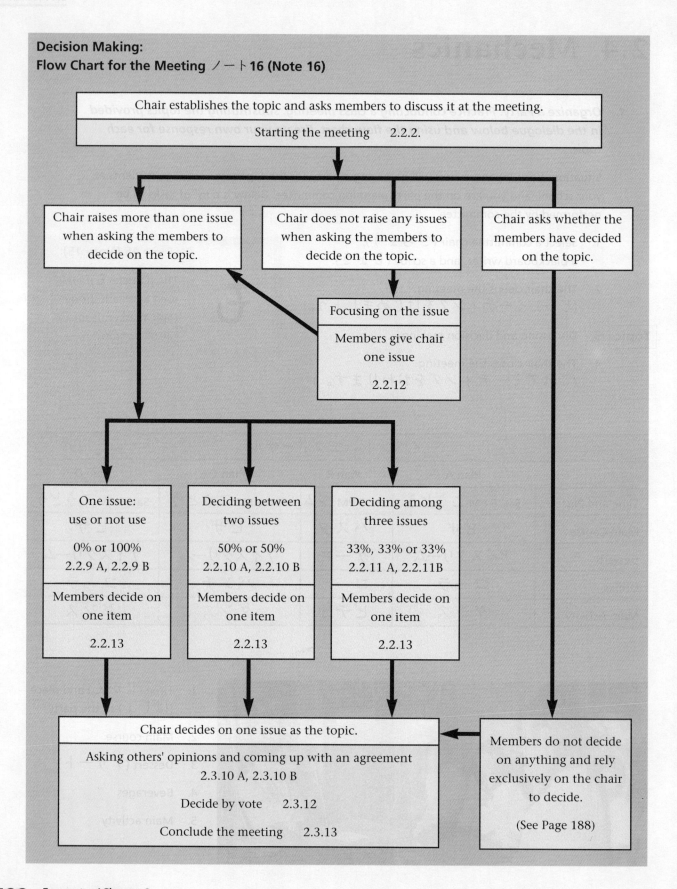

Chair establishes the topic and asks members to discuss it at the meeting.

Starting the meeting   2.2.2.

Chair raises more than one issue when asking the members to decide on the topic.

Chair does not raise any issues when asking the members to decide on the topic.

Chair asks whether the members have decided on the topic.

Focusing on the issue

Members give chair one issue

2.2.12

One issue:
use or not use

0% or 100%
2.2.9 A, 2.2.9 B

Members decide on one item

2.2.13

Deciding between two issues

50% or 50%
2.2.10 A, 2.2.10 B

Members decide on one item

2.2.13

Deciding among three issues

33%, 33% or 33%
2.2.11 A, 2.2.11B

Members decide on one item

2.2.13

Chair decides on one issue as the topic.

Asking others' opinions and coming up with an agreement
2.3.10 A, 2.3.10 B

Decide by vote   2.3.12

Conclude the meeting   2.3.13

Members do not decide on anything and rely exclusively on the chair to decide.

(See Page 188)

会話の例 **(Sample Dialogue)**

Ex. Day of the week

Chair: じゃ、ミーティングをはじめましょう。

Chair: <u>パーティー</u>は、<u>なんようび</u>がいいですか。

A: <u>どようび</u>がいいです。

Chair: Bさんは？

B: <u>にちようび</u>がいいです。

(C raises her hand)

Chair: Cさん。

C: わたしは、<u>どようび</u>がいいです。

Chair: Dさん、<u>にちようびとどようび</u>と、どちらがいいですか。

D: わたしも、<u>どようび</u>がいいです。

Chair: <u>どようび</u>のひと、てをあげてください。

Chair: <u>10にんです</u>。 *(after counting)*

Chair: <u>にちようび</u>のひと、てをあげてください。

Chair: <u>8にんです</u>。 *(after counting)*

Chair: <u>どようび</u>は<u>10にん</u>です。<u>にちようび</u>は<u>8にん</u>です。

Chair: じゃ、<u>どようび</u>にしましょう。 *(announcing the decision)*

Chair: これでミーティングをおわります。

The Japanese style of indecisive cooperative decision making ノート17 (Note 17):

One type of Japanese decision making is called *omakase*. In *omakase*, one person asks another to be the decision maker. Some expensive Japanese restaurants have a special menu called "*omakase ryoori.*" It is sometimes translated "chef's special," but the customers have no idea what the chef will produce. The customers surrender their roles as decision makers and leave the menu up to the chef. The chef makes his or her best effort to accommodate the customers. Try *omakase* using おまかせします, どちらでもいいです or どれでもいいです (*omakase shimasu, dochira demo ii desu or dore demo ii desu*)

Japanese cooking ノート18 (Note 18):

The basement food market of a Japanese department store is a vast and minutely detailed map of Japan's gastronomic universe. Every visitor will want to investigate one, to watch and to taste, for a whirlwind tour of the world of Japanese food. On the top floor of a Japanese department store, you will find various Japanese restaurants. You must decide which restaurant you want to eat in. If you cannot decide, you should ask your Japanese friend using おかませします, どちらでもいいです or どれでもいいです (*omakase shimasu, dochira demo ii desu or dore demo ii desu*)

2. **Practice asking your classmates' preferences in Japanese food using the model below.**

1, すし、てんぷら、うなぎ
2, とんかつ、すきやき、よせなべ
3, そば、うどん、ラーメン
4, おべんとう、カレーライス、おこのみやき、ハンバーガー

Please see Additional Information at the end of the chapter.

会話の例 **(Sample Dialogue)**

A: すしと てんぷらと うなぎと どれがいいですか。

B: うーん、*(hesitating)* どれでもいいです。
or あのう、*(hesitating)* おまかせします。

The main ingredients in Japanese cooking are seafood, vegetables and rice. The consumption of raw seafood has long been a distinguishing feature of the native cuisine, and its preparation requires that fish be very fresh and that it be skillfully cut with a very sharp knife.

Thousands of American-type fast food chains stores are now in Japan. Many sell Japanese-style hamburgers like teriyaki burgers.

3. *Role Play: Cooperative Decision Making*

Do the role play below using the sample conversation on page 187 as a model. The roles of B, C and D can be further divided into blackboard writer, secretary and regular member.

Card A (Activity Committee chair)

You are the chair of a committee for planning school activities. Today you are talking with other committee members to finalize what day of the week, what time and where you want to have a science fair (サイエンスフェア). Ask the other members' opinions regarding this matter and make decisions as a leader.

**Cards B, C, D
(Activity Committee member)**

You are a member of a committee for planning school activities. Today your committee, under the leadership of its chair, is trying to finalize what day of the week, what time and where a science fair (サイエンスフェア) should be held. Help the chair, contributing as much as you can.

189

4. Find a perfect match (formal and informal speech practice).

Preparation: Look at the chart of categories and items below. Have a class vote on what would be a good sixth category to include, as well as two items to represent that category. Then, go through each of the six categories individually and circle the items in those categories that you prefer.

Activity: Go around the class and ask your classmates what they chose in each of the six categories. If you find someone who made exactly the same choices you made, he or she is your perfect match.

Category	Choice A	Choice B
たべもの (food)	ステーキ	パスタ
のみもの (beverage)	コーラ	ジュース
スポーツ(sport)	サッカー	バスケットボール
ばしょ (place)	ショッピングモール	がっこう
ようび (day of the week)	かようび	すいようび
class category		

会話の例A (Sample Dialogue A) (formal)

A: あのう、(hesitating) すみません。

B: はい、なんでしょう。

A: ステーキ と パスタ と どちら が いいですか。

B: パスタ が いいです。

A: そうですか。(saying in an upbeat way) じゃ、(saying quickly) サッカー と バスケットボール と どちら が いいですか。

B: サッカー が いいです。

A: サッカー ですか。(saying in an agreeable way) じゃ…(etc.)

会話の例B (Sample Dialogue B) (informal)

A: あのう、(hesitating) すいません。

B: あ、なあに。(saying in an upbeat way and downbeat way)

A: ステーキ と パスタ と どっち が いい？

B: パスタ が いい。

A: そう。(saying in an upbeat way) じゃ、(saying quickly) サッカー と バスケットボール と どっち が いい？

B: サッカー が いい。

A: サッカー。(saying in an agreeable way) じゃ…(etc.)

Pronunciation | *Word Accent*

When people talk about an **accented** syllable in an English word, they mean the syllable that feels the most prominent or the most conspicuous. Compare the following examples. The accented syllables are in boldface capital letters.

WASHington   Chi**CA**go   Monte**REY**

This kind of accent is also called **stress**. Stressed syllables in English tend to be longer, louder, and higher in pitch than unstressed syllables. The location of the accent is an important part of an English word's pronunciation. If you put the accent on a different syllable in any of the city names above, the name is still understandable, but it sounds very odd.

Japanese also has a kind of word accent, but it works entirely in terms of the pitch and is often called **pitch accent** (as opposed to the **stress accent** of English). The accent in a Japanese word is a sudden drop from a relatively high pitch to a relatively low pitch. The place in the word where the drop occurs can be marked with symbol $^\phi$. Compare the words below.

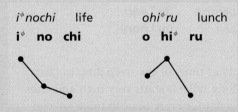

i$^\phi$nochi life   *ohi$^\phi$ru* lunch
i$^\phi$ **no chi**   **o hi**$^\phi$ **ru**

The dots connected by lines are schematic diagrams showing the pitch of a speaker's voice while pronouncing the three syllables in each word. Ask your teacher or another speaker of Japanese to pronounce these two examples and all the examples below for you so that you can compare these diagrams with what you hear. Notice that there's a steep drop in pitch from the first syllable to the second in *i$^\phi$nochi* and from the second syllable to the third in *ohi$^\phi$ru*. The syllable with the highest pitch is traditionally called the **accented syllable**, so *i$^\phi$nochi* is said to have first-syllable accent and *ohi$^\phi$ru* is said to have second-syllable accent. There's also a fairly steep rise from the first syllable to the second in *ohi$^\phi$ru*. A jump from a low first syllable to a high second syllable is the general pattern, but when the first syllable is the accented syllable, there's no room for an upward jump before it, so you don't hear one in *i$^\phi$nochi*.

You're probably wondering whether there are any Japanese words with an accented last syllable. There are, but there are also words with no accent at all. If the final syllable is short, you can't tell the difference between final accent and no accent. See final-accented *kotoba$^\phi$* ("language") and unaccented *sakana* ("fish"), below.

ko to ba$^\phi$ **sa ka na**

The difference between final accent and no accent only emerges when certain other words follow. For instance, the topic particle *wa* can be added to any of the four words diagrammed so far. The pitch patterns on the resulting short phrases are shown below.

The particle *wa* doesn't contribute any accent of its own, but it provides an extra syllable that reveals the difference between the final accent on *kotoba$^\phi$* and the absence of an accent on *sakana*. There's a steep drop in pitch from the third syllable to the fourth syllable in the phrase *kotoba$^\phi$wa*, but not in the phrase *sakana wa*.

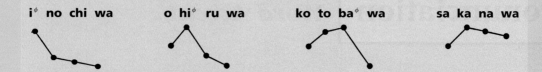

As in these last four examples, short phrases have pitch patterns determined by the words they contain. You'll remember that when *i^φnochi* ("life") is pronounced all by itself, there's no room for the rise in pitch that usually comes at the beginning of a phrase. But *i^φnochi* can combine with the

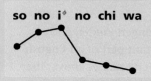

unaccented word *sono* ("that") and the topic particle *wa* into the three-word phrase *sono i^φnochi wa*, and, because *i^φnochi* has first-syllable accent, the entire phrase has third-syllable accent. The pitch pattern on this phrase is diagrammed on the left. Since the accent on the first syllable of *i^φnochi* doesn't get in the way, you see the expected jump from a relatively low first syllable to a relatively high second syllable.

All the words and phrases diagrammed so far consist entirely of short syllables. Now it's time to look at long syllables. When a word has an accent on a long syllable, the^φ symbol is written in the middle of the syllable, between the two beats. The examples below illustrate.

1ST-SYLLABLE ACCENT			2ND-SYLLABLE ACCENT		
ke^φeki	cake	(**kee** | **ki**)	*jiyu^φu*	freedom	(**ji** | **yuu**)
sa^φigo	end	(**sai** | **go**)	*taka^φi*	expensive	(**ta** | **kai**)
ko^φndo	next	(**kon** | **do**)	*Niho^φn*	Japan	(**ni** | **hon**)
sho^φkku	shock	(**shok** | **ku**)			

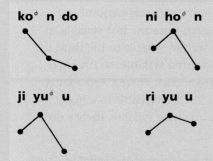

Since a long syllable provides plenty of time for the steep drop in pitch caused by an accent, an accented long syllable starts very high and ends very low. The diagrams below use a dot for every beat, so there are two dots for each long syllable.

It's easy to tell the difference between final accent and no accent in words with long final syllables. The diagrams below show the difference between the pitch patterns on *jiyu^φu* ("freedom"), which ends with an accented long syllable, and *riyuu* ("reason"), which also ends with a long syllable but is unaccented.

In real-life situations, of course, even if you pronounce a word with the wrong accent, people usually understand what you mean, but not always. For example, the word *ka^φki* ("oyster") has first-syllable accent, and the word *kaki* ("persimmon") is unaccented. It's not hard to imagine going into a Japanese supermarket and mistakenly asking where the oysters are when you really want to find the persimmons. On the other hand, if you're in a Japanese restaurant and mistakenly ask for *hashi^φ* ("bridge") instead of *ha^φshi* ("chopsticks"), no waiter will think you want to eat with a bridge.

Even though the chances of real confusion are slim, pronouncing words with the wrong accent sounds strange. Just imagine someone speaking English and saying WashINGton or ChicaGO. There's a lot to get used to at this early stage in your study of Japanese, and it would be silly to say that accent should have the highest priority, but it would be just as silly to say that accent doesn't matter. The most important thing at this point is to pay attention and try to imitate the pitch patterns that Japanese speakers use.

2.5 Mechanics

Listening Exercises

1. **Listening Comprehension (date, time and place)**

   Listen to the conversations and circle the appropriate answers.

   A.   They will watch a movie at:
       1. 8 o'clock   2. 4 o'clock   3. 6 o'clock   4. 3 o'clock

   B.   They will have a dance in:
       1. the class   2. the cafeteria   3. the gym   4. the library

   C.   They will watch a video on:
       1. Monday   2. Sunday   3. Friday   4. Saturday

   D.   They will watch TV:
       1. at 8 o'clock   2. at 4 o'clock   3. on Monday   4. on Saturday

   E.   They will have a party:
       1. on Tuesday   2. on Friday   3. in the gym   4. in the library

   F.   They will have an event:
       1. at 8 o'clock   2. at 4 o'clock   3. in the gym   4. in the library

2. **Listening Comprehension (date, time and place)**

   Listen to the conversations and circle the appropriate answers.

   A.   The person asks for the:
       1. time   2. week   3. month   4. year

   B.   The person asks about the:
       1. grade   2. week   3. age   4. year

   C.   The person asks for the:
       1. time   2. location   3. date   4. price

   D.   The person asks for the:
       1. price   2. activity   3. food   4. drinks

   E.   The person asks about:
       1. location   2. price   3. choice   4. date

3. Listening Comprehension (date, time, and place)

Listen to the dialogues and circle the appropriate answers.

A. The part of the dialogue I heard was
1. the beginning   2. the middle   3. the decisionmaking part   4. the end

B. The part of the dialogue I heard was
1. the beginning   2. the middle   3. the decisionmaking part   4. the end

C. The part of the dialogue I heard was
1. the beginning   2. the middle   3. the decisionmaking part   4. the end

D. The part of the dialogue I heard was
1. the beginning   2. the middle   3. the decisionmaking part   4. the end

4. Listening Comprehension (date, time, and place)

Listen to the conversations and circle the appropriate answers.

A. This dialogue involved
1. confirming a previous statement
2. expressing preference
3. announcing a decision
4. agreeing with a previous statement

B. This dialogue involved
1. confirming a previous statement
2. expressing preference
3. announcing a decision
4. agreeing with a previous statement

C. This dialogue involved
1. confirming a previous statement
2. expressing preference
3. announcing a decision
4. agreeing with a previous statement

D. This dialogue involved
1. confirming a previous statement
2. expressing preference
3. announcing a decision
4. agreeing with a previous statement

FORM

1. Asking someone's preference

A. 〜がいいですか、〜がいいですか。

~ ga ii desu ka, ~ ga ii desu ka.

This construction is used to ask someone's preference by listing possible choices. 〜がいいですか (*~ga ii desu ka*) can be repeated until all the possible items are mentioned. が (*ga*) is a particle used to indicate the subject.

ジャズがいいですか、カントリーがいいですか。

Jazu ga ii desu ka, kantorii ga ii desu ka?

Do you like jazz or do you prefer country music?

ジャズがいいです。 *Jazu ga ii desu.*

I prefer jazz.

B. 〜がいいですか、それとも、〜がいいですか。 *~ga ii desu ka, soretomo, ~ga ii desu ka.*

For added emphasis, the connector それとも (*soretomo*) may be placed before listing the last possible item. With the addition of それとも, the sentence becomes more expressive.

コーヒーがいいですか、それとも、こうちゃがいいですか。

Koohii ga ii desu ka, soretomo, koocha ga ii desu ka?

Would you like coffee or tea?

バナナがいいですか、オレンジがいいですか、それとも、メロンがいいですか。

Banana ga ii desu ka, orenji ga ii desu ka, soretomo, meron ga ii desu ka?

Would you like a banana, an orange or a melon?

C. 〜と〜と、どちらがいいですか。 *~to ~ to dochira ga ii desu ka.*
〜と〜と〜と、どれがいいですか。 *~to ~to ~to dore ga ii desu ka.*

Use of どちら (*dochira*), "which one of the two," also enables you to make a question asking someone's preference, but the choices are limited to two items. For three or more items, どれ (*dore*), "which one," is used. と (*to*) is a particle used to list things in this construction.

レモネードとアイスティーと、どちらがいいですか。

Remoneedo to aisu tii to dochira ga ii desu ka?

Which would you like, lemonade or iced tea?

アイスティーがいいです。

Aisu tii ga ii desu. I prefer iced tea.

ハンバーガーとピザとチキンと、どれがいいですか。

Hanbaagaa to piza to chikin to dore ga ii desu ka?

Which would you like, a hamburger, pizza or chicken?

D. ～と～と、どっちがいいですか。

~to ~ to dotchiga ii desu ka.

Use of どっち (*dotchi*), "which one of the two," enables you to make an informal question asking someone's preference between two items.

レモネードとアイスティーと、どっちがいい？

Remoneedo to aisu tii to dotchi ga ii?

Which would you like, lemonade or iced tea?

アイスティーがいい。

Aisu tii ga ii.　　　　I prefer iced tea.

2. Announcing decisions

～にしましょう。 *~ni shimashoo.*

Let's settle on ~.

に (*ni*) is a particle and しましょう (*shimashoo*) literally means "let's do."
～にします (*~ni shimasu*) means "I will decide on ~."

A: 2じがいいですか、それとも、3じがいいですか。

Niji ga ii desu ka, soretomo, sanji ga ii desu ka?

Is 2 o'clock all right, or would you prefer 3 o'clock?

B: 3じがいいです。

Sanji ga ii desu.　　　　I prefer 3 o'clock

A: そうですか。じゃ、3じにしましょう。

Soo desu ka? Ja, sanji ni shimashoo.

Is that so? Well then, let's say 3 o'clock.

3. Chairing a class meeting (beginning and ending)

～を　はじめましょう。 *~o hajimemashoo.*

Let's start ~.

おわります。 *owarimasu.*

The ~ is over.

A: ミーティングを　はじめましょう。

Miitingu o hajimemashoo.

Let's start the meeting.

B: ミーティングを　おわります。

Mitiingu o owarimasu.

The meeting is over.

4. *Asking questions using question words.*

When a question word (なに *nani* [what], いくら *ikura* [how much], なんじ *nanji* [what time], なんようび *nan'yoobi* [what day of the week], or どこ *doko* [where]) is used, it is inserted in the place where its answer would normally appear.

A. いくらですか。 *Ikura desu ka?*

Use of いくらですか [*ikura desu ka*] enables you to make a question about price.

オレンジは　いくらですか。	*Orenji wa ikura desu ka?*	How much is the orange?
オレンジは１ドルです。	*Orenji wa ichidoru desu.*	The orange is $1.

B. なんじですか。 *Nanji desu ka.*

Use of なんじですか [*nanji desu ka*] enables you to make a question about time.

パーティーはなんじですか。	*Paatii wa nanji desu ka?*	What time does the party start?
６じです。	*Rokuji desu.*	6:00.

C. なんようびですか。 *Nan'yoobi desu ka?*

Use of なんようびですか [*nan'yoobi desu ka*] enables you to make a question about the day of the week.

パーティーはなんようびですか。	*Paatii wa nan'yoobi desu ka?*	What day is the party?
かようびです。	*Kayoobi desu.*	Tuesday.

5. *Requesting objects*

When purchasing or requesting objects, ～をください [*~o kudasai*] is used. ～をおねがいします [*~o onegai shimasu*] is a more polite expression used in the same situation.

オレンジを　ください。	*Orenji o kudasai.*	Please give me an orange.
オレンジを　おねがいします。	*Orenji o onegai shimasu.*	I request an orange.

6. *Indecisive decision*

Sometimes Japanese make indecisive cooperative decisions. どちらでもいいです [*dochira demo ii desu*], どれでもいいです [*dore demo ii desu*], and おまかせします [*omakase shimasu*] are used in these situations.

レモネードとアイスティーと、どちらがいいですか。
Remoneedo to aisu tii to dochira ga ii desu ka?

Which do you prefer, lemonade or iced tea?

どちらでもいいです。	*Dochira demo ii desu.*	Either one is fine. [two items]
どれでもいいです。	*Dore demo ii desu.*	Anything is fine. [three items]
おまかせします。	*Omakase shimasu.*	I leave it up to you.

7. *Cooperative Decision Making*

Roles: Chair
Blackboard Writer
Scribe
Participant(s)

Procedures

1. The blackboard writer writes the topic of the meeting on the board.

    Example: ジャパニーズパーティー

2. The black board writer lists on the board the specific items to be discussed.

    Example:
    ひにち (date)
    じかん (time)
    ばしょ (location)
    たべもの (food) [2-3 items]
    のみもの (drinks) [2-3 items]
    アクティビティー (activities) [2 activities]

3. The chair declares the beginning of the meeting.

    Example: じゃ、ミーティングをはじめましょう。

4. The chair announces the meeting topic.

    Example: トピックはジャパニーズパーティーです。

5. The chair asks participants' preferences regarding the first item of discussion.

    Example: ジャパニーズパーティーはなんにちがいいですか。

6. The blackboard writer lists the participants' preferences on the board.

7. The chair takes a vote. (The chair reads each choice aloud and the participants raise their hands.)

8. The chair narrows the field down to a few choices based on the result of the initial vote and asks the participants to make another choice.

    Example: 2がつ12にちと2がつ15にちとどちらがいいですか。

9. The chair announces the decision based on the result of the second vote.

    Example: 2がつ12にちにしましょう。

10. Both the blackboard writer and the scribe record the final decision.

11. Repeat 5–10 above for the remaining items of discussion.

12. The chair reviews all the decisions made during the meeting.

    Example: ひにちは2がつ15にちです。

13. The chair declares the end of the meeting.

    Example: これで、ミーティングをおわります。

2.6 Application

1. An Afternoon in Town

Introduction

A group of visitors from Japan is in town. They will be having a series of meetings with American business people for the next several days. Since their meeting on the last day is only in the morning, they would like to spend the afternoon in town before leaving for their next destination.

Procedure

1. Designating roles

One-half of your class plays travel agents and the other half plays Japanese visitors.

2. Making packages

Those playing travel agents will receive a list like the one below. There are four different time frames indicated on the sheet, and beside each of these is a list of events, activities, or attractions available during that particular time frame. Your first task as a travel agent is to create an attractive excursion package for 60 dollars or less (per person) for the Japanese visitors. Choose one item from each time frame to create a package you would like to offer and give it a name (such as ゴールドパック "Gold Pack"). Next, create an itinerary to use when presenting your package to the Japanese visitors. Make sure that your package costs no more than 60 dollars.

1:00	えいが	8ドル
	ゆうえんち	22ドル
	ロックコンサート	28ドル
	クラシックコンサート	25ドル
	カントリーミュージックコンサート	14ドル
	インディーカーレース	30ドル
4:30	じゅうどうきょうしつ	13ドル
	テニスきょうしつ	20ドル
	スケートきょうしつ	11ドル
	ゴルフきょうしつ	22ドル
	コンピュータきょうしつ	10ドル
	りょうりきょうしつ	14ドル
6:30	ハンバーガーのみせ	9ドル
	にほんりょうりのみせ	22ドル
	ピザとパスタのみせ	13ドル
	サンドイッチのみせ	7ドル
	ステーキのみせ	25ドル
	ファミリーレストラン	17ドル
8:00	アートフェア	7ドル
	アニメフェスティバル	12ドル
	にほんごスピーチコンテスト	0ドル（ただ）
	サイエンスフェア	5ドル
	タウンミーティング	0ドル（ただ）
	カラオケ	13ドル

3. Exploring choices of attractions

Those playing Japanese visitors will receive a list identical to the one received by the travel agents but without the prices. Look at the list and choose three items (your first, second and third choices) from each time frame.

SAMPLE PACKAGE ITINERARY	
1:00 えいが	8ドル
4:30 じゅうどうきょうしつ	13ドル
6:30 にほんりょうりのみせ	22ドル
8:00 アニメフェスティバル	12ドル

4. **Making presentations**

Each travel agent shows his or her package to the Japanese visitors and tells them the schedule and price of the package.

5. **Preliminary selection**

It's decision-making time for the Japanese visitors. You now have been given presentations by the travel agents about various packages. Since you want to enjoy each other's company as well, you don't want to split into small groups and go for whatever package you choose individually. Dividing the entire delegation into two groups would create a group of a reasonable size. This means that you can choose up to two packages.

6. **Having a quick meeting to make the final selections**
   - Designate a chair and a board writer for the meeting.
   - The chair leads the meeting using the procedure you have practiced in this chapter's Mechanics sections. The topic is ごごのプラン ("the afternoon plan").
   - The blackboard writer lists the names of the packages raised by any participant of the meeting and records the vote count.
   - The participants express their preferences. You may give your first choice in the beginning and your second and third choices when compromise is in order.
   - Decide on one package if the majority is willing to go for it. Pick two packages when it is makes sense to make two groups of roughly equal size.
   - In the case of a tie that appears to allow little room for compromise, deciding by *janken* is a good alternative.

7. **Announcing the decisions**

The chair indicates the group's decision to the travel agents by saying something like:

ゴールドパックをください。 [Give us the Gold Pack.]

ゴールドパックとイーグルパックをください。 [Give us the Gold Pack and the Eagle Pack.]

The agent(s) who created the named package(s) thank the Japanese visitors for their choice. Congratulations to the agents who sold their packages!! And to the Japanese visitors, enjoy your excursion!

8. **Additional activity: reading a menu**

Some of the restaurants listed on the sheet you received in the beginning happen to have written their menus in several different languages, including Japanese. The one on top of Page 201 is such a menu, and it came from a family restaurant. Not specializing in a particular cuisine, the family restaurant offers a wide range of choices.

What should you order if you:

[1] don't want to spend more than $12?
[2] have a $25 dinner coupon but will not get change if your order is under $25?
[3] had rather a heavy lunch and want something light for supper?
[4] are hungry for Japanese food?
[5] are hungry for Italian food?
[6] want something sweet?
[7] like many types of food and enjoy variety?
[8] are a vegetarian?
[9] are a health nut?
[10] have a big appetite?

Practice finding items as efficiently as possible by making adjustments according to the conditions. For example, you may not have to examine every item on the menu if you just want to order dessert. The currency unit of this menu is the dollar.

パインリッジ ファミリー レストラン

スープ＆スナック
トマトスープ	$2.00
クラムチャウダー	$3.00
コーンスープ	$2.50
チキンナゲット	$3.50
オニオンリング	$2.00

サンドイッチ
ハムとチーズ	$6.50
ターキー	$7.00
チキン	$7.00
ベジタリアン	$6.00

サラダ
シーザー	$7.50
グリーク	$7.50
チキン	$8.50
シュリンプ	$9.50
とうふ	$7.50

ステーキ	$24.00
ミニ　ステーキ	$16.00
ハンバーガー	$11.00
ミニ　ハンバーガー	$7.00
ロブスター	$28.00
ミニ　ロブスター	$20.00
さかなフライ	$15.00
グリルサーモン	$16.00
スティームサーモン	$14.50
フライドチキン	$9.00
グリルチキン	$10.00

コンビネーション
ステーキとチキン	$22.00
ステーキとサーモン	$26.00
チキンとサーモン	$21.00

にほんりょうり
てんぷら	$18.00
とんかつ	$9.50
すし	$18.00
すきやき	$15.50
おべんとう	$18.50
カレーライス	$7.50
そば	$6.50
うどん	$6.50

イタリアりょうり
チーズピザ	$9.00
ペパロニピザ	$12.00
チキンパルメザン	$12.50
カラマリ	$15.50
シェルパスタ	$14.00

デザート
ショートケーキ	$4.00
アップルパイ	$3.50

すしはるのメニュー

すし	19ドル
てんぷら	18ドル
やきとり	7ドル
すきやき	15ドル
うどん	5ドル
そば	5ドル
ラーメン	6ドル
とんかつ	12ドル
よせなべ	18ドル
うなぎ	19ドル

VOCABULARY

Functional Vocabulary

Formal		Informal		English
Asking about preference				
〜が いいですか。	ga ii desu ka?	〜が いい。	~ga ii.	Would you like ~?
Asking about preference between two items				
Xがいいですか、	X ga ii desu ka,	Xがいい、	X ga ii,	Is X better or is Y better?
Yがいいですか。	Y ga ii desu ka?	Yがいい。	Y ga ii.	
Expressing a decision				
〜に します。	~ni shimasu.	〜に する。	~-ni suru.	to decide on ~
				to make it ~
Asking for preference between two alternatives				
どちらがいいですか。	Dochira ga ii desu ka?	どっちがいい。	Dotchi ga ii?	Which one is better?
Asking for preference among one of three or more alternatives				
どれがいいですか。	Dore ga ii desu ka?	どれがいい。	Dore ga ii?	Which one is the best?
Asking about time				
なんじですか。	Nanji desu ka?	なんじ？	Nanji?	What time (is it)?
Asking about the day of the week				
なんようびですか。	Nan'yoobi desu ka?	なんようび？	Nan'yoobi?	What day (of week)(is it)?
Asking about place				
どこですか。	Doko desu ka?	どこ？	Doko?	Where (is it)?
Asking about price				
いくらですか。	Ikura desu ka?	いくら？	Ikura?	How much(is it)?
Letting someone else decide				
おまかせします。	Omakase shimasu.	おまかせ。	Omakase.	I leave it up to you.
どちらでもいいです。	Dochira demo ii desu.	どちらでも	Dochira demo.	Either one is fine.
Requesting something				
〜をください。	~o kudasai.	〜をくれ。	~o kure.	Please give me~.
〜をおねがいします。	~o onegai shimasu.	〜をおねがい。	~o onegai.	I request~.

Notional Vocabulary

Beverages

(お)みず	(o)mizu	water
こうちゃ	koocha	black tea
おちゃ	ocha	green tea
ミルク	miruku	milk
コーラ	koora	cola
コーヒー	koohii	coffee
パンチ	panchi	punch
ジュース	juusu	juice
ソーダ	sooda	soda
サイダー	saidaa	cider

Party Activities

ダンス	dansu	dance
ビデオ	bideo	video
カラオケ	karaoke	karaoke
えいが	eiga	movie
パーティー	paatii	party

Food

ピザ	piza	pizza
ハンバーガー	hanbaagaa	hamburger
フライドチキン	furaido chikin	fried chicken
ステーキ	suteeki	steak
ポテトチップ	poteto chippu	potato chip(s)
クッキー	kukkii	cookie
スープ	suupu	soup
ミートローフ	miito roofu	meatloaf
チキン	chikin	chicken
ケーキ	keeki	cake
サラダ	sarada	salad
パスタ	pasuta	pasta

Meeting Words

ばしょ	basho	place
ひにち	hinichi	date
じかん	jikan	time
ねだん	nedan	price
~に しましょう	~ni shimashoo	Let's decide on~.
ただ	tada	free (price)

Miscellaneous

わたし	watashi	I
おかね	okane	money
よさん	yosan	budget
ください	~kudasai	Please give me ~.
ショッピングモール	shoppingu mooru	shopping mall
ぎちょう	gichoo	chairperson
しょき	shoki	scribe
ミーティング	miitingu	meeting
はじめましょう	hajimemashoo	Let's begin ~.
おわります	owarimasu	to end

Time Expressions

いちじ	ichiji	one o'clock
にじ	niji	two o'clock
さんじ	sanji	three o'clock
よじ	yoji	four o'clock
ごじ	goji	five o'clock
ろくじ	rokuji	six o'clock
しちじ	shichiji	seven o'clock
はちじ	hachiji	eight o'clock
くじ	kuji	nine o'clock
じゅうじ	juuji	ten o'clock
じゅういちじ	juuichiji	eleven o'clock
じゅうにじ	juuniji	twelve o'clock
いちじはん	ichijihan	one-thirty
にじはん	nijihan	two-thirty
さんじはん	sanjihan	three-thirty
よじはん	yojihan	four-thirty
ごじはん	gojihan	five -thirty
ろくじはん	rokujihan	six-thirty
しちじはん	shichijihan	seven-thirty
はちじはん	hachijihan	eight-thirty
くじはん	kujihan	nine-thirty
じゅうじはん	juujihan	ten-thirty
じゅういちじはん	juuichijihan	eleven-thirty
じゅうにじはん	juunijihan	twelve-thirty

Days of the Week

げつようび	*getsuyoobi*	Monday
かようび	*kayoobi*	Tuesday
すいようび	*suiyoobi*	Wednesday
もくようび	*mokuyoobi*	Thursday
きんようび	*kin'yoobi*	Friday
どようび	*doyoobi*	Saturday
にちようび	*nichiyoobi*	Sunday
なんようび	*nan'yoobi*	what day

Months

なんがつ	*nangatsu*	what month
いちがつ	*ichigatsu*	January
にがつ	*nigatsu*	February
さんがつ	*sangatsu*	March
しがつ	*shigatsu*	April
ごがつ	*gogatsu*	May
ろくがつ	*rokugatsu*	June
しちがつ	*shichigatsu*	July
はちがつ	*hachigatsu*	August
くがつ	*kugatsu*	September
じゅうがつ	*juugatsu*	October
じゅういちがつ	*juuichigatsu*	November
じゅうにがつ	*juunigatsu*	December

Days of the Month

なんにち	*nannichi*	what day
ついたち	*tsuitachi*	1st day of the month
ふつか	*futsuka*	2nd day of the month
みっか	*mikka*	3rd day of the month
よっか	*yokka*	4th day of the month
いつか	*itsuka*	5th day of the month
むいか	*muika*	6th day of the month
なのか	*nanoka*	7th day of the month
ようか	*yooka*	8th day of the month
ここのか	*kokonoka*	9th day of the month
とおか	*tooka*	10th day of the month
じゅういちにち	*juuichinichi*	11th day of the month
じゅうににち	*juuninichi*	12th day of the month
じゅうさんにち	*juusannichi*	13th day of the month
じゅうよっか	*juuyokka*	14th day of the month
じゅうごにち	*juugonichi*	15th day of the month
じゅうろくにち	*juurokunichi*	16th day of the month
じゅうしちにち	*juushichinichi*	17th day of the month

じゅうはちにち	*juuhachinichi*	18th day of the month
じゅうくにち	*juukunichi*	19th day of the month
はつか	*hatsuka*	20th day of the month
にじゅういちにち		
	nijuuichinichi	21st day of the month
にじゅうににち	*nijuuninichi*	22nd day of the month
にじゅうさんにち		
	nijuusannichi	23rd day of the month
にじゅうよっか	*nijuuyokka*	24th day of the month
にじゅうごにち	*nijuugonichi*	25th day of the month
にじゅうろくにち		
	nijuurokunichi	26th day of the month
にじゅうしちにち		
	nijuushichinichi	
		27th day of the month
にじゅうはちにち		
	nijuuhachinichi	
		28th day of the month
にじゅうくにち	*nijuukunichi*	29th day of the month
さんじゅうにち	*sanjuunichi*	30th day of the month
さんじゅういちにち		
	sanjuuichinichi	31st day of the month

Number of People

なんにん	*nannin*	how many people
ひとり	*hitori*	one person
ふたり	*futari*	two people
さんにん	*sannin*	three people
よにん	*yonin*	four people
ごにん	*gonin*	five people
ろくにん	*rokunin*	six people
しちにん、ななにん		
	shichinin/nananin	
		seven people
はちにん	*hachinin*	eight people
くにん、きゅうにん		
	kunin/kyuunin	nine people
じゅうにん	*juunin*	ten people
じゅういちにん	*juuichinin*	eleven people
じゅうににん	*juuninin*	twelve people
ひと	*hito*	person, man

School Facilities

トイレ	toire	rest room
グランド	gurando	athletic field
じむしつ	jimushitsu	administration office
こうちょうしつ	koochooshitsu	principal's office
プール	puuru	pool
りょう	ryoo	dormitory
メディアルーム		
	media ruumu	media room
カフェテリア	kafeteria	cafeteria
ジム	jimu	gymnasium
コンピュータルーム		
	konpyuuta ruumu	
		computer room
きょうしつ	kyooshitsu	classroom
としょかん	toshokan	library
こうどう	koodoo	auditorium

School Events

アートフェア	aato fea	art fair
アニメフェスティバル		
	anime fesutibaru	
		animation festival
サイエンスフェア		
	saiensu fea	science fair
ジャパニーズナイト		
	japaniizu naito	Japanese night
スピーチコンテスト		
	supiichi kontesuto	
		speech contest
フォークダンス	fooku dansu	folk dance
ロックコンサート		
	rokku konsaato	rock concert

Fruit

バナナ	banana	banana
レモン	remon	lemon
メロン	meron	melon
パイナップル	painappuru	pineapple
キウイ	kyuui	kiwi
グレープフルーツ		
	gureepufuruutsu	grapefruit
マンゴ	mango	mango
オレンジ	orenji	orange
ぶどう	budoo	grape
りんご	ringo	apple
みかん	mikan	mandarin orange
いちご	ichigo	strawberry
なし	nashi	pear

Question Words

どれ	dore	Which one (of three or more alternatives)?
どちら	dochira	Which one (of two alternatives)?
いくら	ikura	How much (is it)?
なんじ	nanji	What time (is it)?
なんようび	nanyoobi	What day of the week (is it)?
どこ	doko	Where (is it)?
なんにち	nannichi	What date (is it)?
なんがつ	nangatsu	What month of the year (is it)?

2.7 Application

1. *Read the following posters and answer the questions*

Everyone makes a poster for a party using the items that were decided on in the Main Activity section. The class later chooses the best poster based on its design, organization, clarity of information and artistic creativity. Now, read the posters and answer the questions.

A.

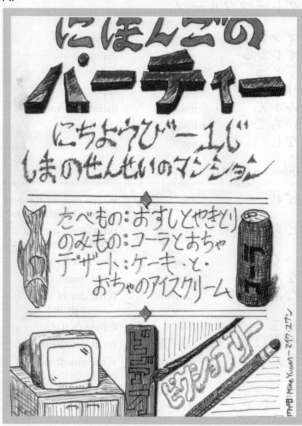

B.

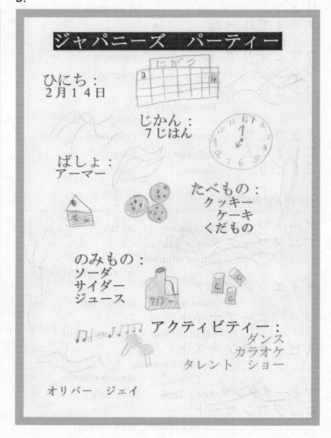

C.

D.

1. Aのパーティーはなんにちですか。デザートはなんですか。

_____

2. Bのパーティーののみものはなんですか。アクティビティーはなんですか。

_____

3. Cのパーティーのたべものはなんですか。パーティーはなんじですか。

_____

4. Dのパーティーはなんじですか。　のみものはなんですか。

_____

p - 漢字
(Kana and Kanji)

Innovative katakana combinations

As you know, the katakana syllabary is used primarily to write words adopted into Japanese from languages other than Chinese. Because many of these words are from English, they're often relatively easy for native English speakers to learn. Since World War II, English and other foreign languages have even influenced Japanese pronunciation to some extent. Several sound combinations that previously didn't exist in Japanese are now part of the language. To write these innovative sound combinations in katakana, a number of new symbol combinations have been devised. All these new combinations involve a full-size symbol followed by a reduced-size symbol. They are shown in the chart below.

	kw	*gw*	*sh*	*j*	*ch*	*ts*	*t*	*d*	*ty*	*dy*	*f*	*fy*	*w*	*y*
a	クァ *kwa*	グァ *gwa*				ツァ *tsa*					ファ *fa*			
i	クィ *kwi*	グィ *gwi*				ツィ *tsi*	ティ *ti*	ディ *di*			フィ *fi*		ウィ *wi*	
u							トゥ *tu*	ドゥ *du*	テュ *tyu*	デュ *dyu*		フュ *fyu*		
e	クェ *kwe*	グェ *gwe*	シェ *she*	ジェ *je*	チェ *che*	ツェ *tse*					フェ *fe*		ウェ *we*	イェ *ye*
o	クォ *kwo*					ツォ *tso*					フォ *fo*		ウォ *wo*	

The list below gives examples of words containing the combinations shown in the chart. These innovative pronunciations aren't all equally well established, though. The ones with more marginal status are marked with asterisks.

* kwa	クァジャレン	*Kwajaren*	Kwajalein
* kwi	クィニョン	*Kwinyon*	Quinhon
* kwe	クェッタ	*Kwetta*	Quetta
* kwo	クォーク	*kwooku*	quark
* gwa	グァリーニ	*Gwariini*	Guarini
* gwi	グィネビア	*Gwinebia*	Guinevere
* gwe	グェルチーノ	*Gweruchiino*	Guercino
she	シェーク	*sheeku*	shake
je	ジェット	*jetto*	jet
che	チェス	*chesu*	chess
tsa	ツァー	*tsaa*	tsar
tsi	エリツィン	*Eritsin*	Yeltsin
tse	ツェッペリン	*Tsepperin*	Zeppelin
tso	カンツォーネ	*kantsoone*	canzone ("Italian song")
ti	パーティー	*paatii*	party
* tu	トゥールーズ	*Tuuruuzu*	Toulouse
di	ディスク	*disuku*	disk
* du	ドゥシャンベ	*Dushanbe*	Dushanbe
dyu	デュエット	*dyuetto*	duet
tyu	テューバ	*tyuuba*	tuba
fa	ファッション	*fasshon*	fashion
fi	フィルム	*firumu*	film
fe	フェルト	*feruto*	felt
fo	フォーク	*fooku*	fork
fyu	フュージョン	*fyuujon*	fusion
* wi	ウィルソン	*Wiruson*	Wilson
* we	ウェールズ	*Weeruzu*	Wales
* wo	ウォード	*Woodo*	Ward
* ye	イェール	*Yeeru*	Yale

Inconsistent spellings

The asterisked combinations on the preceding list above occur mostly in proper names, and at least in some cases, they may be nothing more than spelling conventions rather than reflections of actual pronunciation. In fact, you'll find that many words are spelled inconsistently, sometimes with an innovative symbol combination and sometimes without. The list below shows some katakana words that are typically written with more conservative symbol combinations.

kui	(not kwi)	クイーン	*kuiin*	queen
kue	(not kwe)	クエーサー	*kueesaa*	quasar
kuo	(not kwo)	クオーツ	*kuootsu*	quartz
gua	(not gwa)	グアム	*Guamu*	Guam
tsu	(not tu)	ツアー	*tsuaa*	tour
zu	(not du)	ヒンズー	*Hinzuu*	Hindu
ui	(not wi)	ウイスキー	*uisukii*	whisky
ue	(not we)	ウエスト	*uesuto*	waist
uo	(not wo)	ウオッチ	*uotchi*	watch
ie	(not ye)	イエスマン	*iesuman*	yes man

There's also a set of katakana combinations commonly used to write words adopted from languages that have a *v* sound. These combinations all involve adding dakuten ("voicing dots") to the symbol ウ (u), as shown below.

ヴァ *(va)*   ヴィ *(vi)*   ヴ *(vu)*   ヴェ *(ve)*   ヴォ *(vo)*

But these symbols combinations do **not** reflect a change in actual Japanese pronunciation. In fact, they're pronounced exactly like バ (ba) ビ (bi) ブ (bu) ベ (be) ボ (bo), that is, with the consonant sound *b*. As you've already learned, Japanese doesn't have a *v* sound (at least not yet). Using ヴ to write a word in katakana just shows that the word had a *v* sound in the language that Japanese adopted it from. Since there's no difference in pronunciation, many words like baiorin (from English violin) have two alternative spellings: バイオリン and ヴァイオリン.

To be absolutely accurate, some speakers of Japanese do sometimes pronounce a *v* sound in at least some words, but a person who pronounces a word with a *v* sound is treating that word as foreign rather than as Japanese. This is like an English speaker who knows some Spanish saying burrito with a Spanish rolled **rr** sound instead of an English *r* sound. Once a person decides to pronounce a word with a foreign accent, pretty much anything goes.

2.8 Virtual Reality
I. Warm-Up

A. Match the expressions on the left with the situations on the right.

1. どこが いいですか。 ( ) a. asking for a preference of time

2. はじめましょう。 ( ) b. offering an alternative choice

3. ええと... ( ) c. asking for a preference of location

4. なんじが いいですか。 ( ) d. developing conversation

5. それとも、コーヒーですか。 ( ) e. asking which one of the two is better

6. どれが いいですか。 ( ) f. showing hesitation to respond

7. なんようびが いいですか。 ( ) g. asking for a preference of the day of the week

8. ５じに しましょう。 ( ) h. asking which one among many is the best

9. じゃ... ( ) i. handing over the decision making to somebody else

10. どちらが いいですか。 ( ) j. making a decision

11. いくらですか。 ( ) k. requesting objects

12. おまかせします。 ( ) l. announcing the beginning

13. ～をください。 ( ) m. asking for a price

B. Preliminary suggestion for a party (group work)

Your Japanese class is planning a party for Japanese exchange students. Your group will be expected to find out your classmates' preferences in one of the following areas. Each group will choose the best three items from the date, time and location sections and the best five items from the activity, food and beverage sections. Work with others who are assigned to the same area as you and record the results.

1. Time (-o'clock) of the party (3)

2. Location of the party (3)

3. The best day of the week for the party (3)

4. Activities for the party (5)

5. Food for the party (5)

6. Drinks for the party (5)

II. Main Activity: Class Meeting

A.   Select one student each to serve as the chairperson, the blackboard writer, and the note-taker for a meeting. The rest of the class will play participants in the meeting.

B.   A representative working on each area in Warm-Up Part B reports the results of the preliminary survey. The participants then cooperate under the leadership of the chairperson and make decisions regarding each area. After that, the class makes a comprehensive list of its decisions.

C   The class will make its choices from the date, time, and location sections and will choose two items each from the activity, food, and drinks sections.

Peer Evaluation Form: Class Meeting (Decision-Making Activities)

Name of Person Being Observed: _____ Role: _____

Name of Observer: _____

Performance Rating Chart for the Chair

	poor	fair	good	very good	excellent
Management skills	1	2	3	4	5
Cooperation with the blackboard writer	1	2	3	4	5
Clarity of instructions	1	2	3	4	5
Linguistic accuracy	1	2	3	4	5

Performance Rating Chart for the Blackboard Writer

	poor	fair	good	very good	excellent
Presentation/organization	1	2	3	4	5
Cooperation with the chair	1	2	3	4	5
Accuracy of spelling	1	2	3	4	5
Quality of participation	1	2	3	4	5

Performance Rating Chart for the Scribe

	poor	fair	good	very good	excellent
Presentation/organization	1	2	3	4	5
Cooperation with the chair	1	2	3	4	5
Accuracy of spelling	1	2	3	4	5
Quality of participation	1	2	3	4	5

Performance Rating Chart for the Participant

	poor	fair	good	very good	excellent
Presentation/organization	1	2	3	4	5
Cooperation	1	2	3	4	5
Productivity	1	2	3	4	5
Linguistic accuracy	1	2	3	4	5

Comments

2.9 Virtual Reality

III. Warm-Up: *Making Posters for a party*

Everyone makes a poster for a party using the items that were decided on in the Main Activity section. The class later chooses the best poster based on its design, organization, clarity of information and artistic creativity.

POSTER EVALUATION FORM	
design	
organization	
clarity of information	
artistic creativity	

SUM-UP

1. How well has the required task been carried out? Please rate your performance on a scale of 0 to 5. (0 = performance barely adequate, 5 = excellent performance)

   0   1   2   3   4   5

2. How competently did you interact and/or take the initiative in conversation/dialogue? Please rate your performance on a scale of 0 to 5. (0 = rarely participated; constant prompting is needed, 5 = fully participated and took the initiative in exchanges where appropriate)

   0   1   2   3   4   5

3. How wide was the range of vocabulary and idioms you used? Please rate your range on a scale of 0 to 5. (0 = limited range, 5 = wide range)

   0   1   2   3   4   5

4. Were you able to use the "hesitation noise" when you wanted to say another phrase? Please rate your progress on a scale of 0 to 5. (0 = no progress, 5 = excellent progress)

   0   1   2   3   4   5

5. Were you able to use cooperation strategies when you worked with members of your group? Please rate your progress on a scale of 0 to 5. (0 = no progress, 5 = excellent progress)

   0   1   2   3   4   5

ADDITIONAL VOCABULARY

	Formal	Informal	English
Functional Vocabulary			
Expressing welcome	いらっしゃいませ。 *Irasshaimase.*	いらっしゃい。 *Irasshai.*	Welcome.
Taking an order	なににしますか。 *Nani ni shimasu ka?*	なん(なに)にする。 *Nan (nani) ni suru?*	What would you like?
Requesting items	〜をください。 *o kudasai.*	〜をくれ。 *o kure.*	Please give me~.
Requesting items	〜をおねがいします。 *o onegai shimasu*	〜をおねがい。 *o onegai.*	I request~.
Deciding	〜にします。 *~ni shimasu.*	〜にする。 *~ ni suru.*	I would like~.
Politely prefacing requests with an apology	あのう、すみません。 *Anoo sumimasen.*	あっ、すいません。 *A, suimasen.*	Excuse me.
Acknowledging	はい、なんでしょう。 *Hai, nan deshoo?*	はい、なに。 *Hai, nani?*	Yes, what is it?
Asking the price	いくらですか。 *Ikura desu ka?*	いくら。 *Ikura?*	How much (is it)?
On handing over a requested item	はい、どうぞ。 *Hai, doozo.*	はい。 *Hai.*	Yes, here it is.
Offering food and beverages	〜をどうぞ。 *-o doozo.*	はい。 *Hai.*	Please feel free to eat (it).
Inquiring	あのう、しつもんがあります。 *Anoo, shitsumon ga arimasu.*	あのう、しつもんが *Anoo, shitsumon ga*	Er, I have a question.
Asking for permission	えいごでもいいですか。 *Eigo demo ii desu ka?*	えいごでもいい *Eigo demo ii?*	May I use English?
Requesting	ちょっとまってください。 *Chotto matte kudasai.*	ちょっとまって *Chotto matte.*	Wait a moment, please.
Starting class	きりつ。れい。ちゃくせき。 *Kiritsu. Rei. Chakuseki.*	きりつ。れい。ちゃくせき。 *Kiritsu. Rei. Chakuseki.*	Stand up. Bow. Sit down.
Taking attendance	しゅっせきをとります。 *Shusseki o torimasu.*	しゅっせきをとる。 *Shusseki o toru.*	I will take attendance.
Asking about someone's presence	〜さんはいますか。〜くんはいますか。 *-san wa imasu ka? -kun wa imasu ka?*	〜さんはいる。〜くんはいる。 *-san wa iru? -kun wa iru?*	Is so and so here?
Telling about someone's lateness	やすみです。ちこくです。 *Yasumi desu. Chikoku desu.*	やすみ(だ)。ちこく(だ)。 *Yasumi (da). Chikoku (da).*	He or she is late. He or she is absent.
Extending an offer	はじめましょう。 *Hajimemashoo.*	はじめよう。 *Hajimemeyoo.*	Let's begin
Requesting items	くばってください。 *Kubatte kudasai.*	くばって *Kubatte.*	Please pass these out.
	まわしてください。 *Mawashite kudasai.*	まわして *Mawashite.*	Please pass this around.
Expressing understanding	わかりますか。 *Wakarimasu ka?*	わかる。 *Wakaru?*	Do you understand?
Expressing comprehension	はい、わかります。 *Hai, wakarimasu.*	うん、わかる *Un, wakaru.*	Yes, I understand.
Expressing lack of comprehension	いいえ、わかりません *Iie, wakarimasen.*	ううん、わからない。 *Uun, wakaranai.*	No, I don't understand.
Asking if an action is complete	もういいですか。 *Moo ii desu ka?*	もういい。 *Moo ii?*	All set? Are you all done?
Stating that an action is complete	はい、もういいです。 *Hai, moo ii desu.*	うん、もういい。 *Un, moo ii.*	Yes, I am all set.
Stating that an action is not yet complete	いいえ、まだです。 *Iie, mada desu.*	ううん、まだ。 *Uun, mada.*	No, not yet.
Expressing an apology	おそくなってすみません。 *Osoku natte sumimasen.*	おそくなってすまない。 *Osoku natte sumanai.*	Sorry I'm late.
Giving a warning	これからはきをつけてください。 *Kore kara wa kio tsukete kudasai.*	これからはきをつけて。 *Kore kara wa kio tsukete.*	Please be careful next time.
Expressing praise	たいへんよくできました。 *Taihen yoku dekimashita.*	たいへんよくできた。 *Taihen yoku dekita.*	Very well done.
Expressing thanks	どうもありがとうございます。 *Doomo arigatoo gozaimasu.*	どうもありがとう。 *Doomo arigatoo.*	Thank you very much.
Extending wishes	もうすこしがんばってください。 *Moo sukoshi ganbatte kudasai.*	もうすこしがんばって。 *Moo sukoshi ganbatte.*	You can do a little better. Try your best.
Responding to someone's wishes	はい、がんばります。 *Hai, ganbarimasu.*	うん、がんばる。 *Un, ganbaru.*	Yes, I will do my best.

Notional Vocabulary

Meeting Terms

かいぎ	kaigi	meeting
ぎだい	gidai	topic of a meeting
さんせい	sansei	approval, agreement
はんたい	hantai	opposition

Numbers Representing Quantities

ひとつ	hitotsu	1
ふたつ	futatsu	2
みっつ	mittsu	3
よっつ	yottsu	4
いつつ	itsutsu	5
むっつ	muttsu	6
ななつ	nanatsu	7
やっつ	yattsu	8
ここのつ	kokonotsu	9
とお	too	10

Events

ゆうえんち	yuuenchi	amusement park
クラシックコンサート	kurashikku konsaato	classical concert
カントリーミュージックコンサート	kantorii myuujikku konsaato	country music concert
インディーカーレース	indii kaa reesu	Indy car race
じゅうどうきょうしつ	juudoo kyooshitsu	judo class
りょうりきょうしつ	ryoori kyooshitsu	cooking class
タウンミーティング	taun miitingu	town meeting

Restaurants

すしのみせ	sushi no mise	sushi shop
パスタのみせ	pasuta no mise	pasta shop
ピザのみせ	piza no mise	pizza shop
ハンバーガーのみせ	hanbaaga no mise	hamburger shop
サンドイッチのみせ	sandoitchi no mise	sandwich shop
ステーキのみせ	suteeki no mise	steak shop
ファミリーレストラン	famirii resutoran	family restaurant
イタリアりょうり	Itaria ryoori	Italian cuisine
ちゅうかりょうり	chuuka ryoori	Chinese cuisine
にほんりょうり	nihon ryoori	Japanese cuisine
わしょく	washoku	Japanese cuisine
いらっしゃいませ	irasshaimase	welcome
ショッピングセンター	shoppingu sentaa	shopping center
レストラン街（がい）	resutoran gai	shopping arcade
レストランのなまえ	resutoran no namae	restaurant's name
のみもの	nomimono	drinks, beverages
たべもの	tabemono	food
デザート	dezaato	dessert
メニュー	me'nyuu	menu
やすみのひ	yasumi no hi	day off
スープとスナック	suupu to sunakku	soup and snack
コンビネーション	konbineshon	combination

Japanese Food

すし	sushi	sushi (raw fish with rice)
とんかつ	tonkatsu	pork cutlet
てんぷら	tenpura	tempura
すきやき	sukiyaki	sukiyaki
そば	soba	buckwheat noodles
うどん	udon	white wheat noodles
うなぎ	unagi	eel
おべんとう	obentoo	box lunch
ラーメン	raamen	Chinese-style noodles
やきとり	yakitori	grilled chicken
よせなべ	yosenabe	seafood and chicken in a hot pot

Food

ハンバーガー	hanbaaga	hamburger
チーズバーガー	chiizubaaga	cheeseburger
やさいバーガー	yasai hanbaaga	veggie burger
ピザバーガー	piza hanbaaga	pizzaburger
アップルパイ	appuru pai	apple pie
ピザ	piza	pizza
ペパロニピザ	peparoni	pepperoni
チキンパルメザン	chikin parumezan	chicken parmesan
カラマリ	karamari	fried squid
シェルパスタ	sheru pasuta	shell pasta
フライドチキン	furaido chikin	fried chicken
グリルチキン	guriru chikin	grilled chicken
ミニハンバーガー	mini hanbaagaa	mini hamburger
ソーセージ	sooseeji	sausage
マッシュルーム	masshuruumu	mushroom
シャーベット	shaabetto	sorbet
チーズケーキ	chiizukeeki	cheesecake
ショートケーキ	shooto keeki	shortcake
メロン	meron	melon
まっちゃアイス	maccha aisu	green tea ice cream
トマトスープ	tomato suupu	tomato soup
クラムチャウダー	kuramu chaudaa	clam chowder
コーンスープ	koon suupu	corn soup
チキンナゲット	chikin nagetto	chicken nuggets
オニオンリング	onion ringu	onion rings
ハムとチーズ	hamu to chiizu	ham and cheese
ターキー	taakii	turkey
ベジタリアン	bejitarian	vegetarian
シーザー	shiizaa	Caesar (salad)
グリーク	guriiku	Greek (salad)
チキン	chikin	chicken
シュリンプ	shurinpu	shrimp
とうふ	toofu	tofu
ステーキ	suteeki	steak
ロブスター	robusutaa	lobster
さかなフライ	sakana furai	fried fish
グリルサーモン	guriru saamon	grilled salmon

Japanese Food

にほんのたべもの

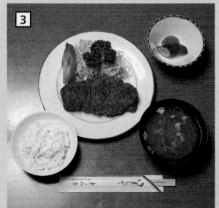

1. すし
2. てんぷら
3. とんかつ
4. すきやき
5. うなぎ
6. よせなべ

<ruby>日本<rt>にほん</rt></ruby>のたべもの

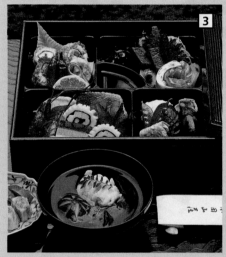

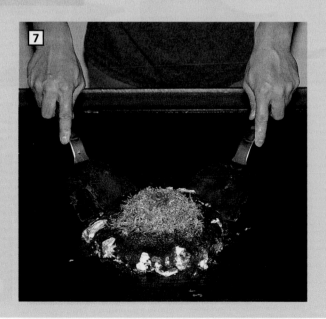

1. そば
2. うどん
3. おべんとう
4. ラーメン
5. ハンバーガー
6. カレーライス
7. おこのみやき

<ruby>日本<rt>にほん</rt></ruby>のレストラン

1. レストランのたべもの
2. ちゃや
3. きっさてん
4. ファーストフードレストラン
5. たちぐいそば

UNIT 1 REVIEW

1. *Let's make mindmaps. Mindmapping helps your make effective use of visual images. Practice making mindmaps for many different categories of things with your partner.*

2. **Read all the katakana words in a TV program listing or an article in a Japanese newspaper. Can you guess what programs are on? Can you guess which college won the NCAA tournament?**

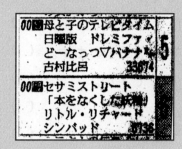

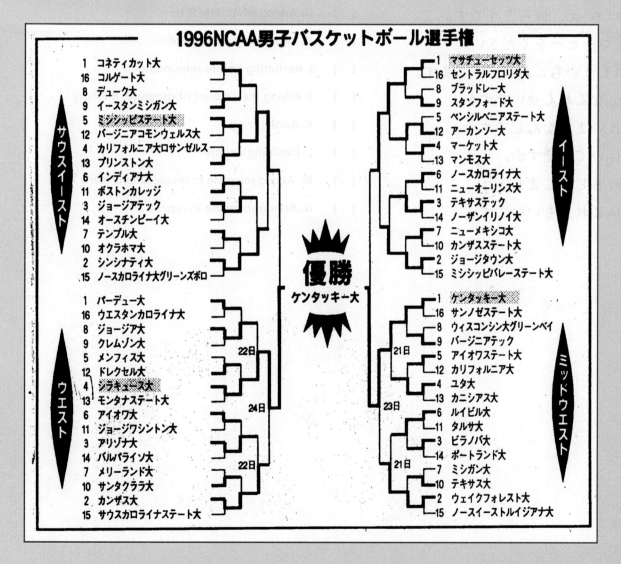

3. *Match the expressions on the left with the situations on the right, filling each ( ) with the appropriate letter.*

1. なんねんうまれですか。 　　(　) 　A. Asking preference about place

2. ハードディスクはなんギガですか。 　(　) 　B. Signaling the beginning

3. あけましておめでとうございます。 　(　) 　C. Asking someone to choose one of two items

4. ジェニーはとらどしですか。 　　(　) 　D. Asking for a show of hands

5. ごめんなさい。 　　　(　) 　E. Announcing a decision

6. どちらがいいですか。 　　(　) 　F. Asking someone's year of birth in the Chinese zodiac

7. いいえ、けっこうです。 　　(　) 　G. Asking what date it is

8. コーヒーをください。 　　(　) 　H. Requesting a beverage

9. もういちどおねがいします。 　(　) 　I. Hesitating before responding

10. なんねんせいですか。 　　(　) 　J. Asking the amount of computer memory

11. いま、なんじですか。 　　(　) 　K. Apologizing

12. いくらですか。 　　　(　) 　L. Declining an offer

13. 8 じにしましょう。 　　(　) 　M. Asking someone to choose among many items

14. どれでもいいです。 　　(　) 　N. Asking someone to repeat

4. *Circle the word you think belongs to a different category from the rest. Then choose the name of the category to which the rest of the words belong from those listed in the box below and write it in the blank.*

1. はる　ねこ　ふゆ　あき　なつ _____

2. うし　いぬ　うさぎ　さる　とり　みず _____

3. コーチ　ぎちょう　てんき　しょき　７ねんせい _____

4. ジャズ　ステーキ　ケーキ　サラダ　チキン _____

5. きょうしつ　ジム　カフェテリア　としょしつ　こうちゃ _____

6. ようか　ふたつ　ここのか　じゅうににち　むいか _____

7. テニス　サッカー　クッキー　ホッケー　ゴルフ _____

8. カラオケ　ダンス　コンサート　パスタ　えいが _____

たべもの	のみもの	がっこう	きせつ	どうぶつ
くだもの	ひと	ばしょ	ひにち	アクティビティー

5. *Rearrange the words in parentheses to make a grammatically correct sentence.*

1. キムさん（せんせい　の　は　にほんご）
   キムさん_____です。

2. マルティネスさん（ばんごう　は　でんわ　の）９２２−４６４６です。
   マルティネスさん_____９２２−４６４６です。

3. ケーキ（どちら　と　が　クッキー　と）いいですか。
   ケーキ_____いいですか。

4. わたし（どようび　も　いい　が）です。
   わたし_____です。

5. スピーチコンテスト（きんようび　に　８じ　の　は）しましょう。
   スピーチコンテスト _____しましょう。

6. （たべもの　を　の　にほん）ください。
   _____ください。

7. リンダ（サッカー　の　スポーツ　の　あき　は）じゃありません。
   リンダ_____じゃありません。

6. Let's role-play.

A. You meet a new exchange student from Japan. Do the following:

- Greet each other
- Introduce each other to a third person
- Exchange information about school, classes, teachers, students and programs.
- Tell each other about your after school activities

B, You are planning a party with your friend. Discuss the following:

- what kind of activities you will have
- what kind of food you will have
- what kind of drinks you will have
- what day you will have the party

C. Take notes as you interview five classmates to find out:

- when their birthday is
- which food they prefer among hamburger, pizza and hot dogs
- which drink they prefer between water and soft drinks
- what animal year they were born

D. You meet a Japanese friend.

Friend	You
Ask which sports he or she plays in the winter.	Say you've decided to play basketball.
Ask which food he or she prefers between sushi and pizza.	Say you prefer sushi.
Ask which drink he or she prefers among milk, juice, and cola.	Say you prefer milk.

7. What do you say in Japanese when:

1. You want to wish someone a happy new year when you part right before the New Year?

_____

2. You want to exchange a New Year greeting with someone?

_____

8. **Find the following countries and cities on the maps.**

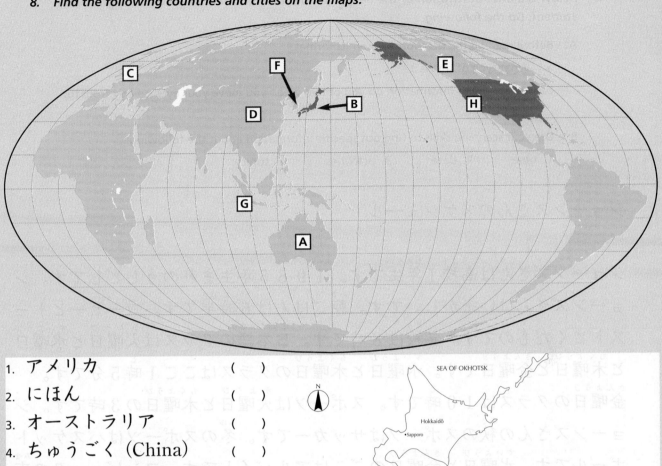

1. アメリカ	( )	
2. にほん	( )	
3. オーストラリア	( )	
4. ちゅうごく (China)	( )	
5. かんこく (South Korea)	( )	
6. インドネシア	( )	
7. イギリス (Great Britain)	( )	
8. カナダ	( )	

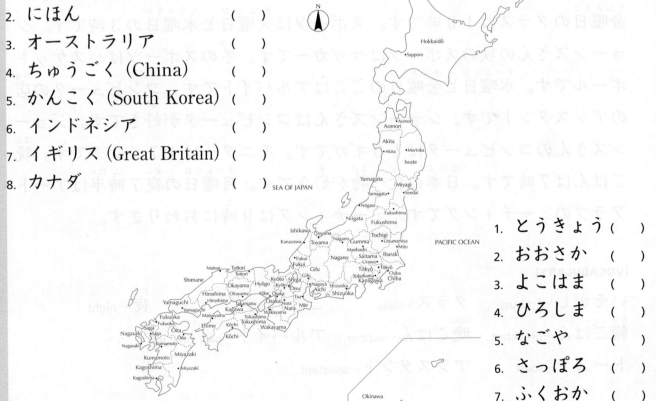

1. とうきょう	( )
2. おおさか	( )
3. よこはま	( )
4. ひろしま	( )
5. なごや	( )
6. さっぽろ	( )
7. ふくおか	( )
8. せんだい	( )

9. *Below is a brief description of the daily activities of Ms. Jones, an American high school student. Do the following.*

A. Before reading the description, scan its format.

   a. What type of text is it?

   b. What type of information do you obtain when you move your eyes quickly from top to bottom?

B. Use your scanning skills to find out specific information about the following:

   1. time   2. date   3. activities   4. topics

ジョーンズさんのスケジュール

ジョーンズさんは高校1年生です。1985年生まれのうしどしです。ジョーンズさんはいそがしいです。朝ごはんは6時半です。コーヒーとトーストとくだものです。学校は8時です。日本語のクラスは火曜日と水曜日と木曜日と金曜日です。水曜日と木曜日のクラスはごご1時5分です。金曜日のクラスは10時です。スポーツは火曜日と木曜日の3時です。ジョーンズさんの秋のスポーツはサッカーです。冬のスポーツはバスケットボールです。水曜日と金曜日のごごはアルバイトです。コンピュータの店のアシスタントです。ジョーンズさんはコンピュータが好きです。ジョーンズさんのコンピュータは10ギガです。モニターは17インチです。晩ごはんは7時です。日本の食べ物が好きです。月曜日の夜7時半はアートクラブのミーティングです。ミーティングは9時におわります。

[VOCABULARY]

いそがしい…busy   クラス…class   ごご…p.m.   夜…night

朝ごはん…breakfast   晩ごはん…supper   アルバイト…part-time job

トースト…toast   アシスタント…assistant

A. Are the following statements TRUE (T) or FALSE (F)?

1. (   ) Ms. Jones' Wednesday schedule includes a Japanese class.
2. (   ) She drinks coffee in the morning.
3. (   ) Her Japanese class on Friday begins at 1:05.
4. (   ) She is in 11th grade.
5. (   ) She attends her art club meeting once a week.
6. (   ) Her art club meeting ends at 9:00 a.m.
7. (   ) She works part-time two afternoons a week.
8. (   ) She has a 17-inch TV set.

B. Answer the following questions in Japanese.

1. ジョーンズさんは何年生まれですか。

   _____

2. ジョーンズさんは何年生ですか。

   _____

3. ジョーンズさんの日本語のクラスは何曜日ですか。

   _____

4. ジョーンズさんの冬のスポーツは何ですか。

   _____

5. ジョーンズさんのアルバイトはどこですか。

   _____

6. ジョーンズさんのコンピューターは何ギガですか。

   _____

7. 晩ごはんは何時ですか。

   _____

10. Today's Youth: Conducting a Survey

Almost every one of you probably has experience answering a survey of some kind. Some of you might even have solicited public opinions or preferences about something. This time all of you will have an opportunity to create and conduct a survey and report its results.

The theme of this survey is "Today's Youth." This theme can cover a wide range of subjects. Your survey should consist of four to six questions in which you ask your classmates to choose their responses from two or three selections you provide.

A. Making and Conducting a Survey

You may use a sheet such as the one below to write down your questions and record the responses during your survey.

	しつもん (Questions)	けっか (Results)		
1	ロックがいいですか。それとも、クラシックがいいですか。	ロック 正正		クラシック 正下
2	コーヒーとこうちゃとココアとどれがいいですか。	コーヒー 正	こうちゃ 正T	ココア 正一
3	かようびともくようびとどちらがすきですか。	かようび 正正		もくようび 正正

Can you guess what those funny symbols in the results column are for? They are for keeping track of the count, the Japanese equivalent of "卌." "正" is actually a kanji meaning "correct."

This is how it works.

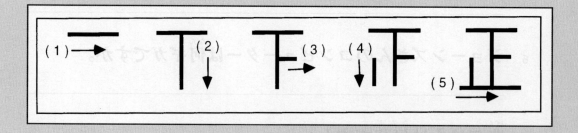

B.   Tallying and Reporting the Results

When reporting, state your question first and then announce the result. An example of this sequence based on the sample given earlier is provided below. You may use visual aids to supplement your oral report as well.

はじめのしつもんは「ロックがいいですか、それとも、クラシックがいいですか」です。ロックの人は１０人です。クラシックの人は８人です。

つぎのしつもんは「コーヒーとこうちゃとココアと、どれがいいですか」です。コーヒーの人は５人です。こうちゃの人は７人です。それから、ココアの人は６人です。つぎのしつもんは「かようびともくようびと、どちらがすきですか」です。かようびの人は９人です。もくようびの人も９人です。つぎのしつもんは「・・・・・

はじめの〜   first〜

つぎの〜   next〜

おわりの〜   final〜

11. **Answer the following questions.**

A.   Japanese white rice and Chinese white rice: which is easier to pick up with chopsticks and why?

B.   Are there any regional differences in the seasoning of food in Japan? If so, what are they?

C.   What sort of Japanese dish or ingredient do you think you'd like to incorporate into your diet and why?

12. Listen to the conversation, transcribe it and extend it using conversation-extension tactics.

1. A: _____   2. A: _____   3. A: _____

    B: _____   B: _____。   B: _____

    A: _____   A: _____   A: _____

    B: _____   B: _____   B: _____

Unit 2: Awareness

The theme of this unit is awareness. Being aware here does not simply mean being knowledgeable about something or being conscious in a general sense. It requires a more active participation and involvement from you in the form of paying attention, monitoring and evaluating situations, seeking and making meanings and paths to further progress, realization, and understanding, as well as searching for answers to problems.

The first chapter in this unit, Chapter 3, focuses on cultivating awareness of both yourself and others. This includes looking at your perception of yourself and others as well as others' perception of you. In Chapter 4 the focus shifts to daily life. You will be comparing your daily activities with those of others. Cultural awareness is an important component of this chapter.

Chapter 3
Getting Better Acquainted

Chapter 3

Getting Better Acquainted

3.1 Introduction

OBJECTIVES

At the end of this chapter, you will be able to:

- exchange basic personal information with others
- handle successfully a variety of situations in which you meet a new acquaintance again
- understand and appreciate the mindset and feelings associated with meeting a new acquaintance again
- establish your identity
- check your comprehension while listening or reading
- use conversation-tactics (analogies and attribution)
- prepare a self-introductory speech
- participate in an oral interview

You will also learn

- how to ask simple personal questions using a polite prefix
- how to ask simple personal questions using interrogatives
- Japanese family terms and names
- words used to describe personality types
- how to use some basic particles
- how to ask questions and respond to requests in the classroom
- how to recognize 15 Chinese characters
- how to read a short composition written both horizontally and vertically
- how to enhance your memorization

KISETSU THEATER

Getting Better Acquainted

Getting Better Acquainted

In Getting Started I and Chapter 1 you learned how to introduce yourself and carry on a brief conversation with someone you just met. In this chapter we will move a step further on this theme and exchange personal information on topics related to school and home–the two places you likely spend the most time in your daily life. You will be talking about yourself, your family members, your classes and your school clubs.

Self-Introduction Speech

Giving speeches is a multifaceted process that involves planning, writing, reading, rehearsing and delivering the speech. You will be guided through the whole process, until you are ready to give your own self-introductory speech. Emphasis here is not only on content but also on the organization of the speech, which typically follows an introduction-body-conclusion sequence. Awareness of this sequence will be useful in both written and oral presentations, both now and in the future.

A Celebrity Interview and a Close-Up: A package for aspiring journalists

The Virtual Reality section of this chapter offers you a taste of what it would be like to be a Japanese-speaking journalist. You will further develop your writing, listening and note-taking skills.

Schools in Japan

What kind of schooling do Japanese children receive? Since the contemporary Japanese school system was established based on its American counterpart, the two are very much alike in some aspects. However, you will certainly find some striking differences when you examine certain aspects, like the classroom environment and teaching techniques. Education is a hot topic in Japan; the Japanese schools are always under the watchful eyes of critics and reformers.

On the other hand, few social institutions are more influenced by the cultural values and traditions of their society than schools. Exploring the educational system in Japan will be a fascinating cultural journey.

Reading: It all begins here

Do you like to read? How would you describe yourself as a reader? Avid, voracious, engaged or reluctant? A "well-read" individual usually means a person who is knowledgeable and well-informed. People read in order to seek new knowledge and information as well as for personal enrichment and enjoyment. What comes to your mind when you think of "reading" in terms of what you have learned in this book so far? It may mean matching kana letters with sounds, pronouncing individual word, or learning how Japanese words line up to form sentences. At any rate, it is far from the kind of reading referred to above, but our goal is to eventually get there–to the stage where you will be engaged not so much in "learning to read" as in "reading to learn" or "reading for pleasure." We encourage you to think of reading in this context. In this chapter you will have opportunities to read materials that consist of more than one sentence. We start with brief personal accounts written in a format similar to that practiced in Japanese composition classrooms. This means that not only will your knowledge of vocabulary and syntax begin to come into play but also your general background knowledge as well as your ability to predict what follows next in your reading. So keep thinking about all the advantages of becoming a bilingual reader and enjoy the challenge!

Kanji: A lifetime friend!

You've already learned that Japanese writing uses both kanji (Chinese characters) and kana (syllabaries). Having become familiar with both sets of kana (katakana and hiragana), we now start incorporating kanji into our studies. How is kanji different from kana? The most conspicuous difference is that each kanji character represents an idea or a thing as well as a sound. The fact that Japanese students learn about 2,000 individual kanji as well as numerous compound words during the course of their twelve years of schooling may sound astonishing. However, building up kanji vocabulary may not be as difficult as you think.

The more you know about kanji, the more capable you will become of mastering the challenges associated with learning them.

WARM-UP

1. **ネームゲーム** *(Name Game)*
The following activity will challenge your memorization skills. It will also make you concentrate and listen carefully to others and help you get to know each other better.

1. **Practice Round: Last Name**
We call this the practice round because you will be dealing with each other's last names only which, we assume, are quite familiar to you already. Everyone sits in a circle and picks a leader (let's assume her last name is Anderson). The leader introduces herself, saying 「アンダーソンです。どうぞよろしく。」. Then the person sitting next to her (let's call him Brown) introduces himself, but he must do so by saying 「アンダーソンさんのとなりのブラウンです。」、which means "I am Brown, who is seated next to Ms. Anderson." The person sitting next to Brown (let's say Smith) then introduces herself by saying 「アンダーソンさんのとなりのブラウンさんのとなりのスミスです。」 "I am Smith, who is sitting next to Mr. Brown, who is seated next to Ms. Anderson." The introduction continues in the same manner until everyone gets a turn.

2. **Round 1: Birth Month and Last Name**
The procedure here is the same as in the practice round, but you will be introducing yourself by giving both your birth month and your last name. See the following example.

> アンダーソン 「８月生まれのアンダーソンです。どうぞよろしく。」
>
> ブラウン 「８月生まれのアンダーソンさんのとなりの２月生まれのブラウンです。」
>
> スミス 「８月生まれのアンダーソンさんのとなりの２月生まれのブラウンさんのとなりの１０月生まれのスミスです。」

3. **Round 2: Describing Your Neighbors**
This round is a little different. You introduce yourself by last name but need to add an adjective when giving the last name of the person who has introduced him- or herself right before you. The class may decide to keep the birth month to make this round even more challenging.

> アンダーソン 「(８月生まれの) アンダーソンです。どうぞよろしく。」
>
> ブラウン 「(８月生まれの) げんきなアンダーソンさんのとなりの (２月生まれの) ブラウンです。」
>
> スミス 「(８月生まれの) げんきなアンダーソンさんのとなりの (２月生まれの) すてきなブラウンさんのとなりの (１０月生まれの) スミスです。」

2. **Let's Play** しんけいすいじゃく

Many of you may be familiar with a card game called Concentration. This game is known as しんけいすいじゃく *in Japan. You will be playing educational versions of* しんけいすいじゃく *here. The procedure is the same as the regular* しんけいすいじゃく, *which is played in the following manner.*

1. A deck of cards is spread on the table facedown.

2. The first player chooses a card and turns it over.

3. The player then chooses another card, attempting to match that card with the first card.

4. If they match, the player keeps the cards and repeat 2 and 3 above until he or she fails to make a match. When the player fails to make a match, the cards are replaced facedown, and the next player's turn begins.

5. When all the cards have been matched, the players count how many pairs they have collected, and the person who has collected the most pairs is the winner.

Versions to try may include:

Katakana しんけいすいじゃく   Hiragana しんけいすいじゃく

Vocabulary しんけいすいじゃく   Picture しんけいすいじゃく

Category しんけいすいじゃく

BASIC VOCABULARY

おくには。

おすまいは。

おとしは。

スポーツは。

たんじょうびは。

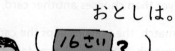

ごしゅっしんは。

たんにんのせんせいは。

どういういみですか。

ごしゅみは。

いみはなんですか。

BASIC VOCABULARY (continued)

にほんじん
にほんご

アメリカじん
えいご

かんこくじん
かんこくご

メキシコじん
スペインご

ちゅうごくじん
ちゅうごくご

カナダじん
えいご
フランスご

いくつ
（なんさい）

どこ

だれ

なに（なん）

いつ

どちら

なんにち

どういう　いみは
いみ　　なに

245

かぞく

1. おとうさん
2. おかあさん
3. おにいさん
4. おねえさん
5. おとうと
6. いもうと

はじめ
なか
おわり

のりもの

1. くるま
2. バス
3. タクシー
4. ちかてつ
5. でんしゃ
6. ひこうき
7. ふね

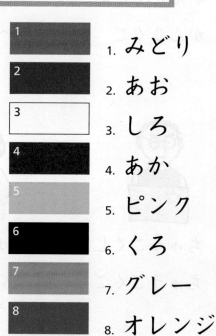

1. みどり
2. あお
3. しろ
4. あか
5. ピンク
6. くろ
7. グレー
8. オレンジ
9. むらさき

かぞくのひとのとくちょう

げんきな	やさしい	きれいな
かわいい	すてきな	おもしろい

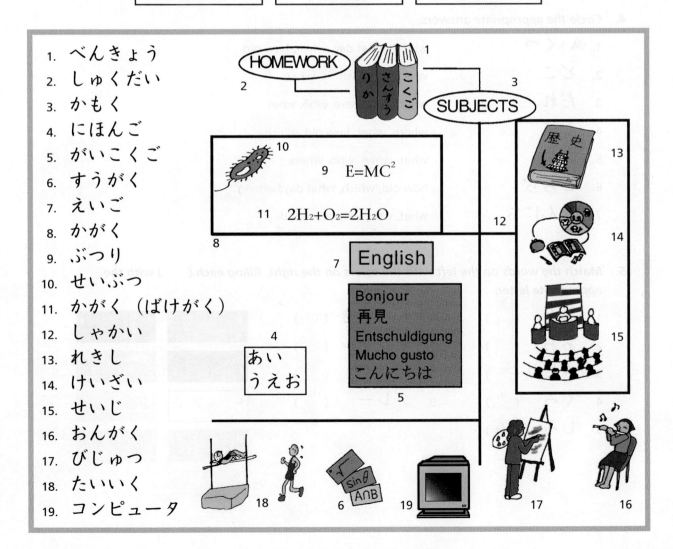

1. べんきょう
2. しゅくだい
3. かもく
4. にほんご
5. がいこくご
6. すうがく
7. えいご
8. かがく
9. ぶつり
10. せいぶつ
11. かがく（ばけがく）
12. しゃかい
13. れきし
14. けいざい
15. せいじ
16. おんがく
17. びじゅつ
18. たいいく
19. コンピュータ

HOMEWORK

SUBJECTS

$9 \quad E=MC^2$

$11 \quad 2H_2+O_2=2H_2O$

7 English

Bonjour
再見
Entschuldigung
Mucho gusto
こんにちは

あい
うえお

MECHANICS

3. **Match the expressions on the left with the situations on the right, filling each ( ) with the appropriate letter.**

1. おとしは   (   ) a. asking someone's name
2. おくには   (   ) b. asking someone's age
3. おなまえは   (   ) c. asking what country someone's from
4. おすまいは   (   ) d. asking what sport someone plays
5. スポーツは   (   ) e. asking someone's place of residence
6. ごしゅっしんは   (   ) f. asking someone's hometown
7. ごしゅみは   (   ) g. asking someone's hobby

4. **Circle the appropriate answers.**

1. いくつ   where, what day, when, how old
2. どこ   which, who, where, when
3. だれ   what day, where, who, what
4. なに   where, what, how old, which
5. いつ   what, when, who, where
6. どちら   how old, which, what day, where
7. なんにち   what, who, where, what day

5. **Match the words on the left with the colors on the right, filling each (   ) with the appropriate letter.**

1. あか   (   )   6. むらさき (   )
2. あお   (   )   7. オレンジ (   )
3. みどり (   )   8. ピンク   (   )
4. くろ   (   )   9. グレー   (   )
5. しろ   (   )

6. **Match the words on the right with the pictures on the left, filling each (   ) with the appropriate letter.**

1. (   )

2. (   )

3. (   )

4. (   )

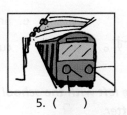
5. (   )

6. (   )

7. (   )

a. くるま
b. バス
c. タクシー
d. ちかてつ
e. でんしゃ
f. ひこうき
g. ふね

7. **Match the expressions on the left with the functions on the right, filling each (   ) with the appropriate letter.**

1. バナナがすきです。   (   ) a. talking about preference

2. バナナがきらいです。   (   ) b. going by a type of vehicle

3. でんしゃでいきます。   (   ) c. going with a certain person

4. せんせいといきます。   (   ) d. talking about dislikes

8. **Draw lines to connect the expressions on the left with the family words on the right.**

はは／おかあさん   •   • father

ちち／おとうさん   •   • younger brother

あに／おにいさん   •   • older brother

あね／おねえさん   •   • mother

おとうと／おとうとさん   •   • older sister

いもうと／いもうとさん   •   • younger sister

9. **Match the words on the left with the functions on the right, filling each (   ) with the appropriate letter.**

   1. かわいいです。   (   ) a. healthy
   2. げんきです。   (   ) b. kind
   3. やさしいです。   (   ) c. wonderful
   4. きれいです。   (   ) d. funny
   5. すてきです。   (   ) e. pretty
   6. おもしろいです。   (   ) f. cute

10. **Match the words on the left with the school subjects on the right, filling each (   ) with the appropriate letter.**

    1. すうがく   (   ) a. music
    2. がいこくご   (   ) b. physical education
    3. おんがく   (   ) c. science
    4. しゃかい   (   ) d. social studies
    5. かがく   (   ) e. English
    6. えいご   (   ) f. art
    7. たいいく   (   ) g. mathematics
    8. びじゅつ   (   ) h. foreign language

11. **Match the words on the left with the school subjects on the right, filling each (   ) with the appropriate letter.**

    1. ぶつり   (   ) a. physics
    2. けいざい   (   ) b. biology
    3. せいぶつ   (   ) c. economics
    4. スペインご   (   ) d. politics
    5. せいじ   (   ) e. Japanese
    6. にほんご   (   ) f. Spanish
    7. フランスご   (   ) g. French
    8. コンピュータ   (   ) h. history
    9. れきし   (   ) i. computer

SONGS

Used by permission of JASRAC
license No.9914305-901

3.2 Mechanics

1. **Fill in the (   ) with the number of the personal question that corresponds to the picture.**

  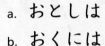

1.(   )   2.(   )   3.(   )

4.(   )   5.(   )   6.(   )

7.(   )   8.(   )

a. おとしは
b. おくには
c. おなまえは
d. おすまいは
e. スポーツは
f. ごしゅっしんは
g. ごしゅみは
h. たんにんのせんせいは

2. **Match the question words on the left with the appropriate picture on the right, filling each (   ) with the appropriate letter.**

1. いくつ　　（   ）
2. どこ　　　（   ）
3. だれ　　　（   ）
4. なに　　　（   ）
5. いつ　　　（   ）
6. どちら　　（   ）
7. なんにち　（   ）

a.   b.   c.

d.   e.   f.

g.   h.

3. **Greet the exchange students from Japan pictured below and ask them simple personal questions, as shown in the example. Practice answering the questions as well, pretending that you are one of the exchange students.**

Name	きむら　ゆか	さとう　けんじ	たなか　まき	もり　みちお
Residence	かごしま	みやざき	ふくおか	おおいた
Age	１７	１５	１６	１８
Birthday	July 11	April 15	September 21	December 7
Birthplace	にいがた	よこはま	ひろしま	ながの

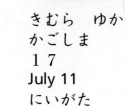

会話の例 (Sample Dialogue)

A:
こんにちは。
あのう、おなまえは。
おすまいは。
おとしは。
じゃ、たんじょうびは。
じゃ、ごしゅっしんは。
にいがたですか。

B:
こんにちは。
きむら　ゆかです。
かごしまです。
１７さいです。
しちがつじゅういちにちです。
にいがたです。
はい。

4. *Continue to ask and answer simple personal questions as shown in the sample dialogue below.*

Name	きむら　ゆか	さとう　けんじ	たなか　まき	もり　みちお
Grade Level	1 1	9	1 0	1 2
Homeroom Teacher	キング	ジョーンズ	ひらの	オマリー
Sport	テニス	じゅうどう	サッカー	フットボール
Club	アート	アニメ	クッキング	コンピュータ

<table>
<tr><td colspan="2">会話の例 (Sample Dialogue)</td></tr>
<tr><td>A:</td><td>B:</td></tr>
<tr>
<td>
きむらさん、がくねんは。
こう２？
あ、こうこう２ねんせいですか。
じゃ、たんにんのせんせいは。
スポーツは　サッカーですか。
クラブは　なんですか。
</td>
<td>
こう２です。
こうこう２ねんせいです。
はい。
キングせんせいです。
いいえ、テニスです
アートクラブです。
</td>
</tr>
</table>

5. **Practice asking for and identifying native countries, as shown in the example.**

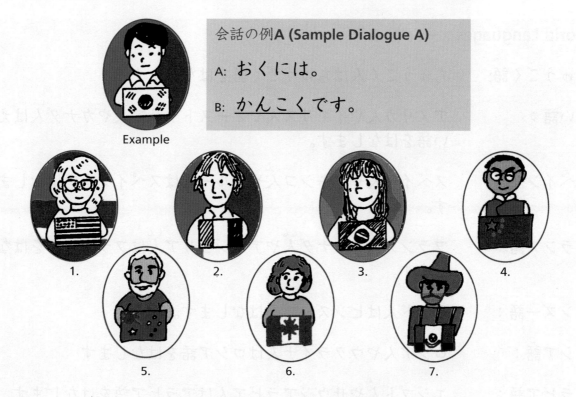

会話の例**A (Sample Dialogue A)**

A: おくには。

B: <u>かんこく</u>です。

Example

1.   2.   3.   4.

5.   6.   7.

6. **Practice asking for and identifying native countries, as shown in the example.**

会話の例**A (Sample Dialogue A)**

A: すみません。<u>アメリカ人</u>ですか。

B: いいえ、ちがいます。<u>オーストラリア人</u>です。

Example

1.   2.   3.   4.

5.   6.   7.

255

7. Practice reading the following sentences.

World Languages ノート1 (Note 1):

ちゅうごく語: ちゅうごく人はちゅうごく語をはなします。

えい語: アメリカ人やイギリス人やオーストラリア人やカナダ人はえい語をはなします。

スペイン語: スペイン人やメキシコ人やペルー人はスペイン語をはなします。

フランス語: フランス人やカナダ人やアルジェリア人はフランス語をはなします。

ヒンズー語: インド人はヒンズー語をはなします。

ロシア語: ロシア人やウクライナ人はロシア語をはなします

アラビア語: エジプト人やサウジアラビア人はアラビア語をはなします。

にほん語: にほん人はにほん語をはなします。

インドネシア語: インドネシア人はインドネシア語をはなします。

ポルトガル語: ポルトガル人やブラジル人はポルトガル語をはなします。

ノート2 (Note 2):

Did you scan the key words in the previous section? The key words are 語 (go) and 人 (jin). Now you can guess the meaning of 語 (go) and 人 (jin). 人 (jin) looks like a person, doesn't it? 語 (go) has many mouths and sound waves. 人 (jin) means "person" and 語 (go) means "language."

---

useful word:

はなします (to speak)

ノート3 (Note 3):

The particle や (ya) is used to connect two or more nouns, similar to と (to). However, と (to) is used to list every item, whereas や (ya) is used to indicate a couple of items in a longer series.

8. Role Play: Follow the models.

<table>
<tr>
<td>

Card A (Japanese)

It's evening and you are attending a get-together sponsored by a local Japanese organization, for Japanese people and those who are learning Japanese at school.

Greet the nearest non-Japanese participant and find out the following from him or her: name, country, school, grade level, age, homeroom teacher, sports, club, birthday and telephone number.

</td>
<td>

Card B (non-Japanese)

It's evening and you are attending a get-together sponsored by a local Japanese organization, for Japanese people and those who are learning Japanese at school.

One of the Japanese participants will greet you and ask you about the following: name, country, school, grade level, age, homeroom teacher, sports, club, birthday and telephone number. Respond appropriately.

</td>
</tr>
</table>

会話の例 (Sample Dialogue)

こんばんは。	こんばんは。
おなまえは。	ロメロです。
ロメロさんですか。おくには。	メキシコです。
がっこうは。	ミドルタウンこうこうです。
１１ねんせいですか。	いいえ、１０ねんせいです。
たんにんの　せんせいは。	ロイドせんせいです。
あのう、スポーツは。	サッカーです。
あ、サッカーですか。	はい。
クラブは　なんですか。	えいがクラブです。
いいですね。ロメロさんの	
たんじょうびは。	６月１６日です。
ああ、そうですか。(*in an upbeat way*)	
でんわ　ばんごうは。	すみません、でんわばんごうですか。
	548-2292 です。
548-2292 ですね。(*raising intonation on ne*)	はい、そうです。

257

Schools in Japan

Schools in Japan and schools in the United States differ in many ways, yet they are similar in many respects as well. One strikingly different aspect of the two school systems is that schools in Japan begin their school year in April and schools in the United States begin theirs in September. Thus the schools in Japan technically start half a year later than the schools in the United States. There have been many books written, debates held, and questions raised about the two school systems, and it is a complex topic, but let us focus here mainly on the division of the school years, the subjects taught, the classroom environment, school uniforms and entrance examinations.

In the United States, it is common to see a 5-3-4 division of the school years, with elementary schools consisting of five grade years (first grade to fifth grade), middle schools consisting of three grade years (sixth grade to eighth grade), and high schools consisting of four grade years (ninth grade to twelfth grade). In Japan, however, the majority of the schools are divided into a 6-3-3 system, with six years in elementary school, three years in middle school and three years in high school. The college years, however, in both countries are the same: four years.

The subjects taught at schools in Japan and schools in the United States are relatively similar. English (Japanese in Japan), mathematics, social studies, science, music, art and physical education are all taught in the schools in both countries. However, there are a few minor differences in what students learn. That is, in the United States, a choice of foreign language courses (French, Spanish, German, Latin, Japanese, etc) is often offered to students from a young age, but in Japan, foreign languages studied before college often only include English, which is a mandatory course for middle school and high school students. Another difference between the subjects taught in the two countries is that, in Japan, *kateika* (home economics) and *dootoku* (moral training) are required. In *kateika*, the students acquire basic knowledge and skills relating to food, clothing and shelter. *Dootoku* classes stress good moral conduct and personal responsibility. These two subjects are seldom mandatory in the United States.

Differences in the classroom environment and teaching techniques in the two countries have given rise to many questions over the years. What is the most effective teaching technique? How does the classroom environment affect a student's progress? A major difference between the two teaching techniques is that while most schools in the United States encourage the expression of individual opinion, schools in Japan emphasize memorization and regurgitation. The differences in the two teaching techniques are reflected in the arrangement of classrooms. Many classrooms in the United States have tables where students sit in groups and discuss issues, while classrooms in Japan have tables arranged in rows facing the blackboard and the teacher. This difference in teaching technique reflects a deep cultural difference.

Many students in the United States go through their school years without ever having to wear a school uniform. For students in Japan, however, wearing a school uniform is almost inescapable. The majority of middle schools and high schools in Japan require them, as do some elementary schools. The uniforms vary, but boys usually wear a pair of dark (often navy blue or black) pants and a matching jacket with a high collar and brass buttons. The girls' uniform, the same color as the boys', is usually a knee-length skirt and a sailor top with white piping.

The pressure of Japanese students to score well on any school entrance exam is outrageously high. This is because, unlike the schools in the United States, the schools in Japan look only at a student's test scores when evaluating that student's abilities. The schools in Japan do not consider other aspects of the student, such as extracurricular activities the student may have been involved in or other nonacademic qualifications that student may have. The importance of these entrance exams is therefore much greater than the SATs in the United States. The pressure for students in Japan to perform well on the entrance exams is so high that there is even a term, *juken jigoku,* which literally translates "examination hell." Students go to "cram" schools, known as *juku,* both during the school year and during vacations, to prepare for these exams. The most important entrance examination for any student in Japan is one for entrance into college or university, but many young students attend *juku* during their elementary school years so that they can attempt to attend a top-class middle school.

As can be seen, the schools in the United States and Japan differ significantly in some respects yet are very much alike in others. This issue of the differences in the two school systems is an issue of great interest but because of cultural influences, it may never be possible to determine which system is better for the students.

3.3 Mechanics

Conversation extension tactics ノート 4 (Note 4):

Have you ever experienced an awkward silence in the middle of a conversation with someone you just met? Or, have you wished that your conversation could always go smoothly? If so, try these tips, which may help you improve your performance.

TACTIC A

Using a word that is either an attribute of or associated with the word just mentioned by the other person

TACTIC B

Using a word bearing a similar or the same meaning to the word just mentioned by the other person

In the example on the left, upon hearing アメリカ, the boy said ウエストコースト, which is a part of the United States. (Attribution/Association)

In the example on the right, the girl said 十一ねんせい upon hearing こうこう二ねんせい. The two words essentially refer to the same thing. (Analogy)

1. **Which conversation-extension tactic introduced in the previous section is used in the following samples: Tactic A (attribution/association) or Tactic B (analogy)?**

1. _____
   A: なんねんせいですか。
   B: 12ねんせいです。
   A: シニアですね。
   B: はい、シニアです。

2. _____
   A: スポーツは。
   B: じゅうどうです。
   A: じゃ、はやしコーチですか。
   B: はい、そうです。

3. _____
   A: くるまは。
   B: アコードです。
   A: じゃ、にほんのくるまですね。
   B: はい、そうです。

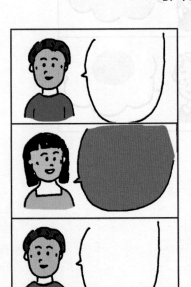

4. _____
   A: おすまいは。
   B: ニューヨークです。
   A: マンハッタンですか。
   B: いいえ、ブルックリンです。

5. _____
   A: たんにんのせんせいは。
   B: かわのせんせいです。
   A: じゃ、じゅうどうのせんせいですね。
   B: はい、そうです。

6. _____
   A: おねえさんですか。
   B: はい、そうです。
   A: おとしはいくつですか。
   B: 22です。

2. **Extend the following dialogues using conversation-extension tactics.**

1. A: あのう、クラブは。　2. A: がくねんは。　3. A: たんじょうびは。

   B: ドラマクラブです。　　 B: 10 ねんせいです。　 B: 7 月 4 日です。

   A: _____　　 A: _____　 A: _____

   B: _____　　 B: _____　 B: _____

Japanese Last Names ノート5 (Note 5):

Japanese last names（みょうじ）and first names consist of one or more kanji. Below are some of the more popular Japanese last names and their literal English translations.

山田（やまだ）	[mountain and rice paddy]	中山（なかやま）	[middle mountain]
木村（きむら）	[tree and village]	林（はやし）	[woods]
鈴木（すずき）	[bell tree]	大山（おおやま）	[big mountain]
川上（かわかみ）	[stream above]	高橋（たかはし）	[tall bridge]
木下（きのした）	[tree below]	小池（こいけ）	[small pond]
青山（あおやま）	[blue mountain]	清水（しみず）	[pure water]

Girls' Names

Mari	真理	truth
Yuri	百合	lily
Mika	美香	beautiful incense
Haruko	春子	spring child
Hiromi	広美	wide and beauty
Erika	恵里花	flowers in a rich village
Naomi	直美	straight and beauty

Boys' Names

Ken	研	truth
Ichiroo	一郎	first son
Akira	明	bright
Kazuki	和樹	peaceful tree
Masao	正男	right man
Hiroyuki	裕幸	rich and happy
Masatoshi	雅俊	sophisticated and bright

Common Japanese Family Names

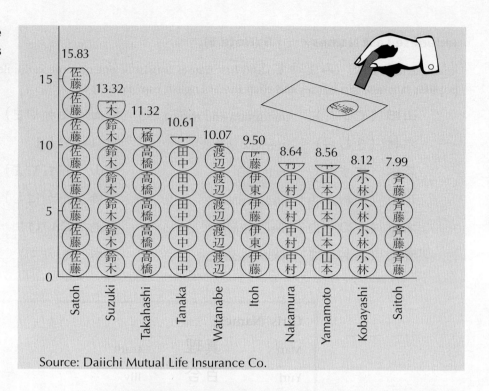

Source: Daiichi Mutual Life Insurance Co.

ノート**6 (Note 6):**

～の　いみは　なんですか or ～は　どういう　いみですか is used to ask someone what something（～）means. Practice asking the following people what their last name means.

3. **Practice asking what it means, as shown in the example.**

| Ex. 大山 | 1. 石川 | 2. 森山 | 3. 木村 | 4. 林 |
| おおやま | いしかわ | もりやま | きむら | はやし |

会話の例 **(Sample Dialogue)**

A: あのう、おおやまさん。

B: はい。

A: おおやまの　いみは　なんですか。

B: "big mountain" です。

4. **Practice asking about preferences. You may answer that you like an item or that you do not.**

会話の例 **(Sample Dialogue)**

A: <u>バナナ</u>がすきですか。

B: <u>はい、すきです。</u>

B: いいえ、すきじゃありません。

5. **Practice asking about preferences. You may answer that you like an item or that you do not.**

会話の例 **(Sample Dialogue)**

A: <u>バナナ</u>がすきですか。

B: <u>はい、バナナがすきです。</u>

B: いいえ、バナナはすきじゃありません。

6. **Practice asking what someone's favorite things are.**

フルーツ

7. **Practice asking what someone's favorite color is.**

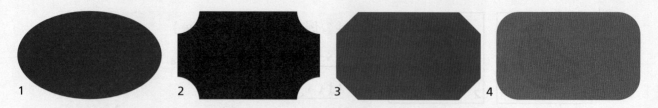

1 2 3 4

会話の例 (Sample Dialogue)

A: なにいろがすきですか。

B: <u>みどり</u>がすきです。

8. **Extend the following dialogue using conversation-extension tactics.**

1. A: なにがすきですか。
   B: オレンジがすきです。
   A: じゃ、＿＿＿＿＿＿＿
   がすきですか。

   B: ＿＿＿＿＿＿＿＿

4. A: おなまえは。
   B: まりです。
   A: じゃ、みょうじは

   ＿＿＿＿＿＿＿＿

   B: ＿＿＿＿＿＿＿＿

2. A: おなまえは。
   B: こやまです。
   A: じゃ、こやまのいみは

   ＿＿＿＿＿＿＿＿

   B: ＿＿＿＿＿＿＿＿

5. A: すしがすきですか。
   B: はい、すきです。
   A: じゃ、＿＿＿＿＿＿
   がすきですか。

   B: ＿＿＿＿＿＿＿＿

3. A: なにいろがすきですか。
   B: みどりがすきです。
   A: じゃ、＿＿＿＿＿＿
   がすきですか。

   B: ＿＿＿＿＿＿＿＿

6. A: すしがすきですか。
   B: いいえ、すしはすきじゃ
   ありません。
   A: じゃ、＿＿＿＿＿＿
   がすきですか。

   B: ＿＿＿＿＿＿＿＿

Language Note

Standard Languages

During the last 200 years or so, the world has been organized into nation-states, which we usually call countries. At least in theory, every person has an attachment to a political unit that is much larger than a family or a village or a region. One result of this change in political organization has been the development of what are called **standard languages**. As you've already learned, every language with more than a few speakers has regional and social dialects, but in most modern countries a particular dialect is recognized as the standard language. Not surprisingly, the standard is typically based on the speech of a powerful elite who live in the capital city.

Most people think of standard languages as the only "real" languages; they consider other dialects **substandard**—not just different but inferior. In fact, though, there's nothing inherently superior about a dialect that becomes a standard; the prestige of the dialect is just a reflection of the prestige of its speakers. That's why linguists generally say **standard dialect** instead of standard language and **nonstandard** dialect instead of substandard dialect. In practical terms, of course, a standard dialect's special status does make it more important than other dialects. You can expect the written language in a country's textbooks, magazines and newspapers to be based on the standard dialect. You can also expect that formal classes for non-native learners will teach the standard.

Tokyo Japanese

Standard Japanese is the dialect of the elite residents of Tokyo. These people typically (but not always) live in the newer, western part of the city known as Yamanote (literally, "foothills") rather than in the older, eastern part known as Shitamachi (literally, "downtown"). Japanese people typically refer to the standard dialect as 標準語 *hyoojungo* ("standard language"), but this same word is often used to mean something rather different. Instead of a real dialect spoken by real people, *hyoojungo* can also mean a kind of artificial, "ideal" Japanese that excludes things like slang and unconventional grammatical patterns.

Although regional dialects of Japanese differ dramatically, in modern Japan virtually everyone goes through at least nine years of schooling, and in the classroom teachers are expected to use a variety of Japanese that approximates the Tokyo standard. The written language studied is based on the same standard. There's some diversity in the language heard on television, but the standard dialect still dominates. As a result, most people in Japan master a variety of Japanese that's close to the Tokyo standard no matter where they grow up. In other words, most Japanese people are **bidialectal** (as opposed to bilingual); they can switch back and forth between the dialect of their hometown and a near-standard variety. In fact, as in most industrialized countries, there's a clear trend toward dialect homogenization in Japan, and many young people today aren't really very proficient in their traditional hometown dialects.

3.4 Mechanics

Japanese Family Terms ノート7 (Note 7):

The vocabulary used to refer to family members in Japanese is quite different from that of English. There are two distinct sets of family terms, depending on whether you are referring to someone from the *soto* group ("out-group") or the *uchi* group ("in-group"). For example, ちち (chichi) is used to refer one's own father with *soto* group members. おとうさん (otoosan) is used to refer to one's own father among *uchi* group members. People in the following three categories will generally belong to your *uchi* group ("in-group"); all others to your *soto* group ("out-group").

1. Members of your family and relatives, especially those with whom you stay in touch.

2. Your friends, especially those in the same age group as you or younger than you.

3. Any other persons with whom you have established a close and congenial relationship.

Japanese Family Terms				
	Humble (Plain)	**Neutral (Casual)**	**Exalted (Polite)**	**Attention-Seeking**
(Use)	Referring to your own family members among people in your そと group	Referring to your own as well as someone else's family members among people in your うち group	Referring to someone else's family members among people in your そと group	Calling one of your family members to draw his or her attention.
Yourself	わたし わたくし	わたし、あたし (female) ぼく (male)		
Father	ちち	おとうさん パパ	おとうさん	おとうさん パパ
Mother	はは	おかあさん ママ	おかあさん	おかあさん ママ
Elder brother	あに	おにいさん	おにいさん	おにいさん
Elder sister	あね	おねえさん	おねえさん	おねえさん
Younger brother	おとうと	おとうと	おとうとさん	(first name)
Younger sister	いもうと	いもうと	いもうとさん	(first name)
Situation	usually formal	unually informal	usually formal	formal/informal

Japanese Family Terms ノート8 (Note 8):

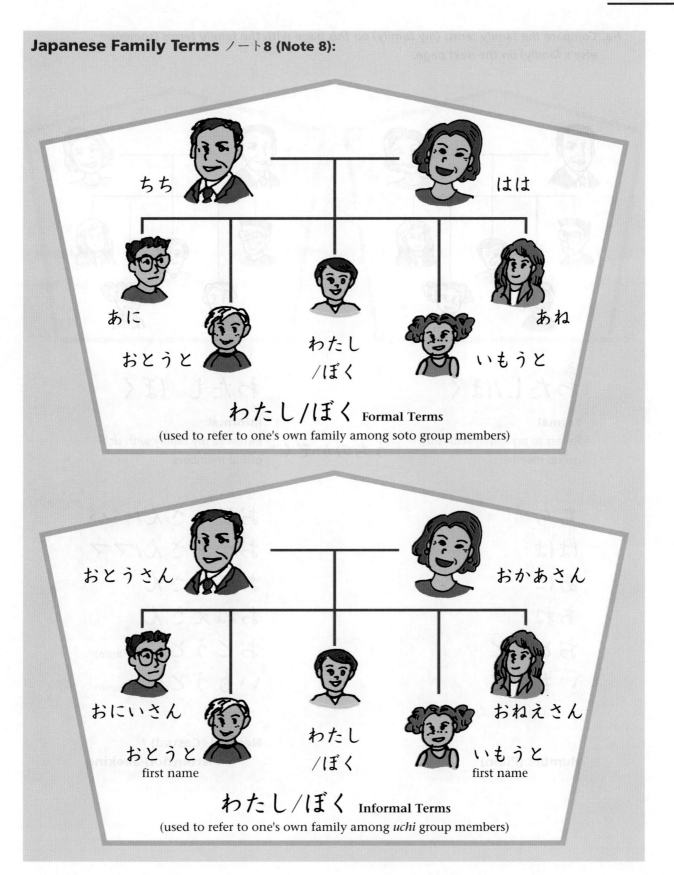

ちち　　　　　　　　　　はは

あに　　　　　　　　　　　　　　あね

おとうと　　わたし　　いもうと
　　　　　　／ぼく

わたし/ぼく Formal Terms
(used to refer to one's own family among *soto* group members)

おとうさん　　　　　　おかあさん

おにいさん　　　　　　　　　おねえさん

おとうと　　わたし　　いもうと
first name　　／ぼく　　first name

わたし/ぼく Informal Terms
(used to refer to one's own family among *uchi* group members)

I-a. **Compare the family terms (my family) on this page with the family terms (someone else's family) on the next page.**

わたし/ぼく

Formal:
Refers to my family with *soto* group members

ちち
はは
あに
あね
おとうと
いもうと

Humble (Plain)

うちのかぞく

わたし/ぼく

Informal:
Refers to my family with *uchi* group members

おとうさん/パパ
おかあさん/ママ
おにいさん
おねえさん
おとうと/(first name)
いもうと/(first name)

Neutral (Casual) /
Attention-Seeking

I-b. *Compare the family terms (someone else's family) on this page with the family terms (my family) on the previous page.*

ともだち

Formal:
Refers to someone else's family
with *soto* group members

おとうさん
おかあさん
おにいさん
おねえさん
おとうとさん／
   (first name + さん)
いもうとさん／
   (first name + さん)

Exalted (Polite)

ともだちの
ごかぞく

ともだち

Informal:
Refers to someone else's family
with *uchi* group members

おとうさん
おかあさん
おにいさん
おねえさん
おとうと／
   (first name + さん)
いもうと／
   (first name + さん)

Neutral (Casual)

2. **Practice answering the following questions about family members and their number, keeping in mind what you have learned about the different family terms used in different situations.**

おおやま　　サム　　　ニコール　　ホゼ　　ヒュンジュン　アヤナ

会話の例 (Sample Dialogue)

(Referring to your own family members among people in your そと group.)

A: あのう、おおやまさんのごかぞくはなんにんですか。

B: ははとちちといもうととわたしのよにんです。

(Referring to someone else's family members among people in your そと group.)

A: あのう、おおやまさんのごかぞくはなんにんですか。

B: おおやまさんのかぞくはおかあさんとおとうさんといもうとさんとおおやまさんのよにんです。

3. **Practice the following expression using the model below.**

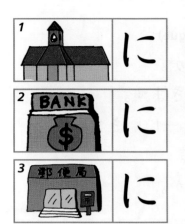

ノート **9 (Note 9):**

The particle に (*ni*) is used to express direction with motion verbs such as **いきます。**(*ikimasu.*) For example, **にほんに にいきます。**(*Nihonni ni ikimasu.*) means "I am going to Japan."

会話の例 (Sample Dialogue)

A: どこにいきますか。

B: がっこうにいきます。

4. **Practice using family terms to refer to your own family. The speaker refers to his or her family members with soto-group or uchi-group members. Red represents the uchi group; blue represents the soto group.**

ノート **10 (Note 10):**

The particle と (*to*) is used to express an activity performed with another person. For example, **あねと いきます** (*Ane to ikimasu.*) means "I am going with my older sister."

会話の例 (Sample Dialogue)

A: だれとがっこうにいきますか。

B: あねといきます。

5. **Practice the following expression using family terms. Red represents the uchi group; blue represents the soto group.**

会話の例 (Sample Dialogue)

A: だれとがっこうにいきますか。

B: ともだちのおとうとさんといきます。

273

6. Practice the following conversation using transportation words.

会話の例 (Sample Dialogue)

A: どこにいきますか。

B: パーティーにいきます。

A: なんで パーティーにいきまか。

B: <u>バス</u>でいきます。

A: ああ、そうですか。

ノート**11 (Note 11):**

で

The particle で (*de*) is used to refer to travel by means of a particular type of transportation. For example, **バスでいきます** (*Basu de ikimasu.*) means "I am going by bus."

7. Practice the following conversation using transportation words.

会話の例 (Sample Dialogue)

A: なんでがっこうにいきますか。

B: <u>でんしゃ</u>でいきます。

A: ああ、そうですか。だれとでんしゃでがっこうにいきますか。

B: <u>ともだちのおとうとさんとでんしゃ</u>でがっこうにいきます。

Kanji and Kana

Writing Hiragana

As mentioned earlier, the hiragana syllabary is thought to have been invented by aristocratic women in the 10th century. Each hiragana symbol evolved from a cursive version of a kanji, which is why people often describe hiragana as curvy and loopy. The examples below show the kanji from which あ (*a*), い (*i*), and う (*u*) developed.

安 → **安** → あ

以 → **以** → い

宇 → **宇** → う

Writing hiragana requires discipline, because there are so few strokes and because many of the strokes are curved. As with kanji and katakana, the aesthetic principles of proportion and balance are very important, and you have to pay careful attention to the length, shape, and curvature of each stroke and to the balance between the writing and the blank space. Mastering hiragana will help you a lot in writing kanji in the future. Look at the hiragana symbol い (*i*) and the kanji it came from. Both symbols take up about the same amount of total space, but since い has fewer stokes than 以, much of it is empty white space.

波 ▸ 波 ▸ 㪫 ▸ は

Stroke Order in Hiragana

As with kanji and katakana, the strokes that make up each hiragana have to be written in a certain order. This order is based on a set of principles that also apply to writing kanji. By learning the correct stroke order for hiragana you'll automatically learn many of the principles that govern writing kanji, and that will make writing them easier.

Take hiragana あ (*a*). How many strokes does it have? And what order do the strokes come in? The diagram below is one common way of showing stroke order. Since あ has three strokes, the diagram shows three stages to the right of the colon. These stages show how the symbol develops as each stroke is added in order.

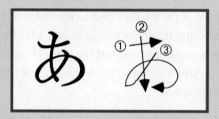

In most cases, higher strokes are written before lower ones, and left before right.

In addition to stroke order, the direction in which each stroke is written is also important. A stage-by-stage diagram like the one above doesn't tell you anything about direction. One common way of showing direction is with arrows, as in the diagram below.

In general, strokes that are basically vertical are written top to bottom, and strokes that are basically horizontal are written left to right. In looped or angled strokes, top to bottom usually takes precedence over left to right. For example, the looped third stroke in あ begins at its highest point, curves down to the left, loops up to the right, and finally curves down to the right.

3.5 Mechanics

1. Practice asking for a description of the character of a person. Choose one or two of the following words using the example.

おとうと

1.

げんき
うるさい
かわいい
おもしろい
まじめ

あね

2.

げんき
うるさい
きれい
おもしろい
まじめ

おかあさん

3.

やさしい
きびしい
すてき
いそがしい
おもしろい

おとうさん

4.

やさしい
きびしい
すてき
いそがしい
おもしろい

例文 **(Sample Sentence)**

おとうとはげんきです。

Describing Persons or Things

I (い)-type Adjectives

Na (な)-type Adjectives

ノート**12 (Note 12):**

When describing persons or things in Japanese, there are several ways of modifying nouns. Here we focus on two types of adjectives. One is called an い *i-adjectives* and the other a な *na-adjectives*. For example, あにはおもしろいひとです。 *Ani wa omoshiroi hito desu.* (My older brother is a funny person), and あにはすてきなひとです。 *Ani wa sutekina hito desu.* (My older brother is an attractive person.)

Adjectives do not always precede nouns. For example, あにはおもしろいです。 *Ani wa omoshiroi desu.* (My older brother is funny), and あにはすてきです。 *Ani wa suteki desu.* (My older brother is attractive.)

Note: When the *na-adjectives* is used as a predicte, *na* is deleted.

2. *Practice describing your friends' personalities. Choose three words from the list.*

1. げんきな
2. うるさい
3. かわいい
4. おもしろい
5. まじめな
6. やさしい
7. きびしい
8. すてきな
9. いそがしい
10. こせいてきな
11. しょうじきな
12. クールな

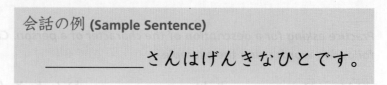

会話の例 **(Sample Sentence)**

＿＿＿＿＿＿さんはげんきなひとです。

ノート**13 (Note 13):**

The *i*-adjectives all end with *-i*. However, there are several *na*-adjectives (like きれい、"kirei"、and きらい "kirai"), which also end with *-i*. You must memorize which adjectives are which.

Adjective Chart	
(い) *i*-adjective	
Adjective + Noun Use	おもしろいひと
Predicate Use	あにはおもしろいです。
(な) *na*-adjective	
Adjective + Noun Use	すてきなひと
Predicate Use	ちちはすてきです。

3. *Describe the character of your family members using an adjective from the list on the previous page. Write two sentences. In the first sentence, use the cause and effect conjunction to tell why you like the family member you describe. In the second sentence, use the contrast conjunction to show that you like this person.*

1. あに   2. あね   3. おとうと   4. いもうと   5. はは   6. ちち

例文 (Sample Sentences)

あにはすてきなひとです。　だから、すきです。

あにはうるさいひとです。　でも、すきです。

ノート14 (Note 14):

A conjunction connects two clauses. There are two different classes of conjunctions. The cause-effect conjunction is だから *dakara* (therefore). The contrasting conjunction is でも *demo* (but). For example, あにはすてきなひとです。　だから、すきです。 *Ani wa sutekina hito desu. Dakara, suki desu.* (My elder brother is attractive. Therefore, I like him.) あにはうるさいひとです。でも、すきです。 *Ani wa urusai hito desu. Demo, suki desu.* (My older brother is picky. But, I like him.)

だから
でも

4. *Practice asking about preferences.*

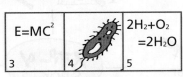

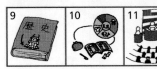

すうがく、　コンピュータ
1.　　　　　　2.

かがく、　せいぶつ、　ぶつり
3.　　　　4.　　　　5.

たいいく、　おんがく、　びじゅつ
6.　　　　7.　　　　8.

れきし、　けいざい、　せいじ
9.　　　　10.　　　　11.

1. えいご
2. フランスご
3. ちゅうごくご
4. ドイツご
5. スペインご
6. にほんご

1. English
2. Bonjour
3. 再見
4. Entschuldigung
5. Mucho gusto
6. こんにちは

会話の例 (Sample Dialogue)

A:　すきなかもくはなんですか。

B:　にほんごです。

5. Practice asking someone's strong subject and weak subject.

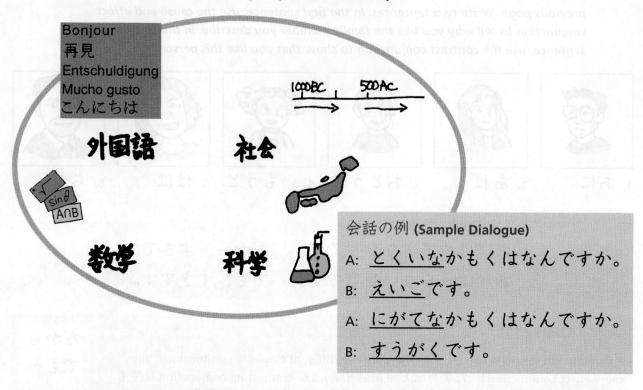

会話の例 (Sample Dialogue)

A: とくいなかもくはなんですか。

B: えいごです。

A: にがてなかもくはなんですか。

B: すうがくです。

6. Practice asking about preferences.

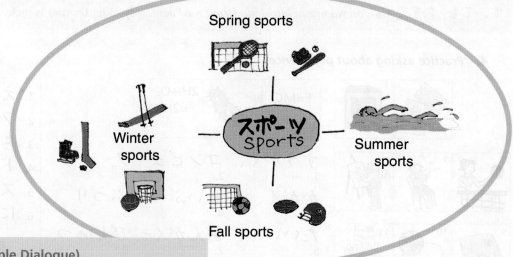

会話の例 (Sample Dialogue)

A: とくいなスポーツはなんですか。

B: テニスです。

A: にがてなスポーツはなんですか。

B: すいえいです。

7. Practice asking about preferences.

会話の例 **(Sample Dialogue)**

A: <u>すきなたべもの</u>はなんですか。

B: <u>すし</u>です。

A: <u>すきなのみもの</u>はなんですか。

B: <u>ミルク</u>です。

8. Practice asking for a description of the character of a subject. Choose one or two of the following descriptions using the example.

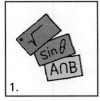   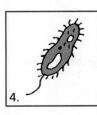  

1. すうがく　　2. びじゅつ　　3. おんがく　　4. せいぶつ　　5. けいざい　　6. たいいく

おもしろい
つまらない
むずかしい
やさしい
たのしい
じゅうよう（な）
たいへん（な）

例文A **(Sample A)**

すうがくはおもしろいです。
すうがくはじゅうようです。

例文B **(Sample B)**

すうがくはおもしろいかもくです。
すうがくはじゅうようなかもくです。

281

9. **Describe a characteristic of a school subject using an adjective from the list on the previous page. Write two sentences. In the first sentence, use the cause-effect conjunction to tell why you like the school subject you describe. In the second sentence, use the contrast conjunction to show that you like this school subject.**

  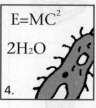  

にほんご　　すうがく　　たいいく　　かがく　　れきし　　コンピュータ

例文 (Sample Sentences)

にほんごはおもしろいです。だから、すきです。

すうがくはむずかしいです。でも、すきです。

10. **Role play**

Card A

You ask person B what subject she or he likes and if it is interesting.

Card B

You answer person A's questions. You tell person A why you like the subject.

会話の例 (Sample Dialogue)

A:

すきなかもくはなんですか。

にほんごはおもしろいですか。

すうがくはむずかしいです。

B:

にほんごです。

にほんごはおもしろいです。

だから、すきです。

でも、すきです。

Profile

Sahe Kawahara

When I was younger, I used to ask: "Where is my home? Am I Japanese or am I American? Is English my first language, or is it Japanese?" Back then, I did not know the answers to these questions. I didn't think I had a home country or a first language. Although I often asked these questions, my parents never needed to. They are both Japanese and call Japan "home"; English, obviously, is their second language. For myself, I can answer these questions now, too, but when I was younger, I could not.

From the time I was two years old, until the time I was twelve, I spent half the year in the United States and half the year in Japan. Each year, I attended school in both countries. For those eleven years, I was exposed to not only two languages, but two cultures. I hated that my parents were constantly moving me from one place to another. I also was extremely upset and angry that I never got a summer vacation like all my other friends! But truth be told, it wasn't the fact that I never had a summer vacation or had to sit through twelve-hour plane rides that bothered me the most. The problem was the constant switching between the two cultures and the two languages.

子供の時、私はしょっちゅう、「私の家はどこ。」、「私は日本人、それともアメリカ人。」、「私の母国語は英語、それとも日本語」などと聞いた。今までは、その答えが分からなかった。自分には母国と母国語はないかと思っていた。私は、こう言う疑問を持ったが、親は持つ必要がなかった。両親は日本生まれの日本人で日本を「家」と呼んでいる。もちろん、英語が彼らの第二言語である。私も今ならこういう質問に答えることができるが、子供の時は答えられなかった。

二才から十二才まで私は半年間アメリカで過ごし半年間日本で過ごした。毎年両方の国で学校へ通った。十一年間、私は二つの言語と二つの文化の中に生きていた。両親に毎年移動させられることが嫌だった。その上、友達の様に夏休みがもらえなかったことに対する怒りもあった。だが実際は、夏休みがなかったことや十二時間も飛行機に乗っていなければいけなかったことが一番困難だったわけではない。問題は二つ

It was very hard for me to be a student in two different countries. When I was in the United States, I was taught to have an opinion and to state it clearly and concisely. When I was in Japan, I was taught to be the opposite, to hide my true thoughts and feelings. As a student in the United States, I was encouraged to participate in group works where I would interact with other students to manipulate and understand what was being taught by the teachers. I found myself handling the information given by the teachers like a piece of clay; I was able to twist it and turn it around in order to try to understand what was being said. In Japan, however, the desks were arranged in rows and I didn't get to communicate and discuss topics with my classmates. I was encouraged to listen attentively and to memorize what was said. I didn't get to play with the "clay" but simply had to store the information inside my brain like a computer. It could get very confusing.

As if the difference in the educational systems wasn't puzzling me enough, the difference in the customs was more puzzling still. As a child I would make mistakes and be unintentionally impolite in Japan when I didn't mean to be. Like I might be offered a drink and without thinking accept readily, when the proper thing to do was to resist the offering, even if I was really thirsty. This was not only true of drinks but of any offering. And since I am desirous of many things, I would often accept them before catching myself. Not only did this extreme difference confuse me, but it also made me feel misplaced wherever I was.

の文化と二つの言語の切り替えだった。

　両方の国で生徒になることは、私にとって、とても難しかった。アメリカにいた時は、自分の意見を持ち、それをはっきりと簡潔に表現する様に教わったが、日本ではアメリカの反対で、自分の意見を隠す様に教わった。アメリカの学校では、先生から受け取った情報を他の生徒たちと一緒に協力し理解しようとした。先生から受け取った情報を粘土の様に私は扱えた。自分が理解するためにその粘土の形を自由に変えることができた。だが、日本の学校では、机が列に並べてあり、私はクラスの生徒たちと相談することはできなかった。注意深く、先生の言うことを聞き、それを暗記してきた。粘土で遊ぶことは可能ではなく、ただ、コンピュータの様に先生の言うことを脳の中に保存していた。

　教育制度の違いだけでなく、生活習慣の違いにも惑わされた。日本で故意でなく無礼なことをしてしまったことは何度もある。例えば、飲み物を差し出された時、遠慮せず堂々と受け取ってしまったことなど。習慣の非常な違いで混乱しただけでなく、どこの国にいても私は居場所を間違えた様に思われた。

日本人は麺類を食べる時、おいしさを示す

In Japan, noodles are not eaten quietly. They are slurped to show the host gratitude for the fine cooking. When I would slurp noodles in the United States, people would look at me with disgust or bluntly tell me, "Eeeeeeuuuuuu. You're disgusting." In Japan, I might forget to slurp and be seen as ungrateful.

Having to switch between English and Japanese often confused me as well. When speaking to my family members, I use both languages. So, many times when speaking to others, I automatically, without thinking, switch from one language to the other before I realize what I have done. Although I am sure that everybody understands what's happening, I still feel embarrassed.

Now that I look back at my early years moving between the United States and Japan, I feel fortunate and appreciate the richness of my experience. A language can be learned from a book, but a culture can only be understood through experience. I realize now that this experience has given me equal footing in two countries and has not made me homeless as I once thought. Back then, I felt that I was floating in mid-air, being pushed to one side of the world and then the opposite side. Now, I know that instead of having one home country or one language which I can feel a close connection to, I have two homes and two primary languages. There is no one place I can call "home." For me, it will always be that my one foot is in the United States and my other is in Japan.

ために「ズルズル」と音を立てて食べるが、アメリカでは静かに食べないと行儀悪いと思われる。アメリカで思わず「ズルズル」と音を立ててしまいいやがられたことがある。そして、日本で静かに食べてしまい、まずそうに食べていると思われたこともある。

英語から日本語への切り替えでもかなり混乱させられた。両親とは両方の言語を使い話し合うが、他の人と話す時、しょっちゅう自然に一つの言語からもう一つの言語へ切り替えてしまうのだ。この現象をみんなから理解されていると思うのだが、まだ少しはずかしい。

やはり今自分の子供時代を振り返って見るとなんてすばらしい経験をさせてもらえたかと感謝している。言語は本から習えるが、文化は経験からしか理解できないものなのだ。今実感できることは私には「家」がないのではなく、私はアメリカと日本、両方の国に足場があるのだ。前は自分が宙に浮いていて地球上の片側から反対側に押し回されていた。でも今は、一つの母国と一つの言語があるのではなく、私には二つの母国があり二つの母国語がある。私には「家」と呼べる一つの場所はない。私の場合、いつまでも、片足がアメリカで、片足が日本なのだ。

3.6 Mechanics
Preparing an Oral Presentation

ノート**15 (Note 15):**

In this exercise you will begin preparing an oral presentation of a self-introduction.

First you should think about the following:

How should I organize my presentation?

How do I begin and end?

What's the best sequence of ideas or events?

What style should I use for my presentation?

How do I use hesitation noises and connectors?

はじめ	なか	おわり

The concept of はじめ (*hajime*), なか (*naka*) and おわり (*owari*) will be helpful with your preparation of the structure of your oral presentation. はじめ means beginning or introduction, なか means main body, and おわり means ending or conclusion. You must organize several groups of sentences in the main body and also identify the sub-tilte of each group of sentence.

Japanese speakers often use special strategies when delivering a monologue. In particular, they use a lot of "connector words." Sometimes the connectors are used to fill in pauses when they're not quite sure what to say. Sometimes these connectors are used to make speech sound more hesitant and soft. Still other times they are used to smoothly connect one sentence to the next.

ええと	"getting started" marker (let's see...)
あのう	The phrase *anoo* is pronounced hesitantly. It is used to get someone's attention gently.
じゃ	connector that relates the current topic to what follows
それから	additional connector
ああ、それから	additional connector and hesitation marker
あのう、それから	additional connector with *anoo*
あのう、でも	juxtaposition with *anoo*

1. *Self-introduction formula. Practice reading the following self-introduction using monologue strategies and "connector words."*

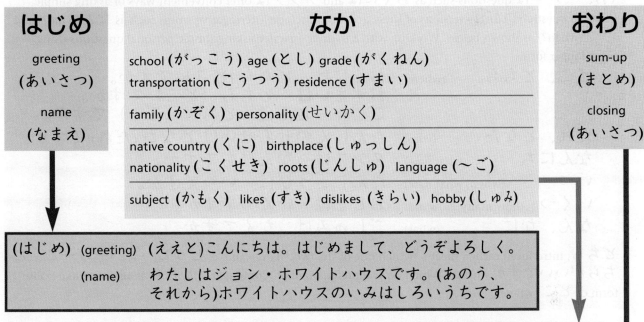

はじめ

greeting
（あいさつ）

name
（なまえ）

なか

school （がっこう） age （とし） grade （がくねん）
transportation （こうつう） residence （すまい）

family （かぞく） personality （せいかく）

native country （くに） birthplace （しゅっしん）
nationality （こくせき） roots （じんしゅ） language （〜ご）

subject （かもく） likes （すき） dislikes （きらい） hobby （しゅみ）

おわり

sum-up
（まとめ）

closing
（あいさつ）

（はじめ） (greeting) （ええと）こんにちは。はじめまして、どうぞよろしく。

（name） わたしはジョン・ホワイトハウスです。（あのう、それから）ホワイトハウスのいみはしろいうちです。

（なか）

school (school) （ええと）、がっこうはニューヘブンこうこうです。
(grade, age) こうこうさんねんです。じゅうろくです。
(transportation) いつもおとうととでんしゃでがっこうにいきます
(residence) （あのう）うちはニュージャージーです。

family (family) かぞくはちちとははとあねとおとうととわたしのごにんです。
(personalities) あねはやさしいです。だから、すきです。
（でも）、おとうとはうるさいです。でも、すきです。

personal information
(birthplace) （それから）しゅっしんはボストンです。
(native country) くにはアメリカです。
(nationality/roots) （あのう、でも）、ドイツ人です。
(language) （でも）、ドイツごをはなしません。でも、えいごをはなします。

preference (subject) （あのう、それから）にほんごはおもしろいです。だから、
(likes) にほんごがすきです。（ええと）すしがすきです。
（ああ、それから）さしみもすきです。
(dislikes) （でも）、たこはすきじゃありません。
(hobbies) （ああ、それから）しゅみはテニスとスキーです。

（おわり） (sum-up) まいにちがんばってべんきょうします。

（closing) （じゃ）、どうぞよろしくおねがいします。

287

Interrogative words: a longer version of （お、ご）～は？**(formal)** ノート16 (Note 16):

（お、ご）～は questions such as おくには and クラブは offer convenient ways of asking simple personal questions. Longer versions of these questions include interrogative words such as なん(what?) and いつ (when?) as shown below. Working with a partner, practice asking simple personal questions using these longer forms.

どこ、どちら	(where)	おくには　どちら（どこ）ですか。 おすまいは　どちら（どこ）ですか。 ごしゅっしんは　どちら（どこ）ですか。
だれ、どなた	(who)	たんにんのせんせいはどなた（だれ）ですか。
なんにち	(what date)	ダンスは　なんにちですか。
いつ	(when, what date)	たんじょうびは　いつですか。
いくつ	(how many, how old)	おとしは　いくつですか。
なん、なに	(what)	ごしゅみは　なんですか。

どちら, introduced earlier, means "which one of the two." For example, ピザとハンバーガーと　どちらがいいですか means "Which do you prefer, pizza or hamburger?" どちら is also used as a polite form of どこ (where).

Interrogative words: a longer version of （お、ご）～は？**(informal)** ノート17 (Note 17):

The prefixes お and ご are used to create polite forms of nouns. As seen above, you can ask questions using these forms with interrogative words and ですか。 You make informal questions by dropping the お and ご. Working with a partner, practice asking simple personal questions using interrogatives and dropping お、ご, and ですか.

どこ、どちら	(where)	くにはどこ（どちら）？ すまいはどこ（どちら）？ しゅっしんはどこ（どちら）？
だれ、どなた	(who)	たんにんのせんせいはだれ（どなた）？
なんにち	(what date)	ダンスはなんにち？
いつ	(when, what date)	たんじょうびはいつ？
いくつ	(how many, how old)	としはいくつ？
なに、なん	(what)	しゅみはなに？

会話の例 (Sample Dialogue)

A: おくにはどちらですか。

B: アメリカです。

A: じゃ、おすまいはどこですか。

B: コロラドです。

A: ああ、そうですか。いいですね。

会話の例 (Sample Dialogue)

A: くにはどこ？

B: アメリカです。

A: じゃ、すまいはどこ？

B: コロラドです。

A: ああ、そう。いい（わ）ね。

Pronunciation

Syllable-Final Consonants

One of the two consonants that can come at the end of a syllable in Japanese is always written *n* in romanization. The pronunciation of this syllable, which always counts as a separate beat, depends on the sound that follows. For example, before a *p*, as in *konpyuutaa* ("computer"), the syllable-final *n* sounds like the English *m* sound in *simple*, but before a *k*, as in *ginkoo* ("bank"), it sounds like the English *n* sound in *tank*. These two pronunciations of the syllable-final *n* are easy for English speakers, but others are hard. To give just one example, English doesn't have the sound that the syllable-final *n* makes in *dansu* ("dance"). Incidentally, if a final *n* comes right before a pause (in other words, if nothing follows it), it's pronounced close to (although not exactly the same as) the English *ng*, as in the word "sing." In some cases, just writing *n* in romanization isn't sufficient to distinguish the syllable-final *n* sound from the *n* sound that comes at the beginning of a syllable. There's no problem at the beginning of a word, of course, since the beginning of a word has to be the beginning of a syllable.

neko	**ne | ko**	2 syllables
cat	**ne·ko**	2 beats

There's no problem at the end of a word, either, since the end of a word has to be the end of a syllable.

sumimasen	**su |mi |ma | sen**	4 syllables
excuse me	**su·mi·ma·se·n**	5 beats

It's in the middle of a word that things get a little complicated. If an *n* in the middle of a word is followed by *y* or by a vowel, it could be either the beginning or the end of a syllable. An apostrophe is written after the *n* in romanization if it's at the end of a syllable. The examples below illustrate.

zeni	**ze | ni**	2 syllables	*kinyuu*	**ki | nyuu**	2 syllables
money	**ze·ni**	2 beats	recording	**ki·nyu·u**	3 beats
zen'i	**zen | i**	2 syllables	*kin'yuu*	**kin | yuu**	2 syllables
good will	**ze·n·i**	3 beats	finance	**ki·n·yu·u**	4 beats

If **n** in the middle of a word is followed by a consonant other than *y*, it has to be at the end of a long syllable, so no apostrophe is necessary, as in the example below.

denwa	**den | wa**	2 syllables
telephone	**de·n·wa**	3 beats

Syllable-final **n** is always written with the same symbol in kana: ン in katakana and ん in hiragana.

The other consonant that can come at the end of a syllable is spelled in a wide variety of ways in romanization, as in the following examples. Notice in particular how it's spelled before **sh**, **ch**, and **ts**. (You've already learned that **sh**, **ch**, and **ts** spell single consonants). You get s before **sh** (as in *hassha*), **t** before **ch** (as in *matchi*), and **t** before **ts** (as in *mittsu*).

*hi**pp**aru*	pull	*gu**zz**u*	goods
*mo**bb**u*	mob	*ha**ss**ha*	departure
*wa**ff**uru*	waffle	*ma**tc**hi*	match
*mi**tt**o*	mitt	*ja**jj**i*	judge
*he**dd**oraito*	headlight	*ga**kk**oo*	school
*mi**tt**su*	three	*ba**gg**u*	bag
*ke**ss**eki*	absence	*Ba**hh**a*	Bach

In every one of these examples, the boldface consonant counts as a separate beat and represents the end of a syllable as well as the first half of a long consonant. For instance, *mittsu* has two syllables (**mit**\|**tsu**) and three beats (**mi·t·tsu**). In spite of all the different spellings in romanization, each of the words above has the same consonant at the end of the first syllable, and in fact, this syllable-final consonant is always written with the same symbol in kana: ッ in katakana and っ in hiragana. Like syllable-final **n**, this consonant is a chameleon sound; that is, its pronunciation depends on the sound that follows. It stretches out the beginning of whatever consonant comes next to provide an extra beat.

3.7 Mechanics

Listening Exercises

1. **Listen to the dialogue and choose the topic of the question.**

   A. (   )   B. (   )   C. (   )   D. (   )

   1. native country
   2. place of residence
   3. grade level
   4. homeroom teacher
   5. club
   6. sports

2. **Listen to the dialogues and determine which of the two conversation-extension tactics (A or B) introduced in this unit is being used in each.**

   A. (   )   B. (   )   C. (   )   D. (   )

   Tactic A: attribution/association   Tactic B: analogy

3. **Listen to the dialogue and circle the appropriate verbs.**

   A.   This person likes/dislikes coffee.
   B.   This person likes/dislikes studying.
   C.   This person likes/dislikes sports.
   D.   This person likes/dislikes hamburgers.
   E.   This person likes/dislikes blue.
   F.   This person likes/dislikes sushi.

4. **Listen to the dialogue and choose the topic of the question.**

   A. (   )   B. (   )   C. (   )   D. (   )

   1. mother
   2. father
   3. younger brother
   4. younger sister
   5. older brother
   6. older sister

5. **Listen to the dialogue and circle the appropriate adjectives.**

   A.   This person is attractive
   B.   This person is healthy
   C.   This person is funny.
   D.   This person is picky.
   E.   This person is kind.

6. Listen to the dialogue and choose the topic of the question.

    A. The woman asked for:
        1. the time
        2. the place
        3. the date
        4. the age

    B. The woman asked for:
        1. the time
        2. to where
        3. with whom
        4. which day

    C. The woman asked for:
        1. the time
        2. the place
        3. what time
        4. with whom

    D. The woman wanted to find out:
        1. what time the movie starts
        2. where the movie is shown
        3. how to get to the movie
        4. how much the movie costs

FORM

1. *Asking simple personal questions using* （お、ご）〜は

In conversation, simple personal questions can be asked by stating the category of information you're looking for, followed by the particle は *wa*. Suppose you want to know your partner's telephone number. All you have to say is でんわばんごうは *denwa bangoo wa*. Some words customarily require either お *o* or ご *go* to be added to the beginning. These prefixes make the entire sentence polite, but not every word requires such prefixes. See the following examples.

Information sought			Questions
Prefix お			
なまえ	(name)	おなまえは。	What is you name?
くに	(home country)	おくには。	What country are you from?
とし	(age)	おとしは。	How old are you?
すまい	(place of residence)	おすまいは。	Where do you live?
たんじょうび	(birthday)	おたんじょうびは。	When is your birthday?
Prefix ご			
しゅっしん	(birthplace)	ごしゅっしんは。	Where are you from?
しゅみ	(hobby)	ごしゅみは。	What is your hobby?
きょうだい	(siblings)	ごきょうだいは。	Do you have any siblings?
No prefix			
がくねん	(grade level)	がくねんは。	What grade are you in?
クラブ	(school club)	クラブは。	What club do you belong to?
がっこう	(school)	がっこうは。	Where do you go to school?
スポーツ	(school sports)	スポーツは。	What sport do you play?
せんせい	(teacher)	せんせいは。	Who is your teacher?

2. *Asking simple personal questions using interrogatives*

You can ask the same questions as above in complete sentence form by using question words such as "what," "where," and "when." You can make such a sentence by simply adding the appropriate question word + ですか to （お、ご）〜は. See below.

What?	なん	ごしゅみは なんですか。
Where?	どこ、どちら (polite)	おくには どちらですか。
Who?	だれ、どなた (polite)	せんせいは だれですか。
When?	いつ	おたんじょうびは いつですか。
How many, how old?	いくつ	おとしは いくつですか。

3. *Describing personalities and things with adjectives*

There are two types of adjectives in Japanese. One is called an い *i*-adjective and the other is called a な *na*-adjective. The majority of adjectives belong to the first category. It should be noted that some English adjectives cannot be replaced by い or な adjectives when they are translated into Japanese. For example, there are no い or な adjective equivalents of the English words "wet," "dry," "trustworthy" and "understanding." You will learn more about this in later chapters.

A. い *i*-adjectives

As its name suggests, this type of adjective ends with い *i*. やさしい (kind), おもしろい (funny), and いい (good) are all examples of い *i*-adjectives. Just like verbs, Japanese adjectives conjugate according to style (plain/polite), tense (nonpast/past), and affirmative/negative. The examples above represent a plain nonpast affirmative form. Like their English counterparts, Japanese adjectives can be used immediately before the noun they modify or in the predicate.

やさしいおかあさん　　　　a kind mother

おもしろいおにいさん　　　a funny older brother

やさしい is in plain style, so you must add です *desu* to make the entire sentence polite when the adjective is used in the predicate.

おかあさんはやさしい。　　Mother is kind. (plain)

おかあさんはやさしいです。Mother is kind. (polite)

B. な *na-adjectives*

な *na*-adjectives end with な *na* when they modify a noun. A な *na*-adjective used in the predicate is followed by だ in a plain-style statement, です in a polite-style statement.

げんきないもうと。 　a healthy young sister

ミミは げんきだ。 　Mimi is healthy. (plain)

ミミはげんきです。 　Mimi is healthy. (polite)

4. *Telling what one likes and dislikes.*

〜が すきです (I like -)、
〜は すきじゃありません (I don't like -)

〜が きらいです (I dislike -)、
〜は きらいじゃありません (I don't dislike -

すき and きらい are the Japanese equivalents of "like" and "dislike," respectively, even though both are な-adjectives.

バレーボールとじゅうどうがすきです。
でも、テニスは すきじゃありません。

I like volleyball and judo. However, I don't like tennis.

A: バナナが すきですか。 　Do you like bananas?

B: はい、すきです。 　Yes, I do. (affirmative)

B: いいえ、すきじゃありません。
　　　　　　　　　No, I don't. (negative)

The particle が is usually used to mark the liked or disliked object. However, the particle は is preferred in a negative construction.

A: バナナが すきですか。 　Do you like bananas?

B: はい、バナナがすきです。 Yes, I like bananas. (affirmative)

B: いいえ、バナナはすきじゃありません。
　　　　　　　　　No, I don't like bananas. (negative)

5   *Asking for a description of something/somebody with*
とくいな、すきな、きらいな

Q: すきなたべものはなんですか。   What's your favorite food?

A: すしです。   It's sushi.

Q:: きらいなかもくはなんですか。   What's your weak subject?

A: すうがくです。   It's mathematics.

Q: とくいなかもくはなんですか。   What's your strong subject?

A: にほんごです。   It's Japanese.

3.8 Application

1. ***"Finding a Pen Pal"***

   A. All students in the class will seek pen pals. Students first provide their basic personal information by filling out a "Pen Pal Request Form: the First Form."

   B. They will receive a "Pen Pal Request Form: the Second Form" next and follow the flow chart according to their preferences. The flow chart will lead them to a certain katakana letter. After that, they follow the flow chart again but without taking exactly the same route as before. This means that everyone will have two different katakana letters.

   C. Students will receive a "Pen Pal List" of prospective pen pals with information regarding their names, places of residence, age, grade levels, sports, favorite academic subjects (すきなかもく), and favorite types of music (すきなおんがく).

   D. Students check the list and find out if their katakana letters from the flow chart are on the list. If so, they read the profiles of people listed next to their letters and fill in "The Third Form" based on the listed information.

   E. If one or both of their katakana characters could not be found on the list, the students will try the flow chart again, obtain another katakana letter(s), and complete their "Third Form."

   F. Students look at the information on their "Third Form" and compare the two prospective pen pals. They then decide which one is their number 1 (いちばん) and which one is their number 2(にばん) candidate for a pen pal. other categories on the lists.

ペンパル　リクエスト　フォーム　第一（だいいち）フォーム

（わたし、ぼく）

たんじょうび	とし
がくねん	スポーツ
すきな　かもく	すきな　おんがく
すきな　いろ	すきな　きせつ

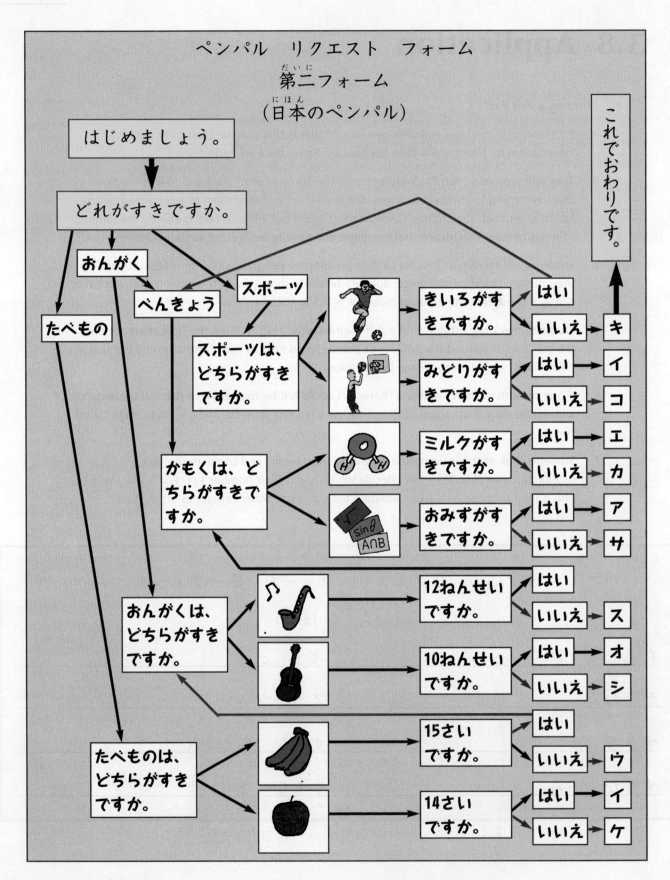

ペンパル　リクエスト　フォーム
第二フォーム
（日本のペンパル）

はじめましょう。

どれがすきですか。

おんがく

べんきょう

スポーツ

たべもの

これでおわりです。

スポーツは、どちらがすきですか。

きいろがすきですか。　はい　／　いいえ　→　キ

みどりがすきですか。　はい　→　イ　／　いいえ　→　コ

かもくは、どちらがすきですか。

ミルクがすきですか。　はい　→　エ　／　いいえ　→　カ

おみずがすきですか。　はい　→　ア　／　いいえ　→　サ

おんがくは、どちらがすきですか。

12ねんせいですか。　はい　／　いいえ　→　ス

10ねんせいですか。　はい　→　オ　／　いいえ　→　シ

たべものは、どちらがすきですか。

15さいですか。　はい　／　いいえ　→　ウ

14さいですか。　はい　→　イ　／　いいえ　→　ケ

	なまえ	すまい	とし	がくねん	スポーツ	すきなかもく	すきなおんがく

ペンパルリスト

	なまえ	すまい	とし	がくねん	スポーツ	すきなかもく	すきなおんがく
ウ	さかい ゆうじ	よこはま	15	9 th	バレーボール	えいご	ロック
エ	なかざと えみ	おおさか	17	11th	テニス	かがく	ジャズ
キ	うえの こういち	やまぐち	13	7th	サッカー	えいご	クラシック
ア	やまだ ようこ	ひろしま	14	8th	すいえい	すうがく	ロック
コ	きむら かおり	あきた	17	12th	バスケットボール	すうがく	ロック
オ	かわはら まさお	とうきょう	18	12th	ラグビー	おんがく	フォーク
ス	きたじま さとこ	さっぽろ	16	10th	サッカー	れきし	クラシック
カ	みわ かずひこ	ながの	15	10th	やきゅう	かがく	ジャズ
イ	さえき ゆか	きょうと	16	11th	バスケットボール	びじゅつ	ロック
シ	あいかわ はじめ	ながさき	14	8 th	りくじょう(track)	えいご	クラシック

ケ ク サ　ちょっとまってください。

ペンパル　リクエスト　フォーム　第三(だいさん)フォーム

ペンパルのなまえ	ペンパルのなまえ
すまい	すまい
とし	とし
がくねん	がくねん
すきなスポーツ	すきなスポーツ
すきなかもく	すきなかもく
すきなおんがく	すきなおんがく
（いちばん、にばん）	（いちばん、にばん）

3. Mirror Image–Warm-Up:

A. Students form groups of 4 or 5.

B. Each member of the group receives the sheet below.

C. Describe your friends' personalities, choosing three words from the following list.

わたしからみた (from my point of view)				
ともだちのせいかく	_____ さん	_____ さん	_____ さん	_____ さん
1. げんきな				
2. すてきな				
3. かわいい				
4. おもしろい				
5. まじめな				
6. やさしい				
7. きれいな				
8. きびしい				
9. いそがしい				
10. こせいてきな				
11. しょうじきな				
12. クールな				

例文 (Sample Sentences)

_____ さんはおもしろいひとです。

_____ さんはクールなひとです。

_____ さんはまじめなひとです。

4. *Mirror Image–Main Application: Each member of the group, including yourself, must choose at least three words from the following list. Each member of the group should tell you his or her description of you. After choosing words to describe your own character, compare your self description with the description of you made by the other members of your group.*

例文 **(Sample Sentences)**

(From my friends' point of view)

_____ (your name) さんはおもしろいひとです。

_____ (your name) さんはクールなひとです。

_____ (your name) さんはまじめなひとです。

_____ (your name) さんは おもしろいひとです。

(From my point of view) わたし（ぼく）はまじめです。

わたしのせいかく まえ(your name):	ともだちからみた (From my friends' point of view) ともだちのなまえ(friends' name)				わたしからみた (From my point of view)
	____ さん	____ さん	____ さん	____ さん	わたし
1. げんきな					
2. すてきな					
3. かわいい					
4. おもしろい					
5. まじめな					
6. やさしい					
7. きれいな					
8. きびしい					
9. いそがしい					
10. こせいてきな					
11. エネルギッシュな					
12. クールな					

5. *Wrap-Up: Each member of the group shares the differences between his or her description of him- or herself and that of the other members of the group. After sharing these descriptions with the members of their own group, students share them with the other groups.*

301

Kanji

Learning Kanji

Kanji ("Chinese characters") first came to Japan when Japanese aristocrats began to study the Chinese language, around 400 A.D. This was a time when Buddhism and many other elements of Chinese culture began to have a major influence on the Japanese upper classes. You've already learned how certain kanji developed into katakana and hiragana. Although Japanese could be written entirely in either katakana or hiragana, the modern writing system uses a complex mixture of kanji and both types of kana. You'll learn more about how kanji were incorporated into the Japanese writing system in the next chapter. In addition to Japan, Chinese characters are still used today in China itself (including Hong Kong and Taiwan) and, to some extent, in South Korea.

For most people, trying to learn kanji outside the context of known vocabulary words is ineffective, so most of the kanji introduced in this chapter are used to write words you've already learned. Most kanji can be analyzed into component parts (graphic elements) that appear in many other kanji. For example, look carefully at three of the kanji introduced below: 一, 二 and 三. You'll notice that each contains the element 一. If you pay attention to various graphic elements as you learn kanji, the more common ones will get to be like old friends.

Each kanji introduced below is accompanied by a story about the graphic elements it contains. A few of these stories are historically accurate accounts of how the kanji originated, but most of them are fanciful. Such stories are commonly used in teaching kanji to beginners, and they're intended only as mnemonic devices. A mnemonic device is just something that helps you remember, and if a story about a kanji does the job, whether or not it's historically accurate is beside the point. How effective such stories are depends on your learning style. For most people, it's probably harder to remember the stories than to just memorize the kanji. If that's the way you feel, don't worry, you're not alone. On the other hand, if the stories help you, there's no reason not to take advantage of them.

Principals of Kanji Stroke Order and Stroke Direction

Just as in katakana and hiragana, the strokes of a kanji are usually written high before low and left before right. For every new kanji introduced in this book, a stage-by-stage diagram is provided to show the correct stroke order. Vertical strokes are written top to bottom, and horizontal strokes are written left to right. In curved or angled strokes, top to bottom takes precedence over left to right.

Chinese Readings

Words adopted into Japanese from languages other than Chinese are normally written in katakana, but words adopted from Chinese are normally written in kanji. Of course, the Chinese pronunciations had to be modified to fit the Japanese sound system. Modifying pronunciation is just part of the process of adopting vocabulary from another language; you've already seen lots of examples of it in Japanese words that have been adopted from English. It's also important to remember that both Japanese and Chinese have changed a lot in the many centuries since the large-scale importations of Chinese vocabulary into Japanese, so if you compare a word in modern Mandarin Chinese with its adopted counterpart in modern Japanese, they often don't sound very much like each other. For example, modern Mandarin *ren* corresponds to modern Japanese *jin* ("people"); both are written with the kanji 人. When a kanji is used to write a Chinese-based Japanese word, that word is called an *on'yomi* ("sound reading") of the kanji, because it is based on an original Chinese pronunciation. The conventional English translation of *on'yomi* is **Chinese reading**. In this book, we'll use the partial translation **On reading**, always capitalizing *On* so that it doesn't get confused with the English preposition on.

Since words were adopted at different times and from different places in China, many kanji have more than one *On* reading. For example, 人 has the two *On* readings *nin* (which is older) and *jin*. *Nin* occurs in numbers used for counting people, as in 三人 *sannin* ("three people"), and *jin* occurs in words used for nationalities , as in カナダ人 *kanadajin* ("Canadian person").

Japanese Readings

When the Japanese of long ago began using kanji, they not only used them to write words adopted from Chinese, but also to write native Japanese words. The basic method was to consider the meaning of the Chinese word written with a particular kanji and assign that same kanji to a native Japanese word with a similar meaning. Consider the kanji 人 again. You've already seen that it's used to write *nin* and *jin*, both of which were adopted from Chinese. But 人 is also used to write the word *hito* ("person") and the suffix *-ri* that appears in the first two numbers for counting people, 一人 *hitori* ("one person") and 二人 *futari* ("two people"). Vocabulary items like *hito* and *-ri* are called native because they already existed in Japanese before the intense contact with China began. When an item like this is written with a kanji, it's called a *kun'yomi* ("meaning reading") of the kanji, because its only connection to Chinese is based on its meaning. The conventional English translation of *kun'yomi* is "Japanese reading", but in this book we'll use the partial translation *Kun* reading, capitalizing *Kun* to make it parallel with *On*.

Incidentally, there are some kanji that don't have any *Kun* readings at all, which just means that they were never assigned to any native Japanese words. The first kanji in 電話 *denwa* ("telephone") is an example. It has the *On* reading *den* ("electric"), but no *Kun* reading. At the same time, there are many kanji, like 人, that have more than one *Kun* reading (*hito* and *-ri*) as well as more than one *On* reading (*nin* and *jin*). Using a single symbol to write different words may seem confusing, but there are a few examples of a similar phenomenon in English: You could say that the numeral *1* has two readings: it's *one* in *#1*, but it's *fir* in *1st*.

Numbers

All the kanji introduced in this lesson, except for the last two (円 and 人), are used to write words or parts of words that mean numbers. Memorizing the first three is easy; "one" is one line, "two" is two lines, and "three" is three lines. After that, things get a little harder, but these kanji all have a small number of strokes. For each kanji, the commonly used *On* and *Kun* readings are listed, although not all of them occur in words that you've learned so far. The readings are followed by examples of words that each kanji is used to write.

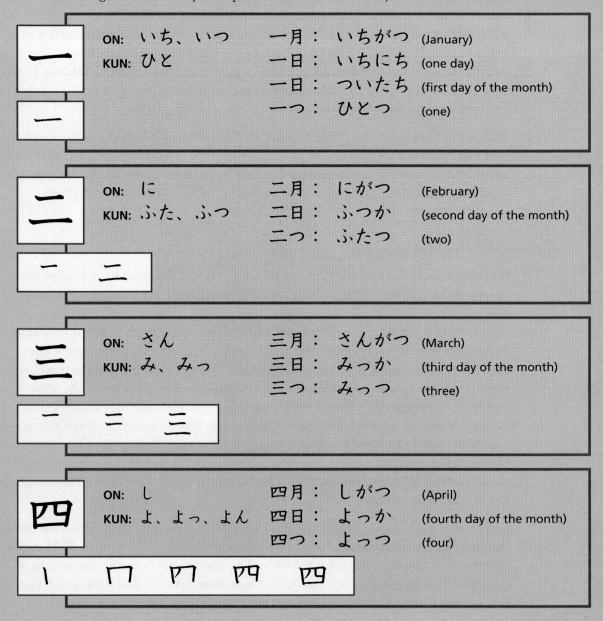

一	ON: いち、いつ	一月：	いちがつ	(January)
	KUN: ひと	一日：	いちにち	(one day)
		一日：	ついたち	(first day of the month)
一		一つ：	ひとつ	(one)

二	ON: に	二月：	にがつ	(February)
	KUN: ふた、ふつ	二日：	ふつか	(second day of the month)
		二つ：	ふたつ	(two)
一　二				

三	ON: さん	三月：	さんがつ	(March)
	KUN: み、みっ	三日：	みっか	(third day of the month)
		三つ：	みっつ	(three)
一　二　三				

四	ON: し	四月：	しがつ	(April)
	KUN: よ、よっ、よん	四日：	よっか	(fourth day of the month)
		四つ：	よっつ	(four)
丨　冂　冂　四　四				

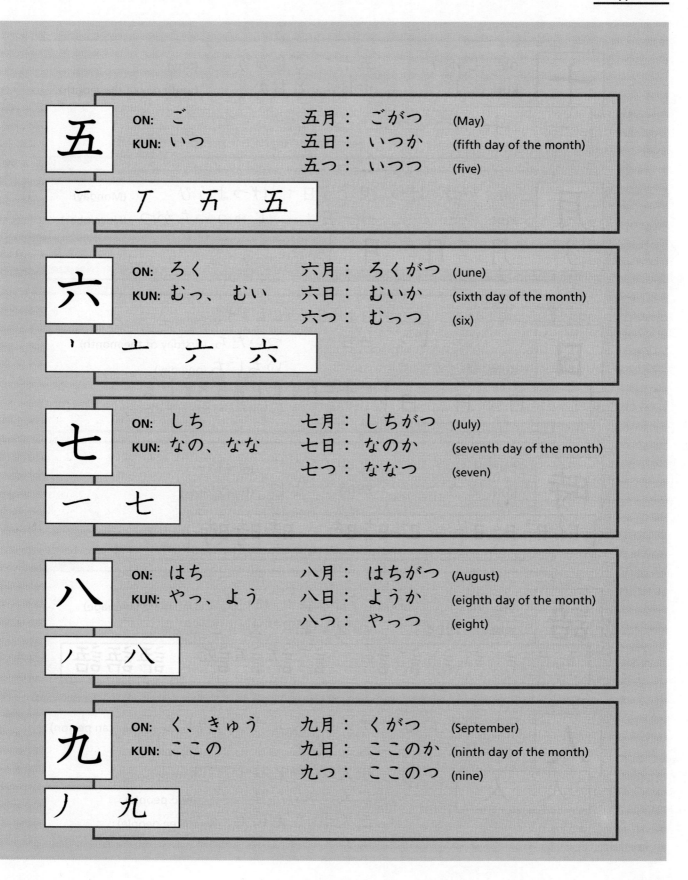

五	ON: ご	五月： ごがつ	(May)
	KUN: いつ	五日： いつか	(fifth day of the month)
		五つ： いつつ	(five)

一 丁 五 五

六	ON: ろく	六月： ろくがつ	(June)
	KUN: むっ、むい	六日： むいか	(sixth day of the month)
		六つ： むっつ	(six)

亠 六 六

七	ON: しち	七月： しちがつ	(July)
	KUN: なの、なな	七日： なのか	(seventh day of the month)
		七つ： ななつ	(seven)

一 七

八	ON: はち	八月： はちがつ	(August)
	KUN: やっ、よう	八日： ようか	(eighth day of the month)
		八つ： やっつ	(eight)

ノ 八

九	ON: く、きゅう	九月： くがつ	(September)
	KUN: ここの	九日： ここのか	(ninth day of the month)
		九つ： ここのつ	(nine)

ノ 九

| 十 | ON: じゅう | 五十： ごじゅう | (fifty) |
| | KUN: とお | 十日： とおか | (tenth day of the month) |

一 十

| 月 | ON: がつ、げつ | 月よう日： げつようび | (Monday) |
| | KUN: つき | 十一月： じゅういちがつ | (November) |

月 月 月 月

日	ON: にち、に、 にっ、じっ	日よう日： にちようび	(Sunday)
		一日： ついたち	(firstday of the month)
	KUN: ひ、か	いちにち	(one day)
		二十三日： にじゅうさんにち	
		(twenty-third day of the month)	

日 日 日 日

| 時 | ON: じ | 九時： くじ | (nine o'clock) |
| | KUN: とき | 四時： よじ | (four o'clock) |

時時時時　時時時　時時時

| 語 | ON: ご | ほん 日本語： にほんご | (Japanese language) |
| | KUN: かた(る) | えい語： えいご | (English) |

語語語語語語語　語語語語　語語語

人	ON: じん,にん	アメリカ人： アメリカじん	(American person)
	KUN: ひと	人： ひと	(people)
		一人： ひとり	(one person)
		二人： ふたり	(two people)
		三人： さんにん	(three people)

人 人

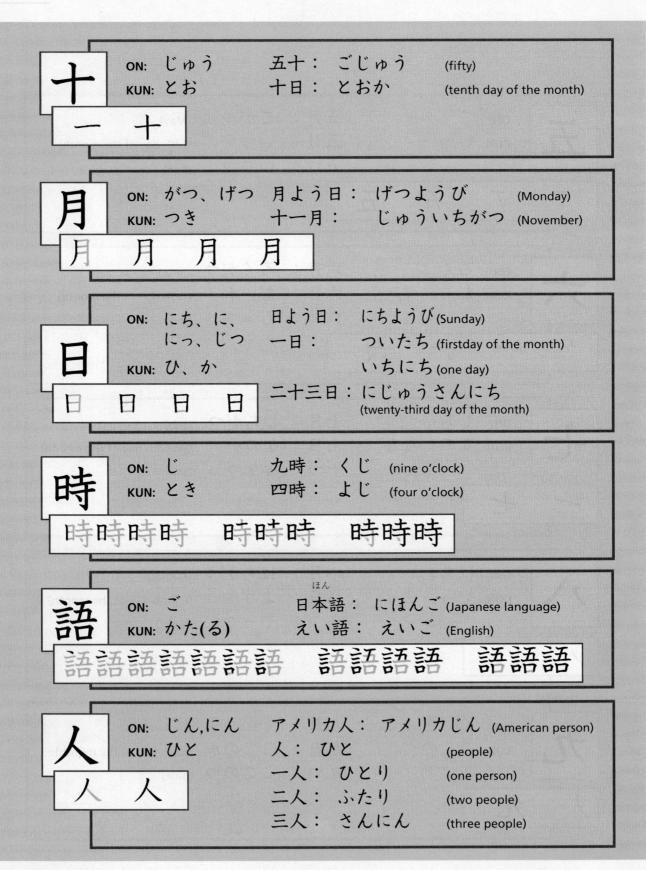

3.9 Application

1. *Create a self-introduction speech using the form you studied in the Mechanics section.*

A. Fill in your information in the blanks in the form on the next page. If you want to create your own sentences, have your teacher check them.

B. After filling in the blanks, add Japanese connectors and hesitation sounds.

C. After writing your draft, practice reading it aloud.

Practicing Your Self-Introduction Speech

1. Read the monologue to yourself to get an overall sense of it.

2. Look up any unfamiliar words.

3. Read the monologue aloud using connectors and hesitation sounds.

4. Check the relationship between the connectors and hesitation sounds and the monologue.

5. Check your body language.

6. Tape record yourself reading the monologue.

7. Listen to the tape carefully, noting any errors.

8. Start memorizing the monologue.

9. Tape yourself again and listen to it with your classmates.

1-A. Fill in the blanks with information about yourself.

(はじめ)	(greeting)	こんにちは。はじめまして、どうぞよろしく。
	(name)	わたしは_____です。

(なか)	(school)	がっこうは_____です。
	(grade)	_____です。 (age)_____です。
	(transportation)	いつも (with whom)_____と (transportation)_____で
		がっこうにいきます。
	(residence)	うちは_____です。

	(family)	かぞくは_____です。
		_____だから、_____
		_____
		_____。

	(birthplace)	しゅっしんは_____です。
	(native country)	くには_____です。
	(nationality)	_____人です。
	(language)	_____をはなします。

	(subject)	_____はおもしろいです。だから、
	(likes)	_____がすきです。
		_____がすきです。
		_____もすきです。
	(dislikes)	_____はすきじゃありません。
	(hobbies)	しゅみは_____です。

(おわり)	(sum-up)	まいにちがんばってべんきょうします。
	(closing)	どうぞよろしくおねがいします。

1-B. After drafting your self-introduction, outline, add the connectors and hesitation

(はじめ)	(greeting)	(ええと)こんにちは。はじめまして、どうぞよろしく。
	(name)	わたしは＿＿＿＿＿＿＿＿＿＿＿＿＿です。
		(あのう、それから)＿＿＿＿＿のいみは＿＿＿＿＿です(if you need)

(なか)	(school)	(ええと) がっこうは＿＿＿＿＿＿＿＿＿です。
	(grade, age)	＿＿＿＿＿＿＿です。＿＿＿＿＿＿＿です。
	(transportation)	いつも＿＿＿＿＿と＿＿＿＿＿でがっこうにいきます。
	(residence)	(あのう) うちは＿＿＿＿＿＿＿＿＿＿＿です。

	(family)	かぞくは＿＿＿＿＿＿＿＿＿＿＿です。
	(personalities)	＿＿＿＿＿＿＿＿＿＿＿＿＿＿＿＿＿

	(birthplace)	(それから) しゅっしんは＿＿＿＿＿＿＿＿＿です。
	(native country)	くには＿＿＿＿＿＿＿＿＿＿＿です。
	(nationality/roots)	(あのう, でも) ＿＿＿＿＿＿＿＿＿人です。
	(language)	(でも) ＿＿＿＿＿ごをはなしません。でも、＿＿＿＿＿をはなします。

	(subject)	(あのう、それから) ＿＿＿＿＿はおもしろいです。だから、
	(likes)	＿＿＿＿＿がすきです。(ええと)＿＿＿＿＿がすきです。
		(ああ、それから)＿＿＿＿＿＿＿もすきです。
	(dislikes)	(でも) ＿＿＿＿＿＿＿はすきじゃありません。
	(hobby)	しゅみは＿＿＿＿＿＿＿＿＿＿＿です。

(おわり)	(sum-up)	まいにちがんばって＿＿＿＿＿＿＿＿＿＿＿。
	(closing)	(じゃ) どうぞよろしくおねがいします。

1-C. Practice giving your self-introduction speech aloud using the nine tips on page 307. GOOD LUCK!

1-D. Checkpoints.

1. Is the content of your self-introduction speech interesting?
2. Is your self-introduction speech lively?
3. Do you use a variety of sentences, grammatical patterns and vocabulary words? Is your presentation error-free?

2. *Now, write a Japanese-style composition based on your self-introduction speech and read it.*

Regular Japanese composition paper (げんこうようし) requires you to write vertically. Japanese can also be written horizontally, like English. Write this exercise vertically. Each line has 20 characters. Each page has 20 lines and 400 characters. On the first line, write the title of the composition. On the second line write only your name. The third line is skipped to create a space. Start your introduction on the fourth line, indenting one character space. Note that Japanese periods and commas are counted as one character each.

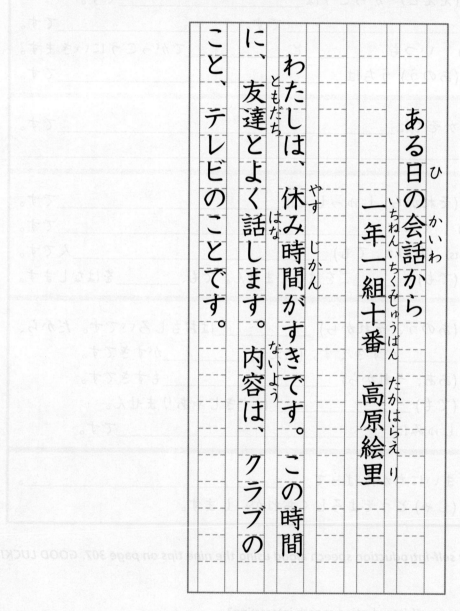

ある日の会話から

一年一組十番　高原絵里

　わたしは、休み時間がすきです。この時間に、友達とよく話します。内容は、クラブのこと、テレビのことです。

3-A. Review this list of useful words that you may want to include in your composition.

1. 放課後 (ほうかご) — after school
2. 夏休み (なつやすみ) — summer vacation
3. 休み時間 (やすみじかん) — recess
4. 昼休み (ひるやすみ) — lunchtime
5. 友達 (ともだち) — friends
6. 練習の内容 (れんしゅうのないよう) — practice material
7. この時間 (じかん) — during this time
8. 食堂 (しょくどう) — cafeteria
9. 勉強 (べんきょう) — study
10. ときどき — sometimes
11. よく — often
12. 塾のあと (じゅくのあと) — after cram school

3-B. Fill in the blanks with the name of the writer of the Japanese-style composition that corresponds to the person who is described .

A.

ある日 (ひ) の会話 (かいわ) から
一年二組七番 (いちねんにくみななばん)
田村奈緒 (たむらなお)

わたしは、放課後 (ほうかご) の時間 (じかん) がすきです。この時間 (じかん) に、友達 (ともだち) とよくテニスの練習 (れんしゅう) に行きます。練習の内容 (れんしゅうのないよう) は、サーブと、バック ハンドです。練習 (れんしゅう) のあと、だいすきなアイスクリームの店 (みせ) へ行きます。

B.

ある日 (ひ) の会話 (かいわ) から
三年五組八番 (さんねんごくみはちばん)
高山康男 (たかやまやすお)

ぼくは、夏休み (なつやすみ) がすきです。夏休み (なつやすみ) には、友達 (ともだち) とよく山 (やま) へ行きます。よるはときどきキャンプ・ファイヤーに行きます。山 (やま) はおもしろいです。

C.

ある日の会話から
２年２組２番　大山春子

　わたしは、昼休みの時間がすきです。この時間に、友達とよく食堂へ行きます。よく友達と話します。

D.

ある日の会話から
3年5組13番　中山里美

　わたしは、塾の時間がすきです。塾の勉強はおもしろいです。友達や塾の先生とよく話します。塾のあとラーメンの店へときどき行きます。

高原絵里
田村奈緒
高山康男
大山春子
中山里美

1. ＿＿高原絵里＿＿ はテレビがすきです。
2. ＿＿＿＿＿＿＿ はあきにU.S. Open にいきます。
3. ＿＿＿＿＿＿＿ はあきに大学 にいきます。
4. ＿＿＿＿＿＿＿ はふゆにスキー にいきます。
5. ＿＿＿＿＿＿＿ は友達とレストランにいきます。

4. **You have finished writing the draft for your self introduction speech and have presented it in front of many people. Now, write a Japanese-style composition based on your self -introduction speech.**

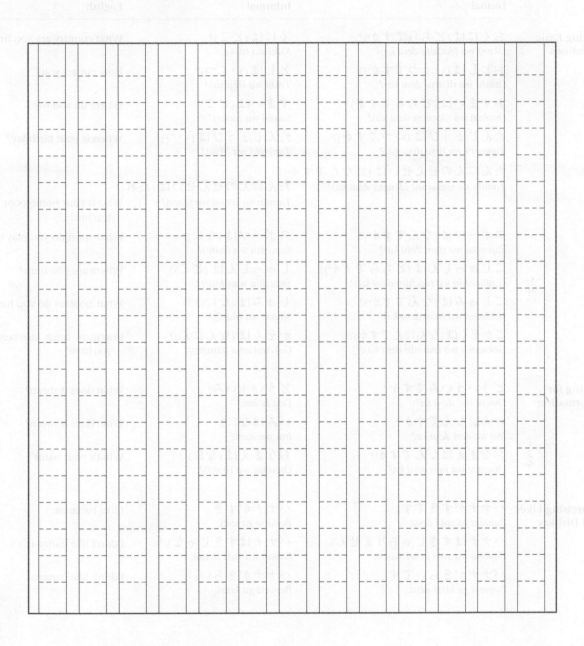

VOCABULARY

Functional Vocabulary

	Formal	Informal	English
Asking Basic Questions	おくには (どちらですか)? *Okuni wa (dochira desu ka)?*	くには (どこ)? *Kuni wa (doko)?*	What country are you from?
	おとしは (いくつですか)? *Otoshi wa (ikutsu desu ka)?*	としは (いくつ)? *Toshi wa (ikutsu)?*	How old are you?
	おすまいは (どちらですか)? *Osumai wa (dochira desu ka)?*	すまいは (どこ)? *Sumai wa (doko)?*	Where do you live?
	たんじょうびは (いつですか)? *Tanjoobi wa (itsu desu ka)?*	たんじょうびは (いつ)? *Tanjoobi wa (itsu)?*	When is your birthday?
	たんにんのせんせいは (どなたですか)? *Tannin no sensei wa (donata desu ka)?*	たんにんのせんせいは (だれ)? *Tannin no sensei wa (dare)?*	Who is your homeroom teacher?
	スポーツは (なんですか)? *Supootsu wa (nan desu ka)?*	スポーツは (なに)? *Supootsu wa (nani)?*	What sport do you play?
	ごしゅっしんは (どちらですか)? *Goshusshin wa (dochira desu ka)?*	しゅっしんは (どこ)? *Shusshin wa (doko)?*	Where are you from?
	ごしゅみは (なんですか)? *Goshumi wa (nan desu ka)?*	しゅみは (なに)? *Shumi wa (nani)?*	What hobbies do you have?
	ごかぞくは (なんにんですか)? *Gokazoku wa (nannin desu ka)?*	かぞくは (なんにん)? *Gokazokuwa (nannin)?*	How many family members do you have?
Asking for Information	どういういみですか? *Doo iu imi desu ka?*	どういういみ? *Doo iu imi?*	What does it mean?
	いみはなんですか? *Imi wa nan desu ka?*	いみはなに? *Imi wa nani?*	What does it mean?
	おなまえはなんですか? *Onamae wa nan desu ka?*	おなまえは (なに)? *Onamae wa (nani)?*	What's your name?
Expressing Likes and Dislikes	バナナがすきです。 *Banana ga suki desu.*	バナナがすき。 *Banana ga suki.*	I like bananas.
	バナナはすきじゃありません。 *Banana wa suki ja arimasen.*	バナナはすきじゃない。 *Banan wa suki ja nai.*	I don't like bananas.
	バナナがきらいです。 *Banana ga kirai desu.*	バナナがきらい。 *Banana ga kirai.*	I don't like bananas.

	Formal	Informal	English
Means (*de*)	バスでいきます。 *Basu de ikimasu.*	バスでいく。 *Basu de iku.*	I am going by bus.
Accompaniment (*to*)	ともだちといきます。 *Tomodachi to ikimasu.*	ともだちといく。 *Tomodachi to iku.*	I am going with my friend.
Connector Sequence (*ya*)	アメリカやにほん *Amerika ya Nihon*	アメリカやにほん *Amerika ya Nihon*	America, Japan, etc.
Connector Sequence (*sorekara*)	それから *sorekara*	それから *sorekara*	and then
Pause (*eeto*)	ええと *eeto*	ええと *eeto*	Let's see
Pause (*anoo*)	あのう *anoo*	あのう *anoo*	uh
Connector Cause-effect (*dakara*)	だから *dakara*	だから *dakara*	therefore, so
Connector Juxtaposition (*demo*)	でも *demo*	でも *demo*	however, but
Connector implying a favor without openly expressing it	リサですが... *Risa desu ga...*		I am Lisa, but...
Expressing Politeness (*o-*, *go-*)	おくに、ごしゅみ *Okuni, goshumi*	くに、しゅみ *Kuni, shumi*	country, hobby
Describing People	あねはおもしろいです。 *Ane wa omoshiroi desu.*	あねはおもしろい。 *Ane wa omoshiroi.*	My elder sister is funny.
Describing People	おもしろいひとです。 *Omoshiroi hito desu.*	おもしろいひとだ。 *Omoshiroi hito da.*	She is a funny person.
Numeral Classifiers	かぞくはよにんです。 *Kazoku wa yonin desu.*	かぞくはよにんだ。 *Kazoku wa yonin da.*	There are four people in my family.

VOCABULARY *(continued)*

	Formal	Informal	English
Simple Questions	だれですか？ *Dare desu ka?*	だれ？ *Dare?*	Who is it?
Asking about likes	すきですか？ *Suki desu ka?*	すき？ *Suki?*	Do you like (it)?
Asking about dislikes	きらいですか？ *Kirai desu ka?*	きらい？ *Kirai?*	Do you dislike (it)?
Asking about destination	どこへいきますか？ *Doko e ikimasu ka?*	どこへいく？ *Doko e iku?*	Where is he going?

Notional Vocabulary

Family Terms

ちち	chichi	(my) father
おとうさん	otoosan	(someone's) father/(my) father
はは	haha	(my) mother
おかあさん	okaasan	(someone's) mother/(my) mother
あに	ani	(my) older brother/
おにいさん	oniisan	(someone's) older brother/(my~)
あね	ane	(my) older sister
おねえさん	oneesan	(someone's) older sister/(my~)
おとうと	otooto	(my) younger brother
おとうとさん	otootosan	(someone's) younger brother/ (my~)
いもうと	imooto	(my) younger sister
いもうとさん	imootosan	(someone's) younger sister/(my~)
うち	uchi	my house
かぞく	kazoku	my family
ごかぞく	gokazoku	(someone's) family
ともだち	tomodachi	friend

Countries

アメリカ	Amerika	America
カナダ	Kanada	Canada
メキシコ	Mekishiko	Mexico
かんこく	Kankoku	Korea
ちゅうごく	Chuugoku	China
タイ	Tai	Thailand
オーストラリア	Oosutoraria	Australia
ニュージーランド	Nyuujiirando	New Zealand
イギリス	Igirisu	Great Britain
フランス	Furansu	France
ドイツ	Doitsu	Germany
イタリア	Itaria	Italy
スペイン	Supein	Spain
ロシア	Roshia	Russia
インド	Indo	India
エジプト	Ejiputo	Egypt
イスラエル	Isuraeru	Israel
サウジアラビア	Sauji Arabia	Saudi Arabia
ペルー	Peruu	Peru
アルジェリア	Arujeria	Algeria
インドネシア	Indoneshia	Indonesia

ポルトガル	Porutogaru	Portugal
ブラジル	Burajiru	Brazil
シンガポール	Shingapooru	Singapore
にほん	Nihon	Japan

Language and People

〜ご	~go	~language
〜じん	~jin	~person (nationality)

Personal Questions

おくには。	Okuni wa?	What country are you from?
おとしは。	Otoshi wa?	How old are you?
おすまいは。	Osumai wa?	Where do you live?
たんじょうびは。	Tanjoobi wa?	When is your birthday?
たんにんのせんせいは	Tanin no sensei wa?	Who is your homeroom teacher?
スポーツは。	Supootsu wa?	What sport do you play?
しゅっしんは。	Shusshin wa?	Where is your birthplace?
ごしゅみは	Goshumi wa?	What are your hobbies?

Colors

あか	aka	red
あお	ao	blue
きいろ	kiiro	yellow
みどり	midori	green
くろ	kuro	black
しろ	shiro	white
ちゃいろ	chairo	brown
オレンジ	orenji	orange
ピンク	pinku	pink
むらさき	murasaki	purple

Names

ファースト・ネーム	faasuto neemu	first name
あおき	Aoki	Japanese family name
おおやま	Ooyama	Japanese family name
やまだ	Yamada	Japanese family name
かわかみ	Kawakami	Japanese family name
はやし	Hayashi	Japanese family name
たかはし	Takahashi	Japanese family name
きのした	Kinoshita	Japanese family name
みょうじ	miyooji	last name
ニックネーム	nikkuneemu	nickname

VOCABULARY

Transportation

でんしゃ	*densha*	train
タクシー	*takushii*	taxi
じてんしゃ	*jitensha*	bicycle
バス	*basu*	bus
ちかてつ	*chikatetsu*	subway
ひこうき	*hikooki*	airplane
ふね	*fune*	ship
あるいて	*aruite*	on foot, by foot

School

ちゅう1	*chuu-ichi*	7th grader
ちゅう2	*chuu-ni*	8th grader
ちゅう3	*chuu-san*	9th grader
こう1	*koo-ichi*	10th grader
こう2	*koo-ni*	11th grader
こう3	*koo-san*	12th grader

Descriptions of Personality

げんき（な）	*genki (na)*	healthy
うるさい	*urusai*	noisy
かわいい	*kawaii*	cute
おもしろい	*omoshiroi*	funny
きれい（な）	*kirei (na)*	pretty
まじめ（な）	*majime (na)*	serious
やさしい	*yasashii*	kind, gentle, nice
きびしい	*kibishii*	strict, demanding
すてき（な）	*suteki (na)*	attractive
いそがしい	*isogashii*	busy
こせいてき（な）	*koseiteki (na)*	individual
しょうじき（な）	*shoojiki (na)*	honest
クール（な）	*kuuru (na)*	cool

Counters for People

ひとり	*hitori*	one person
ふたり	*futari*	two people
さんにん	*sannin*	three people
よにん	*yonin*	four people
ごにん	*gonin*	five people
ろくにん	*rokunin*	six people
しちにん	*shichinin*	seven people
はちにん	*hachinin*	eight people
きゅうにん	*kyuunin*	nine people
じゅうにん	*juunin*	ten people

School Subjects

べんきょう	*benkyoo*	study
しゅくだい	*shukudai*	homework
かもく	*kamoku*	subjects
にほんご	*nihongo*	Japanese language
がいこくご	*gaikokugo*	foreign language
すうがく	*suugaku*	mathematics
えいご	*eigo*	English language
かがく	*kagaku*	science
ぶつり	*butsuri*	physics
せいぶつ	*seibutsu*	biology
かがく（ばけがく）	*kagaku (bakegaku)*	chemistry
しゃかい	*shakai*	social studies
れきし	*rekishi*	history
けいざい	*keizai*	economics
せいじ	*seiji*	politics
おんがく	*ongaku*	music
びじゅつ	*bijutsu*	art
たいいく	*taiiku*	physical education
コンピュータ	*konpyuuta*	computer
とくい（な）かもく	*tokui (na) kamoku*	strong subject, skilled, favored
にがて（な）かもく	*nigate (na) kamoku*	weak subject, unskilled,

3.10 Virtual Reality

I. Warm-Up

A. **Match the expressions on the left with the situations on the right, filling each (   ) with the appropriate letter.**

Then, choose the appropriate expression from those listed below to form a longer version of each question, filling each [   ] with the appropriate katakana character.

1. おとしは。   (   ) [   ] a. asking someone's grade level
2. たんじょうびは。   (   ) [   ] b. asking someone's favorite type of music
3. がくねんは。   (   ) [   ] c. asking someone's age
4. おくには。   (   ) [   ] d. asking who someone's homeroom teacher is
5. すきな　かもくは。   (   ) [   ] e. asking someone's name
6. スポーツは。   (   ) [   ] f. asking where someone's place of residence is
7. ごしゅっしんは。   (   ) [   ] g. asking what sport someone plays
8. たんにんの　せんせいは。
                                        (   ) [   ] h. asking what club someone belongs to
9. おなまえは。   (   ) [   ] i. asking the meaning of something
10. いみは。   (   ) [   ] j. asking what someone's favorite subject is
11. おすまいは。   (   ) [   ] k. asking where someone's native country is
12. すきな　おんがくは。 (   ) [   ] l. asking where someone's birthplace is
13. クラブは。   (   ) [   ] m. asking what someone's hobby is
14. ごしゅみは。   (   ) [   ] n. asking when someone's birthday is

ア. なんですか　　　イ. いつですか　　　ウ.　だれですか
エ. どちらですか　　　オ. いくつですか

B. **Preparation for Main Activity: Creating School Celebrities**

Students work in groups of three. Each group creates a fictitious student character who is well known in his or her school for some reason, then furnishes personal information about the character. In the Main Activity, one group member will play the character they created in a mock interview setting.

II. Main Activity: Student Celebrity Interview

Procedure for celebrity close-up

A. The same groups of three from section B in the Warm-Up continue to work together.

B. Each member of the group chooses a character and becomes the "interviewee." The character can be anyone other than himself or herself (e.g., a movie star, professional sports figure, fictitious person or other student in the school).

C. The class later votes on the best close-up or Web page based on its design, organization, clarity of information and artistic creativity.

Procedure for interview

A. One student is interviewed within his or her group by the other two members.

B. Next, each interviewee is matched with a pair of interviewers from a group other than his or her own. The interviewers are encouraged to try different strategies, such as repeating, half-repeating, developing conversation with じゃ, and conversation-extension using attribution/association and analogy. They also take notes and record personal information about the interviewee.

C. The interviewers are encouraged to ask questions such as "How old are you", "When is your birthday", and so on.

D. Use the form below to prepare questions for the inteviewee and note the answers.

E. Use the form on the next page to evaluate the interview.

インタビュー（しつもん）シート	こたえのシート
1. おくには＿＿＿＿＿＿＿＿＿＿。	1. おくには＿＿＿＿＿＿＿＿＿＿。
2. おとしは＿＿＿＿＿＿＿＿＿＿。	2. おとしは＿＿＿＿＿＿＿＿＿＿。
3. ごしゅみは＿＿＿＿＿＿＿＿。	3. ごしゅみは＿＿＿＿＿＿＿＿。
4. ＿＿＿＿＿＿＿＿＿＿＿＿＿＿	4. ＿＿＿＿＿＿＿＿＿＿＿＿＿＿
5. ＿＿＿＿＿＿＿＿＿＿＿＿＿＿	5. ＿＿＿＿＿＿＿＿＿＿＿＿＿＿
6. ＿＿＿＿＿＿＿＿＿＿＿＿＿＿	6. ＿＿＿＿＿＿＿＿＿＿＿＿＿＿
7. ＿＿＿＿＿＿＿＿＿＿＿＿＿＿	7. ＿＿＿＿＿＿＿＿＿＿＿＿＿＿
8. ＿＿＿＿＿＿＿＿＿＿＿＿＿＿	8. ＿＿＿＿＿＿＿＿＿＿＿＿＿＿
9. ＿＿＿＿＿＿＿＿＿＿＿＿＿＿	9. ＿＿＿＿＿＿＿＿＿＿＿＿＿＿
10. ＿＿＿＿＿＿＿＿＿＿＿＿＿＿	10. ＿＿＿＿＿＿＿＿＿＿＿＿＿＿
11. ＿＿＿＿＿＿＿＿＿＿＿＿＿＿	11. ＿＿＿＿＿＿＿＿＿＿＿＿＿＿
12. ＿＿＿＿＿＿＿＿＿＿＿＿＿＿	12. ＿＿＿＿＿＿＿＿＿＿＿＿＿＿
13. ＿＿＿＿＿＿＿＿＿＿＿＿＿＿	13. ＿＿＿＿＿＿＿＿＿＿＿＿＿＿
14. ＿＿＿＿＿＿＿＿＿＿＿＿＿＿	14. ＿＿＿＿＿＿＿＿＿＿＿＿＿＿
15. ＿＿＿＿＿＿＿＿＿＿＿＿＿＿	15. ＿＿＿＿＿＿＿＿＿＿＿＿＿＿
16. ＿＿＿＿＿＿＿＿＿＿＿＿＿＿	16. ＿＿＿＿＿＿＿＿＿＿＿＿＿＿
17. ＿＿＿＿＿＿＿＿＿＿＿＿＿＿	17. ＿＿＿＿＿＿＿＿＿＿＿＿＿＿
18. ＿＿＿＿＿＿＿＿＿＿＿＿＿＿	18. ＿＿＿＿＿＿＿＿＿＿＿＿＿＿
19. ＿＿＿＿＿＿＿＿＿＿＿＿＿＿	19. ＿＿＿＿＿＿＿＿＿＿＿＿＿＿
20. ＿＿＿＿＿＿＿＿＿＿＿＿＿＿	20. ＿＿＿＿＿＿＿＿＿＿＿＿＿＿

Self-Evaluation Form: Interviewing (Interviewer, interviewee)

Name of interviewer:_____   Name of interviewee: _____

Purpose and Organization	poor	fair	good	very good	excellent
Clarity of purpose	1	2	3	4	5
Organization of thoughts	1	2	3	4	5
Structure (beginning, middle and end)	1	2	3	4	5
Choice of words	1	2	3	4	5

Presentation and Participation	poor	fair	good	very good	excellent
Clarity of communication	1	2	3	4	5
Performance	1	2	3	4	5
Collaboration	1	2	3	4	5
Quality of participation	1	2	3	4	5

Word/sentence use	poor	fair	good	very good	excellent
New vocabulary	1	2	3	4	5
Complete sentences	1	2	3	4	5
Word order	1	2	3	4	5

Comment:

3.11 Virtual Reality

III. Wram-Up

Making a student celebrity close-up or Web page.

Those who played interviewers share the information they gathered with the other group members. Based on the information they collected, each group then creates a "student celebrity close-up page" for a magazine or Web page for teenagers. Include two types of information: written information, such as an article or interview, and visual information, such as a photo or illustration.

The class later votes on the best close-up page or Web page based on design, organization, clarity of information, and creativity.

サウスハイ じゅうどう チーム キャプテン

佐々木 伸治

11月8日生　17さい
11ねんせい
くまもと

Self-Evaluation Form: Close-up					
Name of interviewer:_____			Name of interviewee: _____		
Close-up or Web page	poor	fair	good	very good	excellent
Clarity of purpose	1	2	3	4	5
Choice of words	1	2	3	4	5
Writing of kana or kanji	1	2	3	4	5
Spelling acccuracy	1	2	3	4	5
Illustrations/photos/design	1	2	3	4	5

がっこう

がっこうのなまえは
グレート　レイク
スクールです。
こうこう２ねんせい
です。いつもおとう
ととバスでがっこう
にいきます。

がぞく

かぞくはちちとはは
とおとうとの４にん
です。
ちちはいつもいそが
しいです。ははやや
さしいです。おとう
とはげんきです。

ニーナ

すき／きらい

サッカーがすきです。で
も、バレーボールはすき
じゃありません。
アイスクリームがだいす
きです。　だから、よく
アイスクリームのみせに
いきます。

しゅっしん

なまえはニーナです。
１７さいです。
くにはアメリカです。
しゅっしんはバーモン
トです。すまいはニュ
ーヨークです。

SUM-UP

1. *How well has the required task been carried out? Please rate your performance on a scale of 0 to 5. (0 = performance barely adequate, 5 = excellent performance)*

   0　　　　1　　　　2　　　　3　　　　4　　　　5

2. *How competently did you interact and/or take the initiative in conversation/dialogue? Please rate your performance on a scale of 0 to 5. (0 = rarely participated; constant prompting is needed, 5 = fully participated and took the initiative in exchanges where appropriate)*

   0　　　　1　　　　2　　　　3　　　　4　　　　5

3. *How wide was the range of vocabulary and idioms you used? Please rate your range on a scale of 0 to 5. (0 = limited range, 5 = wide range)*

   0　　　　1　　　　2　　　　3　　　　4　　　　5

4. *Have you been able to use the self-introduction strategy when you wanted to say something? Rate your progress on a scale of 0 to 5. (0 = no progress, 5 = excellent progress)*

   0　　　　1　　　　2　　　　3　　　　4　　　　5

5. *Were you able to use cooperation strategies when you worked with members of your group? Please rate your progress on a scale of 0 to 5. (0 = no progress, 5 = excellent progress)*

   0　　　　1　　　　2　　　　3　　　　4　　　　5

ADDITIONAL VOCABULARY

Functional Vocabulary

	Formal	Informal	English
Asking about colors	どんないろですか？ *Donna iro desu ka?*	どんないろ？ *Donna iro?*	What color is it?
Asking about weather	どんなてんきですか？ *Donna tenki desu ka?*	どんなてんき？ *Donna tenki?*	What kind of weather is it?

Notional Vocabulary

Additional Place Names

ニューヨーク	*Nyuu Yooku*	New York
ボストン	*Bosuton*	Boston
フィラデルフィア	*Firaderufia*	Philadelphia
ハートフォード	*Haatofoodo*	Hartford
ピッツバーグ	*Pittsubaagu*	Pittsburgh
バッファロー	*Baffaroo*	Buffalo
アトランタ	*Atoranta*	Atlanta
シカゴ	*Shikago*	Chicago
ロスアンジェルス	*Rosu Anjerusu*	Los Angeles
ワシントン	*Washinton*	Washington
マイアミ	*Maiami*	Miami
サンフランシスコ	*San Furanshisuko*	San Francisco
シアトル	*Shiatoru*	Seattle
デンバー	*Denbaa*	Denver
いいところ	*ii tokoro*	good place/location
マンハッタン	*Manhattan*	Manhattan
タイムズ・スクエア	*Taimuzu Sukuea*	Times Square
セントラル・パーク	*Sentoraru Paaku*	Central Park
バンクーバー	*Bankuubaa*	Vancouver
トロント	*Toronto*	Toronto

Celebrity

スポーツせんしゅ	*supootsu senshu*	sports figure
えいがスター	*eiga sutaa*	movie star
テレビはいゆう	*terebi haiyuu*	TV actor, actress
バスケットボールのプロ	*basukettobooru no puro*	professional basketball player
やきゅうのプロ	*yakyuu no puro*	professional baseball player
フットボールのプロ	*futtobooru no puro*	professional football player
せいじか	*seijika*	politician
やきゅうのせんしゅ	*yakyuu no senshu*	baseball player
フットボールのせんしゅ	*futtobooru no senshu*	football player
かしゅ	*kashu*	singer
ロックのスター	*rokku no sutaa*	rock 'n roll star
じょゆう	*joyuu*	actress
だんゆう	*dan'yuu*	actor
げいじゅつか	*geijutsuka*	artist
おんがくか	*ongakuka*	musician
さっか	*sakka*	writer
テレビのアナウンサー	*terebi no anaunsaa*	TV announcer
だいとうりょう	*daitooryoo*	president
ファーストレディー	*faasuto redii*	first lady
しゅしょう	*shushoo*	prime minister
おうじ	*ooji*	prince
おうじょ	*oojo*	princess

School Staff

こうちょう	*koochoo*	principal
カウンセラー	*kaunseraa*	counselor
コーチ	*koochi*	coach
キャプテン	*kyaputen*	captain
りゅうがくせい	*ryuugakusei*	foreign student
せいとかいちょう	*seito kaichoo*	chair of student council
クラブのぶちょう	*kurabu no buchoo*	head of club
としょかんいん	*toshokan'in*	librarian

School Items

ほうかご	*hookago*	after school
なつやすみ	*natsu yasumi*	summer vacation
やすみ　じかん	*yasumi jikan*	break time
ひる　やすみ	*hiru yasumi*	lunch break
ともだち	*tomodachi*	friend
れんしゅうのあと	*renshuu no ato*	after practice
じゅくのあと	*juku no ato*	after cram school
しょくどう	*shokudoo*	cafeteria
べんきょう	*benkyoo*	study
やま	*yama*	mountain
キャンプファイヤー	*kyanpu faiyaa*	campfire
れんしゅうのないよう	*renshuu no naiyoo*	practice material
ときどき	*tokidoki*	sometimes
よく	*yoku*	often
いつも	*itsumo*	always
このじかん	*kono jikan*	during this time

Classroom

こくばん	*kokuban*	blackboard
ホワイトボード	*howaitoboodo*	whiteboard
ほん	*hon*	book
ノート	*nooto*	notebook
えんぴつ	*enpitsu*	pencil
ボールペン	*boorupen*	ballpoint pen
ふでばこ	*fudebako*	pencil case
けしごむ	*keshigomu*	eraser
テーブル	*teeburu*	table
コンピュータ	*konpyuuta*	computer
ちず	*chizu*	map
ドア	*doa*	door

Family Terms

おじいさん	*ojiisan*	someone else's grandfather
そふ	*sofu*	my grandfather
おばあさん	*obaasan*	someone else's grandmother
そぼ	*sobo*	my grandmother
おじさん	*ojisan*	someone else's uncle
おじ	*oji*	my uncle
おばさん	*obasan*	someone else's aunt
おば	*oba*	my aunt
ごしんせき	*goshinseki*	someone else's relatives
しんせき	*shinseki*	my relatives
おいとこさん	*oitokosan*	someone else's cousin
いとこ	*itoko*	my cousin
おいごさん	*oigosan*	someone else's nephew
おい	*oi*	my nephew
めいごさん	*meigosan*	someone else's niece
めい	*mei*	my niece
ごきょうだい	*gokyoodai*	someone else's siblings
きょうだい	*kyoodai*	my siblings
ぎりのおとうさん	*giri no otoosan*	someone else's father-in-law
ぎりのちち	*giri no chichi*	my father-in-law
ぎりのおかあさん	*giri no okaasan*	someone else's mother-in-law
ぎりのはは	*giri no haha*	my mother-in-law

Descriptions of Personality

あかるい	*akarui*	cheerful
くらい	*kurai*	gloomy
あたたかい	*atatakai*	warm
つめたい	*tsumetai*	cold
しんせつ（な）	*shinsetsu (na)*	kind
しょうじき（な）	*shoojiki (na)*	honest
かっこいい	*kakkoii*	attractive
かっこわるい	*kakkowarui*	unattractive
しゃこうてき（な）	*shakooteki (na)*	sociable
きどらない	*kidoranai*	not affected
こわい	*kowai*	fearful, awful
ゆうかん（な）	*yuukan (na)*	brave
れいせい（な）	*reisei (na)*	calm, cool
たよりになる	*tayori ni naru*	reliable
おもいやりのある	*omoiyari no aru*	warm-hearted, thoughtful
ユーモアのある	*yuumoa no aru*	humorous
せきにんかんのある	*sekininkan no aru*	responsible
けつだんりょくのある	*ketsudanryoku no aru*	decisive
エネルギッシュ（な）	*enerugisshu (na)*	energetic

School Clubs

クラブかつどう

きゅうどうぶ
弓道部

じゅうどうぶ
柔道部

たっきゅうぶ
卓球部

水泳部の画像

すいえいぶ
水泳部

やきゅうぶ
野球部

ぶ
バレー部

ぶ
テニス部

ほうそうぶ
放送部

さどうぶ
茶道部

しょどうぶ
書道部

びじゅつぶ
美術部

かどうぶ
華道部

えんげきぶ
演劇部

ぶ
コーラス部

しゃしんぶ
写真部

すもうぶ
相撲部

しんぶんぶ
新聞部

ぶ
バスケット部

えいごぶ
英語部

けんどうぶ
剣道部

ぶ
バトミントン部

サッカー部

すいそうがくぶ
吹奏楽部

Chapter 4

Planning Japanese Culture Week

Chapter 4

Planning Japanese Culture Week

4.1 Introduction

OBJECTIVES

At the end of this chapter, you will be able to:

- conduct basic communication by telephone

- indicate time, place, and frequency of action

- extend conversation with ja or jaa

- describe your daily activities

- check your comprehension while listening or reading

- understand basic sentence structure in Japanese

- plan a Japanese culture week by scheduling activities, conducting committee meetings, arranging speakers and presenters, reserving rooms and equipment, writing budgets and proposals, and making posters and flyers

You will also learn:

- basic Japanese verbs

- how to answer yes-no questions negatively

- how to use the verbs arimasu and masu to express existence as well as occurrence

- relative time expression

- about 15 kanji

- how to solve conflicts and problems associated with planning a Japanese culture week

Planning Japanese Culture Week

Planning and executing an event successfully is a well-regarded skill in both schools and workplaces. In most instances you are bound by many factors such as deadlines, budgetary limitations, and the availability of people and facilities. In addition, you have to cooperate well with your fellow planners and present a clear and persuasive proposal to the individual or institution that holds the key to approval. In this final chapter of the book you will be working with your classmates to plan a Japanese culture week from start to finish. It involves writing proposals, making telephone calls to potential guest demonstrators and speakers, coordinating schedules, and making posters and flyers. Did you imagine doing all this in Japanese at the beginning of this school year? We certainly have come a long way, haven't we? Let's tap into and mobilize all the resources you have accumulated so far and plan a wonderful Japanese culture week.

Your Daily Activities: Describe, Compare and Reflect.

Is your daily life well planned and well organized? Do you spend your time wisely and productively? Or do you think you are wasting or spending too much time on something unintentionally? In this chapter you will have opportunities to equip yourself with the words and expressions necessary to describe basic human activities and actions as well as to indicate the time, place and frequency of such actions. Furthermore, you will be comparing your own daily life with that of not only your classmates but also a wider circle of American teenagers and their Japanese counterparts. So take advantage of this opportunity and describe, compare and reflect! You may well end up improving the quality of your daily life.

Japanese Sports and Martial Arts
Where training of the body meets training of the mind.

The popularity of Japanese sports and martial arts has been on the steady rise around the world. Sumo has attracted many non-Japanese fans and spectators, and judo has been an Olympic sport for quite some time. Demonstrations of karate or judo have been popular attractions in Japanese cultural events all over the world. There are other Japanese sports and martial arts which are rich in both tradition and popularity even though they are lesser-known outside Japan than those mentioned above. Since you will be planning a Japanese culture week in this chapter, it is timely that you learn more about these sports and martial arts.

Communicating by Telephone

Are you one of those compulsive telephone users like many others your age? Or do you prefer non-simultaneous and less impulsive ways of communication such as letters and e-mail? Either way, the telephone adds an important dimension to your ability to interact with others, and you may as well expand it by learning how to communicate by phone in Japanese. There are several procedures to follow and expressions to use when making a phone call in Japanese. It may be a challenging task for you to communicate with another person in an indirect situation. However, you have learned the basics already so why not give it a try?

WARM-UP

1. *In your daily life you come across many different types of spoken or written language. We listen and read for a variety of purposes. We can check our comprehension while listening or reading with different strategies to fit our purposes, such as self-monitoring. Listen to the following texts and choose the appropriate description of the context.*

1. The text was
   a. a self-introduction
   b. an introduction of someone else
   c. an announcement
   d. an advertisement

2. The text was
   a. telling the topic of the meeting
   b. announcing the beginning of the meeting
   c. announcing the end of the meeting
   d. asking questions

3. The text was
   a. a self-introduction
   b. an introduction of someone else
   c. an announcement
   d. an advertisement

2. *Self-monitoring is used in a variety of ways to check comprehension. You can monitor your comprehension at different levels, such as the word, phrase or sentence level, and also monitor for style, for your plan, and for the effectiveness of your choice of strategy. You can also check to determine whether personal learning or performance goals have been realized. Fill in the blanks with the letter of the English category of the thing being described in Japanese.*

( ) こんにちは。はじめまして、どうぞよろしく。

( ) わたしは あさいはなです。

( ) がっこうはうえだこうこうです。

( ) １５です。

( ) いつもおとうととでんしゃでがっこうにいきます。

( ) うちはまつもとです。

( ) かぞくはおとうさんとおかあさんとおとうとのよにんです。

( ) しゅっしんはながのです。

( ) にほんごをはなします。

( ) えいががすきです。

( ) しゅみはテニスです。

( ) まいにちがんばってべんきょうします。

A. name	H. age
B. ending	I. residence
C. greetig	J. hobby
D. transportation	K. anguage
E. like	L. birthplace
F. family	
G. school	

Useful words:

予約 (よやく) : reservation

発表 (はっぴょう) : presentation

3. *Read the following and choose the appropriate answer for each item below.*

A: 中村先生（なかむらせんせい）の発表（はっぴょう）は八時（じ）からです。場所（ばしょ）はこうどうです。予約（よやく）が必要（ひつよう）です。発表（はっぴょう）は日本語です。ノートは必要（ひつよう）じゃありません。

B: 田中先生（たなかせんせい）の発表（はっぴょう）は七時半（じはん）からです。場所（ばしょ）はコンサートホールです。予約（よやく）は必要（ひつよう）じゃありません。発表（はっぴょう）は英語（えいご）です。ノートが必要（ひつよう）です。

time	A: 1) 8:00	2) 7:00	B: 1) 8:30	2) 7:30
place	A: 1) concert hall	2) auditorium	B: 1) concert hall	2) auditorium
reservation	A: 1) you need	2) you don't need	B: 1) you need	2) you don't need
presentation	A: 1) English	2) Japanese	B: 1) English	2) Japanese
notebook	A: 1) you need	2) you don't need	B: 1) you need	2) you don't need

BASIC VOCABULARY

もしもし

もしもし、りかさんいますか。　　　　いいえ、ちがいます。

1. おきます
2. がっこうへいきます
3. てがみをかきます
4. ほんをよみます
5. スキーをします
6. バレーボールをします
7. バスケットボール
　 をします
8. じゅうどうをします
9. うちへかえります
10. テレビをみます
11. ごはんをたべます
12. べんきょうします
13. のみます
14. おんがくをききます
15. ねます

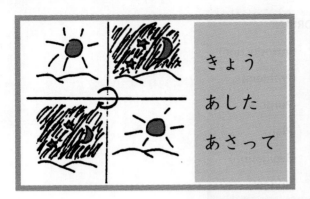

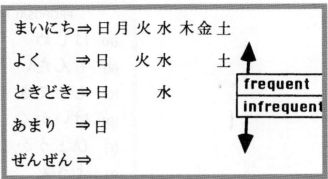

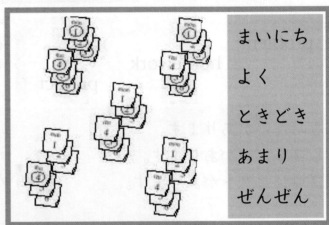

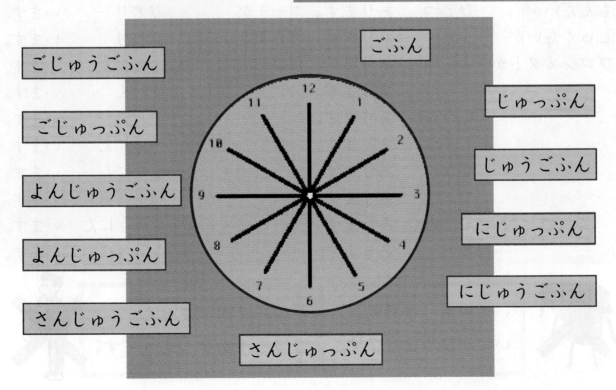

PROPOSAL FORMAT

(A)	はじめ	(Introduction)
(B)	もんだい	(Problem)
(C)	もくてき	(Purpose)
(D)	けいかく	(Plan)
(E)	ひょうか	(Evaluation)
(F)	よさん	(Budget)

problem
homework
project

coach
counselor
professional

もんだいがあります。
しゅくだいがあります。
プロジェクトがあります。

コーチがいます。
カウンセラーがいます。
プロがいます。

もんだいが	ひとつ	あります。
しゅくだいが	ふたつ	あります。
プロジェクトが	みっつ	あります。
	よっつ	あります。
	いつつ	あります。
	むっつ	あります。
	ななつ	あります。
	やっつ	あります。
	ここのつ	あります。
	とお	あります。

コーチが	ひとり	います。
カウンセラーが	ふたり	います。
プロが	さんにん	います。
	よにん	います。
	ごにん	います。
	ろくにん	います。
	しちにん／ななにん	います。
	はちにん	います。
	くにん／きゅうにん	います。
	じゅうにん	います。

いすがありません。
いすがひつようです。

コーチがいません。
コーチがひつようです。

MECHANICS

4. *Circle the phrase that correctly completes each sentence below.*

1. When you call Rika Tanaka at her home, Rika's mother picks up the phone and says:
   （あのう、もしもし）

2. You ask if you have reached the Tanaka residence.
   たなかさんの（おたく、おでんわ）ですか。

3. Rika's mother responds affirmatively.
   はい、（そうじゃありません、そうです。）

4. You ask her if Rika is there.
   りかさん（ですか、いますか。）

5. *Fill in the blanks with the letter of the action verb that corresponds to the picture.*

A.(　　)

B.(　　)

C.(　　)

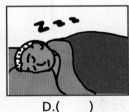
D.(　　)

E.(　　)

F.(　　)

G.(　　)

H.(　　)

1. べんきょうします
2. いきます
3. たべます
4. みます
5. よみます
6. おきます
7. ねます
8. かきます

6. *Fill in the blanks with the letter of the frequency expression.*

(never)	(not much)	(sometimes)	(often)	(always)	(every day)

A. ときどき

B. ぜんぜん

C. あまり

D. まいにち

E. よく

F. いつも

あまり
ぜんぜん

ノート **1 (Note 1):**
あまり and ぜんぜん are used with negative statements. They are similar to the English "not so much" and "not at all/never."

7. *Fill in the blanks with the letter of the Japanese day of the month below.*

１２がつカレンダー (December)						
(1st)	(2nd)	(3rd)	(4th)	(5th)	(6th)	(7th)
(8st)	(9nd)	(10rd)	(11th)	(12th)	(13th)	(14th)

A. ついたち   H. とおか

B. じゅうよっか   I. なのか

C. よっか   J. いつか

D. むいか   K. じゅうににち

E. ふつか   L. ようか

F. みっか   M. じゅうさんにち

G. ここのか   N. じゅういちにち

8. **Fill in the blanks with the letter of the time expression that corresponds to the picture.**

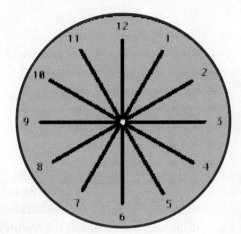

1. (　　) A. じっぷん／じゅっぷん
2. (　　) B. ごふん
3. (　　) C. さんじゅうごふん
4. (　　) D. さんじっぷん／さんじゅっぷん
5. (　　) E. にじっぷん／にじゅっぷん
6. (　　) F. じゅうごふん
7. (　　) G. にじゅうごふん
8. (　　) H. よんじっぷん／よんじゅっぷん

9. **Fill in the blanks with the number of the English proposal term that corresponds to the proposal term in Japanese.**

(1) Introduction　　(2) Problem　　(3) Purpose　　(4) Plan　　(5) Evaluation　　(6) Budget

はじめ	もくてき	もんだい	けいかく	よさん	ひょうか
(　　)	(　　)	(　　)	(　　)	(　　)	(　　)

10. **Circle the word that correctly completes each sentence.**

1. 先生（せんせい）が (います、あります)。
2. もんだいが (います、あります)。
3. しゅくだいが (います、あります)。
4. リンダさんが (います、あります)。
5. いすが (います、あります)。
6. リンダの猫（ねこ）が (います、あります)。

11. **Determine whether the following expressions correspond to the existential expressions by circling** ほんとう *(True) or* うそ *(False).*

1. 先生（せんせい）が ひとり　あります。　　　　ほんとう (True) or うそ (False).
2. もんだいが ふたつ　あります。　　　　ほんとう (True) or うそ (False)
3. しゅくだいが　ふたり　います。　　　　ほんとう (True) or うそ (False)
4. リンダさんが　ひとり　います。　　　　ほんとう (True) or うそ (False)

343

Traditional Japanese Board Games

Fukuwarai

A New Year's game for children. A blindfolded player tries to place pieces of paper in the shape of eyebrows, eyes, nose, and mouth within the outlines of an otafuku, the face of a homely woman with round cheeks and a flat nose. The disorderly placement of the features creates amusing expressions.

Sugoroku

A board game similar to backgammon that is played by two or more persons using dice. *Sugoroku* was introduced from China in the 6th century. Today *sugoroku* have illustrations of popular tourist spots or celebrities. The game is played mainly by children at New Year's.

Let's play fukuwarai

1. Materials; object of the game

Fukuwarai literally means "happy and laugh" in Japanese. The following materials are needed to play *fukuwarai:* a sheet of paper on which a facial outline is drawn with the essential features missing; pieces of paper in the shape of those missing features. Blindfolded players attempt to make a "perfect face" by placing the missing features on the face. The player who has made the best such attempt is the winner.

2. How to play

1. Choose a player. She is given a blindfold to wear.

2. Designate a person to hold the pieces of paper depicting facial features.

3. The player asks the holder for a facial feature by saying, for example, *kuchi o kudasai*, or *me o kudasai*.

4. The holder responds to her request.

5. The player then tries to place the facial feature in the appropriate spot on the facial outline sheet. The onlookers may give her advice and let her know which direction she has to move her piece to reach the appropriate spot on the sheet by saying *hidari* (left), *migi* (right), *ue* (up), or *shita* (down).

6. After placing the facial feature, the player asks for another one. Repeat actions 3-5 until all the facial features are placed on the sheet.

7. The player removes her blindfold and looks at the completed face.

8. Choose another player and holder and start a new game.

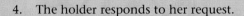
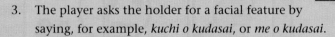
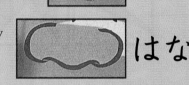
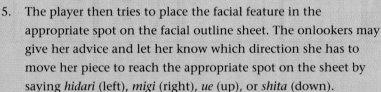

まゆ

め

くち

はな

Let's play picture-matching

1. Materials; object of the game

Cards depicting a particular weather condition or season are used in this game. The cards must be assembled in a sequence of three to make a complete picture set (see sample cards on the following page). The player who has assembled the most sets by the end of the game is the winner. The ideal number of players is five.

2. How to play

1. Choose a dealer. He distributes all the cards face down evenly among the players, including himself.

2. Decide the order of play, either clockwise or counterclockwise. In either case, the dealer goes first.

3. Look at your cards to see if you have a complete set of three. If so, put it on the table, saying " [name of set] 〜があります."

4. Players try to accumulate as many sets as possible by asking other players if they have a certain card (see flow chart). If you fail to thank the player upon receiving the card requested or if the player does not have the card requested, you lose your turn.

[Sample Cards]

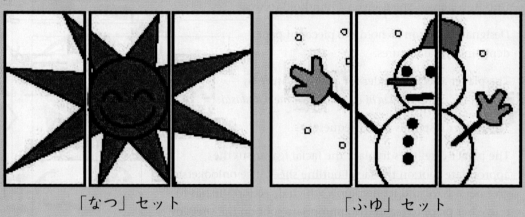

「なつ」セット   「ふゆ」セット

[A starts his turn by asking B (a player A has chosen) if she has a card he is looking for. In this example it happens to be Summer #2 .]

A：Bさん、なつの２はありますか。

[B has the card.]
B：はい、あります。

[B does not have the card.]
B：いいえ、ありません。

loss

of

turn

[A receives the card saying:]
A：ありがとうございます。

[A receives the card without thanking B.]

A continues to ask for cards from anyone he chooses until he loses his turn.

4.2 Mechanics

1 . Fill in the blanks with the letter of the action verb that corresponds to the picture.

1. (　)

2. (　)

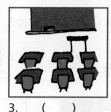
3. (　)

A. カフェテリアへいきます。

B. プールへいきます。

C. きょうしつへいきます。

D. こうどうへいきます。

E. ジムへいきます。

F. コンピュータルームへいきます。

ノート2 (Note 2):

〜へいきます (*e ikimasu.*) is used to express direction with motion verbs such as いきます (*ikimasu*) "to go," きます (*kimasu*) "to come," かえります (*kaerimasu*) "to return," For example, (*Nihon e ikimasu*) "to go to Japan." 〜にいきます (*ni ikimasu.*) is used in the same way. In the most instances the two particles can be used interchangeably with motion verbs. Exceptions include phrases such as べんきょうにいきます (*Benkyoo ni ikimasu*) "to go to stud," and かいものにいきます (*Kaimono ni ikimasu*) "to go shopping," in which *ni*, rather than *e*, is used exclusively.

---

2 . Match the letter of the action verb with the corresponding picture.

1. (　)

2. (　)

3. (　)

4. (　)

5. (　)

6. (　)

7. (　)

8. (　)

ア　たべます

イ　のみます

ウ　べんきょうします

エ　かきます

オ　よみます

カ　ねます

キ　おきます

ク　みます

ケ　いきます

コ　かえります

サ　きます

シ　じゅどうをします

3. **Practice having simple conversations like those in the models below, substituting the places in the illustrations under the dialogues.**

会話の例 (Sample Dialogue)

A: あのう、どこへいきますか。

B: あ (quickly)、<u>としょかん</u>へいきます。

1.

2.

3.

4.

5.

6.

7.

8.

9.

10.

4. **Practice having simple conversations like those in the models below.**

会話の例 (Sample Dialogue)

A: あのう、なんじに<u>カフェテリア</u>へ　いきますか。

B: あ (quickly)、<u>にじ</u>にいきます。

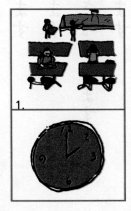
1.

2.

3.

4.

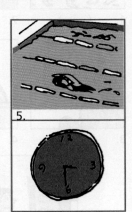
5.

5. **Practice having simple conversations like those in the models below.**

会話の例 **(Sample Dialogue)**

A: あのう、なんようびにえいがにいきますか。

B: そうですね。*(saying in a downbeat way)* <u>きんようび</u>にいきます。

6. **Practice having simple conversations like those in the models below.**

会話の例 **(Sample Dialogue)**

A: あのう、どこへ／にいきますか。

B: あ *(quickly)*、<u>すうがく</u>にいきます。

B: あ *(quickly)*、<u>すうがく</u>のきょうしつへ／にいきます。

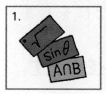 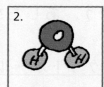   

7. **Practice having simple conversations like those in the models below.**

会話の例 **(Sample Dialogue)**

A: あのう、<u>にじ</u>に<u>としょかん</u>へ
いきますか。

B: <u>はい、いきます。</u>

B: <u>いいえ、にじにいきません。</u>
<u>さんじにいきます。</u>

A: ああ、そうですか。

2:00/3:00   12:00/12:45   4:30/5:15

7:30/8:00   9:10/10:10

8. Practice asking and answering questions using the dialogue below as a model.

1.

2.

3.

4.

5.

6.

7.

会話の例 (Sample Dialogue)

A: あのう、Bさん、まいにちなにを
   しますか。

B: そうですね。 *(speaking in a downbeat way)*
   まいにち<u>バスケットボール</u>をします。

9. Practice asking and answering questions based on the schedules using the dialogue below as a model.

あしたのスケジュール	
go to school	return home
go to Japanese class	do homework
go to science class	eat dinner
go to history class	watch TV
eat lunch	call a friend
write a letter	read a book
play basketball	listen to music

会話の例 (Sample Dialogue)

A: あのう、あしたなにをしま
   すか。

B: <u>バスケットボール</u>をします。

10. Tell what the Japanese students in the picture below are doing in the morning.

11. **Practice asking and answering questions based on the schedule given using the model below.**

まいにちのスケジュール	
6:45	wake up
7:00	wash face
7:10	eat breakfast
8:00	go to school
9:00	go to Japanese class
10:30	go to science class
12:00	go to history class
12:30	eat lunch
1:00	go to math class
2:30	play basketball
4:00	return home
4:45	do homework
6:00	eat dinner
7:00	watch TV
9:00	call a friend
9:30	read a book
10:30	listen to music
11:00	go to bed

会話の例 (Sample Dialogue)

A: あのう、まいにち なんじに おきますか。

B: ろくじよんじゅうごふんに おきます。

ノート3 (Note 3):

The particle に is used to indicate the point in time at which an action takes place. For example, ろくじにおきます (*Rokujini okimasu*) "I get up at 6:00."

12. **Practice frequency expressions using the chart below.**

会話の例 (Sample Dialogue A)

A: すいようびに コンサートに いきますか。

B: はい、いきます。

会話の例 (Sample Dialogue B)

A: かようびに コンサートに いきますか。

B: いいえ、いきません。

一日	二日	三日	四日	五日	六日	七日
ついたち	ふつか	みっか	よっか	いつか	むいか	なのか
にちようび	げつようび	かようび	すいようび	もくようび	きんようび	どようび
パーティー	バレーボール	フットボール	コンサート	ダンス	クラブミーティング	えいが

13. Practice asking and answering questions based on the infomation given using the model below.

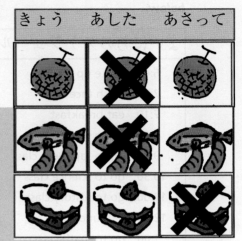

きょう	あした	あさって

会話の例 (Sample Dialogue)

A: あした　メロンをたべましょうか。

B: はい、そうしましょう。 *(agree softly)*

B: はい、たべましょう。 *(agree strongly)*

B: あのう *(hesitating)*、ちょっと………すみません。
　　(refuse softly)

B: いいえ、たべません。 *(refuse strongly)*

きょう
あさ

ノート4 (Note 4.):
Some time expressions such as あさ
(asa) "morning," and きょう *(kyoo)* "today," do not
take the particle に *(ni)*. For example きょういきま
す *(Kyoo ikimasu)* "I am going today."

14. Pair work: Practice asking and answering questions based on the information given using the model below.

(never)	(not much)	(sometimes)	(often)	(always)	(everyday)
ピクニック	コンサート	としょかん	えいが	にほんご	がっこう.

ときどき
ぜんぜん
あまり
まいにち
よく
いつも

会話の例 (Sample Dialogue)

A: よく コンサートに いきますか。

B: いいえ、あまりいきません。

15. Practice frequency expressions using the schedule below.

にちようび	げつようび	かようび	すいようび	もくようび	きんようび	どようび
うち	がっこう	がっこう	がっこう	がっこう	がっこう	としょかん
パーティー	フットボール	フットボール	コンサート	フットボール	クラブミーティング	えいが
スパゲティ	フライドチキン	スパゲティ	ミートローフ	スパゲティ	フライドチキン	すし
コーク	ミルク	みず	コーヒー	みず	みず	コーヒー

会話の例 (Sample Dialogue)

A: <u>よく</u> <u>としょかんに</u> <u>いきますか</u>。

B: <u>いいえ、あまりいきません</u>。

16. Practice frequency expressions using the schedule below.

会話の例 (Sample Dialogue)

A: <u>すいようび</u>に <u>コンサート</u>に いきますか。

B: はい、いきます。

A: じゃ、いっしょにいきましょう。

B: はい、いきましょう。

会話の例 (Sample Dialogue)

A: <u>かようび</u>に <u>コンサート</u>に いきますか。

B: いいえ、いきません。どうも、すみません(hesitating)。

一日	二日	三日	四日	五日	六日	七日
ついたち	ふつか	みっか	よっか	いつか	むいか	なのか
にちようび	げつようび	かようび	すいようび	もくようび	きんようび	どようび
パーティー	バレーボール	フットボール	コンサート	ダンス	クラブミーティング	えいが

Traditional Japanese Arts

Most likely you have already heard a little bit about traditional Japanese arts such as calligraphy and Kabuki theater. This is your chance to get to know a little bit more about these arts. The next two pages will cover flower arrangement, tea ceremony, calligraphy, and the three major classical theaters of Japan: No, Kabuki, and the Bunraku puppet theater.

Ikebana (flower arrangement) literally means, "flowers kept alive." It is also called *kadoo*, or the Way of flowers. Japanese flower arrangement had its origins in early Buddhist flower offerings and developed into a distinctive art form from the 15th century. The attention given to the choice of plant material and container, the placement of branches, and the relationship of the branches to the container and the surrounding space distinguishes this art from purely decorative uses of flowers.

Sadoo, known as tea ceremony in the West, means the Way of tea. It is a highly structured method of preparing powdered green tea in the company of guests. The ideal number of guests is four. The tea is prepared in a specially designated room, the *chashitsu*, which has hardly any decoration except for a hanging scroll and flowers in a vase. Before welcoming the guests, the host purifies their hands and mouth in a stone basin. This ritual is meant to cleanse the host of mundane concerns. The guests do the same before entering the gate to the tea house, which separates the mundane world from the spiritual world of tea. Inside the tea house, the host serves the tea meal before the tea itself. Each guest is served a tray set with three courses: cooked white rice, miso soup, and fish or vegetables. After the meal, the tea is served, and the first guest takes the bowl, drinks, and passes it to the others. The quiet atmosphere of harmony and respect for people and objects in the tea house, with its emphasis on cleanliness and order, is designed to bring peace to the body and the spirit.

Shodoo, the Way of writing, is Japanese-style calligraphy. Japanese calligraphy was influenced by Chinese culture; China is the birthplace of the East Asian tradition of calligraphy. There are various kinds of scripts used in calligraphy. *Kaisho*, or block-style script, is perhaps the most popular style, since the characters are easily recognizable. *Gyosho*, or running-style script, is created by a faster movement of the brush and some consequent abbreviation of the characters. *Shosho*, or grass writing, is a true cursive style that abbreviates and links parts of the characters, resulting in a fluid and curvilinear writing. The history of calligraphy in Japan is very long, starting with the first introduction of the Chinese writing system in the 5th century, and still continues today.

No, a form of musical dance-drama that originated in the 14th century, is the oldest professional theater still in existence. No preserves what all other important contemporary theater has lost: its origin in ritual, reflecting an essentially Buddhist view of existence. There are basically two types of No plays: those dealing with "real people" and those portraying supernatural beings. The language used in No is largely poetic. The costumes are rich and heavy, with multiple layers of brilliantly colored stiff brocades that serve both to create a sense of elegance and to make the actors larger than life. Masks are worn only by the leading character. The masks fall into general categories, including holy old man, god, demon, man and woman. Even though there are masks that represent women, all the No performers are male.

Although No consists only of male actors, the creation of Kabuki is ascribed to a female attendant who, documents record, led her company of mostly women in light theatrical performances featuring dancing and comic sketches. This "women's Kabuki" became extremely popular. However, due to its sensual dances, erotic scenes, and the frequent fights that broke out among the spectators, women were banned from appearing in Kabuki performances from around the 17th century. Thereafter, "young men's Kabuki" achieved great success. However, the spectacular success of Kabuki during the late 17th century was followed by a period of diminished popularity due to the flourishing of the Bunraku puppet theater. Today, half the plays presented on the Kabuki stage are adaptations of Bunraku plays.

Bunraku is the professional puppet theater of Japan. The Bunraku theater presents dramas, both serious and entertaining, as well as beautifully choreographed dances, for a primarily adult audience. The performance is composed of four elements: the puppets, which are approximately one-half to two-thirds life-size; the movement given to the puppets by their operators; the vocal delivery by the chanter; and the rhythmical musical accompaniment provided by the player of the three-stringed shamisen instrument. Bunraku puppets are not operated by strings. With his left arm and hand, the principal operator supports the puppet and manipulates the mechanisms that control the movable eyelids, eyeballs, eyebrows and mouth; with his right hand, he operates the puppet's right arm. One assistant operator operates the puppet's left arm, and another assistant operator operates the puppet's legs. Traditionally, a puppeteer must spend 10 years operating the legs and 10 years the left arm before he may become a principal operator. Bunraku may be enjoying a mild revival because of a new appreciation of tradition among younger Japanese, but its future is uncertain.

4.3 Mechanics

Practice having telephone conversations like those in the models below, substituting Japanese students' names. A will be the caller. B will be the person whom A asks to speak with. R will be the person who answers the phone but not the person A wants to speak with.

1. The caller has reached the right number.

 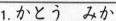  

1. かとう　みか　　2. さだ　ひでき　　3. はやし　りか　　4. さとう　ひろし

会話の例 **(Sample Dialogue)**

A: もしもし。 *(rising intonation)*

B: あのう、<u>かとう</u>さんのおたくですか。

A: はい、そうです。

2. The intended party answers the phone.

1. みか　　2. やすお　　3. かなえ　　4. まさあき

会話の例 **(Sample Dialogue)**

A: もしもし。 *(rising intonation)*

B: あのう、<u>かとう</u>さんのおたくですか。

A: はい、そうです。

B: <u>みか</u>さんいますか。 *(rising intonation)*

A: はい、わたしです。

A: こんばんは。<u>リサ</u>です。

B: こんばんは。

3. **The intended party is present but does not answer the phone.**

会話の例 (Sample Dialogue)

A: もしもし、みかさんいますか。 *(rising intonation on "moshi moshi")*

R: はい、います。ちょっとまってください。

B: もしもし、どなたですか。 *(rising intonation on "moshi moshi")*

A: あ、*(quickly)*わたしは<u>リサ</u>です。こんばんは。

B: こんばんは。

4. **The intended party is present but does not answer the phone. The caller gives her name and affiliation.**

会話の例 (Sample Dialogue)

A: もしもし、<u>みか</u>さんいますか。 *(rising intonation on "moshi moshi")*

R: はい、います。どなたですか。

A: <u>ニューヘブンこうこう</u>の<u>リサ</u>ですが...

B: あっ、ちょっとまってください。

A: <u>リサ</u>です。こんばんは。

B: あ、<u>リサ</u>さん、こんばんは。

ノート5 **(Note 5):**

The conjunction *ga* has several functions. One of these is to indicate one's desire for a favor without actually expressing it. For example, ニューヘブンこうこうの<u>リサ</u>ですが (*nyuuhebun kookoo no Risa desu ga*) (I am Lisa, a student at New Haven High School and [I would like to talk to my friend Mika.)

5. **Calling a wrong number.**

会話の例 (Sample Dialogue)

R: もしもし。 *(rising intonation on "moshi moshi")*

A: あのう、かとうさんのおたくですか。

R: いいえ、ちがいます。

A: ああ、どうもすみません。

R: いいえ。

6.   The intended party is not present. The caller offers to call again.

会話の例 (Sample Dialogue)

A: もしもし、<u>みか</u>さんいますか。 *(rising intonation on "moshi moshi")*

R: みかですか。<u>みか</u>は<u>がっこう</u>ですが。

A: あっ、そうですか。じゃ、あとででんわします。

R: すみません。

A: いいえ。

7.   The time and place of an event are confirmed.

どようび	にちようび
がっこう	うち
パーティー	テニス
９じ	１０じ

会話の例 (Sample Dialogue)

A: <u>パーティー</u>は<u>９じ</u>です。

B: そうですか。がっこうの<u>カフェテリア</u>ですね。

A: そうです。じゃ、<u>どようび</u>に。

B: はい、どうもありがとう。

A: さようなら。

B: さようなら。

8.   The person's attendance at an event is confirmed.

会話の例 (Sample Dialogue)

A: あのう、<u>どようびのパーティー</u>のことですが...

   (falling intonation on "koto desu ga")

B: はい。

A: <u>みかさん</u>はいきますか。

B: はい、<u>いきます</u>。

ノート６ (Note 6):

いきます (*ikimasu*) and きます (*kimasu*) mean "to go" and "to come," respectively. However, in some situations they are used diferently from their English equivalents. いきます is always used when a person travels from his or her starting point to another destination. きます is used only when another person travels from his or her starting point to your location. Compare the Japanese and English in the following dialogue:

いきます
きます

A: *Paatii ni kimasu ka?*   Are you <u>coming</u> to (my) party?
B: *Hai, <u>ikimasu</u>.*   Yes, I'm <u>coming</u>.

ノート７ (Note 7):

～のこと
ですが

<u>～のことですが</u> (*~no koto desu ga.*) is used to broach a topic of conversation. If you want to tell the other party you are calling about tomorrow 's math test you say あしたのすうがくのテストのことですが (*Ashita no suugaku no tesuto no koto desu ga...*) "About tomorrow's math test..."

9.   Reaching an answering machine and hanging up.

会話の例 **(Sample Dialogue)**

A: こちらは<u>かとう</u>です。
 ただいま、がいしゅつちゅうです。

B: (Hang up)

10. Leaving a message that you'll call again.

会話の例 **(Sample Dialogue)**

A: こちらは<u>かとう</u>です。
 ただいま、がいしゅつちゅうです。
 おなまえ、おでんわばんごうをおのこしください。

B: <u>みか</u>です。またでんわします。

11. Leaving a message with your name and number.

会話の例 **(Sample Dialogue)**

A: こちらは<u>かとう</u>です。
 ただいま、がいしゅつちゅうです。
 おなまえ、おでんわばんごうをおのこしください。

B: <u>みか</u>です。すみませんが、でんわしてください。
 でんわばんごうは<u>７３４－３４７５</u>です。
 よろしくおねがいします。

Telephone Flow Chart ノート 8 (Note 8):

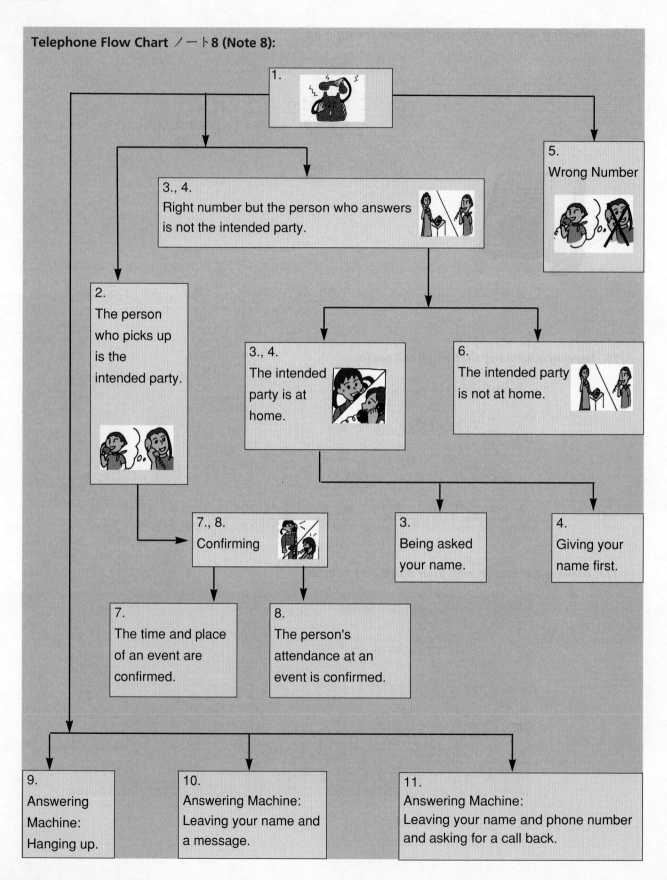

12. In this role play, you and your clasmates each choose one card. Be sure to use the telephone flow chart and the appropriate intonation.

A.	B.	C.
You are Toshio. It's evening, and you call John. His brother answers the phone, and you ask for John. When John comes to the phone, you identify yourself.	You are John's younger brother. The phone rings and you answer it. The caller asks if John is there. You tell the caller that he is and ask him to wait a moment.	You are John. It's evening. Your brother has answered the phone and hands it over to you. Ask the caller who is speaking and greet him.

会話の例 **(Sample Dialogue)**

A: もしもし、ジョンさん いますか。*(rising intonation on "moshi moshi")*

B: はい、ジョンはいます。ちょっとまってください。

C: もしもし、どなたですか。

B: あ、*(quickly)* わたしは としおです。こんばんは。

C: あ、*(quickly)* こんばんは。

13. In this role play, you and your clasmate each choose one card. Be sure to use the telephone flow chart and the appropriate intonation.

A	**B**
You are John, an American high school student. It's 1:00 p.m. and you call Kaori, an exchange student from Japan. You ask her if she's going to the party tomorrow.	You are Kaori, a Japanese exchange student. It's 1:00 p.m. John calls you and asks if you're going to the party tomorrow.

会話の例 **(Sample Dialogue)**

ジョン： もしもし。かとうさんのおたくですか。
かおり： はい、そうです。
ジョン： あのう、 *(hesitating)* かおりさんいますか。
かおり： はい、わたしです。
ジョン： こんにちは。ジョンです。
かおり： こんにちは。
ジョン： あのう、 *(hesitating)* すみません。
　　　　 あしたのパーティーのことですが。
かおり： はい。
ジョン： かおりさんはいきますか。
かおり　 はい、いきます。

Japanese Traditional Sports

Japan is well known for its martial arts. Also called *bugei*, the term martial arts is now usually called *budoo* or "the martial Way". The Japanese terms encompass such martial arts as *kendoo* (fencing), judo, *aikidoo*, and *kyuudoo* (archery). *Karate* is not actually considered one of the traditional Japanese martial arts, although it is sometimes referred to as such outside of Japan. Let us now examine these art forms in some more depth.

Modern *budoo* seek the development of skills through physical exercise and, by establishing objective standards of skills, provide opportunities for competition. In this sense they can be considered a form of sport. Yet behind the martial arts lie the philosophies of Confucianism, Buddhism and Taoism.

Kendoo (the Way of the sword) is the term used for Japanese fencing based on the techniques of the two-handed sword of the samurai. The weapon is a hollow cylinder made of four shafts of split bamboo. It is bound with a leather grip and cap connected by a silk or nylon cord and a leather thong wound three times around the bamboo cylinder and knotted. Fencers are protected by the *men* (face mask) and the trunk of the body is protected by the *do* (chest protector). The thighs are protected with five overlapping quilted panels, the *tare*, and the hands with padded mittens (*kote*). The most fundamental movements of attack and defense are stance, footwork, cuts, thrusts, feints and parries.

Judo (the Way of softness) is a form of unarmed combat that stresses quick motions, clever mental judgment, and rigorous form rather than sheer physical strength. A system of ranks (*dan*) and classes (*kyuu*) has been established. The ranks go from 1 to 10, with 10 being the highest. Those in ranks 1 to 5 wear a black belt, ranks 6 to 8 have a scarlet and white striped belt, and those in ranks 9 to 10 have a scarlet belt. The classes are below the ranks and range from the fifth class to the first, and highest, class. Adults in the first to third class wear a brown belt; children in the first to third class wear a purple belt. Those in the fourth and fifth class wear a white belt.

Aikidoo is derived from judo and is a system of pure self-defense. It is derived from the traditional weaponless fighting techniques of judo, using immobilizing holds and twisting throws whereby an attacker's own momentum and strength are turned against him. Practice usually takes an established form, or *kata*: one partner takes the offensive role, dealing blows or holds, and the other deflects these using *aikidoo* moves. Since two people cannot practice defensive techniques against each other, *aikidoo* does not lend itself to a contest situation. Students are, instead, ranked according to skill level.

Kyuudoo (the Way of the bow) is Japanese archery. The bow is usually 7 feet 3 inches in length. It is an eccentric bow, that is, two-thirds of its length is above the grip and one-third below. Two target distances are used in modern *kyuudoo*. Usually the archer stands 92 feet from a circular target 14 inches in diameter. In contrast to Western archery, in *kyuudoo* the emphasis is on form rather than accuracy.

Karate literally means "empty hand" and is an art of self-defense that uses no weapons and relies instead on three main techniques: arm strikes (*uchi*), thrusts (*tsuki*), and kicks (*keri*). Current forms of karate developed from a style of Chinese boxing called *quanfa* (rules of the fist), known as kung fu in the West. After World War II, *karate* and the martial arts mentioned above experienced a decline that lasted until around 1955. After that, however, the sports increased in popularity, and they are more wide-spread now than ever before.

4.4 Mechanics

じゃ

ノート9 **(Note 9):**

Ja and *jaa* are shortened versions of *de wa*. They are use to develop or extend conversation by taking what the other person has said and linking it with an idea that would logically follow.

Ja and *jaa* function in the following three ways:

(A)   To develop the conversation
       じゃ、こうこうせいですね   *Jaa, kookoosei desu ne.*
       Then, you're a high school student, aren't you?

(B)   To change the topic of the conversation
       じゃ、なんじにいきますか。   *Ja, nanji ni ikimasu ka?*
       So, what time are you going?

(C)   To wrap up the conversation
       じゃ、7じはんにいきましょう。   *Ja, shichijihan ni ikimashoo.*
       So, let's make it 7:30.

会話の例 **(Sample Dialogue)**

A: けんじさんは　なんさいですか。   *Kenji san wa nansai desu ka?*
      How old are you, Kenji?

B: じゅうろくさいです。   *Juurokusai desu*
      I'm 16.

A: じゃ(a)、こうこうせいですね。   *Jaa, kookoosei desu ne.*
      Then, you're a high school student, aren't you?

B: ええ、そうです。   *Ee, soo desu.*
      Yes, I am.

A: パーティーにいきますか。   *Paatii ni ikimasu ka?*
      Are you going to the party?

B: はい、いきます。   *Hai, ikimasu.*
      Yes, I'm going.

A: じゃ(b)、なんじにいきますか。   *Ja, nanji ni ikimasu ka?*
      So, what time are you going?

A: あのう、しちじはんがいいです。   *Anoo, shichijihan ga ii desu.*
      Well, I would like to go at 7:30.

B: じゃ(c)、しちじはんにいきましょう。 *Ja, shichijihan ni ikimashoo.*
      So, let's make it 7:30.

365

1. In this role play, you and your clasmate each choose one card. Be sure to use the telephone flow chart and the appropriate intonation.

A.

You are John, an American high school student. It's 1:00 p.m. and you call Kaori, an exchange student from Japan. You ask her what she's doing tomorrow and the time of that activity.

B.

You are Kaori, a Japanese exchange student. It's 1:00 p.m. John calls you and asks what you're doing tomorrow and the time of the activity.

会話の例 **(Sample Dialogue)**

ジョン:	もしもし。かとうさんのおたくですか。
かおり:	はい、そうです。
ジョン:	あのう、 *(hesitating)* かおりさんいますか。
かおり:	はい、わたしです。
ジョン:	こんにちは。ジョンです。
かおり:	こんにちは。
ジョン:	あのう、 *(hesitating)* すみません。あしたはなにをしますか。
かおり:	バレーボールをします。
ジョン:	じゃ、4じですね。 *(rising intonation on "ja")*
かおり:	はい、そうです。
ジョン:	どうもありがとう。

2. Group Activity: Information Gap

スケジュール

7じに	おきます
7じはんに	あさごはんをたべます
8じに	がっこうに いきます
8じはんに	クラスに いきます
9じに	にほんごを べんきょうします
12じに	ひるごはんを たべます
3じに	としょかんにいきます
4じに	クラブに いきます
6じに	うちに かえります
7じに	ゆうごはんを たべます
8じに	にほんごを べんきょうします
9じに	ほんを よみます
10じに	しゅくだいをします
11じに	テレビを みます
12じに	ねます

A. A group of five students forms a team.
B. Each team receives a daily schedule with different information missing.
C. Team members gather information from the other groups regarding their schedules.
D. The team that completes the list accurately first is the winner.

会話の例 **(Sample Dialogue)**

A:	なんじにあさごはんをたべますか。
B:	＿＿＿じにたべます。
A:	じゃ、8じになにをしますか。
B:	8じに＿＿＿＿をします。

3. Group Activity: Information Gap

A. A group of five students forms a team.
B. Each team receives a daily schedule with different information missing.
C. The teacher flashes a completed daily schedule for 30 seconds.
D. Team members work with each other to complete their schedules.
E. Completed schedules wll be judged in class based on accuracy, time and clarity.

わたしの月曜日（げつようび）のスケジュール

7じから7じはんまで

8じから8じはんまで

9じから10じまで

10じはんから11じまで

12じから12じはんまでひるごはんをたべます

3じから4じまで

5じから6じまで

7じから8じに

9じから10じまで

11じから6じまでねます

会話の例 (Sample Dialogue)

A: テレビをみますか。
B: はい、みます。
A: じゃ、なんじからなんじまでテレビをみますか。
B: そうですね。9じから10じまでみます。

ノート10 (Note 10):

～から
～まで

「～から～まで」 (~kara) "from" (~made) "until, to." The particle から (kara) "from" is used to mark the starting point of a duration of time. The particle まで (made) "until, to" is used to indicate the ending point of the duration. For example, 8じから10じまでテレビをみます。 (Hachiji kara juuji made terebi o mimasu.) "I will watch TV from 8:00 to 10:00."

4. Pair work: Practice asking and answering questions based on the schedule, using the model below.

会話の例 (Sample Dialogue)

A: なんにちにいきますか。
B: 十月十日（じゅうがつとおか）にいきます。
A: じゃ(A)、木曜日（もくようび）ですね。
B: はい、そうです。
A: ごじにいきますか。それとも、ろくじにいきますか。
B: ええと…
A: じゃ(B)、 (rising intonation on "ja") なんじにいきますか。
B: ごじはんがいいです。
A: じゃ(C)、ごじはんにしましょう。

Oct. 10th	April 7th	May 21st
もくようび	どようび	かようび
5じ or 6じ	8じ or 9じ	1じ or 2じ
5じはん	9じはん	1じはん
1.	2.	3.

367

5. Pair Activity (Formal and Informal)

You and your partner have the schedule below. Practice asking and answering questions based on the schedule, as in the examples.

一日	二日	三日	四日	五日	六日	七日
にちようび	げつようび	かようび	すいようび	もくようび	きんようび	どようび
パーティー	バレーボール	フットボール	コンサート	ダンス	クラブミーティング	えいが
ピザ	フライドチキン	ハンバーグ	ミートローフ	スパゲティ	ホットドッグ	すし
コーク	ミルク	オレンジジュース	コーヒー	パンチ	みず	おちゃ

会話の例 (Sample Dialogue)

A: げつようびにパーティーにいきますか。
B: はい、いきます。
A: どこですか。
B: がっこうです。
A: じゃ、なんじに　いきますか。
B: ９じに　いきます。

会話の例 (Sample Dialogue)

A: げつようびにパーティーにいく。
B: うん、いく。
A: どこ。
B: がっこう。
A: じゃ、なんじ。
B: ９じ。

Language Note

Related languages

What does it mean to say that two or more languages are related to each other? It just means that they were the same language at some time in the past. In other words, they are now changed forms of a common ancestor language. The Romance language family is an example of a set of related languages, and you probably already know that their common ancestor is Latin. Since Latin was the language of the Roman empire, it spread to many parts of Europe about 2,000 years ago. But languages are always changing, and the varieties of Latin spoken in separate communities all over Europe gradually diverged from one another. As a result, we now have a whole family of related but distinct languages, including French, Spanish, Portuguese, Italian and Romanian.

Vocabulary resemblances

You expect vocabulary items in related languages to resemble each other. English and German are related to each other in the same way as French and Spanish, and if you look at words with similar meanings in English and German, you find lots of obvious resemblances. For example, the English "drink" and German "trinken" ("to drink") resemble each other in pronunciation because both words are descended from a common ancestor word. In technical terminology, words that developed from a common ancestor word (like drink and *trinken*) are called cognates.

It's important to realize, though, that a resemblance in pronunciation between words with similar meanings doesn't necessarily mean that they're cognates. There are four possible reasons a word in one language might resemble a word with a similar meaning in another language:

(1) descent from the same word in a common ancestor language

(2) adoption from one language into the other

(3) sound symbolism (onomatopoeia)

(4) sheer coincidence

Let's consider adoption first. The English "escalator" and Japanese "esukareetaa" ("escalator") resemble each other, but they aren't cognates because we know that the Japanese word was adopted from English. English and Japanese aren't related languages. Many people mistakenly assume that Japanese must be related to Chinese, but in this case too, the vocabulary resemblances are almost all due to adoption, mostly from Chinese into Japanese.

Now let's consider sound symbolism, which means a natural connection between a word's pronunciation and its meaning. The most familiar kind of sound symbolism is onomatopoeia, that is, words that mimic sounds. The English "moo moo" and Japanese "muu muu" are familiar examples of onomatopoeia, and both mimic the sound a cow makes. This resemblance has nothing to do with language relationship or vocabulary adoption. Since cows sound the same all over the world, you expect words that mimic that sound to have similar pronunciations in different languages.

Finally, no matter what two languages you pick, you can always find a few words with similar meanings that resemble each other just by coincidence. You may have noticed that the English "name" and Japanese "namae" ("name") have pretty similar pronunciations, but in this case, the resemblance is just an accident.

Japanese and Ryuukyuuan

Japanese isn't related to English or to Chinese, but it isn't an orphan. You learned a little about the languages spoken in the Ryuukyuu island chain (Okinawa Prefecture) in Chapter 2, and there's no doubt that they're related to Japanese. In other words, Japanese and the languages of the Ryuukyuu islands are all descended from a common ancestor language, and they're sometimes referred to collectively as the Japanese-Ryuukyuuan language family. The two lists below show some cognates from a dialect of Japanese (the standard Tokyo dialect) and a dialect of one of the Ryuukyuuan languages (from the island of Okinawa).

JAPANESE	RYUUKYUUAN	Meaning
hone	funi	bone
hoshi	fushi	star
kimo	chimu	liver
kiri	chiri	fog
kore	kuri	this
kubi	kubi	neck
kumo	kumu	cloud
kusa	kusa	grass

Other possible relatives

It seems likely that Japanese-Ryuukyuuan and Korean are related to each other, but it isn't easy to find cognates. If Korean is in fact a related language, it must be a fairly distant relative. Some linguists believe that languages such as Turkish and Mongolian are also related to Japanese-Ryuukyuuan, but this idea is controversial.

4.5   Mechanics

1. Make sentences using the appropriate existence verb based on the information in the pictures below.

例文 **(Sample Expression)**

<u>もんだい</u>があります。

例文 **(Sample Expression)**

<u>もんだい</u>が<u>あります</u>。or <u>コーチ</u>が<u>います</u>。

ノート11 **(Note 11):**

あります
います

The verb あります is used to express the existence of all inanimate objects ranging from concrete things such as clocks and umbrellas to abstractions such as ideas and plans. います, on the other hand, is used to express the existence of animate beings such as people and animals. Both verbs are preceded by the particle が. います and あります may express either mere existence ("there is") or existence and possession ("I have"), depending on the context. For example, にほんごのワープロがあります may mean either "There is a Japanese word processor (somewhere)." or "I have/own a Japanese word processor."

ノート12 (Note 12)

Counting using ひとつ、ふたつ、みっつ、よっつ・・

As previously mentioned, the Japanese counting system goes up to 10 and can be used to count various things. After 10, the Chinese system is used.

ひとつ	一つ	one item	むっつ	六つ	six items
ふたつ	二つ	two items	ななつ	七つ	seven items
みっっつ	三つ	three items	やっつ	八つ	eight items
よっつ	四つ	four items	ここのつ	九つ	nine items
いつつ	五つ	five items	とお	十	ten items
			じゅういち	十一	eleven items

2. **Circle the appropriate answer.**

    A. （ふたつ、みっっつ、ここのつ、ひとつ）は一つです。

    B. （よっつ、みっっつ、むっつ、ひとつ）は三つです。

    C. （ふたつ、やっつ、ななつ、よっつ）は八つです。

    D. （やっつ、みっっつ、ここのつ、むっつ）は六つです。

    E. （ななつ、みっっつ、いつつ、ひとつ）は五つです。

3. *Make sentences using number based on the information in the pictures below.*

> 例文 (Sample Expression)
>
> <u>ふたつ</u>あります。

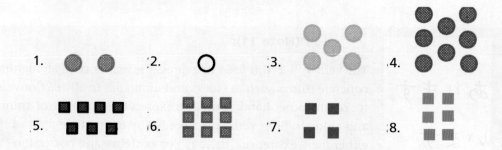

4. **Make sentences using the appropriate existence verb and number based on the information in the pictures below.**

例文 (Sample Expression)

<u>もんだい</u>が<u>ふたつあります</u>。or <u>コーチ</u>が<u>ふたりいます</u>。

5. **Make negative sentences using the appropriate existence verb based on the information in the pictures below.**

例文 (Sample Expression)

<u>いすとつくえ</u>が<u>ありません</u>。 or <u>コーチ</u>が<u>いません</u>。

373

6. *Make sentences using the appropriate words based on the information in the pictures below.*

例文 **(Sample Expression)**

いすとつくえがひつようです。

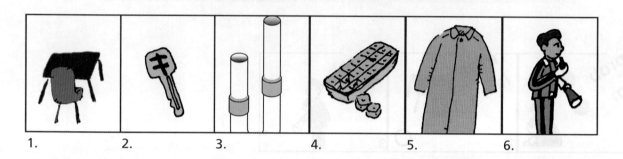

1.　　2.　　3.　　4.　　5.　　6.

7. *Make sentences using the appropriate words and existence verbs based on the information in the pictures below.*

1.　　2.　　3.　　4.　　5.　　6.

例文 **(Sample Expression)**

もんだいがあります。いすとつくえがありません。
いすとつくえがひつようです。

もんだいがあります。コーチがいません。
コーチがひつようです。

Preparation for Japanese Culture Week

In the Virtual Reality section of this chapter, you and your classmates will be engaged in planning Japanese Culture Week. It involves a wide range of activities, from information gathering to production, from proposal writing to decision-making. The following sections are designed to help you prepare for Japanese Culture Week.

8. Japanese culture has many aspects to it. Here are several.

にほんのでんとう
Japanese tradition

にほんのでんとうスポーツ
Japanese traditional sports

1.	おはなのせんせい
2.	おちゃのせんせい
3.	おしゅうじの せんせい
4.	かぶきのせんせい
5.	にほんりょうりの せんせい

6.	じゅうどうの せんせい
7.	からてのせんせい
8.	けんどうの せんせい
9.	きゅうどうの せんせい
10.	すもうのせんせい

9. Use the picture and sample sentences below to make your own sentences about Japanese culture.

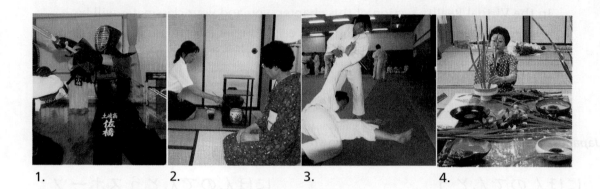

1.   2.   3.   4.

5.   6.   7.   8.

例文 **(Sample Expression)**

A. けんどうの先生がいます。

B. けんどうは日本のぶどうです。

C. けんどうのどうぐがありません。

D. けんどうのどうぐがひつようです。

A. おちゃの先生がいます。

B. おちゃは日本のでんとうげいじゅつです。

C. おちゃのどうぐがありません。

D. おちゃのどうぐがひつようです。

かな－漢字: Kana and Kanji

Long vowels in hiragana

As you have seen, Japanese has both short and long vowels. In romanization, long vowels are spelled with double letters (*aa, ii, uu, ee, oo*), and in katakana, the second half of a long vowel is written with the symbol ー. In hiragana, things are a bit more complicated.

The long vowel sounds ***aa, ii,*** and ***uu*** are written in hiragana by adding あ, い, or う after the syllable that contains that vowel. For example:

おばあさん	*obaasan*	grandmother	ば (*ba*) + あ (*a*) = ***baa***
おじいさん	*ojiisan*	grandfather	じ (*ji*) + い (*i*) = ***jii***
ぴゅうぴゅう	*pyuupyuu*	a whistling sound	ぴゅ (*pyu*) + う (*u*) = ***pyuu***

Most long ***oo*** sounds are written in hiragana by adding う (rather than お) after a syllable that includes the vowel ***o***, as in the following examples.

おはよう	*ohayoo*	good morning	よ (*yo*) + う (*u*) = ***yoo***
きょう	*kyoo*	today	きょ (*kyo*) + う (*u*) = ***kyoo***

In a very small number of words, though, the second half of a long ***oo*** sound is written with お rather than with う. These words aren't predictable: You just have to memorize them as you learn them. The four words below are the most common words that follow this pattern:

おおきい	*ookii*	big	お (*o*) + お (*o*) = ***oo***
おおい	*ooi*	numerous	お (*o*) + お (*o*) = ***oo***
とお	*too*	ten	と (*to*) + お (*o*) = ***too***
とおい	*tooi*	far	と (*to*) + お (*o*) = ***too***

The combination ***ei*** sounds almost exactly like a long ***ee*** sound. Even so, when you have ***ei*** in romanization, the ***i*** is written in hiragana with い, as in the examples below.

せんせい	*sensei*	teacher
えいご	*eigo*	English language

Except for words normally written in katakana, very few words are written with ***ee*** in romanization. Those that are have the hiragana え in the second half of the long ***ee*** sound, as shown in the following examples.

377

えぇ	*ee*	yes	え (*e*) + え (*e*) = ***ee***
おねえさん	*oneesan*	older sister	ね (*ne*) + え (*e*) = ***nee***

The second half of a long vowel is also the second half of a long syllable. Here is how some of the words above divide into syllables and beats.

ぴゅうぴゅう	***pyuu|pyuu***	2 syllables		きょう	***kyoo***	1 syllable
ぴゅ・う・ぴゅ・う	***pyu·u·pyu·u***	4 beats		きょ・う	***kyo·o***	2 beats
おおきい	***oo|kii***	2 syllables		えいご	***ei|go***	2 syllables
お・お・き・い	***o·o·ki·i***	4 beats		え・い・ご	***e·i·go***	3 beats
えぇ	***ee***	1 syllable				
え・え	***e·e***	2 beats				

Syllable-final consonants in hiragana

As you've already learned, a Japanese long syllable can end with a long vowel or with either one of two consonants. One of these syllable-final consonants is always written as ***n*** in romanization and as ん in hiragana.

にほん	*Nihon*	Japan
どんな	*donna*	what kind
せんせい	*sensei*	teacher
たんぼ	*tanbo*	rice paddy

Since ん represents the second half of a long syllable, these words divide into syllables and beats as follows.

にほん	***ni | hon***	2 syllables		どんな	***don |na***	2 syllables
に・ほ・ん	***ni·ho·n***	3 beats		ど・ん・な	***do·n·na***	3 beats
せんせい	***sen | sei***	2 syllables		たんぼ	***tan | bo***	2 syllables
せ・ん・せ・い	***se·n·se·i***	4 beats		た・ん・ぼ	***ta·n·bo***	3 beats

The other syllable-final consonant is romanized in a variety of ways, but it's always written in hiragana with the symbol っ, which is just the symbol つ (*tsu*) reduced in size. Just as in katakana, this *chiisai tsu* ("small tsu") doubles the beginning of whatever consonant comes right after it, as the following words below illustrate.

みっか	*mikka*	3rd of the month
やっつ	*yattsu*	8
あさって	*asatte*	day after tomorrow
ろっぴゃく	*roppyaku*	600

Since っ represents the second half of a long syllable, the words above divide into syllables and beats as follows.

みっ|か	**mik | ka**	2 syllables	あ|さっ|て	**a | sat | te**	3 syllables
み・っ・か	**mi・k・ka**	3 beats	あ・さ・っ・て	**a・sa・t・te**	4 beats
やっ|つ	**yat | tsu**	2 syllables	ろっ|ぴゃ|く	**rop | pya | ku**	3 syllables
や・っ・つ	**ya・t・tsu**	3 beats	ろ・っ・ぴゃ・く	**ro・p・pya・ku**	4 beats

Irregular hiragana spellings

The topic particle *wa* (see Chapter 1) is written は (not わ). Except in this one word, the symbol は represents the sound *ha*. The greetings *konnichi wa* ("good afternoon") and *konban wa* ("good evening") contain the topic particle, so they're written in hiragana with は (こんにちは and こんばんは).

The direct object particle *o* (see Chapter 2) is written を (not お). This is the only word in the entire Japanese language in which the symbol を is used.

The direction particle *e* (see Chapter 2) is written へ (not え). Except in this one word, the symbol へ represents the sound ***he***.

4.6 Mechanics

Preparing an Oral Presentation

Writing even a simple proposal can be a real challenge. Virtually all institutions, agencies, foundations and businesses require a proposal to contain the same generic elements, whether it is a multimillion dollar proposal to the National Science Foundation or a small proposal to a school. In this unit, you are going to write a proposal for a Japanese culture week. Let us briefly explore the standard elements.

1. The Introduction (はじめ) (*hajime*)

    Every proposal begins with an introduction, which sets the stage for the remainder of the document. In this part you present the context of main problem that you intend to solve. For example 〜にち にパーティをします。〜でパーティをします。

2. A Need or Problem (もんだい) (*mondai*)

    The next basic element is a statement of the need being addressed or problem being solved. In this part you will use the expression がひつようです。(*ga hitsuyoo desu.*) "It is necessary that ..."

3. Goals and Objectives (もくてき) (*mokuteki*)

    List your goals next. This is a list of the exact objectives that you intend to accomplish. In this part of the proposal you will use the expression もくてきは〜のためです。(*Mokuteki wa.... no tame desu.*) The goal is for sake of ..."

4. Procedures Activities or Work Plans (けいかく) (*keikaku*)

    In this section of the proposal you will use the expression 〜をします。(*o shimasu.*) "We will do ..."

5. Evaluation (ひょうか) (*hyooka*)

    The fifth basic element of a proposal is usually a description of the evaluation model that you will employ. You will use the peer assessment and self-assessment models described later in this chapter.

6. Budget (よさん) (*yosan*)

    Next is the budget. This section provide a general expenditure plan followed by specific details on how the costs were determined. In this stage you will use the expression 〜は〜ドルです。(*--wa -- doru desu.*) "-- is $ --"

Practice composing the various elements of a proposal based on the examples below, substituting the times, places and items listed in the charts.

1. The Introduction: （はじめ） *(hajime)*

例文 **(Sample Expression)**

21にちに パーティーをします。(date and activity)
きょうしつでパーティーをします。(place and activity)
ピザとコーラがひつようです。(necessary items)

21にち	22にち	23にち	24か	25にち	26にち	27にち
きょうしつ	ジム	グランド	こうどう	カフェテリア	きょうしつ	こうどう
パーティー	バレーボール	フットボール	コンサート	ダンス	クラブミーティング	えいが
ピザ	フライドチキン	ハンバーグ	ミートローフ	スパゲティ	ホットドッグ	すし
コーラ	ミルク	オレンジジュース	コーヒー	パンチ	みず	おちゃ

ノート14 (Note 14):

The particle で (de) is a locative marker, indicating where an action takes place. For example, *Gakkoo de benkyoo shimasu.* がっこうでべんきょうします。I'll study at school.

2. A Need or Problem（もんだい）*(mondai)*

例文 **(Sample Expression)**

21にちにきょうしつで パーティーをします。
(date, place and activity)
いすとつくえがひつようです。 *(necessary items)*

21にち	２２にち	２３にち	24か	25にち	26にち	28にち
きょうしつ	ジム	グランド	こうどう	カフェテリア	きょうしつ	こうどう
パーティー	バレーボール	フットボール	コンサート	ダンス	クラブミーティング	えいが
いす	ボール	ボール	マイク	スピーカー	こくばん	スクリーン
つくえ	ネット	ヘルメット	ライト	CDプレーヤー	チョーク	ビデオプレーヤー

3. Goals and Objectives（もくてき）*(mokuteki)*

例文 **(Sample Expression)**

21にちにきょうしつで パーティーをします。
(date, place and activity)
もくてきはともだちのためです。 *(objective)*

21にち	２２にち	２３にち	24か	25にち	26にち	28にち
きょうしつ	ジム	グランド	こうどう	カフェテリア	きょうしつ	こうどう
パーティー	バレーボール	フットボール	コンサート	ダンス	クラブミーティング	えいが
ともだち	からだ	しあい	おんがくのれんしゅう	ダンスのれんしゅう	ボランティア	フェスティバル

4. Procedures, Activities, or Work Plans （けいかく）*(keikaku)*

例文 **(Sample Expression)**

パーティーのけいかくは：
ダンスをします。
ピザをたべます。
コーラをのみます。

パーティー	バレーボール	フットボール	コンサート	ダンス	クラブミーティング	フェスティバル
ダンス	バレーボール	フットボール	コンサート	ダンス	クラブミーティング	えいが
ピザをたべます	しあいをします	ボールをあらいます	ステージをつくります	れんしゅうをします	けいかくをたてます	おんがくをききます
コーラをのみます	ネットをたてます	ラインをかきます	ライトをつくります	はっぴょうします	ボランティアをします	ダンスをします

5. Budget （よさん）*(yosan)*

例文 **(Sample Expression)**

パーティーのよさんは50ドルです。ピザは28ドルです。
コーラは15ドルです。コップは2ドルです。さらは５ドルです。

パーティー	よさん $50	ピザ $28	コーラ $15	コップ $2	さら $5	きょうしつ $0
コンサート	よさん $200	おんがく $75	ライト $30	マイク $55	チケット $15	コピー $25
フェスティバル	よさん $1000	コピー $225	コンサート $275	ダンス $390	ボランティア $0	でんわ $110

6 Practice simple mathematics using the Japanese format.

例文 **(Sample Expression)**

1	+	3	=	4
（いち）	（たす）	（さん）	（は）	（よん）
(ichi)	(tasu)	(san)	(wa)	(yon)

例文 **(Sample Expression)**

3	−	1	=	2
（さん）	（ひく）	（いち）	（は）	（に）
(san)	(hiku)	(ichi)	(wa)	(ni)

1.	1+2=3	2.	5+4=9	3.	3+4=7
4.	2+4=6	5.	3+1=4	6.	6+2=8
7.	9+3=12	8.	8+7=15	9.	9+8=17
10.	18+7=25	11.	9+19=28	12.	23+15=38

1.	2-1= 1	2.	5-2=3	3.	13-4=11
4.	22-5=17	5.	23-1=22	6.	76-22=54
7.	89-23=66	8.	100-7=93	9.	109-8=101
10.	256-7=243	11.	539-19=520	12.	237-115=122

7. Practice simple mathematics for your budget plan using the Japanese format.

例文 **(Sample Expression)**

ピザの２８ドルたす、コーラの１５ドルたす、コップの２ドルたす、さらの５ドルは５０ドルです。だから、パーティーのよさんは５０ドルです。

パーティー	よさん？	ピザ $２８	コーラ $１５	コップ $２	さら $５	きょうしつ $０
コンサート	よさん？	おんがく $７５	ライト $３０	マイク $５５	チケット $１５	コピー $２５
フェスティバル	よさん？	コピー $２２５	コンサート $２７５	ダンス $３９０	ボランティア $０	でんわ $１１０
サイエンスフェアー	よさん？	ピザ $３８	コーラ $２５	コップ $４	さら $９	きょうしつ $０

8. In order to write you proposal in Japanese, you will need to use a Japanese word processor. One way to get Japanese word-processing capability is to add Japanese Language kit™ to your computer. Your teacher can tell you how to install it. However, you also need to learn how to do Japanese typing with your English keyboard. Practice hiragana using the following chart.

あ a	い i	う u	え e	お o
か ka	き ki	く ku	け ke	こ ko
さ sa	し shi	す su	せ se	そ so
		su		
た ta	ち chi	つ tsu	て te	と to
	ti	tu		
な na	に ni	ぬ nu	ね ne	の no
は ha	ひ hi	ふ fu	へ he	ほ ho
	hi			
ま ma	み mi	む mu	め me	も mo
や ya		ゆ yu		よ yo
ら ra	り ri	る ru	れ re	ろ ro
	li	lu	le	lo
わ wa	ゐ wi	う wu	ゑ we	を wo
ん nn	xn	mn		

が ga	ぎ gi	ぐ gu	げ ge	ご go
ざ za	じ zi	ず zu	ぜ ze	ぞ zo
	ji			
だ da	ぢ di	づ du	で de	ど do
ば ba	び bi	ぶ bu	べ be	ぼ bo
ぱ pa	ぴ pi	ぷ pu	ぺ pe	ぽ po

きゃ kya	きゅ kyu	きょ kyo
しゃ sha	しゅ shu	しょ sho
ちゃ cha	ちゅ chu	ちょ cho
cya	cyu	cyo
tya	tyu	tyo
にゃ nya	にゅ nyu	にょ nyo
ひゃ hya	ひゅ hyu	ひょ hyo
みゃ mya	みゅ myu	みょ myo
りゃ rya	りゅ ryu	りょ ryo
lya	lyu	lyo

ぎゃ gya	ぎゅ gyu	ぎょ gyo
じゃ ja	じゅ ju	じょ jo
jya	jyu	jyo
zya	zju	zyo
ぢゃ dha	ぢゅ dhu	ぢょ dho
びゃ bya	びゅ byu	びょ byo
ぴゃ pya	ぴゅ pyu	ぴょ pyo

ぁ xa	ぃ xi	ぅ xu	ぇ xe	ぉ xo
うぁ wha	うぃ whi			うぇうぉ who
	いぇ yhe			
くぁ qa	くぃ qi	くぇ qu		くうくぉ qe qo
ぐゎ gwa	ぐぃ gwi	ぐぅ gwu	ぐぇ gwe	ぐぉ gwo
っ xtu				
つぁ tsa	つぃ tsi			つぇつぉ tse tso
ぢゃ dya	ぢぃ dyi	ぢゅ dyu	ぢぇ dye	ぢょ dyo
ゔぁ va	ゔぃ vi	ゔ vu	ゔぇ ve	ゔぉ vo
ぢゃ dya	ぢぃ dyi	ぢゅ dyu	ぢぇ dye	ぢょ dyo
わ xwa	ぃ xwi	う xwu	ぇ xwe	お xwo

9. Now, try to change to katakana and kanji using the space bar and return key. Type what appears below.

1. ボストン   2. ワシントン   3. シアトル   4. シカゴ   5. サンフランシスコ
6. ハワイ   7. オレゴン   8. イリノイ   9. テキサス   10. コロラド
11. ニューヨーク 12. ウィスコンシン   13. カルフォルニア   14. ヴァージニア
15. 一月一日   16. 三月三日   17. 五月五日   18. 九月九日   19. 月火水木金土日

10. *It is time to start typing your proposal in Japanese using the sample below.*

例文 (Sample Expression)

プロポーザル

パーティー

四月十五日
ジョン　スミス

21にちに パーティーをします。きょうしつでパーティーをします。

ピザとコーラがひつようです。

もくてきはともだちのためです。

パーティーのけいかくは：
ダンスをします。
ピザをたべます。
コーラをのみます。

パーティーのよさんは50ドルです。ピザは28ドルです。コーラは
15ドルです。コップは2ドルです。さらは5ドルです。

Pronunciation | *Vowel quality*

You already know that the difference between long and short vowels is very important in Japanese. Here we're going to consider **vowel quality** rather than vowel length. If two people who speak the same language pronounce the same vowel, the two versions will probably be different in several respects. One person's vowel might be longer than the other person's, or it might be louder, or it might be on a higher pitch. Also, every individual has a distinctive voice quality, which is why you can recognize a familiar person's voice. Vowel quality is what's left when you ignore all these other differences. In other words, vowel quality is what makes a Japanese *a* sound an "*a*" as opposed to some other vowel.

The vowel system of standard Tokyo Japanese is pretty simple, with only five different qualities: *a, i, u, e, o*. There aren't any noticeable quality differences between Japanese long and short vowels; a long vowel really is just like a short vowel except for the difference in duration, as the double-letter romanization suggests. Now let's describe the five Japanese vowel qualities by comparing them to English vowels. For these comparisons to work, you have to think in terms of a dialect of English that you might call standard United States English.

Japanese *a* has a quality like the *a* in English "father," and Japanese *i* has a quality like the "ee" in English "see." Native English speakers usually don't have much trouble with these two Japanese vowel qualities.

Japanese *u* is harder. The closest English sound is probably the "*oo*" in "too", but the English lip action isn't right for Japanese. In standard United States English, the "*oo*" sound is made with the lips rounded and protruding forward a little. The Japanese *u* doesn't have this kind of rounding and protrusion. In very careful pronunciation, the upper and lower lips do get pressed together on both sides, but they stay apart in the middle. In less careful pronunciation, there's often no discernible lip action at all in the Japanese *u*. You should ask a native speaker of Japanese to pronounce *u* for you a few times so that you can pay careful attention to the lip position.

Native English speakers often pronounce the Japanese *e* like the "*a*" in the English "mace," but this isn't a very good approximation. The reason is that this English vowel is a **diphthong**, which means that it starts out as one quality and ends up as a different quality rather than maintaining a steady quality all the way through. If you listen carefully to this vowel in standard United States English, you'll notice that it begins almost like the "*e*" in "mess" but ends almost like the "*ee*" in "see." The Japanese *e* has a steady quality that's like the beginning of this English diphthong.

Native English speakers often pronounce the Japanese *o* like the "*o*" in English "tone," but this English vowel is another diphthong. In standard United States English, it starts out like the Japanese *o* but ends almost like the *oo* in the English "too." The Japanese *o* has a steady quality that's like the beginning of this English diphthong.

4.7 Mechanics

Listening Exercises

1. Listen to the following dialogues and circle the correct answers.

1. The person does something (every day, always, sometimes, often, not much, not at all).

2. The person does something (every day, always, sometimes, often, not much, not at all).

3. The person does something (every day, always, sometimes, often, not much, not at all).

4. The person does something (every day, always, sometimes, often, not much, not at all).

5. The person does something (every day, always, sometimes, often, not much, not at all).

2. Listen to your teacher or tape while looking at the following schedule.

じに　あさごはんを　たべます。
じに　がっこうに　いきます。
じに　にほんごを　べんきょうします。
じに　ほんを　よみます。
じに　うちに　かえります。
じに　しゅくだいを　します。
じに　テレビを　みます。
じに　ねます。

Answer the following questions.

1. なんじに　あさごはんを　たべますか。
2. なんじに　がっこうに　いきますか。
3. なんじに　にほんごを　べんきょうしますか。
4. なんじに　ほんを　よみますか。

3. Listening and identifying categories

Listen to the tape and choose the appropriate day and activity for each dialogue.
Write the day of the week and the activity in the blanks.

一日	二日	三日	四日	五日	六日	七日
月 (げつ)	火 (か)	水 (すい)	木 (もく)	金 (きん)	土 (ど)	日 (にち)
	パーティー	えいが			ダンス	

4. Listening and identifying categories using a flow chart.

Listen to the tape and choose the appropriate pattern for each dialogue.

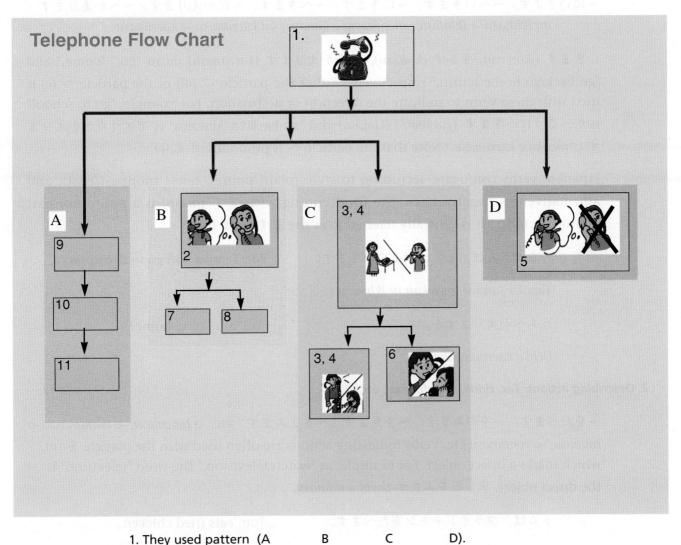

1. They used pattern (A   B   C   D).
2. They used pattern (A   B   C   D).
3. They used pattern (A   B   C   D).
4. They used pattern (A   B   C   D).

FORM

1. Describing motions: Go, come, and return

〜にいきます／〜へいきます、〜にきます／〜へきます、〜にかえります／〜へかえります
-ni ikimasu/-e ikimasu, -ni kimasu/-e kimasu, -ni kaerimasu/-e kaerimasu

いきます (*ikimasu*)、きます (*kimasu*)、and かえります (*kaerimasu*) mean "go," "come," and "go back/go home/return," respectively. Either the particle に (*ni*) or the particle へ (*e*) is used with these verbs to indicate the direction or destination. For example, "go to school" is がっこうにいきます (*gakkoo ni ikimasu*) and "go back to America" is アメリカへかえります (*Amerika e kaerimasu.*) Note that the particle へ is pronounced え (*e*).

Japanese verbs conjugate according to style (plain/polite), tense (nonpast/past), and affirmativeness/negativeness. The form ending with ます (*masu*) is a polite nonpast affirmative form. It is generally referred to as the ます *masu* form.

たなかさんは、としょかんにいきます。	Mr. Tanaka will go to the library.
Tanaka san wa toshokan ni ikimasu.	
うちへかえりますか。	Are you going home?
Uchi e kaerimasu ka?	

2. Describing actions: Eat, drink, watch, read, etc.

〜をたべます、〜をのみます、〜を見ます、〜をよみます　etc. *-o tabemasu, -o nomimasu, -o mimasu, -o yomimasu* etc. Verbs indicating actions are often used with the particle を (*o*), which marks a direct object. For example, in "watch television," the word "television" is the direct object: テレビをみます *terebi o mimasu.*

トムは、フライドチキンをたべます。	Tom eats fried chicken.
Tomu wa furaido chikin o tabemasu.	
あさごはんをたべてください。	Please eat breakfast.
Asagohan o tabete kudasai.	

3. Negatives

〜へいきません、〜をたべません、〜をしません　etc.

-e ikimasen, -o tabemasen, -o shimasen etc.

The negative of 〜ます (*-masu*) is formed by replacing ます (*masu*) with ません (*masen*).

リサは、ダンスへいきません。	Lisa will not go to the dance.
Risa wa dansu e ikimasen.	
ジョンは、ゴルフをしません。	John does not play golf.
Jon wa gorufu o shimasen.	
かんじをよみますか。	Do you read kanji?
Kanji o yomimasu ka?	
いいえ、よみません。	No, I don't (read)
Iie, yomimasen.	

4. Indicating time of action with に (ni)

8じに (at 8 o'clock)	どようびに (on Saturday)	5がつに (in May)
hachiji ni	*doyoobi ni*	*gogatsu ni*

You learned earlier that the particle に (*ni*) is used to indicate the direction of movement. It is also used to indicate the time of action. に (*ni*) marks absolute time expressions such as "6 o'clock," "Wednesday," and "July," but it is not used with relative time expressions like "yesterday," "this week," and "next year."

6じにゆうごはんをたべます。	I eat supper at 6 o'clock.
Rokuji ni yuugohan o tabemasu.	
すいようびにパーティーをします。	We will have a party on Wednesday.
Suiyoobi ni paatii o shimasu.	
8がつに、にほんへいきます。	I will go to Japan in August.
Hachigatsu ni Nihon e ikimasu.	
なんじにねますか。	What time do you go to bed?
Nanji ni nemasu ka?	

FORM (continued)

5. Indicating the existence of something/somebody

〜が あります(〜=inanimate objects) and 〜が います(〜=animate being)

The verb あります is used to express the existence of any inanimate objects ranging from things concrete such as a "clock" and an "umbrella" to things abstract such as "ideas" and "plans." います on the other hand, is used to express the existence of animate beings, such as people and animals. Both あります and います are marked by the particle が.

せんせいが います。	*Sensei ga imasu.*	There is a teacher.
つくえが あります。	*Tsukue ga arimasu.*	There is a desk.

います and あります may also express the following depending on the context.
A. Possession and ownership (I have-)

あおいくるまが あります。	There is a blue car.
aoi kuruma ga arimasu.	or I have/own a blue car.

B. Occurrence (take place, happen)

サッカーのしあいがあります。	There is a soccer game.
sakkaa no shiai ga arimasu.	or A soccer game will take place.

6. Counting people and things

When counting people にん is placed after each number. However, as you already know, the first two ,ひとり (one person) and ふたり (two people), are irregular. For counting things, the Japanese counting system (ひとつ、ふたつ、みっつ、よっつ、いつつ・・・) may be used. This system goes up to 10.

カウンセラーがごにんいます。	There are five counselors.
kaunseraa ga gonin imasu.	
おとうとがひとりいます。	I have one younger brother.
otooto ga hitori imasu.	
いすがよっつあります。	There are four chairs.
isu ga yottsu arimasu.	
しゅくだいがふたつあります。	I have two homework assignments.
shukudai ga futatsu arimasu.	

7. Basic particles I

は   Establishing the topic (Chapter 1)
> *Paatii wa sushi ga ii desu.*
> party Topic sushi Subject good Predicate
> パーティーはすしがいいです。
> [Literally, As for the party, sushi is good.]
> It would be good to have sushi at the party.

の   Linking two nouns to establish relationships (C1)
> • expressing the hyphenated part of telephone numbers and addresses
> > *Denwa bangoo wa san san nii no yon goo roku nana desu.*
> > でんわばんごうは３３２の４５６７です。
> > The telephone number is 332-4567.
>
> • descriptive
> > *Haru no supootsu wa tenisu desu.*
> > はるのスポーツはテニスです。
> > My spring sport is tennis.
>
> • possessive
> > *Tanaka san no hon desu.*
> > たなかさんのほんです。
> > It is Mr./Ms. Tanaka's book.

を   Marking the direct object (C2)
> • situation 1   x *o kudasai*   (requesting something)
> > *Miruku o kudasai.*
> > ミルクをください
> > Can I have some milk?
>
> • situation 2   doing x   (performing actions)
> > *Merii ga terebi o mimasu.*
> > メリーがテレビを見ます
> > Mary watches TV.

と   Listing things (C2)
> > *Higashisan to Nishisan to ikimasu.*
> > ひがしさんとにしさんと行きます。
> > I'm going with Mr./Ms. Higashi and Mr./Ms. Nishi.
>
> • Indicating a person with whom you do something (C3)
> > *Higashisan to ikimasu.*
> > ひがしさんと行きます。
> > I'm going with Mr./Ms. Higashi.

FORM (continued)

が   Marking the subject
- Expressing preference (C2)
  Sushi ga ii desu.
  すしがいいです。
  I prefer sushi.
- Marking a question word (C2)
  Dare ga terebi o mimasu ka?
  だれがテレビを見ますか。
  Who watches TV?
- Indicating existence of:

something/someone
    Tanaka san ga imasu.
    たなかさんがいます。
    There is Mr./Ms. Tanaka.

ownership
    Terebi ga arimasu.
    テレビがあります。
    I have a TV.

availability
    Arubaito ga arimasu.
    アルバイトがあります。
    There is a part-time job.

events and happenings
    Paatii ga arimasu.
    パーティーがあります。
    There is a party.

も   Establishing the topic to indicate "also" or "too" (C2)
    Nishi san mo kimasu.
    にしさんもいきます。
    Mr./Ms. Nishi will also go.

や   Listing representative items (C3)
    Higashisan ya Nishisan to ikimasu.
    ひがしさんやにしさんと行きます。
    I'm going with Mr./Ms. Higashi and Mr./Ms. Nishi among others.

に   Indicating direction and destination (C3)
    Gakkoo ni ikimasu.
    学校に行きます。
    I'm going to school.

Indicating a point in time (C4)
    Hachiji ni ikimasu.
    八時に行きます。
    I'll go at eight o'clock.

で   Indicating means of transportation (C3)
Basu de ikimasu.
バスで行きます。
I'll go to school by bus.

・Indicating a place of action (C4)
Gakkoo de benkyoo shimasu.
学校で勉強します。
I'll study at school.

へ   Indicating direction and destination (C4)
Gakkoo e ikimasu.
学校へ行きます。
I'm going to school.

から Marking the starting point of a duration of time (C4)
Ashita kara natsuyasumi desu.
あしたからなつやすみです。
Summer vacation starts tomorrow.

まで Marking the ending point of a duration of time (C4)
Ashita made natsuyasumi desu.
あしたまでなつやすみです。
It'll be summer vacation until tomorrow.

か   Marking the end of a question (C1)
Denwa bangoo wa san san nii no yon goo roku nana desu ka?
でんわばんごうは３３２の４５６７ですか？
Is the telephone number 332-4567?

ね   Marking the end of a sentence for agreement (C1)
Un, soo da ne.
うん、そうだね。
Yes, that's right、isn't it.

よ   Marking the end of a sentence for persuasion (C1)
Un, soo da yo.
うん、そうだよ。
Yes, that's right.

4.8 Application

1. *Role Play : Telephone Conversation*

A group of six students forms a team. Each team is divided into three different roles. Role A students will be American students. Role B students will be Japanese students. Role C students will be Japanese family members. Each member receives a role card, with complete information on the characters he or she will play and incomplete information on the other characters' roles. Role A students must call the Japanese family. Role C students pick up or do not pick up the phone, according to the information on their card. Role B students answer the phone and answer Role A students' questions to complete the information needed. Role C students ask their siblings what was said on the telephone and report to their parents.

Card A

Your name is Nancy Smith. A party will be held Thursday night, October 7th. Party activities to be chosen by the Japanese student are: dancing, karaoke, and card games. Party drinks and food to be chosen are: cola, milk, and orange juice and pizza, spaghetti or sushi. After calling the Japanese students, you will report back to your club regarding the decisions made.

Card B

Your name is Akio Noda. You will be asked to choose one of the following activities for a party: dancing, karaoke, or card games. You will also be asked to choose among cola, milk and orange juice for drinks and among pizza, spaghetti and sushi for food.

Card B

You are a member of the Noda family who picks up the telephone. After your brother gets off the phone, you ask him questions about the party. Later you tell your parents about it.

2. How are we spending our time?

In this exercise you will examine how much time you spend doing certain things each day. You will also conduct a survey to find out how your classmates are spending their time, and compare the findings with your own time distribution as well as other American and Japanese teenagers' time distribution.

A. Preparation
You will receive a sheet like the one below. Fill in the blanks.

Allocation of My Time

テレビのじかん	じから	じまで
べんきょうのじかん	じから	じまで
スポーツのじかん	じから	じまで
レジャーのじかん	げつようびからきんようびまでの	
	じから	じまで
	どようびの	
	じから	じまで
	にちようびの	
	じから	じまで

アメリカと日本のティーンエージャーのサーベー

	アメリカ	日 本
テレビのじかん	5じから9じまで	8じから9じまで
べんきょうのじかん	10じから11じまで	5じから8じまで
		10じから12じまで
スポーツのじかん	3じから5じまで	3じから5じまで
レジャーのじかん	どようびの	にちようびの
	1じから6じまで	1じから5じまで
	にちようびの	
	1じから6じまで	

B. Survey

Go around the classroom and ask your classmates the questions you studied in the Mechanics section. Using the survey sheet form, record their answers in the columns below their names.

Survey Sheet Form

しつもん	じぶん	なまえ		アメリカの せいと	日本の せいと
テレビの じかん	から まで	から まで	から まで	から まで	から まで
べんきょう のじかん	から まで	から まで	から まで	から まで	から まで
スポーツ のじかん	から まで	から まで	から まで	から まで	から まで
レジャー のじかん	から まで	から まで	から まで	から まで	から まで

C. Results

Report the results of your survey. Compare your results with the results of the American and Japanese students' surveys on the previous page and share your findings with the rest of the class.

Kanji

The first ten kanji introduced in this lesson are used to write words or parts of words that refer to times or time periods. For these and for the other five kanji below, the commonly used On and Kun readings are listed, although not all of them occur in words that you've learned so far. The readings are followed by examples of words that each kanji is used to write.

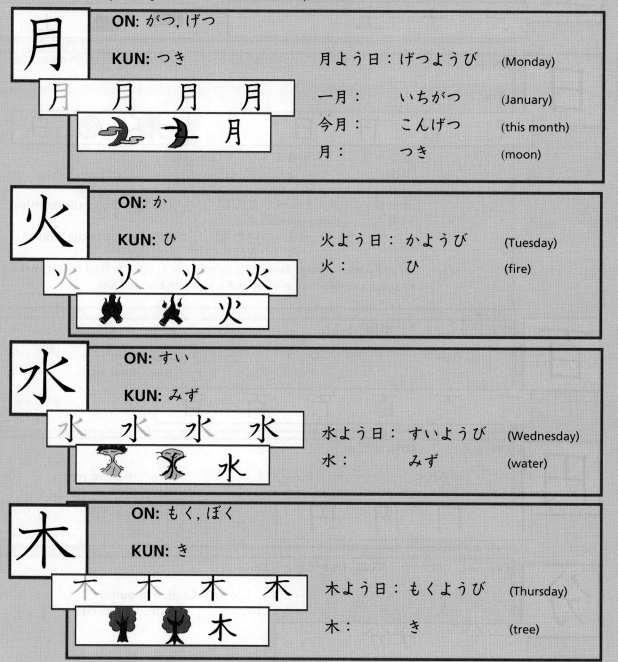

ON: がつ, げつ

KUN: つき

月よう日：げつようび		(Monday)
一月：	いちがつ	(January)
今月：	こんげつ	(this month)
月：	つき	(moon)

ON: か

KUN: ひ

火よう日：	かようび	(Tuesday)
火：	ひ	(fire)

ON: すい

KUN: みず

水よう日：	すいようび	(Wednesday)
水：	みず	(water)

ON: もく, ぼく

KUN: き

木よう日：もくようび		(Thursday)
木：	き	(tree)

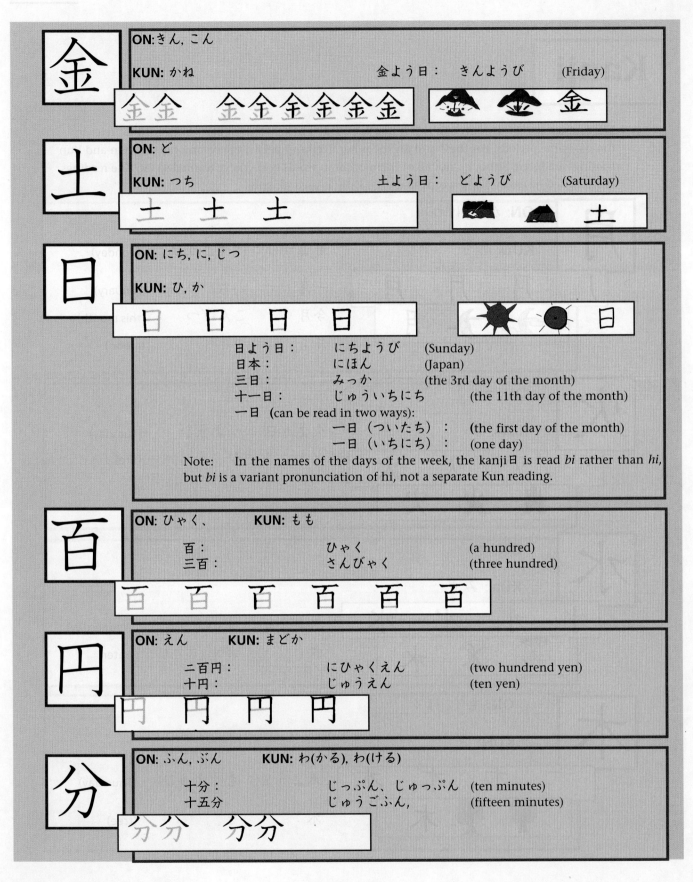

金

ON: きん, こん

KUN: かね

金よう日: きんようび (Friday)

金金　金金金金金金

土

ON: ど

KUN: つち

土よう日: どようび (Saturday)

土　土　土

日

ON: にち, に, じつ

KUN: ひ, か

日　日　日　日

日よう日:	にちようび	(Sunday)
日本:	にほん	(Japan)
三日:	みっか	(the 3rd day of the month)
十一日:	じゅういちにち	(the 11th day of the month)
一日 (can be read in two ways):		
	一日 (ついたち):	(the first day of the month)
	一日 (いちにち):	(one day)

Note:　In the names of the days of the week, the kanji 日 is read *bi* rather than *hi*, but *bi* is a variant pronunciation of hi, not a separate Kun reading.

百

ON: ひゃく、　　KUN: もも

百:	ひゃく	(a hundred)
三百:	さんびゃく	(three hundred)

百　百　百　百　百　百

円

ON: えん　　KUN: まどか

二百円:	にひゃくえん	(two hundrend yen)
十円:	じゅうえん	(ten yen)

円　円　円　円

分

ON: ふん, ぶん　　KUN: わ(かる), わ(ける)

十分:	じっぷん、じゅっぷん	(ten minutes)
十五分	じゅうごふん、	(fifteen minutes)

分分　分分

年

ON: ねん　　　**KUN**: とし

学年：　がくねん　　　　（grade）

| 年 | 年 | 年 | 年 | 年 | 年 |

本

ON: ほん　　　**KUN**: もと

本：　　ほん　　　　　（book）

| 本 | 本 | 本 | 本 | 本 |

学

ON: がく　　　**KUN**: まな(ぶ)

学生：　がくせい　　　（student）

| 学学学学学 | 学学学 |

先

ON:せん　　　**KUN**: さき

先生：　せんせい　　　（teacher）

| 先 | 先 | 先 | 先 | 先 | 先 |

生

ON:せい　　　**KUN**: う(む), う(まれる), い(きる)

先生：　せんせい　　　（teacher）

| 生 | 生 | 生 | 生 | 生 |

千

ON: せん　　　**KUN**: ち

千：　　せん　　　　　（a thousand）

| 千 | 千 | 千 |

万

ON:まん、ばん　　　**KUN**:よろず

一万：　いちまん　　　（ten thousand）

| 万 | 万 | 万 |

4.9 Application
Preparing to write a simple proposal

1. Each of the numbered Japanese sentences below expresses one aspect of a proposal. Match the sentences with the letters on the left naming the elements required in a simple proposal.

(A) はじめ　（　　）	(1)　ベークセールのけいかくは：
(B) もんだい（　　）	(2)　ベークセールのもくてきはエイズウォークのためです。
(C) もくてき（　　）	(3)　１０日にカフェテリア でベークセールをします。
(D) けいかく（　　）	(4)　ベークセールのよさんは５０ドルです。
(E) ひょうか（　　）	(5)　いすとテーブルとよさんがひつようです。
(F) よさん　（　　）	

2. As before, match the sentences with the letters representing the parts of a proposal. This time, state the reason for the matches you make.

order reason

1. だから、いすとテーブルと予算が必要です。 ( ) ( )

2. ベークセールの計画は：
・ケーキを作ります。　・話します。
・ケーキを売ります。　・お金を集めます。 ( ) ( )

3. ベークセールの予算は２５ドルです。ケーキのお金は
１０ドルです。飲み物は５ドルです。コップは2ドル
です。さらは３ドルです。 ( ) ( )

4. ベークセールの目的はエイズウォークのためです。
２２日にニューヨークに行きます。 ( ) ( )

5. １０日にカフェテリアでベークセールをします。 ( ) ( )

(A) もくてき　(B) けいかく　(C) はじめ　(D) もんだい　(E) よさん　(F) ひょうか

A. Simple Proposal

(Date, Place, and Activity)	１０日にカフェテリアでベークセールをします。
(Necessary Items)	だから、いすとテーブルと予算が必要です。
(Objective)	ベークセールの目的はエイズウォークのためです。２２日にニューヨークに行きます。
(Work Plan)	ベークセールの計画は： ・ケーキを作ります。　・話します。 ・ケーキを売ります。　・お金を集めます。
(Total Budget)	ベークセールの予算は２５ドルです。ケーキのお金は１０ドルです。飲み物は５ドルです。コップは２ドルです。さらは３ドルです。

A. Introduction (はじめ)

B. Need or Problem (もんだい)

C. Goals and Objectives

D. Procedures, Activities, or Work Plans (けいかく)

E. Budget (よさん)

3. **Read the following four proposals and fill in the blanks at the end with the letter of the proposal that corresponds to the description of the person making it.**

A

１０日に英語の教室ではるのタレントショーのオーディションをします。だから、マイクとスピーカーといすとテーブルと予算が必要です。オーディションの目的は春のタレントショーのためです。

２２日に講堂で春のタレントショーをします。

オーディションの計画は：

　　　楽器をひきます。

　　　ダンスをします。

　　　音楽を聞きます。

　　　ダンスを見ます。

オーディションの予算は２０ドルです。飲み物のお金は１０ドルです。プログラムのコピーは１０ドルです。

B

５日にカフェテリアでアートショーをします。だから、いすとテーブルと予算が必要です。アートショーの目的はユニセフのボランティアのためです。

２０日にアジアに行きます。

アートショーの計画は：

　　　アートをみせます。

　　　アートを売ります。

　　　おかねを集めます。

アートショーの予算は４５ドルです。プログラムのお金は２５ドルです。ピンは５ドルです。テープは５ドルです。

C.

5日に体育館で秋のサイエンス・コンテストをします。だからマイクとスピーカーといすとテーブルと電気と予算が必要です。サイエンス・コンテストの目的はナショナル・サイエンスフェアーのためです。２２日にナショナル・サイエンス・フェアーがあります。サイエンス・コンテストの計画は：

コンテストをします。

優勝者を決めます。

コンテストを見ます。

サイエンス・コンテストの予算は２５ドルです。ポスターのお金は１５ドルです。プログラムのコピーは１０ドルです。

D.

5日にカフェテリア でダンスパーティーをします。だからいすと予算が必要です。ダンスパーティーの目的はユニセフのボランティアのためです。７月にアフリカでボランティアをします。ダンスパーティーの計画は：

ダンスをおどります。

のみものを売ります。

おかねを集めます。

ダンスパーティーの予算は４５ドルです。DJのお金は２５ドルです。コーラは５ドルです。コップは５ドルです。ポテトチップスは５ドルです。おさらは５ドルです。

1) うたがすきなひと　　（　　）
2) ボランティアがすきなひと　（　　）
3) かがくがすきなひと　　（　　）
4) えがすきなひと　　（　　）

4 *Before attempting to write your own proposal, fill in the blanks in the one below.*

１０日にはるのスピーチ・コンテストをします。だから、
マイクとスピーカーといすとテーブルと予算（よさん）が（　　　　　　）
です。春（はる）のスピーチ・コンテストの（　　　　　　）は日本語
の勉強（べんきょう）の（　　　　　　）です。
春（はる）のスピーチ・コンテストの（　　　　　　）は、スピーチ・
コンテストをします。スピーチ・コンテストの（　　　　　　）
は２５ドルです。切符（きっぷ）のお金（かね）は１５ドルです。コピーは
１０ドルです。

5. *Now, following the format given above, write your proposal for a school activity. It can be for a party for Japanese exchange students or anything you wish. If you can, use a Japanese word processor or word-processing software to write the proposal.*

VOCABULARY

Functional Vocabulary

	Formal	Informal	English
Using the telephone	もしもし *Moshi moshi*	もしもし *Moshi moshi*	Hello (on the phone)
Confirming that the caller has reached the right number	～さんのおたくですか。 *~san no otaku desu ka.*	～さんのうち *~san no uchi*	Is this the ~residence?
Bringing up a topic	～のことですが。 *~no koto desu ga.*	～のこと。 *~no koto.*	I am calling about ~.
For the sake [benefit, good] of	～のためです。 *~no tame desu.*	～のためだ。 *~no tame da.*	It is for
Necessity	～がひつようです。 *~ga hitsuyoo desu.*	～がひつようだ。 *~ga hitsuyoo da.*	It is necessary.
Asking about existence	～がいますか？ *~ga imasu ka?*	～がいる？ *~ ga iru?*	Is (someone) there?
Correcting information	いいえ、ちがいます。 *Iie, chigaimasu.*	いや、ちがう（よ／わ）。 *Iya, chigau (yo/wa)*	That is incorrect.
Asking questions	たべますか？ *Tabemasu ka?*	たべる？ *Taberu?*	Do (you)eat(it)? Will (you) eat (it)?
	いきますか？ *Ikimasu ka?*	いく？ *Iku?*	Are you going? Do (you) go?/Will (you) go
	べんきょうしますか？ *Benkyoo shimasu ka?*	べんきょうする？ *Benkyoo suru?*	Do you study? Will (you) study?
	かえりますか？ *Kaerimasu ka?*	かえる？ *Kaeru?*	Are (you) going home? Will (you) go home?
	しますか？ *Shimasu ka?*	する？ *Suru?*	Are you going to do (it)? Will (you) do (it)?
	みますか？ *Mimasu ka?*	みる？ *Miru?*	Do you watch/see (it)? Will (you) watch/see (it)?
	よみますか？ *Yomimasu ka?*	よむ？ *Yomu?*	Do you read(it)? Will (you) read (it)?
	ねますか？ *Nemasu ka?*	ねる？ *Neru?*	Are you going to sleep?
Negation	いきません。 *Ikimasen.*	いかない。 *Ikanai.*	(I) am not going. (I) will not go.
Asking (someone) to perform an action	ちょっとまってください。 *Chotto matte kudasai.*	ちょっとまって。 *Chotto matte.*	Wait a moment (please).
Starting point and ending point in time	～から～まで *~kara-~made*	～から～まで *~kara~made*	From~ to (until)~
Asking about the place of an action	どこでしますか？ *Doko de shimasu ka?*	どこでする？ *Doko de suru?*	Where do you do it?

National Vocabulary

Time Expression

あした	*ashita*	tomorrow
あさって	*asatte*	the day after tomorrow
きょう	*kyoo*	today
あさ	*asa*	morning

Verbs

います／いる	*imasu/iru*	to exist
たべます／たべる	*tabemasu/taberu*	to eat
のみます／のむ	*nomimasu/nomu*	to drink
します／する	*shimasu/suru*	to do
よみます／よむ	*yomimasu/yomu*	to read
みます／みる	*mimasu/miru*	to see/watch
べんきょうします	*benkyoo shimasu*	to study
べんきょうする	*benkyoo suru*	to study
ねます／ねる	*nemasu/neru*	to go to sleep
いきます／いく	*ikimasu/iku*	to go
きます／くる	*kimasu/kuru*	to come
かえります／かえる	*kaerimasu/kaeru*	to go home
ちがいます／ちがう	*chigaimasu/chigau*	to be incorrect
きめます／きめる	*kimemasu/kimeru*	to decide
でんわします／する	*denwa shimasu/suru*	to telephone
ミーティングします	*miitingu shimasu*	to have a meeting
ミーティングする	*miitingu suru*	to have a meeting
（かお）をあらいます	*(kao) o araimasu*	to wash one's face
（かお）おあらう	*(kao) o arau*	to wash one's face
（は）をみがきます／	*(ha) o migakimasu*	to brush one'steeth
みがく	*(ha)o migaku*	to brush one'steeth

Meal

あさごはん	*asagohan*	breakfast
ひるごはん	*hirugohan*	lunch
ばんごはん	*bangohan*	dinner

Useful Words

テレビ	*terebi*	television
ほん	*hon*	book
うち	*uchi*	home/house
てがみ	*tegami*	letter
おんがく	*ongaku*	music
かお	*kao*	face
は	*ha*	teeth
クラブ	*kurabu*	club
クラス	*kurasu*	class
としょかん	*toshokan*	library
コンサート	*konsaato*	concert
ダンス	*dansu*	dance
クラブ・ミーティング	*kurabu miitingu*	club meeting
こうこうせい	*kookoosei*	high school student
どうぐ	*doogu*	equipment/tool
ゆうしょうしゃ	*yuushoosha*	winner/champion

Proposal Pronouns

わたし	*watashi*	I (for girls and adults)
ぼく	*boku*	I (for boys)
どなた	*donata*	who

Telephone Conversation Words

ちょっとまってください	*Chotto matte kudasai.*	Just a moment, please
どうもすみません	*Doomo sumimasen*	I am sorry/excuse me.
もしもし	*Moshi moshi*	Hello (on the phone)
おたく	*otaku*	residence
あとで	*ato de*	later

Frequency Words

ときどき	*tokidoki*	sometimes
よく	*yoku*	often
まいにち	*mainichi*	every day
あんまり	*anmari*	not so much
ぜんぜん	*zenzen*	not at all

Proposal Words

はじめ	*hajime*	introduction
もんだい	*mondai*	problem
もくてき	*mokuteki*	objective
けいかく	*keikaku*	plan
ひょうか	*hyooka*	evaluation
よさん	*yosan*	budget
〜のためです	*~ no tame desu*	for sake of --
ひつようです	*hitsuyoo desu*	it is necessary

Japanese Sports

ぶどう	*budoo*	martial art
すもう	*sumoo*	sumo
けんどう	*kendoo*	kendo
あいきどう	*aikidoo*	aikido
からて	*karate*	karate
じゅうどう	*juudoo*	judo
きゅうどう	*kyuudoo*	Japanese archery

Japanese Culture

でんとうげいじゅつ	*dentoo geijutsu*	traditional art
おはな	*ohana*	flower arrangement
いけばな	*ikebana*	flower arrangement
おちゃ	*ocha*	te ceremony
おどり	*odori*	Japanese dance
にほんりょうり	*Nihon ryoori*	Japanese cooking
ぜん	*zen*	Zen
かぶき	*kabuki*	kabuki (Japanese theater)
のう	*noo*	No (Japanese theater)
（お）しゅうじ	*(o) shuuji*	Japanese calligraphy

School Events

エイズ・ウォーク	*eizu wooku*	AIDS walk
ベーク・セール	*beeku seeru*	bake sale
ボランティア	*borantia*	volunteer
オーディション	*oodishon*	audition
ユニセフ	*yunisefu*	UNISEF
タレント・ショー	*tarento shoo*	talent show
スピーチ・コンテスト	*supiichi kontesuto*	speech contest
うた	*uta*	song
え	*e*	picture
おかね	*okane*	money
せいとかい	*seitokai*	student council
がっき	*gakki*	instrument
プログラム	*puroguramu*	program
アートショー	*aato shoo*	art show
DJ	*diijee*	disc jockey
スピーカー	*supiikaa*	speaker
マイク	*maiku*	mike
コップ	*koppu*	cup
かみざら	*kamizara*	paper plate
いす	*isu*	chair
つくえ	*tsukue*	desk
ネット	*netto*	net
ボール	*booru*	ball
ヘルメット	*herumetto*	helmet
こくばん	*kokuban*	blackboard
チョーク	*chooku*	chalk
スクリーン	*sukuriin*	screen
ともだち	*tomodachi*	friends
ビデオプレーヤー	*bideo pureeyaa*	video player
CDプレーヤー	*CD pureeyaa*	CD player
ライト	*raito*	light
しあい	*shiai*	game/match
からだ	*karada*	body
れんしゅう	*renshuu*	practice
コピー	*kopii*	copy
ステージ	*suteeji*	stage
ライン	*rain*	line
ゆうしょうしゃ	*yuushoosha*	winner

Time Expressions (Minutes)

いっぷん	*ippun*	one minute
にふん	*nifun*	two minutes
さんぷん	*sanpun*	three minutes
よんぷん	*yonpun*	four minutes
ごふん	*gofun*	five minutes
ろっぷん	*roppun*	six minutes
ななふん	*nanafun*	seven minutes
はっぷん	*happun*	eight minutes
きゅうふん	*kyuufun*	nine minutes
じっぷん／じゅっぷん	*jippun/juppun*	ten minutes
じゅういっぷん	*juuippun*	eleven minutes

Time Expressions (Minutes Past the Hour)

にじごふん	*niji gofun*	2:05
さんじじゅっぷん	*sanji juppun*	3:10
よじじゅうごふん	*yoji juugofun*	4:15
ごじにじゅっぷん	*goji nijuppun*	5:20
ろくじにじゅうごふん	*rokuji nijuugofun*	6:25
しちじさんじゅっぷん	*shichiji sanjuppun*	7:30
はちじさんじゅうごふん	*hachiji sanjuugofun*	8:35
くじよんじゅっぷん	*kuji yonjuppun*	9:40
じゅうじよんじゅうごふん	*juuji yonjuugofun*	10:45
じゅういちじごじゅっぷん	*juuichiji gojuppun*	11:50
じゅうにじごじゅうごふん	*juuniji gojuugofun*	12:55

School Events (Verbs)

あつめます／あつめる	*atsumemasu/ atsumeru*	to collect
おどります／おどる	*odorimasu/odoru*	to dance
あらいます／あらう	*araimasu/arau*	to wash
つくります／つくる	*tsukurimasu/tsukuru*	to make
たてます／たてる	*tatemasu/tateru*	to stand
かきます／かく	*kakimasu/kaku*	to write
ききます／きく	*kikimasu/kiku*	to listen to
れんしゅう（を）します／れんしゅう（を）する		
renshuu (o) shimasu/renshuu (o) suru		to practice
しあい（を）します／しあい（を）する		
shiai (o) shimasu/shiai (o) suru		to play a match
はっぴょう（を）します／はっぴゅう（を）する		
happyoo (o) shimasu/happyoo (o) suru		to present
ダンス（を）します／ダンス（を）する		
dansu (o) shimasu/dansu (o) suru		to dance

4.10 Virtual Reality

I. Warm-Up

A. Match the expressions on the left with the situations on the right.

1. もしもし。 ( )　　a. asking someone to wait

2. りかさんはいますか。 ( )　　b. asking who someone is

3. ちょっとまってください。 ( )　　c. asking what time someone is going

4. どなたですか。 ( )　　d. asking about what someone will do

5. コンサートにいきますか。 ( )　　e. asking whether someone is present

6. いきません。 ( )　　f. greeting someone on the phone

7. なんじにいきますか。 ( )　　g. asking if someone is going to a concert

8. なにをしますか。 ( )　　h. confirming the time someone is going

9. じゃ、よじからですね。 ( )　　i. making a negative statement

B. Preliminary survey for a telephone conversation

Your Japanese class is planning some special events for Japanese Culture Week. To get some assistance, you will call the Japanese families who live nearby. You will be expected to gather information from them on one of the topics below. Work with others who are assigned to the same topic as you, making a list of the various possibilities in each category. The list should be

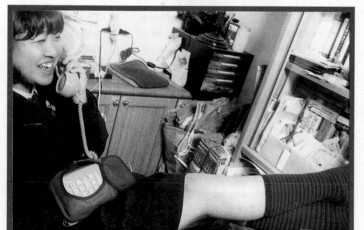

written on large paper and will be pasted up in front of the class when it is completed.

1. Telephone strategies
2. Confirming strategies
3. Meeting strategies
4. Activities and events (Japanese sports, Japanese culture, Japanese business)
5. Location of events
6. Time and date of the event

II. Main Activity: Japanese Culture Week

The following series of tasks relates to the planning of a Japanese culture week in your Japanese class or your school. These tasks involve sustained work and often take several days in and out of class. You need discipline to deal with a task of this nature. It illustrates the major concepts you learned this year. You must define the problem and construct a strategy for solving it. Use group discussion and "brainstorming," in which the problem is considered from multiple perspectives. These tasks require you to determine what data is needed, collect the data, report it, and analyze it to discuss possible sources of error. You will make connections and generalizations that will increase your understanding of important concepts and processes. You will use a variety of skills for acquiring information and for communicating your strategies and data. You and your group will evaluate your individual performance and your group performance, monitoring your progress in order to determine how you might improve your individual and group investigational and processing skills.

Follow this flow chart to plan Japanese Culture Week.

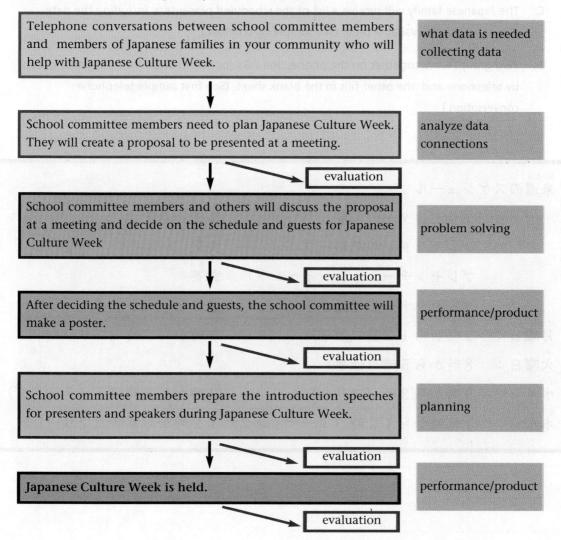

Telephone conversations between school committee members and members of Japanese families in your community who will help with Japanese Culture Week.	what data is needed collecting data
School committee members need to plan Japanese Culture Week. They will create a proposal to be presented at a meeting.	analyze data connections
evaluation	
School committee members and others will discuss the proposal at a meeting and decide on the schedule and guests for Japanese Culture Week	problem solving
evaluation	
After deciding the schedule and guests, the school committee will make a poster.	performance/product
evaluation	
School committee members prepare the introduction speeches for presenters and speakers during Japanese Culture Week.	planning
evaluation	
Japanese Culture Week is held.	performance/product
evaluation	

411

III. Main Activity: Part I

Telephone conversations between school committee members and members of Japanese families in your community who are helping with Japanese Culture Week.

A. Select three students to serve as Japanese family members. The rest of the class will play members of the Japanese Culture Week committee.

B. The committee members will decide on the presenters' schedules at three events from three categories: Japanese sports (*sumoo,* judo*, kendoo, aikidoo, karate*), Japanese culture (flower arrangement, tea ceremony, Zen, Japanese calligraphy, *Kabuki, No*), and Japanese business (car, camera, audio, game, watch). Members will make flyers, including the date, day of week and location of the representatives' appearances, as well as the telephone number of the sponsoring organizations. (See sample on next page.)

C. The Japanese family will receive a list of the scheduled presenters, including the date, day of week and available time. (See sample card below.)

D. Two groups work together on the phone: one asks for information from the other group by telephone and the other fills in the blank sheet. (See first sample telephone conversation.)

来週のスケジュール

	プレゼンターの名前	山田　春子
プレゼンターのグループ	文化
プレゼンテーション（イベント）	お茶
プレゼンターの電話番号	２２２－７８９４

月曜日：　９時から１２時（仕事）　　　　３時から５時（フリー）

火曜日：　８時から５時（仕事）

水曜日：　９時から２時（フリー）　　　　３時から８時（ミーティング）

木曜日：　１０時から１２時（ミーティング）　１２時から６時（フリー）

| スケジュールのドラフト | ちらしのサンプル |

Japanese Culture Week Events Schedule

月曜日　3:00－7:00
（レセプション）

火曜日　3:00－5:00
(スポーツ、文化、会社^{かいしゃ})
イベント：
名前：

水曜日　3:00－5:00
(スポーツ、文化、会社)
イベント：
名前：

木曜日　3:00－5:00
(スポーツ、文化、会社)
イベント：
名前：

金曜日　3:00－8:00
（ダンス）

Japanese Culture Week Schedule

月：　三時から七時まで
　　　レセプション

火：　三時から五時まで
　　　からてのデモンストレーション

水：　三時から五時まで
　　　田中^{たなか}さんのはなし（カメラ）

木：　三時から五時まで
　　　おちゃのデモンストレーション

金:　三時から五時まで
　　　ダンスパーティー

Sample Telephone Conversation Ⅰ

(John is an American high school student and a member of the committee. Kaori Kato is a member of a Japanese family who is living in the community and is helping with Japanese Culture Week. Kaori already received the information from a Japanese tea ceremony expert.)

(beginning the call)

かおり： もしもし。

(confirming that the caller has reached the right number)

ジョン： もしもし。かとうさんのおたくですか。

かおり： はい、そうです。

(getting the right person on the phone)

ジョン： かおりさんいますか。

かおり： はい。わたしです。

ジョン： あ、こんばんは。ジョンです。

かおり： あ、ジョンさん。こんばんは。

(bringing up the general topic)

ジョン： あのう、ジャパニーズカルチャーウィークのことで
すが。

かおり： はい。

(bringing up a subtopic)

ジョン： あのう、日本文化グループのことですが。

(asking someone's preference)

かおり： ああ、禅がいいですか。それとも、習字がいいでか。

(considering)

ジョン： ええと。

(asking someone's preference)

かおり： じゃ、かぶきがいいですか。能がいいですか。それ
とも、お茶がいいですか。

(indicating one's preference)

ジョン： お茶がいいです。

(indicating who the presenter will be)

かおり： プレゼンターは山田春子先生です。

(asking about the duration of the presentation)

ジョン： ああ、そうですか。お茶のプレゼンテーションは何時<ruby>何時<rt>なんじ</rt></ruby>から何時までですか。

(indicating when the presenter is free)

かおり： 山田先生は月曜日<rt>げつようび</rt>は３時<rt>じ</rt>から５時までフリーです。
水曜日<rt>すいようび</rt>は９時から２時までフリーです。
木曜日<rt>もくようび</rt>は３時から６時までフリーです。

(asking someone's preference)

かおり： どれがいいですか。

(indicating that the information gathered will be relayed at a committee meeting and that the speaker will call back later)

ジョン： ちょっとまってください。３時からミーティングをします。じゃ、あとででんわします。

かおり： ああ、そうですか。

(responding to the above)

ジョン： どうもありがとうございます。よろしくおねがいします。さようなら。

かおり： さようなら。

Sample Telephone Conversation II

(After the meeting, John calls Kaori about the presentation. (The beginning part of the telephone conversation is like the previous one.)

(bringing up a topic)

ジョン： あのう、ジャパニーズカルチャーウィークの日本文化グループのことですが。

かおり： はい。

(announcing their decision)

ジョン： お茶のプレゼンテーションは木曜日にします。

(requesting the presenter's schedule)

ジョン： 山田先生のスケジュールをおねがいします。

(indicating the presenter's schedule)

かおり： ああ、山田先生は１２時３０分に学校にいきます。

１２時半から１時までおひるごはんをたべます。

１時から３時までプリパレーションをします。

３時から５時までデモンストレーションをします。

５時から５時半までそうじをします。

６時にうちにかえります。

(confirming the schedule)

ジョン： 山田先生は１２時半に学校にきますね。

かおり： はい、いきます。

ジョン： ３時から５時までデモンストレーションをしますね。

かおり： はい、３時から５時までします。

(asking for the telephone number)

ジョン： あのう、すみません。山田先生のでんわ番号は何番ですか。

かおり： はい、２１２－３９３９です。

(The final part of the telephone conversation is like the previous one.)

IV. Main Activity: Part II

Writing a Proposal for Japanese Culture Week

Students will work in groups of five. Each group will write its own proposal using information that members of the group collected by telephone. Each group will decide on the presenters' schedules at three events from three categories: Japanese sports (*sumoo*, judo, *kendoo, aikidoo, karate*), Japanese culture (flower arrangement, tea ceremony, Zen, Japanese calligraphy, *Kabuki*, *No*), and Japanese business (car, camera, audio, game, watch). Each group will submit its proposal to all committee members and will have a meeting in order to decide the schedule and guests. Each group will make a proposal containing the folllowing elements:

A. Introduction: (はじめ) (*hajime*)

B. Need or Problem （もんだい）(*mondai*)

C. Goals and Objectives （もくてき）(*mokuteki*)

D. Procedures, Activities or Work Plans （けいかく）(*keikaku*)

E. Evaluation （ひょうか）(*hyooka*)

F. Budget （よさん）(*yosan*)

Sample Cover

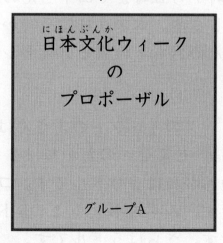

日本文化ウィーク
の
プロポーザル

グループA

Sample Proposal

１日から７日までがっこうで日本文化（にほんぶんか）ウィークをします。(*Date, Place, and Activity*)　だから、１０日にカフェテリアでベークセールをします。(*Date and Activity*)

いすとテーブルとマットとマイクとスピーカーがひつようです。(*Necessary Items*)

日本文化（にほんぶんか）ウィークのもくてきは日本文化（にほんぶんか）のべんきょうのためです。(*Objective*)

日本文化（にほんぶんか）ウィークのけいかくは：

火よう日は三時から五時までおおやま先生のからてのデモンストレーションをします。水よう日は三時から五時まで田中（たなか）さんのはなし（カメラ）をします。木よう日は三時から五時まではやしさんのおちゃのデモンストレーションをします。

日本文化（にほんぶんか）ウィークのイベントのよさんは３５０ドルです。(*Total Budget*)　せんせいのおかねは２５０ドルです。プログラムのおかねは５０ドルです。コピーのおかねは２５ドルです。みずのボトルは１５ドルです。コップは５ドルです。さらは５ドルです。

Peer Evaluation Form: Proposal

Name of Person Being Observed: _____ Role:_____

Name of Observer: _____

The introduction provides a clear and logical lead into the problem	poor	fair	good	very good	excellent
Clear statement	1	2	3	4	5
Logical	1	2	3	4	5
Linguistic accuracy	1	2	3	4	5

The problem is explicitly stated	poor	fair	good	very good	excellent
Clear statement	1	2	3	4	5
Logical coherence to the objectives	1	2	3	4	5
Accuracy of spelling	1	2	3	4	5

The procedure relates to the objectives	poor	fair	good	very good	excellent
Clear statement	1	2	3	4	5
Logical coherence to the objectives	1	2	3	4	5
Accuracy of spelling	1	2	3	4	5

Evaluation is oriented toward project objectives	poor	fair	good	very good	excellent
Clear statement	1	2	3	4	5
Logical coherence to the objectives	1	2	3	4	5
Accuracy of spelling	1	2	3	4	5

Budget is adequate or realistic for the project	poor	fair	good	very good	excellent
Clear statement	1	2	3	4	5
Adequate or realistic for the project	1	2	3	4	5
Linguistic accuracy	1	2	3	4	5

Comments

V. Main Activity: Part III Committee Meeting

School committee members will decide on the schedule and the guests for Japanese Culture Week

The committee will discuss the information their members collected from the Japanese families. They will decide the schedule and tell the Japanese families their decision. Select one student each to serve as chairperson of the meeting, blackboard writer, and note-taker. The rest of the class will play participants in the meeting. A representative working on each area in Warm-Up Part B reports the results of the preliminary survey. The participants then cooperate under the leadership of the chairperson and make decisions regarding each area. After that, the class makes a list of its decisions. The committee will make its choice of time, location and date and will choose two items from the activity, food and drinks sections. The groups then check the other groups' work for accuracy.

Sample Meeting

Chair:	じゃ、ミーティングをはじめましょう。 日本文化(にほんぶんか)のしゅうはなんにちからなんにちがいいですか。
A:	ついたちからむいかがいいです。
Chair:	Bさんは？
B:	なのかからじゅうさんにちがいいです。
[C raises her hand]	
Chair:	Cさん。
C:	わたしは、ついたちからむいかがいいです。
Chair:	Dさん、ついたちからむいかと　なのかからじゅうさんにちと、どちらがいいですか。
D:	わたしも、ついたちからむいかがいいです。
Chair	ついたちからむいかのひと。 １０。 なのかからじゅうさんにちのひと。 ８。 ついたちからむいかは１０。

なのかからじゅうさんにちは8。

じゃ、ついたちからむいかにしましょう。

[*announcing the decision*]

Chair: じゃ、A グループのプロポーザルをはじめましょう。

A グループのプロポーザルをよんでください。

それから、こくばんにかいてください。

A: じゃ、A グループのプロポーザルをよみます。

[*presenting Group A's proposal*]

Chair: B グループのプロポーザルをよんでください。

それから、こくばんにかいてください。

[*presenting Group B's proposal*]

Chair: 日本文化のしゅうはA グループのプロポーザルとB グループのプロポーザルとどちらがいいですか。

A: A グループのプロポーザルがいいです。

Chair: Bさんは。

B: B グループのプロポーザルがいいです。

[*C raises her hand*]

Chair: Cさん。

C: わたしは、B グループのプロポーザルがいいです。

Peer Evaluation Form: Committee Meeting (Decision-Making Activities)

Name of Person Being Observed:_____   Role:_____

Name of Observer:_____

Performance Rating Chart for Chairperson

	poor	fair	good	very good	excellent
Management skills	1	2	3	4	5
Cooperation with the board writer	1	2	3	4	5
Clarity of instructions	1	2	3	4	5
Linguistic accuracy	1	2	3	4	5

Performance Rating Chart for Board Writer

	poor	fair	good	very good	excellent
Presentation/organization	1	2	3	4	5
Cooperation with the chair	1	2	3	4	5
Accuracy of spelling	1	2	3	4	5
Quality of participation	1	2	3	4	5

Performance Rating Chart for Scribe

	poor	fair	good	very good	excellent
Presentation/organization	1	2	3	4	5
Cooperation with the chair	1	2	3	4	5
Accuracy of spelling	1	2	3	4	5
Quality of participation	1	2	3	4	5

Performance Rating Chart for Participant

	poor	fair	good	very good	excellent
Participation/involvement	1	2	3	4	5
Cooperation	1	2	3	4	5
Productivity	1	2	3	4	5
Linguistic accuracy	1	2	3	4	5

Comments:

4.11 Virtual Reality
VI. Wrap-Up: Part I

Making a Poster for Japanese Culture Week

1. *Types of posters*

   Everyone makes a poster for the party using the items that were decided on in the Main Activity section. The class later chooses the best poster based on design, organization, clarity of information and artistic creativity.

2. *Selection of posters*

   Upon the completion of the covers, the class will compare the creations and choose one of each type for use in the poster.

にほん　ぶんか
日本の文化とスポーツ

ひにち：５月２４日から５月２８日まで
じかん：９時から６時まで
ばしょ：マジソンスクエアーガーデン
ひよう：ただ

Peer Evaluation

Rate the design and content of a segment made by another group according to the criteria below. Use a 5-point scale, with 5 being the highest score. Write additional comments at the end.

Segment evaluated: _____

Evaluator: _____

1. *Layout: every component, including title and subtitle, well coordinated.*

    0   1   2   3   4   5

2. *Description*

    0   1   2   3   4   5

    Structure: well structured overall and topic sentence well supported by examples.

    0   1   2   3   4   5

    Content: message well deliverd and persuasive.

    0   1   2   3   4   5

    accuracy: no spelling or grammatical errors.

    0   1   2   3   4   5

3. *Graphs/Charts: clear and easy to read*

    0   1   2   3   4   5

4. *Map: well designed and easy to use*

    0   1   2   3   4   5

5. *Photos/Illusrations: attractive and blend in well with the overall design*

    0   1   2   3   4   5

6. *Overall*

    0   1   2   3   4   5

VII. *Wrap-Up: PartII*

Preparing to introduce speakers and introducing them during Japanese Culture Week

The Student Committee will prepare introductory speeches for presenters and speakers during Japanese Culture Week. If the committee has not already collected information from them, they should call them now and get their information. The committee should prepare various questions, such as what kind of job does the presenter have, when is his or her birthday, and so on, in order to introduce him or her. The draft introduction should have a beginning, middle and end, with a clear message(See Chapter3). One of the committee members will present this introduction. Be sure to make use of *aizuchi* (connection words) to make the presentation flow naturally.

Self-Evaluation

Self-Evaluation Form: Planning introductory speeches for presenters					
Name:_____					
Name of Presenter:_____					

Purpose and organization	poor	fair	good	very good	excellent
Clarity of purpose	1	2	3	4	5
Organization of thought	1	2	3	4	5
Structure (begining, middle and end)	1	2	3	4	5
Use of right words	1	2	3	4	5

Word/Sentence use	poor	fair	good	very good	excellent
New vocabulary	1	2	3	4	5
Completed sentences	1	2	3	4	5
Word order	1	2	3	4	5
Quality of participation	1	2	3	4	5

Mechanics/Format

	poor	fair	good	very good	excellent
Accuracy of spelling	1	2	3	4	5
Using periods correctly	1	2	3	4	5
Writing of kana and kanji	1	2	3	4	5
Indenting of paragraphs	1	2	3	4	5

Editing

	poor	fair	good	very good	excellent
Monitoring	1	2	3	4	5
Peer monitoring	1	2	3	4	5

Self-Evaluation Form: Introductory speeches for presenters

Name:_____   Name of Presenter:_____

Purpose and organization

	poor	fair	good	very good	excellent
Clarity of message	1	2	3	4	5
Grasp of main point	1	2	3	4	5
Completed task	1	2	3	4	5
Use of right words	1	2	3	4	5

Presentation

	poor	fair	good	very good	excellent
Fluency of presentation	1	2	3	4	5
Interaction	1	2	3	4	5
Response of audience	1	2	3	4	5

Language

	poor	fair	good	very good	excellent
Vocabulary	1	2	3	4	5
Accuracy	1	2	3	4	5
Pronunciation	1	2	3	4	5

Comments:

SUM-UP

1. *How clear and/or effective was the message? How appropriate were the responses?*
   Please rate them on a scale of 0 to 5.   (0 = difficult to understand or inappropriate, 5 =
   appropriate and easy to understand, interesting, clear and imaginatively presented)

   0   1   2   3   4   5

2. *Did your conversation flow logically? Please rate your performance on a scale of 0 to 5.*
   (0 = telephone conversation dialogue disjointed, 5 = telephone conversation dialogue
   flowed freely and coherently)

   0   1   2   3   4   5

3. *To what extent were the use of grammatical structures accurate and varied? Please rate*
   them on a scale of 0 to 5.   (0 = a high proportion of errors, 5 = utterances almost error-
   free)

   0   1   2   3   4   5

4. *Have you been able to use the ja tactic when you wanted to say another phrase? Please*
   rate your progress on a scale of 0 to 5.   (0 = no progress , 5 = excellent progress)

   0   1   2   3   4   5

5. *Have you been able to use the memorization strategy when you worked with members*
   of your group? Please rate your progress on a scale of 0 to 5.   (0 =no progress, 5 =
   excellent progress)

   0   1   2   3   4   5

ADDITIONAL VOCABULARY

Functional Vocabulary

	Formal	Informal	English
Asking Questions	デモンストレーションしますか。	デモンストレーションする?	Do (you) demonstrate (it)?
	Demonsutoreeshon shimasu ka?	*Demonsutoreeshon suru?*	Will (you) demonstrate (it)?
	プレゼンテーションしますか。	プレゼンテーションする?	Do (you) present (it)?
	Purezenteeshon shimasu ka?	*Purezenteeshon suru?*	Will (you) present (it)?
	プレパレーションしますか	プレパレーションする?	Do (you) prepare for (it)?
	Purepareeshon shimasu ka?	*Purepareeshon suru?*	Will (you) prepare for (it)?
	シャワーをあびますか。	シャワーをあびる?	Do (you) take a shower?
	Shawaa o abimasu ka?	*Shawaa o abiru?*	Will (you) take a shower?
	しんぶんをよみますか。	しんぶんをよむ?	Do (you) read a newspaper?
	Shinbun o yomimasu ka?	*Shinbun o yomu?*	Will (you) read a newspaper?
	ケーキをつくりますか。	ケーキをつくる?	Do (you) make a cake?
	Keeki o tsukurimasu ka?	*Keeki o tsukuru?*	Will (you) make a cake?
	デートをしますか。	デートをする?	Do (you) date?
	Deeto o shimasu ka?	*Deeto o suru?*	Will (you) date?
	かいものをしますか。	かいものをする?	Do (you) go shopping?
	Kaimono o shimasu ka?	*Kaimono o suru?*	Will (you) go shopping?
	せんたくをしますか。	せんたくをする?	Do (you) do laundry?
	Sentaku o shimasu ka?	*Sentaku o suru?*	Will (you) do laundry?
	そうじをしますか。	そうじをする?	Do (you) clean up?
	Sooji o shimasu ka?	*Sooji o suru?*	Will (you) clean up?
	インターネットしますか。	インターネットする?	Do (you) surf the Internet?
	Intaanetto shimasu ka?	*Intaanetto suru?*	Will (you) surf the Internet?
	アルバイトしますか。	アルバイトする?	Do (you) have a part-time job?
	Arubaito shimasu ka?	*Arubaito suru?*	Will (you) have a part-time job?
	あそびますか。	あそぶ?	Do (you) play?
	Asobimasu ka?	*Asobu?*	Will (you) play?
	ともだちにあいますか。	ともだちにあう?	Do (you) meet a friend?
	Tomodachi ni aimasu ka?	*Tomodachi ni au?*	Will (you) meet a friend?
	ボランティアしますか。	ボランティアする?	Do (you) volunteer?
	Borantia shimasu ka?	*Borantia suru?*	Will (you) volunteer?
	りょうりしますか。	りょうりする?	Do (you) cook?
	Ryoori shimasu ka?	*Ryoori suru?*	Will (you) cook?
	さんぽしますか。	さんぽする?	Do (you) go for a walk?
	Sanpo shimasu ka?	*Sanpo suru?*	Will (you) go for a walk?
	はなしますか。	はなす?	Do (you) talk?
	Hanashimasu ka?	*Hanasu?*	Will (you) talk?
	ちこくしますか。	ちこくする?	Do (you) come late?
	Chikoku shimasu ka?	*Chikoku suru?*	Will (you) come late?
Simple Question Words	だれですか。 *(Dare desu ka?)*	だれ? *(Dare?)*	Who is (he)?
	いくらですか。 *(Ikura desu ka?)*	いくら? *(Ikura?)*	How much is (it)?
	どこですか。 *(Doko desu ka?)*	どこ? *(Doko?)*	Where is (it)?
	なんじですか。 *(Nanji desu ka?)*	なんじ? *(Nanji?)*	What time is (it)?
	なんようびですか。	なんようび?	What day of the week is (it)?
	(Nan'yoobi desu ka?)	*(Nan'yoobi?)*	
	なんにちですか。	なんにち?	What day of the month is (it)?
	(Nannichi desu ka?)	*(Nannichi?)*	

Functional Vocabulary

Verbs

シャワーをあびます	*shawaa o abimasu*	to take
シャワーをあびる	*shawaa o abiru*	a shower
しんぶんをよみます	*shinbun o yomimasu*	to read
しんぶんをよむ	*shinbun o yomu*	a newspaper
ケーキをつくります	*keeki o tsukurimasu*	to make
ケーキをつくる	*keeki o tsukuru*	a cake
デートをします	*deeto o shimasu*	to date
デートをする	*deeto o suru*	
かいものをします	*kaimono o shimasu*	to go shopping
かいものをする	*kaimono o suru*	
せんたくをします	*sentaku o shimasu*	to do
せんたくをする	*sentaku o suru*	laundry
そうじをします	*sooji o shimasu*	to clean up
そうじをする	*sooji o suru*	
インターネットします	*intaanetto shimasu*	to surf the
インターネットする	*intaanetto suru*	Internet
アルバイトします	*arubaito shimasu*	to have a
アルバイトする	*arubaito suru*	part-time job
あそびます	*asobimasu*	to play
あそぶ	*asobu*	
ともだちにあいます	*tomodachi ni aimasu*	to meet a
ともだちにあう	*tomodachi to au*	friend
ボランティアします	*borantia shimasu*	to volunteer
ボランティアする	*borantia suru*	
りょうりします	*ryoori shimasu*	to cook
りょうりする	*ryoori suru*	
さんぽします	*sanpo shimasu*	to go for a walk
さんぽする	*sanpo suru*	
はなします	*hanashimasu*	to talk
はなす	*hanasu*	
ちこくします	*chikoku shimasu*	to be late
ちこくする	*chikoku suru*	

Public Facilities

こうえん	*kooen*	park
びょういん	*byooin*	hospital
ゆうびんきょく	*yuubinkyoku*	post office
デパート	*depaato*	department store
えいがかん	*eigakan*	movie theater
えき	*eki*	train station

Japanese Sports

すもう	*sumoo*	sumo
けんどう	*kendoo*	kendo
あいきどう	*aikidoo*	aikido
からて	*karate*	karate
じゅうどう	*juudoo*	judo

Japanese Culture

いけばな	*ikebana*	flower arrangement
おちゃ	*ocha*	tea ceremony
ぜん	*zen*	Zen
かぶき	*kabuki*	Kabuki (Japanese theater)
のう	*noo*	No (Japanese theater)
しゅうじ	*shuuji*	Japanese calligraphy

Japanese Business

くるま	*kuruma*	car
カメラ	*kamera*	camera
オーディオ	*oodio*	audio
とけい	*tokei*	watch
ゲーム	*geemu*	game

Japanese Culture Week Events

ぶんか	*bunka*	culture
かいしゃ	*kaisha*	company/business
はなし	*hanashi*	story
しごと	*shigoto*	job/work
らいしゅう	*raishuu*	next week
ミーティング	*miitingu*	meeting
フリー	*furii*	free
スケジュール	*sukejuuru*	schedule
プレゼンター	*purezentaa*	presenter
グループ	*guruupu*	group
レセプション	*resepushon*	reception
ドラフト	*dorafuto*	draft
サンプル	*sanpuru*	sample
デモンストレーション	*demonsutoreeshon*	demonstration
プレゼンテーション	*purezenteeshon*	presentation
プレパレーション	*purepareeshon*	preparation
イベント	*ibento*	event
ちらし	*chirashi*	flyer
レジャーのじかん	*rejaa no jikan*	leisure time
すいみんのじかん	*suimin no jikan*	sleep time
プロポーザル	*puropoozaru*	proposal
ひよう	*hiyoo*	expense
しゅう	*shuu*	week
マジソンスクエアガーデン	*majison sukuea gaaden*	Madison Square Garden

Actions and Attractions

きもの

もちつき

ちゃのゆ

1. おきます／おきる
2. たべます／たべる
3. はをみがきます／
   はをみがく
4. かおをあらいます／
   かおをあらう
5. がっこうへいきます／
   がっこうへいく
6. べんきょうします／
   べんきょうする
7. じてんしゃにのります／
   じてんしゃにのる
8. テレビをみます／
   テレビをみる
9. かきます／かく
10. おんがくをききます／
    おんがくをきく
11. よみます／よむ
12. はなします／はなす

1. かえります／かえる
2. でんわします／でんわする
3. あそびます／あそぶ
4. うります／うる
5. かいます／かう
6. ぎゅうにゅうをのみます／
   ぎゅうにゅうをのむ
7. しゅくだいをします／
   しゅくだいをする
8. りょうりします／
   りょうりする
9. そうじします／
   そうじする
10. おふろにはいります／
    おふろにはいる
11. くつをはきます／
    くつをはく
12. アルバイトをします／
    アルバイトをする
13. ねます／ねる

1. れんしゅうします／
   れんしゅうする
2. かいぎをします／
   かいぎをする
3. うんどうします／
   うんどうする
4. しごとをします／
   しごとをする
5. やすみます／やすむ
6. つくります／つくる
7. おしえます／おしえる
8. わらいます／わらう
9. およぎます／およぐ
10. つかいます／つかう
11. はなします／はなす
    あいます／あう
12. うたいます／うたう

UNIT 2 REVIEW

1. Let's make mindmaps. Focus on the larger picture, and see how you can start building up cues clues, and tactics that are useful in your own communication and learning.

2. **Match the expressions on the left with the situations on the right, filling each (   )**
    with the appropriate letter.

1.	おとしは。	( )	a.	asking someone's grade level
2.	たんじょうびは。	( )	b.	asking someone's favorite type of music
3.	もしもし….	( )	c.	asking someone to wait
4.	りかさんはいますか。	( )	d.	asking who someone is
5.	がくねんは。	( )	e.	asking someone's age
6.	おくには。	( )	f.	asking someone's homeroom teacher
7.	すきなかもくは。	( )	g.	asking someone's name
8.	ちょっとまってください。	( )	h.	asking what time someone is going
9.	どなたですか。	( )	i.	asking about what someone will do
10.	スポーツは。	( )	j.	asking someone's place of residence
11.	ごしゅっしんは。	( )	k.	asking someone's sport
12.	コンサートにいきますか。	( )	l.	asking whether someone is present
13.	いきません。	( )	m.	greeting someone on the phone
14.	なんじにいきますか。	( )	n.	asking someone if he or she is going to a concert
15.	たんにんのせんせいは。	( )	o.	asking someone's club
16.	おなまえは。	( )	p.	asking the meaning of something
17.	いみは。	( )	q.	asking someone's favorite subject
18.	おすまいは。	( )	r.	asking someone's native country
19.	すきなおんがくは。	( )	s.	asking someone's birthplace
20.	クラブは。	( )	t.	asking someone's hobby
21.	ごしゅみは。	( )	u.	asking someone's birthday
22.	なにをしますか。	( )	v.	confirming the time someone is going
23.	じゃ、よじからですね。	( )	w.	making a negative statement

3. *Circle the word that you think belongs to a different category from the rest. Then choose the name of the category to which the rest of the words belong from the ones below and write it in the blank.*

1. ちち　あに　みせ　あね　おとうと　おかあさん　　　　＿＿＿＿＿＿＿

2. むらさき　みどり　しろ　あか　ピンク　プール　　　　＿＿＿＿＿＿＿

3. せんせい　ぎちょう　しょき　もんだい　コーチ　カウンセラー

    　　　　　　　　　　　　　　　　　　　　　　　＿＿＿＿＿＿＿

4. ピザ　パイナップル　チーズケーキ　フライドチキン　コンピューター

    　　　　　　　　　　　　　　　　　　　　　　　＿＿＿＿＿＿＿

5. きょうしつ　ジム　こうどう　ダンス　カフェテリア　グランド

    　　　　　　　　　　　　　　　　　　　　　　　＿＿＿＿＿＿＿

6. みっか　ここのか　ふたつ　いつか　ついたち　じゅうごにち

    　　　　　　　　　　　　　　　　　　　　　　　＿＿＿＿＿＿＿

7. ふね　しゅみ　タクシー　ちかてつ　でんしゃ　くるま

    　　　　　　　　　　　　　　　　　　　　　　　＿＿＿＿＿＿＿

8. こうどう　だいがく　ちゅうがく　しょうがっこう　こうこう

    　　　　　　　　　　　　　　　　　　　　　　　＿＿＿＿＿＿＿

9. びじゅつ　すうがく　きょうしつ　にほんご　れきし　かがく

    　　　　　　　　　　　　　　　　　　　　　　　＿＿＿＿＿＿＿

10. じゅうどう　きゅうどう　けんどう　やきゅう　からて　あいきどう

    　　　　　　　　　　　　　　　　　　　　　　　＿＿＿＿＿＿＿

たべもの	のみもの	どうぶつ	いろ		かもく	かぞく
くだもの	ひと	がっこう	きせつ		おんがく	てんき
ばしょ	ひにち	ようび	ぶどう／ぶげい			

4. *How many kanji compounds can you make? Circle as many as you can. You may go in any direction and use the same kanji as often as you like. However, each compound circled should be read from either left to right or top to bottom, not the other way around. (You may begin with those compounds consisting of two kanji and then expand your search later to include those consisting of three or more kanji.)*

七	金	四	十	日
水	九	時	一	本
八	年	五	月	語
木	六	分	土	先
火	人	二	学	生

5. *Circle the most appropriate word in parentheses.*

1. ちちはドイツ人です。（だから、でも、それから）ドイツごをはなしません。

2. 飲み物はコーラがいいですか、（だから、じゃ、それとも）ジュースがいいですか。

3. ダンスをします。（だから、でも、それから）DJと音楽が必要です。

4. 秋のスポーツはサッカーです。（だから、それとも、それから）冬のスポーツはスキーです。

5. [The Chair is announcing the result of a vote and the subsequent decision.]

金曜日の人は１０人です。土曜日の人は６人です。（それから、じゃ、それとも）金曜日にしましょう。

6. [A phone caller is bringing up the topic of conversation.]

あのう、あしたのパーティーの（こと、ため、から）ですが・・・。

7. 日本ウィークの目的は日本語や日本文化の勉強の（こと、ため、から）です。

6. **Transcribe the conversation you hear. Then extend it using conversation-extension tactics.**

1. A: _____

   B: _____

   A: _____

   B: _____

2. A: _____

   B: _____

   A: _____

   B: _____

3. A: _____

   B: _____

   A: _____

   B: _____

7.   *Let's role play.*

A   You are on the phone with a friend:

Friend	You
Ask what the other person is going to do tonight.	Say you have a lot of homework.
Ask the other person to go to a movie tonight.	Say you have to do your science homework.
Ask the other person to come to a party.	Say you will go to the party and ask your friend to bring food and drinks.

B.   You meet an exchange student from Japan. Do the following:

• Greet each other

• Tell each other of your studies and which classes you like and dislike.

• Name your favorite teachers.

• Discuss your favorite movie stars.

• Exchange information about summer vacation.

• Tell where you are going and what you plan to do after school.

• Say good-bye.

C.   Take notes as you interview five classmates to find out:

• when their birthday is

• what their favorite food is

• what their favorite sport is

• where their hometown is

D.   Interview five students about where they go and what they eat and drink when they are hungry and thirsty. Ask how much they usually spend and how many hours they spend hanging out. Write down their responses and report to the class the most popular places, food, and drinks, as well as the average your classmates spend per day on food and how much time they spend hanging out each day.

8. Below is a brief description of the daily activities of Ms. Jones, an American high school student.

A. Before reading the description, scan the format and answer the following questions.

a. What type of text is it?

b. What type of imformation do you see when you move your eyes quickly from top to bottom?

B. Find out specific information about time, date, topics, and activities.

1. time 　　　　2. date　　　　3. topics　　　　4. action verbs

ジョーンズさんの一日
　ジョーンズさんは、まいにち、6時に起きます。6時半に朝ごはんを食べます。ときどきコーヒーを飲みますが、ぜんぜん牛乳を飲みません。7時半に電車で学校へ行きます。ジョーンズさんのクラスは、日本語と数学とラテン語と科学と美術です。日本語のクラスは、火曜日と水曜日と木曜日と金曜日にあります。　火曜日のクラスは、ごご1時5分から1時50分までです。金曜日のクラスは、10時から11時20分までです。数学のクラスは、まいにち、2時からです。スポーツは火曜日と木曜日の3時から5時までです。ジョーンズさんの冬のスポーツは、アイスホッケーです。　いちばん好きなスポーツは、バレーボールです。月曜日と水曜日と金曜日に図書館へ行きます。6時ごろうちへ帰ります。7時に晩ごはんを食べます。7時半から10時まで、勉強をします。あまりテレビを見ません。まいにち10時半ごろ音楽を聞きます。いちばん好きな音楽は、クラシックです。ジョーンズさんは11時ごろ寝ます。

[VOCABULARY]　クラス…class　　　　　　　ごご… p.m.
いちばん好きな〜…favorite(No.1)〜　　晩ごはん…supper
[1]. Are the following statements TRUE(T) or FALSE(F) ?

1. (　　) Ms. Joneꞏs Wednesday schedule includes a Japanese class.
2. (　　) She drinks coffee everyday.
3. (　　) Her Japanese class on Friday ends at 1:50.
4. (　　) She goes to school by train.
5. (　　) Her math class happens on Tuesdays and Thursdays only.

6. (　　) Her favorite class is music.

7. (　　) Her Tuesday schedule includes a trip to the library.

8. (　　) She studies two and a half hours a day at her home.

[2]. Answer the following questions in Japanese.

1. ジョーンズさんは何時ごろ寝ますか。

_____

2. ジョーンズさんは牛乳を飲みますか。

_____

3. ジョーンズさんは火曜日の何時に日本語のクラスへ行きますか。

_____

4. ジョーンズさんの冬のスポーツは何ですか。

_____

9. Write a paragraph for your diary describing your activities.

A. Before writing, make an outline and answer the following questions.

a. What am I writing about ?

b. What kind of mindmap can I create to discover my main idea?

c. What type of text do you use to write in a letter?

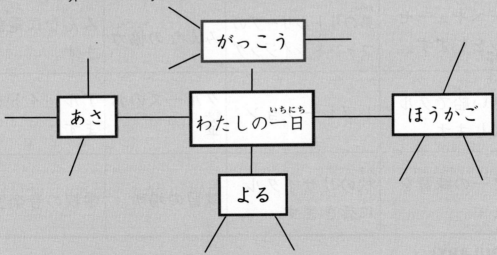

B. Before writing, create a mindmap of your activities.

C. Share a first draft of your diary with your friends and compare it with the paragraph on the previous page. Collect suggestions for possible improvements to your paragraph.

D. Rewrite the first draft and submit it to your teacher.

441

10. 夏休みの計画
<ruby>夏休<rt>なつやす</rt></ruby>み <ruby>計画<rt>けいかく</rt></ruby>

We are steadily approaching the end of this book, and many of you may be doing this section with your mind already wandering into the world of summer sun and fun filled with visits to malls, movie theaters, and beaches. But wait, if you plunge into your summer vacation with a fidgety mindset like that, you may look back later and regret how poorly it was spent or how many things you wanted to do during your time off from school were left undone. So doing a little advance planning is not be a bad idea. Let's see if you can do it using a format similar to the one you used when writing a proposal in Chapter 4. After all, what you are making is a proposal for your own enjoyable and productive summer.

A. Making a "table of plans"

1. A table such as the following will be helpful for listing plans, identifying purposes, assessing needs and finding ways to make them happen.

	計画 (plan)	目的 (purpose)	必要 (needs)	行動 (action)
1	サッカーのキャンプに行きます。	秋のサッカーシーズン	体力	いつもたくさん食べます。
2	バーベキューセールをします。	弟のリトルリーグのファンドレイジング	みんなの協力	みんなに電話します。
3	大きい船でクルーズします。	レクレーション	クルーズのお金	アルバイトをします。
4	ギターの練習をします。	秋のリサイタルに行きます。	練習の場所	学校の音楽室

[VOCABULARY]

キャンプ…camp   サッカーシーズン…soccer season   クルーズ…cruise
みんな…everyone   体力…physical strength, stamina   協力…cooperation
リトルリーグ…Little League バーベキューセール…berbecue sale   ギター…guitar
レクリエーション…recreation ファンドレイジング…fund raising   リサイタル…recital

2   Writing a "statement of plans"

Now you can put together all the information in your table in paragraph form. The following are based on 1-3 from the sample table above.

夏休みにサッカーのキャンプに行きます。秋のサッカーシーズンのためです。体力が必要です。だから、いつもたくさん食べます。バーベキューセールもします。目的は弟のリトルリーグのファンドレイジングです。みんなの協力が必要です。だから、みんなに電話します。
夏休みに大きい船でクルーズをします。レクリエーションのためです。クルーズのお金が必要です。だから、アルバイトをします。

Table of Plans

	計画 (plan)	目的 (purpose)	必要 (needs)	行動 (action)
1				
2				
3				
4				

Appendices

Roman letters are permitted in italics throughout the book when they are used to indicate the following:

        * instructions and directions for frills and activities

        * the readings of Japanese words and sentences

Boldface in the glossary indicates the section of the textbook in which the given word or expression first appears.

Numbers in the credit section correspond to the photographs shown throughout the textbook. Photographs are numbered and listed according to its layout. Photographs without a number will be read from up to down or from left to right.

Advanced Study
1. Workout

日本語ワークアウト

おはようございます。体操の時間です。

はじめはストレッチです。

ひざを曲げます。2回曲げます。

うでを伸ばします。
上に伸ばします。
前に伸ばします。
下に伸ばします。

足を開いて腰を回します。

左、右、左、右

つぎはシェイクです。

1 2 3 4 1 2 3 4 ・・・・・

日本語ワークアウト	Vocabulary	**Japanese Workout**
体操（たいそう）	exercise	Good morning, it is exercise time.
ストレッチ	stretch	First, stretch.
ひざ	knee	Bend your knees two times.
曲（ま）げます	bent	Stretch your arms.
2回（かい）	2 times	Raise them.
うで	arm	Extend them toward the front.
伸（の）ばします	stretch	Let them down.
上（うえ）	up	Spread your legs apart and twist.
前（まえ）	front	Left, right, left, right
下（した）	down	Next shake your body.
足（あし）	leg	1 2 3 4 1 2 3 4 · · · · ·
開（ひら）いて	open	
腰（こし）	twist	
回（まわ）します	turn	
左（ひだり）	left	
右（みぎ）	right	
つぎ	next	
シェイク	shake	

Advanced Study
2. Sanbiki no Kobuta

季節版：三匹の子ぶた

配役 (CAST)
お母さん (mother pig)
ブー (oldest pig – male)
フー (second oldest pig – male)
ウー (youngest pig – female)
おおかみ (wolf)
マーケットの店員 (clerk at the market)

ＰＡＲＴＩ：シーン１［ぶたのうちの中］

お母さん： みんながいなくなると、さびしいわ。
ブー： お母さん、だいじょうぶです。
まいにち電話しますから。
フー： ぼくはまいにち手紙を書きます。
お母さん： そう。ありがとう。
ウー： わたしもさびしいです。お母さんはいつもやさしいから。
これまで、ほんとうにありがとう。
お母さん： がんばってね。それから、おおかみに気をつけてね。
ウー： おおかみ？
ブー： だいじょうぶです。
お母さん： おおかみが来たら、みんなで協力するのよ。わかった？
ブーとフーとウー：はーい！
お母さん： じゃ、がんばってね。さようなら。
ブーとフーとウー：さようなら。

ＰＡＲＴＩ：シーン２　［道で］

ブー： 楽しみだなあ、これからのまいにちが。
フー： でも、ちょっとこわいなあ。
ウー： どうしてこわいの？

おもしろいことがたくさんあるわよ。

ブー： ぼうもそう思う。

フー： みんな元気だなあ。それで、まず、何が必要なの。

ウー： そうねえ、うちが必要ね。
それから、食べ物や飲み物やベッドも必要ね。

ブー： じゃ、はじめに材料を買って、うちを作りましょう。

ウー： 材料はなあに？　わら、木、それとも、れんが？

ブー： ぼくはわらだ。予算が少ないから。

フー： ぼくは木。ウーは？

ウー： わたしはれんがのうち。れんがはじょうぶだから。

ブー： え、れんが？　れんがはたかいよ。お金あるの？

ウー： ええ、ちょきんがあるのよ。
小学校１年生のときからの。

フー： え、小学校１年生のときから？
えらいなあ。

ウー： 計画よ、計画。

ブー： 計画ねえ・・・、あ、お店がある。

ＰＡＲＴＩ：シーン３［森の中］

おおかみ： あー、おなかがすいた。食べ物はどこかなあ。
おいしい肉はどこかなあ。あー、おなかがすいた。
あ、ぶたがいる！　わたしはぶたが好きです。

ＰＡＲＴＩ：シーン４［マーケット］

ブー： あのう、すみません。

店員： はい、何でしょう。

ブー： わらはいくらですか。

店員： 目的はなんですか。

ブー： うちを作るためです。

店員： うち。じゃ、８パック必要です。
１パック５ドルです。

ブー： １パック５ドル。
じゃ、えーと（５×８＝４０）、
４０ドルね。

店員： はい、ありがとうございます。

フー： あのう、木をください。ぼくは木でうちを作ります。

店員： 木のうちですか。じゃ、５パック必要です。
５パック１２５ドルです。くぎはありますか。

フー： いいえ、ありません。

店員： くぎは８ドルです。

フー： 木が１２５ドル、くぎが８ドル。
えーと（１２５＋８＝１３３）、
ぜんぶで１３３ドルか。じゃ、１３３ドル。

店員： はい、ありがとうございます。

ウー： れんがは１パック６０ドル・・、
ちょっと高いなあ。

(She looks at the store clerk.)

店員： お客さんもうちですか。じゃ、６パック必要です。

ウー： え、６パック？（６０×６＝３６０）３６０ドル。
ちょっと安くならない？

店員： そうですねえ。じゃ、３４０ドルは。

ウー： もうちょっと。

店員： うーん、じゃ、３２０ドル。安いですよ。

ウー： じゃ、６パックください。

(She gives the clerk 350 dollars.)

店員：　　　　　はい、３５０ドルから。
　　　　　　　　えーと（３５０－３２０＝３０）
　　　　　　　　３０ドルのおつりです。
　　　　　　　　ありがとうございました。すばら
　　　　　　　　しいうちを作ってください。

PARTⅡ：シーン１［子ぶたのうちの近く］

(Pigs have built their houses. Wolf comes out of the bushes, from where he had been watching the pigs.)

おおかみ：　　　もうすぐおいしいごはんの時間だ
　　　　　　　　ぞ。
　　　　　　　　はじめにだれを食べようか。ブー
　　　　　　　　はやせているからダイエットにも
　　　　　　　　いい。

PARTⅡ：シーン１［わらのうちの中］

(Knocks on door.)

おおかみ：　　　ごめんください。
ブー：　　　　　どなたですか。
おおかみ：　　　おおかみです。おいしそうですね
　　　　　　　　え。
ブー：　　　　　あっち行け。
おおかみ：　　　ドアをあけないと、うちをふきと
　　　　　　　　ばすぞ！

(House is destroyed. ブーruns away.)

ブー：　　　　　助けて！

PARTⅡ：シーン２［木のうちの中］

ブー：　　　　　フー、中に入れて。おおかみだ
よ、　　　　　　おおかみ。
フー：　　　　　え、おおかみ？　はやく入って、
　　　　　　　　お兄さん。

(Phone rings and フー answers.)

フー：　　　　　もしもし。
おおかみ：　　　もしもし。子ぶたさんのおたくで
　　　　　　　　すか。

フー：　　　　　はい、そうです。
おおかみ：　　　フーさんいますか。
フー：　　　　　はい、わたしです。どなたです
　　　　　　　　か。
おおかみ：　　　ひつじです。食べ物がありませ
ん。　　　　　　食べ物をください。
フー：　　　　　かわいそうに。じゃ、うちへ来て
　　　　　　　　ください。
おおかみ：　　　(in disguise)ごめんください。
ブー：　　　　　大きい口ですねえ。
おおかみ：　　　気にしない、気にしない。はやく
　　　　　　　　中へ入れてください。
ブー：　　　　　わあ、おおかみだ。

(Pigs run away. Wolf burns down house.)

PARTⅡ：シーン３［れんがのうちの中］

ウー：　　　　　これからぶたのミーティングを始
　　　　　　　　めます。
　　　　　　　　きょうのトピックはおおかみたい
　　　　　　　　じです。
　　　　　　　　サジェスチョンはありますか。
フー：　　　　　おおかみに肉屋のギフトけんをあ
　　　　　　　　げましょう。
ブー：　　　　　いけどりにしましょう。
ウー：　　　　　肉屋のギフトけんといけど
　　　　　　　　り・・・、ほかにありますか。
ブーとフー：　　いいえ。
ウー：　　　　　じゃ、きめましょう。ギフトけん
　　　　　　　　の人、手をあげてください。

(フー raises his hand.)

　　　　　　　　いけどりの人、手をあげてくださ
　　　　　　　　い。

(ブー and ウー raise their hands.)

　　　　　　　　じゃ、いけどりにしましょう。

つぎのミーティングは何曜日がいいですか。

場所はわたしのうちです。

ブー： ええと、水曜日がいいです。

フー： ぼくも水曜日がいいです。

ウー： じゃ、水曜日にしましょう。
時間は7時と8時とどちらがいいですか。

フー： 8時がいいです。

ブー： ぼくは7時がいいです。

フー： え、7時はちょっとはやいですよ。

ウー： じゃ、7時半はどうですか。

ブーとフー： はい、いいです。

ウー： じゃ、7時半にしましょう。
これできょうのミーティングをおわります。

(Later, ウー is talking to her mother on the phone.)

お母さん： え、いけどり？

ウー： うん、きょうのミーティングできめました。

お母さん： それはあぶないわよ。それから、おおかみがかわいそうよ。

ウー： そうですかねえ、でも・・・・。

お母さん： おおかみをベジタリアンにしなさい。
野菜が好きなおおかみは問題がないでしょう？

ウー： 野菜が好きなおおかみ。たしかに、問題がありませんね。

(ウー reports the outcome of her conversation with mother to her brothers.)

ブーとフー： え？　ベジタリアン？　それはいいアイデアだ。

(Knock at door.)

おおかみ： 子ぶたちゃん、子ぶたちゃん、中に入れて。

ブーとフーとウー： いいえ、入れません。

おおかみ： そうか。じゃ、うちをふきとばすぞ！

(Wolf unsuccessfully tries to destroy the house.)

よし、じゃ、まどから入るぞ。

(Wolf enters through the window. Anticipating this move, pigs immediately stuff food into wolf's mouth.)

おいしいねえ。これ、なあに？

ブー： それは、ソイビーンカードベジースシです。

おおかみ： すみません。もういちどおねがいします。

ブーとフーとウー： ソイビーンカードベジースシ。

おおかみ： ソイビーンカード・・・。

フー： ベジースシです。

おおかみ： ソイビーンカードベジースシね。
あのう、意味は何ですか。

ウー： とうふと野菜のおすしです。

おおかみ： え、とうふと野菜のおすし？
これ、肉じゃないの？

ブー： ちがいます。肉じゃありません。

おおかみ： へえ、おいしいねえ、これは。
ほんとうにおいしい。ダイエットにもいい。

ブーとフーとウー： あーよかった。
ソイビーンカードベジーロールばんざい！
ダイエットがんばってね。

おわり

三匹の子ぶた　**Vocabulary**

PART I : シーン1

マーケット	market
店員	store clerk
みんな	everyone, all of you
いなくなる	disappear
さびしい	lonely
だいじょうぶ	all right
いつも	always
これまで	up to now
ほんとうに	truly, really
がんばる	give one's best
～に気をつける	be careful with~
来たら	if one comes
協力する	cooperate
道	road

PART I : シーン2

楽しみ	something to look forward to
こわい	scary
こと	thing
ぼく	I (male)
思う／思います	think
まず	first of all
必要（な）	necessary
材料	material, ingredient
うち	house
作る／作ります	make

作りましょう	let's make
わら	straw
れんが	brick
予算	budget
少ない	a little, a few
じょうぶ（な）	sturdy, well-built
ちょきん	deposit, savings
～のとき	at the time of~
えらい	great, admirable
計画	plan
店	store
森	forest
中	inside, middle

PART I : シーン3

おなかがすいた	hungry
おいしい	delicious

PART I : シーン4

目的	purpose
～（の）ため	for the purpose of~
パック	pack, package
くぎ	nail
ぜんぶで	altogether
高い	expensive
客	customer
安くなる／安くなります	become cheaper
もうちょっと	a little more
安い	inexpensive
おつり	change

すばらしい　　　　wonderful

PART I : シーン5

もうすぐ　　　　　soon

ごはんの時間　　　mealtime

はじめに　　　　　at first

やせている／やせています

　　　　　　　　　skinny

ダイエット　　　　diet

PART II : シーン1

おいしそう　　　　look delicious

あっち行け　　　　go away, get lost

ドア　　　　　　　door

あける／あけます　to open

ふきとばす／ふきとばします

　　　　　　　　　blow away

助ける／助けます　rescue, help

PART II : シーン2

入れる／入れます　put in

はやく　　　　　　quickly

入る／入ります　　enter

ひつじ　　　　　　sheep

かわいそう　　　　pitiful

ごめんください　　Hello (at the door)

口　　　　　　　　mouth

気にしない　　　　never mind

PART II : シーン3

おおかみたいじ　　wolf conquest

サジェスチョン　　suggestion

肉屋　　　　　　　meat shop, butcher

ギフト券　　　　　gift certificate

あげる／あげます　give

いけどり　　　　　catch (an animal)

ほか　　　　　　　else, other

きめる／きめます　decide

手をあげる／手をあげます

　　　　　　　　　raise one's hand

つぎの〜　　　　　next~

はやい　　　　　　early

おわる／おわります

　　　　　　　　　to end

あぶない　　　　　dangerous

ベジタリアン　　　vegetarian

野菜　　　　　　　vegetables

問題　　　　　　　problem

問題がない　　　　no problems

たしかに　　　　　without doubt

まど　　　　　　　window

意味　　　　　　　meaning

とうふ　　　　　　tofu, soybean curd

ばんざい　　　　　Hurray! Cheers!

Kisetsu Version of "The Three Little Pigs"

CAST
Mother   (mother pig)
Buu   (eldest pig – male)
Fuu   (second eldest pig – male)
Uu   (youngest pig – female)
Wolf   (wolf)
Clerk   (clerk at the market)

Part I, Scene 1: Inside the Pigs' House

Mother: I'm going to be so lonely when you all leave.

Buu: Don't worry, I'll call you every day.

Fuu: And I'll write you every day.

Mother: Oh, thank you.

Uu: I'm sad too because Mommy is always so kind. Thank you so much for everything.

Mother: Good luck! But be very cautious, there are wolves out there.

Uu: Wolves?

Buu: Don't worry.

Mother: If a wolf does come out, then you all watch out for each other, okay?

Buu, Fuu, and Uu: Yes, Mother!

Mother: Well, good luck. So long.

Buu, Fuu, and Uu: Goodbye!

Part I, Scene 2: On the Road

Buu: I'm so excited! I wonder what the days are going to be like from now on.

Fuu: But I'm feeling a little scared about this.

Uu: Why are you scared, Fuu? There are going to be so many interesting things on the way.

Buu: Yeah, I think so too.

Fuu: Gee, you both have so much energy. So, what's the first thing we need?

Uu: Let's see, well, we each need a house to begin with. And we also need food, drinks, and beds.

Buu: So let's first buy the necessary materials and build our houses.

Uu: What kind of materials? Straw? Wood? Bricks?

Buu: I'm going to buy some straw because my budget is low.

Fuu: I'm going to go for wood. What about you, Uu?

Uu: I'm going to build a brick house because brick houses are sturdy.

Buu: What? A brick house? Bricks are very expensive. Do you have the money for it?

Uu: Yes, I have been saving up since first grade.

Fuu: Since first grade? Wow, that's really impressive.

Uu: It's all about planning ahead.

Buu: Planning ahead, huh? Hey, look! There's a store over there.

Part I, Scene 3: In the Woods

Wolf: Oh, I'm starting to get hungry. Where can I find some food? Where can I find some tasty meat? Ah, I'm starving! Oh, perfect! I see some pigs! I love pigs!

Part I, Scene 4: At the Market

Buu: Um, excuse me.

Clerk: Yes, what is it?

Buu: How much is the straw?

Clerk: What is the straw for?

455

Buu:	It will be used for building a house.
Clerk:	A house . . . I see. Well then, you'll need 8 packs. 1 pack is 5 dollars.
Buu:	1 pack is 5 dollars. Well then, um, 5 multiplied by 8 equals 40, so 40 dollars, right?
Clerk:	That is correct. Thank you very much.
Fuu:	Um, can you give me some wood, please? I'm going to build a house as well.
Clerk:	A wooden house? Well then, you'll need 5 packs. 5 packs is 125 dollars. Do you have nails?
Fuu:	No, I do not.
Clerk:	Nails are 8 dollars.
Fuu:	The wood is 125 dollars and the nails are 8 dollars. Um, 125 plus 8 equals 133, so the total is 133 dollars. Well then, here is 133 dollars.
Clerk:	Yes, thank you very much.
Uu:	1 pack of bricks is 60 dollars . . . that's a little expensive. (*Uu looks at the clerk.*)
Clerk:	Will you be building a house as well? Well, then, you'll need 6 packs.
Uu:	What? 6 packs? 60 multiplied by 6 equals 360, so 360 dollars. Do you think that you can lower the price a little?
Clerk:	Let's see. Well, then, how is 340 dollars?
Uu:	A little more.
Clerk:	Um, well, then, 320 dollars.
Uu:	Well, then, please give me 6 packs. (*Uu hands 350 dollars to the clerk.*)
Clerk:	Okay from 350 dollars . . . um, 350 minus 320 equals 30, so 30 dollars' change. Thank you very much. I hope you all can build wonderful houses.

Part I, Scene 5: Near the Little Pigs' Houses

(*The three little pigs have built their houses. The wolf comes out from the bushes, where he has been hiding, watching the pigs.*)

Wolf:	It's almost time for a delicious meal! Who should I eat first? The oldest pig is skinny, so that would be good for my diet.

Part II, Scene 1: Inside the Straw House

Wolf:	(*knocks on the door*) Excuse me.
Buu:	Who is it?
Wolf:	I'm the wolf. You look very tasty, don't you?
Buu:	Go away!
Wolf:	If you don't open the door, I'll blow your house down!

(*The straw house is destroyed and Buu runs away.*)

Buu:	Help me!

Part II, Scene 2: Inside the Wooden House

Buu:	Fuu, let me in! The wolf, the wolf!
Fuu:	What? The wolf? Hurry up and come in, Elder Brother. (*The phone rings and Fuu answers.*) Hello?
Wolf:	Hello. Is this the little pig's residence?
Fuu:	Yes, it is.
Wolf:	Is Fuu there?
Fuu:	Yes, that's me. Who is this?
Wolf:	I am a sheep. I do not have any food. Please give me some food.
Fuu:	Oh, I feel so bad. Well, then, please come to my house.
Wolf:	(*In disguise*) Excuse me.
Buu:	You have a very big mouth.
Wolf:	Never mind that , new mind that. Please, hurry up and let me inside.
Buu:	Ah! It's the wolf!

(*Buu and Fuu run away and the wolf burns the house down.*)

Part II, Scene 3: Inside the Brick House

Uu: Let us now begin the pig meeting. Today's topic is how to get rid of the wolf. Do any of you have any suggestions?

Fuu: Let's give the wolf gift certificates to the meat shop.

Buu: Let's capture him alive.

Uu: Gift certificates to the meat shop and capturing him alive . . . any other ideas?

Buu and Fuu: No.

Uu: Well, then, let us decide. Whoever agrees with the gift certificate idea, please raise your hand. (*Fuu raises his hand.*) Whoever agrees with capturing the wolf alive, please raise your hand. (*Buu and Uu raise their hands.*) Well, then, let us capture the wolf alive. What day of the week should we have our next meeting? It will be at my house.

Buu: Um, Wednesday would be good for me.

Fuu: Wednesday is good for me too.

Uu: Well, then, let us have it Wednesday. For the time, 7 o'clock or 8 o'clock, which of the two would be better?

Fuu: I would like to have it at 8 o'clock.

Buu: I would like 7 o'clock.

Fuu: What? 7 o'clock is a little too early.

Uu: Well, then, how about 7:30?

Buu and Fuu: Yes, that is fine.

Uu: Well, then, let us say 7:30. Now we will end today's meeting.

(*Later, Uu is talking to her mother on the phone.*)

Mother: What? Capturing him alive?

Uu: Yeah, we decided at today's meeting.

Mother: That is dangerous. And I feel bad for the wolf.

Uu: That's true, but . . .

Mother: Make the wolf a vegetarian. There'd be no problem with a wolf who likes vegetables, right?

Uu: A wolf who likes vegetables . . . that's true, there would not be a problem.

(*Uu reports the outcome of her conversation with her mother to her two brothers.*)

Buu and Fuu: What? A vegetarian? That's a good idea.

Wolf: (*knocks on the door*) Little pig, little pig, let me in!

Buu, Fuu, and Uu: No, we will not let you in.

Wolf: I see. Well, then, I will blow your house down! (*The wolf unsuccessfully tries to blow the house down.*) Okay, then, I will come in through the window! (*The wolf enters through the window. Anticipating this move, the pigs immediately stuff food into the wolf's mouth.*) This tastes good! What is it?

Buu: That is soy bean curd veggie sushi.

Wolf: Excuse me, can you say that one more time?

Buu, Fuu, and Uu: Soy bean curd veggie sushi.

Wolf: Soy bean curd . . .

Fuu: It is veggie sushi.

Wolf: Soy bean curd veggie sushi. Um, what does that mean?

Fuu: It is a tofu and vegetable sushi.

Wolf: What? Tofu and vegetable sushi? This isn't meat?

Buu: No, it is not meat.

Wolf: Wow, it's pretty tasty, this thing. It's really delicious. It's also good for my diet.

Buu, Fuu, and Uu: Phew! Hurray for soy bean curd veggie sushi! Good luck on your diet.

THE END

Appendix
1. Expressions for Getting Started I and II

Daily Expressions Notes for Getting Started I

Step 1-1: はじめまして。〜です。どうぞよろしく。
(Hajimemashite. 〜desu. Doozo yoroshiku.)
[How do you do? My name is 〜.
Nice to meet you.]

"*Hajimemashite*" and "*doozo yoroshiku*" are the two expressions used most commonly when people meet for the first time. Their literal translations are "It's first time (for us to meet) isn't it?" and "Please take care of me kindly (and I will do the same for you)," respectively. You may simply say "*Yoroshiku*" instead of "*doozo yoroshiku*" when introducing yourself to someone in your own age group in casual situations, but you may want to use a longer version, "*doozo yoroshiku onegai shimasu or (onegai itashimasu),*" when introducing yourself to a group of people in formal situations or to someone older than yourself. "*〜desu*" corresponds to "*I am~.*"

Step 1-2: さんですか。 (*〜san desu ka?*)
[Are you Mr./Ms. etc.〜?]

はい、そうです。／いいえ、ちがいます。
(Hai, soo desu.) / *(Iie, chigaimasu.)*
[Yes, I am./ Yes, that's correct.]
[No, I am not./No, that's incorrect.]

さん "*san*" is the Japanese equivalent of Mr., Miss, Mrs. etc., though it is not used when the speaker is referring to him- or herself. It sounds perfectly appropriate in English for someone to say "My name is Mrs. so and so." or "I am Ms. so and so." However, that is not the case in Japanese. Just say your name and do not attach さん "*san*" when referring to yourself. On the other hand, you must attach さん "*san*" to someone else's name when addressing that person unless it is a sibling or close friend. スミスさんですか "*Sumisusan desu ka?*" means "Are you Ms.(Mrs./Mr.) Smith?" The response may be "*Hai, sòo desu,*" or "*Iie, chigaimasu,*" which literally mean "*Yes, that is right,*" and "*No, that*

is wrong" respectively.

Step 2-1: さようなら。 (*Sayoonara.*) [Goodbye.]

Step 2-2: じゃ、また。(じゃ。バイバイ。バーイ。)
(Ja mata./Ja. baibai. baai.) [See you. Bye.]

"*Sayoonara*" is used when people part. Like "*Konnichi wa*" and "*Konban wa,*" it is not used among family members unless they expect that they will not see each other again for a long time. "*Sayoonara*" is customarily exchanged between teachers and students in schools. "*Ja, mata.,*" "*Ja,*" "*Baibai,*" and "*Baai.*" are expressions used commonly among close friends or coworkers when parting. "*Ja, mata*" can be considered as the Japanese equivalent of "*See you later.*"

Step 2-3: しつれいします。 (*Shitsurei shimasu.*)
[Excuse me./Good bye.]

This expression can be used in situationssimilar to those calling for its English equivalents. "*Shitsurei shimasu*" literally means "I am going to be rude," and Japanese people use it whenever they think their own "rudeness" must be acknowledged. In contrast to Western greetings, Japanese greetings tend to sound more, especially as they become more formal. See the following examples.

(A) "*Shitsureei shimasu.*" as "Excuse me."
   1. A college student who has an appointment with a professor may enter his or her office saying: "*Shitsurei shimasu..*"
   2. Someone who is trying to pass in front of people who are seated in a theater row will say "*Shitsurei shimasu.*"

(B) "*Shitsurei shimasu*" as "Goodbye"
This is used in formal leave-taking situations. It is also used by someone younger when addressing older acquaintances.

Step 2-4: おやすみ。／おやすみなさい。
(*Oyasumi/Oyasuminasai.*) [Good night.]

"*Oyasumi*" and its more polite equivalent "*oyasuminasai*" are used to say "Good night" before going to bed. It is also used among friends and coworkers when they part at night.

Step 3-1: おはよう。／おはようございます。
(*Ohayoo.*) / (*Ohayoo gozaimasu.*)
[Good morning.]

Step 3-2: こんにちは。 (*Konnichi wa.*)
[Hello. Good afternoon.]

Step 3-3: こんばんは。 (*Konban wa.*) [Good evening.]

"*Ohayoo*" and its formal equivalent "*Ohayoo gozaimasu*" are used as greetings up to around 10 a.m. They literally mean "It's early, isn't it?" "*Konnichw a.*" is used to greet someone after around 10 in the morning and during the afternoon until it becomes dark. "*Konban wa*" is exchanged after dark. Both "*Konnichi wa*" and "*Konban wa*" can be regarded as Japanese equivalents of "Hello" or "Hi," but it should be noted that these expressions are not used among family members unless they live apart and don't see each other on a daily basis.

Step 3-4: いいおてんきですね。 (*Ii otenki desu ne.*)
そうですね。 (*soo desu ne.*)
[It's a beautiful day, isn't it?] [Yes, indeed.]

Step 3-5: あついですね。 (*Atsui desu ne.*)
[It's hot, isn't it?]

Step 3-6: むしあついですね。 (*Mushiatsui desu ne.*)
[It's hot and humid, isn't it?]

Step 3-7: さむいですね。 (*Samui desu ne.*)
[It's cold, isn't it?]

Step 3-8: よくふりますね。 (*Yoku furimasu ne.*)
[It rains a lot, isn't it?]

"*Ii otenki desu ne*" literally means "It's nice weather, isn't it?" Japanese often make some reference to the weather when they come across their neighbors or acquaintances on the street and exchange greetings. A typical response is "*Soo desu ne*" or "*Soo desu nee*," which literally mean "That's right."

Step 4-1: どうも。／ありがとう。／どうもありがとう。
（どうも）ありがとうございます／ーました。
(*Doomo./Arigatoo./Doomo arigatoo.*)
[Thanks./Thank you./Thank you very much.]
([*Doomo*]*arigatoo gozaimasu/-mashita.*)

いいえ。／いいえ、どういたしまして。(*Iie./Iie, doo itashimashite.*) [You are welcome.]

"*Doomo*" and "*arigatoo*" are the most casual ways of expressing gratitude when used by themselves. "*Doomo arigatoo*" is less casual than the first two, but "*gozaimasu*" or "*gozaimashita*" must be added in slightly more formal situations. Since "*gozaimashita*" is in the past tense, "*Doomo arigatoo gozaimashita*" is more suitable than "*doomoarigatoogozaimasu*" when expressing for an activity already completed. "*Iie, doo itashimashite*" is a polite, formal reply to an expression of gratitude. Just saying "*Iie*" is sufficient in most informal situations.

Step 4-2: 〜をください。 (*〜o kudasai.*) [Please give me〜.]

はい、どうぞ。 (*Hai, doozo.*) [Here you are.]

"*〜o kudasai*" is used when requesting something. You can use this expression when ordering in a restaurant, "*Koohii o kudasai*" ("Coffee. please"), when purchasing something "*Aoi boorupen o kudasai*" (Give me a blue ballpoint pen), or when asking someone to pass something to you, "*Bataa o kudasai*" (Pass the butter, please). "*Hai, doozo*" corresponds to "Here you are (Please take it)." in English and may be used as in response to such requests.

Step 5-1: 〜をどうぞ。 (*〜o doozo.*)
はい、いただきます。／いいえ、けっこうです。
(*Hai, itadakimasu.*) (*Iie, kekkoo desu.*)
[No, thank you.]

"*〜o doozo*" is a simple and useful expression used when you are offering something to someone. For example, if you offer some cookies to your guest, you say "*Kukkii o doozo*" (Please have some cookies) "*Doozo*" literally means "please" and is used when you want to encourage someone to accept your offer. One may respond to such an offer by saying "*Hai, itadakimasu*" (Yes, I will take it. Thank you.) or "*Iie, kekkoo desu.*" (No, thank you.).

Step 5-2: いただきます。
ごちそうさま。／ごちそうさまでした。
(*itadakimasu.*)
(*gochisoosama/gochisoosama deshita.*)

"*Itadakimasu*" and "*Gochisoosama (deshita)*" are said customarily before eating and after eating, respectively. In Japan children are trained at home to say these phrases before and after all meals and snacks. Both are expressions of gratitude for everyone and everything that has made the meal possible. This custom is not always strictly observed when people eat out, especially when an adult eats out alone. When you are invited to lunch or supper at someone's house, you should not forget to say both phrases as a way of thanking your host.

Step 6-1: いってまいります。（いってきます。）
いってらっしゃい。
(*Itte mairimasu/itte kimasu.*) (*Itte rasshai*)

When Japanese people leave home for work, school, etc., they customarily say "*Itte mairimasu*" or its slightly less formal equivalent, "*Ittekimasu.*" to the rest of the family. Both expressions literally mean "I will go and come back." Those remaining in the house will then say "*Itte rasshai.*" These expressions are used among people working in the same office as well, when, for example, one of them leaves for an errand.

Step 6-2: ただいま。 (*Tadaima.*) [I'm home./I'm back.]
おかえりなさい。 (*Okaerinasai.*)
[Welcome home./Welcome back.]

The expression "*Tadaima*" (I'm home) is used by someone who has just arrived home from school, work, or an errand to inform the rest of the family that he or she has returned. The family members respond with "*Okaeri*" or "*Okaerinasai.*" (Welcome home).

Step 6-3: おげんきですか。 (*O genki desu ka?*)
[Are you well?]

はい、おかげさまで。 (*Hai, okagesamade.*)
[Yes, thank you.]

げんき。 (*Genki?*) [Are you well?]
うん、げんき。 (*Un, genki.*) [Yes, I am.]

"*Ogenki desu ka*" literally means "Are you in good spirits?" The effect of this expression is

somewhat similar to that of "How are you?" in English, though the latter is used far more frequently and routinely than the former. A typical response to "*Ogenki desu ka.*" is "*Hai, okagesamade,*" or its slightly casual equivalent "*Ee, okagesamade.*" Both of these expressions literally mean "Yes, thanks to you." You will be thanked in this way even if you haven't done anything personally to keep this person healthy. The phrase is a general expresssion of gratitude for everything that has contributed to the person's good health, including your friendship, your hospitality, or even your mere existence. "*Genki*" is a casual version of "*Ogenkid esu ka,*" and "*Un, genki,*" means "Yes, I am fine." "*Un*" is casual equivalent of "*hai*" or "*ee.*"

Step 7-1: あのう、すみません。 (*Anoo, sumimasen.*)

はい、なんでしょう。 (*Hai, nan deshoo?*)

"*Sumimasen*" is used when you want to attract someone's attention. It corresponds to "Excuse me." One may say "*Hai, nandeshoo.*" (Yes, what is it?) in response.

Step 7-2: あのう、しつもんがあります。
(*Anoo, shitsumon ga arimasu.*)
[Er, I have a question.]

えいごでもいいですか。
(*Eigo demo ii desu ka?*) [May I use English?]

ちょっとまってください。
(*Chotto matte kudasai.*) [Wait a moment, please.]

Step 8-1: きりつ。れい。ちゃくせき。 (*Kiritsu.*)
[Stand up.] (*Rei.*) [Bow.] (*Chakuseki.*) [Sit down.]

The sequence above is a kind of ritualistic exchange of greetings between students and teacher at the beginning of a class. A student leader will say "*Kiritsu*" as the teacher comes into the classroom and the rest of the class immediately stands up. The students then bow to the teacher following the leader's directions to do so ("*Rei*"), and the teacher bows back to them. Finally, the leader says "*Chakuseki,*" and the students sit down.

Step 8-2: しゅっせきをとります。 (*Shusseki o torimasu.*)
[I will take attendance.]
〜さんはいますか。〜くんはいますか。
(*-san wa imasu ka?*) (*-kun wa imasu ka?*)
[Is so-and-so here?]

やすみです。ちこくです。
(*Yasumi desu.*) [She or he is absent.]
(*Chikoku desu.*) [She or he is late.]

Both "*-san wa imasu ka?*" and "*-kun wa imasu ka*" mean "Is so-and-so here?" "*San*" and "*kun*" are the Japanese equivalents of "Mr." "Miss," etc. but they can be attached to either the first name or the last name. The use of "*kun*" is usually limited to occasions in which an older person is addressing a younger colleague or acquaintance, and many occasions the addressee is a male. In Japanese schools, a teacher typically calls his or her students by their last name, attaching "*san*" when addressing female students and "*kun*" when addressing a male students.

Step 8-3: しつれい。 (*Shitsurei*) [Excuse me./I'm sorry.]

This is the same "*Shitsurei*" in "*Shitsurei shimasu*" introduced earlier. As indicated after, "*Shiturei*" implies rudeness, making this an appropriate form apology in spontaneous situations such as when you have stepped on someone's foot in a train.

Step 9-1: はじめましょう。 (*Hajimemashoo.*) [Let's begin.]

くばってください。 (*Kubatte kudasa.*)
[Please pass these out.]

まわしてください。 (*Mawashite kudasai.*) [Please pass this around.]

Step 9-2: わかりますか。 (*Wakarimasu ka?*) [Do you understand?]

はい、わかります。 (*Hai, wakarimasu.*) [Yes, I understand.]

いいえ、わかりません。 (*Iie, wakarimasen.*) [No, I don't understand.]

Step 9-3: もういいですか。 (*Moo ii desu ka?*)
[All set? Are you all done?]

はい、もういいです。 (*Hai, moo ii desu.*)
[Yes, I am all set.]

いいえ、まだです。 (*Iie, mada desu*) [No, not yet.]

You may hear your teacher say "*Moo ii desu ka?*" when he or she wants to find out if you have finished with whatever task you are engaged in so that onto the next scheduled activity can begin. Respond by saying "*Hai, moo ii desu,*" if you are done and "*Iie, mada desu,*" if you need more time.

Step 10-1: すいません。すみません。 (*Suimasen. Sumimasen.*)
どうもすいません。どうもすみません。
(*Doomo suimasen.Doomo sumimasen.*)
[I am sorry.]

いいえ。 (*Iie.*) [That's all right. Never mind.]

"*Suimasen*" and "*sumimasen*" are common expressions of apology. The former is the contracted, less formal equivalent, both are often preceded by "*doomo,*" which adds politeness. These expressions are used often to express gratitude as well. When a person chooses to thank someone by saying "*Sumimasen*" rather than "*Arigatoo,*" it is usually a stituation in which he or she feels the gratitude should include a note of apology for causing trouble or inconvenience. For example, you may say "*Doomo sumimasen*" to someone who picked up a pen you just dropped. "*Iie*" is an appropriate response to "*Sumimasen.*"

Step 10-2: ごめんなさい。ごめん。ごめんね。 (*Gomennasai. Gomen. Gomen ne.*) [I am sorry.]

いいえ。 (*Iie.*) [That's all right. Never mind.]

These are casual expressions of apology. They are commonly used among family members and close friends.

Step 10-3: おそくなってすみません。 (*Osoku natte sumimasen.*) [Sorry I'm late.]
これからはきをつけてください。 (*Kore kara wa ki o tsukete kudasai.*) [Please be careful next time.]

Step 10-4: たいへんよくできました。 (*Taihen yoku dekimashita.*) [Very well done.]
どうもありがとうございます。 (*Doomo arigatoo gozaimasu.*) [Thank you very much.]

もうすこしがんばってください。
(*Moo sukoshi ganbatte kudasai.*) [You can do a little better. Try your best.]

はい、がんばります。 (*Hai, ganbarimasu.*) [Yes, I will do my best.]

Simple Q&A Notes for Getting Started II

The question and answer sequences given in parentheses are the plain/casual equivalents of those outside the parentheses. Keep in mind that your choice of a situation-appropriate speech level will be influenced by many factors,

461

including the age and seniority of the addressee. Plain/casual style questions do not necessarily draw responses in the same style. In your Japanese class your may want to address your teacher and answer questions in the polite style regardless of how you are addressed.

Step 1:   なんですか。　～です。 *Nan desu ka?*
[What is that?] (~desu) [It is ~.]

(なに？／なあに？　～。) *(Nani/Naani?)* (-.)

Step 2:   いくらですか。　～ドル／えん(etc.)です。
Ikura desu ka? [How much is it?] (~doru/en desu.) [It's ~dollars/yen.]

(いくら？　～ドル／えん。) *(Ikura?)* (~doru/en.)

Store clerks, especially those who work in department stores and upscale specialty shops, are trained to be polite to their customers and will answer questions politely no matter how you are addressed.

Step 3:   どこですか。　～です。 *Doko desu ka?* [Where is it?] (-desu.) [It is (in) such and such a place.]

(どこ？　～。) *(doko?)* (~.)

Step 4-1:   なんじですか。　～じです。 *Nanji desu ka?* [What time is it?] (~ji desu.) [It's such and such o'clock.]
(なんじ？　～じ。) *(Nanji?)* (~ji.)

Step 4-2:   なんようびですか。 *Nanyoobi desu ka?* [What day of the week is it?]

～ようびです。　*~yoobi desu.* [It's such and such day of the week.]

(なんようび？　～ようび。) *Nan'yoobi? ~yoobi.*

Step 4-3:   なんにちですか。 *Nannichi desu ka?*
[What date is it?]

～がつ～にちです。 *~gatsu~nichi desu.*
[It's ~month ~day.]

～にちです。　*~nichidesu.*
[It's ~day of the month.]

((なんにち？　～がつ～にちです。／～にちです。)
Nannichi? (~gatsu ~nichi.)(~nichi.)

Remember the variations in vocabulary in the days of the month:The first through tenth do not end with "*nichi*". There are several other exceptions later in the month as well.

Step 5:   だれですか。～さん／せんせい(etc.)です。
Dare desu ka? [Who is he/she?] (~san/sensei desu.) [He/she is ~.]

(だれ？　～さん／せんせいetc.。) *Dare?*
(~san/sensei.)

Titles comes after the name in Japanese.

Step 6-1:   すきですか。はい、すきです。 *Suki desu ka?* [Do you like it?] *Hai, sukidesu.* [Yes, I like it.]

いいえ、すきじゃありません。 *Iie, suki ja arimasen.* [No, I don't like it.]

いいえ、きらいです。 *Iie, kiraidesu.*
[No, I dislike it.]

(すき？　うん、すき。) *Suki. (Un, suki.)*
(ううん、すきじゃない。) *Uun, suki ja nai.*
(ううん、きらい。) *Uun, kirai.*

Step 6-2:   きらいですか。はい、きらいです。
Kirai desu ka? [Do you dislike it?]
Hai, kiraidesu. [Yes, I dislike it.]

いいえ、きらいじゃありません。
Iie, kirai ja arimasen. [No, I don't dislike it.]

いいえ、すきです。 *Iie, sukidesu.* [No, I like it.]
(きらい？　うん、きらい。) *Kirai. (un, kirai.)*
(ううん、きらいじゃない。) *Uun, kirai ja nai.*
(ううん、すき。) *Uun, suki.*

When answering the question "*Suki desu ka*" negatively, "*Suki ja arimasen*" sounds somewhat softer and gentler than "*Kirai desu.*" because it is less direct. This "softening" factor becomes important depending upon the situation in which you have to give your response. Even "*Suki ja arimasen*" can be a bit too strong in some situations. Instead people may hesitantly say something like "*Anoo, X wa chotto...*" meaning something like "Well, I am not that keen on X...." You may want to try this last option when, say, your Japanese host mother asks you if you like a certain food that you feel you canot eat.

Step 7-1:   ありますか。 *Arimasu ka?*
[Do you have it?/Is it available?]

はい、あります。 *Hai, arimasu.*
[Yes, we do./Yes, it's available.]

いいえ、ありません。 *Iie, arimasen.*
[No, we don't./No, it's not available.]

（ある？）（うん、ある。）（ううん、ない。）
Aru. Un, aru. Uun, nai.

"*Arimasu*" means "*exist*," and its use is limited to the existence of inanimate items. Such inanimate items can either be concrete (e.g., a store, a desk) or abstract (e.g., an idea, a plan). Furthermore, "*arimasu*" can be used to indicate either mere existence ("There is -.") or the possession/availability ("I have -.") of something. This means that you can use its interrogative form, "*Arimasu ka?*" in stores and restaurants when you want to find out the availability of a certain item. For example, if you want to ask a store clerk if the store carries videotapes, you may say "*Bideo teepu arimasu ka*" or "*Bideo teepu wa arimasu ka.*"

Step 8-1: いますか。 *Imasu ka?*
[Is so and so here?/Is so and so available?]

はい、います。 *Hai, imasu.*
[Yes, she/he is./Yes, she/he is available.]

いいえ、いません。 *Iie, imasen.*
[No, she/he isⁿt./No, she/he is not available.]

（いる？）（うん、いる。）（ううん、いない。）
Iru. Un, iru. Uun, inai.

"*Imasu*" also means "*exist*" and functions the same as "*arimasu*," except that it can only indicate of the existence of animate beings such as humans and animals.

Step 9: やさしいせんせいはだれですか。
Yasashii sensei wa dare desu ka?
[Which teacher is nice?]

おもしろいせんせいはだれですか。
Omoshiroi sensei wa dare desu ka?
[Which teacher is interesting?]

げんきなせんせいはだれですか。
Genkina sensei wa dare desu ka?
[Which teacher is enthusiastic?]

すてきなせんせいはだれですか。
Sutekina sensei wa dare desu ka?
[Which teacher is attractive?]

まじめなせんせいはだれですか。
Majimena sensei wa dare desu ka?
[Which teacher is serious?]

～せんせいです。 (*-senseidesu.*) [It is so-and-so.]

（やさしいせんせい（は）だれ？）
Yasashii sensei (wa) dare?

（おもしろいせんせい（は）だれ？）
Omoshiroi sensei (wa) dare?

げんきなせんせい（は）だれ？
Genkina sensei (wa) dare?

（すてきなせんせい（は）だれ？）
Sutekina sensei (wa) dare?

（まじめなせんせい（は）だれ？）
Majimena sensei (wa) dare?

（～せんせい。）(*-sensei.*)

(See Page 294 for further information on adjectives.)

Step 10-1: どこへいきますか。 *Doko e ikimasu ka?*
[Where are you going?]

～へいきます。 *~e ikimasu*
[I (will/am going to) go to~.]

（どこ（へ）いく（の）？ ～。）
Doko(e)iku(no)? ~.

Step 10-2: だれといきますか。 *Dare to ikimasu ka?*
[Who are you going with?]

～といきます。 *~to ikimasu*
[I (will/am going to) go with~.]

（だれといく（の）？ ～（と）。）*Dare to iku(no)?*
~(to).

Step 10-3: なにをしますか。 *Nani o shimasu ka?*
[What do/will you do?]

～をします。 *~o shimasu*
[I (will/am going to) do~.]

（なに（を）する（の）？ ～。）
Nani(o)suru(no)? ~.

Step 10-4: どこでしますか。 *Doko de shimasu ka?*
[Where do/will you do it?]

～でします。 *-de shimasu*
[I (will/am going to) do it in/at-.]

（どこでする（の）？ ～（で）。）
(*Doko de suru(no).*) (*-(de).*)

(See Page 390 for further information on vorbs)

Appendix
2. Romanization and Translation

Chapter 1

1.1 Warm-Up

Kore wa nan desu ka? (What is this?) Try to guess.
The answers are: 1 leaf 2 camera eye 3 octopus

1.1.3 A: *mi ru ku* (milk) B: *ba na na* (banana)
C: *ko o ra* (coke) D: *chi ki n* (chicken)

1.1.4 **Conversation 1**
A: *Okadasan wa nansai desu ka?*
(Ms. Okada, how old are you?)
A: *Anoo, juuyonsai desu.* (Um, I am 14 years old.)

Conversation 2
A: *Okadasan wa nannensei desu ka?*
(Ms. Okada, what grade are you in?)
B: *Anoo, nananensei desu.* (Um, I am a 7th grader.)

Conversation 3
A: *Okadasan, ichidoru wa nanen desu ka?*
(Ms. Okada, how many yen is 1 dollar?)
B: *Anoo, ichidoru wa hyakujuunien desu?*
(Um, 1 dollar is 112 yen.)

Conversation 4
A: *Okudasan wa ikutsu.*
(Ms. Okuda, how old are you?)
B: *Anoo, juurokusai desu.* (Um, I am 16 years old.)

Conversation 5
A: *Okudasan no gakunen wa?*
(Ms. Okuda, what grade are you in?)
B: *Anoo, juuichinensei desu.*
(Um, I am an 11th grader.)

Conversation 6
A: *Okuda san, nannen umare desu ka?*
(Ms. Okuda, What year were you born?)
B: *Anoo, senkyuuhyakuhachijuukyuunen desu.*
(Um, 1 was born in 1989.)

1.1 Basic Vocabulary

Ohayoo. (Good morning.)
Ohayoo gozaimasu. (Good morning.)

Konnichi wa. (Good afternoon.)
Konnichi wa. (Good afternoon.)

Konban wa. (Good evening.)
Konban wa. (Good evening.)

Hajimemashite. (It's nice to meet you.)
Hajimemashite. Doozo yoroshiku. (It's nice to meet you. Please look with favor upon me.)

Hajimemashite. (It's nice to meet you.)
Doozo yoroshiku onegai shimasu. (Please look with favor upon me.)

Hai, doozo. (Please take it.)
Hai, arigatoo gozaimasu. (Yes, thank you.)
Iie, kekkoo desu. (No, thank you.)

Ogenki desu ka? (How are you?)
Hai, arigatoo gozaimasu. (Yes, thank you.)

Sayoonara. (Good bye.)
Sayoonara. (Good bye.)

denwa (telephone)

denwa bangoo (telephone number)

denwa bangoo (telephone number.)

rei/zero (0)	*shichi/nana* (7)	*juu shi/yon* (14)
ichi (1)	*hachi* (8)	*juu go* (15)
ni (2)	*kyuu/ku* (9)	*juu roku* (16)
san (3)	*juu* (10)	*juu shichi/nana* (17)
shi/yon (4)	*juu ichi* (11)	*juuhachi* (18)
go (5)	*juu ni* (12)	*juu kyuu/ku* (19)
roku (6)	*juu san* (13)	*nijuu* (20)

1.1 Basic Vocabulary

juu ninensei (12th grader)
kookoo sannensei (3rd year high school student)
juu ichinensei (11th grader)
kookoo ninensei (2nd year high school student)
juunensei (12th grader)
kookoo ichinensei (1st year high school student)
kyuunensei (9th grader)
chuugaku sannensei (3rd year junior high school student)
hachinensei (8th grader)
chuugaku ninensei (2nd year junior high school student)
nananensei (7th grader)
chuugaku ichinensei (1st year junior high school student)
rokunensei (6th grader)
shoogaku rokunensei (6th year elementary school student)
gonensei (5th grader)
shoogaku gonensei (5th year elementary school student)
yonensei (4th grader)
shoogaku yonensei (4th year elementary school student)
sannensei (3rd grader)
shoogaku sannensei (3rd year elementary school student)
ninensei (2nd grader)
shoogaku ninensei (2nd year elementary school student)
ichinensei (1st grader)
shoogaku ichinensei (1st year elementary school student)
kyuunensei (9th grader)
chuugaku sannensei (3rd year junior high school student)
rokunensei (6th grader)
shoogaku rokunensei (6th year elementary school student)
juu ichinensei (11th grader)
kookoo ninensei (2nd year high school student)
sannensei (3rd grader)
shoogaku sannensei (3rd year elementary school student)

1.1 Basic Vocabulary

nijuu (20)
nijuuichi (21)
nijuuni (22)
nijuusan (23)
nijuushi/nijuuyon (24)
nijuugo (25)
nijuuroku (26)
nijuushichi/nijuunana (27)
nijuuhachi (28)
nijuukyuu/nijuuku (29)
sanjuu (30)
yonjuu (40)
gojuu (50)
rokujuu (60)

shichijuu/nanajuu (70)
hachijuu (80)
kyuujuu (90)
kyuujuukyuu/kyuujuuku (99)
hyaku (100)
nihyaku (200)
sanbyaku (300)
yonhayku (400)
gohyaku (500)
roppyaku (600)
nanahyaku (700)
happyaku (800)
kyuuhyaku (900)
sen (1,000)

Nannen umare desu ka? (What year were you born in?)

Tsuda Umeko, senhappyakurokujuuyonen umare.
(Umeko Tsuda, born in 1864)

Ozawa Seiji, senkyuuhyakusanjuugonen umare.
(Seiji Ozawa, born in 1935)

Tezuka Osamu, senkyuuhyakunijuurokunen umare.
(Osamu Tezuka, born in 1926)

senhappyakurokujuuhachinen (1868)
senkyuuhyakuyonjuugonen (1945)
senkyuuhyakukyuujuukyuunen (1999)
nisennen (2000)
nisenichinen (2001)
nisenhyakujuuichinen (2111)

1.1.5 1. *Konnichi wa. Ohayoo. Konban wa.*
(Good afternoon. Good morning. Good evening.)

2. *Konnichi wa. Ohayoo. Konban wa.*
(Good afternoon. Good morning. Good evening.)

3. *Konnichi wa. Ohayoo. Konban wa.*
(Good afternoon. Good morning. Good evening.)

1.1.6 1. *Sayoonara.* (Good bye.)

2. *Ogenki desu ka?* (How are you?)

3. *Doozo. Hai, arigatoo gozaimasu.*
(Please. Yes, thank you.)

4. *Iie, kekkoo desu.* (No, thank you.)

5. *Ii tenki desu ne.* (It's a fine day, isn't it?)

1..7 A. *ichi* (1)   C. *kyuu* (9)   E. *roku* (6)
B. *go* (5)   D. *juuichi* (11)

1.1.8 *kookoo sannesei* (3rd year high school student)
juuninensei (12th grader)
kookoo (high school)
kookoo ichinensei (1st year high school student)
juunensei (10th grader)
kookoo ninensei (2nd year high school student)
juu ichinensei (11th grader)

1.1.9 *chuugakkoo* (junior high school)
shoogakkoo (elementary school)

1.1.10 1. *Chuugaku ninensei wa (roku, nana, hachi, kyuu) nensei desu.*
(A 2nd year junior high school student is in (6th, 7th, 8th, 9th) grader.)

2. *Kookoo ichinensei wa (hachi, kyuu, juu, juu ichi) nensei desu.*(A 1st year high school student is a (8th, 9th, 10th, 11th) grader.)

3. *Shoogaku ninensei wa (ichi, ni, san, yo) nensei desu.*(A 2nd year elementary school student is in (1st, 2nd, 3rd, 4th)

grader.)

4. *Kookoo sannensei wa (kyuu, juu, juuichi, juuni) nensei desu.*(A 3rd year high school student is in (9th, 10th, 11th, 12th) grader.)

5. *Chuugaku sannensei wa (roku, nana, hachi, kyuu) nensei desu.*(A 3rd year junior high school student is in (6th, 7th, 8th, 9th) grader.)

1.1.11 1. *San, yon, nana no hachi, ichi, kyuu, roku wa (san, yon, nana no hachi, ichi, kyuu, roku) desu. (Hontoo)* or *(uso).*
(347-8196 is 347-8196. True or false.)

2. *Senhappyakukyuujuunannen wa (sen, happyaku, kyuujuu, nananen) desu. (Hontoo)* or *(uso).*
(The year 1897 is the year 1897. True or false.)

3. *Sanbyaku wa (sanhyaku) desu. (Hontoo)* or *(uso).*
(300 is 300. True or false.)

4. *Kookoo ichinensei wa (kyuunensei) desu. (Hontoo)* or *(uso).*
(A 1st year high school student is a 9th grader. True or false.)

5. *Nisenhyakugonen wa (nisen, hyaku, gonen) desu. (Hontoo)* or *(uso).*
(The year 2105 is 2105. True or false.)

1.2. Mechanics

1.2.1 1. *Konnichi wa* (Good afternoon.)
2. *Ohayoo* (Good morning.)
3. *Konban wa* (Good evening).
4. *Yoroshiku.* (It's nice to meet you.)

1.2.2 A: *Sensei ohayoo gozaimasu.*
(Good morning, teacher.)
B: *A, ohayoo.* (Oh, good morning.)

1.2.3 A: *Ohayoo.* (Good morning.)
B: *Ohayoo gozaimasu.* (Good morning.)

1.2.4 A: *Hajimemashite. X desu. Doozo yoroshiku.* (It's nice to meet you. I am X. Please look with favor upon me.)
B: *Hajimemashite. Y desu. Doozo yoroshiku.* (It's nice to meet you. I am Y. Please look with favor upon me.)
or B: *Hajimemashite. Y desu. Doozo yoroshiku onegai shimasu.* (It's nice to meet you. I am Y. Please look with favor upon me.)

1.2.5 A: *Konnichi wa.*(Hello.)
B: *Konnichi wa.* (Hello.)
A: *Anoo, onamae wa.* (Um, what is your name?)
B: _____ *desu.* ((My name is _____.)

1.2.5 Note 4

rei, zero (0)   *ichi* (1)
ni (2)   *san* (3)
shi, yon (4)   *go* (5)
roku (6)   *shichi, nana* (7)
hachi (8)   *kyuu, ku* (9)
juu (10)   *juuichi* (11)
juuni (12)   *juusan* (13)
juushi,juuyon (14)   *juugo* (15)
juuroku (16)   *juushichi, juunana* (17)
juuhachi (18)   *juukyuu, juuku* (19)
nijuu (20)

1.2.6 1* *ni* (2)   4* *juusan* (13)
2* *juukyuu* (19)   18* *juuhachi* (18)

465

19*	*nana	13*	*yon
	(7)		(4)
7*	*ichi	20*	*nijuu
	(1)		(20)

1.2.7 Note 5

reisai, zerosai (0 years old)	issai (1 year old)
nisai (2 years old)	sansai (3 years old)
yonsai (4 years old)	gosai (5 years old)
rokusai (6 years old)	nanasai (7 years old)
hassai (8 years old)	kyuusai (9 years old)
jissai/jussai (10 years old)	juuissai (11 years old)
juunisai (12 years old)	juusansai (13 years old)
juuyonsai (14 years old)	juugosai (15 years old)
juurokusai (16 years old)	juunanasai (17 years old)
juuhassai (18 years old)	juukyuusai (19 years old)
hatachi /nijissai (20 years old)	

1.2.8
1. *Naokosan wa 7 (nana) sai desu.*
   (Naoko is 7 years old.)
2. *Sayakasan wa 11 (is) sai desu.*
   (Sayaka is 11 year old.)
3. *Gorookun wa 18 (juu has) sai desu.*
   (Goroo is 18 years old.)

1.2.9

Jenifaa (Jennifer)	Nikooru (Nicole)
Samu (Sam)	Hoze (Jose)
Hyun Jun (Hyuun-Jun)	Rosa (Rosa)
Ayana (Ayana)	

A: *Jenii san wa nansai desu ka?*
   (How old are you, Jenny?)
B: *Juu nanasai desu.*
   (I am 17 years old.)

1.2.10 A
1. *Gochisoosama deshita.* 2. *Gomennasai.*
   (Thank you for the meal.]) (I'm sorry.)
3. *Iie, kekkoo desu.* 4. *Hai, arigatoo gozaimasu.*
   (No, thank you.) (Yes, thank you.)
5. *Itadakimasu.*
   (Thank you for the meal.)

1.2.10 B
1. *Oyasuminasai* 2. *Ii tenki desu ne?*
   (Good night.) (It's a fine day, isn't it?)
3. *Anoo, sumimasen.* 4. *Arigatoo gozaimasu.*
   (Um, excuse me.) (Thank you.)

1.2.10 C
1. *Gochisoosama deshita.* 2. *Sayoonara.*
   (Thank you for the meal.) (Goodbye.)
3. *Genki?* 4. *Okagesamade.*
   (How are you?) (I am fine. Thank you.)
5. *Itadakimasu.*
   (Thank you for the meal.)

1.2.11 A
A: *Anoo, sumimasen.* (Um, excuse me.)
B: *Hai, nan deshoo?* (Yes, what is it?)
or B: *Nan deshoo ka?* (Yes, what is it?)

1.2.11 B
A: *Ii tenki desu ne.* (It's a fine day, isn't it?)
B: *Hai, soo desu ne.* (Yes, that's right.)

1.2.11 C
A: *Hai, doozo.* (Please take it.)
B: *Hai, arigatoo gozaimasu.* (Yes, thank you.)
or B: *Hai, itadakimasu.* (Yes, thank you.)
or B: *Hai, sumimasen.* (Yes, thank you [I am sorry].)

1.2.11 D
A: *Hai, doozo.* (Please, take it.)
B: *Iie, kekkoo desu.* (No, thank you.)

1.2.11 E
A: *~o onegai shimasu.* (I would like to request~.)
   ~ o kudasai. (Please, give me~.)

B: *Hai, doozo.* (Please take it.)

1.2.11 F
A: *Arigatoo gozaimasu.* (Thank you.)
B: *Dooitashimashite.* (You're welcome.)
A: *Iie.* (No problem.)

1.2.11 G
A: *Sumimasen. Gomennasai.* (Excuse me. I'm sorry.)
B: *Iie.* (No.)

1.2.11 H
A: *Itadakimasu.* (Thank you for the meal.)

1.2.11 I
A: *Gochisoosama deshita.* (Thank you for the meal.)

1.2.11 J
A: *Oyasumi nasai.* (Good night.)
B: *Oyasumi nasai.* (Good night.)

1.2.11 K
A: *Shitsurei shimasu.* (Excuse me.)

1.2.11 L
A: *Sayoonara.* (Good bye.)

1.2.12
A: *Ii tenki desu ne.* (It's a fine day, isn't it?)
B: *Hai, soo desu ne.* (Yes, that's right.)

1.2.13 A
A: *Ogenki desu ka?* (How are you?)
B: *Okagesamade.* (I am fine.Thank you.)
A: *Sayoonara.* (Good bye.)
B: *Shitsurei shimasu.* (I should be leaving.)

1.2.13 B
A: *Genki?* (How are you?)
B: *Un, genki.* (I'm fine.)
A: *Ja, mata.* (See you later.)
B: *Ja.* (See you.)

1.2 Note 8

nijuu (20)	nijuuichi (21)
nijuuni (22)	nijuusan (23)
nijuushi/yon (24)	nijuugo (25)
nijuuroku (26)	nijuushichi/nijuunana (27)
nijuuhachi (28)	nijuukyuu/ku (29)
sanjuu (30)	yonjuu (40)
gojuu (50)	rokujuu (60)
shichijuu/nanajuu (70)	hachijuu (80)
kyuujuu (90)	kyuujuuroku (96)
kyuujuu shichi/nana (97)	kyuujuu hachi (98)
kyuujuu kyuu/ku (99)	hyaku (100)

1.2.14

A: *21 wa (ni ichi juu, nijuu ichi, juu ni ichi) desu.*
B: *40 wa (yonjuu, yo juu, sanjuu, gojuu) desu.*
C: *100 wa (haku, byaku, ichi juu, hyaku, juu juu) desu.*

1.2.16

Hoshi Masako (Masako, Hoshi)
Suzuki Yoshio (Yoshio, Suzuki)
Kebin Buraun (Kevin Brown)
Kita Shiroo (Shiroh, Kita)

A: *Hoshisan wa nansai desu ka?*
   (How old are you, Miss Hoshi?)
B: *Nijuuyonsai desu.*
   (I am 24 years old.)
A: *Arigatoo gozaimasu.*
   (Thank you.)

1.3 Note 9

zero, san no san, nana, hachi no kyuu, goo, yon, nii
(03-378-9542)

0 zero/rei (zero)	2 nii (two)
4 yon (four)	5 goo (five)
7 nana (seven)	9 kyuu (nine)

1.3.1

1. *407-8196 wa (yon, rei, nan, hachi, ichi, kyuu, roku) desu.*
   (hontoo) or (uso).
   (407-8196 is 407-8196. True or false.)
2. *425-8376 wa (yon, nii, goo no hachi, san, nana, roku) desu.*
   (hontoo) or (uso).
   (425-8376 is 425-8376. True or false.)
3. *212-374-5190 wa (nii, ichi, nii no san, nana, yon no goo, ichi, kyuu, rei) desu.*
   (hontoo) or (uso).
   (212-374-5190 is 212-374-5190. True or false.)
4. *202-448-2200 wa (ni, zero, ni no shi, shi, hachi, ni, ni, rei, rei) desu.*
   (hontoo) or (uso).
   (202-448-2200 is 202-448-2200. True or false.)

1.3.3

BOY: *Denwa bangoo wa nanban desu ka?*
(What is your phone number?)
GIRL: *Yon, san hachi no goo, goo, nii, nana desu.*
(It's 438-5527.)

1.3.4

A: *Gifuto sentaa wa nan ban desu ka?.*
(What is the gift center's phone number?)
B: *Roku, hachi, zero no sa, nii, hachi, hachi desu.*
(It's 680-3288.)

1.3.4 Note 12

hyaku (100)	*nihyaku* (200)
sanbyaku (300)	*yonhyaku* (400)
gohyaku (500)	*roppyaku* (600)
nanahyaku (700)	*happyaku* (800)
kyuuhyaku (900)	
sen (1,000)	*nisen* (2,000)

1.3.5

A: *(Nisen, sen, ichi sen, sanzen) wa 1,000 desu.*
B: *(Hachihyaku, shichisen, shissen, happyaku) wa 800 desu.*
C: *(Sanhyaku, sanbyaku, sanpyaku, sappyaku) wa 300 desu.*
D: *(Rokuhaku, rokuhyaku, roppyaku, rokubyaku) wa 600 desu.*
E: *(Gohaku, goppyaku, gohyaku, gobyaku) wa 500 desu.*

1.3.7

Ichidoru wa hyakuen desu. (one dollar is hundred yen.)
1. *Nidoru wa ikura (nan'en) desu ka?*
   (How many yen is two dollars?)
2. *Hachidoru wa ikura (nan'en) desu ka?*
   (How many yen is eight dollars?)
3. *Juudoru wa ikura (nan'en) desu ka?*
   (How many yen is ten dollars?)
4. *Roppyakuen wa ikura (nandoru) desu ka?*
   (How many dollars is six hundred yen?)
5. *Kyuuhyakuen wa ikura (nandoru) desu ka?*
   (How many dollars is nine hundred yen?)

1.3.7 Note 14

A: *Nidoru wa ikura (nan'en) desu ka?*
(How many yen is two dollars?)
B: *Nidori kakeru hyakukyuuen wa nihyaku juuhachien desu.*
(Two dollar multiplied by 109 yen is 218 yen.)
A: *Nihyakuen wa ikura (nandoru) desu ka?*
(How many dollars is two hundredyen?)
B: *Nihyakuen waru hyakuen wa nidoru desu.*
(Two hundredyen divided by hundredyen is 2 dollars.)

1.3.7 Note 15

GIRL: *Goo, zero, kyuu no yon, roku, ichi, hachi desu.*
(It's 509-4618.)

Partial Repeating

BOY: *Goo, zero, kyuu no...* (509-...)
GIRL: *Yon, roku, ichi, hachi desu.* (4618.)

Confirming

BOY: *Goo, zero, kyuu no yon, roku, ichi, hachi desu ne.*
(It's 509-4618, right?)
GIRL: *Hai, soo desu.*
(Yes, that's correct.)

Asking Again

BOY: *Moo ichido onegai shimasu.*
(Could you say it again?)
GIRL: *Goo, zero, kyuu no yon, roku, ichi, hachi desu.*
(It's 509-4618.)

1.3.8

A: *Anoo denwa bangoo wa nanban desu ka ?*
(Um, what is your phone number?)
B: *Roku, kyuu, goo no ichi, rei, hachi, nii desu.*
(It's 695-1082.)
A: *Roku, kyuu, goo no ...* (695- ...)
B: *Ichi, rei, hachi, nii desu.* (1082.)
A: *Arigatoo gozaimashita.* (Thank you.)

1.3.9

A: *Jeniisan wa nannensei desu ka?*
(What grade is Jenny in?)
B: *Juuichinensei desu. Kookoo ninensei desu.*
(She is an 11th grader. She is second year high school student.)

1.3.9 Note 16

sen (1,000)	*nisen* (2,000)
sanzen (3,000)	*yonsen* (4,000)
gosen (5,000)	*rokusen* (6,000)
shichi/nanasen (7,000)	*hassen* (8,000)
kyuusen (9,000)	*ichiman* (10,000)

1.3.10

1. *8,496 wa (hassen yohyaku kyuujuu roku) desu.*
   (hontoo) or (uso).
   (8,496 is 8,496. true or false.)
2. *3,375 wa (sansen, sanbyaku, nanajuu, go) desu.*
   (hontoo) or (uso.)
   (3,375 is 3,375. true or false.)
3. *5,190 wa (gosen hyaku kyuujuu) desu.*
   (hontoo) or (uso).
   (5,190 is 5,190. true or false.)
4. *12,200 wa (ichiman nisen nihyaku) desu.*
   (hontoo) or (uso).
   (12,200 is 12,200. true or false.)
5. *17,050 wa (ichiman nanazen gojuu) desu.*
   (hontoo) or (uso).
   (17,050 is 17,050. true or false.)

1.3.12

Ichi giga wa sen mega desu.
(1 gigabyte is 1,000 megagabytes.)
Ichi kei wa sen baito desu.
(1 kilobyte is 1,000 bytes.)
1. *Ni giga wa nanmega desu ka?*
   (How many megabyte is 2 gigabytes?)
2. *Hachi mega wa nankei desu ka?*
   (How many k is 8 megabytes?)
3. *Jukkei wa nanbaito desu ka?*
   (How many byte is 10 kilobytes?)
4. *Hyaku giga wa nanmega desu ka?*
   (How many megabyte is 100 gigabytes?)
5. *Nisen mega wa nangiga desu ka?*
   (How many gigabyte is 2,000 megabytes?)
6. *Sanzen kei wa nanmega desu ka?*
   (How many megabyte is 3,000 kilobytes?)
7. *Gosen baito wa nankei desu ka?*
   (How many kilobyte is 5,000 bytes?)
8. *Hassen mega wa nangiga desu ka?*
   (How many gigabyte is 8,000 megabytes?)

9. *Sen giga wa ikura desu ka?*
(How much is 1,000 gigabytes?)

1.3.12 Note 17

1970 nen: senkyuuhyakunanajuunen (1970)
1980 nen: sen kyuuhyaku hachijuunen (1980)
1990 nen: senkyuuhyakukyuujuunen (1990)
2000 nen: nisennen (2000)
2010 nen: nisenjuunen (2010)
1868 = Meiji gannen (Meiji era 1st year)
1900 = Meiji sanjuu ninen (Meiji era 33rd year)
1912 = Taishoo gannen (Taisho era 1st year) *1917*
= Tiashoo nananen (Taisho era 6th year)
1926 = Shoowa gannen (Showa era 1st year) *1945*
= Shoowa nijuu nen (Showa era 20th year)
1980 = Shoowa gojuugonen (Showa era 55th year)
1989= Heisei gannen (Heisei era 1st year)
2000 = Heisei juuninen (Heisei era 12th year)

1.3.8

Tezuka Osamu 1928nen umare.
(Osamu Tezuka, born in 1928.)
Ozawa Seiji 1935 nen umare.
(Seiji Ozawa, born in 1935.)
Tsuda Umeko 1864nen umare.
(Umeko Tsuda, born in 1864.)
A: *Tezuka san wa nannen umare desu ka?*
(What year were you born in, Mr. Tezuka?)
B: *1928nen umare desu.*
(I was born in 1928.)
A: *Aa, soo desu ka.*
(Oh, I see.)

1.4.1

A: *Kookoo ichinensei desu ka?*
(Are you a 1st year high school student?)
B: *Hai, soo desu.*
(Yes, I am.)
A: *Ja, juunensei desu ne.*
(Well then, you must be a 10th grader.)
B: *Hai, soo desu.*
(Yes, that's correct.)

1.4.2

A: *Nikoorusan chuugaku sannensei desu ka?*
(Nicole, are you a 3rd year junior high school student?)
B: *Hai, soo desu.*
(Yes, I am.)
A: *Ja, juugosai desu ne.*
(Well then, you must be 15 years old.)
B: *Iie, chigaimasu. Juuyonsai desu.*
(No, I am not. I am 14 years old.)
A: *Aa, soo desu ka?*
(Oh, I see.)

1.4.2 Note 18

nezumi/nedoshi
(Year of the rat)
toradoshi
(Year of the tiger)
tatsudoshi
(Year of the dragon)
umadoshi
(Year of the horse)
sarudoshi
(Year of the monkey)
inudoshi
(Year of the dog)

ushidoshi
(Year of the cow)
usagidoshi/udoshi
(Year of the rabbit)
hebidoshi/midoshi
(Year of the snake)
hitsujidoshi
(Year of the sheep)
toridoshi
(Year of the bird)
inoshishidoshi/idoshi
(Year of the boar)

1.4.3

1. *uma* (horse)
3. *neko* (cat)
5. *inu* (dog)
2. *saru* (monkey)
4. *ushi* (cow)

6. *nezumi* (rat)
8. *tori* (bird)
10. *tora* (tiger)
7. *hebi* (snake)
9. *hitsuji*(sheep)

1.4.4

A: *Ushidoshi desu ka?*
(Were you born in the year of the cow?)
B: *Hai, soo desu.*
(Yes, I was.)
A: *Ja, senkyuuhyakuhachijuugonen umare desu ne.*
(Well, then, you must have been born in1985.)
B: *Hai, soo desu.*
(Yes, that's correct.)

1.4.5

A: *Senkyuuhyakuhachijuuninen umare desu ka?*
(Were you born in 1982?)
B: *Hai, soo desu.*
(Yes, I was.)
A: *Ja, toridoshi desu ne.*
(Well, then, you must have been born in the year of
the bird.)
B: *Iie, chigaimasu. Inudoshi desu.*
(No, It was n't. I was born in the year of the dog.)
A: *Aa, soo desu ka?*
(Oh, I see.)

1.4.6

A: *Aki no supootsu wa baree booru desu ka?*
(Is your fall sport volleyball?)
B: *Iie, chigaimasu.*
(No, it is not.)
A: *Ja, sakkaa desu ka?*
(Well, then, is it soccer?)
B: *Hai, soo desu.*
(Yes, it is.)

1.4.7 A

A: *Anoo, ichidoru wa nanen desu ka?*
(Um, how many yen is 1 dollar?)
B: *Ichidoru wa hyakujuunien desu.*
(1 dollar is 112 yen.)
A: *Ja, nijuudoru wa nisennihyakuyonjuuen desu ne.*
(Well, then, 20 dollars must be 2,240 yen.)
B: *Hai, soo desu.*
(Yes, that is correct.)

1.4.7 B

A: *Anoo, haado disuku wa nanmega desu ka?*
(Um, how many megabytes is your hard disk?)
B: *Kyuugiga desu.*
(It is 9 gigabytes.)
A: *Ja, kyuusenmega desu ne.*
(Well, then, it must be 9,000 megabytes.)
B: *Hai, soo desu.*
(Yes, that is correct.)

1.4.8 Case 1

Sensei: *Maakusan/Reecherusan, aki no supootsu wa
nan desu ka?*
(Mark/Rachel, what is your fall sport?)
Maaku/Reecheru: *Bareebooru desu.*
(It is volleyball.)
Sensei: *Ja, koochi wa Shimano sensei desu ka?*
(Well then, is your coach Mr. Shimano?)
Maaku/Reecheru: *Hai, soo desu.*
(Yes, it is.)

1.4.8 Case 2

Hiroko: *Maaku/Reecheru, aki no supootsu naani?*
(Mark/Rachel, what's your fall sport?)
Maaku/Reecheru: *Bareebooru.*
(Volleyball.)
Hiroko: *Ja, koochi wa Shimano sensei?*
(Well, then, is your coach Mr. Shimano?)

Maaku: *Un, soo da yo.*
(Yeah, it is.)
Reecheru: *Un, soo yo.*
(Yeah, it is.)

1.4.9

dorama kurabu
(drama club)
gakunen
(grade year)

namae
(name)
denwabangoo
(telephone number)

1.6 Application 1

Desktop name sign:
Yokoyama Misako
(Misako Yokoyama)

Risa Yungu
(Lisa Jung)

Name tag:
Dai Ichi Shoogakkoo, Ichi nen ni kumi, Ono Jun
(Elementary School Number 1, 1st grade, 2nd section, Jun Ono)
Risa Yungu, Ribaa kookoo
(Lisa Jung, River High School)

Business card:
Yamaguchi Kootoo gakkoo,
(Yamaguchi High School)
kyooyuu, Murakami Haruji
(Instructor, Haruji Murakami)
Yamaguchi-ken, Kawaguchi-shi, Ichi ban-choo 3-2-8
(Yamaguchi prefecture, Kawaguchi-city, ichi banchoo 3-2-8)
Denwa: 0839-22-6111
(Tel: 0839-22-6111)
Ribaa Kookoo
(River High School)
Risa Yungu
(Lisa Jung)

1.6 Application 2

namae (name)
kurabu (club)
denwabangoo (telephone number)
guruupu ichi (group 1)
guruupu san (group 3)
guruupu go (group 5)

gakunen (grade year)
supootsu (sports)

guruupu ni (group 2)
guruupu yon (group 4)

1.7 Note 22

Akemashite omedetoo gozaimasu.
(Happy New Year.)
Kinga shinnen
(I humbly wish you a Happy New Year.)
Gashoo.
(Celebrating a new year.)
Gei shun.
(Welcoming Spring = New Year)
Kotoshi mo yoroshiku onegai shimasu.
(I wish our cordial relationship to continue this year.)
Kotoshi mo ogenki de.
(Have a healthy and happy year.)
eto
(twelve signs of the Chinese zodiac)
nezumi/nedoshi
(Year of the rat)
toradoshi
(Year of the tiger)
tatsudoshi
(Year of the dragon)
umadoshi
(Year of the horse)
sarudoshi

ushidoshi
(Year of the cow)
usagidoshi/udoshi
(Year of the rabbit)
hebidoshi/midoshi
(Year of the snake)
hitsujidoshi
(Year of the sheep)
toridoshi

(Year of the monkey)
inudoshi
(Year of the dog)

(Year of the bird)
inoshishidoshi/idoshi
(Year of the boar)

1.7 Application

A: *Akemashite omedetoo gozaimasu. Kotoshi mo yoroshiku onegai shimasu. Nisennen, gantan.*
(Happy New Year. I wish our cordial relationship to continue this year. January 1, 2000.)
B: *Kinga shin nen. Kotoshi mo ogenki de. Nisennen, gantan.*
(I humbly wish you a Happy New Year. Have a healthy and happy year. January 1, 2000.)
C: *Gashoo. Heisei juu go nen, ichi gatsu tsuitachi.*
(Celebrating a new year. January 1st., Heisei 15)
D: *Geishun.*
(Welcoming Spring.)

1.8.1 Virtual Reality 1 A

1. *Konban wa.*
(Good evening.)
3. *Ohayoo gozaimasu.*
(Good morning.)
5. *Onamae wa?*
(What is your name?)
7. *Denwa bangoo wa nanban desu ka?.*
(What is your phone number?)
8. *Ohayoo.*
(Good morning.)
9. *Hai, soo desu.*
(Yes, that is correct.)
11. *Hajimemashite.*
(It's nice to meet you.)

2. *Nannensei desu ka?*
(What grade are you in?)
4. *Konnichi wa.*
(Good afternoon.)
6. *Iie, chigaimasu.*
(No, that is incorrect.)

10. *Anoo...*
(Um...)
12. *Ja,...*
(Well then, ...)

1.8 Virtual Reality 1 B

1. *Anoo, sumimasen.*
(Um, excuse me.)
3. *Hai, doozo.*
(Please take it.)
5. *Arigatoo gozaimasu.*
(Thank you.)
7. *Iie, kekkoo desu.*
(No, thank you.)
9. *~o kudasai.*
(Please give me~.)
11. *Itadakimasu.*
(Thank you for the meal.])
13. *Nansai desu ka?.*
(What's your age?)
15. *Gomennasai.*
(I am sorry.)
17. *Shitsurei shimasu.*
(Excuse me.)
19. *Ogenki desu ka?*
(How are you?)
21. *Ja, mata.*
(See you later.)

2. *Ii tenki desu ne.*
(It's a nice day, isn't it?)
4. *Hai, itadakimasu.*
(Yes, I will receive food/drink.)
6. *Hai, sumimasen.*
(Excuse me.)
8. *~o onegai shimasu.*
(I request ~.)
10. *Dooitashimashite.*
(You're welcome.)
12. *Gochisoosama deshita.*
(Thank you for the meal. [after eating])
14. *Nannen umare desu ka?*
(What year were you born?)
16. *Oyasuminasai.*
(Good night.)
18. *Sayoonara.*
(Goodbye.)
20. *Nanidoshi desu ka?*
(What's your animal year?)

Chapter 2

2.1.0 Warm-Up

furuutsu   fruit

2.1.3 Basic Vocabulary

dochira (which one)   *dore* (which one)

soretomo (or)
banana (banana)
kukkii (cookie)
rokku (rock)
tenisu (tennis)
dansu (dance)
koocha (black tea)
sarada (salad)
piza (pizza)
chikin (chicken)
sooda (soda)
ichiji (one o'clock)
sanji (three o'clock)
goji (five o'clock)
shichiji/nanaji (seven o'clock)
kuji (nine o'clock)
juu ichiji (eleven o'clock)
nan'yoobi (what day)
getsuyoobi (Monday)
suiyoobi (Wednesday)
kin'yoobi (Friday)

painappuru (pineapple)
keeki (cake)
jazu (jazz)
sakkaa (soccer)
eiga (movie)
koohii (coffee)
suupu (soup)
hanbaagaa (hamburger)
suteeki (steak)
aisu tii (ice tea)
nanji (what time)
niji (two o'clock)
yoji (four o'clock)
rokuji (six o'clock)
hachiji (eight o'clock)
juuji (ten o'clock)
juuniji (twelve o'clock)
nichiyoobi (Sunday)
kayoobi (Tuesday)
mokuyoobi (Thursday)
doyoobi (Saturday)

2.1.3 Basic Vocabulary

doko (where)
ikura (how much)
(one thirty)
~o kudasai (Please give me~)
jimu (gymnasium)
kyooshitsu (classroom)
konsaato hooru
(concert hall)
media ruumo (media room)
gurando (athletic field)
ichigatsu (January)
sangatsu (March)
gogatsu (May)
shichigatsu (July)
kugatsu (September)
juuichigatsu (November)

nanji (what time)
~ni shimashou
(Let's decide on~)
kafeteria (cafeteria)
toshoshitsu (library)
koodoo (auditorium)
konpyuutaa ruumu
(computer room)
puuru (pool)

nigatsu (February)
shigatsu (April)
rokugatsu (June)
hachigatsu (August)
juugatsu (October)
juunigatsu (December)

2.1.3 Basic Vocabulary

tsuitachi
(1st day of the month)
mikka
(3rd day of the month)
itsuka
(5th day of the month)
nanoka
(7th day of the month)
kokonoka
(9th day of the month)
juuichinichi
(11th day of the month)
juusannichi
(13th day of the month)
juugonichi
(15th day of the month)
juushichinichi/juunananichi
(17th day of the month)
juukunichi
(19th day of the month)
nijuuichinichi
(21st day of the month)
nijuusannichi
(23rd day of the month)
nijuugonichi
(25th day of the month)
nijuunananichi/nijuushichinichi
(27th day of the month)

futsuka
(2nd day of the month)
yokka
(4th day of the month)
muika
(6th day of the month)
yooka
(8th day of the month)
tooka
(10th day of the month)
juuninichi
(12th day of the month)
juuyokka
(14th day of the month)
juurokunichi
(16th day of the month)
juuhachinichi
(18th day of the month)
hatsuka
(20th day of the mo nth)
nijuuninichi
(22nd day of the month)
nijuuyokka
(24th day of the month)
nijuurokunichi
(26th day of the month)
nijuuhachinichi
(28th day of the month)

2.1.4

nijuukunichi
(29th day of the month)
sanjuuichinichi
(31st day of the month)
Topikku wa paatii desu.
(The topic is the party.)
Ja, nijuu yokka no kin'yoobi ni shimashoo.
(Well, let's have it on Friday, the 24th.)
Kore de miitingu o owarimasu.
(This is the end of our meeting.)
nannin
(how many people)
hitori
(one person)
sannin
(three people)
gonin
(five people)

sanjuunichi
(30th day of the month)
Miitingu o hajimemashoo.
(Let's begin the meeting.)

futari
(two people)
yonin
(four people)

1. doko (where)
3. dore (which one)
5. nanji (what time)

2. dochira (which one)
4. ikura (how much)
6. nan yoobi (what day)

2.1.5

tabemono (food)
akutibitii (activity)
meron (melon)
piza (pizza)
koohii (coffee)
koora (cola)
banana (banana)
karaoke (karaoke)

nomimono (beverage)
bideo (video)
panchi (punch)
keeki (cake)
dansu (dance)
poteto chippusu (potato chips)
miruku (milk)

2.1.6

1. niji (two o'clock)
3. hachiji (eight o'clock)
5. nanji (what time)

2. yoji (four o'clock)
4. kuji (nine o'clock)
6. juuniji (twelve o'clock)

2.1.7

Ichigatsu karendaa (January calendar)
A. kin'yoobi (Friday)
C. getsuyoobi (Monday)
E. doyoobi (Saturday)
G. nichiyoobi (Sunday)

B. kayoobi (Tuesday)
D. mokuyoobi (Thursday)
F. suiyoobi (Wednesday)

2.1.8

A. tsuitachi
(1st day of the month)
C. yokka
(4th day of the month)
E. futsuka
(2nd day of the month)
G. kokonoka
(9th day of the month)
I. nanoka
(7th day of the month)
K. juuninichi
(12th day of the month)
M. juusannichi
(13th day of the month)

B. juuyokka
(14th day of the month)
D. muika
(6th day of the month)
F. mikka
(3rd day of the month)
H. tooka
(10th day of the month)
J. itsuka
(5th day of the month)
L. yooka
(8th day of the month)
N. juuichinichi
(11th day of the month)

2.1.9

1. Miitingu o hajimemashou.
(Let's begin the meeting.)
2. Kore de owarimasu.
(This marks the end of the meeting.)
3. Tatte kudasai.
(Please stand up.)
4. Te o agete kudasai.
(Please raise your hand.)
5. Ii otenki desu ne.
(It's nice day, isn't it?)
6. Itadakimasu.

(Thank you for the food.)
7. *Dore ga ii desu ka?*
(Which one is best?)

2.1.9 Game and Song

Janken de kimemashoo.
(Let's solve the problem by doing *jan-ken -pon*?)

2.2.0 Note 1

nanji (what time)	*ichiji* (one o'clock)
niji (two o'clock)	*sanji* (three o'clock)
yoji (four o'clock)	*goji* (five o'clock)
rokuji (six o'clock)	*shichiji/nanaji* (seven o'clock)
hachiji (eight o'clock)	*kuji* (nine o'clock)
juuji (ten o'clock)	*juuichiji* (eleven o'clock)
juuniji (twelve o'clock)	*ichijihan* (one thirty)
nan'yoobi (what day of the week)	
nichiyoobi (Sunday)	*getsuyoobi* (Monday)
kayoobi (Tuesday)	*suiyoobi* (Wednesday)
mokuyoobi (Thursday)	*kin'yoobi* (Friday)
doyoobi (Saturday)	

2.2.1

A. *kin'yoobi*
(Friday)
B. *kayoobi*
(Tuesday)
C. *getsuyoobi*
(Monday)
D. *mokuyoobi*
(Thursday)
E. *doyoobi*
(Saturday)
F. *suiyoobi*
(Wednesday)
G. *nichiyoobi*
(Sunday)
H. *niji*
(two o'clock)
I. *yoji*
(four o'clock)
J. *hachiji*
(eight o'clock)
K. *rokuii*
(six o'clock)
L. *kuji*
(nine o'clock)
M. *juunijihan*
(twelve-thirty)
N. *ichijihan*
(one thirty)
O. *sanji*
(three o'clock)
P. *sanjihan*
(three-thirty)
Q. *nijihan*
(two-thirty)
R. *nanji*
(what time)
S. *nan'yoobi*
(what day of the week)

2.2.2

ibento karendaa (event calendar)

ibento (event)	*yoobi* (day)	*jikan* (time)	*basho* (place)
aato fea (art fair)	*suiyoobi* (Wednesday)	*sanji* (three o'clock)	*aato sentaa* (art center)
anime fesutibaru (animation festival)	*kayoobi* (Tuesday)	*hachiji* (eight o'clock)	*gurando* (athletic field)
saiensu fea (science fair)	*getsuyoobi* (Monday)	*yoji* (four o'clock)	*koodoo* (auditorium)
japaniizu naito (Japanese night)	*doyoobi* (Saturday)	*kuji* (nine o'clock)	*kafeteria* (cafeteria)

2.2.3

A: *Ima nanji desu ka?* (What time is it now?)
B: *Juujihan desu.* (It's 10:30.)
A: *Aa, soo desu ka? Doomo arigatoo.*
(Oh, I see. Thank you.)

2.2.4

A: *Ashita no paatii wa doko desu ka?*
(Where will tomorrow's party be?)
B: *Kafeteria desu.*
([In] the cafeteria.)
A: *Aa, soo desu ka? paatii wa rokuji desu ne?*
(Oh, I see. The party is at 6:00, isn't it?)
B: *Iie, chigaimasu. rokujihan desu.*
(No, that's incorrect. It's at 6:30.)

2.2.5

A: *Anoo, dansu paatii no kippu wa ikura desu ka?*

(Um, how much is a ticket for the dance party?)
B: *Eeto, nidoru desu.*
(Um, it's 2 dollars.)
A: *Ja, kippu o kudasai./kippu o onegai shimasu.*
(Well then, please give me a ticket.)
1. *dansu paatii* (dance party) *nidoru* (2 dollars)
2. *tarento shoo* (talent show) *godoru* (5 dollars)
3. *eiga* (movie) *nanadoru* (7 dollars)
4. *futtobooru* (football) *nijuudoru* (20 dollars)
5. *aato shoo* (art show) *juunidoru* (12 dollars)

2.2.6

A: *Paatii wa nanyoobi desu ka?* (What day is the party?)
B: *Suiyoobi desu.* (It's Wednesday.)
A; *Aa, soo desu ka? Doomo arigatoo.*
(Oh, I see. Thank you.)

2.2.7

A: *Nan' yoobi no nanji desu ka?*
(What day and what time is the party?)
B: *Suiyoobi no niji desu.*
(It's Wednesday at 2:00.)
A; *Aa, soo desu ka? Doomo arigatoo.*
(Oh, I see. Thank you.)

2.2.8

ibento karendaa (event calendar)

ibento (event)	*yoobi* (day)	*jikan* (time)	*nedan* (price)	*basho* (place)	*denwa* (phone)
aato fea (art fair)					*aato sentaa* (art center)
anime fesutibaru (animation festival)					
saiensu fea (science fair)					
japaniizu naito (Japanese night)			*tada* (free)	*kafeteria* (cafeteria)	
supiichi kontesuto (speech contest)					
fooku dansu (folk dance)				*gurando* (athletic field)	
rokku konsaato (rock concert)				*koodoo* (auditorium)	

2.2.8

A: *Anoo, aato fea wa nan'yoobi desu ka?*
(Um, what day is the art fair?)
B: *Suiyoobi desu.* (It's Wednesday.)
A: *Nanji desu ka?* (What time is it?)
B: *Eeto, sanji desu.* (Well, it is at 3:00.)
A: *Anoo, aato fea wa nanji desu ka?*
(Um, what time is the art fair?)
B: *Sanji desu.* (It's at 3:00.)
A: *Anoo, aato fea wa ikura desu ka?*
(Um, how much is the art fair?)
B: *Nidoru desu.* (It's two dollars.)
A: *Sorekara, aato fea wa doko desu ka?*
(Also, where is the art fair?)
B: *Aato sentaa desu.* (It's at the art center.)
A: *Sore kara, aato sentaa no denwa bangoo wa nanban desu ka?*
(Also, what is the art center's phone number?)
B: *277-4589 desu.* (It's 277-4589.)

2.2.9 A

A: *Doyoobi ga ii desu ka?*
(Do you prefer Saturday?)
B: *Soo desu ne. Doyoobi ga ii desune.*
(That's right. I prefer Saturday.)

2.2.9 B

A: *Kayoobi ga ii desu ka?*
(Do you prefer Tuesday?)

B: *Soo desu nee. Kayooobi wa chotto.*
(Uh, no, Tuesday is a little.)

2.2.10 A

A: *Banana ga ii desu ka. Soretomo, ringo ga ii desu ka?*
(Would you like a banana or would you prefer an apple?)
B: *Ringo ga ii desu.*
(I'd prefer an apple.)

2.2.10 B

A: *Hanbaagaa to piza to dochira ga ii desu ka?*
(Which do you prefer, hamburgers or pizza?)
B: *Piza ga ii desu.*
(I prefer pizza.)

2.2.11 A

A: *Koora ga ii desu ka? Aisu tii ga ii desu ka? Soretomo, sooda ga ii desu ka?*
(Do you prefer cola or do you prefer ice tea? Or do you prefer iced cola?)
B: *Anoo, aisu tii ga ii desu.*
(Well, I prefer iced tea.)

2.2.11 B

A: *Koora to aisu tii to soo da to dore ga ii desu ka?*
(Which would you like, cola, iced tea or soda?)
B: *Aisu tii ga ii desu.*
(I would like iced tea.)

2.2.12

A: *dansu wa kuji ga ii desu ka? Soretomo, juuji ga ii desu ka?*
(As for the dance,is 9 o'clock good or would you prefer 10 o'clock?)
B: *Eeto...*
(Well...)
A: *Ja, nanji ga ii desu ka?*
(Then, what time would you like to have it?)
B: *Anoo, hachiji ga Ii desu.*
(Well, I would like to have it at 8 o'clock.)
Ex.1 *kuji, juuji, nanji*
(9:00, 10:00, what time)
Ex.2 *sanji, goji, nanji*
(3:00, 5:00, what time)
Ex.3 *getsuyoobi, suiyoobi, nan'yoobi*
(Monday, Wednesday, what day)
Ex.4 *mokuyoobi, kin'yoobi, nan'yoobi*
(Thursday, Friday, what day)
Ex. 5 *kafeteria, jimu, doko*
(cafeteria, gymnasium, where)
Ex. 6 *toshokan, kyooshitsu, doko*
(library, classroom, where)

yoobi	*~yoobi*
(day of the week)	(day of the week)
jikan	*~ji*
(time)	(~o'clock)
basho	
(place)	

2.2.13

A: *Koora ni shimasu ka.?*
(Will you have cola?)
B: *Soo desu ne, koora ni shimashoo.*
(That's right. I'll have cola.)

2.2.14

A: *Meron ga ii desu ka, sore tomo, orenji ga ii desu ka?*
(Would you prefer a melon or would you prefer an orange?)
B: *Meron ga ii desu.*
(I prefer a melon.)
A: *Koora to juusu to koohii to dore ga ii desu ka?*
(Which would you like, coke, juice, or coffee?)
B: *Eeto, koohii ga ii desu.*
(Well, I'd like coffee.)
A: *Bideo to karaoke to dochira ga ii desu ka?*
(Which do you prefer, video or karaoke?)
B: *Karaoke ga ii desu.*
(I prefer karaoke.)

2.2.15

A: *Supiichi kontesuto wa, getsuyoobi ga ii desu ka?*
(Is Monday a good day for the speech contest?)
B: *Iie...*
(Um...)
A: *Ja, nanyoobi ga ii desu ka?*
(Well then, what day would you like to have it?)
B: *Mokuyoobi ga ii desu.*
(Thursday is good.)
A: *C san wa nanyoobi ga ii desu ka?*
(What day would you like to have it, Mr. C?)
C: *Mokuyoobi ga ii desu.*
(Thursday is fine.)
A: *Ja, mokuyoobi ni shimashoo.*
(Let's make it on Thursday then?))

2.3.1

Miitingu o hajimemashoo.
(Let's begin the meeting.)
Kore de owari desu.
(This marks the end of meetings.)
Te o agete kudasai.
(Please raise your hand.)
Toppikku wa paatii desu.
(The topic is the party.)
Ja, doyoobi ni shimashoo.
(Let's make it on Saturday, then.)

2.3.2

paatii (party)	*konsaato* (concert)
dansu (dance)	*fesutibaru* (festival)
asuretikku dee (athletics day)	

C: *Ja, miitingu o hajimemashoo.*
(Ok, let's begin the meeting.)
C: *Topikku wa paatii desu.*
(The topic is the party.)

2.3.2 Note 11

nangatsu (what month)	*ichigatsu* (January)
nigatsu (February)	*sangatsu* (March)
shigatsu (April)	*gogatsu* (May)
rokugatsu (June)	*shichigatsu* (July)
hachigatsu (August)	*kugatsu* (September)
juugatsu (October)	*juuichigatsu* (November)
juunigatsu (December)	

2.3.2 Note 11

nannichi(what date)	
tsuitachi	*futsuka*
(1st day of the month)	(2nd day of the month)
mikka	*yokka*
(3rd day of the month)	(4th day of the mo nth)
itsuka	*muika*
(5th day of the month)	(6th day of the mo nth)
nanoka	*yooka*
(7th day of the month)	(8th day of the month)
kokonoka	*tooka*
(9th day of the month)	(10th day of the month)

2.3.3

gogatsu	*ichigatsu*
(May)	(January)
juu gatsu	*hachigatsu*
(October)	(August)
sangatsu	*kugatsu*

(March)　　　　　　　　(September)
shichigatsu　　　　　　*shigatsu*
　(July)　　　　　　　　　(April)
yokka　　　　　　　　　*tooka*
　(4th day of the month)　　(10th day of the month)
tsuitachi　　　　　　　*itsuka*
　(1st day of the month)　　(5th day of the month)
muika　　　　　　　　　*mikka*
　(6th day of the month)　　(3rd day of the month)
yooka　　　　　　　　　*nanoka*
　(8th day of the month)　　(7th day of the month)

2.3.4
A: *Paatii wa nannichi desu ka?*
　(What is the date of the party?)
B: *Ichigatsu tsuitachi desu.*
　(January 1st.)

2.3.4 Note 12
nannichi desu ka?　　　(What is the date of ~?)

2.3.4 Note 13
juuichinichi　　　　　　*juuninichi*
　(11th day of the month)　(12th day of the month)
juusannichi　　　　　　*juuyokka*
　(13th day of the month)　(14th day of the month)
juugonichi　　　　　　　*juurokunichi*
　(15th day of the month)　(16th day of the month)
juushichinichi　　　　　*juuhachinichi*
　(17th day of the month)　(18th day of the month)
juukunichi　　　　　　　*hatsuka*
　(19th day of the month)　(20th day of the month)
nijuuichinichi　　　　　*nijuuninichi*
　(21st day of the month)　(22nd day of the month)
nijuusannichi　　　　　*nijuuyokka*
　(23rd day of the month)　(24th day of the month)
nijuugonichi　　　　　　*nijuurokunichi*
　(25th day of the month)　(26th day of the month)
nijuushichinichi/　　　　*nijuuhachinichi*
　(27th day of the month)　(28th day of the month)
nijuukunichi　　　　　　*sanjuunichi*
　(29th day of the month)　(30th day of the month)
sanjuuichinichi
　(31st day of the month)

2.3.5
kugatsu nijuusannichi　　*kugatsu nijuugonichi*
　(September 23rd)　　　　(September 25th)
kugatsu nijuuyokka　　　*kugatsu nijuuninichi*
　(September 24th)　　　　(September 22nd)

2.3.6
kugatsu juusannichi　　　*sangatsu tooka*
　(September 13th)　　　　(March 10th)
rokugatsu nijuugonichi　　*shigatsu nanoka*
　(July 25th)　　　　　　(April 7th)
A: *Dansu wa nannichi desu ka?*
　(What is the date of the dance?)
B: *Kugatsu juusannichi desu.*
　(It's September 13th.)

2.3.7
A: *Harowiin paatii wa nannichi desu ka?*
　(What is the date of the Halloween party?)
B: *Juugatsu sanjuuichinichi.*
　(It's October 31st.)
Uerukamu Dansu　　　　*kugatsu juusannichi*
　(Welcome Dance)　　　　(September 13th)
Posutaa Seeru　　　　　*kugatsu nijuuyokka*
　(Poster Sale)　　　　　(September 24th)
Dorama Naito　　　　　*juugatsu itsuka*
　(Drama Night)　　　　　(October 5th)

Supootsu Dee　　　　　*juugatsu tooka*
　(Sports Day)　　　　　(October 10th)
Harowiin Paatii　　　　*juugatsu sanjuuichinichi*
　(Halloween Party)　　　(October 31st)
Sunoo Fesutibaru　　　*nigatsu yooka*
　(Snow Festival)　　　　(February 8th)
Sukii Toonamento　　　*sangatsu muika*
　(Ski Tournament)　　　（March 6th)
Supiichi Kontesuto　　　*shigatsu tsuitachi*
　(Speech Contest)　　　(April 1st)
Essee Kontesuto　　　　*gogatsu juushichinichi*
　(Essay Contest)　　　　(May 17th)

2.3.8
Hinichi:　　　　　　　*nigatsu juusannichi*
　(Date:)　　　　　　　(February 13)
Jikan:　　　　　　　　*niji*
　(Time:)　　　　　　　(2:00)
Basho:　　　　　　　　*koodoo*
　(Place:)　　　　　　　(auditorium)
1.　*Hinichi:*　　　　　*ichigatsu juugonichi*
　　(Date:)　　　　　　(January 15)
　Jikan:　　　　　　　*rokuji*
　　(Time:)　　　　　　(6:00)
　Basho:　　　　　　　*gakkoo*
　　(Place:)　　　　　　(school)
2.　*Hinichi:*　　　　　*gogatsu nijuuichinichi*
　　(Date:)　　　　　　(May 21)
　Jikan:　　　　　　　*goji*
　　(Time:)　　　　　　(5:00)
　Basho:　　　　　　　*kyooshitsu*
　　(Place:)　　　　　　(classroom)
3.　*Hinichi*　　　　　　*shigatsu mikka*
　　(Date:)　　　　　　(April 3)
　Jikan:　　　　　　　*ichiji*
　　(Time:)　　　　　　(1:00)
　Basho:　　　　　　　*koodoo*
　　(Place:)　　　　　　(auditorium)

2.3.9
Hinichi:　　　　　　　*kugatsu futsuka*
　Date:　　　　　　　　September 2
Jikan:　　　　　　　　*yoji*
　Time:　　　　　　　　4:00
Basho:　　　　　　　　*koodoo*
　Place:　　　　　　　　auditorium
1.　*Hinichi:*　　　*Jikan:*　　　*Basho:*
　　(Date):　　　(Time):　　　(Place):
2.　*Hinichi:*　　　*Jikan:*　　　*Basho:*
　　(Date):　　　(Time):　　　(Place):

2.3.10 A
Kanin: mokuyoobi　　　(Kanene: Thursday)
Joan: suiyoobi　　　　(Joanne: Wednesday)
Jon: kayoobi　　　　　(John: Tuesday)
Kaori: kin'yoobi　　　(Kaori: Friday)
C: *Paatii wa nan'yoobi ga ii desu ka?*
　(What day is a good day to have the party?)
X: *Doyoobi ga ii desu.*
　(I would like to have it on Saturday.)
C: *Kanin wa?*
　(What day would you like to have it, Kanin?)
Y: *Mokuyoobi ga ii desu.*
　(I suggest Thursday.)

2.3.10 B
Janetto　　　　　　　*Jooji*
　(Janet)　　　　　　　(George)
Sun Yun　　　　　　　*Jakku*
　(Soung Yoon)　　　　　(Jack)
C: *Paatii wa nanyoobi ga ii desu ka?*
　(What day is a good day to have the party?)
X: *Doyoobi ga ii desu.*

473

(Saturday is good.)
C: *Janetto san wa?*
(What day would you like to have it, Janet?)
Y: *Watashi mo doyoobi ga ii desu.*
(I go with Saturday, too.)

2.3.10 Note 14

hitori (one person)	*futari* (two people)
sannin (three people)	*yonin* (four people)
gonin (five people)	*rokunin* (six people)
nananin/shichinin (seven people)	*hachinin* (eight people)
kunin (nine people)	*juunin* (nine people)

2.3.11

C: *Piza no hito. Te o agete kudasai.*
(Those people who would like pizza, please raise your hand.)
C: *Futari desu.*
(Two people.)

2.3.12

C: *Doyoobi no hito. Te o agete kudasai.*
(Those people who vote for Saturday, Please raise your hand.)
C: *Juunin desu.*
(10 people.)
C: *Kin'yoobi no hito .te o agete kudasai.*
(Those people who vote for Friday, please raise your hand.)
C: *Hachinin desu.*
(8 people.)

2.3.13

C: *Doyoobi wa juu nin desu. Kin yoobi wa hachi nin desu.*
(10 people for Saturday, 8 people for Friday.)
C: *Ja, doyoobi ni shimashoo.*
(Well, let's make it on Saturday then.)
C: *Kore de, miitingu o owarimasu.*
(This marks the end of the meeting.)

2.4.1

ibento puropoorazu   (event proposal)

(Time and location)

Sat. 6PM *koodoo* (auditorium)	Fri. 7PM *jimu* (gymnasium)	Sat. 6PM *koodoo* (auditorium)	Sat. 6PM *koodoo* (auditorium)

(Main course)

piza (pizza)	*pasuta* (pasta)	*piza* (pizza)	*piza* (pizza)

(Dessert)

aisu kuriimu (ice cream)	*keeki* (cake)	*aisu kuriimu* (ice cream)	*aisu kuriimu* (ice cream)

(Beverage)

koora (coke)	*koora* (coke)	*panchi* (punch)	*koora* (coke)

(Main activity)

dansu (dance)	*bideo* (video)	*dansu* (dance)	*dansu* (dance)

C: *Ja, miitingu o hajimemashoo.*
(Ok, let's begin the meeting.)
C: *Paatii wa, nanyoobi ga ii desu ka?*
(What day would be a good day to have the party?)
A: *Do yoobi ga ii desu.*
(I would like to have it on Saturday.)
C: *B san wa?*
(What about you, Mr. B?)
B: *Nichiyoobi ga ii desu.*

(I suggest Sunday.)
C: *C san wa?*
(How about you, Ms. C?)
C: *Watashi wa, doyoobi ga ii desu.*
(I would like to have it on Saturday.)
C: *D san nichiyoobi to doyoobi to dochira ga ii desu ka?*
(How about you, Ms.D ? Which day is better for you, Saturday or Sunday?)
D: *Watashi mo, doyoobi ga ii desu.*
(I would also like to have it on Saturday.)
C: *Doyoobi no hito. Te o agete kudasai.*
(People who vote for Saturday, please raise your hand.)
C: *Juunin desu.*
(10 people.)
C: *Nichiyoobi no hito. Te o agete kudasai.*
(People who vote for Sunday, please raise your hand.)
C: *Hachinin desu.*
(8 people.)
C: *Doyoobi wa juunin desu. Nichiyoobi wa hachinin desu.*
(10 people for Saturday, 8 people for Sunday.)
C: *Ja, doyoobi ni shimashoo.*
(Well, let's make it on Saturday.)
C: *Kore de miitingu o owarimasu.*
(This marks the end of the meeting.)

2.4.2

1. *sushi* (sushi)   *tenpura* (tempura)
   unagi (eel)
2. *tonkatsu* (pork cutlet)   *sukiyaki* (sukiyaki)
   yosenabe (seafood and chicken in a hot pot)
3. *soba* (buckwheat noodles)   *udon* (white wheat noodles)
   raamen (Chinese-style noodles)
4. *obentoo* (box lunch)   *kareeraisu* (curry and rice)
   okonomiyaki (savory pancakes)   *hanbaagaa* (hamburger)
A: *Sushi to tenpura to unagi to dore ga ii desu ka?*
(Which do you like, sushi, tempura, or eel?)
B: *Anoo, dore demo ii desu.* (Um, anything is fine.)

or

B: *Anoo, omakase shimasu.*   (Um, I'll leave it up to you.)

2.4.4

tabemono (food)
   suteeki (steak)   *pasuta* (pasta)
nomimono (beverage)
   koora (coke)   *juusu* (juice)
supootsu (sports)
   sakkaa (soccer)   *basukettobooru* (basketball)
basho (place)
   shoppingu mooru (shopping mall)   *gakkoo* (school)
yoobi (day of the week)
   kayoobi (Tuesday)   *suiyoobi* (Wednesday)

2.4.4 A

A: *Anoo, sumimasen.*
(Um, excuse me.)
B: *Hai, nan deshoo.*
(Yes, what is it?)

A: *Suteeki to pasuta to dochira ga ii desu ka?*
(Which do you like better, steak or pasta?)
B: *Pasuta ga ii desu.*
(I prefer pasta.)
A: *Soo desu ka? Ja, sakkaa to basukettobooru to dochira ga ii desu ka?*
(Is that so. Well then, which do you like better, soccer or basketball?)
B: *Sakkaa ga ii desu.*
(I prefer soccer.)
A: *Sakkaa desu ka? Ja,...*
(Soccer, I see. Well then,...)

2.4.4 B

A: *Anoo, suimasen.*
(Um, excuse me.)
B: *A, naani?*
(Yes, what is it?)
A: *Suteeki to pasuta to docchi ga ii?*
(Which do you like better, steak or pasta?)
B: *Pasuta ga ii.*
(I prefer pasta.)
A: *Soo. Ja, sakkaa to basukettobooru to docchi ga ii?*
(Is that so? Well then, which do you like better, soccer or basketball?)
B: *Sakkaa ga ii.*
(I prefer soccer.)
A: *Sakkaa. Ja,...*
(Soccer, I see. Well then,...)

2.6.1 Application

eiga (movie) *hachidoru* (8 dollars)
yuuenchi (amusement park) *nijuunidoru* (22 dollars)
rokku konsaato (rock concert) *nijuuhachidoru* (28 dollars)
kurashikku konsaato *nijuugodoru*
(classic concert) (25 dollars)
kantorii muujikku konsaato *juuyondoru*
(country music concert) (14 dollars)
indii caa reesu (India car race) *sanjuudoru* (30 dollars)
juudoo kyooshitsu (judo class) *juusandoru* (13 dollars)
tenisu kyooshitsu (Tennis class) *nijuudoru* (20 dollars)
sukeeto kyooshitsu (skate class) *juuichidoru* (11 dollars)
gorufu kyooshitsu (golf class) *nijuunidoru* (22 dollars)
konpyuuta kyooshitsu *juudoru*
(computer class) (10 dollars)
ryoori kyooshitsu *juuyondoru*
(cooking class) (14 dollars)
hanbaagaa no mise *hachidoru*
(hamburger shop) (8 dollars)
nihon ryoori no mise *nijuunidoru*
(Japanese cuisine) (22 dollars)
piza to pasuta no mise *juusandoru*
(pizza shop) (13 dollars)
sandoitchi no mise *nanadoru*
(sandwich shop) (7 dollars)
suteeki no mise *nijuugodoru*
(steak shop) (25 dollars)
famirii resutoran *juunanadoru*
(family restaurant) (17 dollars)
aato fea (art fair) *nanadoru* (7 dollars)
anime fesutibaru *juunidoru*
(animation festival) (12 dollars)
nihongo supiichi kontesuto *reidoru*
(Japanese speech contest) *(tada)* (0 dollars) (free)
saiensu fea (science fair) *godoru* (5 dollars)
toun miitingu (town meeting) *reidoru (tada)* (0 dollars) (free)
karaoke (karaoke) *juusandoru* (13 dollars)

2.6.1.3

eiga (movie) *hachidoru* (8 dollars)
juudoo kyooshitsu (judo class) *juusandoru* (13 dollars)

nihonryoori no mise *nijuunidoru*
(Japanese cuisine) (22 dollars)
anime fesutibaru *juunidoru*
(animation festival) (12 dollars)

2.6.1.6

gogo no puran (The afternoon plan)

2.6.1.7

goorudo pakku o kudasai.
(Give us the Gold Pack.)
goorudo pakku to iiguru pakku o kudasai.
(Give us the Gold Pack and the Eagle Pack.)

2.6.1.8

suupu to sunakku (soup and snacks)
tomato suupu (tomato soup)
kuramu chaudaa (clam chowder)
koon suupu (corn soup)
chikin nagetto (chicken nugget)
onion ringu (onion lings)
hamu to chiizu (ham and cheese)
taakii (turkey)
chikin (chicken)
bejitariann (vegetarian)
sarada (salad)
shiizaa (Caesar (salad))
guriiku (greek (salad))
chikin (chicken)
toofu (tofu)
surinpu (shrimp)
suteeki (steak)
mini suteeki (mini steak)
hanbaaga (hamburger)
mini hanbaaga (mini hamburger)
robusutaa (lobster)
mini robusutaa (mini lobster)
sakana furai (fried fish)
guriru saamon (grill salmon)
sutoomu saamon (steamed salmon)
furaido chikin (fried chicken)
guriru chikin (grilled chicken)
suteeki to chikin (steak and chicken)
suteeki to saamon (steak and salmon)
saamon to chikin (salmon and chicken)
nihon ryoori (Japanese cuisine)
tenpura (tempura)
tonkatsu (pork cutlet)
sushi (sushi (raw fish with rice))
sukiyaki (sukiyaki)
obentoo (box lunch)
soba (buckwheat noodles)
udon (white wheat noodles)
unagi (eel)
Itaria ryoori (Italian cuisine)
chiizu piza (cheese pizza)
peparoni piza (pepperoni)
chikin parumezan (cheese parmesan)
karamari (fried squid)
sheru pasuta (shell pasta)
dezaato (desert)
shooto keeki (short cake)
appuru pai (apple pie)

2.6 Application

Sushi Haru no menyuu (Sushi Haru's menu)
sushi (sushi (raw fish with rice))
tenpura (tempura)
yakitori (grilled chicken)
sukiyaki (sukiyaki)
udon (white wheat noodles)

soba	(buckwheat noodles)
raamen	(Chinese Style noodles)
tonkatsu	(pork cutlet)
yosenabe	(seafood and chicken in a hot pot)
unagi	(eel)

2.7.1.A Application

nihongo no paatii	(Japanese language party)
nichiyoobi	(Sunday)
ichji	(one o'clock)
shinamo sensei no manshonn	(Mr. Shimano's mansion)
tabemono	(food)
osushi to yakitori	(sushi and grilled chicken)
nominomo	(beverage)
koora to ocha	(cola and tea)
dezaato	(dessert)
keeki to ocha no aisukuriimu	(cake and tea ice cream)
bideo	(video)
pikushonarii	(pictionary™)

2.7.1.B

japaniizu paatii	(Japanese party)
hinichi	(date)
nigatujuuyokka	(February 24th)
jikan	(time)
shichiji han	(seven-thirty)
basho	(place)
aamaa	(the name of a dormitory)
tabemono	(food)
kukkii	(cookie)
keeki	(cake)
kudamono	(fruit)
nominomo	(beverage)
sooda	(soda)
saida	(cider)
juusu	(juice)
akutibitii	(activities)
dansu	(dance)
karaoke	(karaoke)
tarentoshoo	(talents show)

2.7.1.C

suiyoobi	(Wednesday)
shichiji	(7 o'clock)
kafeteria	(cafeteria)
paatii	(party)
sushi/pizza	(sushi and pizza)
ocha/koora	(tea and cola)

2.7.1.D

nihongo no paatii	(Japanese language party)
furaido chikin	(fried chicken)
piza	(pizza)
koora · juusu	(cola and juice)
kin'yoobi	(Friday)
rokuji	(six o'clock)
jimu	(gymnasium)

A no paatii wa nannichi desu ka?
　(What day is the A's party?)
dezaato wa nan desuka?
　(What desserts are there?)
B no paatii no nominono wa nan desu ka?
　(What food is there at B's party?)
akutebitii wa nan desu ka?
　(What activities are there?)
C no paatii no tabemono wa nan desu ka?
　(What food is there at C's party?)
paattii wa nanji desu ka?
　(What time will the party begin?)
D no paatii wa nanji desu ka?
　(What time will the D's party begin?)
nomimono wa nan desu ka?
　(What beverages are there?)
[Which] do you like better, steak or pasta?

2.8.1 Virtual Reality

1. *Doko ga ii desu ka?*
　(Where is a good location?)
2. *Hajimemashoo.*
　(Let's begin.)
3. *Eeto...*
　(Um...)
4. *Nanji ga ii desu ka?*
　(What time should we do it?)
5. *Sore tomo koohii desu ka?*
　(Or would you prefer coffee?)
6. *Dore ga ii desu ka?*
　(Which one among these do you like?)
7. *Nan'yoobi ga ii desu ka?*
　(What day of the week should we do it?)
8. *Goji ni shimashoo.* (Let's make it on 5:00.)
9. *Ja...* (Well then...)
10. *Dochira ga ii desu ka?*
　(Which [of the two] do you prefer?)
11. *Ikura desu ka?* (How much is it?)
12. *Omakase shimasu.* (I'll let you decide.)
13. *~o kudasai.* (Please give me~.)

Chapter 3

3.1.1.1 Warm Up 1

Neemu geemu (Name game)
1. Andaason desu. Doozo yoroshiku. Andaason san no tonari no Buraun desu.
　(I am Anderson. Please look with favor upon me.)(I am Brown, seated next to Ms. Anderson.)
Andaasonsan no tonari no Buraunsan no tonari Sumisu desu.]
　(I am Smith, seated next to Mr. Brown who is seated next to Ms. Anderson.)

3.1.1.2 Warm Up 2

Andaason: Hachigatsu umare no Andaason desu. Doozo yoroshiku.
　(Anderson: I am Anderson, born in August. Please look with favor upon me.)
Buraun: Hachigatsu umare no Andaasonsan no tonari no nigatsu umare no Buraun desu.
　(Brown: I am Brown, born in February, seated next to Ms. Anderson who was born in August.)
Sumisu: Hachigatsu umare no Andaasonsan no tonari no nigatsu umare no Buraunsan no tonari no juugatsu umare no Sumisu desu.
　(Smith: I am Smith, born in October, seated next to Mr. Brown who was born February, who is seated next to Ms. Anderson who was born in August.)

3.1.1.3 Warm Up 3

Andaason: (Hachigatsu umare no) Andaason desu. Doozo yoroshiku.
　(Anderson: I am Anderson (born in August). Please look with favor upon me.)
Buraun: (Hachigatsu umare no) genki na Andaasonsan no tonari no (nigatsu umare no) Buraun desu.
　(Brown: I am Brown (born in February), seated next to healthy Ms. Anderson (born in August).
Sumisu: (Hachigatsu umare no) genki na Andaasonsan no tonari no (ni gatsu umare no) suteki na Buraunsan no tonari no (juugatsu umare no) Sumisu desu.
　(Smith: I am Smith (born in October), seated next to wonderful Mr. Brown (born in February), who is seated next to Ms. Anderson (born in August).

3.1.2 Warm-Up

Shinkei suijyaku (Concentration game)

3.1.2 Basic Vocabulary

Okuni wa?.
(What country are you from?)
Supootsu wa?
(What sport do you play?)
Doo iu imi desu ka?
(What does it mean?)
Tanjoobi wa?
(When is your birthday?)

Goshumi wa?
(What hobbies do you have?)
Nihonjin
(Japanese person)
Amerikajin
(American person)
Kankokujin
(Korean person)
Mekishikojin
(Mexican person)
Chuugokujin
(Chinese person)
Kanadajin
(Canadian person)
Furansugo
(French language)
doko
(where)
nani/nan
(what)
dochira
(which one)
Doo iu imi?
(What does it mean?.)

Osumai wa?
(Where is your residence?)
Goshusshin wa?
(Where is your birthplace?)
Otoshi wa?
(What is your age?)
Tannin no sensei wa?
(Who is your homeroom teacher?)
Imi wa nan desu ka?
(What does it mean?)
Nihongo
(Japanese language)
Eigo
(English language)
Kankokugo
(Korean language)
Supeingo
(Spanish language)
Chuugokugo
(Chinese language)
Eigo
(English language)
ikutsu/nansai
(how old)
dare
(who)
itsu
(when)
nannichi
(what date)
Imi wa nan desuka?
(What does it mean?)

3.1.2 Basic Vocabulary

kazoku (family)
otoosan
(father)
oniisan
(elder brother)
otooto
(younger brother)
norimono (forms of transportation)
kuruma
(car)
takushii
(taxi)
densha
(train)
fune
(ship)
naka
(middle)
midori
(green)
shiro
(white)
pinku
(pink)
guree
(gray)
murasaki
(purple)
kazoku no hito no tokuchoo

okaasan
(mother)
oneesan
(elder sister)
imooto
(younger sister)

basu
(bus)
chikatetsu
(subway)
hikooki
(airplane)
hajime
(introduction)
owari
(conclusion)
ao
(blue)
aka
(red)
kuro
(black)
orenji
(orange)

(family member's characteristic)
genki-na
(healthy)
kirei-na
(beautiful)
suteki-na
(wonderful)
benkyoo
(study)
shukudai
(homework)
Nihongo
(Japanese language)
suugaku
(mathematics)
kagaku
(science)
seibutsu
(biology)
shakai
(social studies)
keizai
(economics)
ongaku
(music)
taiiku
(physical education)

yasashii
(kind)
kawaii
(cute)
omoshiroi
(funny)

kamoku
(school subject)
gaikokugo
(foreign language)
Eigo
(English language)
butsuri
(physics)
kagaku/bakegaku
(chemistry)
rekishi
(history)
seiji
(politics)
bijutsu
(art)
konpyuutaa
(computer)

3.1.3 Mechanics

1. *Otoshi wa?*
(What is your age?)
3. *Onamae wa?*
(What is your name?)
5. *Supootsu wa?*
(What sport do you play?)
7. *Goshumi wa?*
(What hobbies do you have?)

2. *Okuni wa?*
(What country are you from?)
4. *Osumai wa?*
(Where is your residence?)
6. *Goshusshin wa?*
(Where is your birthplace?)

3.1.4

ikutsu (how old)
dare (who)
itsu (when)
nan nichi (what date)

doko (where)
nani (what)
dochira (which one)

3.1.5

aka (red)
midori (green)
shiro (white)
orenji (orange)
guree(gray)

ao (blue)
kuro (black)
murasaki (purple)
pinku(pink)

3.1.6

kuruma (car)
takushii (taxi)
densha (train)
fune (ship)

basu (bus)
chikatetsu (subway)
hikooki (airplane)

3.1.7

1. *Banana ga suki desu.*
(I like bananas)
3. *Densha de ikimasu.*
(I go by train.)

2. *Banana ga kirai desu.*
(I hate bananas.)
4. *Sensei to ikimasu.*
(I go with the teacher.)

3.1.8

1. *haha/okaasan*
(mother)
3. *ani/oniisan*
(elder brother)
5. *otooto/otootosan*
(younger brother)

2. *chichi/otoosan*
(father)
4. *ane/oneesan*
(elder sister)
6. *imooto/imootosan*
(younger sister)

3.1.9

1. *Kawaii desu.*
(He/she is cute.)
3. *Yasashii desu.*

2. *Genki desu.*
(He/she is healthy.)
4. *Kirei desu.*

(He/she is kind.) (He/she is beautiful.)
5. *Suteki desu.* 6. *Omoshiroi desu.*
(He/she is wonderful.) (He/she is funny.)

3.1.10

1. *suugaku* 2. *gaikokugo*
(mathematics) (foreign language)
3. *ongaku* 4. *shakai*
(music) (social studies)
5. *kagaku* 6. *Eigo*
(science) (English language)
7. *taiiku* 8. *bijutsu*
(physical education) (art)

3.1.11

1. *butsuri* 2. *keizai*
(physics) (economics)
3. *seibutsu* 4. *Supeingo*
(biology) (Spanish language)
5. *seiji* 6. *Nihongo*
(politics) (Japanese language)
7. *Furansu go* 8. *konpyuutaa*
(French language) (computer)
9. *rekishi*
(history)

3.2.1 Mechanics

a. *Otoshi wa?* b. *Okuni wa?*
(What is your age?) (What country are you from?)
c. *Onamae wa?* d. *Osumai wa?*
(What is your name?) (Where is your residence?)
e. *Supootsu wa?* f. *Goshusshin wa?*
(What sport do you play?) (Where is your birthplace?)
g. *Goshumi wa?* h. *Tannin no sensei wa?*
(What hobbies do you have?) (Who is your homeroom teacher?)

3.2.2

1. *ikutsu* (how old) 2. *doko* (where)
3. *dare* (who) 4. *nani* (what)
5. *itsu* (when) 6. *dochira* (which one)
7. *nannichi* (what date)

3.2.3

Kimura Yuka	Satoo Kenji	Tanaka Maki	Mori Michio
(Yuka Kimura)	(Kenji Sato)	(Maki Tanaka)	(Michio Mori)
Kagoshima	*Miyazaki*	*Fukuoka*	*Ooita*
(Kagoshima prefecture)	(Miyazaki prefecture)	(Fukuoka prefecture)	(Oita prefecture)
juunana	*juugo*	*juuroku*	*juuhachi*
(17)	(15)	(16)	(18)
shichigatsu juuichinichi	*shigatsu juugonichi*	*kugatsu nijuuichinichi*	*juunigatsu nanoka*
(July 11)	(April 15)	(September 21)	(December 7)
Niigata	*Yokohama*	*Hiroshima*	*Nagano*
(Niigata prefecture)	(Yokohama prefecture)	(Hiroshima prefecture)	(Nagano prefecture)

A: *Konnichi wa.* (Good afternoon.)
B: *Konnichi wa.* (Good afternoon.)
A: *Anoo, onamae wa?* (Um, what is your name?)
B: *Kimura Yuka desu.* (Yuka Kimura.)
A: *Osumai wa?* (Where is your residence?)
B: *Kagoshima desu.* (Kagoshima prefecture.)
A: *Otoshi wa?* (What is your age?)
B: *Juu nana sai desu.* (17.)
A: *Ja, tanjoobi wa?* (Well then, when is your birthday?)
B: *Shichigatsu juu ichi nichi desu.*
(July 11th.)
A: *Ja, goshusshin wa?* (Well then, where is your birthplace?)
B: *Niigata desu.* (Niigata prefecture.)

A: *Niigata desu ka?* (Niigata prefecture?)
B: *Hai.* (Yes.)

3.2.4

Kimura Yuka	Satoo Kenji	Tanaka Maki	Mori Michio
(Yuka Kimura)	(Kenji Sato)	(Maki Tanaka)	(Michio Mori)
juuichi	*kyuu*	*juu*	*juu ni*
(11)	(9)	(10)	(12)
Kingu	*Joonzu*	*Hirano*	*Omarii*
(King)	(Jones)	(Hirano)	(Omari)
tenisu	*juudoo*	*sakkaa*	*futto booru*
(tennis)	(judo)	(soccer)	(football)
aato	*anime*	*kukkingu*	*konpyuuta*
(art)	(animation)	(cooking)	(computer)

A: *Kimura san, gakunen wa?* (What grade are you in, Ms. Kimura?)
B: *Koo ni desu.* (2nd year of high school.)
A: *Koo ni?* (2nd year of high school?)
B: *Kookoo ninensei desu.* (I am a 2nd year high school student.)
A: *A, kookoo ninensei desu ka?*
(Oh, a 2nd year high school student.)
B: *Hai.* (Yes.)
A: *Ja, tannin no sensei wa?* (Well then, who is your homeroom teacher?)
B: *Kingu sensei desu.* (Ms. King.)
A: *Supootsu wa sakkaa desu ka?*
(What sport do you play?)
B: *Iie, tenisu desu.* (No, it is tennis.)
A: *Kurabu wa nan desu ka?* (What club do you belong to?)
B: *Aato kurabu desu.* (The art club.)

3.2.5

A: *Okuni wa?* (What country [are you from?])
B: *Kankoku desu.* ([I am fom] Korea.)

3.2.6 Mechanics

A: *Sumimasen. Amerikajin desu ka?* (Excuse me. Are you an American?)
B: *Iie, chigaimasu. Oosutorariajin desu.* (No, I'm not. I am an Australian.)

3.2.7

Chuugokugo (Chinese language)
Chuugokujin wa Chuugokugo o hanashimasu.
(Chinese people speak the Chinese language.)
Eigo (English language)
Amerikajin ya Igirisujin ya Oosutorariajin ya Kanadajin wa Eigo o hanashimasu.
(American people, British people Australian people, and Canadian people etc. speak the English language.)
Supeingo (Spanish language)
Supeinjin ya Mekishikojin ya Peruujin wa Supeingo o hanashimasu.
(Spanish people, Mexican people, Perusian people , etc. speak the Spanish language.)
Furansugo (French language)
Furansujin ya Kanadajin ya Arujeriajin wa Furansugo o hanashimasu.
(French people, Canadian people, Algerian people etc. speak the French language.)
Hinzuugo (Hindi language)
Indojin wa Hinzuugo o hanashimasu. (Indian people speak the Hindi language.)
Roshiago (Russian language)
Roshiajin ya Ukurainajin wa Roshiago o hanashimasu.
(Russian people, Ukrainian people, etc. speak the Russian language.)
Arabiago (Arabic language)

Ejiputojin ya Sauji Arabiajin wa Arabiago o hanashimasu.
  (Egyptian people, Saudi Arabian people etc. speak the Arabic language.)
Nihongo (Japanese language)
Nihonjin wa Nihongo o hanashimasu.
  (Japanese people speak the Japanese language.)
Indoneshiago (Indonesian language)
Indoneshiajin wa Indoneshiago o hanashimasu.
  (Indonesian people speak the Indonesian language.)
Porutogarugo (Portuguese language)
Porutogarujin ya Burajirujin wa Porutogarugo o hanashimasu.
  (Portuguese people, Brazilian people etc. speak the Portuguese language.)

3.2.8

A: *Konban wa.*   (Good afternoon.)
B: *Konban wa.*   (Good afternoon.)
A: *Onamae wa?*   (What is your name?)
B: *Romero desu.*   (It is Romero.)
A: *Romero san desu ka? Okuni wa?*
  (Romero, I see. What country are you from?)
B: *Mekishiko desu.*   (Mexico.)
A: *Gakkoo wa?*   (What school do you attend?)
B: *Midorutaun kookoo desu.* (Middle Town High School.)
A: *Juu ichinensei desu ka?* (Are you an eleventh grader?)
B: *Iie, juunensei desu.* (No, I am a tenth grader.)
A: *Tannin no sensei wa?* (Who is your homeroom teacher?)
B: *Roido sensei desu.* (Mr. Lloyd.)
A: *Anoo, supootsu wa?* (Um, what sport do you play?)
B: *Sakkaa desu.* (Soccer.)
A: *A, sakkaa desu ka?* (Oh, you play soccer.)
B: *Hai.* (Yes.)
A: *Kurabu wa nan desu ka?* (What club do you belong to?)
B: *Eiga kurabu desu.* (The film club.)
A: *Ii desu ne. Romero san no tanjoobi wa?*
  (That's great. When is your birthday, Mr. Romero?)
B: *Roku gatsu juurokunichi desu.*
  (June 16th.)
A: *Aa, soo desu ka? Denwa bangoo wa?*
  (Oh, I see. What is your phone number?)
B: *Sumimasen, denwa bangoo desu ka? Goo, yon, hachi no nii, nii, kyuu, nii desu.*
  (My phone number? It is 548-2292.)
A: *Goo, yon, hachi no nii, nii, kyuu, nii desu ne.*
  (548-2292, right?)
B: *Hai, soo desu.* (Yes, that is correct.)

3.3.0 Mechanics

Note 4 Tactic A
BOY: *Okuni wa?* (What country are you from?)
GIRL: *Amerika desu.* (America.)
BOY: *Uesuto koosuto desu ka?* (The west coast?)
GIRL: *Iie, Nyuu Ingurando desu.*
  (No, the New England area.)

3.3.0

Note 4 Tactic B
GIRL: *Gakunen wa?* (What grade are you in?)
BOY: *Juu ichinensei desu.* (I am an 11th grader.)
GIRL: *Ja, kookoo ninensei desu ka?*
  (Well then, you must be in your third year high school, aren't you?)

BOY: *Hai, soo desu.* (Yes, that's right.)

3.3.1

1. A: *Nannensei desu ka?* (What grade are you in?)
B: *Juuninensei desu.* (I am a 12th grader.)
A: *Shinia desu ne.* (You must be a senior.)
B: *Hai, Shinia desu.* (Yes, I am a senior.)

2. A: *Supootsu wa?* (What sport do you play?)
B: *Juudoo desu.* (Judo.)
A: *Ja, Hayashi koochi desu ka?* (Well then, do you have coach Hayashi?)
B: *Hai, soo desu.* (Yes, that is correct.)

3. A: *Kuruma wa?* (What car do you have?)
B: *Akoodo desu.* (An Accord.)
A: *Ja, Nihon no kuruma desu ne.* (Well then, it must be a Japanese car.)
B: *Hai, soo desu.* (Yes, that is correct.)

4. A: *Osumai wa?* (Where is your residence?)
B: *Nyuu Yooku desu.* (New York.)
A: *Manhattan desu ka?* (Manhattan?)
B: *Iie, Burukkurin desu.* (No, Brooklyn.)

5. A: *Tannin no sensei wa?* (Who is your homeroom teacher?)
B: *Kawano sensei desu.* (Mr. Kawano.)
A: *Ja, juudoo no sensei desu ne.* (Well then, he must be the judo instructor.)
B: *Hai, soo desu.* (Yes, that is correct.)

6. A: *Oneesan desu ka?* (Is she your older sister?)
B: *Hai, soo desu.* (Yes, she is.)
A: *Ikutsu desu ka?* (How old is she?)
B: *Nijuuni desu.* (22.)

3.3. 2

1. A: *Anoo, kurabu wa?* (Um, what club do you belong to?)
B: *Dorama kurabu desu.* (The drama club.)

2. A: *Gakunen wa?* (What grade are you in?)
B: *Juunensei desu.* (I am a 10th grader.)

3. A: *Tanjoobi wa?* (When is your birthday?)
B: *Shichigatsu yokka desu.* (July 4th.)

3.3.2 Note 5

myooji (last name)

Yamada (Yamada [last name])	*Kimura* (Kimura [last name])
Suzuki (Suzuki [last name])	*Kawakami* (Kawakami [last name])
Kinoshita (Kinoshita [last name])	*Aoyama* (Aoyama [last name])
Nakayama (Nakayama [last name])	*Hayashi* (Hayashi [last name])
Ooyama (Ooyama [last name])	*Takahashi* (Takahashi [last name])
Koike (Koike [last name])	*Shimuzu* (Shimizu [last name])

3.3.3 Note 6

~no imi wa nan desu ka? (What is the meaning of~?)
A: *Anoo, Ooyama san.* (Um, Ms. Ooyama?)
B: *Hai.* (Yes?)
A: *Ooyama no imi wa nan desu ka?*
B: *"Big mountain" desu.*

~wa doo iu imi desu ka? (What does ~ mean?)
  (What is the meaning of Ooyama?)
  (It means "big mountain".)

3.3.4

A: *Banana ga suki desu ka?*
(Do you like banana?)
B *Hai, suki desu.* (Yes, I do.)
B: *Iie, suki ja arimasen,* (No, I do n't.)

3.3.5

A: *Banana ga suki desu ka?*
(Do you like banana?)
B *Hai, bana na ga suki desu.* (Yes, I like banana.)
B: *Iie, sbanana ga suki ja arimasen,* (No, I do n't
like banana.)

3.3.6

furuutsu (fruits)

3.3.7

A: *Naniiro ga suki desuka ?*
(What color do you like?)
B: *Midori ga suki desu.*
(I like green.)

3.4.0 Mechanics Note 7

watashi, watashikushi (I)

chichi	*haha*
(father)	(mother)
ani	*ane*
(older brother)	(older sister)
otooto	*imooto*
(younger brother)	(younger sister)

watashi/atashi (I)

otoosan/papa	*okaasan/mama*
(father)	(mother)
oniisan	*oneesan*
(older brother)	(older sister)
otooto	*imooto*
(younger brother)	(younger sister)
otoosan	*okaasan*
(father)	(mother)
oniisan	*oneesan*
(older brother)	(older sister)
otootosan	*imootosan*
(younger brother)	(younger sister)
otoosan, papa	*okaasan, mama*
(father)	(mother)
oniisan	*oneesan*
(older brother)	(older sister)
kazoku	
(family)	

3.4.0 Note 8

chichi (father)	*haha* (mother)
ani (older brother)	*ane* (older sister)
watashi/boku (I)	
otooto (younger brother)	*imooto* (younger sister)
otoosan (father)	*okaasan* (mother)
oniisan (older brother)	*oneesan* (older sister)
watashi/boku (I)	
otooto (younger brother)	*imooto* (younger sister)

3.4.1 A

watashi/boku (I)	
chichi (father)	*haha* (mother)
ani (older brother)	*ane* (older sister)
otooto (younger brother)	*imooto* (younger sister)
uchi no kazoku (my family)	*watashi/boku* (I)
otoosan, papa (father)	*okaasan, mama* (mother)

oniisan (older brother)	*oneesan* (older sister)
otooto (younger brother)	*imooto* (younger sister)

3.4.1 B

tomodachi (friend)	
otoosan (father)	*okaasan* (mother)
oniisan (older brother)	*oneesan* (older sister)
otootosan (younger brother)	*imootosan* (younger sister)
tomodachi no gokazoku (friend's family)	
tomodachi (friend)	
otoosan (father)	*okaasan* (mother)
oniisan (older brother)	*oneesan* (older sister)
otooto (younger brother)	*imooto* (younger sister)

3.4.2

Ooyama	*Samu*
(Ooyama)	(Sam)
Nikooru	*Dariru*
(Nicole)	(Daril)
Hyub jun	*Ayana*
(Hyun Jun)	(Ayana)

A: *Anoo, Ooyamasan no gokazoku wa nannin desu ka?*
(Um, how many people are you in your family, Ms.
Ooyama?)
B: *Haha to chichi to imooto to watashi no yonin desu.*
(My family consists of four people: my father, my
mother, my younger sister, and myself.)
A: *Anoo, Ooyamasan no gokazoku wa nannin desu ka?*
(Um, how many people are in Ms. Ooyama's family?)
B: *Ooyamasan no kazoku wa okaasan to otoosan to imootosan
to Ooyama san no yonin desu.*
(Ooyama's family consists of four people: her mother,
her father, her younger sister, and her.)

3.4.3

A: *Doko ni ikimasu ka?* (Where do you go?)
B: *Gakkoo ni ikimasu.* (I go to school.)

3.4.4

A: *Dare to gakkoo ni ikimasu ka?* (Who do you go to school
with?)
B: *Ane to ikimasu.* (I go with my older sister.)

3.4.5

A: *Dare to gakkoo ni ikimasu ka?* (Who do you go to school
with?)
B: *Tomodachi no otoosan to ikimasu.*
(I go with my friend's
younger brother.)

3.4.6

A: *Doko ni ikimasu ka?* (Where are you going?)
B: *Paatii ni ikimasu.* (I am going to a party.)
A: *Nan de paatii ni ikimasu ka?* (How are you going to the
party?)
B: *Basu de ikimasu.* (I am going by bus.)
A: *Aa, soo desu ka?* (Oh, I see.)

3.4.7

A: *Nan de gakkoo ni ikimasu ka?* (How do you go to
school?)
B: *Densha de ikimasu.* (I go by train.)
A: *Aa, soo desu ka? Dare to densha de gakkoo ni ikimasu ka?*
(Oh, I see. Who do you go
to school with by train?)
B: *Tomodachi no otootosan to densha de gakkoo ni ikimasu.*
(I go to school with my
friend's younger brother
by train.)

3.5.1 Mechanics

otooto	*ane*	*okaasan*	*otoosan*
(younger brother)	(older sister)	(mother)	(father)
1. *genki*	2. *genki*	3. *yasashii*	4. *yasashii*
(healthy)	(healthy)	(kind)	(kind)

urusai	*urusai*	*kibishii*	*kibishii*
(noisy)	(noisy)	(strict)	(strict)
kawaii	*kirei*	*suteki*	*suteki*
(cute)	(beautiful)	(wonderful)	(wonderful)
omoashiroi	*omoshiroi*	*isogashii*	*isogashii*
(funny)	(funny)	(busy)	(busy)
majime	*majime*	*omoshiroi*	*omoshiroi*
(serious)	(serious)	(funny)	(funny)

Otooto wa genki desu.
(My younger brother is healthy.)

3.5.2

____ *san wa genki na hito desu.*
(---[Mr., Mrs., Ms., Miss] ____ is a healthy person.)
1. *genki-na* (a healthy~)   2. *urusai* (a noisy~)
3. *kawaii* (a cute~)   4. *omoshiroi* (a funny~)
5. *majime-na* (a serious~)   6. *yasashii* (a kind~)
7. *kibishii* (a strict~)   8. *suteki-na* (an attractive~)
9. *isogashii*   10. *koseiteki-na*
(a busy~)   (an individual~)
11. *shoojiki-na*   12. *kuuru-na*
(an honest~)   (a cool~)

3.5.2 Note 12

omoshiroi hito   *Ani wa omoshiroi desu.*
(a funny person)   (My elder brother is funny.)
suteki-na hito   *Chichi wa suteki desu.*
(an attractive person)   (My father is a wonderful person.)

3.5.3

1. *ani* (older brother)   2. *ane* (older sister)
3. *otooto* (younger brother)   4. *imooto* (younger sister)
5. *haha* (mother)   6. *chichi* (father)

Ani wa suteki-na hito desu. Dakara, suki desu.
(My older brother is a wonderful person. That is why I like him.)
Ani wa urusai hito desu. Demo, suki desu.
(My older brother is a noisy person. However, I like him.)

3.5.4

1. *suugaku* (mathematics)   2. *konpyuutaa* (computer)
3. *kagaku* (chemistry)   4. *seibutsu* (biology)
5. *butsuri* (physics)   6. *taiiku* (physical education)
7. *ongaku* (music)   8. *bijutsu* (art)
9. *rekishi* (hisotry)   10. *keizai* (economics)
11. *seiji* (politics)

Eigo   *Furansugo*
(English language)   (French language)
Chuugokugo   *Doitsugo*
(Chinese language)   (German language)
Supeingo   *Nhongo*
(Spanish language)   (Japanese language)

A: *Suki-na kamoku wa nan desu ka?*
(What is your favorite subject? .)
B: *Nihongo desu.*
(It is Japanese.)

3.5.5

A: *Tokui-na kamoku wa nan desu ka?*
(What is your strong subject? .)
B: *Eigo desu.*
(It is English.)
A: *Nigate-na kamoku wa nan desu ka?*
(What is your weak subject? .)
B: *Suugaku desu.*
(It is mathematics.)

3.5.6

A: *Tokui-na spootsu wa nan desu ka?*
(What is your strong sport? .)

B: *Tenisu desu.*
(It is tennis.)
A: *Nigate-na supootsu wa nan desu ka?*
(What is your weak sport? .)
B: *Suiei desu.*
(It is swimming.)

3.5.7

A: *Suki-na tabemono wa nan desu ka?*
(What is your favorite food? .)
B: *Sushi desu.*
(It is sushi.)
A: *Suki-na nomimono wa nan desu ka?*
(What is your favorite beverage? .)
B: *Miruku desu.*
(It is milk.)

3.5.8

suugaku (mathematics)   *bijutsu* (art)
ongaku (music)   *seibutsu* (biology)
keizai (economics)   *taiiku* (physical education)
omoshiroi (interesting)   *tsumaranai* (boring)
muzukashii (difficult)   *yasashii* (easy)
tanoshii (fun)   *juuyoo-na* (important)
taihen-na (great deal)

A: *Suugaku wa omoshiroi desu.* (Mathematics is interesting.)
Suugaku wa jyuuyoo desu. (Mathematics is important.)
B: *Suugaku wa omoshiroi kamoku desu.*
(Mathematics is an interesting subject.)
Suugaku wa jyuuyoo na kamoku desu.
(Mathematics is an important subject.)

3.5.9

Nihongo (Japanese language)   *suugaku* (mathematics)
taiiku (physical education)   *kagaku* (chemistry)
rekishi (history)   *konpyuuta* (computer)

Nihongo wa omoshiroi desu. Dakara, suki desu.
(Japanese language is interesting. That's why I like it.)
Suugaku wa muzukashii desu. Demo, suki desu.
(Mathematics is difficult. However, I like it.)

3.5.10

A: *Suki-na kamoku wa nan desu ka?*
(What school subject do you like?)
B: *Nihongo desu.*
(Japanese language.)
A: *Nihongo wa omoshiroi desu ka?*
(Is Japanese language interesting?)
B: *Nihongo wa omoshiroi desu. Dakara, suki desu.*
(Japanese language is interesting. That's why I like it.)
A: *Suugaku wa muzukashii desu.*
(Mathematics is difficult.)
B: *Demo, suki desu.*
(But, I like it..)

3.6.1 Mechanics

aisatsu   *namae*
gakkoo   *toshi*
gakunen   *kootsuu*
sumai   *kazoku*
seikaku   *kuni*
shusshin
(greeting)   (name)
(school)   (age)
(grade year)   (transportation)
(residence)   (family)
(personality)   (country)
(birth place)
kokuseki   *~go*
kamoku   *suki*

kirai   shumi
matome   aisatsu
(nationality)   (~language)
(school subject)   (likes)
(dislikes)   (hobby)
(sum up)   (greeting)

Hajime: (Introduction):
(Eeto) konnichi wa.
     (Um) good afternoon.
Hajimemashite, doozo yoroshiku.
     It's nice to meet you. Please look with favor upon me.
(Anoo) watashi wa Jon Howaitohausu desu.
     (Um) I'm John Whitehouse.
(Aa, sorekara) Howaitohausu no imi wa shiroi uchi desu.
     (Oh, and also) the meaning of "Whitehouse" is white house.

Naka: (Main body):
(Eeto), gakkoo wa Nyuuhebun kookoo desu.
     (Um), my school is New Haven High School.
Kookoo sannen desu.
     I am a 3rd year high school student.
Juu roku desu.
     I am 16 years old.
Itsumo otooto to densha de kookoo ni ikimasu.
     I always go to school by train with my younger brother.
(Anoo) uchi wa Nyuu Jaajii desu.
     (Um) my home is in New Jersey.
Kazoku wa chichi to haha to ane to otooto to watashi no gonin desu.
     My family consists of five people: my father, my mother, my elder sister, my younger brother, and myself.
Ane wa yasashii desu. Dakara, suki desu.
     My older sister is nice. So I like her.
(Demo), otooto wa urusai desu. Demo, suki desu.
     (However), my younger brother is noisy. However, I like him.
(Aa, sorekara) shusshin wa Bosuton desu.
     (Oh, and also) my birth place is Boston.
Kuni wa America desu.
     My country is America.
(Anoo, demo), Doitsujin desu.
     (Um, however), I am German.
(Demo), Doitsugo o hanashimasen.
     (However), I do not speak German.
Demo, Eigo o hanashimasu.
     However, I speak English.
(Anoo, sorekara) Nihongo wa omoshiroi desu.
     (Um, also) Japanese is interesting.
Dakara, Nihongo ga suki desu.
     That's why I like Japanese.
(Eeto) sushi ga suki desu.
     (Um) I like sushi.
(Aa, sorekara) sashimi mo suki desu.
     (Oh, and also) I like sashimi too.
(Demo), tako wa suki ja arimasen.
     (However), I do not like octopus.

Owari: Conclusion:
(Ja), mainichi ganbatte benkyou shimasu.
     (Well), I study as hard as I can everyday.
Doozo yoroshiku onegai shimasu.
     Please look with favor upon me.

3.6.1 Note 16

doko (where)   dochira (where)
dare (who)   donata (who)
nan nichi (what date)   itsu (when)
ikutsu (how many, how old)   nan/nani (what)

Okuni wa dochira (doko) desu ka?
     (What country are you from?)
Osumai wa dochira (doko) desu ka?
     (Where is your residence?)
Goshusshin wa dochira (doko) desu ka?
     (Where is your birthplace?)
Tannin no sensei wa donata (dare) desu ka?
     (Who is your homeroom teacher?)
Dansu wa nannichi desu ka?
     (What is the date of the dance?)
Tanjoobi wa itsu desu ka?
     (When is your birthday?)
Otoshi wa ikutsu desu ka?
     (What is your age?)
Goshumi wa nan desu ka?
     (What hobbies do you have?)

3.6.1 Note 17

doko (where)   dochira (where)
dare (who)   donata (who)
nan nichi (what date)   itsu (when)
ikutsu (how many, how old)   nan/nani (what)

Kuni wa doko (dochira)?
     (What country are you from?)
Sumai wa doko(dochira)?
     (Where is your residence?)
Shusshin wa doko(dochira)?
     (Where is your birthplace?)
Tannin no sensei wa dara (donata)?
     (Who is your homeroom teacher?)
Dansu wa nannichi?
     (What is the date of the dance?)
Tanjoobi wa itsu?
     (When is your birthday?)
Toshi wa ikutsu?
     (What is your age?)
Shumi wa nani?
     (What hobbies do you have?)

A: Okuni wa dochira desu ka? (What country are you from?)
B: Amerika desu. (America.)
A: Ja, osumai wa doko desu ka? (Well then, where is your residence?)
B: Kororado desu. (Colorado.)
A: Aa, soo desu ka? Ii desu ne. (Oh, I see. How nice.)
A: Kuni wa doko? (What country are you from?)
B: Amerika desu. (America.)
A: Ja, sumai wa doko? (Well then, where is your residence?)
B: Kororado desu. (Colorado.)
A: Aa, soo . Ii (wa) ne. (Oh, I see. How nice.)

3.8 Application

penparu rikuesuto foomu (penpal) (request) (form)

dai ichi foomu (number one) (form)

watashi (I/me)   boku (I/me)
tanjoobi (birthday)
toshi (age)
gakunen (grade)
supootsu (sports)
suki-na kamoku (school subject I like)
suki-na ongaku (music I like)
suki na iro (color I like)
suki na kisetsu (season I like)

Hajimemashoo   (Let's begin.)

Dore ga suki desu ka?	(Which one do you like?)
supootsu	(sports)
Supootsu wa dochira ga suki desu ka?	
	(Which sport do you like?)
benkyoo	(study)
Kamoku wa dochira ga suki desu ka?	
	(Which school subject do you like?)
ongaku	(music)
Ongaku wa dochira ga suki desu ka?	
	(Which type of music do you like?)
tabemono	(food)
Tabemono wa, dochira ga suki desu ka?	
	(Which food do you like?)
Kiiro ga suki desu ka?	(Do you like yellow?)
Midori ga suki desu ka?	(Do you like green?)
Miruku ga suki desu ka?	(Do you like milk?)
Omizu ga suki desu ka?	(Do you like water?)
Juuninensei desu ka?	(Are you a 12th grader?)
Juunensei desu ka?	(Are you a 10th grader?)
Juugosai desu ka?	(Are you 15 years old?)
Juuyonsai desu ka?	(Are you 14 years old?)
Hai	(Yes)
Iie	(No)
Kore de owari desu.	(This marks the end of the meeting.)

3.9.1 A Application

Hajime:	Introduction:
Konnichi wa.	Good afternoon.
Hajimemashite, doozo yoroshiku	It's nice to meet you. Please look with favor upon me.
Watashi wa ____ desu.	I am ____.
Naka: Main body:	
Gakkoo wa ____ desu.	My school is ____.
____ desu.	I am ____.
____ desu.	I am ____.
Itsumo ____ to ____ de gakkoo ni ikimasu.	I always go to school with ____ by ____.
Uchi wa ____ desu.	My home is in ____.
Kazoku wa ____ desu.	My family consists of ____.
____ dakara, ____.	____ therefore, ____.
(Aa, sorekara) shusshin wa ____ desu.	(Oh, and also) my birthplace is ____.
Kuni wa ____ desu.	I'm from ____.
____ jin desu.	I am ____.
____ o hanashimasu.	I speak ____.
(Anoo, sorekara) ____ wa omoshiroi desu.	(Oh, and also) ____ is funny.
Dakara, ____ ga suki desu.	Therefore, I like ____.
(Eeto), ____ ga suki desu.	(Um), I like ____.
____ mo suki desu.	I like ____ too.
____ wa suki ja arimasen.	I do not like ____.
Shumi wa ____ desu.	My hobbies are ____.
Owari: Conclusion:	
(Ja) mai nichi ganbatte benkyoo shimasu.	(Well then) I will study as hard as I can everyday.
Doozo yoroshiku onegai shimasu.	Please look with favor upon me.

3.9.1 B

Hajime: Introduction:	
(Eeto) konnichi wa.	(Um) good afternoon.
Hajimemashite, doozo yoroshiku	It's nice to meet you. Please look with favor upon me.
(Anoo) watashi wa ____ desu.	

(Um) I am ____.	
(Aa, sorekara), ____ no imi wa ____ desu.	(Oh, and also), the meaning of ____ is ____.
Naka: Main body:	
(Eeto) gakkoo wa ____ desu.	(Um) my school is ____.
____ desu.	I am ____.
____ desu.	I am ____.
Itsumo ____ to ____ de gakkoo ni ikimasu.	I always go to school with ____ by ____.
(Anoo) uchi wa ____ desu.	(Um) my home is in ____.
Kazoku wa ____ desu.	My family consists of ____.
____ dakara,	
____ therefore, ____.	
(Aa, sorekara) shusshin wa ____ desu.	(Oh, and also) my birth place is ____.
Kuni wa ____ desu.	I'm from ____.
(Anoo, demo) ____ jin desu.	(Um, however) I am ____.
(Demo) ____ o hanashimasen.	(However) I do not speak ____.
Demo, ____ o hanashimasu.	However, I speak ____.
(Anoo, sorekara) ____ wa omoshiroi desu.	(Oh, and also) ____ is funny.
Dakara, ____ ga suki desu.	Therefore, I like ____.
(Eeto), ____ ga suki desu.	(Um), I like ____.
(Aa, sorekara) ____ mo suki desu.	(Oh, and also) I like ____ too.
(Demo) ____ wa suki ja arimasen.	(However) I do not like ____.
Shumi wa ____ desu.	My hobbies are ____.
Owari: Conclusion:	
(Ja) mai nichi ganbatte ____.	(Well then) I ____ as hard as I can everyday.
Doozo yoroshiku onegai shimasu.	Please look with favor upon me.

3.9.2

Aru hi no kaiwa kara.
(From a conversation on a certain day.)
Rei nen, rei kumi, rei ban   Takahara Eri
(grade zero, class zero, number zero)   (Eri Takahara)
Watashi wa yasumi jikan ga suki desu.
(I like break time.)
Kono jikan ni, tomodachi to yoku hanashimasu.
(During this time, I often chat with my friend.)
Naiyoo wa, kurabu no koto, terebi no kotodesu.
(The content of the conversation is about our clubs and about television.)

3.9.3 A

1. *hookago*	2. *natsu yasumi*
(after school)	(summer vacation)
3. *yasumi jikan*	4. *hiru yasumi*
(break time)	(lunch time)
5. *tomodachi*	6. *renshuu no naiyoo*
(lunch time)	(content of practice)
7. *kono jikan*	8. *shokudoo*
(during this time)	(cafeteria)
9. *benkyoo*	10. *tokidoki*
(study)	(sometimes)
11. *yoku*	12. *juku no ato*

483

(often)   (after cram school)

3.9.3 B

A.

Aru hi no kaiwa kara.
(From a conversation on a certain day.)
Ichi nen, ni kumi, nana ban   Tamura Nao
(1st grade, class 2, number 7)(Nao Tamura)
Watashi wa, hookago no jikan ga suki desu.
(I like after school time.)
Kono jikan ni, tomodachi to yoku tenisu no renshuu ni ikimasu.
(During this time, I often go to tennis practice with my friend.)
Renshuu no naiyoo wa, saabu to, bakku hando desu.
(The content of the practices are serving and back-hand shots.)
Renshuu no ato, daisuki na aisu kuriimu no mise e ikimasu.
(After practice, I go to my favorite ice cream shop.)

B.

Aru hi no kaiwa kara.
(From a conversation on a certain day.)
San nen, go kumi, hachi ban   Takayama Yasuo
(3rd grade, class 5, number 8) (Yasuo Takayama)
Boku wa, natsu yasumi ga suki desu.
(I like summer vacations.)
Natsu yasumi ni wa, tomodachi to yoku yama e ikimasu. Yama wa omoshiroi desu.
(During summer vacations, I go to the mountain with my friend.)
Tokidoki yoru wa kyampu faiyaa ni ikimasu.
(The mountains are fun.) (Sometimes at night we go to a camp fire.)

C.

Aru hi no kaiwa kara.
(From a conversation on a certain day.)
Ni nen, ni kumi, ni ban   Ooyama Haruko
(2nd grade, class 2, number 2)(Haruko Ooyama)
Watashi wa hiru yasumi no jikan ga suki desu.
(I like lunch time.)
Kono jikan ni, tomodachi to yoku shokudoo e ikimasu.
(During this time, I often go to the cafeteria with my friend.)
Yoku tomodachi to hanashimasu.
(I often chat with my friend.)

D.

Aru hi no kaiwa kara.
(From a conversation on a certain day.)
San nen, go kumi, juu san ban Nakayama Satomi
(3rd grade, class 5, number 13) (Satomi Nakayama)
Watashi wa juku no jikan ga suki desu.
(I like cram school time.)
Juku no benkyoo wa omoshiroi desu.
(What we study in cram school is fun.)
Tomodachi ya juku no sensei to yoku hanashimasu.
(I often chat with my friend and my cram school teacher.)
Juku no ato raamen no mise he tokidoki ikimasu.
(After cram school, I sometimes go to a Ramen noodle shop.)

Takahara Eri (Eri Takahara)
Tamura Nao (Nao Tamura)
Takayama Yasuo (Yasuo Takayama)
Ooyama Haruko (Haruko Ooyama)
Nakayama Satomi (Satomi Nakayama)

1. *Takahara Eri wa terebi ga suki desu.*
   (Eri Takahara likes television.)
2. ____ *wa aki ni Yuu-Esu Oopun ni ikimasu.*
   (____ will go to the U.S. Open in the fall.)

3. ____ *wa aki ni daigaku ni ikimasu.*
   (____ will go to college ni the fall.)
4. ____ *wa fuyu ni sukii ni ikimasu.*
   (____ will go skiing in the winter.)
5. ____ *wa tomodachi to resutoran ni ikimasu.*
   (____ will go to a restaurant with a friend.)

3.10.1 Virtual Reality 1

1. *Otoshi wa?*	(What is your age?)
2. *Tanjoobi wa?*	(When is your birthday?)
3. *Gakunen wa?*	(What grade are you in?)
4. *Okuni wa?*	(What country are you from?)
5. *Suki na kamoku wa?*	(What school subject do you like?)
6. *Supootsu wa?*	(What sport do you play?)
7. *Goshusshin wa?*	(What is your birthplace?)
8. *Tannin no sensei wa?*	(Who is your homeroom teacher?)
9. *Onamae wa?*	(What is your name?)
10. *Imi wa?*	(What does it mean?)
11. *Osumai wa?*	(Where is your residence?)
12. *Suki na ongaku wa?*	(What type of music do you like?)
13. *Kurabu wa?*	(What club do you belong to?)
14. *Goshumi wa?*	(What hobbies do you have?)
a. *Nandesu ka?*	(What is it?)
i. *Itsu desu ka?*	(When is it?)
u. *Dare desu ka?*	(Who is it?)
e. *Dochira desu ka?*	(Which one is it?)
o. *Ikutsu desu ka?*	(How old are you?)

3.11.3 Virtual Reality

gakkoo (school)
Gakkoo no namae wa Gureeto Reiku sukuuru desu.
(The name of my school is Great Lake School.)
Kookoo ninensei desu.
(I am a 2nd year high school student.)
Otooto to gakko ni itsumo basu de ikimasu.
(I always go to school with my younger brother by bus.)
kazoku (family)
Kazoku wa chichi to haha to otooto no yo nin desu.
(My family consists of four people: my father, my mother, my younger brother, and myself.)
Chichi wa itsumo isogashii desu.
(My father is always busy.)
Haha wa yasashii desu.
(My mother is kind.)
Otooto wa genki desu.
(My younger brother is healthy.)
suki/kirai (likes/dislikes)
Sakkaa ga suki desu.
(I like soccer.)
Demo, baree booru wa suki ja arimasen.
(However, I do not like volleyball.)
Aisu kuriimu ga daisuki desu.
(I like ice cream a lot.)
Dakara, yoku aisu kuriimu no mise ni ikimasu.
(That's why I often go to the ice cream shop.)
shusshin (birth place)
Namae wa Niina desu.
(My name is Nina.)
Kuni wa Amerika desu.
(My country is America.)
Shusshin wa Baamonto desu.
(My birthplace is Vermont.)
Sumai wa NyuuYooku desu.

(My residence is in New York.)

Chapter 4

4.1.2 Warm-Up

Konnichi wa. Hajimemashite, doozo yoroshiku.
(Good afternoon. It's nice to meet you. Please look with favor upon me.)
Watashi wa Asai Hana desu.
(I am Hana Asai.)
Gakkoo wa Ueda kookoo desu.
(My school is Ueda High School.)
Juu go desu.
(I am 15 years old.)
Itsumo otooto to densha de gakkoo ni ikimasu.
(I always go to school with my younger brother by train.)
Uchi wa Matsumoto desu.
(My residence is Matsumoto City.)
Kazoku wa otoosan to okaasan to otooto no yonin desu.
(My family consists of 4 people: my father, my mother, and my younger brother, and myself.)
Shusshin wa Nagano desu.
(My birth place is Nagano prefecture.)
Nihon go wo hanshimasu.
(I speak Japanese.)
Eiga ga suki desu.
(I like movies.)
Shumi wa tenisu desu.
(My hobby is tennis.)
Mai nichi ganbatte benkyoo shite imasu.
(I study as hard as I can everyday.)

4.1.3 A;

Nakamura sensei no happyoo wa hachiji kara desu.
(Mrs. Nakamura's presentation will begin at 8:00.)
Basho wa koodoo desu.
(The presentation will be at the auditorium.)
Yoyaku ga hitsuyoo desu.
(Reservations are required.)
Happyoo wa nihongo desu.
(Her presentation will be in Japanese.)
Nooto ga hitsuyoo ja arimasen.
(Notebook is not required.)

4.1.3 B;

Tanaka sensei no happyoo wa shichijihan kara desu.
(Mrs. Nakamura's presentation will begin at 7:30.)
Basho wa konsaato hooru desu.
(The presentation will be at the concert hall.)
Yoyaku ga hitsuyoo ja arimasen.
(Reservations are not required.)
Happyoo wa eigo desu.
(Her presentation will be in English.)
Nooto ga hitsuyoo desu.
(Notebook is required.)

4.1.3 Basic Vocabulary

Moshi moshi, Rika san imasu ka?
(Hello, is Rika there/?)
Iie, chigaimasu.
(You have the wrong number.)

1. *okimasu*
2. *gakkoo e ikimasu*
3. *tegami o kakimasu*
4. *hon o yomimasu*
5. *sukii o shimasu*
6. *bareebooru o shimasu*
(wake up)
(go to school)
(write a letter)
(read a book)
(ski)
(play volleyball)
7. *basuketto booru o shimasu*
8. *juudoo o shimasu*

9. *uchi e kaerimasu*
10. *terebi o mimasu*
11. *gohan o tabemasu*
12. *benkyoo o shimasu*
(play basketball)
(play judo)   (return home)
(watch television)
(eat a meal)   (study)
13. *nomimasu.*
14. *ongaku o kikimasu.*   15. *nemasu.*
kyoo   *ashita*
asaatte
(drink)
(go to bed)
(listen to music)
(the day after tomorrow)
(today)   (tomorrow)
mainichi   *yoku*
tokidoki   *amari*
zenzen   *asagohan*
(everyday)   (often)
(sometimes)   (seldom)
(never)   (breakfast)
hirugohan   *bangohan*
mainichi   *yoku*
tokidoki   *amari*
(lunch)   (dinner)
(everyday)   (often)
(sometimes)   (seldom)
gofun   *juppun*
jugofun   *nijuppun*
nijuugofun   *sanjuppun*
(5 minutes)   (10 minutes)
(15 minutes)   (20 minutes)
(25 minutes)   (30 minutes)
sanjuugofun   *yonjuppun*
yonjuugofun   *gojuppun*
gojuugofun   *hajime*
(35 minutes)   (40 minutes)
(45 minutes)   (50 minutes)
(55 minutes)   (introduction)
mondai   *mokuteki*
keikaku   *hyooka*
yosan   *Mondai ga arimasu.*
(problem)   (purpose)
(plan)   (evaluation)
(budget)   (There is a problem.)
Shukudai ga arimasu.   *Purojekuto ga arimasu.*
Koochi ga imasu.   *Kaunseraa ga imasu.*
Puro ga imasu.   *Isu ga arimasu.*
(There is homeroom.)   (There is a project.)
(There is a coach.)   (There is a counselor.)
(There is a professional.) (There is a chair.)
Mondai ga hitotsu arimasu.   *Shukudai ga futatsu arimasu.*
Purojekuto ga mittsu arimasu.   *Yottsu arimasu.*
(There is one problem.)   (There are two homeworks.)
(There are three projects.)   (There are four.)
Itsutsu arimasu.   *Muttsu arimasu.*
Nanatsu arimasu.   *Yattsu arimasu.*
Kokonotsu arimasu.   *Too arimasu.*
(There are five.)   (There are six.)
(There are seven.)   (There are eight.)
(There are nine.)   (There are ten.)
Koochi ga hitori imasu.   *Kaunseraa ga futari imasu.*
Puro ga sannin imasu. *Yonin imasu.*
Gonin imasu.
(There is one coach.)   (There are two counselors.)
(There are three professionals.)   (There are four people.)
(There are five people.)
Rokunin imasu.   *nananin/shichinin imasu*
Hachinin masu.   *Kunin imasu Juunin masu.*
(There are six people.) (There are seven people.)
(There are eight people.)   (There are nine people.)
(There are ten people.)

Isu ga arimasen.
(There is no chair.)
Isu ga hitsuyoo desu.
(We need a chair.)
Koochi ga imasen.
(There is no coach.)
Koochi ga hitsuyoo desu.
(We need a coach.)

4.1.4

1. *Anoo, moshi moshi* (Um, hello?)
2. *Tanaka san no (otaku, odenwa) desu ka?*
   (Is this the Tanaka residence?)
3. *(Hai, iie) (soo desu, soo ja arimsen.)*
   (Yes, it is/No, it is not.)
4. *Rikasan (desu ka?, imasu ka?)*
   (Is this Rika?/Is Rika there?)

4.1.5

1. *benkyoo shimasu*	2. *Ikimasu*
3. *tabemasu*	4. *mimasu*
5. *yomimasu*	6. *okimasu*
7. *nemasu*	8. *kakimasu*
(to study)	(to go)
(to eat)	(to watch)
(to read)	(to wake up)
(to sleep)	(to write)

4.1.6

A. *tokidoki*	B. *zenzen*
C. *amari*	D. *mai nichi*
E. *yoku*	F. *itsumo*
(sometimes)	(never)
(seldom)	(everyday)
(often)	(always)

4.1.7

A. *tsuitachi*	B. *juuyokka*
C. *yokka*	D. *muika*
E. *futsuka*	F. *mikka*
(1st day of the month)	(14th day of the month)
(4th day of the month)	(6th day of the month) (2nd
day of the month)	(3rd day of the month)
G. *kokonoka*	H. *tooka*
I. *nanoka*	J. *itsuka*
K. *juuninichi*	L. *yooka*
(9th day of the month)	(10th day of the month)
(7th day of the month)	(5th day of the month)
(12th day of the month)	(8th day of the month)
M. *juusannichi*	N. *juuichinichi*
(13th day of the month)	(11th day of the month)

4.1.8

A. *jippun/juppun*	B. *gofun*
(10 minutes)	(5 minutes)
C. *sanjuugofun*	D. *sanjippun/sanjuppun*
(35 minutes)	(30 minutes)
E. *nijippun/nijuppun*	F. *juugofun*
(20 minutes)	(15 minutes)
G. *nijuugofun*	H. *yonippun/yonjuppun*
(25 minutes)	(40 minutes)

4.1.9

hajime (introduction)	*mokuteki* (purpose)
mondai (problem)	*keikaku* (plan)
yosan (budget)	*hyooka* (evaluation)

4.1.10

1. *Sensei ga (imasu, arimasu.)* (There is a teacher.)
2. *Mondai ga (imasu, arimasu.)* (There is a problem.)
3. *Shukudai ga (imasu, arimasu.)* (There is homework.)
4. *Rindasan ga (imasu, arimasu.)* (There is Linda.)
5. *Isu ga (imasu, arimasu.)* (There is a chair.)
6. *Rinda no neko ga (imasu, arimasu.)*
   (There is Linda's cat.)

4.1.11

1. *Sensei ga hitoti arimasu.* *hotoo* or *uso*
   (There is a teacher.) (true or false)
2. *Mondai ga futatsu arimasu.* *hotoo* or *uso*
   (There is two problems.) (true or false)
3. *Shukudai ga futari imasu.* *hotoo* or *uso*
   (There is two homeworks.) (true or false)
4. *Rindasan ga hitori imasu.* *hotoo* or *uso*
   (There is one Linda.) (true or false)

4.2.1 Mechanics

A. *Kafeteria e ikimasu.* (I am going to cafeteria.)
B. *Puuru e ikimasu.* (I am going to pool.)
C. *Kyooshitsu e ikimasu.* (I am going to classroom.)
D. *Koodoo e ikimasu.* (I am going to auditorium.)
E. *Jimu e ikimasu.* (I am going to gymnasium.)
F. *Konpyuuta ruumu e ikimasu.*
(I am going to computer room.)

4.2.2

a. *Tabemasu.* (I eat [it].) (true or false)
i. *Nomimasu.* (I drink [it].)
u. *Benkyoo o shimasu.* (I study.)
e. *Kakimasu.* (I write [it].)
o. *Okimasu.* (I wake up.)
ka. *Yomimasu.* (I read [it].)
ki. *Nemasu.* (I go to bed)
ku. *Mimasu.* (I watch.)
ke. *Ikimasu.* (I go.)
ko. *Kaerimasu.* (I return home.)
sa. *Kimasu.* (I come.)
shi. *Juudoo o shimasu.* (I play judo.)

4.2.3

A: *Anoo, doko e ikimasu ka?* (Um, where are you going?)
B: *A, toshokan e ikimasu.* (Oh, I'm going to the library.)

4.2.4

A: *Anoo, nanji ni kafeteria e ikimasu ka?*
(Um, what time are you going to the cafeteria?)
B: *A, niji ni ikimasu.*
(Oh, I'm going at 2:00.)

4.2.5

A: *Anoo, nan'yoobi ni eiga ni ikimasu ka?*
(Um, what day of you the week are you going to the movies?)
B: *Soo desu ne. Kin'yoobi ni ikimasu.*
(Let's see. I'm going on Friday.)

4.2.6

A: *Anoo, doko e/ni ikimasu ka?*
(Um, where are you going?)
B: *A, suugaku ni ikimasu.*
(Oh, I'm going to math.)
B: *A, suugaku no kyooshitsu e/ni ikimasu.*
(Oh, I'm going to math class.)

4.2.7

A: *Anoo, niji ni toshokan e ikimasu ka?*
(Um, are you going to library at two o'clock?)
B: *Hai, ikimasu.*
(Yes, I'm going.)
B: *Iie, niji ni ikimasen. sanji ni ikimasu.*
(No, I'm not going at two o'clock. I'm going at three o'clock)
A: *Aa soo desu ka?*
(Oh, Is it really?)

4.2.8

A: *Anoo, B san, mainichi nani o shimasu ka?*
(Um, Mr. B, what do you do everyday?)
B: *Soo desu ne. Mainichi basukettobooru o shimasu.*
(Let's see. I play basketball everyday.)

4.2.9

A: *Anoo, ashita nani o shimasu ka?*
(Um, what are you doing tomorrow?)
B: *Basukettobooru o shimasu.*
(I'm playing basketball.)

4.2.11

A: *Anoo, mainichi nanji ni okimasu ka?*
(Um, what time do you wake up everyday?)
B: *Rokuji yonjuugofun ni okimasu.*
(I wake up at 6:45.)

4.2.12

tsuitachi (the first day)   *futsuka* (the second)
mikka (the third)   *yokka* (the fourth)
itsuka (the fifth)   *muika* (the sixth)
nanoka(the seventh)
nichiyoobi (Sunday)   *getsuyoobi* (Monday)
kayoobi (Tuesday)   *suiyoobi* (Wednesday)
mokuyoobi (Thursday)   *kin'yoobi* (Friday)
doyoobi (Saturday)   *paatii* (party)
baree booru (volleyball)   *futto booru* (football)
konsaato (concert)   *dansu* (dance)
kurabu miitingu   *eiga*
(club meeting)   (movie)

A: *Suiyoobi ni konsaato ni ikimasu ka?*
(Are you going to the concert on Wednesday?)
B: *Hai, ikimasu.*
(Yes, I am.)
A: *Kayoobi ni konsaato ni ikimasu ka?*
(Are you going to the concert on Tuesday?)
B: *Iie, ikimasen.*
(No, I'm not.)

4.2.13

kyoo (today)   *ashita* (tomorrow)
asatte (the day after tomorrow)
A: *Ashita meron o tabemashoo ka?*
(Shall we eat a melon tomorrow?)
B: *Hai, soo shimashoo.*
(Yes, let's do that.)
B: *Hai, tabemashoo.*
(Yes, let's eat it.)
B: *Anoo, chotto . . . sumimasen . . .*
(Um, [no I'm] a bit [afraid of eating] sorry.)
B: *Iie, tabemasen.*
(No, I won't eat it.)

4.2.14

pikunikku (picnic)   *konsaato* (concert)
toshokan (library)   *eiga* (movie)
Nihongo (Japanese language) *gakkoo* (school)

tokidoki (sometimes)   *zen zen* (never)
amari (seldom)   *mai nichi* (everyday)
yoku (often)   *itsumo* (always)

A: *Yoku konsaato ni ikimasu ka?*
(Do you often go to the concert?)
B: *Iie, amari ikimasen.*
(No, I seldom go.)

4.2.15

nichiyoobi (Sunday)	*uchi* (home)	*paatii* (party)	*supagettii* (spaghetti)	*kooku* (coke)
getsuyoobi (Monday)	*gakkoo* (school)	*futto booru* (football)	*furaido chikin* (fried chicken)	*miruku* (milk)
kayoobi (Tuesday)	*gakkoo* (school)	*futto booru* (football)	*supagettii* (spaghetti)	*mizu* (water)
suiyoobi (Wednesday)	*gakkoo* (school)	*konsaato* (concert)	*miito roofu* (meat loaf)	*koohii* (coffee)
mokuyoobi (Thursday)	*gakkoo* (school)	*futto booru* (football)	*supagettii* (spaghetti)	*mizu* (water)
kn'yoobi gakkoo		*kurabu miitingu*	*furaido chikin*	*mizu*

(Friday)	(school)	(club meeting)	(fried chicken)	(water)
doyoobi (Saturday)	*toshokan* (library)	*eiga* (movie)	*sushi* (sushi)	*koohii* (coffee)

A: *yokutoshokan e ikimasu ka?* (Do you often go to the library?)
B: *Iie, amari ikimasen.*   (No, I seldom go.)

4.2.16

tsuitachi (1st day of the month)	*nichiyoobi* (Sunday)	*paatii* (party)
futsuka (2nd day of the month)	*getsuyoobi* (Monday)	*baree booru* (volleyball)
mikka (3rd day of the month)	*kayoobi* (Tuesday)	*futto booru* (football)
yokka (4th day of the month)	*suiyoobi* (Wednesday)	*konsaato* (concert)
itsuka (5th day of the month)	*mokuyoobi* (Thursday)	*dansu* (dance)
muika (6th day of the month)	*kn'yoobi* (Friday)	*kurabu miitingu* (club meeting)
nanoka (7th day of the month)	*do yoobi* (Saturday)	*eiga* (movie)

A: *Suiyoobi ni konsaato ni ikimasu ka?*
(Are you going to the concert on Wednesday?)
B: *Hai, ikimasu.*
(Yes, I'm going.)
A: *Ja, issho ni ikimashoo.*
(Well then, let's go together.)
B: *Hai, ikimashoo.*
(Yes, let's go.)
A: *Kayoobi ni konsaato ni ikimasu ka?*
(Are you going to the concert on Tuesday?)
B: *Iie, ikimasen. Doomo, sumimasen.*
(No, I'm not going. I'm very sorry.)

4.3.1 Mechanics

Katoo Mika (Mika Kato)   *Sada Hideki* (Hideki Sada)
Hayashi Rika (Rika Hayashi)   *Satoo Hiroshi* (Hiroshi Sato)

R: *Moshi moshi.*   (Hello.)
A: *Anoo, Katoo san no otaku desu ka?*
(Um, is this the Kato residence?)
R: *Hai, soo desu.*   (Yes, it is.)

4.3.2

Mika (Mika)   *Yasuo* (Yasuo)
Kanae (Kanae)   *Masaaki* (Masaaki)

B: *Moshi moshi.*   (Hello.)
A: *Anoo, Katoo san no otaku desu ka?*
(Um, is this the Kato residence?)
B: *Hai, soo desu.*   (Yes, speaking.)
A: *Mika san imasu ka?*   (Is Mika there?)
B: *Hai, watashi desu.*   (Yes, it is I.)
A: *Konban wa. Risa desu.*   (Good evening. This is Lisa.)

4.3.3

A: *Moshi moshi, Mika san imasu ka?*
(Hello. Is Mika there?)
R: *Hai, imasu. Chotto matte kudasai.*
(Yes, she is. Please wait a moment.)
B: *Moshi moshi, donata desu ka?* (Hello. Who is this?)
A: *A, watashi wa Risa desu. Konban wa.*
(Oh, it's me, Lisa. Good evening.)
B: *Konban wa.*   (Good evening.)

4.3.4

A: *Moshi moshi Mika san imasu ka?* (Hello is Mika there?)
R: *Hai, imasu. Donata desu ka?* (Yes, she is. Who is this?)
A: *Nyuu Hebun kookoo no Risa desu ga . . .*
(This Lisa from New Haven High School [but].)
R: *A, chotto matte kudasai.* (Oh, please wait a moment.)
A: *Risa desu. Konban wa.* (This is Lisa. Good evening.)
B: *A, Risa san, konban wa.* (Oh, Lisa, good evening.)

4.3.5

R: *Moshi moshi.* (Hello.)
A: *Anoo, Katoo san no otaku desu ka?*
(Um, is this the Kato resident?)
R: *Iie, chigaimasu.* (No, it is n't.)
A: *Aa, doomo sumimasen.* (Oh, I'm sorry.)
R: *Iie.* (No problem.)

4.3.6

A: *Moshi moshi, Mika san imasu ka?*
(Hello. Is Mika there?)
R: *Mika desu ka? Mika wa gakkoo desu ga.*
(Mika?. She is at school, (but...))
A: *A, soo desu ka?. Ja, ato de denwa shimasu.*
(Is that right? Well then, I will call again later.)
R: *Sumimasen.* (Sorry about that.)
A: *Iie.* (No problem.)

4.3.7

paatii (party)   *dance* (dance)
kuji (9:00)   *shichijihan*(7:30)
kafeteria (cafetera)   *jimu*(gym)
doyoobi (Saturday)   *kinyoobi* (Friday)

A: *Paatii wa kuji desu.* (The party is at 9:00.)
B: *Soo desu ka? Gakkoo no kafeteria desu ne?*
(Oh, I see. It's at the school cafeteria, right?)
A: *Soo desu. Ja, doyoobi ni.* (Yes. Well then, I will see you on Saturday.)
B: *Hai, doomo arigatoo.* (Yes, thank you very much.)
A: *Sayoonara. Baibai.* (Goodbye.)
B: *Sayoonara. Baibai.* (Goodbye.)

4.3.8

A: *Anoo, doyoobi no paatii no koto desu ga.*
(Um, I'm calling about the party on Saturday [but].)
B: *Hai.* (Yes.)
A: *Mika san wa ikimasu ka?* (Are you going to the party, Mika?)
B: *Hai, ikimasu.* (Yes, I'm going.)

4.3.9

A: *Kochira wa Katoo desu. Tadaima gaishutsuchuu desu.*
(This is Kato. I'm not at home.)

4.3.10

A: *Kochira wa Katoo desu. Tadaima gaishutsuchuu desu. Onamae, odenwa bagoo o onokoshi kudasai.*
(This is Kato. I'm not at home. Please leave your name and number.)
B: *Mika desu. Mata denwa shimasu.*
(This is Mika. I will call back.)

4.3.11

A: *Kochira wa Katoo desu. Tadaima gaishutsu chuu desu. Onamae, odenwa bangoo wo onokoshi kudasai.*
(This is Kato. I am currently away. Please leave your

name and number.)
B: *Mika desu. Sumimasen ga, denwa shite kudasai. Denwa bangoo wa nan, san, yon no san, yon, nana, goo desu. Yoroshiku onegai shimasu.*
(This is Mika. I'm sorry but please call me back. My phone number is 734-3475. Thank you.)

4.3.12

A: *Moshi moshi, Jon san imasu ka?*
(Hello. Is John there?)
B: *Hai, imasu. Chotto matte kudasai.*
(Yes, John is here. Please wait a moment.)
C: *Moshi moshi, donata desu ka?*
(Hello. Who is this?)
B: *A, Toshio desu. Konban wa.*
(Oh, this is Toshio. Good evening.)
C: *A, konban wa.*
(Oh, good evening.)

4.3.13

John: *Moshi moshi. Katoo san no otaku desu ka?*
(Hello. Is this the Kato residence?)
Kaori: *Hai, soo desu.* (Yes, it is.)
John: *Anoo, kaori san imasu ka?*
(Um, is Kaori there?)
Kaori: *Hai, watashi desu.* (Yes, speaking.)
John: *Konnichi wa. Jon desu.* (Good afternoon. This is John.)
Kaori: *Konnichi wa.* (Good afternoon.)
John: *Anoo, sumimasen. Ashita no paatii no koto desu ga.*
(Um, excuse me. I'm calling about tomorrow's party but .)
Kaori: *Hai.* (Yes.)
John: *Kaori san wa ikimasu ka?*
(Are you going, Kaori?)
Kaori: *Hai, ikimasu.* (Yes, I'm going.)

4.4.1 Mechanics

John: *Moshi moshi. Katoo san no otaku desu ka?*
(Hello. Is this the Kato residence?)
Kaori: *Hai, soo desu.* (Yes, it is.)
John: *Anoo, Kaori san imasu ka?*
(Um, is Kaori there?)
Kaori: *Hai, watashi desu.* (Yes, speaking.)
John: *Konnichi wa. Jon desu.* (Good afternoon. This is John.)
Kaori: *Konnichi wa.* (Good afternoon.)
John: *Anoo, sumimasen. Ashita wa nani o shimasu ka?*
(Um, excuse me. What are you doing tomorrow?)
Kaori: *Bareebooru o shimasu.* (I am playing volleyball.)
John: *Ja, yoji desu ne.* (So, are you playing at 4:00?)
Kaori: *Hai, soo desu.* (Yes, I am.)
John: *Doomo arigatoo.* (Thanks.)

4.4.2

sukejuuru (schedule)
Shichiji ni okimasu. (I wake up at 7:00.)
Shichijihan ni asagohan o tabemasu.
(I eat breakfast at 7:30.)
Hachiji ni gakkoo ni ikimasu. (I go to school at 8:00.)
Hachijihan ni kurasu ni ikimasu. (I go to class at 8:30.)
Kuji ni Nihongo o benkyoo shimasu.
(I study Japanese at 9:00.)
Juuniji ni hirugohan o tabemasu. (I eat lunch at 12:00.)
Sanji ni toshokan ni ikimasu. (I go to the library at 3:00.)
Yo ji ni kurabu ni ikimasu. (I go to my club at 4:00.)
Rokuji ni uchi ni kaerimasu. (I go home at 6:00.)
Shichiji ni yuugohan o tabemasu. (I eat dinner at 7:00.)

Hachiji ni Nihongo o benkyoo shimasu.
(I study Japanese at 8:00.)
Kuji ni hon o yomimasu. (I read a book at 9:00.)
Juuji ni shukudai o shimasu. (I do my homework at 10:00.)
Juuichiji ni terebi o mimasu. (I watch television at 11:00.)
Juuniji ni nemasu. (I go to sleep at 12:00.)

A: *Nanji ni asagohan o tabemasu ka?*
(What time do you eat breakfast?)
B: ____ *ji ni.* (At ____ o'clock.)
A: *Hachiji ni nani o shimasu ka?* (What do you do at 8:00?)
B: *Hachiji ni ____ o shimasu.* (I ____ at 8:00.)

4.4.3

Watashi no getsuyoobi no sukejuuru
(My schedule for Monday)

Shichiji kara shichijihan made (from 7:00 to 7:30)
Hachiji kara hachijihan made (from 8:00 to 8:30)
Kuji kara juuji made (from 9:00 to 10:00)
Juujihan kara juuichiji made (from 10:30 to 11:00)
Juuniji kara juunijihan made hirugohan o tabemasu.
(I eat lunch from 12:00 to 12:30.)
Sanji kara yoji made (from 3:00 to 4:00)
Goji kara rokuji made (from 5:00 to 6:00)
Shichiji kara hachiji made (from 7:00 to 8:00)
Kuji kara juuji made (from 9:00 to 10:00)
Juuichiji kara rokuji made nemasu. (I sleep from 11:00 to 6:00.)

A: *Terebi o mimasu ka?*
(Do you watch TV?)
B: *Hai, mimasu.*
(Yes, I do.)
A: *Nanji kara nanji made terebi o mimasu ka?*
(From what time to time do you watch TV?)
B: *Soo desu ne. Kuji kara juuji made mimasu.*
(Let's see. I watch TV from 9:00 to 10:00.)

4.4.4

A: *Nannichi ni ikimasu ka?* (What day are you going?)
B: *Juugatsu tooka ni ikimasu.* (I'm going on October 10th.)
A: *Ja, mokuyoobi desu ne.* (Well then, that must be a Thursday.)
B: *Hai, soo desu.* (Yes, it is.)
A: *Goji ni ikimasu ka? Soretomo, rokuji ni ikimasu ka?*
(Are you going at 5:00? Or are you going at 6:00?)
B: *Eeto.* (Um.)
A: *Ja, nanji ni ikimasu ka?* (Well then, what time are you going?)
B: *Gojihan ga ii desu.* (I would like to go at 5:30.)
A: *Ja, gojihan ni shimashoo.* (Ok, let's make it 5:30.)

4.4.5

tsuitachi	*nichiyoobi*	*paatii*	*piza*	*kooku*
(The 1st day)	(Sunday)	(party)	(pizza)	(coke)
futsuka	*getsuyoobi*	*baree booru*	*furaido chikin*	*miruku*
(The 2nd day)	(Monday)	(volleyball)	(fried chicken)	(milk)
mikka	*kayoobi*	*futto booru*	*hanbaagaa*	*orenjijuusu*
(The 3rd day)	(Tuesday)	(football)	(hamburger)	(orange juice)
yokka	*suiyoobi*	*konsaato*	*miito roofu*	*koohii*
(The 4th day)	(Wednesday)	(concert)	(meat loaf)	(coffee)
itsuka	*mokuyoobi*	*dansu*	*supagettii*	*panchi*
(The 5th day)	(Thursday)	(dance)	(spaghetti)	(punch)
muika	*kin'yoobi*	*kurabu miitingu*	*hotto doggu*	*mizu*
(The 6th day)	(Friday)	(club meeting)	(hot dog)	(water)
nanoka	*doyoobi*	*eiga*	*sushi*	*ocha*
(The 7th day)	(Saturday)	(movie)	(sushi)	(tea)

A: *Getsuyoobi ni paatii ni ikimasu ka?*
(Are you going to the party on Monday?)
B: *Hai, ikimasu.* (Yes, I'm going.)
A: *Doko desu ka?* (Where is it?)
B: *Gakkoo desu.* (It's at school.)
A: *Ja, nanji ni ikimasu ka?* (What time are you going?)
B: *Kuji ni ikimasu.* (I'm going at 9:00.)
A: *Getsuyoobi ni paatii ni iku?* (Are you going to the party on Monday?)
B: *Un, iku.* (Yes, I'm going.)
A: *Nanji?* (What time are you going?)
B: *Kuji.* (I'm going at 9:00.)
A: *Doko?* (Where is it?)
B: *Gakkoo.* (It's at school.)

4.5.1.1 Mechanics
Mondai ga arimasu. (There is a problem.)

4.5.1.2
Mondai ga arimasu. (There is a problem.)
Koochi ga imasu. (There is a coach.)

4.5.2 Note 12
hitotsu (one item) *futatsu* (two items)
mittsu (three items) *yottsu* (four items)
itsutsu (five items) *muttsu* (six items)
nanatsu (seven item) *yattsu* (eight items)
kokonotsu (nine items) *too* (ten items)
juuichi (eleven items)

4.5.2
A. (*Futatsu, mittsu, kokonotsu, hitotsu*) *wa hitotsu desu.*
(Two items, three items, nine items, one item) is one item.)
B. (*Yottsu, mittsu, muttsu, nanatsu*) *wa mittsu desu.*
(Four items, three items, six items, one item) are three items.)
C. (*Futatsu, yattsu, nanatsu, Yottsu*) *wa yattsu desu.*
(Two items, eight items, seven items, four items) are eight items.)
D. (*Yattsu, mittsu, kokonotsu, muttsu*) *wa muttsu desu.*
(Eight items, three items, nine items, six items) are six items.)
E. (*Nanatsu, mittsu, itsutsu, hitotsu*) *wa itsutsu desu.*
(Seven items, three items, nine items, one item) are five items.)

4.5.3
Futatsu arimasu. (There are two items.)

4.5.4
Mondai ga futatsu arimasu. (There are two problems.)
Koochi ga futari imasu. (There are two coaches.)

4.5.5
Isu to tsukue ga arimasen. (There is no chair or table.)
Koochi ga imasen. (There is no coach.)

4.5.6
Isu to tsukue ga hitsuyoo desu. (We need a chair and a table.)

4.5.7
Mondai ga arimasu. Isu to tsukue ga arimasen. Isu to tsukue ga hitsuyoo desu.
(There is a problem. There is no chair or table. We need a chair and a table.)
Mondai ga arimasu. Koochi ga imasen. Koochi ga hitsuyoo desu.
(There is a problem. There is no coach. We need a coach.)

4.5.8
Nihon no dentoo (Japanese tradition)
ohana no sensei (flower arrangement master)

ocha no sensei	(tea ceremony master)
oshuuji no sensei	(calligraphy master)
kabuki no sensei	(Kabuki master)
Nihon ryoori no sensei	(Japanese cooking master)
Nihon no dentoo supootsu	(Japanese traditional sport)
juudoo no sensei	(judo master)
karate no sensei	(karate master)
kendoo no sensei	(Japanese fencing master)
kyuudoo no sensei	(Japanese archery master)
sumoo no sensei	(sumo master)

4.5.9

A. *Kendoo no sensei ga imasu.*
(There is a kendo master.)
B. *Kendoo wa Nihon no dentoo supootsu (budoo) desu.*
(Kendo is a Japanese traditional sport (martial art.).)
C. *Kendoo no doogu ga arimasen.*
(There is no kendo equipment.)
D. *Kendoo no doogu ga hitsuyoo desu.*
(We need kendo equipment.)
A. *Ocha no sensei ga imasu.*
(There is a tea ceremony master.)
B. *Ocha wa Nihon no dentoo (geijutsu) desu.*
(Tea ceremony is a traditional Japanese art.)
C. *Ocha no doogu ga arimasen.*
(There is no tea ceremony equipment.)
D. *Ocha no doogu ga hitsuyoo desu.*
(We need tea ceremony equipment.)

4.6.1 Mechanics

nijuuichinichi	*kyooshitsu*	*paatii*
(21st day of the month)	(classroom)	(party)
nijuuninichi	*jimu*	*baree booru*
(22nd day of the month)	(gymnasium)	(volleyball)
nijuusannichi	*gurando*	*futto booru*
(23th day of the month)	(athletic field)	(football)
nijuuyokka	*koodoo*	*konsaato*
(24th day of the month)	(auditorium)	(concert)
nijuugonichi	*kafeteria*	*dansu*
(25th day of the month)	(cafeteria)	(dance)
nijuurokunichi	*kyooshitsu*	*kurabu miitingu*
(26th day of the month)	(classroom)	(club meeting)
nijuushichinichi	*koodoo*	*eiga*
(27th day of the month)	(auditorium)	(movie)

nijuuichinichi	*piza*	*koora*
(21st day of the month)	(pizza)	(coke)
nijuuninichi	*furaido chikin*	*miruku*
(22nd day of the month)	(fried chicken)	(milk)
nijuusannichi	*hanbaagaa*	*orenji juusu*
(23th day of the month)	(hamburger)	(orange juice)
nijuuyokka	*miito roofu*	*koohii*
(24th day of the month)	(meat loaf)	(coffee)
nijuugonichi	*supagetti*	*panchi*
(25th day of the month)	(spaghetti)	(punch)
nijuurokunichi	*hotto doogu*	*mizu*
(26th day of the month)	(hot dog)	(water)
nijuushichinichi	*sushi*	*ocha*
(27th day of the month)	(sushi)	(tea)

Nijuu ichi nichi ni paatii o shimasu.
(We will have a party on the 21st.)
Kyooshitsu de paatii o shimasu.
(We will have a party in the classroom.)
Piza to koora ga hitsuyoo desu.
(We need Pizza and coke.)

4.6.2

nijuuichinichi	*kyooshitsu*	*paatii*
(21st day of the month)	(classroom)	(party)
nijuuninichi	*jimu*	*baree booru*

(22nd day of the month)	(gymnasium)	(volleyball)
nijuusannichi	*gurando*	*futto booru*
(23th day of the month)	(athletic field)	(football)
nijuuyokka	*koodoo*	*konsaato*
(24th day of the month)	(auditorium)	(concert)
nijuugonichi	*kafeteria*	*dansu*
(25th day of the month)	(cafeteria)	(dance)
nijuurokunichi	*kyooshitsu*	*kurabu miitingu*
(26th day of the month)	(classroom)	(club meeting)
nijuuhachinichi	*koodoo*	*eiga*
(28th day of the month)	(auditorium)	(movie)

nijuuichinichi	*isu*	*tsukue*
(21st day of the month)	(chair)	(table)
nijuuninichi	*booru*	*netto*
(22nd day of the month)	(ball)	(net)
nijuusannichi	*booru*	*herumetto*
(23th day of the month)	(ball)	(helmet)
nijuuyokka	*maiku*	*raito*
(24th day of the month)	(mike)	(light)
nijuugonichi	*supiikaa*	*siidii pureiyaa*
(25th day of the month)	(speaker)	(CD player)
nijuurokunichi	*kokuban*	*chooku*
(26th day of the month)	(black board)	(chalk)
nijuuhachinichi	*sukuriin*	*bideo pureiyaa*
(28th day of the month)	(screen)	(video player)

Nijuu ichi nichi ni kyooshitsu de paatii o shimasu.
(We will have a party in the classroom on the 21St.)
Isu to tsukue ga hitsuyoo desu.
(Chairs and tables are necessary.)

4.6.3

nijuuichinichi	*kyooshitsu*	*paatii*	*tomodachi*
(21st day)	(classroom)	(party)	(friend)
nijuuninichi	*jimu*	*baree booru*	*karada*
(22nd day)	(gymnasium)	(volleyball)	(body)
nijuusannichi	*gurando*	*futto booru*	*shiai*
(23th day)	(athletic field)	(football)	(tournament)
nijuuyokka	*koodoo*	*konsaato*	*ongaku no renshuu*
(24th day)	(auditorium)	(concert)	(music practice)
nijuugonichi	*kafeteria*	*dansu*	*dansu no renshuu*
(25th day)	(cafeteria)	(dance)	(dance practice)
nijuurokunichi	*kyooshitsu*	*kurabu miitingu*	*borantia*
(26th day)	(classroom)	(club meeting)	(volunteer)
nijuuhachinichi	*koodoo*	*eiga*	*fesutibaru*
(28th day)	(auditorium)	(movie)	(festival)

Nijuu ichi nichi ni kyooshitsu de paatii o shimasu.
(We will have a party in the classroom on the 21st.)
Mokuteki wa tomodachi no tame desu.
(The purpose is for my friend.)

4.6.4

paatii	*dansu*	*piza o tabemasu*	*koora o nomimasu*
(party)	(dance)	(eat pizza)	(drink coke)
baree booru	*baree booru*	*shiai o shimasu*	*netto o tatemasu*
(volleyball)	(volleyball)	(have a tournament)	(set a net up)
futto booru	*futto booru*	*booru o araimasu*	*rain o kakimasu*
(football)	(football)	(wash a ball)	(write lines)
konsaato	*konsaato*	*suteeji o tsukurimasu*	*raito o tsukurimasu*
(concert)	(concert)	(build a stage)	(set lights)
dansu	*dansu*	*renshuu o shimasu*	*happyoo shimasu*
(dance)	(dance)	(practice)	(make presentations)
kurabu miitingu	*kurabu miitingu*	*keikaku o tatemasu*	*borantia o shimasu*
(club meeting)	(club meeting)	(make a plan)	(volunteer)
fesutibaru	*eiga*	*ongaku o kikimasu*	*dansu o shimasu*
(festival)	(movie)	(listen to music)	(dance)

Paatii no keikaku wa: Dansu o shimasu. Piza o tabemasu.
Koora o nomimasu.

(The plan of the party: We will dance, eat pizza, and drink cola.)

4.6.5

Paatii no yosan wa gojuudoru desu.

(The budget for the party is $50.)

Piza wa nijuuhachidoru desu.	(Pizza is $28.)
Koora wa juugodoru desu.	(Cola is $15.)
Koppu wa nidorudesu.	(Cups are $2.)
Sara wa godoru desu.	(Plates are $5.)

paatii (party)

yosan gojuudoru	*piza nijuuhachidoru*
(budget $50)	(pizza $28)
koora juugodoru	*koppu nidoru*
(cola $15)	(cups $2)
sara godoru	*kyooshitsu zerodoru*
(plates $5)	(classroom $0)

konsaato (concert)

yosan nihyakudoru	*ongaku nanajuugodoru*
(budget $200)	(concert $75)
raito sanjuudoru	*maiku gojuu godoru*
(lights $30)	(mike $50)
chiketto juugodoru	*kopii nijuugodoru*
(ticket $15)	(copies $25)

fesutibaru (festival)

yosan sendoru	*kopii nihyakunijuugodoru*
(budget $1,000)	(copies $225)
konsaato nihyakunanajuugodoru	
(concert $275)	
dansu sanbyakukyuujuudoru	
(dance $390)	
borantia zerodoru	*denwa hyakujuudoru*
(volunteer $0)	(telephone $110)

4.6.6

Ichi tasu san wa yon.	*San hiku ichi wa ni*
(One plus three equals four.)	(Three minus one equals two.)

4.6.7

Piza no nijuuhachidoru tasu, Koora no juugodoru tasu, koppu no nidoru tasu, sara no godoru wa gojuudoru desu. Dakara, Paatii no yosan wa gojuudoru desu.

($28.for piza plus $15 for cola plus $2 for cups plus $5 for paper plates equals $50. Therefore, the budget for the party is $50.)

paatii (party)

yosan ?	*piza nijuuhachidoru*
(budget ?)	(pizza $28)
koora juugodoru	*koppu nidoru*
(cola $15)	(cups $2)
sara godoru	*kyooshitsu zerodoru*
(plates $5)	(classroom $0)

konsaato (concert)

yosan ?	*ongaku nanajuugodoru*
(budget ?)	(music $75)
raito sanjuudoru	*maiku gojuu godoru*
(lights $30)	(mike $50)
chiketto juugodoru	*kopii nijuugodoru*
(ticket $15)	(copies $25)

fesutibaru (festival)

yosan sendoru	*kopii nihyakunijuugodoru*
(budget ?)	(copies $225)
konsaato nihyakunanajuugodoru	
(concert $275)	

dansu sanbyakukyuujuudoru
(dance $390)

borantia zerodoru	*denwa hyakujuudoru*
(volunteer $0)	(telephone $110)

saiensu faa (science fair)

yosan ?	*piza sanuuhachidoru*
(budget ?)	(pizza $38)
koora juugodoru	*koppu yondoru*
(cola $25)	(cups $4)
sara kyuudoru	*kyooshitsu zerodoru*
(plates $9)	(classroom $0)

4.6.9

1. *Bosuton* (Boston)	2. *Washinton* (Washigton)
3. *Shiatoru* (Seattle)	4. *Shikago* (Chicago)
5. *San Furanshisuko* (San Francisco)	6. *Hawai* (Hawaii)
7. *Oregon* (Oregon)	8. *Irinoi* (Illinois)
9. *Tekisasu* (Texas)	10. *Kororado* (Colorado)
11. *Nyuuyooku* (New York)	12. *Wisukonshin* (Wisconsin)
13. *Kariforunia*(California)	14. *Vaajinia* (Virginia)

15. *Ichigatu tsuitachi* (January first)
16. *Sangatsu mikka* (March third)
17. *Gogatsu itsuka* (May fifth)
18. *Kugatsu kokonoka* (September 9th)
19. *Getsu, Ka, Sui, Moku, Kin, Do, Nichi*
    (Monday, Tuesday, Wednesday, Thursday, Friday, Saturday, Sunday)

4.6.10

Puro pozaru	(Proposal)
Paatii	(Party)
Shigatsu juugonichi	(April 15th)
Jon Sumisu	(John Smith)

Nijuuninichi ni paatii o shimasu. Kyooshitsu de paatii o shimasu.

(We will have a party on the 21st. We will have a party in the classroom.)

Piza to koora ga hitsuyoo desu.

(We need Pizza and coke.)

Mokuteki wa tomodachi no tame desu.

(The purpose is for my friend.)

Paatii no keikaku wa: Dansu o shimasu. Piza o tabemasu. Koora o nomimasu.

(The plan of the party: We will dance, eat pizza, and drink cola.)

Paatii no yosan wa gojuudoru desu. Piza wa nijuuhachidoru desu.Koora wa juugodoru desu..

(The budget for the party is $50. Pizza is $28. Coke is $15.)

Koppu wa nidorudesu.Sara wa godoru desu

(Cups are $2. Plates are $5.)

4.7.2 Mechanics

____ *ji ni asa gohan o tabemasu.*
    (I eat breakfast at ____ o'clock.)
____ *ji ni gakkoo ni ikimasu.*
    (I go to school at ____ o'clock.)
____ *ji ni Nihongo o benkyoo shimasu.*
    (I study Japanese at ____ o'clock.)
____ *ji ni hon o yomimasu.*
    (I read a book at ____ o'clock.)
____ *ji ni shukudai o shimasu.*
    (I do my homework at ____ o'clock.)
____ *ji ni terebi o mimasu.*
    (I watch television at ____ o'clock.)
____ *ji ni uchi ni kaerimasu.*
    (I go home at ____ o'clock.)
____ *ji ni nemasu.*
    (I go to bed at ____ o'clock.)

1. *Nanji ni asa gohan o tabemasu ka?*
   (What time do you eat breakfast?)
2. *Nanji ni gakkoo ni ikimasu ka?*
   (What time do you go to school?)
3. *Nanji ni Nihon go o benkyoo shimasu ka?*
   (What time do you study Japanese?)
4. *Nanji ni hon o yomimasu ka?*
   (What time do you read a book?)

4.7.3

tsuitachi (1st day of the month)   *getsu* (Mon.)   *paatii* (party)
futsuka (2nd day of the month)   *ka* (Tues.)
mikka (3rd day of the month)   *sui* (Wed.)   *eiga* (movie)
yokka (4th day of the month)   *moku* (Thurs.)
itsuka (5th day of the month)   *kin* (Fri.)
muika (6th day of the month)   *do* (Sat.)   *dansu* (dance)
nanoka (7th day of the month)   *nichi* (Sun.)

4.8.2 Application 1

terebi no jikan (television time)
   ____ *ji kara* ____ *ji made* (from____o'clock to____'clock)
benkyoo no jikan (study time)
   ____ *ji kara* ____ *ji made* (from____o'clock to____'clock)
supootsu no jikan (sports time)
   ____ *ji kara* ____ *ji made* (from____o'clock to____'clock)
rejaa no jikan (leisure time)
getsuyoobi kara kin'yoobi made no jikan (Monday through Friday)
   ____ *ji kara* ____ *ji made* (from____o'clock to____'clock)
doyoobi no (Saturday)
   ____ *ji kara* ____ *ji made* (from____o'clock to____'clock)
nichiyoobi no (Sunday)
   ____ *ji kara* ____ *ji made* (from____o'clock to____'clock)

Amerika to Nihon no tiineijaa no saabee
   (American and Japanese teenager survey)
Amerika   *Nihon*
(America)   (Japan)
terebi no jikan (television time)
benkyoo no jikan (study time)
supootsu no jikan (sports time)
rejaa no jikan (leisure time)

4.8.3

namae (name)   *jibun* (self)
shitsumon (question)
kurasu no seito   *Nihon no seito*
(students in class)   (students in Japan)

terebi no jikan   *kara* (from)
(television time)   *made* (until)

benkyoo no jikan   *kara* (from)
(study time)   *made* (until)

supootsu no jikan   *kara* (from)
(sports time)   *made* (until)

rejaa no jikan   *kara* (from)
(leisure time)   *made* (until)

4.9.1 Application

A. *hajime* (introduction)   B. *mondai* (problem)
C. *mokuteki* (purpose)   D. *keikau* (plan)
E. *hyooka* (evaluation)   F. *yosan* (budget)

1. *Beeku seeru no keikaku wa:*
   (The plan for the bake sale is:)
2. *Beeku seeru no mokuteki wa Eizu wooku no tame desu.*
   (The purpose of the blake sale is to raise money for an AIDS walk.)

3. *Tooka ni kafeteria de beeku seeru o shimasu.*
   (We will have a bake sale at the cafeteria on the 10th.)
4. *Beeku seeru no yosan wa gojuudoru desu.*
   (The budget for the bake sale is $50.)
5. *Isu to teeburu to yosan ga hitsuyoo desu.*
   (Chairs, tables, and a budget are necessary.)

4.9.2

1. *Dakara, isu to teeburu to yosan ga hitsuyoo desu.*
   (That's why chairs, tables, and a budget are necessary.)
2. *Beeku seeru no keikaku wa: Keeki o tsukuri masu.*
   Keeki o urimasu. Hanashimasu. Okane o atsumemasu.
   (The plan for bake sale is: We will bake a cake. We will sell the cake. We will talk. We will collect money.)
3. *Beeku seeru no yosan wa nijuugodoru desu. Keeki no okane wa juudoru desu. Nomimono wa godoru desu. Koppu wa nidoru desu. Sara wa sandoru desu.*
   (The budget for the bake sale will be $25. The cake will cost $10. The beverages will cost $5. The cups will cost $2. The plates will cost $3.)
4. *Beeku seeru no mokuteki wa Eizu wooku no tame desu. Nijuuninichi ni Nyuu Yooku ni ikimasu.*
   (The purpose of the bake sale is to raise money for the AIDS walk. We will be going to New York on the 22nd.)
5. *Tooka ni kafeteria de beeku seeru o shimasu.*
   (We will hold a bake sale in the cafeteria on the 10th.)

A. *mokuteki* (Objectives)   B. *keikaku* (plan)
C. *hajime* (introduction)   D. *mondai* (problem)
E. *yosan* (budget)   F. *hyooka* (evaluation)

4.9.2.A

Tooka ni kafeteria de beeku seeru o shimasu.
   (We will have a bake sale in the cafeteria on the 10th)
Dakara, isu to teeburu to yosan ga hitsuyoo desu.
   (That's why chairs, tables, and a budget are necessary.)
Beeku seeru no mokuteki wa Eizu wooku no tame desu.
   (The purpose of the bake sale is to raise money for the AIDS walk.)
Nijuuninichi ni Nyuu Yooku ni ikimasu.
   (We will be going to New York on the 22nd.)
Beeku seeru no keikaku wa:
   (The plans for the bake sale are:)
Keeki o tsukimasu.
   (We will bake a cake.)
Keeki o urimasu.
   (We will sell the cake.)
Hanashimasu.
   (We will talk.)
Okane o atsumemasu.
   (We will collect money.)
Beeku seeru no yosan wa nijuugodoru desu.
   (The budget for the bake sale is $25.)
Keeki no okane wa juudoru desu.
   (The cake will cost $10.)
Nomimono wa godoru desu.
   (The beverages will cost $5.)
Koppu wa nidoru desu.
   (The cups will cost $2.)
Sara wa sandoru desu.
   (Plates will cost $3.)
hajime (introduction)   *mondai* (problem)
mokuteki (purpose)   *keikaku* (plan)
yosan (budget)

4.9.3.A

Tooka ni Eigo no kyooshitsu de haru no tarento shoo no oodishon o shimasu.
   (We will hold an audition for the spring talent show on the 10th.)

Dakara, maiku to supiikaa to isu to teeburu to yosan ga hitsuyoo desu.
    (That's why a mikes, speakers, chairs, tables, and a budget are necessary.)
Oodishon no mokuteki wa haru no tarento shoo no tame desu.
    (The auditions will be for the Spring Talent Show.)
Nijuuninichi ni koodoo de haru no tarento shoo o shimasu.
    (We will have the Spring Talent Show in the auditorium on the 22nd.)
Oodishon no keikaku wa:
    (The plan for the audition is as follows:)
Gakki o hikimasu.
    (We will play instruments.)
Dansu o shimasu.
    (We will dance.)
Ongaku o kikimasu.
    (We will listen to music.)
Dansu o mimasu.
    (We will watch dances.)
Oodishon no yosan wa nijuudoru desu.
    (The budget for the audition is $20.)
Nomimono no okane wa juudoru desu.
    (The beverages will cost $10.)
Puroguramu no kopii wa juudoru desu.
    (The making copies of the program will cost $10.)

4.9.3.B

Itsuka ni kafeteria de aato shoo o shimasu.
    (We will hold an art show in the cafeteria on the 5th.)
Dakara, isu to teeburu to yosan ga hitsuyoo desu.
    (That's why chairs, tables, and a budget are necessary.)
Aato shoo no mokuteki wa Unisefu no borantia no tame desu.
    (The purpose of the art show is to send the Unicef volunteers to Asia.)
Hatsuka ni Ajia ni ikimasu.
    (The volunteers will go to Asia on the 20th.)
Aato shoo no keikaku wa:
    (The plan for the art show is as follows:)
Aato o misemasu.
    (We will exhibit art.)
Aato o urimasu.
    (We will sell art.)
Okane o atsumemasu.
    (We will collect money.)
Aato shoo no yosan wa yonjuu godoru desu.
    (The budget for the art show is $45.)
Puroguramu no okane wa nijuu godoru desu.
    (The making the programs will cost $25.)
Pin wa godoru desu.
    (The pins will cost $5.)
Teepu wa godoru desu.
    (The tape will cost $5.)

4.9.3.C

Itsuka ni taiikukan de aki no saiensu kontesuto o shimasu.
    (We will hold the fall science contest at the gymnasium on the 5th)
Dakara maiku to supiikaa to isu to teeburu to denki to yosan ga hitsuyoo desu.
    (That's why makes, speakers, chairs, tables, electricity, and a budget are necessary.)
Saiensu kontesuto no mokuteki wa nashonaru saiensu feaa no tame desu.
    (The purpose of the science fair is [to choose entrants] for the national science fair.)
Nijuu ni nichi ni nashonaru saiensu feaa ga arimasu.
    (The national science fair will be on the 22nd.)
Saiensu kontesuto no keikaku wa:
    (The plan for the science contest is as follows)
Kontesuto o shimasu.
    (We will have a contest.)

Yuushoosha o kimemasu.
    (We will choose winners.)
Kontesuto o mimasu.
    (We will watch the science contest.)
Saiensu kontesuto no yosan wa nijuu godoru desu.
    (The budget for the science contest is $25.)
Posutaa no okane wa juu godoru desu.
    (The making the posters will cost $15.)
Puroguramu no kopii wa juudoru desu.
    (The making copies of the program will cost $10.)

4.9.3.D

Itsuka ni kafeteria de dansu paatii o shimasu.
    (We will hold a dance party in the cafeteria on the 5th.)
Dakara isu to yosan ga hitsuyoo desu.
    (That's why chairs, and a budget are necessary.)
Dansu paatii no mokuteki wa yunisefu no borantia no tame desu.
    (The purpose of the dance party is for the Unicef volunteers.)
Shichi gatsu ni Afurika de borantia o shimasu.
    (We will be volunteering in Africa in July.)
Dansu paatii no keikaku wa:
    (The plans for the dance party is as follows:)
Odorimasu.
    (We will dance.)
Nomimono o urimasu.
    (We will sell beverages.)
Okane o atsumemasu.
    (We will collect money.)
Dansu paatii no yosan wa yonjuu godoru desu.
    (The budget for the dance party is $45.)
Diijee no okane wa nijuu godoru desu.
    (The DJ will cost $25.)
Koora wa godoru desu.
    (The cola will cost $5.)
Koppu wa godoru desu.
    (The cups will cost $5.)
Poteto chippusu wa godoru desu.
    (The potato chips will cost $5.)
Osara wa godoru desu.
    (The paper plates will cost $5.)
1. *uta ga suki na hito* (people who like songs)
2. *borantia ga suki na hito* (people who like volunteering)
3. *kageku ga suki na hito* (people who like science)
4. *e ga suki na hito* (people who like pictures)

4.9.4

Tooka ni haru no supiichi kontesuto o shimasu.
    (We will have the spring speech contest on the 10th.)
Dakara, maiku to supiikaa to isu to teeburu to yoasan ga ( ) desu.
    (That's why mikes, speakers, chairs, tables, and budget are ( ).)
Haru no supiichi kontesuto no ( ) wa Nihongo no benkyoo no ( ) desu.
    (The ( ) of the spring speech contest is ( ) Japanese studies.)
Haru no supiichi kontesuto no ( ) wa, supiichi kontesuto o shimasu.
    (The ( ) for the spring speech contest is as follows: We will hold a speech contest.)
Supiichi kontesuto no ( ) wa nijuu godoru desu.
    (The ( ) for the speech contest is $25.)
Kippu no okane wa juu godoru desu.
    (The tickets will cost $15.)
Kopii wa juudoru desu.
    (The photocopying will cost $10.)

4.10.1 Virtual Reality 1

1. *Moshi moshi*
(Hello.)

2. *Rika san wa imasu ka.?*
(Is Rika there?)

3. *Chotto matte kudasai.*
(Just a moment, please)

4. *Donata desu ka?*
(Who is this?)

5. *Konsaato ni ikimasu ka?*
(Are you going to the concert?)

6. *Ikimasen.*
(I'm not going.)

7. *Nan ji ni ikimasu ka?*
(What time are you going?)

8. *Nani o shimasu ka?*
(What are you going to do?)

9. *Ja, yoji kara desu ne?*
(Ok, It's 4:00, isn't it?.)

4.10.3

Raishuu no sukejuuru
(schedule for next week)

Purezentaa no Namae
(Name of Presenter)

Yamada Haruko
(Haruko Yamada)

Purezentaa no Guruupu
(Group of Presenter)

Bunka
(Culture)

Purezenteeshon (ibento)
(Presentation [event])

Ocha
(Tea Ceremony)

Purezentaa no denwa bangoo nii, nii, nii no nana, hachi, kyuu, yon
(Telephone Number of Presenter) (222-7894)

Getsuyoobi (Monday)
kuji kara juuni ji (shigoto) *sanji kara goji (furii)*
(from 9:00 to 12:00 [work]) (from 3:00 to 5:00 [free])

Kayoobi (Tuesday)
hachiji kara goji (shigoto)
(from 8:00 to 5:00 [work])

Suiyoobi (Wednesday)
kuji kara niji (furii) *sanji kara hachiji (miitingu)*
(from 9:00 to 2:00 [free]) (from 3:00 to 8:00 [meeting])

Mokuyoobi(Thursday)
juuji kara juuniji (miitingu) *juuniji kara rokuji (furii)*
(from 10:00 to 2:00 [meeting]) (from 12:00 to 6:00 [free])

4.10.3 *Sukejuuru no Dorafuto* (Draft Schedule)

Getsuyoobi (Monday)
sanji kara shichiji *resepushon*
(from 3:00 to 7:00) (reception)

Kayoobi (Tuesday)
sanji kara goji *supootsu, bunka, kaisha*
(from 3:00 to 5:00) (sports, culture, company
ibento *namae*
(event) (name)

Suiyoobi (Wednesday)
sanji kara goji *supootsu, bunka, kaisha*
(from 3:00 to 5:00) (sports, culture, company
ibento *namae*
(event) (name)

Mokuyoobi (Thursday)
sanji kara goji *supootsu, bunka, kaisha*
(from 3:00 to 5:00) (sports, culture, company
ibento *namae*
(event) (name)

Kin'yoobi (Friday)
sanji kara hachiji *dansu*

(from 3:00 to 8:00) (dance)

4.10.3 *Chirashi no Sanpuru* (Sample Leaflet)

Getsu (Mon.)
sanji kara shichiji made *resepushon*
(from 3:00 to 7:00) (reception)

Ka (Tues.)
sanji kara goji made *karate no demonsutoreeshon*
(from 3:00 to 5:00) (karate demonstration)

Sui (Wed.)
sanji kara goji made *Tanaka san no hanashi (kamera)*
(from 3:00 to 5:00) (Mr. Tanaka's lecture [camera])

Moku (Thurs.)
sanji kara goji made *ocha no demonsutoreeshon*
(from 3:00 to 5:00) (tea ceremony demonstration)

Kin (Fri.)
sanji kara goji made *dansu paatii*
(from 3:00 to 5:00) (dance party)

4.10.3 Sample Telephone Conversation

Kaori: *Moshi moshi.* (Hello.)
John: *Moshi moshi. Katoo san no otaku desu ka?*
(Hello. Is this the Kato residence?)
Kaori: *Hai, soo desu.* (Yes, it is.)
John: *Kaori san imasu ka?* (Is Kaori there?)
Kaori: *Hai, watashi desu.* (Yes, speaking.)
John: *A, konban wa. John desu.*
(Oh, good evening. This is John.)
Kaori: *A, John san. Konban wa.*
(Oh, John. Good evening.)
John: *Anoo, Japaneezu Karuchaa Wiiku no koto desu ga.*
(Um, I'm calling about the Japanese Culture Week [but].)
Kaori: *Hai.* (Yes.)
John: *Anoo, Nihon bunka guruupu no koto desu ga.*
(Um, it's about the Japanese culture group.)
Kaori: *Aa, zen ga ii desu ka? Soretomo, shuuji ga ii desu ka?*
(Oh, would you like Zen? Or would you prefer calligraphy?)
John: *Eeto.* (Um.)
Kaori: *Ja, kabuki ga ii desu ka? Noo ga ii desuka? Soretomo, ocha ga ii desu ka?*
(Well then, would you like kabuki? Or No? Or would you prefer a tea ceremony?)
John: *Ocha ga ii desu.* (I prefer a tea ceremony.)
Kaori: *Purezentaa wa Yamada Haruko sensei desu.*
(The presenter is Haruko Yamada.)
John: *Aa, soo desu ka? Ocha no purezenteeshon wa nanji kara nanji made desu ka?*
(Oh, I see. From what time towhat time will the tea ceremony presenter's presentation last?)

Kaori: *Yamada sensei wa getsuyoobi wa sanji kara goji made furii desu.*

(On Mondays, Ms. Yamada is free from 3:00 to 5:00.

Sui yoobi wa kuji kara niji made furii desu. Mokuyoobi wa sanji kara rokuji made furii desu.

(On Wednesdays, Ms. Yamada is free from 9:00 to 2:00. On Thursdays, Ms. Yamada is free from 3:00 to 6:00.)

Dore ga ii desu ka? When would be good for you?)

John: *Chotto matte kudasai. Sanji kara miitungu o shimasu. Ja, atode denwa shimasu.*

(Please wait a moment. We will have a meeting starting at 3:00. Well then, I will call you later.)

Kaori: *Aa, soo desu ka?* (Oh, I see.)

John: *Doomo arigatoo gozaimasu. Yoroshiku onegai shimasu. Sayoonara.*

(Thank you very much. We appreciate your help. Goodbye.)

Kaori: *Sayoonara.* (Goodbye.)

4.10.3 sample telephone conversation II

John: *Anoo, Japaneezu Karuchaa Wiiku no Nihon bunka guruupu no koto desu ga.*

(Um, I'm calling about the Japanese Culture Week [but].)

Kaori: *Hai.* (Yes.)

John: *Ocha no purezenteeshon wa mokuyoobi ni shimasu. Yamada sensei no sukejuuru o onegai shimasu.*

(We've decided to have the tea ceremony presentation on Thursday. Please tell me Ms. Yamada's schedule.)

Kaori: *Aa, Yamada sensei wa juuniji sanjuppun ni gakkoo ni ikimasu. Juuniji han kara ichiji made ohiru gohan o tabemasu. Ichiji kara san ji made puripareeshon o shimasu.*

(Well, Ms. Yamada will go to school at 12:30. From 12:30 to 1:00, she will eat lunch. From 1:00 to 3:00, she will prepare.)

Sanji kara goji made demonsutoreeshon o shimasu. Goji kara goji han made sooji o shimasu. Rokujini uchi ni kaerimasu.

(From 3:00 to 5:00, she will have her demonstration. From 5:00 to 5:30, she will clean up. At 6:00, she will go home.)

John: *Yamada sensei wa juuniji han ni gakkoo ni kimasu ne?*

(Ms. Yamada will come to school at 12:30, right?)

Kaori: *Hai, ikimasu.* (Yes, she will.)

John: *Sanji kara goji made demonsutoreeshon o shimasu ne?*

(From 3:00 to 5:00, she will have her demonstration, right?)

Kaori: *Hai, sanji kara goji made shimasu.*

(Yes, she will from 3:00 to 5:00.)

John: *Anoo, sumimasen. Yamada sensei no denwa bangoo wa nanban desu ka?* (Um, excuse me. What is Ms. Yamada's telephone number?)

Kaori: *Hai, nii, ichi, nii no san, kyuu, san, kyuu desu.*

(Yes, it is 212-3939.)

4.10.4 Sample Proposal

Tsuitachi kara nanoka made gakkoo de Nihon Bunka Wiiku o shimasu.

(We will have the Japanese Culture Week at school from the 1st until the 7th.)

Dakara, tooka ni kafeteria de beeku seeru o shimasu.

(That's why we will have a bake sale in the cafeteria on the 10th.)

Isu to teeburu to matto to maiku to supiikaa ga hitsuyoo desu.

(Chairs, tables, mats, mikes, and speakers are necessary.)

Nihon Bunka Wiiku no mokuteki wa Nihon bunka no benkyoo no tame desu.

(The purpose of the Japanese Culture Week is for Japanese cultural studies.)

Nihon Bunka Wiiku no keikaku wa.

(The plan for the Japanese Culture Week is as follows:)

Kayoobi wa sanji kara goji made Ooyama sensei no karate no demonsutoreeshon o shimasu.

(On Tuesday from 3:00 to 5:00, Mr. Ooyama will have his karate demonstration.)

Suiyoobi wa sanji kara goji made Tanaka san no hanashi (kamera) o shimasu.

(On Wednesday from 3:00 to 5:00, Mr. Tanaka will have her lecture [camera].)

Mokuyoobi wa sanji kara goji made Hayashi san no ocha no demonsutoreeshon o shimasu.

(On Thursday from 3:00 to 5:00, Ms. Hayashi will have her tea ceremony demonstration.)

Nihon Bunka Wiiku no ibento no yosan wa sanbyaku gojuudoru desu.

(The budget for the events during the Japanese Culture Week is $350.)

Sensei no okane wa nihyakugojuudoru desu.

(The teachers will cost $250.)

Puroguramu no okane wa gojuudoru desu.

(Making the programs will cost $50.)

Kopii no okane wa nijuugodoru desu.

(Making copies will cost $25.)

Mizu no botoru wa juugodoru desu.

(Bottled water will cost $15.)

Koppu wa godoru desu.

(Cups will cost $5.)

Sara wa godoru desu.

(Plates will cost $5.)

4.10.5 Sample meeting

Chair: *Ja, miitingu o hajimemashoo. Nihon Bunka no Shuu wa nannichi kara nannichi ga ii desu ka?*

(Ok, let's start the meeting. From what day to what day should we hold the Japanese Culture Week?)

A: *Tsuitachi kara muika ga ii desu.*

(I would like it to be from the 1st to the 6th.)

Chair: *B san wa?* (What about you, Mr. B?)

B: *Nanoka kara juusannichi ga ii desu.*

(From the 7th to the 13th.)

Chair: *C san.* (Ms. C.)

C: *Watashi wa, tsuitachi kara muika ga ii desu.*

(From the 1st to the 6th.)

Chair: *D san, tsuitachi kara muika to nanoka kara juu sannichi to dochira ga ii desu ka?*

(Ms. D, would you rather it be from the 1st to the 6th or from the 7th to the 13th?)

D: *Watashi mo, tsuitachi kara muika ga ii desu.*

(I would also like to have it from the 1st to the 6th.)

Chair: *Tsuitachi kara muika no hito? Juu. Nanoka kara juusannichi no hito? Hachi. Tsuitachi kara muika wa juu. Nanoka kara juusannichi wa hachi.*

(People who vote for the 1st to the 6th? 10. People who vote for the 7th to the 13th? 8. 10 people for the 1st to the 6th. 8 people for the 7th to the 13th.

Ja, tsuitachi kara muika ni shimashoo. Ja, A guruupu no purupoozaru o hajimemashoo. A guruupu no puropoozaru wo yonde kudasai. Sore kara, kokuban ni kaite kudasai.

(Well then, let's have it from the 1st to the 6th. Well then, let's start with Group A's proposal. Please read Group A's proposal. Also, please write it on the black board.)

A: *Ja, A guruupu no puropoozaru o yomimasu.*

(Well then, I will read Group A's proposal.)

Chair: *B guruupu no puropoozaru o yonde kudasai. Sorekara, kokuban ni kaite kudasai.*

(Please read Group B's proposal. Also, please write it on the black board.)

Nihon Bunka no Shuu wa A guruupu no puropoozaru to B guruupu no puropoozaru to dochira ga ii desu ka?

(For the Japanese Culture Week, would you rather use Group A's proposal or Group B's proposal?)

A: *A guruupu no puropoozaru ga ii desu.*

(I would prefer to use Group A's proposal.)

Chair: *B san wa?* (What about you, Mr. B?)

B: *B guruupu no puropoozaru ga ii desu.*

(I would prefer to use Group B's proposal.)

Chair: *C san.* (Ms. C.)

C: *Watashi wa, B guruupu no puropoozaru ga ii desu.*

(I would prefer to use Group B's proposal.)

Glossary
English – Japanese

a little	ちょっと	2.2, 4.8, 4.10
a person who is quick in decision making		
	けつだんりょくのあるひと	
		3.11A
a person with a sense of responsibility		
	せきにんかんのあるひと	
		3.11A
about ~	~のことですが	4.3, 4.8, 4.10
Accord	アコード	3.3
activity	アクティビティー	2.1, 2.5, 2.7, 3.2
activity	かつどう	3.11
actor	だんゆう	3.11A
actress	じょゆう	3.11A
address	じゅうしょ	3.8
administration office		
	じむしつ	2.6
Africa	アフリカ	4.9
after	あと	3.9
after cram school	じゅくのあと	3.11A
after practice	れんしゅうのあと	3.11A
after school	ほうかご	3.9, 3.11A
age	（お）とし	3.1B, 3.1, 3.2, 3.6, 3.7, 3.9, 3.10
age	とし	3.6, 3.8, 4.9
age, ~year(s) old	さい	1.1, 1.2, 1.4, 1.5, 1.6
AIDS Walk	エイズウォーク	4.9
Aikawa, Hajime (name of person)		
	あいかわ　はじめ	3.8
aikido	あいきどう	4.9, 4.11A
air conditioner	エアコン	0.2.08G
airplane	ひこうき	3.1B, 3.1, 3.9
Akira (name of person)		
	あきら	3.3
Akita prefecture	あきた	3.8
Algeria	アルジェリア	3.9
Algerian person	アルジェリアじん	3.02
all	ぜんぶ	4.7
all set? are you all done?		
	もういいですか	0.1.09G,1.9A
also/then	それから	2.2, 3.9, 4.10
always	いつも	3.5, 3.6, 3.9, 3.11, 3.11A, 4.1, 4.2
ambulance	きゅうきゅうしゃ	1.3, 1.6, 1.9A
America	アメリカ	0.2.05G, 3.2, 3.3, 3.6, 3.8, 3.9, 3.11, 4.8
American football		

	アメフト	0.2.08G
American person	アメリカじん	3.1B, 3.2, 3.9, 4.7
Ami Katoh (name of person)		
	かとう　あみ	1.2
and	と	3.6, 4.5. 4.7. 4.9
animation	アニメ	3.2
animation festival		
	アニメフェスティバル	
		2.1, 2.2, 2.6
answer	こたえ	3.10
Aoki (Japanese family name)		
	あおき	3.9
Aoyama (name of person)		
	あおやま	3.3
apple	りんご	0.2.09G, 1.9A, 2.2, 2.6,
apple pie	アップルパイ	2.6, 2.9A
approval, agreement		
	さんせい	2.9A
April	しがつ	2.1B, G, 2.3, 2.6, 3.2, 3.9
Arabic language	アラビアご	3.02
archery club	きゅうどうぶ	3.11
are you Mr./Ms. etc~.?		
	~さんですか	0.1.01G
are you well?	おげんきですか	0.1.06G, 1.6, 1.8, 2.9A
art	げいじゅつ	4.5
art	びじゅつ	3.1B, 3.1, 3.5, 3.8, 3.9
art	アート	3.2, 4.9
art center	アートセンター	2.1
art club	びじゅつぶ	1.9A, 3.11
art fair	アートフェア	2.1, 2.2, 2.6
art show	アートショー	2.2, 4.9
artist	げいじゅつか	3.11A
Asai Hana (name of person)		
	あさい　はな	4.1
Asia	アジア	4.9
at	に	4.7, See. p393~395
at	で	0.2.10G, 4.7, See. p393~395
at eighth thirty	はちじはんに	4.4
at eleven o'clock	じゅういいちじに	4.4
at home	うちに	4.4
at ten o'clock	じゅうじに	4.4
Atlanta	アトランタ	3.11A
attractive	かっこいい	3.11A
attractive	すてき(な)	0.2.09G, 3.1B, 3.5, 3.8, 3.9

audio	オーディオ	4.11A
audition	オーディション	4.8, 4.9
auditorium	こうどう	2.1B, 2.1, 2.3, 2.4, 2.6, 3.6, 4.2, 4.6, 4.9
August	はちがつ	2.1B, G2.3, 2.6, 3.9, 4.7
aunt	おばさん	3.11A
aunt	おば	3.11A
Australia	オーストラリア	3.9
Australian person	オーストラリアじん	3.02
away from (location)	がいしゅつちゅう	4.3
Ayana	アヤナ	1.2, 1.3, 1.4, 3.4
be (is, am, are)~~?	～は～ですか	1.6
be (is, am, are)~~? (informal) ～は～か		1.6
Babe Ruth	ベーブルース	0.2.05G
back hand (in sports) バックハンド		3.9
badminton club	バトミントンぶ	3.11
bag	バッグ	0.1.06G
bake sale	ベークセール	4.9, 4.10
bakery	パンや	3.11A
ball	ボール	4.9
ballpoint pen	ボールペン	3.11A
banana	バナナ	1.1, 1.9A, 2.1B, 2.2, 2.5, 2.6, 3.1, 3.3, 3.9
base	ベース	0.1.06G
baseball	やきゅう	1.6, 3.8
baseball player	やきゅうのせんしゅ	3.11A
baseball team	やきゅうぶ	1.9A, 3.11
basketball	バスケットボール	1.6, 2.4, 3.5, 3.8, 4.1B, 4.2
basketball club	バスケットぶ	3.11
[Be~]~?	～ですか	1.6
[Be~]~? (informal)	～か	1.6
~be (is, am, are)~	～は～です	1.6
~be (is, am, are)~	～は～だ	1.6
beautiful	きれい	3.1B, 3.1, 3.5, 3.8, 3.9
bed	ベッド	3.11A
bicycle	じてんしゃ	3.9
big	おおきい	3.7, 4.5
biology	せいぶつ	3.1B, 3.1, 3.5, 3.9
birthday	たんじょうび	3.01B, 3.2, 3.3, 3.6, 3.8, 3.9, 3.10, 4.6
birthday	（お）たんじょうび	3.7
black	くろ	1.9A G, 3.1B, 3.1, 3.9
blackboard	こくばん	3.11A, 4.6, 4.8
black tea	こうちゃ	1.9A, 2.1B, 2.1, 2.5, 2.6
blue	あお	0.2.01G, 1.9A, 3.1B, 3.1, 3.9
boar	いのしし	0.2.05G, 1.4
boat	ボート	0.1.06G, 4.6, 4.8
body	からだ	4.6, 4.9
book	ほん	0.2.09G, 3.7, 3.11A, 4.1B, 4.4, 4.7 4.8, 4.9
boots	ブーツ	0.1.06G

boring	つまらない	3.5
born	うまれる	4.9
born in year~	～ねんうまれ	1.1B, 1.3 1.4, 1.6, 1.8
Boston	ボストン	3.6, 3.11A, 4.6
bottle	ボトル	4.9, 4.10
Bow	れい	0.1.08G, 1.1B, 1.2, 1.3, 1.5
box lunch	おべんとう	2.4, 2.9A, 2.9
brass band club	ブラスバンドぶ	3.11
brave	ゆうかん	3.11A
Brazil	ブラジル	3.9
Brazilian person	ブラジルじん	3.02
bread	パン	1.7, 3.2
breakfast	あさごはん	4.1B, 4.4, 4.7, 4.8, 4.9
broadcasting club	ほうそうぶ	1.9A
Brooklyn	ブルックリン	3.3
brown	ちゃいろ	1.9A, G3.9
brush	ふで	1.2
buck wheat noodles	そば	2.4, 2.6, 2.9A, 2.9
Buddhist temple	おてら	1.2
budget	よさん	4.1B, 4.1, 4.6, 4.9, 4.10
Buffalo	バッファロー	3.11A
bus	バス	3.01B, 3.1, 3.4, 3.9, 3.11, 4.9
busy	いそがしい	3.5, 3.8, 3.8, 3.11
by	で	3.1, 3.6, 3.9, 3.11, 4.7 See. p393-395
by why/with what	なんで	3.4
Bye	バイバイ	0.1.02G, 1.9A, 4.3
Bye	バーイ	0.1.02G
bye	では	1.9A
byte	バイト	1.3, 1.5, 1.6
cacao	カカオ	0.1.02G
cafe	カフェ	0.1.10G
cafeteria	カフェテリア	2.1B, 2.2, 2.6, 4.2, 4.6, 4.9, 4.10
cafeteria	しょくどう	3.9, 3.11A
cake	ケーキ	0.1.02G, 1.7, 2.1B, 2.1, 2.4, 2.6, 3.2
calendar	カレンダー	2.1, 2.2
California	カリフォルニア	4.6
calligraphy club	しょどうぶ	3.11
calligraphy master	おしゅうじのせんせい	4.5
calm/cool	れいせい	3.11A
camera	カメラ	4.10, 4.11A
campfire	キャンプファイヤー	0.1.10G, 3.9, 3.11A
Canada	カナダ	3.2, 3.9
Canadian person	カナダじん	3.1B, 3.2
cannot speak	はなしません	3.6, 3.9
canoe	カヌー	0.1.05G
canzone	カンツォーネ	2.7
captain	キャプテン	3.11A
car	くるま	3.1B, 3.1, 3.3, 3.7, 4.11A

car navigation	カーナビ	0.2.08G
carefully	そっと	0.2.04G
cash service	キャッシュサービス	2.9A
cat	ねこ	0.2.05G, 1.1, 4.1
CD player	CD（シーディー）プレーヤー	
		4.6 4.9
cent	セント	1.5, 1.6
Central Park	セントラルパーク	3.11A
chair	いす	3.11A, 4.1B, 4.1, 4.5, 4.6, 4.8, 4.9, 4.10
chair of student council		
	せいとかいちょう	3.11A
chalk	チョーク	4.6, 4.8
chapter one	いっか	0.2.04G
characteristics	とくちょう	3.1B
cheerful	あかるい	3.11A
cheese cake	チーズケーキ	2.6, 2.9A
chemistry	ばけがく	3.01B, 3.9
chemistry	かがく	3.01B
chess	チェス	2.7
chess team	チェスクラブ	1.9A
Chicago	シカゴ	0.1.03G, 3.11A, 4.6
chicken	チキン	0.2.06G, 1.1, 2.1B, 2.5, 2.6
China	ちゅうごく	3.9
Chinese cuisine	ちゅうかりょうり	2.9A
Chinese language	ちゅうごくご	3.1B, 3.2, 3.5
Chinese person	ちゅうごくじん	3.1B, 3.2
Chinese-style noodles		
	ラーメン	0.1.09G, 0.2.06G, 2.4, 2.6, 2.9A, 3.9
chorus	コーラスぶ	3.11
cider	サイダー	2.6
circus	サーカス	0.1.03G
clam sauce	クラムソース	2.6, 2.9A
class	くみ	1.5, 1.6, 3.9
class	クラス	0.2.07G, 4.8
class 2	にくみ	1.6, 3.9
class 5	ごくみ	3.9
classical music	クラシック	3.8
classroom	きょうしつ	2.1B, 2.2, 2.3, 2,.6, 4.2, 4.6, 4.9
clean up	そうじをします/そうじをする	
		4.10, 4.11A
cloudy	くもり	3.11A
club	クラブ	3.2, 3.3, 3.7, 3.9, 3.10, 3.11, 4.4, 4.8
club meeting	クラブミーティング	3.5, 4.2, 4.4, 4.6, 4.8,
coach	コーチ	0.1.04G, 1.4, 3.11A, 4.1B, 4.5
coach Hayashi	はやしコーチ	3.3
coat	コート	0.1.04G
cocoa	ココア	0.1.02G
coffee	コーヒー	0.1.06G, 1.9A, 2.1B, 2.2, 2.5, 2.6, 3.2, 4.2, 4.4, 4.6

coke	コーク	3.5, G, 4.2, 4.5
cola	コーラ	0.2.06G, 1.1, 1.9A, 2.2, 2.4, 2.6, 3.2, 4.6, 4.9
cold	つめたい	3.11A
cold	さむい	0.2.07G, 1.6, 1.9A
college	だいがく	1.9A, 3.2, 3.9
color	いろ	0.2.09G, 3.2, 3.8, 3.11A
Colorado	コロラド	3.6, 4.6
come late	ちこくします/ちこくする	
		4.11A
comments	コメント	2.6, 2.9A
company/business	かいしゃ	4.10, 4.11A
computer	コンピュータ	0.2.07G, 1.2, 1.6, 1.8, 3.1B, 3.9, 3.11A
computer room	コンピュータルーム	2.1B, 2.6, 4.2
concert	コンサート	3.5, 4.2, 4.4, 4.6, 4.8, 4.10
concert hall	コンサートホール	2.1B, 4.1
content of practice	れんしゅうのないよう	
		3.11A
contents	ないよう	3.9
contest	コンテスト	4.9
conversation	かいわ	3.9
cook	りょうりします/りょうりする	
		4.11A
cookie	クッキー	2.1B, 2.6
cooking	クッキング	3.02
cool~	クール（な）	3.5, 3.8, 3.9
copy	コピー	4.6, 4.9, 4.10
could you say it one more time?		
	もういちどおねがいします	
		1.6, G, 1.9A
counselor	カウンセラー	3.11A, 4.1B
country music	カントリー	2.5
country	（お）くに	3.1B, 3.1, 3.2, 3.6, 3.7, 3.9, 3.10, 3.11
cow	うし	1.1, 1.4
cram school	じゅく	3.9
culture	ぶんか	4.10, 4.11A
cup	コップ	4.6, 4.8, 4.9, 4.10
curry and rice	カレーライス	0.1.09G, 0.2.06G, 2.4, 2.9
cut	カット	0.1.04G
cute	かわいい	3.01B, 3.1, 3.5, 3.8, 3.9
dance	ダンス	1.7, 2.1B, 2.2., 2.3, 2.4, 2.5, 2.6, 3.5, 3.6, 4.2. 4.4, 4.6, 4.7, 4.8, 4.9, 4.10
dance party	ダンスパーティー	2.2, 4.9, 4.10
dance practice	ダンスのれんしゅう	4.6
Daryl	ダリル	1.2, 1.3, 1.4, 3.4,
date	ひにち	2.3, 2.5, 2.6, 4.11
date	デートをします/デートをする	
		4.11A
day	ひ	2.6
day after tomorrow		
	あさって	4.1B, 4.5, 4.8

English	Japanese	References
~day of the month	〜にち	0.2.04G, 2.1B
day of the week	ようび	2.1, 2.2, 2.4, 2.5
day off	やすみのひ	2.9A
December	じゅうにがつ	2.1B, G, 2.1, 2.3, 2.6
demonstrate	デモンストレーションします/デモンストレーションする	4.10, 4.11A
demonstration	デモンストレーション	4.10, 4.11A
Denver	デンバー	3.11A
department store	デパート	4.11A
desk	つくえ	0.2.04G, 3.11A, 4.5, 4.6, 4.9
dessert	デザート	2.4, 2.6, 2.7, 2.9A
dialects	ほうげん	2.3
difficult	むずかしい	3.5
difficult/serious	たいへん	3.5
dinner	ばんごはん	4.1B, 4,9
dinner	ゆうごはん	4.4, 4.7, 4.9
disk	ディスク	2.7
divide	わる	1.3, 1.6
do laundry	せんたくをします/せんたくをする	4.11A
do your best/hang in there!	がんばってください	1.9A, G
do your best/hang in there! (informal)	がんばって	1.9A, 3.6, 3.9, 4.1
do you have any questions?	しつもんがありますか	1.9A, G
do you have any questions? (informal)	しつもんがあるか	1.9A
do you understand?	わかりますか	0.1.09G, 1.9A
do you understand? (informal)	わかるか	1.9A
dog	いぬ	0.2.05G, 1.4
dollar	ドル	1.1, 1.3, 1.4, 1.5, 1.6, 2.2, 4.6, 4.9, 4.10
donut	ドーナツ	0.1.05G
door	ドア	3.11A
dormitory	りょう	2.6
draft	ドラフト	4.10, 4.11A
dragon	たつ	1.4
drama club	ドラマクラブ	1.4, 1.6, 3.3
drama club	えんげきぶ	1.9A, 3.11
drama night	ドラマナイト	0.2.04G, 2.3
drinks	のみもの	2.1, 2.4, 2.5, 2.6, 2.7, 2.9A, 3.2, 4.9
duet	デュエット	2.7
during this time	このじかん	3.11A
Dushanbe	ドゥシャンベ	2.7
economics	けいざい	3.1B, 3.1, 3.5, 3.9
eel	うなぎ	2.4, 2.6, 2.9, 2.9A
Egypt	エジプト	3.9
Egyptian person	エジプトじん	3.02
eight	はち	1.1B, G, 1.1, 1.2, 1.3, 1.5, 1.6, 3.9
eight hundred	はっぴゃく	1.1B, G, 1.1, 1.3, 1.5, 1.6
eight minutes	はっぷん	4.8
eight o'clock	はちじ	2.1B, G, 2.1, 2.2, 2.6, 4.1, 4.4, 4.7, 4.8, 4.10
eight people	はちにん	2.3, 2.6, 3.7, 4.1
eight (quantity)	やっつ	2.9A, G, 4.1b, 4.5
eight thirty	はちじはん	2.6
eight thousand	はっせん	1.3, 1.5, 1.6
eight years old	はっさい	1.2
eight thirty five	はちじさんじゅうごふん	4.8
eighteen	じゅうはち	1.1B, G, 1.2, 1.5, 1.6,
eighteen years old	じゅうはっさい	1.2
eighteenth day of the month	じゅうはちにち	2.1B, G, 2.3, 2.6
eighth day of the month	ようか	2.1B, G, 2.1, 2.3, 2.6, 3.9, 4.1
eighth grade	はちねんせい	1.6, 3.1B
eighty	はちじゅう	1.1B, G, 1.2, 1.5, 1.6
elder brother	あに	3.1, 3.4, 3.5, 3.9
elder brother	おにいさん	0.2.10G, 3.01B, 3.1, 3.4, 3.9
elder sister	あね	3.1, 3.4, 3.5, 3.6, 3.9
elder sister	おねえさん	0.2.10G, 3.1B, 3.1, 3.4, 3.5, 3.9, 4.5
electricity	でんき	4.9
elementary school	しょうがく	1.1B
elementary school	しょうがっこう	1.1, 1.6
elephant	ぞう	0.2.03G
eleven	じゅういち	1.1B, G, 1.1, 1.2, 1.5, 1.6
eleven minutes	じゅういっぷん	4.9
eleven o'clock	じゅういちじ	2.1B, G, 2.2 , 2.6, 4.8
eleven thirty	じゅういちじはん	2.6, 4.1, 4.8
eleven years old	じゅういっさい	1.2
eleven fifty	じゅういちじごじゅっぷん	4.9
eleventh day of the month	じゅういちにち	2.1B, G, 2.1, 2.3, 2.6, 4.1, 4.9
eleventh grade	じゅういちねんせい	1.6, 3.2, 3.3
eleventh grade	こうに	3.9
end	おわり	3.1B, 3.6, 3.9
England	イギリス	3.9
English language	えいご	0.2.02G, 3.1B, 3.2, 3.5, 3.8, 3.9. 4.1, 4.5, 4.9
English language club	えいごぶ	3.11
English person	イギリスじん	3.02
enjoyable	たのしい	3.5
equals	は	1.3, 4.6.
equipment	どうぐ	4.5, 4.9
eraser	けしごむ（けしゴム）	3.11A
Erika (name of person)	えりか	3.3

essay contest	エッセイコンテスト	0.2.04G, 2.3
evaluation	ひょうか	4.1B, 4.1, 4.6, 4.9, 4.10
events	ぎょうじ	0.2.01G, 0.2.05G, 1.2
events	できごと	0.2.05G
events	イベント	2.1, 2.2, 4.11A
every day	まいにち	4.1B, 3.5, 3.6, 3.9, 4.2, 4.9
excuse me but	すみませんが	1.6, 4.3
excuse me but (informal)	すまないが	1.6
excuse me/good bye	しつれいします	0.1.02G, 1.2, 1.6, 1.8, 1.9A, 2.9A
excuse me./I'm sorry	しつれい	0.1.08G, 1.6, 1.9A, 2.9A, 4.11A
expense	ひよう	
extra-curricular activities	かがいかつどう	1.9A
eye	め	0.2.07G, 4.1
eyebrow	まゆ	0.2.08G, 4.1
face	かお	0.2.02G, 4.9
fall	あき	1.4, 1.6, 2.4, 3.9, 4.9
false	うそ	1.1, 1.3
family	（ご）かぞく	3.4, 3.9
family	かぞく	0.2.03G, 3.1B, 3.4, 3.9, 3.11, 4.1
far	とおい	4.5
fashion	ファッション	2.7
father	ちち	3.1, 3.4, 3.5, 3.6, 3.9, 3.11
father	パパ	3.4
father	おとうさん	0.2.10G, 3.1B, 3.1, 3.4, 3.5, 3.9, 4.1
father-in-law	ぎりのおとうさん	3.11A
father-in-law	ぎりのちち	3.11A
favor	おねがい	1.2, 1.3, 1.5, 1.6,
fearful/awful	こわい	3.11A
February	にがつ	2.1B, G, 2.3, 2.6, 3.5, 3.9,
felt	フェルト	2.7
festival	フェスティバル	4.6
fettuccini	フェタチーニ	2.6, 2.9A
field	グランド	2.1B, 2.2, 2.6, 4.6
fifteen	じゅうご	1.1B, G, 1.2, 1.5, 1.6,
fifteen minutes	じゅうごふん	4.1B, 4.1
fifteen years old	じゅうごさい	1.2, 3.8
fifteenth day of the month	じゅうごにち	2.1B, G, 2.3, 2.6
fifteenth year of the Heisei eara	へいせいじゅうごねん	1.7
fifth day of the month	いつか	2.1B, G, 2.1, 2.3, 2.6, 3.5, 3.9, 4.1, 4.2, 4.4, 4.7, 4.9
fifth grade	ごねんせい	1.6
fifty	ごじゅう	1.1B, G, 1.2, 1.5, 1.6, 3.9
fifty five minutes	ごじゅうごふん	4.1B
fifty minutes	ごじゅっぷん	4.1B

fifty years	ごじゅうねん	1.3
fifty yen	ごじゅうえん	1.9
film	フィルム	2.7
fine weather	いいてんき	1.6, 1.9A
fire	ひ	4.9
fire	かじ	1.3, 1.6, 1.9A
fire engine	しょうぼうしゃ	1.9A
first	さき	4.9
first calligraphy writing of the year	かきぞめ	1.2
first day of the month	ついたち	1.7, 2.1B, 2.3, 2.6, 3.2, 3.5, 3.9, 4.1, 4.2, 4.4. 4.7, 4.9
first day of the year	がんじつ／がんたん	1.2, 1.7, 1.9
first lady	ファーストレディー	3.11A
ffirst year (of an era)	がんねん	1.3, 1.6
first grade	いちねんせい	1.6
first name	ファーストネーム	3.9
first year, second class	いちねんにくみ	1.6
fish	さかな	0.2.05G
five	ご	1.1B, G, 1.1, 1.2, 1.5, 1.6, 3.9
five	ごう	1.3
five hundred	ごひゃく	1.1B, G, 1.3, 1.5, 1.6
five hundred yen	ごひゃくえん	1.9
five minutes	ごふん	4.1B, 4.1 ,4.9
five o'clock	ごじ	2.1B, G, 2.2, 2.6, 4.3, 4.10
five people	ごにん	2.1B, G, 2.3, 2.6, 3.6, 3.7, 3.9. 4.1
five (quantity)	いつつ	2.9A, 4.1B, 4.5,
five thirty	ごじはん	2.6, 4.1, 4.3
five thousand	ごせん	1.3, 1.5, 1.6,
five thousand yen	ごせんえん	1.9
five years old	ごさい	1.2
five yen	ごえん	1.9
five ten	ごじにじゅっぷん	4.9
flower	はな	0.2.06G
flower arrangement	おはな	4.9
flower arrangement	いけばな	4.9, 4.11A
flower arrangement club	かどうぶ	1.9A, 3.11
flower arrangement master	おはなのせんせい	4.5
flower viewing	はなみ	0.1.07G
flyer	ちらし	4.10, 4.11A
folk dance	フォークダンス	2.2, 2.6
folk music	フォーク	3.8
food	たべもの	2.1, 2.4, 2.5, 2.6, 2.7, 2.9A, 3.2, 3.5, 3.8
football	フットボール	1.6, 2.2, 3.2, 3.5, 4.2, 4.4 4.6,
football team	フットボールぶ	1.9A
for the sake of~	～のためです	4.6, 4.9

foreign language	がいこくご	3.1B, 3.1, 3.9
foreign student	りゅうがくせい	3.11A
fork	フォーク	0.1.10G, 2.7
form	フォーム	3.8
fort five minutes	よんじゅうごふん	4.1B
forty minutes	よんじゅっぷん	4.1B
forty minutes	よんじっぷん／よんじゅっぷん	4.1
four	し	1.1B, G, 1.2, 1.3, 1.5, 1.6, 3.9
four	よん	1.1B, G, 1.2, 1.3, 1.5, 1.6, 4.6
four-five	よじごふん	4.9
four hundred	よんひゃく	1.1B, G, 1.3, 1.5, 1.6
four minutes	よんぷん	4.9
four o'clock	よじ	2.1B, G, 2.1, 2.2, 2.6, 3.9, 4.3, 4.4, 4.8, 4.10
four people	よにん	2.1B, G, 2.3, 2.6, 3.4, 3.7, 3.9, 3.11, 4.1
four (quantity)	よっつ	2.9A, G, 4.1B, 4.5
four thirty	よじはん	2.6
four thousand	よんせん	1.3, 1.5, 1.6
four years old	よんさい	1.2
fourteen	じゅうし	1.1B, G, 1.2, 1.5, 1.6,
fourteen	じゅうよん	1.1B, G, 1.2, 1.5, 1.6,
fourteen years old	じゅうよんさい	1.2, 3.8
fourteenth day of the month		
	じゅうよっか	2.1B, G, 2.1, 2.3, 2.6
fourth day of the month		
	よっか	2.1B, G, 2.1, 2.3, 2.6, 3.3, 3.5, 3.9, 4.1, 4.2, 4.4, 4.7
fourth grade	よねんせい	1.6
forty	よんじゅう	1.1B, G, 1.2, 1.5, 1.6
France	フランス	3.1B, 3.1, 3.9
free	フリー	4.10, 4.11A
free (price)	ただ	2.6, 4.10
French cuisine	フランスりょうり	2.9A
French language	フランスご	3.1B, 3.1, 3.2, 3.5,
French person	フランスじん	3.02
Fri.	きん	4.7
Friday	きんようび	2.1B, G, 2.1, 2.2, 2.3, 2.6, 3.5, 4.2, 4.4, 4.9, 4.10
fried chicken	フライドチキン	4.2, 2.6, 3.5, 4.4, 4.6,
friend	ともだち	3.4, 3.8, 3.9, 3.11A, 4.6, 4.9
from	から	3.8, 3 9, 4.1, 4.7, 4.10
from~to~	～から～まで	4.4, 4.8, 4.11, See. p393-395
fruit store	くだものや	3.11A
fruits	フルーツ	2.1
fruits	くだもの	3.02, G
Fukuoka prefecture	ふくおか	3.02
funny	おもしろい	0.2.09G, 3.1B, 3.1, 3.5, 3.6, 3.8, 3,9
fusion	フュージョン	2.7

game	しあい	4.6, 4.9
game	ゲーム	2.9A, 4.1, 4.6, 4.11A
German language	ドイツご	3.5, 3.6
German person	ドイツじん	3.6
Germany	ドイツ	3.9
gift center	ギフトセンター	1.3
giga	ギガ	1.3, 1.4, 1.5, 1.6
gloomy	くらい	3.11A
go for a walk	さんぽします／さんぽする	4.11A
go shopping	かいものをします／かいものをする	4.11A
golf	ゴルフ	1.6, 4.7
good	いいです	4.3, 4.7
good	いい	1.1, 1.2, 1.8, 2.2, 2.3, 2.4, 3.6, 3.7
good afternoon, Hello.		
	こんにちは	0.1.03G, 1.1B, 1.1, 1.2, 1.6, 1.8, 3.2, 3.5, 3.6, 3.9, 4.3
good evening	こんばんは	0.1.03G, 1.1B, 1.1, 1.6, 1.8, 3.2, 4.3
good morning	おはよう	0.1.03G, 1.1B, 1.1, 1.2, 1.6, 1.8, 4.5
good morning	おはようございます	0.1.03G, 1.1B, 1.1, 1.2, 1.6, 1.8
good night	おやすみ	0.1.02G, 1.6, 1.9A, 2.9A
good night	おやすみなさい	0.1.02G, 1.2, 1.6, 1.8, 1.9A, 2.9A
good place/location	いいところ	3.11A
good-bye	さようなら	0.1.02G, 1.1, 1.2, 1.6, 1.8, 1.9A, 4.3, 4.10
grade year	がくねん	1.1, 1.4, 3.3, 3.6, 3.7, 3.8, 3.10, 4.9
grade year	～ねんせい	1.1B, 1.1, 1.3, 1.4, 1.5, 1.6,
graduate school	だいがくいん	1.9A
grandfather	おじいさん	3.11A, 4,5
grandfather	そふ	3.11A
grandmother	おばあさん	3.11A, 4,5
grandmother	そぼ	3.11A
grape	ぶどう	1.9A, 2.6 4.5, 4.8
grapefruit	グレープフルーツ	1.9A, 2.6
gray	グレー	1.9A, G, 3.1B, 3.1,
Great Lake School		
	グレートレイクスクール	3.11
green	みどり	1.9A, G, 3.1B, 3.1, 3.2, 3.8, 3.9
green tea ice cream	まっちゃアイス	2.6, 2.9A
greeting	あいさつ	3.6
grilled chicken yakitori		
	やきとり	2.6
group	グループ	1.6, 4.10, 4.11A
Guam	グアム	2.7
Guarini	グァリーニ	2.7

Guercino	グェルチーノ	2.7
Guinevere	グィネビア	2.7
guitar	ギター	1.5, 1.7
gymnasium	ジム	2.1B, 2.2, 2.4, 2.6, 4.2, 4.6
gymnasium	たいいくかん	4.9
Halloween party	ハロウィーンパーティー 0.2.04G, 2.3	
ham	ハム	0.1.07G, 0.2.06G
hamburger	ハンバーグ	4.4, 4.6
hamburger	ハンバーガー	2.1B, 2.2, 2.4, 2.5, 2.6, 2.9A, 2.9, 3.2, 3.6
hamburger shop	ハンバーガーのみせ	2.9A
hand	て	0.2.04G
Happy New Year	あけましておめでとうございます 1.2, 1.6, 1.7, 1.9	
hard disk	ハードディスク	1.4, 1.6
Hartford	ハートフォード	3.11A
Haruko (name of person)	はるこ	3.3
have a part-time job	アルバイトします/アルバイトする 4.11A	
have a safe trip (when someone else is leaving)	いってらっしゃい	0.1.06G, 1.9A
Hawaii	ハワイ	4.6
Hayashi (name of person)	はやし（さん）	1.5, 3.3 3.9
Hayashi Rika (name of person)	はやし　りか	4.3
head of club	クラブぶちょう	3.11A
healthy	げんき(な)	0.2.09G, 1.1B, 1.1, 1.2, 1.6, 1.7, 2.9A, 3.1B, 3.1, 3.5, 3.8, 3.9
Heisei era	へいせい	1.3, 1.6
Helen Keller	ヘレン ケラー	0.2.05G
hello	もしもし	4.1B, 4.3, 4.4, 4.9, 4.10
helmet	ヘルメット	4.6, 4.9
here	ここ	4.7
here you are.	はい、どうぞ	0.1.04G, 1.6, 1.8, 2.9A
Higashi (name of person)	ひがしさん	4.7
high school	こうとうがっこう	1.6
high school	こうこう	0.2.02G, 1.1B, 1.1, 1.3, 1.4, 3.2
high school student	こうこうせい	4.4, 4.9
high/expensive	たかい	3.7
Hindi	ヒンズーご	3.02
Hindu	ヒンズー	2.7
Hirano (name of person)	ひらの	3.02
Hiromi (name of person)	ひろみ	3.3
Hiroshima	ひろしま	3.2, 3.8

Hiroyuki (name of person)	ひろゆき	3.3
history	れきし	0.2.09G, 3.1B, 3.1, 3.5, 3.8, 3.9
hobby	（ご）しゅみ	3.1B, 3.1, 3.2, 3.6, 3.7, 3.9, 3.10
hobby	しゅみ	3.6, 3.8, 3.9, 4.1
hockey	ホッケー	1.6
homeroom teacher	たんにんのせんせい	3.1B, 3.1, 3.2,3.3 3.6, 3.9, 3.10,
homework	しゅくだい	0.2.08G, 3.1B. 3.9. 4.1B. 4.4, 4.7, 4.8
honest	しょうじき	3.8, 3.9, 3.11A
horse	うま	0.2.07G, 1.1, 1.4
hospital	びょういん	4.11A
hot	あつい	1.6, 1.9A, 1.9A
hot and humid	むしあつい	1.6, 1.9A
hot dog	ホットドッグ	4.4, 4.6
house	いえ	0.2.01G
house	うち	3.5, 3.9, 4.1B, 4.2, 4.3, 4.7, 4.8, 4.9, 4.10
how do you do?	はじめまして	0.1.01G, 1.1B, 1.2, 1.6, 1.8, 3.6, 3.9
how many people	なんにん	2.1B, 2.6, 3.4, 3.9
how many yen	なんえん	1.3, 1.4, 1.6
how many/how old	いくつ	1.1, 1.6, 3.1B, 3.1, 3.2, 3.3, 3.6, 3.7, 3.9, 3.10
how much is it?	いくらですか	2.5, 2.6, 2.8
how much is it? (informal)	いくら	2.6
how much (price)	いくら	1.3, 2.1B, 2.2, 2.6, 3.2
however	でも	3.5, 3.6, 3.9
humorous~	ユーモアのある～	3.11A
Hyun Jun	ヒュンジュン	1.2, 1.3, 1.4, 3.4
I accept the food/thing with gratitude (informal)	あっ、ありがとう	1.6
I accept whatever you suggest	どっちでもいい	2.5
I accept whatever you suggest	どちらでもいいです	2.4, 2.5, 2.6
I accept whatever you suggest (informal)	どちらでも	2.6
I am calling about~	～のことですが	4.3, 4.8
I am fine.	はい、げんきです	2.9A
I am sorry.	すいません	0.1.10G, 1.6, 2.4, 2.9A
I am sorry.	どうもすいません	0.1.10G
I am sorry.	どうもすみません	0.1.10G, 2.9A, 3.5, 4.2, 4.3, 4.8
I am sorry.	ごめんなさい	0.1.10G, 1.1, 1.2, 1.6, 1.8, 2.9A
I am sorry.	ごめんね	0.1.10G
I am sorry./excuse me	すみません	0.1.10G, 1.2, 1.6, 1.8, 2.4, 3.2, 4.3

I am sorry/excuse me (informal) すまない	1.6	
I am sorry/excuse me (informal) ごめん	0.1.10G, 1.6, 2.9A	
I am sorry/thank you はい、すみません	1.6, 1.8	
I am sorry/thank you (informal) あっ、すまない	1.6	
I (for girls and adults) わたし	2.4, 2.6, 3.4, 3.6, 3.8, 3.9, 4.1, 4.3, 4.8	
I rely on your suggestion (informal) おまかせ	2.6	
I request~ おねがいします／する（を）	1.2, G, 1.6, 1.8, 2.2, 2.5, 2.6, 4.10	
I request~ (informal) おねがい（を）	2.6	
I see (with agreeable tone) (informal) そうか	1.9A	
I see/oh really (with agreeable tone) そうですか	1.9A, 2.4, 4.3	
I will go and come back いってまいります	0.1.06G, 1.9A	
I will go and come back いってきます	0.1.06G, 1.9A	
I will leave it up to you おまかせします	2.4, 2.5, 2.6, 2.8	
I will receive the food/thing (informal) あっ、いただき	1.6	
I will take attendance しゅっせきをとります	0.1.08G	
I would like~ ～がいいです	2.5	
I'm home./I'm back ただいま	0.1.06G, 1.9A, 4.3	
I/me あたし	3.4	
I/me (boys) ぼく	3.4, 3.9, 4.9	
I/me (formal) わたくし	3.4	
iced coffee アイスコーヒー	1.9A	
ice cream アイスクリーム	0.1.09G, 0.2.06G, 2.4, 2.6, 3.9, 3.11	
ice hockey アイスホッケー	1.6	
iced tea アイスティー	0.2.06G, 1.9A, 2.1B, 2.2, 2.5	
Ichiro (name of person) いちろう	3.3	
Illinois イリノイ	4.6	
important じゅうよう	3.5, 3.9	
incorrect ちがいます／ちがう	1.4, 4.1 B, 4.9	
India インド	3.9	
Indian ink すみ	1.2	
Indian person インドじん	3.02	
individual~ こせいてき(な)	3.5, 3.8, 3.9	
Indonesia インドネシア	3.9	
Indonesian language インドネシアご	3.02	
Indonesian person インドネシアじん	3.02	
inside うち	3.4, 3.6, 3.9	

instrument がっき	4.9	
internet インターネット	0.2.07G	
interview インタビュー	3.10	
introduction/beginning はじめ	3.01B, 3.6, 3.9, 4.1B, 4.1, 4.6, 4.9, 4.10	
is ~ ～です	0.1.01G	
is (animate thing) there? いますか	0.2.08G, 3.11A, 4.1B, 4.3, 4.10	
is (inanimate thing) there? ありますか	0.2.07G, 3.11A, 4.1B, 4.3, 4.10	
is Kaori there? かおりさんいますか	4.3	
is so and so here? ～さんはいますか	0.1.08G	
is so and so here? ～くんはいますか	0.1.08G	
is this the ~ residence? ～さんのおたくですか	4.3, 4.4, 4.9, 4.10	
is that so? あ、そうですか	1.6	
is that so? (informal) あ、そう	1.6	
Israel イスラエル	3.9	
it is a cold day, isn't it? (informal) さむいね	1.6	
it is a fine day, isn't it? いいてんきですね	1.6, G, 1.9A	
it is a fine day, isn't it? (informal) いいてんき（だ）ね	1.6, 1.9A	
it is a hot day, isn't it? (informal) あついね	1.6	
it is a humid and hot day, isn't it? (informal) むしあついね	1.6	
it is~isn't it? ～ですね	1.6	
it is~isn't it? (informal) ～（だ）ね	1.6	
it is not ~ ～じゃありません	1.5, 3.2, 3.6, 3.9	
it rains あめがふります／ふる	1.6	
it rains a lot あめがよくふります／ふる	1.6	
it rains a lot, doesn't it? (informal) よくふるね	1.6	
it rains a lot, doesn't it? よくふりますね	0.1.03G, 1.6, 1.9A	
it's a beautiful day, isn't it? いいおてんきですね	0.1.03G, 2.1	
it's cold, isn't it? さむいですね	0.1.03G, 1.6, 1.9A	
it's cold, isn't it? (informal) さむい（わ）ね	1.9A	
it's hot and humid, isn't it? むしあついですね	0.1.03G, 1.6, 1.9A,	
it's hot and humid, isn't it? (informal) むしあつい（わ）ね	1.9A	
it's hot, isn't it? あついですね	0.1.03G, 1.6, 1.9A	

it's hot, isn't it? (informal)		
	あつい（わ）ね	1.9A
it's raining hard, isn't it? (informal)		
	よくふる（わ）ね	1.9A
Italian ice	イタリアンアイス	2.6, 2.9A
Italy	イタリア	3.9
Janet	ジャネット	2.3
January	いちがつ	1.7, 2.1B, 2.3, 2.6, 3.9, 4.9
Japan	にほん	3.2, 3.3, 3.8, 3.9, 4.5, 4.7, 4.8, 4.9
Japanese archery	きゅうどう	4.9
Japanese archery master		
	きゅうどうのせんせい	4.5
Japanese calligraphy	おしゅうじ	4.9, 4.10
Japanese cooking	にほんりょうり	4.9
Japanese cooking mater		
	にほんりょうりのせんせい	4.5
Japanese cuisine	わしょく	2.9A
Japanese fair	ジャパニーズフェア	2.1
Japanese fencing club		
	けんどうぶ	3.11
Japanese fencing master		
	けんどうのせんせい	4.5
Japanese food	にほんのたべもの	2.9
Japanese language	にほんご	3.1B, 3.1, 3.2, 3.5, 3.7, 3.8, 3.9, 4.1, 4.2, 4.7, 4.8, 4.9
Japanese night	ジャパニーズナイト	2.2, 2,6
Japanese party	ジャパニーズパーティー	2.5
Japanese person	にほんじん	3.1B, 3.2, 4.7
jazz	ジャズ	2.1B, 2.5, 3.8
Jenny	ジェニー	1.2, 1.3, 1.4
jet	ジェット	2.7
job/work	しごと	4.11A
John	ジョン	4.3, 4.7,4.10
John Kennedy	ジョン ケネディー	0.2.05G
John Whitehouse	ジョン ホワイトハウス	3.6
Jones	ジョーンズ	3.02
Jose	ホゼ	1.2, 1.3, 1.4
judo	じゅうどう	1.6, 3.2, 3.3, 4.1B, 4.8, 4.11A
judo club	じゅうどうぶ	3.11
judo instructor	じゅうどうのせんせい	1.5, 4.5
juice	ジュース	1.9A, 2.2, 2.4, 2.6, 3.2
July	しちがつ	2.1B, G, 2.3, 2.6, 3.5, 3.9
Jun Ono (name of person)		
	おの じゅん	1.6
June	ろくがつ	2.1B, G, 2.3, 2.6. 3.2, 3.9
k	ケイ	1.3, 1.5, 1.6
kabuki (Japanese theater)		
	かぶき	4.9, 4.10, 4.11A

Kabuki master		
	かぶきのせんせい	4.5
Kagoshima		
	かごしま	3.2
kana	かな	4.5, 4.9
Kanae (name of person)		
	かなえ	4.3
Kanene	カニン	2.3
kanji	かんじ	3.8, 4.5, 4.7, 4.9
Kaori (name of person)		
	かおりさん	4.3, 4.10
karaoke	カラオケ	0.2.08G, 2.2, 2.6, 4.6
karate	からて	1.6, 4.10, 4.11A
karate master	からてのせんせい	4.5
Katoh (name of person)		
	かとうさん	4.3
Katsuyama High School		
	かつやまこうこう	3.11
Kawahara, Masao (name of person)		
	かわはら まさお	3.8
Kawakami (name of person)		
	かわかみ	3.3, 3.9
Kazuki (name of person)		
	かずき	3.3
Ken (name of person)		
	けん	3.3
kendo	げんどう	4.8, 4.11A
Kevin Brown (name of person)		
	ケビン ブラウン	1.2
key	キー	0.1.02G
kick	キック	0.1.04G
kimono	きもの	4.11A
Kimura, Kaori (name of person)		
	きむら かおり	3.8
Kimura (name of person)		
	きむら	3.3
Kimura Yuka (name of person)		
	きむら ゆか	3.02
kind	しんせつ	3.11A
kind	やさしい	0.2.09G, 3.1B, 3.1, 3.5, 3.6, 3.8, 3.9. 3.11
kindergarten	ようちえん	1.9A
King (name of person)		
	キング	3.2
Kinoshita (name of person)		
	きのした	3.3, 3.9
kiss	キス	0.1.03G
Kita (name of person)		
	きたさん	4.7
Kitajima, Satoko (name of person)		
	きたじま さとこ	3.8
kiwi	キウイ	1.9A, 2.6
Koike (name of person)		
	こいけ	3.3
Korea	かんこく	3.2, 3.9

Korean language	かんこくご	3.1B
Korean person	かんこくじん	3.1B
Kwajalein	クァジャレン	2.7
Kyoto	きょうと	3.8
~language	～ご	3.6, 3.9
lap top	ラップトップ	0.2.07G
last name	みょうじ	3.3, 3.9
later	あとで	4.3, 4.9, 4.10
leisure	レジャー	4.8
leisure time	レジャーのじかん	4.11A
lemon	レモン	1.9A, 2.6
lemonade	レモネード	0.1.09G, 2.5
let's begin~	はじめましょう（～を）	0.1.09G, 2.1B, 2.1, 2.3, 2.4, 2.5, 2.6, 2.8, 3.8 4.10
let's decide on~	～にしましょう	2.1B, 2.2, 2.3, 2.4, 2.5, 2.6, 2.8, 4.10
let's do that	そうしましょう	4.2
let's eat	たべましょう	4.2
let's go	いきましょう	4.2
let's see	そうですね	3.5, 4.2, 4.4
letter	てがみ	4.1B, 4.7, 4.9
librarian	としょかんいん	3.11A
library	としょしつ	2.1B
library	としょかん	2.2, 3.2, 2.6, 3.2, 3.5, 4.2, 4.4, 4.7, 4.9
light	ライト	4.6, 4.9
like a lot	だいすき	3.9, 3.11
Linda	リンダさん	4.1
line	ライン	4.9
Lisa	リサ	1.6, 3.8, 3.9, 4.7
list	リスト	3.8
lit: Celebrating a New Year	がしょう	1.6, 1.7
lit: Have a healthy and well spirited year	ことしもおげんきで	1.6, 1.7, 1.9
lit: I humbly wish you a Happy New Year	きんがしんねん	1.6, 1.7
lit: I wish our cordial relationship to continue this year	ことしもどうぞよろしく	1.6
lit: Please continue to be kind to me this year	ほんねんもどうぞよろしくおねがいします	1.2
lit: Please continue to be kind to me this year	ことしも（どうぞよろしくおねがいします	1.2, 1.7, 1.9
lit: We are happy to have the new year	しんねんおめでとうございます	1.2
lit: Welcoming Spring=New Year	げいしゅん	1.6, 1.7
literary club	ぶんげいぶ	1.9A
live	いきる	4.9
Lloyd	ロイド	3.02

location/place	ばしょ	0.2.10G, 2.1, 2.2, 2.3, 2.4, 2.5, 2.6, 3.2, 3.7, 4.1,4.11
Los Angeles	ロスアンジェルス／ロサンゼルス	3.11A
love	あい	0.2.01G
lunch	ひるごはん	4.1B, 4.4, 4.8, 4.9
lunch time	ひるやすみ	3.11A, 3.9
Madison Square Garden	マジソンスクエアガーデン	4.11A
Lyons	リヨン	3.01B
make a cake	ケーキをつくります／ケーキをつくる	4.11A
make-up	メーク	0.1.07G
mandarin orange, clementine	みかん	1.9A, 2.6
mango	マンゴ	1.9A, 2.6
Manhattan	マンハッタン	3.3, 3.11A
map	ちず	3.11A
March	さんがつ	2.1B, G, 2.3, 2.6, 3.9
Mari (name of person)	まり	3.3
Marilyn Monroe	マリリン モンロー	0.2.05G
Mark	マークさん	1.4
Mary	メリー	4.7
Masaaki (name of person)	まさあき	4.3
Masako Hoshi (name of person)	ほし　まさこ	1.2
Masao (name of person)	まさお	3.3
Masatoshi (name of person)	まさとし	3.3
mat, mattress	マット	4.10
match	あわせ	4.1
match	マッチ	1.7
mathematics	すうがく	0.2.03G, 3.1B, 3.1, 3.2, 3.5, 3.8, 3.9, 4.2
Matsumoto (name of place)	まつもと	4.1
May	ごがつ	2.1B, G, 2.3, 2.6, 3.9, 4.7
may I use English?	えいごでもいいですか	0.1.07G
me too	わたしも	2.3, 2.4
meal	ごはん	4.1B, 4.8
meaning	いみ	3.3, 3.6, 3.9, 3.10
meat	にく	0.2.05G
meat loaf	ミートローフ	3.5
meat sauce	ミートソース	2.6, 2.9A
media room	メディアルーム	2.1B, 2.6
meet a friend	ともだちにあいます／ともだちにあう	4.11A
meeting	ミーティング	0.1.10G, 2.1B, 2.3, 2.4, 2.5, 2.6, 4.10, 4.11A

meeting	かいぎ	0.2.07G, 2.9A
megabyte	メガ	1.3, 1.4, 1.5, 1.6
Meiji era	めいじ	1.3, 1.6
melon	メロン	1.9A, 2.1, 2.2, 2.5, 2.6, 2.9A. 3.5, 4.2
memo	メモ	1.3
menu	メニュー	2.6, 2.9A
Mexican person	メキシコじん	3.1B, 3.2
Mexico	メキシコ	3.2, 3.9
Miami	マイアミ	3.11A
middle	なか	3.1B, 3.6, 3.9
middle school	ちゅうがく	1.1B, 3.2
middle school	ちゅうがっこう	1.1, 1.6
Middle Town High School		
	ミドルタウンこうこう	
		3.2
Mika (name of person)		
	みか	3.3, 4.3
mike	マイク	0.1.07G, 4.6, 4.9, 4.10
milk	ミルク	1.1, 1.9A, 2,6, 3.5, 3.8, 4.2, 4.4, 4.6
Milwaukee	ミルウォーキー	0.1.10G
Minami (name of person)		
	みなみさん	4.7
Misako Yokoyama (name of person)		
	よこやま　みさこ	1.6
mit	ミット	0.1.07G
Miwa, Kazuhiko (name of person)		
	みわ　かずひこ	3.8
Miyazaki	みやざき	3.02
Mon.	げつ	4.7
Monday	げつようび	2.1B, G, 2.1, 2.2, 2.6, 3.5, 4.2, 4.4, 4.8, 4.9, 4.10
money	おかね	4.7, 2.5, 3.2, 4.6, 4.9, 4.10
monitor	モニター	0.1.07G, 0.2.07G
monkey	さる	0.2.09G, 1.1, 1.4
month of ~	～がつ	0.2.04G, 2.3
moon	つき	3.9, 4.9
Mori Michio (name of person)		
	もり　みちお	3.02
morning	あさ	3.5, 4.2, 4.9
mother	はは	3.1, 3.4, 3.5, 3.6, 3.9, 3.11
mother	ママ	3.4
mother	おかあさん	0.2.10G, 3.1B. 3.1, 3.4, 3.5, 3.9, 4.1
mother-in-law	ぎりのおかあさん	3.11A
mother-in-law	ぎりのはは	3.11A
mountain	やま	3.9, 3.11A
mouth	くち	0.2.04G, 4.1
movie	えいが	2.1B, 2.2, 2.6, 3.2, 3.5, 4.1, 4.2, 4.4, 4.6, 4.7
movie star	えいがスター	3.11A
movie theater	えいがかん	4.11A

Mr., Ms., Mrs., Miss	なまえ＋さん	1.6
multiply	かける	1.3, 1.6
mushroom	マッシュルーム	2.6, 2.9A
music	おんがく	3.1B, 3.1, 3.2, 3.5, 3.8, 3.9, 3.10, 4.1B, 4.6, 4.8, 4.9
musician	おんがくか	3.11A
music practice	おんがくのれんしゅう	
		4.6
my	わたしの	4.8
my family	うちのかぞく	3.4
Nagano	ながの	3.2, 3.8, 4.1
Nagasaki	ながさき	3.8
Nakamura (name of person)		
	なかむら	4.1
Nakayama (name of person)		
	なかやま	3.3
Nakayama, Satomi (name of person)	なかやま　さとみ	3.9
Nakazato, Emi (name of person)		
	なかざと　えみ	3.8
name	なまえ	1.2, 1.4, 3.6, 3.8, 3.11, 4.8, 4.10
name (formal)	おなまえ	1.2, 1.8, 3.1B, 3.1, 3.2, 3.7, 3.9, 3.10, 4.3
Naomi (name of person)		
	なおみ	3.3
nationality	こくせき	3.6
nature	しぜん	3.11A
necessary	ひつよう	4.1B, 4.1, 4.5, 4.6,4.8, 4.9, 4.10
Nelson Mandela	ネルソン　マンデラ	0.2.05G
net	ネット	0.1.05G, 4.6 4.9
never	ぜんぜん	3.5, 4.2, 4.9
New Haven High School		
	ニューヘブンこうこう	
		3.6, 4.3
New Jersey	ニュージャージー	3.6
New Year	しょうがつ	1.2
New Year's card	ねんがじょう	1.2, 1.7, 1.9
New Year's Eve	おおみそか	1.2
New Year's money gift from parent to child		
	おとしだま	1.2
New York	ニューヨーク	3.3, 3.11A, 4.7, 4.9
New Zealand	ニュージーランド	3.9
news club	ほうどうぶ	3.11
newspaper club	しんぶんぶ	1.9A, 3.11
next week	らいしゅう	4.10, 4.11A
nice to meet you	どうぞよろしく	0.1.01G, 1.1B, 1.2, 3.6. 3.9
nice to meet you	よろしく	1.1, 1.6
nick name	ニックネーム	3.9
Nicole	ニコール	1.2, 1.3, 1.4, 3.4
Niigata	にいがた	3.02
night	よる	3.9

Nina	ニーナ	0.1.05G, 3.11
nine	きゅう	1.1B, G, 1.1, 1.2, 1.3, 1.5, 1.6, 3.9
nine	く	1.1B, G, 1.5, 1.6, 3.9
nine hundred	きゅうひゃく	1.1B, G, 1.3, 1.5, 1.6
nine minutes	きゅうふん	4.9
nine o'clock	くじ	2.1B, G, 2.1 ,2.2, 2.6, 3.9, 4.4, 4.8, 4.10
nine people	くにん	2.3, G, 2.6, 3.7, 4.1
nine people	きゅうにん	2.6, G, 3.9
nine (quantity)	ここのつ	2.9A, G, 4.1B, 4.5
nine thirty	くじはん	2.6
nine thousand	きゅうせん	1.3, 1.5, 1.6,
nine years old	きゅうさい	1.2
nine forty	くじよんじゅっぷん	4.9
nineteen	じゅうきゅう	1.1B, G, 1.2, 1.5, 1.6,
nineteen eighty	せんきゅうひゃくはちじゅうねん	1.3
nineteen seventy	せんきゅうひゃくななじゅうねん	1.3
nineteen years old	じゅうきゅうさい	1.2
nineteenth day of the month		
	じゅうくにち	2.1B, G, 2.3, 2.6,
nineteen ninety	せんきゅうひゃくきゅうじゅうねん	1.3
ninth day of the month		
	ここのか	2.1B, G, 2.1, 2.3, 2.6, 3.9, 4.1
ninth grade	きゅうねんせい	1.6
ninth grade	ちゅうさん	3.9
ninety	きゅうじゅう	1.1B, G, 1.1, 1.2, 1.5, 1.6
ninety eight	きゅうじゅうはち	1.2, G
ninety nine	きゅうじゅうく	1.1B, G, 1.2
ninety nine	きゅうじゅうきゅう	1.1B, G, 1.2
ninety seven	きゅうじゅうしち	1.2, G
ninety seven	きゅうじゅうなな	1.2, G
ninety six	きゅうじゅうろく	1.2, G
nineteen	じゅうく	1.1B, G, 1.2, 1.5, 1.6,
Nishi (name of person)		
	にしさん	4.7
no	いいえ	1.2, 1.4, 1.6, 4.1B, 4.2, 3.2, 3.3, 3.8
no, I do not have	いいえ、ありません	1.9A, G
no, I do not have (informal)		
	ううん、ない	1.9A
no, I do not understand (informal)		
	ううん、わからない	1.9A
no, I do not understand.		
	いいえ、わかりません	0.1.09G, 1.9A, G
no (informal)	ううん	1.6
no it is not	そうじゃありません	4.1
no, it is not so	いいえ、そうじゃありません	1.6
no, it is not so (informal)		
	ううん、そうじゃない	1.6

no, not yet.	いいえ、まだです	0.1.09G
no thank you	いいえ、けっこうです	
		0.1.05G. 1.1, 1.2, 1.6, 1.8, 2.9A
no, thank you	けっこうです	1.1B, 1.1, 1.2
no, thank you (informal)		
	いえ、けっこう	1.6
no, thank you (informal)		
	いいえ	2.9A
no, that is incorrect (informal)		
	ううん、ちがう	1.6
no, that's incorrect./No, I'm not.		
	いいえ、ちがいます	0.1.01G, 1.4, 1.5, 1.6, 1.8, 2.2, 3.2, 4.3
noh (Japanese theater)		
	のう	4.9, 4.10, 4.11A
noisy	うるさい	3.5, 3.6, 3.9
nose	はな	4.1
not affected	きどらない	3.11A
not at all	いいえ	1.2, 1.6
not at all (informal)	いや	1.6
note	ノート	0.1.05G, 3.11A, 4.1
November	じゅういちがつ	2.1B, G, 2.3, 2.6
now	いま	2.2
number	ばんごう	1.1B, 1.3, 1.4, 1.5, 3.7
number	ばん	3.9
number 13	じゅうさんばん	3.9
number 2	にばん	3.9
number 7	ななばん	3.9
number 8	はちばん	3.9
number one	だいいち	1.6
number three	だいさん	3.8
number two	だいに	3.8
numerous	おおい	4.5
October	じゅうがつ	2.1B, G, 2.3, 2.6, 4.3
octopus	たこ	3.6
often	よく	3.5, 3.9, 3.11, 3.11A, 4.1B, 4.2, 4.8
oh	ああ	1.4
oh	あ	3.02
oh, and also~	ああ、それから	3.6, 3.9
oh, really, oh, I see	ああ、そうですか	1.3, 1.4, 2.2, 3.2, 3.4, 3.6
Oita	おおいた	3.02
Okada (name of person)		
	おかださん	1.1
Okuda (name of person)		
	おくださん	1.1
old	ふるい	3.7
O'Malley	オマリー	3.2
on foot/by foot	あるいて	3.9
one	いち	1.1B, G.,1.1, 1.2, 1.3, 1.4, 1.5, 1.6, 3.9, 4.6
one day	いちにち	4.9
one day	あるひ	3.9

one hundred	ひゃく	**1.1B**, G, 1.1, 1.2, 1.3, 1.5, 1.6, 4.7
one hundred yen	ひゃくえん	**1.9**
one minute	いっぷん	**4.9**
one more time	もういちど	**1.3**, 1.5
one o'clock	いちじ	**2.1B**, G, 2.2, 2.6, 3.2, 4.9
one person	ひとり	**2.1B**, G, 4.12.3, 2.6, 3.7, 3.9
one (quantity)	ひとつ	**2.9A**, 3.9, 4.1B, 4.5
one thirty	いちじはん	**2.2**, 2.6
one thousand	せん	**1.1B**, G, 1.1, 1.3, 1.5, 1.6
one thousand yen	せんえん	**1.9**
one year	いちねん	**1.3**, 3.9
one year old	いっさい	**1.2**
Ooyama, Haruko (name of person) おおやま はるこ		**3.9**
Ooyama (name of person) おおやま		**3.3**, 3.4, 3.9
opposition	はんたい	**2.9A**
or	それとも	**2.2**, 2.5, 2.8, 4.4
or/and so on	や	**3.9**, 4.7, See. p393-395
orange	オレンジ	**1.9A**, G, 2.2, 2.5, 2.6, 3.1B, 3.1, 3.2, 3.9
orange juice	オレンジジュース	**4.4**, 4.6
Oregon	オレゴン	**4.6**
origami club	おりがみぶ	**1.9A**
Osaka	おおさか	**3.8**
Osamu Tezuka (name of person) てづか おさむ		**1.1B**, 1.3
outside	そと	**3.4**
Pablo Picasso	パブロ ピカソ	**0.2.05G**
pager/beeper	ポケベル	**0.2.08G**
paper plate	かみざら	**4.9**
Paris	パリ	**3.01B**
park	こうえん	**3.4**, G, 4.11A
particle e	～へ	**4.7**, See. p393-395
particle o	～を	**4.7**, See. p393-395
particle wa	～は	**4.7**, See. p393-395
party	パーティー	**0.2.04G**, 2.1B, 2,2, 2.3, 2.4, 2.5, 2.6, 2.7, 3.2, 3.4, 4.2, 4.3, 4.4, 4.6, 4.7
pasta	パスタ	**0.2.01G**, 2.4, 2.6, 2.9A
pasta shop	パスタのみせ	**2.9A**
pear	なし	**1.9A**, 2.6
pencil	えんぴつ	**3.11A**
pencil case	ふでばこ	**3.11A**
pen pal	ペンパル	**3.8**
pepperoni	ペパロニ	**2.6**, 2.9A
person	ひと	**0.2.06G**, 0.2.08G, 0.2.09G, 2.3, 2.4, 2.6, 3.1B, 3.4, 3.5, 3.8, 3.9, 4 .9, 4.10
~person (nationality) ～じん		**3.9**
personal computer	パソコン	**0.2.07G**

personality	せいかく	**3.1B**, 3.8
Peru	ペルー	**3.9**
Peru person	ペルーじん	**3.02**
Philadelphia	フィラデルフィア	**3.11A**
photo club	しゃしんぶ	**1.9A**, 3.11
physical education	たいいく	**0.2.04G**, 3.1B, 3.1, 3.5, 3.9
physical exercise	たいそう	**3.5**
physics	ぶつり	**3.1B**, 3.1, 3.5, 3.9
picnic	ピクニック	**3.5**, 4.2
picture	え	**0.2.01G**, 4.1, 4.9
pin	ピン	**4.9**
pineapple	パイナップル	**1.9A**, 2.1B, 2.6
ping-pong	ピンポン	**1.7**
pink	ピンク	**1.9A**, 3.1B, 3.1, 3.9
Pittsburgh	ピッツバーグ	**3.11A**
pizza	ピザ	**2.1B**, 2.1, 2.2, 2.3, 2.4, 2.5, 2.6, 2.9A, 3.2, 3.6, 4.4, 4.6
pizza burger	ピザバーガー	**2.6**, 2.9A
pizza shop	ピザのみせ	**2.9A**
plan	けいかく	**0.2.02G**, 4.1B4.1, 4.6, 4.9, 4.10
plate	さら	**4.6**, 4.9, 4.10
play	あそびます/あそぶ	**4.11A**
play an instrument がっきをひきます／ひく		**4.9**
please	どうぞ	**1.1B**, 1.1, 1.2
please be careful next time これからはきをつけてください		**0.1.10G**
please be quiet	しずかにしてください	**1.9A**, G
please be quiet (informal) しずかにして		**1.9A**
please call me	でんわしてください	**4.3**
please close your book ほんをとじてください		**1.9A**, G
please close your book (informal) ほんをとじて		**1.9A**
please give me~ (informal) くれ（～を）		**1.6**, 2.6, 2.9A
Please give me/I would like to have~ ください（～を）		**0.1.04G**, 1.2, 1.6, 1.8, 2.1B, 2.2, 2.5, 2.6, 2.9A, 4.7, 4.8, 4.10
please (informal)	はい	**1.6**, 2.9A
please leave	おのこしください	**4.3**
please listen	きいて（いて）ください	**1.9A**, G
please listen (informal) きいて（いて）		**1.9A**
please look	みてください	**1.9A**, G
please look (informal) みて		**1.9A**

English	Japanese	Reference
please look with favor upon me	どうぞよろしくおねがいします	1.6, G, 3.6, 3.9
please make a pair	ペアーをつくってください	1.9A, G
please make a pair (informal)	ペアーをつくって	1.9A
please open your book	ほんをあけてください	1.9A, G
please open your book (informal)	ほんをあけて	1.9A
please pass these out	くばってください	0.1.09G
please pass this around.]	まわしてください	0.1.09G
please raise your hand	てをあげてください	2.1, 2.3
please read	よんでください	1.9A, G, 4.10
please read (informal)	よんで	1.9A
please say	いってください	1.9A, G
please say (informal)	いって	1.9A
please say it clearly	はっきりいってください	1.9A, G
please say it clearly (informal)	はっきりいって	1.9A
please say it slowly	ゆっくりいってください	1.9A, G
please say it slowly (informal)	ゆっくりいって	1.9A
please say it together	みんなでいってください	1.9A, G
please sit down	すわってください	1.9A, G
please sit down (informal)	すわって	1.9A
please stand up	たってください	1.9A, G, 2.1
please stand up (informal)	たって	1.9A
please wait a moment (informal)	ちょっとまって	1.9A, G
please write	かいてください	1.9A, G, 4.10
please write (informal)	かいて	1.9A
plus/add	たす	1.6, 4.6
police	けいさつ	1.3, 1.6, 1.9A
politics	せいじ	3.1B, 3.1, 3.5, 3.9
politician	せいじか	3.11A
pool	プール	1.7, 2.1B, 2.6, 4.2
pork chops	とんかつ	2.4, 2.6, 2.9, 2.9A,
Portugal	ポルトガル	3.9
Portuguese language	ポルトガルご	3.02
Portuguese person	ポルトガルじん	3.02
post box	ポスト	0.1.06G
post office	ゆうびんきょく	4.11A
poster	ポスター	3.11A
poster sale	ポスターセール	0.2.04G, 2.3
potato chip(s)	ポテトチップ	2.6
pound	ポンド	1.5, 1.6
practice	れんしゅう	3.9, 4.6, 4.9
prefecture	けん	1.6
preparation	プリパレーション	4.10, 4.11A
prepare for	プレパレーションします/プレパレーションする	4.10, 4.11A
present	プレゼンテーションします/プレゼンテーションする	4.10, 4.11A
presentation	はっぴょう	4.1, 4.8, 4.9
presentation	プレゼンテーション	4.10, 4.11A
presenter	プレゼンター	4.10, 4.11A
president	だいとうりょう	3.11A
price	ねだん	2.2, 2.6
prime minister	しゅしょう	3.11A
prince	おうじ	3.11A
princess	おうじょ	3.11A
principal	こうちょう	3.11A
principal's office	こうちょうしつ	2.6
problem	もんだい	0.2.07G, 4.1B, 4.1, 4.5, 4.6, 4.9, 4.10
professional	プロ	4.1B
professional wrestling	プロレス	0.2.08G
professor	きょうし	1.6
program	プログラム	4.8, 4.9
project	プロジェクト	0.1.10G, 4.1B
proposal	プロポーザル	4.10, 4.11A
punch	パンチ	1.9A, 2.1, 2.6, 4.4, 4.9
purple	むらさき	1.9A, 3.1B, 3.1, 3.9
purpose	ため	4.9, 4.10
purpose/objective	もくてき	4.1B, 4.1, 4.6, 4.8, 4.9, 4.10
quark	クォーク	2.7
quartz	クオーツ	2.7
quasar	クエーサー	2.7
queen	クイーン	2.7
question	しつもん	0.2.07G, 3.10, 4,8
Quetta	クェッタ	2.7
quiet	しずか	3.7
Quinhon	クィニョン	2.7
rabbit	うさぎ	1.1, 1.4
Rachel	レーチェルさん	1.4
rain	あめ	3.11A
read a newspaper	しんぶんをよみます/しんぶんをよむ	4.11A
reception	レセプション	4.10, 4.11A
recess time	やすみじかん	3.9, 3.11A
red	あか	1.9A, 3.1B, 3.1, 3.9
reliable	たよりになる	3.11A
remote control	リモコン	0.2.08G

request	リクエスト	3.8
reserch	リサーチ	0.2.10G
reservation	よやく	4.1
residence	おたく	4.1, 4.3, 4.8
residence	（お）すまい	3.1B, 3.1, 3.2, 3.3, 3.6, 3.7, 3.9, 3.10
residence	すまい	3.6, 3.11
rest	やすみ	2.6
restaurant	レストラン	2.6, 3.9
restaurant's name	レストランのなまえ	2.9A
restroom	トイレ	2.6
rice paddy	たんぼ	4.5
rice pounding	もちつき	4.11A
Rika (name of person)		
	りかさん	4.1B, 4.1, 4.10
River high school	リバーこうこう	1.6
roast beef	ローストビーフ	0.1.09G
rock	ロック	2.1B, 3.8
rock concert	ロックコンサート	2.2, 2.6
rock'n roll star	ロックのスター	3.11A
Romero	ロメロ	3.2
room	へや	0.2.07G, 0.2.08G
Rosa	ロサ	1.2, 1.3, 1.4
rugby	ラグビー	3.8
Russia	ロシア	3.9
Russian language	ロシアご	3.2
Russian person	ロシアじん	3.2
Sachiko Tanaka (name of person)		
	たなか さちこ	1.2
Sada Hideki (name of person)		
	さだ ひでき	4.3
Saeki, Yuka (name of person)		
	さえき ゆか	3.8
Sakai, Yuji (name of person)		
	さかい ゆうじ	3.8
salad	サラダ	2.1B, 2.6
Sam	サム	1.2, 1.3, 1.4, 3.4
sample	サンプル	4.10, 4.11A
San Francisco	サンフランシスコ	3.11A, 4.6
Sapporo	さっぽろ	3.8
sashimi	さしみ	3.6
Sat.	ど	4.7
Satoh Hiroshi (name of person)		
	さとう ひろし	4.3
Satoh Kenji (name of person)		
	さとう けんじ	3.2
Saturday	どようび	0.2.08G, 2.1, 2.2, 2.3, 2.4, 2.6, 3.5, 4.2, 4.3, 4.4, 4.7, 4.9
sauce	ソース	0.1.03G
Saudi Arabia	サウジアラビア	3.9
Saudi Arabian person		
	サウジアラビアじん	3.02
sausage	ソーセージ	0.1.03G, 2.6, 2.9A

savory pancakes	おこのみやき	2.4, 2.9
schedule	スケジュール	0.1.08G, 3.5, 4.4, 4.8, 4.10, 4.11A
school	がっこう	0.2.05G, 0.2.08G, 1.6, 2.3, 2.4, 2.5, 3.2, 3.4, 3.6, 3.7, 3.9, 3.11, 4.1B, 4.2, 4.3, 4.7, 4.8, 4.10
school subject	かもく	0.2.05G, 0.2.07G, 3.1B, 3.2, 3.5, 3.6, 3.7, 3.8, 3.9, 3.10
science	かがく	0.2.02G, 3.1B, 3.1, 3.5, 3.8, 3.9, 4.9
science club	かがくぶ	1.9A
science fair	サイエンスフェア	2.1, 2.2, 2.4, 2.6, 4.9
screen	スクリーン	4.6, 4.9
scribe	しょき	2.6
seafood and chicken	よせなべ	2.4, 2.6, 2.9, 2.9A
seasons	きせつ	0.2.04G, 1.6, 3.8
Seattle	シアトル	3.11A, 4.6
second day of the month		
	ふつか	2.1B, 2.1, 2.3, 2.6, 3.5, 3.9, 4.1, 4.2, 4.4, 4.7
second grade	にねんせい	1.6
second year high school student		
	こうこうにねんせい	1.5, 3.2, 3.3, 3.11
secretary	しょき	2.4
See you	じゃ、また	0.1.02G, 1.2, 1.6, 1.8, 1.9A
See you	じゃ	0.1.02G, 1.6, 1.9A
see you later	それじゃ、また	1.9A
Seiji Ozawa (name of person)		
	おざわ せいじ	1.1B, 1.3
seldom	あんまり	4.8
seldom	あまり	3.5, 4.1B, 4.2
self	じぶん	4.8
senior	シニア	3.3
September	くがつ	2.1B, G, 2.3, 2.6, 3.9, 4.8
serious~	まじめな	3.5
serve (in sports)	サーブ	3.9
service	サービス	4.7
set	セット	0.1.04G, 4.1
seven	しち	1.1B, G, 1.2, 1.5, 1.6, 3.9
seven	なな	1.1B, G, 1.1, 1.2, 1.3, 1.5, 1.6, 3.9
seven hundred	ななひゃく	1.1B, G, 1.3, 1.5, 1.6
seven minutes	ななふん	4.8
seven o'clock	しちじ	2.1B, G, 2.2, 2.6, 4.4, 4.8
seven people	しちにん	2.3, G, 2.6, 3.7, 3.9, 4.1
seven people	ななにん	2.6, G
seven (quantity)	ななつ	2.9A, G, 4.1B, 4.5
seven thirty	しちじはん	2.6, 4.4, 4.9
seven thousand	ななせん／しちせん	1.3, 1.5, 1.6
seven years old	ななさい／しちさい	1.2
seven thirty	しちじさんじゅっぷん	4.8
seventeen	じゅうしち	1.1B, G, 1.2, 1.5, 1.6
seventeen	じゅうなな	1.1B, G, 1.2, 1.5, 1.6

seventeen years old	じゅうしちさい	1.2
seventeen years old	じゅうななさい	1.2, 3.11
seventeenth day of the month		
	じゅうしちにち	2.1B, G, 2.1, 2.3, 2.6
seventh day of the month		
	なのか	2.1B, G, 2.1, 2.3, 2.6, 3.5, 3.9, 4.1, 4.2, 4.4., 4.7
seventh grade	ななねんせい	1.6
seventh grade	しちねんせい	1.6
seventh grade	ちゅうに	3.1B, 3.9
seventh grade	ちゅういち	3.9
seventy	しちじゅう	1.1B, G, 1.2, 1.5, 1.6
seventy	ななじゅう	1.1B, G, 1.2, 1.5, 1.6,
shake	シェーク	2.7
shall we eat~?	たべましょうか	3.5
she or he is absent		
	やすみです	0.1.08G
she or he is late	ちこくです	0.1.08G
sheep	ひつじ	1.4
sheet	シート	3.10
sheets	シーツ	0.1.04G
sherbet	シャーベット	2.6, 2.9A
Shimano (name of person)		
	しまの	1.4
Shimizu (name of person)		
	しみず	3.3
shinto shrine	じんじゃ	1.2
ship	ふね	0.2.06G, 1.6, 3.1B, 3.1, 3.9
Shiroh Kita (name of person)		
	きた　しろう	1.2, 2.4, 2.6
shirt	シャツ	0.1.08G
shop	みせ	2.6, 3.9, 3.11
shopping arcade	レストランがい	2.6, 2.9A
shopping center	ショッピングセンター	
		2.6, 2.9A
shopping mall	ショッピングモール	2.4, 2.6
shorts	ショーツ	0.1.08G
Showa era	しょうわ	1.6
Shunji Muraue (name of person)		
	むらうえ　しゅんじ	1.6
sibling	きょうだい	3.11A
siblings	（ご）きょうだい	3.7
singer	かしゅ	3.11A
Sit down	ちゃくせき	0.1.08G
six	ろく	1.1B, G, 1.1, 1.2, 1.3, 1.5, 1.6, 3.9
six forty five	ろくじよんじゅうごふん	
		3.5, 4.2
six hundred	ろっぴゃく	1.1B, G, 1.3, 1.5, 1.6, 4.5
six minutes	ろっぷん	4.8
six o'clock	ろくじ	2.1B, G, 2.2, 2.6, 4.3, 4.4, 4.7, 4.8, 4.10
six people	ろくにん	2.3, 2.6, 3.7, 3.9, 4.1
six (quantity)	むっつ	2.9A, G, 4.1B, 4.5

six thirty	ろくじはん	2.2, 2.6, 4.8
six thousand	ろくせん	1.3, 1.5, 1.6
six years old	ろくさい	1.2
six fifteen	ろくじにじゅうごふん	
		4.8
sixteen	じゅうろく	1.1B, G, 1.2, 1.5, 1.6, 3.6
sixteen years old	じゅうろくさい	1.2
sixteenth day of the month		
	じゅうろくにち	2.1B, G, 2.3, 2.6, 3.2
sixth day of the month		
	むいか	2.1B, G, 2.1, 2.3, 2.6, 3.5, 3.9, 4.1, 4.2, 4.4, 4.7, 4.10
sixth grade	ろくねんせい	1.6
sixty	ろくじゅう	1.1B, G, 1.2, 1.5, 1.6
skating	スケート	1.6
ski	スキー	1.7, 1.6. 3.6, 3.9, 4.1B
ski tournament	スキートーナメント	0.2.04G, 2.3
skilled, favored	とくい	3.5, 3.7, 3.9
sleep time	すいみんのじかん	4.11A
snake	へび	0.2.06G, 1.4
snow	ゆき	3.11A
snow festival	スノーフェスティバル	
		0.2.04G, 2.3
soccer	サッカー	1.4, G, 1.6, 1.7, 2.1B, 2.4, 3.2, 3.8, 3.11
soccer team	サッカーぶ	1.9A, 3.11
sociable	しゃこうてき	3.11A
social studies	しゃかい	3.1B, 3.1, 3.9
socks	ソックス	0.1.04G
soda	ソーダ	1.7, 2.1B, 2.2, 2.6
sometimes	ときどき	4.1B, 3.5, 3.11A, 3.9, 4.2, 4.9
song	うた	4.8, 4.9
sorry I am late	おそくなってすみません	
		0.1.10G
soup	スープ	2.1B, 2.6
soup with rice cake	おぞうに	1.2
spaghetti	スパゲッティー	3.5, 4.2, 4.4, 4.6
Spain	スペイン	3.9
Spanish language	スペインご	3.1B, 3.1, 3.2, 3.5
Spanish person	スペインじん	3.2
speaker	スピーカー	4.6, 4.9, 4.10
speech contest	スピーチコンテスト	2.2, 2.3, 2.6, 4.8, 4.9
sports	スポーツ	1.4, G, 2.4, 3.1B, 3.2, 3.3, 3.5, 3.7, 3.8, 3.9, 3.10, 4.8
sports day	スポーツデー	0.2.04G, 2.3
sports figure	スポーツのせんしゅ	3.11A
spring	はる	1.6, 4.9
spring storm	はるいちばん	G
stage	ステージ	4.6, 4.9
stamp	きって	0.2.04G
Stand up	きりつ	0.1.08G
stapler	ホッチキス	0.1.06G
star	ほし	0.2.06G

steak	ステーキ	2.1B, 2.4, 2.6,
story	はなし	4.10, 4.11A
strawberry	いちご	1.9A, 2.6
strict	きびしい	3.5, 3.8, 3.9
student	がくせい	4.9
student	せいと	0.2.04G, 4.8, 4.9
student council	せいとかい	4.9
study	べんきょうします／べんきょうする	
		3.6, 3.8, 4.1B, 4.2, 4.4, **4.10**
study	まなぶ	4.9
study	べんきょう	3.1B, 3.8, 3.9, 3.11A, 4.1, 4.7,
		4.8 ,4.9
subtract/minus	ひく	1.6, 4.6
subway	ちかてつ	3.1B, 3.1, 3.9
sukiyaki	すきやき	2.4, 2.6, 2.9, 2.9A
sum up	まとめ	3.6
summer	なつ	1.6, 4.1
summer vacation	なつやすみ	3.9, 3.11A, 4.7
sumo	すもう	1.6, 4.9, 4.11A
Sumo club	すもうぶ	3.11
Sumo master	すもうのせんせい	4.5
Sun.	にち	4.7
Sunday	にちようび	2.1B, G, 2.1, 2.2, 2.4, 2.6,
		3.5, 3.9, 4.2, 4.3, 4.4., 4.9
sunny	はれ	3.11A, 4.1
supermarket	スーパー	3.11A
surf the Internet	インターネットします／	
	インターネットする	
		4.11A
survey	サーベー	4.8
sushi	すし	0.2.03G, 2.4, 2.6, 2.9, 2.9A
		3.2, 3.5, 3.6, 4.2, 4.4, 4.6
Sushi haru (name of restaurant)		
	すしはる	2.6
sushi shop	すしのみせ	2.9A
Suzuki (name of person)		
	すずき	3.3
sweater	セーター	0.1.04G
swimming	すいえい	3.8
swimming club	すいえいぶ	3.11
Switzerland	スイス	0.1.03G
table	テーブル	3.11A, 4.9, 4.10
table tennis club	たっきゅうぶ	3.11
Taisho era	たいしょう	1.3, 1.6
Takahara, Eri (name of person)		
	たかはら　えり	3.9
Takahashi (name of person)		
	たかはし	3.3
Takayama, Yasuo (name of person)		
	たかやま　やすお	3.9
take a shower	シャワーをあびます／	
	シャワーをあびる	4.11A
talent show	タレントショー	2.2, 4.9

Tamura, Nao (name of person)		
	たむら　なお	3.9
Tanaka Maki (name of person)		
	たなか　まき	3.02
Tanaka (name of person)		
	たなか	4.1
Tanaka (name of person)		
	たなかさん	1.5, 4.7
tape	テープ	4.9
taxi	タクシー	3.1B, 3.1, 3.9
tea	（お）ちゃ	1.9A, 2.6, 4.4, 4.6
tea ceremony	おちゃ	4.9, 4.10, 4.11A
tea ceremony	ちゃのゆ	4.11A
tea ceremony club	さどうぶ	1.9A
tea ceremony club	ちゃどうぶ	3.11
tea ceremony master	おちゃのせんせい	4.5
teacher	せんせい	0.2.09G, 1.2, 1.4, 1.5,
		1.6, 3.1, 3.7, 3.8, 3.9, 4.1, 4.5,
		4.9, 4.10
teacher Kawano	かわのせんせい	3.3
teenager	ティーンエージャー	4.8
teeth	は	4.8
telephone	でんわ	0.2.09G, 1.1B, 1.3, 1.4,
		1.5, 1.6, 2.2, 3.7, 4.3, 4.6,
		4.10
telephone (formal)	おでんわ	4.1
telephone number	でんわばんごう	1.6, 1.8, 2.2, 3.2, 3.8, 4.10
telephone number (formal)		
	おでんわばんごう	4.3
television	テレビ	3.9, 4.1B, 4.4, 4.7, 4.9
tempura	てんぷら	2.4, 2.6, 2.9A, 2.9
ten	じゅう	1.1B, G, 1.2, 1.5, 1.6, 3.9
ten minutes	じゅっぷん	4.1B
ten minutes	じっぷん／じゅっぷん	
		4.1, 4.9
ten o'clock	じゅうじ	2.1B, G, 2.2, 2.6, 4.8, 4.10
ten people	じゅうにん	2.3, 2.6, 3.7, 3.9, 4.1
ten (quantity)	とお	2.9A, G, 4.1B, 4.5
ten thirty	じゅうじはん	2.6
ten thousand	いちまん	1.3, 1.5, 1.6
ten thousand yen	いちまんえん	1.9
ten years old	じゅっさい／じっさい	1.2
ten yen	じゅうえん	1.9
ten forty five	じゅうじよんじゅうごふん	
		4.9
tennis	テニス	1.6, 2.1B, 3.2, 3.5, 3.6, 3.8,
		3.9, 3.11, 4.1, 4.3
tennis club	テニスぶ	3.11
tenth day of the month		
	とおか	0.2.10G, 2.1B 2.1, 2.3, 2.6,
		2.7, 3.2, 3.9. 4.3, 4.9
tenth grade	じゅうねんせい	1.6, 3.2, 3.3, 3.8
tenth grade	こういち	3.9
teramisu	ティラミス	2.6, 2.9A

513

Texas	テキサス	0.1.04G, 4.6
Thailand	タイ	3.9
thank you	ありがとう	0.1.04G, 1.6, 2.2
thank you for the meal	ごちそうさま	0.1.05G, 1.1, 1.6, 2.9A,
thank you for the meal	ごちそうさまでした	0.1.05G, 1.2, 1.6, 1.8, 2.9A
thank you for the meal	いただきます	0.1.05G, 1.2
thank you, I can serve myself	いただきます	1.1, 1.6, 1.8, 2.1, 2.9A
thank you very much.	どうもありがとう	0.1.04G, 2.2, 2.9A, 4.3
thank you very much.	（どうも）ありがとうございます	0.1.04G, 0.1.10G, 2.2, 2.9A, 4.10
thank you very much.	（どうも）ありがとうございました	0.1.04G
thank you very much	ありがとうございます	0.1.04G, 1.1B, 1.1, 1.2, 1.6, 1.8, 4.1
thank you very much	ありがとうございました	1.2, 1.3
thanks	どうも	0.1.04G, 2.9A
thanks to you	おかげさまで	1.2, 1.6
that	その	4.7
that is correct (emphasis)	そうね	1.6
that is correct, I see (informal)	そう	1.6, 2,4
that's all right. Never mind	いいえ	0.1.10G
that's correct (informal)	そうだ（わ）ね	1.9A
there is an animate being	～がいます	3.7
there is an inanimate thing	～があります	3.7
there is (living)	います／いる	4.1B, 4.1, 4.5, 4.9
there is no .... (living)	いません	4.5
there is no ... (non-living)	ありません	4.5
there is (non-living)	あります／ある	4.1B, 4.1, 4.5, 4.7
therefore	だから	3.5, 3.6, 3.9, 3.11, 4.9
third day of the month	みっか	2.1B, G, 2.1, 2.3, 2.6, 3.5, 3.9, 4.1, 4.2, 4.4, 4.5, 4.7, 4.9
third grade	さんねんせい	1.6
thirteen	じゅうさん	1.1B, G, 1.2, 1.5, 1.6,
thirteen years old	じゅうさんさい	1.2

thirteenth day of the month	じゅうさんにち	2.1B, G, 2.1, 2.3, 2.6, 3.2, 4.1, 4.10
thirtieth day of the month	さんじゅうにち	2.1B, G, 2.3, 2.6
thirty	さんじゅう	1.1B, G, 1.2, 1.3, 1.5, 1.6
thirty first day of the month	さんじゅういちにち	2.1B, G, 2.3, 2.6
thirty minutes	さんじゅっぷん	4.1B
thirty minutes	さんじっぷん／さんじゅっぷん	4.1
thirty five minutes	さんじゅうごふん	4.1B, 4.1
this	これ	1.1, 4.7
this	この	3.9, 4.7
this is	こちらは	4.3
this is the end	これでおわりです	3.8
this month	こんげつ	4.9
this year	ことし	1.7
three	さん	1.1B, G, 1.1, 1.2, 1.3, 1.5, 1.6, 3.9, 4.6
three hundred	さんびゃく	1.1B, G, 1.1, 1.3, 1.5, 1.6,
three minutes	さんぷん	4.9
three o'clock	さんじ	2.1B, G, 2.1, 2.2, 2.6, 4.4, 4.8, 4.10
three people	さんにん	2.1B, G, 2.3, 2.6, 3.7, 3.9, 4.1
three (quantity)	みっつ	2.9A, G, 4.1B, 4.5
three thirty	さんじはん	2.6
three thousand	さんぜん	1.3, 1.5, 1.6
three years old	さんさい	1.2
three years/third year	さんねん	3.9
three-ten	さんじじゅっぷん	4.9
Thurs.	もく	4.7
Thursday	もくようび	2.1B, G, 2.1, 2.2, 2.3, 2.6, 3.5, 4.2, 4.4, 4.9, 4.10
ticket	チケット	4.6
ticket	きっぷ	2.2, 4.8, 4.9
tiger	とら	0.2.09G, 1.4
time	じかん	2.1, 2.2, 2.3, 2.4, 2.5, 2.6, 3.2, 3.9, 4.8
time	とき	3.9
Times Square	タイムズスクエア	3.11A
tire	タイヤ	0.1.08G
to	へ	0.2.10G, 4.7, See.393-395
to	に	4.7, 3.4, See. p393-395
to be absent	やすみます／やすむ	4.7
to borrow	かります／かりる	4.7
to brush	みがきます／みがく	4.8
to build	たてます／たてる	4.6, 4.9
to come	きます／くる	4.7, 4.8, 4.10
to cut	きります／きる	4.7
to dance	おどります／おどる	4.8, 4.9

to decide on~	～にします／～にする	2.6
to dislike	きらい	3.1, 3.5, 3.6, 3.7, 3.9, 3.11A, 3.11
to do	します／する	0.2.10G, 3.5, 4.1B, 4.2, 4.4, 4.5, 4.6, 4.7, 4.8, 4.9, 4.10
to drink	のみます／のむ	4.1B, 4.2, 4.9
to eat	たべます／たべる	4.1B, 4.1, 4.2, 4.4, 4.6, 4.7, 4.8, 4.9
to end	おわります／おわる	2.1B, 2.1, 2.3, 2.4, 2.5, 2.6
to fall (rain)	ふります／ふる	1.9A
to fall (rain)a lot	よくふります／ふる	1.9A
to gather	あつめます／あつめる	4.8, 4.9
to give	あげる	4.7
to give birth to	うむ	4.9
to go	いきます／いく	0.2.10G, 3.4, 3.6, 3.9, 3.11A, 3.11, 4.1B, 4.1, 4.2, 4.3, 4.4, 4.7, 4.8, 4.10
to have a meeting	ミーティングします／する	4.8
to like	すき（な）	0.2.09G, 3.1, 3.2, 3.5, 3.6, 3.7, 3.8, 3.9, 3.10, 3.11A, 4.1, 4.9
to listen	ききます／きく	4.1B, 4.2, 4.6, 4.8, 4.9
to make	つくります／つくる	4.6, 4.8, 4.9
to make a plan	けいかくをたてます／たてる	4.6
to present	はっぴょうします／する	4.9
to read	よみます／よむ	4.1B, 4.1, 4.2, 4.4, 4,7, 4.9, 4.10
to receive	いただきます／いただく	1.2
to return	かえります／かえる	4.1B, 4.2, 4.4, 4.7, 4.8,
to say	かたる	4.9
to sell	うります／うる	4.9
to show	みせます／みせる	4.9
to sleep	ねます／ねる	4.1B, 4.1, 4.2, 4.4, 4.7, 4.8
to talk	はなします／はなす	3.2, 3.6, 3.9, 4.1, 4.9, 4.11A
to telephone	でんわします／する	4.8
to visit shrines/temples at New Year's	はつもうでします／する	1.2
to wait	まちます／まつ	4.7
to wake up	おきます／おきる	3.5, 4.1B, 4.1, 4.2, 4.4, 4.8, 4.9
to walk	あるきます／あるく	4.9
to wash	あらいます／あらう	4.6, 4.9
to watch	みます／みる	4.1B, 4.1, 4.2, 4.4, 4.6, 4.7, 4.8, 4.9
to write	かきます／かく	4.1B, 4.1, 4.2, 4.6, 4.7, 4.9
today	きょう	3.5, 4.1B, 4.2, 4.5, 4.8
together	いっしょ	4.2
Tokyo	とうきょう	3.2, 3.8
Tom	トム	3.7, 4.7

tomato sauce	トマトソース	2.6, 2.9A
tomorrow	あした	2.2, 3.5, 4.1B, 4.2, 4.3, 4.4, 4.7, 4.8
too	も	1.7, 2.4, 3.6, 3.9, 4.7 See. p393-395
topic	トピック	2.1B, 2.3, 2.5
topic of a meeting	ぎだい	2.9A
Toronto	トロント	3.11A
Toulouse	トゥールーズ	2.7
tour	ツアー	2.7
track and field	りくじょう	3.8
tradition	でんとう	4.5
traditional art	でんとうげいじゅつ	4.9
traditional Japanese new year cuisine	おせちりょうり	1.2
train	でんしゃ	3.01B, 3.1, 3.4, 3.6, 3.9, 4.1
train station	えき	4.11A
transportation	こうつう	3.6
tree/wood	き	0.2.02G, 4.9
true	ほんとう	1.1, 1.3
Tsar	ツァー	2.7
tuba	テューバ	2.7
Tues.	か	4.7
Tuesday	かようび	2.1B, G, 2.1, 2.2, 2.4, 2.5, 2.6, 3.5, 4.2, 4.4, 4.9, 4.10
tunnel	トンネル	1.7
TV actor/actress	テレビはいゆう	3.11A
TV announcer	テレビのアナウンサー	3.11A
twelfth day of the month	じゅうににち	2.1B, G, 2.1, 2.3, 2.6, 4.1
twelve	じゅうに	1.1B, G, 1.2, 1.5, 1.6,
twelve o'clock	じゅうにじ	2.1B, G, 2.2, 2.6, 4.4
twelve people	じゅうににん	2.6
twelve signs of the Oriental zodiac cycle	えと	1.4, 1.6, 1.7
twelve thirty	じゅうにじはん	2.6
twelve years	じゅうにねん	1.3
twelve years old	じゅうにさい	1.2
twelve fifty five	じゅうにじごじゅうごふん	4.9
twelfth grade	じゅうにねんせい	1.6, 3.3, 3.8
twelfth grade	こうこうさんねん	3.6
twelfth grade	こうさん	3.9
twentieth day of the month	はつか	2.1B, G, 2.3, 2.6, 4.9
twenty	にじゅう	1.1B, G, 1.2, 1.5, 1.6
twenty eight	にじゅうはち	1.1B, G, 1.2
twenty eighth day of the month	にじゅうはちにち	2.1B, G, 2.3, 2.6
twenty fifth day of the month	にじゅうごにち	2.1B, G, 2.3, 2.6, 4.6

twenty first day of the month	にじゅういちにち	2.1B, G, 2.3, 2.5, 4.6
twenty five	にじゅうご	1.1B, G, 1.2
twenty five minutes	にじゅうごふん	4.1B, 4.1
twenty four	にじゅうし	1.1B, G, 1.2
twenty four	にじゅうよん	1.1B, G, 1.2
twenty fourth day of the month	にじゅうよっか	2.1B, G, 2.3. 2.6, 4.6
twenty minutes	にじゅっぷん	4.1B
twenty minutes	にじっぷん／にじゅっぷん	4.1
twenty nine	にじゅうきゅう／にじゅうく	1.1B, G, 1.2
twenty ninth day of the month	にじゅうくにち	2.1B, G, 2.3, 2.6
twenty one	にじゅういち	1.1B, G, 1.2, 1.5
twenty second day of the month	にじゅうににち	2.1B, G, 2.3, 2.6, 4.6, 4.9
twenty seven	にじゅうしち	1.1B, G, 1.2
twenty seven	にじゅうなな	1.1B, G
twenty seventh day of the month	にじゅうしちにち	2.1B, G, 2.3, 2.6, 4.6
twenty six	にじゅうろく	1.1B, G, 1.2
twenty sixth day of the month	にじゅうろくにち	2.1B, G, 2.3, 2.6, 4.6
twenty third day of the month	にじゅうさんにち	2.1B, G, 2.3, 2.6, 3.9. 4.6
twenty three	にじゅうさん	1.1B, G, 1.2
twenty two	にじゅうに	1.1B, G, 1.2
twenty years	にじゅうねん	1.3
twenty years old	はたち	1.2
two	に	1.1B, G, 1.1, 1.2, 1.3, 1.5, 1.6, 3.9
two	にい	1.3
two hundred	にひゃく	1.1B, G, 1.3, 1.5, 1.6
two minutes	にふん	4.9
two o'clock	にじ	2.1B, G, 2.2, 2.6, 4.2, 4.8
two people	ふたり	2.1B, G, 2.3, 2.6, 3.7, 3.9, 4.1, 4.5
two (quantity)	ふたつ	2.9A, G, 3.9, 4.1B, 4.5
two thirty	にじはん	2.6
two thousand	にせん	1.1, 1.3, 1.5, 1.7
two years old	にさい	1.2
two years/second year	にねん	3.9
two five	にじごふん	4.9
typhoon	たいふう	3.11A
Ueda High School	うえだ こうこう	4.1
Ueno, Koichi (name of person)	うえの こういち	3.8
Ukrainian person	ウクライナじん	3.02
umbrella	かさ	0.2.03G
Umeko Tsuda (name of person)	つだ うめこ	1.1B, 1.3

umm	あのう	1.1, 1.2, 1.3, 1.8, 2.2, 2.4, 2.9A, 3.2, 3.3, 3.4, 3.5, 3.6, 3.9, 4.1, 4.2, 4.3, 4.4
umm	ええと	2.2, 2.8, 3.6, 3.9, 4.4
umm, also	あのう、それから	3.6
umm, excuse me	あのう、すみません	0.1.07G, 1.2, 2.9A, 4.10
umm, however	あのう、でも	3.6
unattractive	かっこわるい	3.11A
uncle	おじさん	3.11A
uncle	おじ	3.11A
uncooked buck wheat noodles	なまそば	2.9A
UNICEF	ユニセフ	4.8, 4.9
uniform	ユニホーム	0.1.08G
unskilled	にがて	3.5, 3.7, 3.9
until	まで	4.7, 4.8, See. p393-395
up/above	うえ	0.2.01G
um, I have a question	あのう、しつもんがあります	0.1.07G
Vancouver	バンクーバー	3.11A
veggie burger	やさいバーガー	2.6, 2.9A
vehicle	のりもの	3.01B
Vermont	バーモント	3.11
very well done	たいへんよくできました	0.1.10G
video	ビデオ	2.1, 2.2, 2.4, 2.6
video player	ビデオプレーヤー	4.6, 4.9
violin	バイオリン	2.7
Virginia	ヴァージニア	4.6
vocabulary	たんご	1.9
volleyball	バレーボール	1.4, 1.6, 3.5, 3.8, 4.2, 4.3, 4.4, 4.6
volleyball club	バレーぶ	3.11
volleyball team	バレーボールぶ	1.9A
volunteer	ボランティア	4.6, 4.8, 4.9
volunteer	ボランティアします／ボランティアする	4.11A
waffle	ワッフル	0.1.09G, 0.2.06G
waist	ウエスト	2.7
wait	まって	4.8, 4.10
wait a moment, please.	ちょっとまってください	0.1.07G, 1.9A, 4.3, 4.10
Wales	ウェールズ	2.7
Ward	ウォード	2.7
warm	あたたかい	3.11A
warm hearted/thoughtful (person)	おもいやりのある(ひと)	3.11A
Washington	ワシントン	3.11A, 4.6
watch	ウオッチ	2.7
watch	とけい	4.11A
water	(お) みず	1.9A, 3.8

water	みず	0.2.07G, 2.6, 3.2, 4.2, 4.4, 4.6, 4.9, 4.10
weather	てんき	1.1, 1.2, 1.8, 1.9A, 3.11A
Wed.	すい	4.7
Wednesday	すいようび	2.1B, G, 2.1, 2.2, 2.4, 2.6, 3.4, 4.2, 4.4, 4.7, 4.9, 4.10
welcome	いらっしゃいませ	2.9A
welcome dance	ウエルカムダンス	0.2.04G, 2.3
welcome home./welcome back	おかえりなさい	0.1.06G, 1.9A
well then	じゃ	1.4, 1.6, 1.8, 2.1B, 2.2, 2.3, 2.4, 2.5, 2.8, 3.1B, 3.2, 3.3, 3.6, 3.9, 4.3, 4.4, 4.10
West coast	ウエストコースト	3.3
what	なん	0.2.09G, 1.1, 1.3, 1.4, 1.6, 2.7 3.1B, 3.2, 3.5, 3.6, 3.7, 3.9, 3.10
what	なに	0.2.10G, 2.5, 3.1, 3.2, 3.5, 3.6, 3.9, 4.2, 4.3, 4.10
what age	なんさい	1.1, 1.2, 1.6, 1.8, 3.1B
what can I do for you? (informal)	なあに	1.6
what day of the month	なんにち	2.3, G, 2.5, 2.7, 3.1B, 3.2, 3.6, 4.3, 4.10
what day of the week	なんようび	2.1B, G, 2.2, 2.3, 2.4, 2.5 2.6, 2.8, 4.2
what does that mean?	どういういみですか	3.1B, 3.3
what does that mean?	いみはなんですか	3.1B
what grade	なんねんせい	1.5, 1.6, 1.8, 3.1B, 3.3
what is it?	なんでしょう	1.2, 1.6
what is it? (informal)	なあに	1.4, 1.6
what is the meaning of~	～のいみはなんですか	3.3
what is your animal year? (informal)	なにどし	1.6, 1.8
what is your name?	おなまえは	1.2, 1.6, G, 3.9
what is your name? (informal)	なまえは	1.6
what kind	どういう	3.7, 3.9
what kind	どんな	3.11A, 4.5
what month	なんがつ	2.3, G, 2.6
what number	なんばん	1.3, 1.5, 1.6, 1.8 2.2
what number?	なんばんですか	1.6, 4.10
what number group	なんグループ	2.6
what time	なんじ	2.1B, 2.2, 2.5, 2.6, 2.7, 3.5, 4.2, 4.3, 4.4, 4.7, 4.10
what time would you prefer?	なんじがいいですか	2.8

what year	なんねん	1.3
what year were you born in?	なんねんうまれ	1.1, 1.6
when	いつ	3.1B, 3.1, 3.2, 3.6, 3.7, 3.9, 3.10
where	どこ	0.2.10G, 2.1B, 2.2, 2.5, 2.6, 2.8, 3.1B, 3.2, 3.4 3.6, 3.7, 3.9, 3.11A, 4.2, 4.4
where (formal)	どちら	3.1B, 3.1, 3.6, 3.7, 3.9, 3.10
where is it? (informal)	どこ	2.6
where one is from	（ご）しゅっしん	3.1B, 3.1, 3.2, 3.6, 3.7, 3.9, 3.10
where one is from	しゅっしん	3.6, 3.8, 3.9, 3.11, 4.1
which do you prefer?	どれがいいですか	2.1, 2.5, 2.6, 2.8
which ever one does not matter to me	どれでもいいです	2.4
which (more than two items)	どれ	2.1B, 2.2, 2.4, 2.5, 2.6, 3.2, 3.8
which one is better? (informal)	どっちがいい	2.6
which (two items)	どちら	2.1B, 2.2, 2.4, 2.5 2.6, 2.8, 3.2, 3.8
which (two items)	どっち	2.4, 2.5
which would you prefer? (two items)	どちらがいいですか	2.6, 2.8
whisky	ウイスキー	2.7
whistlingly	ぴゅうぴゅう	4.5
white	しろ	1.9A, G, 3.1B, 3.1, 3.9
white~	しろい	3.6
white board	ホワイトボード	3.11A
white wheat noodles	うどん	2.4, 2.6, 2.9, 2.9A
who	どなた	3.6, 4.8, 4.10
who	だれ	0.2.05G, 0.2.09G, 0.2.10G, 3.1, 3.4, 3.6, 3.7, 3.9, 3.10, 4.8
who is this?	どなたですか	4.3
will not eat	たべません	4.2
will not go	いきません	4.2, 4.8, 4.10
will (subject) return?	かえりますか	4.9
will you go?	いきますか	4.2, 4.3, 4.4, 4.8
Wilson	ウィルソン	2.7
wind	かぜ	0.2.03G
winner/champion	ゆうしょうしゃ	4.9
winter	ふゆ	1.6, 3.9, 4.1
Wisconsin	ウィスコンシン	0.1.10G, 4.6
with/and	と	0.2.10G, 3.1 3.9, 3.11 4.7, See. P393~395
woman	おんなのひと	3.7
would you like~	～がいいですか	2.5, 2.7
would you like~? (informal)	～がいい	2.6

writing utensils	かきもの	3.02
yacht	ヨット	0.1.08G
Yale	イェール	2.7
Yamada (name of person)		
	やまだ	3.3, 3.9
Yamada, Yoko (name of person)		
	やまだ ようこ	3.8
Yamada, Haruko (name of person)		
	やまだ はるこ	3.8
Yamaguchi high school		
	やまぐちこうとうがっこう	
		1.6
Yamaguchi prefecture		
	やまぐち	3.8
Yasuo (name of person)		
	やすお	4.3
year 2000	にせんねん	1.3, 1,7, 1,9
year 2001	にせんいちねん	1.7
year 2010	にせんじゅうねん	1.3
year (animal)	とし／どし	1.5
year of the bird	とりどし	1.4, 1,6, 1.7
year of the boar	いのししどし	1.4, 1.6, 1.7
year of the boar	いどし	1.4, 1.6, 1.7
year of the cow	うしどし	1.4, 1.6, 1.7,
year of the dragon	たつどし	1.4, 1.6, 1.7
year of the horse	うまどし	1.4, 1.6, 1.7
year of the monkey	さるどし	1.4, 1.6, 1.7
year of the rabbit	うさぎどし	1.4, 1.6, 1.7
year of the rat	ねずみどし	1.4, 1.6, 1.7
year of the rat	ねどし	1.4, 1.6 1.7
year of the sheep	ひつじどし	1.4, 1.6, 1.7, 1.8
year of the snake	へびどし	1.4, 1.6, 1.7
year of the snake	みどし	1.4, 1.6, 1.7
year of the tiger	とらどし	1.4, 1.6, 1.7
year of the dog	いぬどし	1.4, 1.6, 1.7
yellow	きいろ	1.9A, G, 3.8, 3.9
yellow tuna	イエローツナ	0.2.06G
Yeltsin	エリツィン	2.7
yen	えん	1.1, 1.3, 1.5, 1.6, 4.7
yes	はい	1.2, 1.3, 1.4, 1.6, 3.8, 4.2
yes	ええ	1.6, 4.5
yes, I am all set.	はい、もういいです	0.1.09G
yes, I am fine (informal)		
	うん、げんき	0.1.06G, 1.6, 2.9A
yes, I am./ Yes, that's correct.		
	はい、そうです	0.1.01G, 1.4, 1.5, 1.8, 3.1B, 3.2, 3.3, 4.3
yes, I have	はい、あります	1.9A, G
yes, I have (informal)		
	うん、ある	1.9A
yes, I understand.]	はい、わかります	0.1.09G, 1.9A
yes, I understand (informal)		
	うん、わかる	1.9A
yes, I will do my best	はい、がんばります	0.1.10G

yes, I will take it	はい、いただきます	0.1.05G, 1.6, 1.8, 2.9A
yes. indeed./that is right		
	そうですね	0.1.03G, 1.6, 1.9A, 2.2
yes (informal)	うん	1.4, 1.6
yes, it is me	はい、わたしです	4.3
yes, it is. That is correct		
	そうです	1.2, 1.3, 1.4, 1.6, 4.1, 4.3
yes, let do that	はい、そうしましょう	
		3.5
yes, let's eat	はい、たべましょう	3.5
yes man	イエスマン	2.7
yes, she is here	はい、います	4.3
yes, thank you.]	はい、おかげさまで	0.1.06G, 2.9A
yes, thank you	はい、ありがとうございます	
		1.1, 1.2, 1.6
yes, What is it?)	はい、なんでしょう	0.1.07G, 2.4, 2.9A
yes, what is it? (informal)		
	あ、なあに	2.4
yes, what is it? (informal)		
	はい、なに	2.9A
Yokohama		
	よこはま	3.2, 3.8
Yoshio Suzuki (name of person)		
	すずき よしお	1.2
you are welcome	どういたしまして	1.2, 1.6, 1.8
you are welcome	いいえ、どういたしまして	
		0.1.04G, 2.9A
you are welcome	いいえ	0.1.04G
you are welcome (informal)		
	いいえ	2.9A
you can do a little better. Try your best		
	もうすこしがんばってください	
		0.1.10G
younger brother	おとうと	3.01B, 3.1, 3.4, 3.5, 3.6, 3.9, 3.11 4.1
younger brother	おとうとさん	3.4, 3.9
younger sister	いもうと	3.1B, 3.1 3.4, 3.5, 3.9
younger sister	いもうとさん	3.4, 3.9
Yuji Yamada (name of person)		
	やまだ ゆうじ	1.7
Yumi Katoh (name of person)		
	かとう ゆみ	1.2, 4.3
Yuri (name of person)		
	ゆり	3.3
zen	ぜん	4.9, 4.10, 4.11A
Zeppelin	ツェッペリン	2.7
zero	ゼロ	1.1B, G, 1.2, 1.3, 1.5
zero years old	れいさい	1.2
zero years old	ゼロさい	1.2

Glossary
Japanese – English

あ	oh	**3.02**
ああ	oh	**1.4**
ああ、そうですか	oh, really/oh, I see.	**1.3, 1.4, 2.2, 3.2, 3.4, 3.6**
ああ、それから	oh, and also~	**3.6, 3.9**
アート	art	**3.2, 4.9**
アートショー	art show	**2.2, 4.8, 4.9**
アートセンター	art center	**2.2**
アートフェア	art fair	**2.1, 2.2, 2.6**
あい	love	**0.2.01G**
あいかわ　はじめ	Aikawa, Hajime (name of person) **3.8**	
あいきどう	aikido	**4.9, 4.11A**
あいさつ	greeting	**3.6**
アイスクリーム	ice cream	**0.1.09G, 0.2.06G, 2.4, 2.6, 3.9, 3.11**
アイスコーヒー	iced coffee	**1.9A**
アイスティー	iced tea	**0.2.06G, 1.9A, 2.1B, 2.2, 2.5**
アイスホッケー	ice hockey	**1.6**
あお	blue	**0.2.01G, 1.9A, 3.1B, 3.1, 3.9**
あおき	Aoki (Japanese family name) **3.9**	
あおやま	Aoyama (name of person) **3.3**	
あか	red	**1.9A, 3.1B, 3.1, 3.9**
あかるい	cheerful	**3.11A**
あき	fall	**1.4, 1.6, 2.4, 3.9, 4.9**
あきた	Akita (prefecture)	**3.8**
あきら	Akira (name of person)	**3.3**
アクティビティー	activity	**2.1, 2.5, 2.7, 3.2**
あけましておめでとうございます	Happy New Year	**1.2, 1,6, 1.7, 1.9**
あげる	give	**4.7**
アコード	Accord	**3.3**
あさ	morning	**4.2, 4.9**
あさい　はな	Asai Hana (name of person) **4.1**	
あさごはん	breakfast	**4.1B, 4.4, 4.7, 4.8, 4.9**
あさって	the day after tomorrow	**4.1B, 4.5, 4.9**
アジア	Asia	**4.9**
あした	tomorrow	**2.2, 3.5, 4.1B, 4.2, 4.3, 4.4, 4.7, 4.9**
あ、そう	is that so? (informal)	**1.6**
あ、そうですか	is that so?	**1.6**
あそびます／あそぶ	play	**4.11A**
あたし	I/me	**3.4**
あたたかい	warm	**3.11A**
あっ、ありがとう	I accept the food/thing with gratitude. (informal)	**1.6**
あつい	hot	**1.6, 1.9A, 1.9A**
あっ、いただき	I will receive the food/thing. (informal) **1.6**	
あついですね	It's hot, isn't it?	**0.1.03G, 1.6, 1.9A**
あついね	It is a hot day, isn't it? (informal) **1.6**	
あつい（わ）ね	it's hot, isn't it? (informal) **1.9A**	
あっ、すまない	I am sorry/thank you. (informal) **1.6**	
アップルパイ	apple pie	**2.6, 2.9A**
あつめます／あつめる	to gather	**4.8, 4.9**
あと	after	**3.9**
あとで	later	**4.3, 4.9, 4.10**
アトランタ	Atlanta	**3.11A**
あ、なあに	yes, what is it? (informal) **2.4**	
あに	elder brother	**3.1, 3.4, 3.5, 3.9**
アニメ	animation	**3.2**
アニメフェスティバル	animation festival	**2.1, 2.2, 2.6**
あね	elder sister	**3.1, 3.4, 3.5, 3.6, 3.9**
あのう	umm	**1.1, 1.2, 1.3, 1.8, 2.2, 2.4, 2.9A, 3.2, 3.3, 3.4, 3.5, 3.6, 3.9, 4.1, 4.2, 4.3, 4.4, 4.10**
あのう、しつもんがあります	ur, I have a question.	**0.1.07G**
あのう、すみません	umm, excuse me.	**0.1.07G, 1.2, 1.6, 2.9A, 4.10**
あのう、それから	umm, also	**3.6**
あのう、でも	umm, however	**3.6**
アフリカ	Africa	**4.9**
あまり	seldom	**3.5, 4.1B, 4.2**
あめ	rain	**3.11A**
あめがふります／ふる	it rains.	**1.6**
あめがよくふります／ふる	it rains a lot.	**1.6**
アメフト	American football	**0.2.08G**
アメリカ	America	**0.2.05G, 3.2, 3.3, 3.6, 3.8, 3.9, 3.11, 4.8**
アメリカじん	American person	**3.1B, 3.2, 3.9, 4.7**
アヤナ	Ayana	**1.2, 1.3, 1.4, 3.4**
あらいます／あらう	to wash	**4.6, 4.9**
アラビアご	Arabic language	**3.02**
ありがとう	thank you.	**0.1.04G, 1.6, 2.2**
ありがとうございました	thank you very much.	**1.2, 1.3**

ありがとうございます	thank you very much.	**0.1.04G**, 1.1B, 1.1, 1.2, 1.6, 1.8, 4.1
あります／ある	there is (non-living).	**4.1B**, 4.1, 4.5, 4.7
ありますか	is (inanimate thing) there?	**0.2.07G**, 3.11A
ありません	there is no ... (non-living)	**4.5**
あるいて	on foot/by foot	**3.9**
あるきます／あるく	to walk	**4.9**
アルジェリア	Algeria	**3.9**
アルジェリアじん	Algerian person	**3.02**
アルバイトします／アルバイトする	have a part-time job	**4.11A**
あるひ	one day	**3.9**
あわせ	match	**4.1**
あんまり	seldom	**4.9**
いい	good	**1.1**, 1.2, 1.8, 2.2, 2.3, 2.4, 3.6, 3.7
いいえ	no	**1.2**, 1.4, 1.6, 4.1B, 4.2, 3.2, 3.3, 3.8
いいえ	not at all	**1.2**, 1.6
いいえ	no, thank you. (informal)	**2.9A**
いいえ	you are welcome. (informal)	**2.9A**
いいえ	you are welcome.	**0.1.04G**
いいえ	that's all right. never mind.	**0.1.10G**
いいえ、ありません	no, I do not have.	**1.9A**, G
いいえ、けっこうです	no thank you.	**0.1.05G**, 1.1, 1.2, 1.6, 1.8, 2.9A
いいえ、そうじゃありません	no, it is not so.	**1.6**
いいえ、ちがいます	no, that's incorrect./No, I'm not.	**0.1.01G**, 1.4, 1.5, 1.6, 1.8, 2.2, 3.2, 4.3, 4.9
いいえ、どういたしまして	you are welcome.	**0.1.04G**, 2.9A
いいえ、まだです	no, not yet.	**0.1.09G**
いいえ、わかりません	no, I do not understand.	**0.1.09G**,1.9A, G
いいおてんきですね	It's a beautiful day, isn't it?	**0.1.03G**, 2.1
いいです	good	**4.3**, 4.7
いいてんき	fine weather	**1.6**, 1.9A
いいてんき（だ）ね	It is a fine day, isn't it? (informal)	**1.6**, 1.9A
いいてんきですね	It is a fine day, isn't it?	**1.6**, G, 1.9A
いいところ	good place/location	**3.11A**
いえ	house	**0.2.01G**
イェール	Yale	**2.7**
いえ、けっこう	no, thank you. (informal)	**1.6**

イエスマン	yes man	**2.7**
イエローツナ	yellow tuna	**0.2.06G**
いきましょう	let's go	**4.2**
いきます／いく	to go	**0.2.10G**, 3.4, 3.6, 3.9, 3.11A, 3.11, 4.1B, 4.1, 4.2, 4.3, 4.4, 4.7, 4.8
いきますか	will you go?	**4.2**, 4.3, 4.4, 4.8
いきません	will not go	**4.2**, 4.8, 4.10
イギリス	Great Britain	**3.9**
イギリスじん	English person	**3.02**
いきる	live	**4.9**
いくつ	how many/how old	**1.1**, 1.6, 3.1B, 3.1, 3.2, 3.3, 3.6, 3.7, 3.9, 3.10
いくら	how much is it? (informal)	**2.6**
いくら	how much (price)	**1.3**, 2.1B, 2.2, 2.6, 3.2
いくらですか	how much is it?	**2.5**, 2.6, 2.8
いけばな	flower arrangement	**4.8**, 4.11A
いす	chair	**3.11A**, 4.1B, 4.1, 4.5, 4.6, 4.8, 4.9, 4.10
イスラエル	Israel	**3.9**
いそがしい	busy	**3.5**, 3.8, 3.8, 3.11
いただきます	thank you, I can serve myself.	**1.1**, 1.6, 1.8, 2.1, 2.9A,
いただきます	thank you for the meal.	**0.1.05G**, 1.2
いただきます／いただく	to receive	**1.2**
イタリア	Italy	**3.9**
イタリアンアイス	Italian ice	**2.6**, 2.9A
いち	one	**1.1B**, G, 1.1, 1.2, 1.3, 1.4, 1.5, 1.6, 3.9, 4.6
いちがつ	January	**1.7**, 2.1B, 2.3, 2.6, 3.9, 4.9
いちご	strawberry	**1.9A**, 2.6
いちじ	one o'clock	**2.1B**, G, 2.2, 2.6, 3.2, 4.9
いちじはん	one thirty	**2.2**, 2.6
いちにち	one day	**4.9**
いちねん	one year	**1.3**, 3.9
いちねんせい	first grade	**1.6**
いちねんにくみ	first year, second class	**1.6**
いちまん	ten thousand	**1.3**, 1.5, 1.6,
いちまんえん	ten thousand yen	**1.9**
いちろう	Ichiro (name of person)	**3.3**
いつ	when	**3.1B**, 3.1, 3.2, 3.6, 3.7, 3.9, 3.10
いつか	fifth day of the month	**2.1B**, G, 2.1, 2.3, 2.6, 3.5, 3.9, 4.1, 4.2, 4.4, 4.7, 4.9
いっか	chapter one	**0.2.04G**
いっさい	one year old	**1.2**
いっしょ	together	**4.2**
いつつ	five (quantity)	**2.9A**, 4.1B, 4.5,
いって	please say. (informal)	**1.9A**
いってきます	I will go and come back.	**0.1.06G**, 1.9A
いってください	please say.	**1.9A**, G
いってまいります	I will go and come back	**0.1.06G**, 1.9A
いってらっしゃい	have a safe trip. (when someone else is leaving)	**0.1.06G**, 1.9A
いっぷん	one minute	**4.9**

いつも	always	3.5, 3.6, 3.9, 3.11, 3.11A, 4.1, 4.2
いどし	year of the boar	1.4, 1.6, 1.7
いぬ	dog	0.2.05G, 1.4
いぬどし	year of thedog	1.4, 1.6, 1.7
いのしし	boar	0.2.05G, 1.4
いのししどし	year of the boar	1.4, 1.6, 1.7
イベント	events	2.1, 2.2, 4.10, 4.11A
いま	now	2.2
います／いる	there is (living).	0.2.08G, 4.1B, 4.1, 4.5, 4.8
いますか	is (animate thing) there?	
		3.11A, 4.1B, 4.3, 4.10,
いません	there is no ... (living).	4.5
いみ	meaning	3.3, 3.6, 3.9, 3.10
いみはなんですか	what does that mean?	3.1B
いもうと	younger sister	3.1B, 3.1 3.4, 3.5, 3.9
いもうとさん	younger sister	3.4, 3.9
いや	not at all (informal)	1.6
いらっしゃいませ	welcome	2.9A
イリノイ	Illinois	4.6
いろ	color	0.2.09G, 3.2, 3.8, 3.11A
インターネット	internet	0.2.07G
インターネットします／インターネットする		
	surf the Internet	4.11A
インタビュー	interview	3.10
インド	India	3.9
インドじん	Indian person	3.2
インドネシア	Indonesia	3.9
インドネシアご	Indonesian language	3.2
インドネシアじん	Indonesian person	3.2
ヴァージニア	Virginia	4.6
ウイスキー	whisky	2.7
ウィスコンシン	Wisconsin	0.1.10G, 4.6
ウィルソン	Wilson	2.7
ううん	no (informal)	1.6
ううん、そうじゃない		
	no, it is not so. (informal)	
		1.6
ううん、ちがう	no, that is incorrect. (informal)	
		1.6
ううん、ない	no, I do not have. (informal)	
		1.9A
ううん、わからない		
	no, I do not understand. (informal)	
		1.9A
うえ	up/above	0.2.01G
ウェールズ	Wales	2.7
ウエスト	waist	2.7
ウエストコースト	West coast	3.3
うえだ　こうこう	Ueda High School	4.1
うえの　こういち	Ueno, Koichi (name of person)	
		3.8
ウエルカムダンス	welcome dance	0.2.04G, 2.3
ウォード	Ward	2.7
ウオッチ	watch	2.7
ウクライナじん	Ukrainian person	3.02
うさぎ	rabbit	1.1, 1.4
うさぎどし	year of the rabbit	1.4, 1.6, 1.7

うし	cow	1.1, 1.4
うしどし	year of the cow	1.4, 1.6, 1.7,
うそ	false	1.1, 1.3
うた	song	4.8, 4.9, 4.10
うち	inside	3.4, 3.6, 3.9
うち	house	3.5, 3.9, 4.1B, 4.2, 4.3, 4.7, 4.8
うちに	at home	4.4
うちのかぞく	my family	3.4
うどん	white wheat noodles	2.4, 2.6, 2.9, 2.9A
うなぎ	eel	2.4, 2.6, 2.9, 2.9A
うま	horse	0.2.07G, 1.1, 1.4
うまどし	year of the horse	1.4, 1.6, 1.7
うまれる	born	4.9
うむ	to give birth to	4.9
うります／うる	to sell	4.9
うるさい	noisy	3.5, 3.6, 3.9
うん	yes (informal)	1.4, 1.6
うん、ある	yes, I have. (informal)	1.9A
うん、げんき	yes, I am fine. (informal)	0.1.06G, 1.6, 2.9A
うん、わかる	yes, I understand. (informal)	
		1.9A
え	picture	0.2.01G, 4.1, 4.9
エアコン	air conditioner	0.2.08G
えいが	movie	2.1B, 2.2, 2.6, 3.2, 3.5, 4.1, 4.2, 4.4, 4.6, 4.7
えいがかん	movie theater	4.11A
えいがスター	movie star	3.11A
えいご	English language	0.2.02G, 3.1B, 3.2, 3.5, 3.8, 3.9. 4.1, 4.5, 4.9
えいごでもいいですか		
	may I use English?	0.1.07G
えいごぶ	English language club	3.11
エイズウォーク	AIDS Walk	4.8, 4.9
ええ	yes	1.6, 4.5
ええと	umm	2.2, 2.8, 3.6, 3.9, 4.4
えき	train station	4.11A
エジプト	Egypt	3.9
エジプトじん	Egyptian person	3.02
エッセイコンテスト		
	essay contest	0.2.04G, 2.3
えと	twelve signs of the Oriental zodiac cycle	
		1.4, 1.6, 1.7
えりか	Erika (name of person)	3.3
エリツィン	Yeltsin	2.7
えん	yen	1.1, 1.3, 1.5, 1.6, 4.7
えんげきぶ	drama club	1.9A, 3.11
えんぴつ	pencil	3.11A
おうじ	prince	3.11A
おうじょ	princess	3.11A
おおい	numerous	4.5
おおいた	Oita (prefecture)	3.02
おおきい	big	3.7, 4.5
おおさか	Osaka	3.8
オーストラリア	Australia	3.9
オーストラリアじん		
	Australian person	3.02
オーディーション	audition	4.8, 4.9

521

おーでぃお		
オーディオ	audio	4.11A
おおみそか	New Year's Eve	1.2
おおやま	Ooyama (name of person)	3.3, 3.4, 3.9
おおやま　はるこ	Ooyama, Haruko (name of person)	3.9
おかあさん	mother	0.2.10G, 3.1B. 3.1, 3.4, 3.5, 3.9, 4.1
おかえりなさい	welcome home./Welcome back	0.1.06G, 1.9A
おかげさまで	thanks to you	1.2, 1.6
おかだ	Okada (name of person)	1.1
おかね	money	4.7, 2.5, 3.2, 4.6, 4.9, 4.10
おきます／おきる	to wake up	3.5, 4.1B, 4.1, 4.2, 4.4, 4.8, 4.9
（お）くに	country	3.1B, 3.1, 3.2, 3.6, 3.7, 3.9,3.10
おくだ	Okuda (name of person)	1.1
おげんきですか	are you well?	0.1.06G, 1.6, 1.8, 2.9A
おこのみやき	savory pancakes	2.4, 2.9
おざわ　せいじ	Seiji Ozawa (name of person)	1.1B, 1.3
おじ	uncle	3.11A
おじいさん	grandfather	3.11A, 4,5
おじさん	uncle	3.11A
おしゅうじ	Japanese calligraphy	4.9, 4.10
おしゅうじのせんせい	calligraphy master	4.5
（お）すまい	residence	3.1B, 3.1, 3.2, 3.3, 3.6, 3.7, 3.9, 3.10
おせちりょうり	traditional Japanese New Year cuisine	1.2
おぞうに	soup with rice cake	1.2
おそくなってすみません	sorry I am late	0.1.10G
おたく	residence	4.1, 4.3, 4.4
（お）たんじょうび	birthday	3.7
おちゃ	tea ceremony	4.9, 4.10, 4.11A
（お）ちゃ	tea	1.9A, 2.6, 4.4, 4.6
おちゃのせんせい	tea ceremony master	4.5
おてら	Buddhist temple	1.2
おでんわ	telephone (formal)	4.1
おでんわばんごう	telephone number (formal)	4.3
おとうさん	father	0.2.10G, 3.1B, 3.1, 3.4, 3.5, 3.9, 4.1
おとうと	younger brother	3.01B, 3.1, 3.4, 3.5, 3.6, 3.9, 3.11, 4.1
おとうとさん	younger brother	3.4, 3.9
（お）とし	age	3.1B, 3.1, 3.2, 3.6, 3.7, 3.9, 3.10
おとしだま	New Year's money gift from parent to child	1.2
おどります／おどる	to dance	4.8, 4.9
おなまえ	name (formal)	1.2, 1.8, 3.1B, 3.1, 3.2, 3.7, 3.9, 3.10, 4.3
おなまえは	what is your name?	1.6, G, 3.9
おにいさん	elder brother	0.2.10G, 3.01B, 3.1, 3.4, 3.9
おねえさん	elder sister	0.2.10G, 3.1B, 3.1, 3.4, 3.5, 3.9, 4.5
おねがい	favor	1.2, 1.3, 1.5, 1.6,
おねがい（～を）	I request~ (informal)	2.6
おねがいします／する（～を）	I request~	1.2, G, 1.6, 1.8, 2.2, 2.5, 2.6, 4.10
おのこしください	please leave	4.3
おの　じゅん	Jun Ono (name of person)	1.6
おば	aunt	3.11A
おばあさん	grandmother	3.11A, 4.5
おばさん	aunt	3.11A
おはな	flower arrangement	4.9
おはなのせんせい	flower arrangement master	4.5
おはよう	good morning.	0.1.03G, 1.1B, 1.1, 1.2, 1.6, 1,8, 4.5
おはようございます	good morning.	0.1.03G, 1.1B, 1.1, 1.2, 1.6, 1.8
おべんとう	box lunch	2.4, 2.9A, 2.9
おまかせ	I rely on your suggestion. (informal)	2.6
おまかせします	I will leave it up to you.	2.4, 2.5, 2.6, 2.8
オマリー	O'Malley	3.2
（お）みず	water	1.9A, 3.8
おもいやりのある(ひと)	warm hearted/thoughtful(person)	3.11A
おもしろい	funny	0.2.09G, 3.1B, 3.1, 3.5, 3.6, 3.8, 3,9
おやすみ	good night	0.1.02G, 1.6, 1.9A, 2.9A
おやすみなさい	good night	0.1.02G, 1.2, 1.6, 1.8, 1.9A, 2.9A
おりがみぶ	origami club	1.9A
オレゴン	Oregon	4.6
オレンジ	orange	1.9A, G, 2.2, 2.5, 2.6, 3.1B, 3.1, 3.2, 3.9
オレンジジュース	orange juice	4.4, 4.6
おわり	end	3.1B, 3.6, 3.9
おわります／おわる	to end	2.1B, 2.1, 2.3, 2.4, 2.5, 2.6
おんがく	music	3.1B, 3.1, 3.2, 3.5, 3.8, 3.9, 3.10, 4.1B, 4.6, 4.8, 4.9
おんがくのれんしゅう	music practice	4.6
おんなのひと	woman	3.7
か	Tues.	4.7
～か	[Be~]~? (informal)	1.6
カーナビ	car navigation	0.2.08G
～があります	there is an inanimate thing	3.7
～がいい	would you like~? (informal)	2.6
～がいいです	I would like~.	2.5
～がいいですか	would you like~.	2.5, 2.6, 2.7
かいぎ	meeting	0.2.07G, 2.9A
がいこくご	foreign language	3.1B, 3.1, 3.9
かいしゃ	company/business	4.10, 4.11A

がいしゅつちゅう	away from (location)	4.3
かいて	please write. (informal)	1.9A
かいてください	please write.	1.9A, G, 4.10
〜がいます	there is an animate being.	3.7
かいものをします／かいものをする		
	go shopping	4.11A
かいわ	conversation	3.9
カウンセラー	counselor	3.11A, 4.1B
かえりますか	will (subject) return?	4.9
かえります／かえる		
	to return	4.1B, 4.2, 4.4, 4.7, 4.9, 4.10
かお	face	0.2.02G, 4.9
かおりさん	Kaori (name of person)	4.3, 4.10
かおりさんいますか		
	Is Kaori there?	4.3, 4.10
かがいかつどう	extra-curricular activities	1.9A
カカオ	cacao	0.1.02G
かがく	chemistry	3.01B
かがく	science	0.2.02G, 3.1B, 3.1, 3.5, 3.8, 3.9, 4.9
かがくぶ	science club	1.9A
かきぞめ	first calligraphy writing of the year	1.2
かきます／かく	to write	4.1B, 4.1, 4.2, 4.6, 4.7, 4.9
かきもの	writing utensils	3.02
がくせい	student	4.9
がくねん	grade year	1.1, 1.4, 3.3, 3.6, 3.7, 3.8, 3.10, 4.9
がくねんは	what's your grade?	3.2
かける	muliply	1.3, 1.6
かごしま	Kagoshima (prefecture)	3.2
かさ	umbrella	0.2.03G
かじ	fire	1.3, 1.6, 1.9A
かしゅ	singer	3.11A
がしょう	lit: Celebrating a New Year	1.6, 1.7
かずき	Kazuki (name of person)	3.3
かぜ	wind	0.2.03G
かぞく	family	0.2.03G, 3.1B, 3.4, 3.9, 3.11, 4.1
かたる	to say	4.9
〜がつ	month of ~	0.2.04G, 2.3
がっき	instrument	4.9
がっきをひきます／ひく		
	play an intrument	4.9
かっこいい	attractive	3.11A
がっこう	school	0.2.05G, 0.2.08G, 1.6, G, 2.3, 2.4, 2.5, 3.2, 3.4, 3.6, 3.7, 3.9, 3.11, 4.1B, 4.2, 4.3, 4.7, 4.8, 4.10
かっこわるい	unattractive	3.11A
カット	cut	0.1.04G
かつどう	activity	3.11
かつやまこうこう	Katsuyama High School	3.11
かとう　あみ	Ami Katoh (name of person)	1.2
かとうさん	Katoh (name of person)	4.3
かどうぶ	flower arrangement club	1.9A, 3.11
かとう　ゆみ	Yumi Katoh (name of person)	1.2, 4.3
かな	kana	4.5, 4.9
かなえ	Kanae (name of person)	4.3
カナダ	Canada	3.2, 3.9
カナダじん	Canadian person	3.1B, 3.2
カニン	Kanene	2.3
カヌー	canoe	0.1.05G
カフェ	cafe	0.1.10G
カフェテリア	cafeteria	2.1B, 2.2, 2.6, 4.1, 4.2, 4.6, 4.9, 4.10
かぶき	kabuki (Japanese theater)	4.9, 4.10, 4.11A
かみざら	paper plate	4.9
カメラ	camera	4.10, 4.11A
かもく	school subject	0.2.05G, 0.2.07G, 3.1B, 3.2, 3.5, 3.6, 3.7, 3.8, 3.9, 3.10
かようび	Tuesday	2.1B, G, 2.1, 2.2, 2.4, 2.5, 2.6, 3.5, 4.2, 4.4, 4.9, 4.10
から	from	3.8, 3 9, 4.1, 4.7, 4.10 See. p393-395
カラオケ	karaoke	0.2.08G, 2.2, 2.6, 4.6
からだ	body	4.6, 4.9
からて	karate	1.6, 4.10, 4.11A
からてのせんせい	karate master	4.5
〜から〜まで	from~to~	4.4
かります／かりる	will borrow/to borrow	4.7
カリフォルニア	California	4.6
カレーライス	curry and rice	0.1.09G, 0.2.06G, 2.4, 2.9
カレンダー	calender	2.1, 2.2
かわいい	cute	3.01B, 3.1, 3.5, 3.8, 3.9
かわかみ	Kawakami (name of person)	3.3, 3.9
かわのせんせい	teacher Kawano	3.3
かわはら　まさお	Kawahara, Masao (name of person)	3.8
かんこく	Korea	3.02, 3.9
かんこくご	Korean language	3.1B
かんこくじん	Korean person	3.1B
かんじ	kanji	3.8, 4.5, 4.7, 4.9
がんじつ	first day of the year	1.2, 1.7, 1.9
がんたん	first day of the year	1.2, 1.7, 1.9
カンツォーネ	canzone	2.7
カントリー	country music	2.5
がんねん	first year (of an era)	1.3, 1.6
がんばって	do you best/hang in there! (informal)	1.9A, 3.6, 3.9, 4.1
がんばってください		
	do you best/hang in there!	1.9A, G
き	tree/wood	0.2.02G, 4.9
キー	key	0.1.02G
きいて（いて）	please listen. (informal)	1.9A
きいて（いて）ください		
	please listen.	1.9A, G
きいろ	yellow	1.9A, G, 3.8, 3.9
ギガ	giga	1.3, 1.4, 1.5, 1.6
ききます／きく	to listen	4.1B, 4.2, 4.6, 4.8, 4.9

キス	kiss	0.1.03G
きせつ	seasons	0.2.04G, 1.6, 3.8
ギター	guitar	1.5, 1.7
ぎだい	topic of a meeting	2.9A
きたさん	Kita (name of person)	4.7
きたじま　さとこ	Kitajima, Satoko (name of person)	3.8
きた　しろう	Shiroh Kita (name of person)	1.2, 2.4, 2.6
キック	kick	0.1.04G
きって	stamp	0.2.04G
きっぷ	ticket	2.2, 4.8, 4.9
きどらない	not affected	3.11A
きのした	Kinoshita (name of person)	3.3, 3.9
きびしい	strict	3.5, 3.8, 3.9
ギフトセンター	gift center	1.3
きます／くる	to come	4.7, 4.8, 4.10
きむら	Kimura (name of person)	3.3
きむら　かおり	Kimura, Kaori (name of person)	3.8
きむら　ゆか	Kimura Yuka (name of person)	3.02
きめます／きめる	to decide	4.9
きもの	kimono	4.11A
キャッシュサービス	cash service	2.9A
キャプテン	captain	3.11A
キャンプファイヤー	camp fire	0.1.10G, 3.9, 3.11A
きゅう	nine	1.1B, G, 1.1, 1.2, 1.3, 1.5, 1.6, 3.9
キュウイ	kiwi	1.9A, 2.6
きゅうきゅうしゃ	ambulance	1.3, 1.6, 1.9A
きゅうさい	nine years old	1.2
きゅうじゅう	ninety	1.1B, G, 1.1, 1.2, 1.5, 1.6
きゅうじゅうきゅう	ninety nine	1.1B,G, 1.2
きゅうじゅうく	ninety nine	1.1B, G, 1.2
きゅうじゅうしち	ninety seven	1.2, G
きゅうじゅうなな	ninety seven	1.2, G
きゅうじゅうはち	ninety eight	1.2, G
きゅうじゅうろく	ninety six	1.2, G
きゅうせん	nine thousand	1.3, 1.5, 1.6,
きゅうどう	Japanese archery	4.9
きゅうどうのせんせい	Japanese archery master	4.5
きゅうどうぶ	archery club	3.11
きゅうにん	nine people	2.6, G, 3.9
きゅうねんせい	nineth grade	1.6
きゅうひゃく	nine hundred	1.1B, G, 1.3, 1.5, 1.6
きゅうふん	nine minutes	4.9
きょう	today	3.5, 4.1B, 4.2, 4.5, 4.9
きょうし	professor	1.6
ぎょうじ	events	0.2.01G, 1.2
きょうしつ	classroom	2.1B, 2.2, 2.3, 2,.6, 4.2, 4.6, 4.9
きょうだい	sibling	3.11A

きょうと	Kyoto prefecture	3.8
きらい	(to) dislike	3.1, 3.5, 3.6, 3.7, 3.9, 3.11A, 3.11
きりつ	stand up	0.1.08G
ぎりのおかあさん	mother-in-law	3.11A
ぎりのおとうさん	father-in-law	3.11A
ぎりのちち	father-in-law	3.11A
ぎりのはは	mother-in-law	3.11A
きります／きる	to cut	4.7
きれい	beautiful	3.1B, 3.1, 3.5, 3.8, 3.9
きん	Fri.	4.7
きんがしんねん	lit: I humbly wish you a Happy New Year.	1.6, 1.7
キング	King	3.2
きんようび	Friday	2.1B, G, 2.1, 2.2, 2.3, 2.6, 3.5, 4.2, 4.4, 4.9, 4.10
く	nine	1.1B, G, 1.5, 1.6, 3.9
クァジャレン	Kwajalein	2.7
グアム	Guam	2.7
グァリーニ	Guarini	2.7
クイーン	queen	2.7
クィニョン	Quinhon	2.7
グィネビア	Guinevere	2.7
クール(な)	a cool~	3.5, 3.8, 3.9
クエーサー	quasar	2.7
クェッタ	Quetta	2.7
グェルチーノ	Guercino	2.7
クォーク	quark	2.7
クオーツ	quartz	2.7
くがつ	September	2.1B, G, 2.3, 2.6, 3.9, 4.8
くじ	nine o'clock	2.1B, G, 2.1 ,2,2, 2.6, 3.9, 4.4, 4.8, 4.10
くじはん	nine thirty	2.6
くじよんじゅっぷん	nine forty	4.9
ください(を)	please give me/I would like to have~.	0.1.04G, 1.2, 1.6, 1.8, 2.1B, 2.2, 2.5, 2.6, 2.9A, 4.7, 4.8, 4.10
くだもの	fruits	3.02, G
くち	mouth	0.2.04G, 4.1
クッキー	cookie	2.1B, 2.6
クッキング	cooking	3.02
くに	country	3.6, 3.9, 3.11
くにん	nine people	2.3, G, 2.6, 3.7, 4.1
くばってください	Please pass these out.	0.1.09G
くみ	class	1.5, 1.6, 3.9
くもり	cloudy	3.11A
くらい	gloomy	3.11A
クラシック	classical music	3.8
クラス	class	0.2.07G, 4.8
クラブ	club	3.2, 3.3, 3.7, 3.9, 3.10, 3.11, 4.4, 4.8
クラブぶちょう	head of club	3.11A
クラブミーティング	club meeting	3.5, 4.2, 4.4, 4.6, 4.8,
クラムソース	clam sauce	2.6, 2.9A
グランド	field	2.1B, 2.2, 2.6, 4.6

グループ	group	1.6, 4.10,4.11A
くるま	car	3.1B, 3.1, 3.3, 3.7, 4.11A
～くれ	please give me~. (informal)	1.6, 2.6, 2.9A
グレー	gray	1.9A, G, 3.1B, 3.1,
グレートレイクスクール	Great Lake School	3.11
グレープフルーツ	grapefruit	1.9A, 2.6
くろ	black	1.9A G, 3.1B, 3.1, 3.9
～くんはいますか	Is so and so here?	0.1.08G
ケイ	k	1.3, 1.5, 1.6
けいかく	plan	0.2.02G, 4.1B4.1, 4.6, 4.9,
けいかくをたてます／たてる	to make a plan	4.6
けいざい	economics	3.1B, 3.1, 3.5, 3.9
けいさつ	police	1.3, 1.6, 1.9A
げいじゅつ	art	4.5
げいじゅつか	artist	3.11A
げいしゅん	lit: Welcoming Spring=New Year	1.6, 1.7
ケーキ	cake	0.1.02G, 1.7, 2.1B, 2.1, 2.4, 2.6, 3.2
ケーキをつくります／ケーキをつくる	make a cake	4.11A
ゲーム	game	2.9A, 4.1, 4.6, 4.11A
けしごむ	eraser	3.11A
げつ	Mon.	4.7
けっこうです	no, thank you	1.1B, 1.1, 1.2
けつだんりょくのある（ひと）	a person that is quick in decision making	3.11A
げつようび	Monday	2.1B, G, 2.1, 2.2, 2.6, 3.5, 4.2, 4.4, 4.8, 4.9, 4.10
けん	prefecture	1.6
けん	Ken (name of person)	3.3
げんき(な)	healthy	0.2.09G, 1.1B, 1.1, 1.2, 1.6, 1.7, 2.9A, 3.1B, 3.1, 3.5, 3.7, 3.8, 3.9
けんどう	kendo	4.9, 4.11A
けんどうのせんせい	Japanese fencing master	4.5
けんどうぶ	Japanese fencing club	3.11
ご	five	1.1B, G, 1.1, 1.2, 1.5, 1.6, 3.9
～ご	~language	3.6, 3.9
こいけ	Koike (name of person)	3.3
ごう	five	1.3
こういち	tenth grade	3.9
こうえん	park	3.4, G, 4.11A
こうこう	high school	0.2.02G, 1.1B, 1.1, 1.3, 1.4, 3.2
こうこうせい	high school student	4.4, 4.9
こうこうさんねん	twelveth grade	3.6
こうこうにねんせい	second year high school student	1.5, 3.2, 3.3, 3.11
こうさん	twelveth grade	3.9
こうちゃ	black tea	1.9A, 2.1B, 2.1, 2.5, 2.6
こうちょう	principal	3.11A
こうちょうしつ	principal's office	2.6
こうつう	transportation	3.6
こうどう	auditorium	2.1B, 2.1, 2.3, 2.4, 2.6, 3.6, 4.2, 4.6, 4.9
こうとうがっこう	high school	1.6
こうに	eleventh grade	3.9
ごえん	five yen	1.9
コーク	coke	3.5, G, 4.2, 4.5
コーチ	coach	0.1.04G, 1.4, 3.11A, 4.1B, 4.5
コート	coat	0.1.04G
コーヒー	coffee	0.1.06G, 1.9A, 2.1B, 2.2, 2.5, 2.6, 3.2, 4.2, 4.4, 4.6
コーラ	coke	0.2.06G, 1.1, 1.9A, 2.2, 2.4, 2.6, 3.2, 4.6, 4.9
コーラスぶ	chorus	3.11
（ご）かぞく	family	3.4, 3.9
ごがつ	May	2.1B, G, 2.3, 2.6, 3.9, 4.7
（ご）きょうだい	siblings	3.7
こくせき	nationality	3.6
こくばん	blackboard	3.11A, 4.6, 4.9, 4.10
ごくみ	class 5	3.9
ここ	here	4.7
ココア	cocoa	0.1.02G
ここのか	nineth day of the month	2.1B, G, 2.1, 2.3, 2.6, 3.9, 4.1
ここのつ	nine (quantity)	2.9A, G, 4.1B, 4.5
ごさい	five years old	1.2
ごじ	five o'clock	2.1B, G, 2.2, 2.6, 4.3, 4.10
ごじじゅっぷん	5:10	4.8
ごじはん	five thirty	2.6, 4.1, 4.3
ごじゅう	fifty	1.1B, G, 1.2, 1.5, 1.6, 3.9
ごじゅうえん	fifty yen	1.9
ごじゅうごねん	fifty five years	1.3
ごじゅうごふん	fifty five minutes	4.1B
（ご）しゅっしん	where one is from	3.1B, 3.1, 3.2, 3.6, 3.7, 3.9, 3.10
ごじゅっぷん	fifty minutes	4.1B
（ご）しゅみ	hobby	3.1B, 3.1, 3.2, 3.6, 3.7, 3.9, 3.10
こせいてき(な)	an individual~	3.5, 3.8, 3.9
ごせん	five thousand	1.3, 1.5, 1.6,
ごせんえん	five thousand yen	1.9
こたえ	answer	3.10
ごちそうさま	thank you for the meal.	0.1.05G, 1.1, 1.6, 2.9A
ごちそうさまでした	thank you for the meal.	0.1.05G, 1.2, 1.6, 1.8, 2.9A
こちらは	this is	4.3
コップ	cup	4.6, 4.9, 4.10
ことし	this year	1.7
ことしもおげんきで	lit: Have a healthy and well spirited year.	1.6, 1.7, 1.9
ことしもどうぞよろしく	lit: I wish our cordial relationship to continue this year.	1.6
ことしもどうぞよろしくおねがいします	lit: please continue to be kind to me this year.	1.2, 1.7, 1.9

525

ごにん	five people	**2.1B**, G, 2.3, 2.6, 3.6, 3.7, 3.9, 4.1
ごねんせい	fifth grade	1.6
この	this	3.9, 4.7
このじかん	during this time	**3.11A**
ごはん	meal	**4.1B**, 4.8
コピー	copy	4.6, 4.9, 4.10
ごひゃく	five hundred	**1.1B**, G, 1.3, 1.5, 1.6
ごひゃくえん	five hundred yen	1.9
ごふん	five minutes	**4.1B**, 4.1 ,4.9
ごめん	I am sorry/excuse me (informal)	**0.1.10G**, 1.6, 2.9A
コメント	comments	2.6, 2.9A
ごめんなさい	I am sorry.	**0.1.10G**, 1.1, 1.2, 1.6, 1.8, 2.9A
ごめんね	I am sorry.	**0.1.10G**
ゴルフ	golf	1.6, 4.7
これ	this	1.1, 4.7
これからはきをつけてください		
	please be careful next time.	**0.1.10G**
これでおわりです	this is the end.	3.8
コロラド	Colorado	3.6, 4.6
こわい	fearful/awful	**3.11A**
こんげつ	this month	4.9
コンサート	concert	3.5, 4.2, 4.4, 4.6, 4.8, 4.10
コンサートホール	concert hall	**2.1B**, 4.1
コンテスト	contest	4.9
こんにちは	good afternoon/hello.	**0.1.03G**, **1.1B**, 1.1, 1.2, 1.6, 1.8, 3.2, 3.5, 3.6, 3.9, 4.3
こんばんは	good evening.	**0.1.03G**, **1.1B**, 1.1, 1.6, 1.8, 3.2, 4.3
コンピュータ	computer	**0.2.07G**, 1.2, 1.6, 1.8, **3.1B**, 3.9, **3.11A**
コンピュータルーム		
	computer room	**2.1B**, 2.6, 4.2
サーカス	circus	**0.1.03G**
サービス	service	4.7
サーブ	serve (in sports)	3.9
サーベー	survey	4.8
~さい	age, ~year(s) old	1.1, 1.2, 1.4, 1.5, 1.6
サイエンスフェア	science fair	2.1, 2.2, 2.4, 2.6, 4.9
サイダー	cider	2.6
サウジアラビア	Saudi Arabia	3.9
サウジアラビアじん		
	Saudi Arabian person	3.02
さえき ゆか	Saeki, Yuka (name of person)	3.8
さかい ゆうじ	Sakai, Yuji (name of person)	3.8
さかな	fish	**0.2.05G**
さき	first	4.9
さしみ	sashimi	3.6
さだ ひでき	Sada Hideki (name of person)	4.3
さっか	writer	**3.11A**
サッカー	soccer	1.4, G, 1.6, 1.7, **2.1B**, 2.4, 3.2, 3.8, 3.11
サッカーぶ	soccer team	**1.9A**, 3.11
さっぽろ	Sapporo	3.8
さとう けんじ	Satoh Kenji (name of person)	3.02
さとう ひろし	Satoh Hiroshi (name of person)	4.3
さどうぶ	tea ceremony club	**1.9A**
サム	Sam	1.2, 1.3, 1.4, 3.4
さむい	cold	**0.2.07G**, 1.6, **1.9A**
さむいですね	It's cold, isn't it?	**0.1.03G**, 1.6, **1.9A**
さむいね	It is a cold day, isn't it? (informal)	1.6
さむい（わ）ね	it's cold, isn't it? (informal)	**1.9A**
さようなら	good-bye.	**0.1.02G**, 1.1, 1.2, 1.6, 1.8, **1.9A**, 4.3, 4.10
さら	plate	4.6, 4.9, 4.10
サラダ	salad	**2.1B**, 2.6
さる	monkey	**0.2.09G**, 1.1, 1.4
さるどし	year of the monkey	1.4, 1.6, 1.7
さん	three	**1.1B**, G, 1.1, 1.2, 1.3, 1.5, 1.6, 3.9, 4.6
さんがつ	March	**2.1B**, G, 2.3, 2.6, 3.9
さんさい	three years old	1.2
さんじ	three o'clock	**2.1B**, G, 2.1, 2.2, 2.6, 4.4, 4.8, 4.10
さんじじゅっぷん	3:10	4.9
さんじっぷん／さんじゅっぷん		
	thirty minutes	4.1
さんじはん	three thirty	2.6
さんじゅう	thirty	**1.1B**, G, 1.2, 1.3, 1.5, 1.6
さんじゅういちにち		
	thirty first day of the month	**2.1B**, G, 2.3, 2.6
さんじゅうごふん	thiry five minutes	**4.1B**, 4.1
さんじゅうにち	thirtieth day of the month	**2.1B**, G, 2.3, 2.6
さんじゅっぷん	thirty minutes	**4.1B**
さんせい	approval, agreement	2.9A
さんぜん	three thousand	1.3, 1.5, 1.6
~さんですか	are you Mr./Ms etc.~?	**0.1.01G**
さんにん	three people	**2.1B**, G, 2.3, 2.6, 3.7, 3.9, 4.1
さんねん	three years/third year	3.9
さんねんせい	third grade	1.6
～さんはいますか	is so and so here?	**0.1.08G**
さんびゃく	three hundred	**1.1B**, G, 1.1, 1.3, 1.5, 1.6,
サンフランシスコ	San Francisco	**3.11A**, 4.6
サンプル	sample	4.10, **4.11A**
さんぷん	three minutes	4.9
さんぽします／さんぽする		
	go for a walk	**4.11A**
し	four	**1.1B**, G, 1.2, 1.3, 1.5, 1.6, 3.9
しあい	game	4.6, 4.9
シアトル	Seattle	**3.11A**, 4.6
シーツ	sheets	**0.1.04G**
（シーディー）CDプレイーヤー		
	CD player	4.6, 4.9
シート	sheet	3.10
シェーク	shake	2.7
ジェット	jet	2.7

ジェニー	Jenny	1.2, 1.3, 1.4
シカゴ	Chicago	0.1.03G, 3.11A, 4.6
しがつ	April	2.1B, G, 2.3, 2.6, 3.2, 3.9
じかん	time	2.1, 2.2, 2.3, 2.4, 2.5, 2.6, 3.2, 3.9, 4.8, 4.11
しごと	job/work	4.10, 4.11A
しずか	quiet	3.7
しずかにして	please be quiet. (informal) 1.9A
しずかにしてください		
	please be quiet.	1.9A, G
しち	seven	1.1B, G, 1.2, 1.5, 1.6, 3.9
しちがつ	July	2.1B, G, 2.3, 2.6, 3.5, 3.9
しちさい	seven years old	1.2
しちじ	seven o'clock	2.1B, G, 2.2, 2.6, 4,4, 4.8
しちじさんじゅっぷん		
	7:30	4.8
しちじはん	seven thirty	2.6, 4.4, 4.9
しちじゅう	seventy	1.1B, G, 1.2, 1.5, 1.6
しちせん	seven thousand	1.3, 1.5, 1.6,
しちにん	seven people	2.3, G, 2.6, 3.7, 3.9, 4.1
しちねんせい	seventh grade	1.6
じっさい	ten years old	1.2
じっぷん／じゅっぷん		
	ten minutes	4.1, 4.8
しつもん	question	0.2.07G, 3.10, 4,8
しつもんがありますか		
	do you have any questions?	
		1.9A, G
しつもんがあるか	do you have any questions? (informal)
		1.9A
しつれい	Excuse me./I'm sorry.	0.1.08G, 1.6, 1.9A, 2.9A,
しつれいします	Excuse me./Good bye.	0.1.02G, 1.2, 1.6, 1.8, 1.9A, 2.9A
じてんしゃ	bicycle	3.9
シニア	senior	3.3
じぶん	self	4.8
します／する	to do	0.2.10G, 3.5, 4.1B, 4.2, 4.4, 4.5, 4.6, 4.7, 4.8, 4.9, 4.10
しまの	Shimano (name of person)	
		1.4
しみず	Shimizu (name of person)	
		3.3
ジム	gymnasium	2.1B, 2.2, 2.4, 2.6, 4.2, 4.6
じむしつ	administration office	2.6
じゃ	well then	1.4, 1.6, 1.8, 2.1B, 2,2, 2.3, 2.4, 2.5, 2.8, 3.1B, 3.2, 3.3, 3.6,3.9, 4.3, 4.4, 4.10
じゃ	See you	0.1.02G, 1.6, 1.9A
シャーベット	sherbert	2.6, 2.9A
～じゃありません	it is not~.	1.5, 3.2, 3.6, 3.9
しゃかい	social studies	3.1B, 3.1, 3.9
しゃこうてき	sociable	3.11A
しゃしんぶ	photo club	1.9A, 3.11
ジャズ	jazz	2.1B, 2.5, 3.8
シャツ	shirt	0.1.08G
ジャネット	Janet	2.3
ジャパニーズナイト		
	Japanese night	2.2, 2,6

ジャパニーズパーティー		
	Japanese party	2.5
ジャパニーズフェア		
	Japanese fair	2.1
じゃ、また	See you	0.1.02G, 1.2, 1.6, 1.8, 1.9A
シャワーをあびます／シャワーをあびる		
	to take a shower	4.11A
しゅう	week	4.10, 4.11A
じゅう	ten	1.1B, G, 1.2, 1.5, 1.6, 3.9
じゅういちじに	at eleven o'clock	4.4
じゅういち	eleven	1.1B, G, 1.1, 1.2, 1.5, 1.6
じゅういちがつ	November	2.1B, G, 2.3, 2.6
じゅういちじ	eleven o'clock	2.1B, G, 2.2 , 2.6, 4.8
じゅういちじごじゅっぷん		
	eleven fifty	4.9
じゅういちじはん	eleven thirty	2.6, 4.1, 4.8
じゅういちにち	eleventh day of the month	
		2.1B, G, 2.1, 2.3, 2.6, 4.1, 4.9
じゅういちねんせい		
	eleventh grader	1.6, 3.2, 3.3
じゅういっさい	eleven years old	1.2
じゅういっぷん	eleven minutes	4.9
じゅうえん	ten yen	1.9
じゅうがつ	October	2.1B, G, 2.3, 2.6, 4.3
じゅうきゅう	nineteen	1.1B, G, 1.2, 1.5, 1.6,
じゅうきゅうさい	nineteen years old	1.2
じゅうく	ninteen	1.1B, G, 1.2, 1.5, 1.6,
じゅうくにち	nineteenth day of the month	
		2.1B, G, 2.3, 2.6,
じゅうご	fifteen	1.1B, G, 1.2, 1.5, 1.6,
じゅうごさい	fifteen years old	1.2, 3.8
じゅうごにち	fifteenth day of the month	
		2.1B, G, 2.3, 2.6
じゅうごふん	fifteen minutes	4.1B, 4.1
じゅうさん	thirteen	1.1B, G, 1.2, 1.5, 1.6,
じゅうさんさい	thirteen years old	1.2
じゅうさんにち	thirteenth day of the month	
		2.1B, G, 2.1, 2.3, 2.6, 3.2, 4.1, 4.10
じゅうさんばん	number 13	3.9
じゅうし	fourteen	1.1B, G, 1.2, 1.5, 1.6,
じゅうじ	ten o'clock	2.1B, G, 2.2, 2.6, 4.8, 4.10
じゅうしち	seventeen	1.1B, G, 1.2, 1.5, 1.6,
じゅうしちさい	seventeen years old	1.2
じゅうしちにち	seventeenth day of the month	
		2.1B, G, 2.1, 2.3, 2.6
じゅうじに	at ten o'clock	4.4
じゅうじはん	ten thirty	2.6
じゅうしょ	address	3.8
じゅうじよんじゅうごふん		
	10:45	4.9
しゅうしん	from where one is from	3.9
ジュース	juice	1.9A, 2.2, 2.4, 2.6, 3.2
じゅうどう	judo	1.6, 3.2, 3.3, 4.1B, 4.8, 4.11A
じゅうどうのせんせい		
	judo instructor	1.5, 4.5
じゅうどうぶ	Judo club	3.11
じゅうなな	seventeen	1.1B, G, 1.2, 1.5, 1.6

じゅうななさい	seventeen years old	1.2, 3.11
じゅうに	twelve	**1.1B**, G, 1.2, 1.5, 1.6
じゅうにがつ	December	**2.1B**, G, 2.1, 2.3, 2.6
じゅうにさい	twelve years old	**1.2**
じゅうにじ	twelve o'clock	**2.1B**, G, 2.2, 2.6, 4.4, 4.10
じゅうにじごじゅうごふん	12:55	**4.9**
じゅうにじはん	twelve thirty	2.6, 4.10
じゅうにち	twelfth day of the month	
		2.1B, G, 2.1, 2.3, 2.6, 4.1
じゅうににん	twelve people	**2.6**
じゅうにねん	twelve years	**1.3**
じゅうにねんせい	twelveth grader	1.6, 3.3, 3.8
じゅうにん	ten people	2.3, 2.6, 3.7, 3.9, 4.1
じゅうねんせい	tenth grader	1.6, 3.2, 3.3, 3.8
じゅうはち	eighteen	**1.1B**, G, 1.2, 1.5, 1.6
じゅうはっさい	eighteen years old	**1.2**
じゅうはちにち	eighteenth day of the month	
		2.1B, G, 2.3, 2.6
じゅうよう	important	3.5, 3.9
じゅうよっか	fourteenth day of the month	
		2.1B, G, 2.1, 2.3, 2.6
じゅうよん	fourteen	**1.1B**, G, 1.2, 1.5, 1.6
じゅうよんさい	fourteen years old	1.2, 3.8
じゅうろく	sixteen	**1.1B**, G, 1.2, 1.5, 1.6, 3.6
じゅうろくさい	sixteen years old	**1.2**
じゅうろくにち	sixteenth day of the month	
		2.1B, G, 2.3, 2.6, 3.2
じゅく	cram school	**3.9**
しゅくだい	homework	**0.2.07G**, 3.1B. 3.9. 4.1B. 4.4, 4.7, 4.8
じゅくのあと	after cram school	**3.11A**
しゅしょう	prime minister	**3.11A**
じゅっさい	ten years old	**1.2**
しゅっしん	where one is from	3.6, 3.8, 3.9, 3.11, 4.1
しゅっせきをとります	I will take attendance.	**0.1.08G**
じゅっぷん	ten minutes	**4.1B**
しゅみ	hobby	3.6, 3.8, 3.9, 4.1
しょうがく	elementary school	**1.1B**
しょうがつ	new year	**1.2**
しょうがっこう	elementary school	1.1, 1.6
しょうじき	honest	3.8, 3.9, 3.11A
しょうぼうしゃ	fire engine	**1.9A**
しょうわ	Showa era	**1.6**
ショーツ	shorts	**0.1.08G**
ジョーンズ	Jones	**3.02**
しょき	secretary	**2.4**
しょき	scribe	**2.6**
しょくどう	cafeteria	3.9, 3.11A
ショッピングセンター	shopping center	2.6, 2.9A
ショッピングモール	shopping mall	2.4, 2.6
しょどうぶ	calligraphy club	**3.11**
じょゆう	actress	**3.11A**
ジョン	John	4.3, 4.7

ジョン ケネディー	John Kennedy	**0.2.05G**
ジョン ホワイトハウス	John Whitehouse	**3.6**
しろ	white	**1.9A**, G, 3.1B, 3.1, 3.9
しろい	a white~	**3.6**
～じん	~person (nationality)	**3.9**
じんじゃ	Shinto shrine	**1.2**
しんせつ	kind	**3.11A**
しんねんおめでとうございます	lit: We are happy to have the new year.	
		1.2
しんぶんぶ	newspaper club	1.9A, 3.11
しんぶんをよみます/しんぶんをよむ	read a newspaper	**4.11A**
すい	Wed.	**4.7**
すいえい	swimming	**3.8**
すいえいぶ	swimming club	**3.11**
スイス	Switzerland	**0.1.03G**
すいません	I am sorry.	**0.1.10G**, 1.6, 2.4, 2.9A
すいみんのじかん	sleep time	**4.11A**
すいようび	Wednesday	**2.1B**, G, 2.1, 2.2, 2.4, 2.6, 3.4, 4.2, 4.4, 4.7, 4.9, 4.10
すうがく	mathematics	**0.2.03G**, 3.1B, 3.1, 3.2, 3.5, 3.8, 3.9, 4.2
スーパー	supermarket	**3.11A**
スープ	soup	**2.1B**, 2.6
スキー	ski	1.7, 1.6. 3.6, 3.9, 4.1B
スキートーナメント	ski tournament	**0.2.04G**, 2.3
すき (な)	like	**0.2.09G**, 3.1, 3.2, 3.5, 3.6, 3.7, 3.8, 3.9, 3.10, 3.11A, 4.1, 4.9
すきやき	sukiyaki	2.4, 2.6, 2.9, 2.9A
スクリーン	screen	4.6, 4.9
スケート	skating	**1.6**
スケジュール	schedule	**0.1.08G**, 3.5, 4.4, 4.8, 4.10, 4.11A
すし	sushi	**0.2.03G**, 2.4, 2.6, 2.9, 2.9 A 3.2, 3.5, 3.6, 4.2, 4.4, 4.6
すしのみせ	sushi shop	**2.9A**
すしはる	Sushi haru (name of restaurant)	
		2.6
すずき	Suzuki (name of person) 3.3	
すずき よしお	Yoshio Suzuki (name of person)	
		1.2
ステーキ	steak	**2.1B**, 2.4, 2.6,
ステージ	stage	4.6, 4.9
すてき(な)	attractive	**0.2.09G**, 3.1B, 3.5, 3.8, 3.9
スノーフェスティバル	snow festival	**0.2.04G**, 2.3
スパゲッティー	spaghetti	3.5, 4.2, 4.4, 4.6
スピーカー	speaker	4.6, 4.9, 4.10
スピーチコンテスト	speech contest	2.2, 2.3, 2.6, 4.9
スペイン	Spain	**3.9**
スペインご	Spanish language	**3.1B**, 3.1, 3.2, 3.5
スペインじん	Spanish person	**3.2**

スポーツ	sports	**1.4**, G, 2.4, 3.1B, 3.2, 3.3, 3.5, 3.7, 3.8, 3.9, 3.10, 4.8
スポーツデー	sports day	**0.2.04G**, 2.3
スポーツせんしゅ	sports figure	**3.11A**
すまい	residence	**3.6**, 3.11
すまない	I am sorry/excuse me. (informal) **1.6**	
すまないが	excuse me but (informal) **1.6**	
すみ	Indian ink	**1.2**
すみません	I am sorry./excuse me.	**0.1.10G**, 1.2, 1.6, 1.8, 2.4, 3.2, 4.3
すみませんが	excuse me but	**1.6**, 4.3
すもう	sumo	**1.6**, 4.9, 4.11A
すもうのせんせい	sumo master	**4.5**
すもうぶ	sumo club	**3.11**
すわって	please sit down (informal) **1.9A**	
すわってください	please sit down	**1.9A**, G
せいかく	personality	**3.1B**, 3.8
せいじ	politics	**3.1B**, 3.1, 3.5, 3.9
せいじか	politician	**3.11A**
せいと	student	**0.2.04G**, 4.8, 4.9
せいとかい	student council	**4.9**
せいとかいちょう	chair of student council	**3.11A**
せいぶつ	biology	**3.1B**, 3.1, 3.5, 3.9
セーター	sweater	**0.1.04G**
せきにんかんのある（ひと）	a (person) with a sense of responsibility **3.11A**	
セット	set	**0.1.04G**, 4.1
ゼロ	zero	**1.1B**, G, 1.2, 1.3, 1.5
ゼロさい	zero years old	**1.2**
せん	one thousand	**1.1B**, G, 1.1, 1.3, 1.5, 1.6
ぜん	zen	**4.9**, 4.10, 4.11A
せんえん	one thousand yen	**1.9**
せんきゅうひゃくきゅうじゅうねん 1990		**1.3**
せんきゅうひゃくななじゅうねん 1970		**1.3**
せんきゅうひゃくはちじゅうねん 1980		**1.3**
せんせい	teacher	**0.2.09G**, 1.2, 1.4, 1.5, 1.6, 3.1, 3.7, 3.8, 3.9, 4.1, 4.5, 4.9
ぜんぜん	never	**3.5**, 4.2, 4.9
せんたくをします／せんたくをする	do laundry	**4.11A**
セント	cent	**1.5**, 1.6
セントラルパーク	Central Park	**3.11A**
ぜんぶ	all	**4.7**
そう	that is correct, I see. (informal) **1.6**, 2,4	
ぞう	elephant	**0.2.03G**
そうか	I see. (with agreeable tone) (informal) **1.9A**	
そうしましょう	let's do that.	**4.2**
そうじゃありません	no, it is not	**4.1**

そうじをします／そうじをする	clean up	**4.10**, 4.11A
そうだ（わ）ね	that's correct. (informal) **1.9A**	
そうです	yes, it is. that is correct.	**1.2**, 1.3, 1.4, 1.6, 4.1, 4.3
そうですか	I see (with agreeable tone)/oh really.	**1.9A**, 2.4, 4.3
そうですね	let's see.	**3.5**, 4.2, 4.4
そうですね	yes. indeed./that is right.	**0.1.03G**, 1.6, 1.9A, 2.2
そうね	that is correct. (emphasis)	**1.6**
ソース	sauce	**0.1.03G**
ソーセージ	sausage	**0.1.03G**, 2.6, 2.9A
ソーダ	soda	**1.7**, 2.1B, 2.2, 2.6
ソックス	socks	**0.1.04G**
そっと	carefully	**0.2.04G**
そと	outside	**3.4**
その	that	**4.7**
そば	buck wheat noodles	**2.4**, 2.6, 2.9A, 2.9
そふ	grandfather	**3.11A**
そぼ	grandmother	**3.11A**
それから	also/then	**2.2**, 3.9, 4.10
それじゃ、また	see you later.	**1.9A**
それとも	or	**2.2**, 2.5, 2.8, 4.4
タイ	Thailand	**3.9**
たいいく	physical education	**0.2.04G**, 3.1B, 3.1, 3.5, 3.9
たいいくかん	gynnasium	**4.9**
だいいち	number one	**1.6**
だいがく	college	**1.9A**, 3.2, 3.9
だいがくいん	graduate school	**1.9A**
だいさん	number three	**3.8**
たいしょう	Taisho era	**1.3**, 1.6
だいすき	like a lot	**3.9**, 3.11
たいそう	physical exercise	**3.5**
だいとうりょう	president	**3.11A**
だいに	number two	**3.8**
たいふう	typhoon	**3.11A**
たいへん	difficult/serious	**3.5**
たいへんよくできました	very well done	**0.1.10G**
タイムズスクエア	Times Square	**3.11A**
タイヤ	tire	**0.1.08G**
たかい	high/expensive	**3.7**
たかはし	Takahashi (name of person) **3.3**	
たかはら　えり	Takahara, Eri (name of person) **3.9**	
たかやま　やすお	Takayama, Yasuo (name of person) **3.9**	
だから	therefore	**3.5**, 3.6, 3.9, 3.11, 4.9
タクシー	taxi	**3.1B**, 3.1, 3.9
たこ	octopus	**3.6**
たす	plus/add	**1.6**, 4.6
ただ	free (price)	**2.6**, 4.11
ただいま	I'm home./I'm back.	**0.1.06G**, 1.9A, 4.3
たつ	dragon	**1.4**
たっきゅうぶ	table tennis club	**3.11**

たって	please stand up. (informal)	**1.9A**
たってください	please stand up.	**1.9A, G, 2.1**
たつどし	year of the dragon	**1.4, 1.6, 1.7**
たてます／たてる	to build	**4.6, 4.9**
たなか	Tanaka (name of person)	**4.1**
たなか　さちこ	Sachiko Tanaka (name of person)	**1.2**
たなかさん	Tanaka (name of person)	**1.5, 4.7**
たなか　まき	Tanaka Maki (name of person)	**3.02**
～（だ）ね	it is~isn't it? (informal)	**1.6**
たのしい	enjoyable	**3.5**
たべましょう	let's eat	**4.2**
たべましょうか	let's eat~	**3.5**
たべます／たべる	to eat	**4.1B, 4.1, 4.2, 4.4, 4.6, 4.7 4.8**
たべません	will not eat	**4.2**
たべもの	food	**2.1, 2.4, 2.5, 2.6, 2.7, 2.9A, 3.2, 3.5, 3.8**
たむら　なお	Tamura, Nao (name of person)	**3.9**
ため	purpose	**4.9, 4.10**
たよりになる	reliable	**3.11A**
ダリル	Daryl	**1.2, 1.3, 1.4, 3.4,**
だれ	who	**0.2.05G, 0.2.09G, 0.2.10G, 3.1, 3.4, 3.6, 3,7, 3.9, 3.10, 4.8**
タレントショー	talent show	**2.2, 4.9**
たんご	vocabulary	**4.9**
たんじょうび	birthday	**3.01B, 3.2, 3.3, 3.6, 3.8, 3.9, 3.10, 4.6**
ダンス	dance	**1.7, 2.1B, 2.2., 2.3, 2.4, 2.5, 2.6, 3.5, 3.6, 4.2. 4.4, 4.6, 4.7, 4.8, 4.9, 4.10**
ダンスのれんしゅう	dance practice	**4.6**
ダンスパーティー	dance party	**2.2, 4.9**
たんにんのせんせい	homeroom teacher	**3.1B, 3.1, 3.2, 3.3, 3.6, 3.9, 3.10,**
たんぼ	rice paddy	**4.5**
だんゆう	actor	**3.11A**
チーズケーキ	cheese cake	**2.6, 2.9A**
チェス	chess	**2.7**
チェスクラブ	chess team	**1.9A**
ちがいます／ちがう	incorrect	**1.4, 4.1 B, 4.9**
ちかてつ	subway	**3.1B, 3.1, 3.9**
チキン	chickin	**0.2.06G, 1.1, 2.1B, 2.5, 2.6**
チケット	ticket	**4.6**
ちこくします/ちこくする	come late	**4.11A**
ちこくです	she or he is late.	**0.1.08G**
ちず	map	**3.11A**
ちち	father	**3.1, 3.4, 3.5, 3.6, 3.9, 3.11**
ちゃいろ	brown	**1.9A, G, 3.9**
ちゃくせき	sit down	**0.1.08G**
ちゃどうぶ	tea ceremony club	**3.11**
ちゃのゆ	tea ceremony	**4.11A**
ちゅういち	seventh grade	**3.9**
ちゅうがく	middle school	**1.1B, 3.2**
ちゅうがっこう	middle school	**1.1, 1.6**
ちゅうかりょうり	Chinese cousine	**2.9A**
ちゅうごく	China	**3.9**
ちゅうごくご	Chinese language	**3.1B, 3.2, 3.5**
ちゅうごくじん	Chinese person	**3.1B, 3.2**
ちゅうさん	nineth grade	**3.9**
ちゅうに	seventh grade	**3.1B, 3.9**
チョーク	chalk	**4.6, 4.9**
ちょっと	a little	**2.2, 4.8, 4.10**
ちょっとまって	please wait a moment. (informal)	**1.9A, G**
ちょっとまってください	wait a moment, please.	**0.1.07G, 1.9A, 4.3, 4.10**
ちらし	flyer	**4.10, 4.11A**
ツアー	tour	**2.7**
ツァー	Tsar	**2.7**
ついたち	first day of the month	**1.7, 2.1B, 2.3, 2.6, 3.2, 3.5, 3.9, 4.1, 4.2, 4.4. 4.7, 4.9, 4.10**
ツェッペリン	Zeppelin	**2.7**
つき	moon	**3.9, 4.9**
つくえ	desk	**0.2.04G, 3.11A, 4.5, 4.6, 4.9**
つくります／つくる	to make	**4.6, 4.8, 4.9**
つだ　うめこ	Umeko Tsuda (name of person)	**1.1B, 1.3**
つまらない	boring	**3.5**
つめたい	cold	**3.11A**
て	hand	**0.2.04G**
で	by	**3.1, 3.6, 3.9, 3.11,4.7 See. p393-395**
で	at	**0.2.10G, 4.6, 4,7 See. p393-395**
ティーンエージャー	teenager	**4.8**
ディスク	disk	**2.7**
ディー-ジェー(DJ)	disk jokey	**4.9**
ティラミス	teramisu	**2.6, 2.9A**
デートをします／デートをする	date	**4.11A**
テープ	tape	**4.9**
テーブル	table	**3.11A, 4.9, 4.10**
てがみ	letter	**4.1B, 4.7, 4.9**
テキサス	Texas	**0.1.04G, 4.6**
デザート	dessert	**2.4, 2.6, 2.7, 2.9A**
～です	is ~	**0.1.01G**
～ですか	[Be~]~?	**1.6**
てずか　おさむ	Osamu Tezuka (name of person)	**1.1B, 1.3**
～ですね	it is~isn't it?	**1.6**

テニス	tennis	1.6, 2.1B, 3.2, 3.5, 3.6, 3.8, 3.9, 3.11,4.1, 4.3
テニスぶ	tennis club	3.11
では	bye	1.9A
デパート	department store	4.11A
でも	however	3.5, 3.6, 3.9
デモンストレーション	demonstration	4.11A
デモンストレーションします／デモンストレーションする	demonstrate	4.11A
テューバ	tuba	2.7
デュエット	duet	2.7
テレビ	television	3.9, 4.1B, 4.4, 4.7, 4.9
テレビはいゆう	TV actor, actress	3.11A
テレビのアナウンサー	TV announcer	3.11A
てをあげてください	please raise your hand.	2.1, 2.3
てんき	weather	1.1, 1.2, 1.8, 1.9A, 3.11A
でんき	electricity	4.9
でんしゃ	train	3.01B, 3.1, 3.4, 3.6, 3.9, 4.1
でんとう	tradition	4.5
でんとうげいじゅつ	traditional art	4.9
デンバー	Denver	3.11A
てんぷら	tempura	2.4, 2.6. 2.9A, 2.9
でんわ	telephone	0.2.09G,1.1B, 1.3, 1.4, 1.5, 1.6, 2.2, 3.7, 4.3, 4.6, 4.10
でんわしてください	please call me	4.3
でんわします／する	to telephone	4.8
でんわばんごう	telephone number	1.6, 1,8, 2.2 3.2 3.8, 4.10
と	and	3.6, 4.5. 4.7. 4.9, 4.10 See. p393-395
と	with/and	0.2.10G, 3.1 3.9, 3.11, 4.7, See. p393-395
ど	Sat.	4.7
ドア	door	3.11A
ドイツ	Germany	3.9
ドイツご	German language	3.5, 3.6
ドイツじん	German person	3.6
トイレ	restroom	2.6
どういう	what kind	3.7, 3.9
どういういみですか	what does that mean?	3.1B, 3.3
どういたしまして	you are welcome.	1.2, 1.6, 1.8
トゥールーズ	Toulouse	2.7
とうきょう	Tokyo	3.2, 3.8
どうぐ	equipment	4.5, 4.9
ドゥシャンベ	Dushanbe	2.7
どうぞ	please	1.1B, 1.1, 1.2
どうぞよろしく	nice to meet you.	0.1.01G, 1.1B, 1.2, 3.6. 3.9
どうぞよろしくおねがいします	please look with favor upon me.	1.6, G, 3.6, 3.9
どうも	thanks	0.1.04G, 2.9A
どうもありがとう	thank you very much.	0.1.04G, 2.2, 2.9A, 4.3

（どうも）ありがとうございました	thank you very much.	0.1.04G
（どうも）ありがとうございます	thank you very much.	0.1.04G, 0.1.10G, 2.2, 2.9A, 4.10
どうもすいません	I am sorry.	0.1.10G
どうもすみません	I am sorry.	0.1.10G, 2.9A, 3.5, 4.2, 4.3, 4.8
とお	ten (quantity)	2.9A, G,4.1B, 4.5
とおい	far	4.5
とおか	tenth day of the month	0.2.10G,G, 2.1B 2.1, 2.3, 2.6, 2.7, 3.2, 3.9, 4.1, 4.3, 4.9
ドーナツ	donut	0.1.05G
とき	time	3.9
ときどき	sometimes	4.1B, 3.5, 3.11A, 3.9, 4.2, 4.9
とくい	forte	3.5, 3.7, 3.9
とくちょう	characteristics	3.1B
とけい	watch	4.11A
どこ	where	0.2.10G, 2.1B, 2.2, 2.5, 2.6, 2.8, 3.1B, 3.2, 3.4 3.6, 3.7, 3.9, 3.11A, 4.2, 4.4
とし	age	3.6, 3.8, 4.9
とし／どし	year (animal)	1.5
としょかん	library	2.2, 3.2, 2.6, 3.2, 3.5, 4.2, 4.4, 4.7, 4.8
としょかんいん	librarian	3.11A
としょしつ	library	2.1B
どちら	which (two items)	2.1B, 2.2, 2.4, 2.5 2.6, 2.8, 3.2, 3.8
どちら	where (formal)	3.1B, 3.1, 3.6, 3.7, 3.9, 3.10
どちらがいいですか	which would you prefer? (two items) 2.6, 2.8	
どちらでも	I accept whatever you suggest (informal) 2.6	
どちらでもいいです	I accept whatever you suggest. 2.4, 2.5, 2.6	
どっち	which (two items)	2.4, 2.5
どっちがいい	which one is better? (informal) 2.6	
どっちでもいい	I accept whatever you suggest. 2.5	
どなた	who	3.6, 4.8, 4.10
どなたですか	who is this?	4.3
トピック	topic	2.1B, 2.3, 2.5
トマトソース	tomato sauce	2.6, 2.9A
トム	Tom	3.7, 4.7
ともだち	friend	3.4, 3.8, 3.9, 3.11A, 4.6, 4.9
ともだちにあいます／ともだちにあう	meet a friend	4.11A
どようび	Saturday	0.2.08G, 2.1, 2.2, 2.3, 2.4, 2.6, 3.5, 4.2, 4.3, 4.4, 4.7, 4.9
とら	tiger	0.2.09G, 1.4
とらどし	year of the tiger	1.4, 1.6, 1.7
ドラフト	draft	4.10, 4.11A
ドラマクラブ	drama club	1.4, 1.6, 3.3

にじゅうさん	twenty three	**1.1B**, G, 1.2
にじゅうさんにち	twenty third day of the month	
		2.1B, G, 2.3, 2.6, 3.9. 4.6
にじゅうし	twenty four	**1.1B**, G, 1.2
にじゅうしち	twenty seven	**1.1B**, G, 1.2
にじゅうしちにち	twenty seventh day of the month	
		2.1B, G, 2.3, 2.6, 4.6
にじゅうなな	twenty seven	**1.1B**, G
にじゅうに	twenty two	**1.1B**, G, 1.2
にじゅうににち	twenty second day of the month	
		2.1B, G, 2.3, 2.6, 4.6, 4.9
にじゅうねん	twenty years	**1.3**
にじゅうはち	twenty eight	**1.1B**, G, 1.2
にじゅうはちにち	twenty eighth day of the month	
		2.1B, G, 2.3, 2.6
にじゅうよっか	twenty fourth day of the month	
		2.1B, G, 2.3, 2.6, 4.6
にじゅうよん	twenty four	**1.1B**, G, 1.2
にじゅうろく	twenty six	**1.1B**, G, 1.2
にじゅうろくにち	twenty sixth day of the month	
		2.1B, G, 2.3, 2.6, 4.6
にじゅっぷん	twenty minutes	**4.1B**
にせん	two thousand	**1.1**, 1.3, 1.5, 1.7
にせんいちねん	year 2001	**1.7**
にせんじゅうねん	year 2010	**1.3**
にせんねん	year 2000	**1.3**, 1.7, 1.9
にち	Sun.	**4.7**
～にち	~day of the month	**0.2.04G**
にちようび	Sunday	**2.1B**, G, 2.1, 2.2, 2.4, 2.6, 3.5, 3.9. 4.2, 4.3, 4.4., 4.9
ニックネーム	nick name	**3.9**
にねん	two years/second year	**3.9**
にねんせい	second grade	**1.6**
にばん	number 2	**3.9**
にひゃく	two hundred	**1.1B**, G, 1.3, 1.5, 1.6
にふん	two minutes	**4.8**, 4.9
にほん	Japan	**3.2**, 3.3, 3.8, 3.9, 4.5, 4.7, 4.8, 4.9, 4.10, 4.11
にほんご	Japanese language	**3.1B**, 3.1, 3.2, 3.5, 3.7, 3.8, 3.9, 4.1, 4.2, 4.7, 4.8, 4.9
にほんじん	Japanese person	**3.1B**, 3.2, 4.7
にほんのたべもの	Japanese food	**2.9**
にほんりょうり	Japanese cooking	**4.9**
にほんりょうりのせんせい		
	Japanese cooking mater	**4.5**
ニュージーランド	New Zealand	**3.9**
ニュージャージー	New Jersey	**3.6**
ニューヘブンこうこう		
	New Haven High School	**3.6**, 4.3
ニューヨーク	New York	**3.3**, 3.11A, 4.7, 4.9
ねこ	cat	**0.2.05G**, 1.1, 4.1
ねずみどし	year of the rat	**1.4**, 1.6, 1.7
ねだん	price	**2.2**, 2.6
ネット	net	**0.1.05G**, 4.6 4.8
ねどし	year of the rat	**1.4**, 1.6 1.7
ねます／ねる	to sleep	**4.1B**, 4.1, 4.2, 4.4, 4.7, 4.8
ネルソンマンデラ	Nelson Mandela	**0.2.05G**
～ねんうまれ	born in year~	**1.1B**, 1.3 1.4, 1.6, 1.8

ねんがじょう	New Year's card	**1.2**, 1.7, 1.9
～ねんせい	grade year	**1.1B**, 1.1, 1.3, 1.4, 1.5, 1.6,
～のいみはなんですか		
	what is the meaning of~	
		3.3
のう	noh (Japanese theater)	
		4.9, 4.10, 4.11A
ノート	note	**0.1.05G**, 3.11A, 4.1
～のことですが	I am calling about~	**4.3**, 4.8, 4.11
～のためです	for the sake of~	**4.6**, 4.9
のみます／のむ	to drink	**4.1B**, 4.2, 4.9
のみもの	drinks	**2.1**, 2.4, 2.5, 2.6, 2.7, 2.9A, 3.2, 4.9
のりもの	vehicle	**3.01B**
は	teeth	**4.8**
は	equals	**1.3**, 4.6.
は	topic particle (wa)	**4.7**, See. p393-395
バーイ	bye	**0.1.02G**
パーティー	party	**0.2.04G**, 2.1B, 2,2, 2.3, 2.4, 2.5, 2.6, 2.7, 3.2, 3.4, 4.2, 4.3, 4.4, 4.6, 4.7
ハードディスク	hard disk	**1.4**, 1.6
ハートフォード	Hartford	**3.11A**
バーモント	Vermont	**3.11**
はい	yes	**1.2**, 1.3, 1.4, 1.6, 3.8, 4.2
はい	please (informal)	**1.6**, 2.9A
はい、ありがとうございます		
	yes, thank you	**1.1**, 1.2, 1.6
はい、あります	yes, I have	**1.9A**, G
はい、いただきます		
	yes, I will take it	**0.1.05G**, 1.6, 1.8, 2.9A
はい、います	yes, she is here	**4.3**
はい、おかげさまで		
	Yes, thank you.]	**0.1.06G**, 2.9A
バイオリン	violin	**2.7**
はい、がんばります		
	Yes, I will do my best	**0.1.10G**
はい、げんきです	I am fine.	**2.9A**
はい、すみません	I am sorry/thank you.	**1.6**, 1.8
はい、そうしましょう		
	yes, let do that.	**3.5**
はい、そうです	yes, I am./ Yes, that's correct.	
		0.1.01G, 1.4, 1.5, 1.8, 3.1B, 3.2, 3.3, 4.3
はい、たべましょう		
	yes, let's eat.	**3.5**
バイト	byte	**1.3**, 1.5, 1.6
はい、どうぞ	here you are.	**0.1.04G**, 1.6, 1.8, 2.9A
パイナップル	pineapple	**1.9A**, 2.1B, 2.6
はい、なに	yes, what is it? (informal)	
		9A
はい、なんでしょう		
	yes, what is it?	**0.1.07G**, 2.4, 2.9A
バイバイ	bye	**0.1.02G** 1.9A, 4.3
はい、もういいです		
	yes, I am all set.	**0.1.09G**
はい、わかります	yes, I understand.	**0.1.09G**, 1.9A
はい、わたしです	yes, it is me.	**4.3**

～は～か	Be(is, am, are)~? (informal) 1.6	
ばけがく	chemistry	**3.01B**, 3.9
はじめ	introduction/beginning	**3.01B**, 3.6, 3.9, 4.1B, 4.1, 4.6, 4.9, 4.10
はじめまして	how do you do.	**0.1.01G**, 1.1B, 1.2, 1.6, 1.8, 3.6, 3.9
はじめましょう(～を)		
	let's begin.	**0.1.09G**, 2.1B, 2.1, 2.3, 2.4, 2.5, 2.6, 2.8, 3.8, 4.10
ばしょ	location/place	**0.2.10G**, 2.1, 2.2, 2.3, 2.4, 2.5, 2.6, 3.2, 3.7, 4.1, 4.11
バス	bus	**3.01B**, 3.1, 3.4, 3.9, 3.11, 4.9
バスケットぶ	basketball club	**3.11**
バスケットボール	basketball	**1.6**, 2.4, 3.5, 3.8, 4.1B, 4.2
パスタ	pasta	**2.4**, 2.6, 2.9A
パスタのみせ	pasta shop	**2.9A**
パソコン	personal computer	**0.2.07G**
～は～だ	~be(is, am, are)~.	**1.6**
はたち	twenty years old	**1.2**
はち	eight	**1.1B**, G, 1.1, 1.2, 1.3, 1.5, 1.6, 3.9
はちがつ	August	**2.1B**, G, 2.3, 2.6, 3.9, 4.7
はちじ	eight o'clock	**2.1B**, G, 2.1, 2.2, 2.6, 4.1, 4.4, 4.7, 4.8
はちじさんじゅうごふん		
	8:35	**4.9**
はちじはん	eight thirty	**2.6**
はちじはんに	at eight thirty	**4.4**
はちじゅう	eighty	**1.1B**, G, 1.2, 1.5, 1.6
はちにん	eight people	**2.3**, 2.6, 3.7, 4.1
はちねんせい	eighth grader	**1.6**, 3.1B
はちばん	number 8	**3.9**
はつか	twentieth day of the month **2.1B**, G, 2.3, 2.6, 4.9	
はっきりいって	please say it clearly (informal) **1.9A**	
はっきりいってください		
	please say it clearly	**1.9A**, G
バッグ	bag	**0.1.06G**
バックハンド	back hand (in sports)	**3.9**
はっさい	eight years old	**1.2**
はっせん	eight thousand	**1.3**, 1.5, 1.6
はっぴゃく	eight hundred	**1.1B**, G, 1.1, 1.3, 1.5, 1.6
はっぴょう	presentation	**4.1**, 4.8
はっぴょうします／する		
	to present	**4.9**
バッファロー	Buffalo	**3.11A**
はっぷん	eight minutes	**4.8**
はつもうでします／する		
	to visit shrines/temples at New Year's **1.2**	
～は～です	~be(is, am, are)~	**1.6**
～は～ですか	B(is, am, are)~?	**1.6**
バトミントンぶ	badminton club	**3.11**
はな	flower	**0.2.06G**
はな	nose	**4.1**
はなし	story	**4.11A**

はなします／はなす		
	to talk	**3.2**, 3.6, 3.9, 4.1, 4.9, 4.11A
はなしません	cannot speak	**3.6**, 3.9
バナナ	banana	**1.1**, 1.9A, 2.1B, 2.2, 2.5, 2.6, 3.1, 3.3, 3.9
はなみ	flower viewing	**0.1.07G**
はは	mother	**3.1**, 3.4, 3.5, 3.6, 3.9, 3.11
パパ	father	**3.4**
パブロ ピカソ	Pablo Picasso	**0.2.05G**
ハム	ham	**0.1.07G**, 0.2.06G
はやしコーチ	coach Hayashi	**3.3**
はやし(さん)	Hayashi (name of person) **1.5**, 3.3 3.9	
はやし りか	Hayashi Rika (name of person) **4.3**	
パリ	Paris	**3.01B**
はる	spring	**1.6**, 4.9
はるいちばん	spring storm	**G**
はるこ	Haruko (name of person) **3.3**	
はれ	sunny	**3.11A**, 4.1
バレーぶ	volleyball club	**3.11**
バレーボール	volleyball	**1.4**, 1.6, 3.5, 3.8, 4.2, 4.3, 4.4, 4.6
バレーボールぶ	volleyball team	**1.9A**
ハロウィーンパーティー		
	Halloween party	**0.2.04G**, 2.3
ハワイ	Hawaii	**4.6**
ばん	number	**3.9**
パン	bread	**1.7**, 3.2
バンクーバー	Vancouver	**3.11A**
ばんごう	number	**1.1B**, 1.3, 1.4, 1.5, 3.7
ばんごはん	dinner	**4.1B**, 4.9
はんたい	opposition	**2.9A**
パンチ	punch	**1.9A**, 2.1, 2.6, 4.4, 4.9
ハンバーガー	hamburger	**2.1B**, 2.2, 2.4, 2.5, 2.6, 2.9A, 2.9, 3.2, 3.6
ハンバーガーのみせ		
	hamburger shop	**2.9A**
ハンバーグ	hamburger	**4.4**, 4.6
ひ	fire	**4.9**
ひ	day	**2.6**
ひがしさん	Higashi (name of person) **4.7**	
ひく	subtract/minus	**1.6**, 4.6
ピクニック	picnic	**3.5**, 4.2
ひこうき	airplane	**3.1B**, 3.1, 3.9
ピザ	pizza	**2.1B**, 2.1, 2.2, 2.3, 2.4, 2.5, 2.6, 2.9A, 3.2, 3.6, 4.4, 4.6
ピザのみせ	pizza shop	**2.9A**
ピザバーガー	pizza burger	**2.6**, 2.9A
びじゅつ	art	**3.1B**, 3.1, 3.5, 3.8, 3.9
びじゅつぶ	art club	**1.9A**, 3.11
ひつじ	sheep	**1.4**
ひつじどし	year of the sheep	**1.4**, 1.6, 1.7, 1.8
ピッツバーグ	Pittsburg	**3.11A**
ひつよう	necessary	**4.1B**, 4.1, 4.5, 4.6, 4.8, 4.9, 4.10
ビデオ	video	**2.1**, 2.2, 2.4, 2.6

ビデオプレーヤー	video player	**4.6**, 4.9
ひと	person	**0.2.06G**, 0.2.08G, 0.2.09G, 2.3, 2.4, 2.6, 3.1B, 3.4, 3.5, 3.8, 3.9.4 .9, 4.10
ひとつ	one (quantity)	**2.9A**, 3.9, 4.1B, 4.5
ひとり	one person	**2.1B**, G, 2.6, 3.7, 3.9, 4.1B
ひにち	date	**2.3**, 2.5, 2.6, 4.11
ひゃく	one hundred	**1.1B**, G, 1.1, 1.2, 1.3, 1.5, 1.6, 4.7
ひゃくえん	one hundred yen	**1.9**
ぴゅうぴゅう	whistlingly	**4.5**
ヒュンジュン	HyunJun	**1.2**, 1.3, 1.4, 3.4
ひよう	expense	**4.11A**
びょういん	hospital	**4.11A**
ひょうか	evaluation	**4.1B**, 4.1, 4.6, 4.9, 4.10
ひらの	Hirano (name of person)	3.02
ひるごはん	lunch	**4.1B**, 4.4, 4.8
ひるやすみ	lunch time	**3.11A**, 3.9, 4.9
ひろしま	Hiroshima	**3.2**, 3.8
ひろみ	Hiromi (name of person)	3.3
ひろゆき	Hiroyuki (name of person)	3.3
ピン	pin	**4.9**
ピンク	pink	**1.9A**, 3.1B, 3.1, 3.9
ヒンズー	Hindu	**2.7**
ヒンズーご	Hindi	**3.02**
ピンポン	ping-pong	**1.7**
ファーストネーム	first name	**3.9**
ファーストレディー	first lady	**3.11A**
ファッション	fashion	**2.7**
フィラデルフィア	Philadelphia	**3.11A**
フィルム	film	**2.7**
ブーツ	boots	**0.1.06G**
プール	pool	**1.7**, 2.1B, 2.6, 4.2
フェスティバル	festival	**4.6**
フェタチーニ	fettuccini	**2.6**, 2.9A
フェルト	felt	**2.7**
フォーク	folk music	**3.8**
フォーク	fork	**0.1.10G**, 2.7
フォークダンス	folk dance	**2.2**, 2.6
フォーム	form	**3.8**
ふくおか	Fukuoka(prefecture)	**3.02**
ふたつ	two (quantity)	**2.9A**, G, 3.9, 4.1B, 4.5
ふたり	two people	**2.1B**, G, 2.3, 2.6, 3.7, 3.9, 4.1, 4.5
ふつか	second day of the month	**2.1B**, G. 2.1, 2.3, 2.6, 3.5, 3.9, 4.1, 4.2, 4.4, 4.7
フットボール	football	**1.6**, 2.2, 3.2, 3.5, 4.2, 4.4 4.6,
フットボールぶ	football team	**1.9A**
ぶつり	physics	**3.1B**, 3.1, 3.5, 3.9
ふで	brush	**1.2**
ふでばこ	pencil case	**3.11A**
ぶどう	grape	**1.9A**, 2.6 4.5, 4.8
ふね	ship	**0.2.06G**, 1.6, 3.1B, 3.1, 3.9
ふゆ	winter	**1.6**, 3.9, 4.1
フュージョン	fusion	**2.7**
フライドチキン	fried chicken	**4.2**, 2.6, 3.5, 4.4, 4.6,
ブラジル	Brazil	**3.9**
ブラジルじん	Brazilian person	**3.02**
ブラスバンドぶ	brass band club	**3.11**
フランス	France	**3.1B**, 3.1, 3.9
フランスご	French language	**3.1B**, 3.1, 3.2, 3.5,
フランスじん	French person	**3.02**
フランスりょうり	French cousine	**2.9A**
フリー	free	**4.11A**
プリパレーション	preparation	**4.11A**
ふります／ふる	to fall (rain)	**1.9A**
ふるい	old	**3.7**
フルーツ	fruits	**2.1**
ブルックリン	Brooklyn	**3.3**
プレゼンター	presenter	**4.11A**
プレゼンテーション	presentation	**4.11A**
プレゼンテーションします/プレゼンテーションする	present	**4.11A**
プレパレーションします/プレパレーションする	prepare for	**4.11A**
プロ	professional	**4.1B**
プログラム	program	**4.9**, 4.10
プロジェクト	project	**0.1.10G**, 4.1B, 4.10
プロポーザル	proposal	**4.10**, 4.11A
プロレス	professional wrestling	**0.2.08G**
ぶんか	culture	**4.11A**
ぶんげいぶ	literary club	**1.9A**
へ	to	**0.2.10G**, 4.7, See. p 393-395
ペアーをつくって	please make a pair. (informal)	**1.9A**
ペアーをつくってください	please make a pair.	**1.9A**, G
ヘアムース	hair mousse	**0.1.07G**
へいせい	Heisei era	**1.3**, 1.6
へいせいじゅうごねん	fifteenth year of the Heisei period	**1.7**
ベークセール	bake sale	**4.9**, 4.10
ベース	base	**0.1.06G**
ベーブルース	Babe Ruth	**0.2.05G**
ベッド	bed	**3.11A**
ペパロニ	pepperoni	**2.6**, 2.9A
へび	snake	**0.2.06G**, 1.4
へびどし	year of the snake	**1.4**, 1.6, 1.7
へや	room	**0.2.07G**, 0.2.08G
ペルー	Peru	**3.9**
ペルーじん	Peru person	**3.2**
ヘルメット	helmet	**4.6**, 4.9
ヘレン ケラー	Helen Keller	**0.2.05G**
べんきょう	study	**3.1B**, 3.8, 3.9, 3.11A, 4.1, 4.7, 4.8 ,4.9, 4.10
べんきょうします／べんきょうする	study	**3.6**, 3.8, 4.1B, 4.2, 4.4,
ペンパル	penpal	**3.8**

ほうかご	after school	3.9, 3.11A
ほうげん	dialects	2.3
ほうそうぶ	broad casting club	1.9A
ほうどうぶ	news club	3.11
ボート	boat	0.1.06G, 4.6,
ボール	ball	4.9
ボールペン	ball point pen	3.11A
ぼく	I/me (boys)	3.4, 3.9, 4.9
ポケベル	pager/beeper	0.2.08G
ほし	star	0.2.06G
ほし　まさこ	Masako Hoshi (name of person)	
		1.2
ポスター	poster	3.11A
ポスターセール	poster sale	0.2.04G, 2.3
ポスト	mail box	0.1.06G
ボストン	Boston	3.6, 3.11A, 4.6
ホゼ	Jose	1.2, 1.3, 1.4
ホッケー	hockey	1.6
ホッチキス	stapler	0.1.06G
ホットドッグ	hot dog	4.4, 4.6
ポテトチップ	potato chip(s)	2.6
ボトル	bottle	4.9, 4.10
ボランティア	volunteer	4.6, 4.8, 4.9
ボランティアします/ボランティアする		
	volunteer	4.11A
ポルトガル	Portugal	3.9
ポルトガルご	Portugese language	3.02
ポルトガルじん	Portugese person	3.02
ホワイトボード	white board	3.11A
ほん	book	0.2.09G, 3.7, 3.11A, 4.1B,
		4.4, 4.7, 4.8, 4.9
ポンド	pound	1.5, 1.6
ほんとう	true	1.1, 1.3
ほんねんもどうぞよろしくおねがいします		
	lit: please continue to be kind to me this year.	
		1.2
ほんをあけて	please open your book. (informal)	
		1.9A
ほんをあけてください		
	please open your book.	1.9A, G
ほんをとじて	please close your book. (informal)	
		1.9A
ほんをとじてください		
	please close your book.	1.9A, G
マークさん	Mark	1.4
マイアミ	Miami	3.11A
マイク	mike	0.1.07G, 4.6, 4.9, 4.10
まいにち	every day	4.1B, 3.5, 3.6, 3.9, 4.2, 4.9
まさあき	Masaaki (name of person)	
		4.3
まさお	Masao (name of person)	3.3
まさとし	Masatoshi (name of person)	
		3.3
マジソンスクエアガーデン		
	Madison Square Garden	
		4.11A
まじめな	a serious~	3.5
まちます/まつ	to wait	4.7

マッシュルーム	mushroom	2.6, 2.9A
マッチ	match	1.7
まっちゃアイス	green tea ice cream	2.6, 2.9A
まって	wait	4.8, 4.10
マット	mat, mattress	4.10
まつもと	Matsumoto (name of place)	
		4.1
まで	particle (until)	4.7, 4.8
まとめ	sum up	3.6
まなぶ	study	4.9
ママ	mother	3.4
まゆ	eye brow	0.2.08G, 4.1
まり	Mari (name of person)	3.3
マリリン モンロー		
	Marilyn Monroe	0.2.05G
まわしてください	please pass this around.]	0.1.09G
マンゴ	mango	1.9A, 2.6
マンハッタン	Manhattan	3.3, 3.11A
ミーティング	meeting	0.1.10G, 2.1B, 2.3, 2.4, 2.5,
		2.6, 4.11A
ミーティングします/する		
	to have a meeting	4.8
ミートソース	meat sauce	2.6, 2.9A
ミートローフ	meat loaf	3.5
みか	Mika (name of person)	3.3, 4.3
みがきます/みがく		
	to brush	4.8
みかん	mandarin orange, clementine	
		1.9A, 2.6
みず	water	0.2.07G, 2.6, 3.2, 4.2,
		4.4, 4.6, 4.9, 4.10
みせ	shop	2.6, 3.9, 3.11
みせます/みせる	to show	4.9
みた	saw	3.8
みっか	third day of the month	2.1B, G, 2.1, 2.3, 2.6, 3.5,
		3.9, 4.1, 4.2, 4.4, 4.5, 4.7, 4.9
みっつ	three (quantity)	2.9A, G, 4.1B, 4.5
ミット	mitt	0.1.07G
みて	please look. (informal)	1.9A
ミーティーング	meeting	2.3
みてください	please look.	1.9A, G
みどし	year of the snake	1.4, 1.6, 1.7
みどり	green	1.9A, G3.1B, 3.1, 3.2, 3.8, 3.9
ミドルタウンこうこう		
	Middle Town High School	
		3.2
みなみさん	Minami (name of person)	
		4.7
みます/みる	to watch	4.1B, 4.1, 4.2, 4.4, 4.6, 4.7,
		4.8, 4.9
みやざき	Miyazaki (prefecture)	3.02
みょうじ	last name	3.3, 3.9
ミルウォーキー	Milwaukee	0.1.10G
ミルク	milk	1.1, 1.9A, 2,6, 3.5, 3.8,
		4.2, 4.4, 4.6
みわ　かずひこ	Miwa, Kazuhiko (name of person)	
		3.8
みんなでいってください		
	please say it together.	1.9A, G

むいか	sixth day of the month	**2.1B**, G, 2.1, 2.3, 2.6, 3.5, 3.9, 4.1, 4.2, 4.4, 4.7, 4.10
むしあつい	hot and humid	**1.6**, 1.9A
むしあついですね	It's hot and humid, isn't it?	**0.1.03G**, 1.6, 1.9A,
むしあついね	It is a humid and hot day, isn't it? (informal) **1.6**	
むしあつい（わ）ね	it's hot and humid, isn't it? (informal) **1.9A**	
むずかしい	difficult	**3.5**
むっつ	six (quantity)	**2.9A**, G, 4.1B, 4.5
むらうえ　しゅんじ	Shunji Muraue (name of person) **1.6**	
むらさき	purple	**1.9A**, 3.01B, 3.9
め	eye	**0.2.07G**, 4.1
めいじ	Meiji era	**1.3**, 1.6
メーク	make-up	**0.1.07G**
メガ	megabyte	**1.3**, 1.4, 1.5, 1.6
メキシコ	Mexico	**3.2**, 3.9
メキシコじん	Mexican person	**3.1B**, 3.2
メディアルーム	media room	**2.1B**, 2.6
メニュー	menu	**2.6**, 2.9A
メモ	memo	**1.3**
メリー	Mary	**4.7**
メロン	melon	**1.9A**, 2.1, 2.2, 2.5, 2.6, 2.9A. 3.5, 4.2
も	too	**1.7**, 2.4, 3.6, 3.9, 4.7, See. p393-395
もういいですか	all set? are you all done? **0.1.09G**, 1.9A	
もういちど	one more time	**1.3**, 1.5
もういちどおねがいします	could you say it one more time? **1.6**,G, 1.9A	
もうすこしがんばってください	you can do a little better. Try your best **0.1.10G**	
もく	Thurs.	**4.7**
もくてき	purpose/objective	**4.1B**, 4.1, 4.6, 4.8, 4.9, 4.10
もくようび	Thursday	**2.1B**, G, 2.1, 2.2, 2.3, 2.6, 3.5, 4.2, 4.4, 4.9, 4.10
もしもし	hello	**4.1B**, 4.3, 4.4, 4.9, 4.10
もちつき	rice pounding	**4.11A**
モニター	monitor	**0.1.07G**, 0.2.07G
もり　みちお	Mori Michio (name of person) **3.02**	
もんだい	problem	**0.2.07G**, 4.1B, 4.1, 4.5, 4.6, 4.9
や	or/and so on	3.9, 4.10, See.p393-395
やきとり	grilled chicken yakitori	**2.6**
やきゅう	baseball	**1.6**, 3.8
やきゅうのせんしゅ	baseball player	**3.11A**
やきゅうぶ	baseball team	**1.9A**, 3.11
やさいバーガー	veggie burger	**2.6**, 2.9A
やさしい	kind	**0.2.09G**, 3.1B, 3.1, 3.5, 3.6, 3.8, 3.9. 3.11
やすお	Yasuo (name of person)	**4.3**
やすみ	rest	**2.6**
やすみじかん	recess time	**3.9**, 3.11A
やすみです	she or he is absent.	**0.1.08G**
やすみのひ	day off	**2.9A**
やすみます／やすむ	to be absent	**4.7**
やっつ	eight (quantity)	**2.9A**, G, 4.1b, 4.5
やま	mountain	**3.9**, 3.11A
やまぐち	Yamaguchi(prefecture)	**3.8**
やまぐちこうとうがっこう	Yamaguchi high school	**1.6**
やまだ	Yamada (name of person) **3.3**, 3.9	
やまだ　はるこ	Yamada, Haruko (name of person) **3.8**	
やまだ　ゆうじ	Yuji Yamada (name of person) **1.7**	
やまだ　ようこ	Yamada, Yoko (name of person) **3.8**	
ゆうかん	brave	**3.11A**
ゆうごはん	dinner	**4.4**, 4.7, 4.8
ゆうしょうしゃ	winner	**4.9**
ゆうびんきょく	post office	**4.11A**
ユーモアのある～	a humorous~	**3.11A**
ゆき	snow	**3.11A**
ゆっくりいって	please say it slowly (informal) **1.9A**	
ゆっくりいってください	please say it slowly	**1.9A**, G
ユニセフ	UNICEF	**4.9**
ユニホーム	uniform	**0.1.08G**
ゆり	Yuri (name of person)	**3.3**
ようか	eighth day of the month	**2.1B**, G, 2.1, 2.3, 2.6, 3.9, 4.1
ようちえん	kindergarden	**1.9A**
ようび	day of the week	**2.1**, 2.2, 2.4, 2.5
よく	often	**3.5**, 3.9, 3.11, 3.11A, 4.1B, 4.2, 4.8
よくふりますね	it rains a lot, isn't it?	**0.1.03G**,1.6, 1.9A
よくふります／ふる	to fall (rain)a lot	**1.9A**
よくふるね	it rains a lot, doesn't it? (informal) **1.6**	
よくふる（わ）ね	it's raining hard, isn't it? (informal) **1.9A**	
よこはま	Yokohama	**3.2**, 3.8
よこやま　みさこ	Misako Yokoyama (name of person) **1.6**	
よさん	budget	**4.1B**, 4.1, 4.6, 4.9, 4.10
よじ	four o'clock	**2.1B**, G, 2.1, 2,2, 2.6, 3.9, 4.3,4.4, 4.8, 4.10
よじごふん	4:05	**4.8**
よじはん	four thirty	**2.6**
よせなべ	seafood and chicken	**2.4**, 2.6, 2.9, 2.9A
よっか	fourth day of the month	**2.1B**, G, 2.1, 2.3, 2.6, 3.3, 3.5, 3.9, 4.1, 4.2, 4.4, 4.7
よっつ	four (quantity)	**2.9A**, G, 4.1B, 4.5
ヨット	yacht	**0.1.08G**

よにん	four people	2.1B, G, 2.3, 2.6, 3.4, 3.7, 3.9, 3.11, 4.1
よねんせい	fourth grader	1.6
よみます／よむ	to read	4.1B, 4.1, 4.2, 4.4, 4,7, 4.9, 4.10
よやく	reservation	4.1
よる	night	3.9, 3.11A
よろしく	nice to meet you	1.1, 1.6
よん	four	1.1B, G, 1.2, 1.3, 1.5, 1.6, 4.6
よんさい	four years old	1.2
よんじっぷん／よんじゅっぷん		
	forty minutes	4.1
よんじゅう	forty	1.1B, G, 1.2, 1.5, 1.6
よんじゅうごふん	forty five minutes	4.1B
よんじゅっぷん	forty minutes	4.1B
よんせん	four thousand	1.3, 1.5, 1.6
よんで	please read (informal)	1.9A
よんでください	please read	1.9A, G, 4.10
よんひゃく	four hundred	1.1B, G, 1.3, 1.5, 1.6
よんぷん	four minutes	4.9
ラーメン	Chinese-style noodles	0.1.09G, 0.2.06G, 2.4, 2.6, 2.9A, 3.9
らいしゅう	next weeek	4.10, 4.11A
ライト	light	4.6, 4.8
ライン	line	4.9
ラグビー	rugby	3.8
ラップトップ	lap top	0.2.07G
リヨン	Lyons	3.01B
りかさん	Rika (name of person)	4.1B, 4.1, 4.10
リクエスト	request	3.8
りくじょう	track and field	3.8
リサ	Lisa	1.6, 3.8, 3.9, 4.7
リサーチ	research	4.9
リスト	list	3.8
リバーこうこう	River high school	1.6
リモコン	remote control	0.2.08G
りゅうがくせい	foreign student	3.11A
りょう	dormitory	2.6
りょうりします／りょうりする		
	cook	4.11A
りんご	apple	0.2.09G, 1.9A, 2.2, 2.6,
リンダさん	Linda	4.1
れい	Bow	0.1.08G, 1.1B, 1.2, 1.3, 1.5
れいさい	zero years old	1.2
れいせい	calm/cool	3.11A
レーチェルさん	Rachel	1.4
れきし	history	0.2.09G, 3.1B, 3.1, 3.5, 3.8, 3.9
レジャー	leisure	4.8
レジャーのじかん	leisure time	4.11A
レストラン	restaurant	2.6, 3.9
レストランがい	restaurant row	2.6, 2.9A
レストランのなまえ		
	restaurant's name	2.9A
レセプション	reception	4.11A
レモネード	lemonade	0.1.09G, 2.5
レモン	lemon	1.9A, 2.6
れんしゅう	practice	3.9, 4.6, 4.9

れんしゅうのあと	after practice	3.11A
れんしゅうのないよう		
	content of practice	3.11A
ロイド	Lloyd	3.2
ローストビーフ	roast beef	0.1.09G
ろく	six	1.1B, G, 1.1, 1.2, 1.3, 1.5, 1.6, 3.9
ろくがつ	June	2.1B, G, 2.3, 2.6. 3.2, 3.9
ろくさい	six years old	1.2
ろくじ	six o'clock	2.1B, G, 2.2, 2.6, 4.3, 4.4, 4.7, 4.9, 4.10
ろくじにじゅうごふん		
	6:15	4.8
ろくじはん	six thirty	2.2, 2.6, 4.8
ろくじゅう	sixty	1.1B, G, 1.2, 1.5, 1.6
ろくじよんじゅうごふん		
	six fourty five	3.5, 4.2
ろくせん	six thousand	1.3, 1.5 , 1.6
ろくにん	six people	2.3 , 2.6, 3.7, 3.9, 4.1
ろくねんせい	sixth grade	1.6
ロサ	Rosa	1.2, 1.3, 1.4
ロシア	Russia	3.9
ロシアご	Russian language	3.02
ロシアじん	Russian person	3.02
ロスアンジェルス	Los Angeles	3.11A
ロック	rock	2.1B, 3.8
ロックコンサート	rock concert	2.2, 2.6
ろっぴゃく	six hundred	1.1B, G, 1.3, 1.5, 1.6, 4.5
ろっぷん	six minutes	4.8
ロメロ	Romero	3.02
わかりますか	do you understand?	0.1.09G, 1.9A
わかるか	do you understand? (informal)	
		1.9A
わしょく	Japanese cousine	2.9A
ワシントン	Washington	3.11A, 4.6
わたくし	I/me (formal)	3.4
わたし	I (for girls and adults)	2.4, 2.6, 3.4, 3.6, 3.8, 3.9, 4.1, 4.3, 4.8
わたしの	my	4.8
わたしも	me too	2.3, 2.4
ワッフル	waffle	0.1.09G 0.2.06G
わる	divide	1.3, 1.6
～を	particle 0	4.7

Index

Credits

000, 001 © 小川進、Susumu Ogawa/ The Japan Forum

003 © The Japan Forum

006-1 © 中西祐介、Yusuke Nakanishi/ The Japan Forum

006-2 © 中西祐介、Yusuke Nakanishi/ The Japan Forum

006-3 © The Japan Forum

007 © 島野雅俊、Masatoshi Shimano

024 © 株式会社講談社、Kodansha Ltd., Publishers

025 © 中西祐介、Yusuke Nakanishi/ The Japan Forum

032 © 株式会社講談社、Kodansha Ltd., Publishers

033 © 株式会社講談社、Kodansha Ltd., Publishers

034, 035-1, 6 ©株式会社講談社、Kodansha Ltd., Publishers

034, 035-2 ,7, 11© 君島哲夫、Tetsuo Kimijima/ The Japan Forum

034, 035-3, 4, 8, 12 渡辺裕一、Yuichi Watanabe, Teacher of Toki Shogyo High School/The Japan Forum

034, 035-5 © 小川進、Susumu Ogawa , Teacher of Kanaegaura High School/The Japan Forum

034, 035-9.© 吉新麻由、Mayu Yoshiara/ The Japan Forum

037 © 渡辺裕一、Yuichi Watanabe/ The Japan Forum

040-1 © 中西祐介、Yusuke Nakanishi/ The Japan Forum

040-2 © 毛利圭助、Keisuke Mori/The Japan Forum

041 © UNIS Yearbook

048 © 中西祐介、Yusuke Nakanishi/ The Japan Forum

052-1 © 中西祐介、Yusuke Nakanishi/ The Japan Forum

052-2 © 岩切裕、Yutaka Iwakiri/The Japan Forum

053 © 株式会社講談社、Kodansha Ltd., Publishers

060 © 富士ゼロックス株式会社、Fuji Xerox Co., Ltd.

066-1, 4 © The Japan Forum

066-2, 3, 5, 6, 7, 8 © 株式会社講談社、Kodansha Ltd. Publishers;

067-1, 2, 3, 5, 6, 7 © 株式会社講談社、Kodansha Ltd., Publishers

067-4 © 渡辺裕一、Yuichi Watanabe/ The Japan Forum

067-8 © The Japan Forum

068-1 © 岩瀬三八、Miya Iwase/The Japan Forum

068-2 © 嶋亜希子、Akiko Shima/The Japan Forum

068-3 © 金森亜衣、Ai Kanamori/The Japan Forum

068-4 © 吉田篤史、Atsushi Yoshida/The Japan Forum

068-5 © The Japan Forum

068-6 © 越田純代、Sumiyo Koshida/The Japan Forum

069-1 © 中西祐介、Yusuke Nakanishi/The Japan Forum

069-2 ©那須智之、Tomoyuki Nasu/The Japan Forum

069-3 ©教育出版株式会社、Kyoiku Shuppan

069-4 © 西美有紀、Miyuki Nishi/The Japan Forum

069-5, 6 ©古川鈴子、Suzuko Furukawa/The Japan Forum

070, 071 © Chris Cole/Tony Stone Images; Tony Stone Images

073 © Bob Torrez/Tony Stone Images; Tony Stone Images

076 © Bob Torrez/Tony Stone Images; Tony Stone Images

078 © 岩切裕、Yutaka Iwakiri

078-1, 4, 7 © 中西祐介、Yusuke Nakanishi/The Japan Forum

078-2 © 三上達也、Tatsuya Mikami/The Japan Forum

078-3, 5 © The Japan Forum

078-6 © 松井美緒、Mio Matsui/The Japan Forum

085-1 © 津田塾大学、Tsuda College

085-2 © 株式会社講談社、Kodansha Ltd., Publishers

085-3 © 手塚プロダクション、Tezuka Poroduction Co., Ltd.

091-1, 2, 6 © 中西祐介、Yusuke Nakanishi/The Japan Forum

091-3 © 松井美緒、Mio Matsui/The Japan Forum

091-4 © 古川鈴子、Suzuko Furukawa/The Japan Forum

091-5 © The Japan Forum

101-1 © The Japan Forum

101-3 © Lora Runge

101-2, 4 © 中西祐介、Yusuke Nakanishi/The Japan Forum

102 © 岩切裕、Yutaka Iwakiri/The Japan Forum

103-1 © 岩切裕、Yutaka Iwakiri/The Japan Forum

103-3 © 岩切裕、Yutaka Iwakiri

103-2, 4 © 株式会社講談社、Kodansha Ltd., Publishers

104 © 吉田篤史、Atsushi Yoshida/The Japan Forum

105 © 松井美緒、Mio Matsui/The Japan Forum

108 © 岩切裕、Yutaka Iwakiri/The Japan Forum

110-1 © 古川鈴子、Suzuko Furukawa/The Japan Forum

110-2 © 毛利圭助、Keisuke Mori/The Japan Forum

113-1 © 手塚プロダクション、Tezuka Poroduction Co., Ltd.

113-2 © 株式会社講談社、Kodansha Ltd., Publishers

113-3 © 津田塾大学、Tsuda College

113-4 © UNIS Yearbook

120 © 岩切裕、Yutaka Iwakiri/The Japan Forum

122 © 中西祐介、Yusuke Nakanishi/The Japan Forum

132 © UNIS Yearbook

141 © 島野雅俊、Masatoshi Shimano

143 © UNIS Yearbook

149 © 岩切裕、Yutaka Iwakiri/The Japan Forum

150 © 岩切裕、Yutaka Iwakiri/The Japan Forum

151 © 小川進、Susumu Ogawa/The Japan Forum

155 © 岩切裕、Yutaka Iwakiri

160 © 小川進、Susumu Ogawa/The Japan Forum

175 © 株式会社講談社、Kodansha Ltd., Publishers

183 © UNIS Yearbook

185 © 小川進、Susumu Ogawa/The Japan Forum

188 © 岩切裕、Yutaka Iwakiri

189-1 © 株式会社講談社、Kodansha Ltd., Publishers